# THE CATHOLIC
# PEACE TRADITION

# THE CATHOLIC
# PEACE TRADITION

*Ronald G. Musto*

ORBIS BOOKS

Maryknoll, New York 10545

The Catholic Foreign Mission Society of America (Maryknoll) recruits and trains people for overseas missionary service. Through Orbis Books Maryknoll aims to foster the international dialogue that is essential to mission. The books published, however, reflect the opinions of their authors and are not meant to represent the official position of the society.

Manuscript Editor: Mary Heffron

**Library of Congress Cataloging-in-Publication Data**

Musto, Ronald G.
  The Catholic peace tradition.

  Bibliography: p.
  Includes index.
  1. Peace—Religious aspects—Catholic Church—
History of doctrines.   2. Catholic Church—Doctrine—
History.   I. Title.
BX1795.P43M87   1986        261.8′73        86-12494
ISBN 0-88344-263-9 (pbk.)

*To my Mother and Father*

# CONTENTS

*vii*

# PREFACE

This book is a history of the peace tradition in the Roman Catholic Church from the time of the gospels to the twentieth century. Its purpose is to show that there is a continuing, unbroken, and self-sustaining stream within Catholicism from the the the martyrs and pacifists of the early church to John XXIII and the peacemakers of our time.

In doing the research for this book over the last four years, I talked with many friends and associates who expressed surprise that—given the dangers of a war or a nuclear holocaust—I would spend so much time delving into the Catholic past and ignoring, it seemed, the active Catholic present. Yet this is an age in which personal faith, as rarely before in American history, is dramatically affecting public policy and life. Change will flow from such personal faith and commitment, and only a clear understanding of the workings of Catholic faith in history can provide a firm foundation for the attitudes and actions of Catholics today.

My purposes in writing this book are simple. First, I want to show young Catholic men and women of college and draft age that a peace tradition exists and to point out the different forms that Catholic peacemaking has taken and can take in the future. Like young Catholics of the 1960s and 1970s, today's young men and women need to know that they are neither alone nor abnormal as Catholics in their desire for peace and their opposition to war and militarism. These young people also hope to find that their commitment to, and community in, peacemaking is not a radical departure from the past, nor a loss of their Catholicism, but that it flows from their religious tradition. Second, I hope by this book to reach the teacher, student, or general reader who might want a basic introduction to the Catholic peace tradition or readings for a course on Church or peace history. I have tried to provide a full treatment of as many topics, problems, individuals, and movements within Catholic peace history as possible, with appropriate annotation and bibliography.

This work is a synthesis, a bringing together of the rich findings of many scholars and religious writers who have contributed similar surveys or who have concentrated on smaller, more particular fields of study. The list of such histories is a long one. Perhaps the best known, written from the Protestant point of view, is Roland H. Bainton's *Christian Attitudes Toward War and Peace.* Catholic accounts have, until now, been specialized, focusing on the ethical and theological problems of war and peace, the biblical foundations of peacemaking, or the problem of conscientious objection in the modern world. Excellent examples include Richard McSorley's *New Testament Basis of Peacemaking,* Thomas A. Shannon's *War or Peace?,* Eileen Egan's *The Catholic Conscientious Objector,* all of Gordon Zahn's works, especially *In Solitary Witness,* and, of course, the many writings of Thomas Merton on Christian peacemaking. Unlike these works, however, this book is primarily a *historical* account of peacemaking from the Catholic point of view, and it concentrates solely on the Catholic tradition.

My own field of expertise is the Middle Ages and the Renaissance, periods in the

Catholic past that receive the least attention in accounts of peacemaking and that seem to be the least understood. In these and other areas, I have attempted to be as thorough as possible in my survey of primary peace sources and secondary studies, taking into account the full range of research and interpretation available. In the last four chapters, those dealing with the twentieth century, I have also surveyed the vast field of contemporary Catholic peacemaking and have tried to give a comprehensive and coherent account of all its forms. I hope that I have covered all this material fairly and used good judgment in guiding the reader through it. I trust that my efforts will encourage others to criticize, search further, and fill in the gaps.

This book is the first part of a three-volume study. The second, *The Peace Tradition in the Catholic Church. An Annotated Bibliography* (New York: Garland, 1986), gives detailed information on, and analysis of, the works cited in the notes and bibliography below. It also expands and updates research from November 1984, when work on this book was completed, to mid-1986. The Annotated Bibliography includes some works that were, unfortunately, overlooked in my research but that are no less important than those cited below.

The third, projected, volume is one of readings in Catholic peace history that will include selections from the sources used in this book: the Bible, writings of the early Fathers, canon law and penitential texts, the lives and sayings of the saints, histories of popular peace movements, monastic texts, missionary accounts and plans for conversion, Humanist tracts, accounts of individual witnesses for peace, episcopal and papal letters, and the decrees of church synods and councils.

Finally, I would like to thank those who helped make this project possible. Robert Nee, Ss.Cc., and Professor Gordon Zahn of Pax Christi and Bill Offenloch of the Catholic Peace Fellowship offered advice and encouragement at the early stages of my research. My thanks also go to Philip Scharper and John Eagleson of Orbis Books, who saw the potential of this book and helped guide it to its final form; to Mary Heffron, who edited a long and at times difficult manuscript with professional skill; and to Catherine Costello, Production Coordinator at Orbis, for her expertise and advice. The staffs of the New York Public Library and of the Columbia University Libraries and, most especially, the staff of the Fordham University Library all helped make the necessary resources available to this "unaffiliated" scholar.

Many years ago, as an undergraduate at Fordham College, I was first introduced to the possibility of Catholic peacemaking by Fr. Herbert Rogers, S.J. For that I am ever grateful. Dr. Eileen Gardiner has since then been my companion and inspiration. She is as responsible as anyone for whatever truth or learning emerges from these pages.

# INTRODUCTION

## UNCOVERING THE CATHOLIC PEACE TRADITION

One of the great developments of the past decade has been the reaffirmation among United States Catholics of the Christian call to peacemaking within their community and the world at large. Yet a clearly recognizable peace tradition, such as exists in many Protestant peace churches, that goes beyond Vatican II to the age of the Fathers, has been lost or overlooked by Catholic hierarchy and laity in the face of other pressing social, moral, and theological concerns. Both Catholic and non-Catholic historians have all too willingly accepted the viewpoint expressed by the Protestant historian Roland H. Bainton in his *Christian Attitudes Toward War and Peace*. After establishing the existence of a pacifist tradition in the New Testament and in patristic writings, Bainton goes on to demonstrate that, with isolated exceptions (largely among proto-Protestant pacifist sects), the traditions of the just and holy war dominated Christian history until the Reformation and the emergence of the Protestant peace churches.

Bainton's treatment of both Catholic and Protestant traditions is fair, but he does tend to link the tradition of the just war and the holy war with the Catholic Church and the pacifist tradition of the gospels and the Fathers with the Protestant churches. Surprisingly, even Catholics have generally accepted this view. The *New Catholic Encyclopedia*'s article on pacifism (1967) denied the pacifism of Christ and the Fathers, covered the entire medieval period from Saint Augustine to the Reformation in eight lines, passed off medieval pacifism as the province of "a few heretical sects of relatively late date and minor influence," disassociated modern pacifism from religious belief, and concluded that "it is clear from what has been said that absolute pacifism is irreconcilable with traditional Catholic doctrine." (NCE 10:856).

For many Catholics the effects of this lack of religious tradition, this moral amnesia, were felt in the 1960s and 1970s when many organized Catholic peace groups and individual Catholic peacemakers, forced to explain their beliefs and actions, called on the authority of the gospels and the Fathers but could not point to any recognizable tradition of peacemaking to show their connection, their community with the living past. For Roman Catholics this was especially hard to bear, for their church rests not only on the gospels and the Fathers but also on a continuing tradition of grace granted through the Holy Spirit. To act without tradition as a guide and an aid caused spiritual trauma and alienation for these peacemakers, who sought their place in a Catholic tradition of peacemaking.

Their situation was like that of a man in middle age who can recall the warmth and nurturing of his infancy and early boyhood but who is completely unable to remember his youth, his adolescence, or his young manhood or to explain how he has become the person he now perceives himself to be. He maintains a deep sense of faith that he is that boy, that youth, and a firm desire to act on that faith, but he feels alienated from his spiritual inheritance and his community. He feels abandoned, as if he had been left

*1*

an orphan. Like an orphan, he shifts his love to parents he knows are not his own; he latches on to a tradition outside the church. Yet he feels empty and longs for completeness and community within his own family, his own tradition. He is longing for that which defines any mental or spiritual well-being: a wholeness of person and of purpose that is indeed the most fundamental definition of peace.

This book is a step toward uncovering the Catholic peacemaking tradition. It attempts to show Catholics that their moral and religious commitment to a positive peacemaking based on the gospels can also find nourishment from a long, long history of individuals and groups, clerical and lay, men and women, of all social levels and occupations, who have never let the message of peace be stilled.

## PEACE HISTORY: A THEORY OF DIALOGUE WITHIN THE MYSTICAL BODY

This account attempts to show Catholics not only that peacemaking is a strong tradition that is theirs to inherit and to use but also that it is a continuing process, a continuous call to accept the gift and the challenge of Christ: "Peace I leave with you, my peace I give to you" (Jn 14:27). Peacemaking is a gift because Christ has left us his life, sacrifice, and model to imitate, a challenge because without individuals who continue to make peace an active principle of their lives, Christ's message falls mute. Without Christians to carry out his word, it can never be fulfilled and made perfect.

This truth was expressed clearly by the bishops assembled at the Second Vatican Council in the *Decree on the Apostolate of the Laity:*

> For this the Church was founded: that by spreading the kingdom of Christ everywhere for the glory of God the Father, she might bring all men [*sic*] to share in Christ's saving redemption; and that through them the whole world might in actual fact be brought into relationship with Him. All activity of the Mystical Body directed to the attainment of this goal is called the apostolate, and the Church carries it on in various ways through all her members. For by its very nature the Christian vocation is also a vocation to the apostolate. No part of the structure of a living body is merely passive but each has a share in the functions as well as in the life of the body. So, too, in the body of Christ, which is the Church, the whole body, "according to the functioning in due measure of each single part, derives its increase" (Eph 4:16). Indeed, so intimately are the parts linked and interrelated in this body (cf. Eph 4:16) that the member who fails to make his proper contribution to the development of the Church must be said to be useful neither to the Church nor to himself.
>
> In the Church, there is a diversity of service but unity of purpose. Christ conferred on the apostles and their successors the duty of teaching, sanctifying, and ruling in His name and power. But the laity, too, share in the priestly, prophetic, and royal office of Christ and therefore have their own role to play in the mission of the whole People of God in the Church and in the world.
>
> They exercise a genuine apostolate by their activity on behalf of bringing the gospel and holiness to men, and on behalf of penetrating and perfecting the temporal sphere of things through the spirit of the gospel. In this way, their temporal activity can openly bear witness to Christ and promote the salvation of men. Since it is proper to the layman's state in life for him to spend his days in the midst of the world and of secular transactions, he is called by God to burn with

the spirit of Christ and to exercise his apostolate in the world as a kind of leaven [no. 2].

The role of the layperson, as of the cleric, can no longer be that of the passive recipient of an official dogma developed and handed down by a remote hierarchy. It must be that of an active participant in the work of the Spirit. Through their life and beliefs laypersons help to mold the teachings of the church, of which they are essential members.

The individual Catholic's membership in the church and in Christ's work for peace through the Mystical Body is a central theme of this book and provides a key historical principle for its organization. In a real sense the Mystical Body forms a unit: the head and the members—pope, hierarchy, clergy, and laity—are joined together as one. The Holy Spirit works within the church as a whole, not only through the head but also through the members, to develop and make clear the truth. Thus the developing tradition of peacemaking can be seen in terms of a dialogue within the church—a historical and spiritual dialogue—of the teachings of the hierarchy at one time and place, the response of the laity, and the reaffirmation or alteration of doctrine by the church as a whole.

In any dialogue one person makes a statement that is received and pondered by the other. The other person in turn replies to what has been said and adds a new element to the conversation, based partly on what has been said before, partly on his or her own ideas and experience. This reply is then received and pondered by the first speaker, and a new response is given. We follow this process in any real conversation, any real dialogue. When we are truly communicating we are open to the other person and to his or her ideas in a spirit of cooperation, and this spirit works within and guides the dialogue. If it is missing we enter into a dialectic of point and counterpoint never intended to be reconciled, but only to show the power relationships between the parties involved.

We have a model for dialogue and dialectic in the history of European ideas (see Heer 1968). This history is not linear but is the product of an intellectual exchange between "above" and "below." Ideas are sometimes born from above, from the official or high culture, and sometimes from below, from the mass, or popular culture. They are often forcefully imposed from above; they are sometimes an attempt to imitate high society or civilization, and thus become for a while the official culture of the entire society. At other times, however, ideas are born from below and move up through all levels of a civilization by virtue of their appeal and inner strength. They are then adopted by the upper culture and become part of the official culture or civilization. In turn they are spread throughout the society by official channels, adopted and changed on the popular level, and reemerge as new ideas.

In our society we need only think of certain fashions in dress or music to see how styles are born among the young, the "hip," or the poor, how they become popular at large, and how they are then picked up by the elite to become the new official style. This is then marketed to society as a whole. Think of the progress of blue jeans; of "punk" style in dress, graphic design, and fashion of the 1970s and 1980s; of jazz music and its adoption by classical composers in America and Europe in the 1920s and 1930s. The process works on every level of our lives. Even the nuclear freeze movement of the 1980s progressed from the unnoticed work of a few college students to a massive popular movement to the concern of presidents and Congress.

Throughout history ideas born of the official culture, whether of Imperial Rome, the monasteries of Europe, or the salons of the Enlightenment, run parallel to the ideas and views of slaves and peasants, of merchants and political reformers. These ideas interact in a dialogue or a dialectic to form new ideas that become orthodox opinion, an official view that becomes the dominant opinion of society by authority or by force. The official ideas are then changed by the culture at large to suit particular needs of the time and place until the original idea is transformed. Pressure from below brings the transformed idea to the attention of policy makers, and so the process begins all over again. By "policy makers" I do not necessarily mean those people with political power or authority. More often than not those who make policy have little power or authority other than their creative abilities to give birth to ideas and movements or to mold these ideas in effective ways. Artists, writers, and intellectuals are most often the creators of the official culture that others merely impose or propagate.

Throughout the history of the Catholic Church, from the time of the gospels to our own day, this process of dialogue has been at work. Now a council or pope, now a bishop or synod, now a philosopher or canon lawyer, will receive and bear witness to the message of peace for a particular time and audience. At other times the message of pacifism and peacemaking will come from the lowly, from assemblies of peasants, from solitary hermits and isolated missionaries, from a lonely Austrian farmer in the isolation of a Nazi prison.

Barbarians overwhelm Europe while abbots condemn as murder the shedding of blood, even in a just war, and stop armies singlehandedly with a message of peace; knights wage "holy wars" while friars and missionaries speak of love and toleration of the non-Christian and troubadours mock the ways of the soldier; Renaissance popes lay waste to cities while Humanist scholars move readers to peace and the imitation of Christ; modern bishops bless field artillery while college students seek to live the message of the gospels; nations threaten nuclear destruction and citizens prepare for death or lonely survival while popes and bishops speak for peace and hope. Thus the message of peace found in the gospels and renewed by the Holy Spirit is never to be found in any one person, group, or time. It springs forth now here, now there, and in continuing dialogue it involves us all. It is refined and redefined, sometimes confused, but never lost, and ever growing.

## PEACE HISTORY AND NEW HISTORY

Until the last few decades the church focused on the monologue of the hierarchy; the message of the lowly, of the laity, was overlooked. In parallel fashion, we have traditionally looked at history as the story of the mighty, as a monologue of those with power or authority. This was the "old history" that dealt solely with the dates of battles and treaties, the births and deaths of kings and millionaires, the destruction of towns and the invasion of countries. This was the history that bored us all so much in school, and with good reason. Although these accounts could often excite with deeds or famous words, they lacked the essential element that could draw us into them: the account of how great men and women, significant dates, bloody battles, or brilliant speeches affected the lives of real people, how they touched the ways in which people felt and lived. They were a monologue from above, which never expected or wanted a reply.

In the last few decades a "new history" has emerged. This history gives due credit to important persons, events, and dates, but it also gives serious attention to how people lived and died, how they practiced their trades or arts, how and what they believed about God and the world. This new history has reclaimed much that was previously ignored: the histories of women and minorities, folk traditions, daily life, sickness and healing, social and sexual mores. It has shown that these things are just as important, if not more important in the long view, than the isolated battles and dates we once learned in school. While I cannot claim here to fully incorporate the methods of the new history, I have tried to use the insights it provides to describe the workings of peace in the Catholic tradition.

We will thus discuss popular spirituality and lay religious movements as well as official papal teachings, the thoughts of obscure men and women as well as those of the Fathers of the church, and streams of events not generally considered important along with well-known currents in church history. I have chosen to discuss many topics that do not normally enter into accounts of the Catholic peace tradition: the penitential literature, the early canonical tradition, the popular peace movement behind the Peace and Truce of God, the missionary movements of the early Middle Ages and the period of the Crusades. I also examine the mendicant movement (including the life and work of Saint Francis of Assisi) as an association of peace and poverty that struck at the heart of the militarism and the economic exploitation of the day. I hope to show how late-medieval themes of individual conscience and the limits of authority over that conscience are the seeds of today's Catholic theory of conscientious objection. My discussion of apocalypticism, an important issue today as in the past, runs counter to the accepted interpretations as in Norman Cohn's *Pursuit of the Millennium*. I make the case for a peaceful apocalyptic that can be traced from the time of the early church to the writings of Thomas Merton. My study will also touch on the life and thought of such twentieth-century men and women as Franz Jaegerstaetter, Danilo Dolci and Lanzo del Vasto, the Irish Peace People, and the Solidarity movement in Poland. It concludes with a survey of the progress of Catholic peacemaking in the Third World and in the United States today.

Through this book I hope to encourage my readers to realize their own role in creating peace and in interpreting the message of the gospels; to sustain their part in a continuing dialogue that needs the active participation of all if it is to truly affect all. I trust that I have neither distorted the historical evidence or the theological grounding of the Catholic tradition nor ignored the research of other historians or the strength and reality of certain, often contradictory, traditions of the Catholic past. I invite the reader to share with me the realization that a tradition of peace and peacemaking does indeed exist and that with time this tradition will become stronger and clearer. In the words of St. Paul: "We know in part, and we prophesy in part. But when that which is perfect has come, that which is imperfect will be done away with. . . . For now we see through a mirror in an obscure way, but then face to face." (I Cor 13:9–10, 12).

# CHAPTER 1

# A CATHOLIC DEFINITION OF PEACE: THE MEANING OF PEACEMAKING

We cannot discuss the history of peacemaking in the Catholic tradition without first defining what the word "peace" means today and what it has meant in the past. This is important because "peace" can mean so many things; the word has been exploited and abused by so many who cry "peace" when they intend no peace. We must understand what the word can mean before we can begin to create a new vision of peace in the world today. Thus we will formulate a definition of peace that can meet the criteria of Catholic thought and history and can serve as a basis for the times that will follow.

## SOME DICTIONARY DEFINITIONS

The best place to begin the search for a definition of peace is with the dictionary. *Webster's Dictionary*[1] tells us that "peace" can mean several things. The oldest meaning has an "external" sense: a "state of tranquillity or quiet" as found in "freedom from civil disturbance" (such as war or civil war) or in "a state of security or order within a community provided by law or custom." We generally associate this peace with the expression "law and order." The meaning of peace here is essentially negative: a *freedom from* disorder or an *absence of* war, a quiet much like that of a forest cleared of its songbirds.

The next meaning applied to the word "peace" is internal and individual, but it might also apply to the notion of community: "freedom from disquieting or oppressive thoughts or emotions." In one sense this is what we generally enjoy as "peace and quiet" and describe with the adjective "peaceful."[2] We associate this peace with pleasant weekends with the family at the seashore or with sitting quietly at home enjoying a good book: relaxation from work or social obligations. This sense of peace carries a deep, a fundamental, feeling of ease: a freedom from worry about money, job, or health—what we might call "peace of mind." It might also imply a feeling of security both personal and communal brought about by the absence of civil disturbance or threat of war, violence, or crime.

In a communal or social sense this might mean an absence of the debate or contention found in democratic, open societies. It might mean the repression of dissenting voices in authoritarian or totalitarian societies. The shout of "peace, peace!" as a command to fall silent is evoked by this definition of the word. A military dictator who puts off elections and outlaws political activity in the name of "law and order" will often equate "peace" with this repression. Again, the meaning of peace is essentially negative: it is a freedom from worry, an absence of anxiety, a calming of emotion, an ending of debate.

Our day-to-day definition of peace can also have a positive aspect. *Webster's Dictionary* tells us that "peace" can mean a "harmony in personal relations," implying a smoothly working relationship between individuals, such as between one's peers at work or at school. This relationship recognizes mutually shared goals and the benefits brought to all by working cooperatively toward their achievement.

This sense of the word is close to the political and international definition of peace as "a state or period of mutual concord between governments." This meaning could apply to relations between Germany and France between World War I and World War II as well as to relations between the United States and Vietnam today: an interim between wars marked not so much by friendly and cooperative relations as by a temporary cessation of open hostilities. The term can also refer to "a pact or agreement to end hostilities between those who have been at war or in the state of enmity." Peace in this sense is clearly used in our historical and political vocabulary: the Peace of Paris ended the Seven Years War; another Peace of Paris ended World War I and included the Treaty of Versailles.

On another level political peace can mean the positive "concord" of political allies such as NATO or the Warsaw Pact. Peace can refer to those in economic accord such as the nations of the Common Market, or to the diplomatic relations between the members of the United Nations. "Peace" can thus mean both a period and a state of "being at peace" with one's neighbors. The connotation behind all these political uses of the word "peace" is the negative one of an absence of war. Little else is implied.

The *Oxford English Dictionary* brings us closer to a positive definition: peace can mean a state of friendliness, implying openness and cooperation.[3] Internally it can mean calmness and peace of mind, as we have already seen, but more importantly, peace of soul and of conscience.

The *New Catholic Encyclopedia*[4] offers a theological definition of peace both on a social level as a "state of untroubled tranquillity between persons" (similar to definitions examined above) and on a personal level, "within an individual's own self." "So understood it is the tranquil composure of soul that an individual experiences in the absence of a strong conflict of urge or desire between different elements of his own being." Here again we have barely gone beyond our negative day-to-day definition. But the encyclopedia goes on to add that the theological basis of peace, whether internal or external, is the "virtue of charity," which unites all appetites and desires first with the will of one's neighbors and then with a love of God. This peace is based on grace and is informed by the desire for a positive good.

What elements does this theological definition add? Three essential points become clear. First, peace must have an *external* object. It cannot simply be "peace of mind" or "peace and quiet." Second, it is founded on love for one's neighbor and for God. Finally, it is a positive "work of justice" and has an external end. The desire for a positive good.

What exactly is the positive goal and by what positive process is it attained? In the broad sense we can call this goal and this process "peacemaking."

## PEACEMAKING AND PACIFISM

At its most basic level "making peace" means "enforcing public order" or "enforcing silence."[5] Like "keeping the peace," this means maintaining public order, refraining from or preventing others from disturbing the peace, or preventing or restraining others from causing strife or commotion. A "peacemaker" according to this logic is anyone who imposes, enforces, keeps, or maintains order and silence, or who prevents or restrains others from disrupting order and silence.[6] By a perverse extension of this logic, "peacemaker," from the 1840s on came to mean a weapon: a revolver, a battleship, or an MX missile—anything that could be used to settle a dispute once and for all.[7]

"Peacemaking" can mean more than the imposition of order by force or terror. It can also mean the bringing about of a sense of well-being or calm, the creation of tranquility or peace of mind, peace and quiet, the end of hostilities, and the reconciliation between individuals and nations.[8]

Similarly, the words "pacific" and "pacifist," used to describe individuals who make peace, have an activist meaning. *Webster's* tells us that "pacific applies chiefly to persons or to utterances, acts, influences, or ideas that tend to maintain peace or to conciliate strife."[9] Likewise the oldest definition of "pacifism" is "opposition to war or violence as a means of settling disputes," specifically a "refusal to bear arms on moral or religious grounds." The pacifist, by the same token, is "strongly and actively opposed to conflict, and especially war." Only more recently has pacifism been defined as "an attitude or policy of nonresistance."

According to its definition, pacifism has nothing passive or negative about it, although it is often confused with "passiveness" or described as "passive resistance." Pacifism is active, strong, and committed to maintaining peace or reconciling strife.

How can we explain the shift from the generally negative dictionary meanings of peace, to the positive, external, and active definition of peacemaker or pacifist? The explanation it seems, lies in uncovering the cultural connotation of these words, the tradition of meaning that has been lost in the daily definition of terms.

## THE ETYMOLOGY OF PEACE

### Roman Pax

We can trace the word "peace" back to the Middle, or medieval, English word *pees*. This, in turn, is derived from the French word of the Norman conquerors of England. Their word *pais* ultimately derives from the Latin word *pax*.[10] *Pax* comes from a family of Latin words having the roots *pak, pag,* or *pac,* such as *pango* or *pacisco,* meaning "to determine," "to conjugate," or "to retain."[11] The modern word "pact" has the same ancestor.[12] In fact, the Latin word for peace, *pax,* is a close relative of the Latin *pacisci,* meaning to agree, or to come to some form of *pactum,* agreement, to bring about a condition free of conflict.[13] Here war is absent and reconciliation is achieved. Tranquility, quiet, leisure, repose, and security flourish.[14] *Pax* also implies the agreement to establish this condition. Thus for the ancient Romans, a *pactum* meant a peace treaty or an agreement.[15]

Though the Roman *pax* could mean a reciprocal legal relationship between two parties,[16] the relationship was most often determined by the power relationships between Rome and the city or people with whom Rome was entering into agreement. In the words of one historian, "It generally meant, purely and simply, the unconditional surrender of the defeated state"[17] after one of the interminable series of wars Rome waged against its neighbors.[18] Peace for Rome therefore meant a sense of security and an absence of war brought about by Rome's conquests[19] and the subjugation of its real or perceived enemies.[20] By implication *pax* also meant dominion or empire for the Romans—the "peace" that they had established by the conquest of other peoples.[21] The Romans believed that peace through repression was the only peace possible and that only their power could bring the order necessary for it.[22] We will discuss the implications of this Pax Romana for good and bad in chapter 2.[23]

All this does not exhaust the Roman meaning of peace, however. Besides the absence of conflict, *pax* could also mean the special grace or favor that the gods bestowed on the Roman people. This *pax deorum* (peace of the gods) was the equivalent of a special relationship, a *fides* (faithfulness) between the gods and between women and men. This relationship was not moral or ethical. It was a favor, assistance in its most fundamental sense: the fertility and prosperity enjoyed by a primitive agricultural society; "a balance of nature in which divine powers and human beings worked in harmony . . . secured by meticulous ritual and not so much, as more recent religions would maintain, by good moral behavior."[24] Roman peace thus equals the first *Webster's* definitions: freedom from war and trouble, security, and material comfort. The Pax Americana thus differs little from the Pax Romana.

Even the *pax deorum* rose above the purely materialistic favors bestowed on crops or on children. "This idea of the divine peace indirectly exercised a moral influence, since the respect that it induced for vows made to the gods was extended, in the course of time, to vows made to other human beings as well."[25] *Pax* could therefore mean an agreement to end war based on the sanction of oaths to the gods. Thus in Roman religion there arose a conception of peace that was internal and individual, a *pax animi* (peace of the soul), a tranquility of mind. In the second and first centuries B.C. Roman writers, influenced by Greek Stoic philosophy, used this *pax animi*, the peace of sleep[26] or of death,[27] to mean an internal tranquility, a dominion over the passions, and a peace of the Spirit expressed by conscious serenity.[28] Cicero wrote in his *Tusculan Disputations,* "The wise man is always free from all turbulence of mind . . . always in his mind there reigns the most placid peace."[29]

Stoicism produced a similar change in the meaning of Pax Romana. The imperialism of the Roman Republic embraced little political ideology beyond the principles of expedience, expansionism, and the warrior ethos of its aristocracy.[30] The Stoics, however, gave the Empire and its administration the justification for its repressive policies: the maintenance of the individual's economic and spiritual freedom. Thus Seneca (c. 3 B.C.–A.D. 65) wrote that Rome's mission was to impose law and culture upon the world.[31] Epictetus (A.D. c. 50–c. 138) wrote: "You see that the emperor appears to provide us with profound peace"[32] so that people and business might prosper and individuals find an inner refuge from the disorders of daily life.

Even with this Latin root-meaning of peace, we have still not moved far beyond the English definition that we found so unsatisfactory. How is it that *pax*—meaning the absence of war brought about by domination, material prosperity, or inner tranquility— came to be taken as the symbol of Christ and his church? How did *pax* come to mean a peace based on love that works from within to change the individual and to transform society from the grassroots? The answer lies in the use of the Latin language as a vehicle of Western Christian Scripture.

The Latin Bible, both in its Old Latin version and in the version known to us as St. Jerome's Vulgate[33] derives from the Greek original of the New Testament and the Septuagint Old Testament.[34] In the Latin Bible, *pax* became the vehicle for all the meanings of peace evolved over the history of the Old Testament and encapsulated in the Greek Septuagint's word *eirene*[35] and the Hebrew *šālôm*.

## Eirene: *Peace and the Ancient Greeks*

From the time of Homer (c. 800 B.C.) the word *eirene* meant much the same as the Latin and English terms for peace: the opposite of war,[36] the condition resulting from the end of war,[37] the state of law and order that gives the blessings of prosperity.[38] *Eirene* meant not an inner attitude or condition, but an external state or a time of peace. More explicit than the Roman *pax*, however, the Greek *eirene* implied an interlude in the everyday, natural state of war.[39]

In a social or political sense, *eirene* evolved to mean more than material prosperity and to include everything assured by the Latin *pax* or the English "peace." In the period between 450 and 350 B.C. *eirene* came to mean the conclusion of peace negotiations, the actual treaty of peace with its clauses, the document itself, or a condition or period of peace.[40] Unlike the Pax Romana, however, in which superior force and military skill dictated the terms of peace to the defeated,[41] the Greek *eirene* between states was a relationship between legally equal parties with identical rights, even if one were the clear victor over the other.[42]

In a larger context *eirene* implied the total physical well-being that derives from the absence of war: prosperity, security, and harmony,[43] "the state of peace from which flow all blessings for both land and people."[44] On a deeper level this well-being was seen as the blessing upon the *polis* (the Greek community of the city-state), which was dependent upon the favorable attitude and actions of the gods.[45] Hesiod (c. 700 B.C.) saw peace as the satisfaction of the elemental needs and the insurance of the continuity of the race. In *Works and Days*[46] he paints a vivid and idyllic picture of what peace meant to a primitive Greek society.[47] Fertility of land and people, prosperity, harmony and repose at home was showered upon those who lived in justice, that is, in accordance with the will of the gods. For the ancient Greeks good will derived from the supplication of the faithful through strict ritual offerings and prayer. Even with this primitive religious notion, a new element had already been introduced.

As the Greek consciousness developed, "living in justice" took on the new meaning of "peaceful conduct," the ability to live together in the urban *polis* as a community, much like the modern English meaning of peace as "harmony in personal relations." Thus *eirene* came to mean a state of linkage,[48] of order and coherence that brings about, and results from, prosperity. But *eirene* meant little more than that. Other words were used for related concepts: *filia* for love or friendship,[49] *homonoia* for unity or concord,[50] *galene* for inner calm.[51]

*Eirene* retained a negative meaning: the absence of war. Even the influence of Stoic philosophy and the notion of spiritual, inner peace did not change this. Until as late as the time of the *Meditations* of Marcus Aurelius (A.D. 161–180) the Greek word *galene* meant inner calm, while *eirene* referred to external relationships.[52] Only when *eirene* was used in the Greek Septuagint to translate the Hebrew *šālôm* did the word take on any deeper or more active meaning.

## Šālôm: *Peace in the Old Testament*

The root of the Hebrew word *šālôm*, like the Arabic *salaam*,[53] contains the meaning of order also implied by *pax* or *eirene*. Its root, *slm*, means to be whole, complete, or uninjured.[54] Because the historical process during which the Jewish language evolved was so long, it is difficult to attach any single meaning to the word *šālôm*. The word has twenty-five meanings in the Old Testament.[55] It sometimes has the same meaning as *pax* or *eirene* in the sense of peace, security, or freedom from fear of enemies[56] or of death.[57] It sometimes means a state of good health (Ps 37:4), of well-being (2 Kgs 18:32; Gn 43:27), or of a happy old age.[58] Unlike *pax* and *eirene*, however, *šālôm* did not originally mean the opposite of war,[59] and could in fact mean the harmony of those working together for success in war (2 Kgs 11:7) or victory in war.[60] In a wider context *šālôm* meant fertility (Is. 1:19–20), healing (Jer. 6:14; Léon-Dufour, 412), or success in any daily activity (Gn. 26:29; Dn. 3:98), such as an expedition (Jgs. 18:5). It could mean safety in the sense of escape from battle (Ps. 55:19) or the safety and calm of a dwelling, a place, or a region.[61]

Like *pax* and *eirene*, *šālôm* also meant the prosperous and harmonious condition of a whole personality, family, or community (Jos. 9:15; Jgs. 4:17; 3 Kgs. 5:4), the harmony between lovers[62] or between humans and God. It brought prosperity and order,[63] comradeship,[64] mutual confidence (Nm. 25:12; Sir 45:24), and well-being engendered by mutual trust and a sense of community.[65] This was expressed succinctly in the greeting and blessing *Šālôm* spoken by one friend to another.[66]

Although a spiritual concept of well-being was implied by the word, the Hebrew *šālôm* originally reflected the needs and desires of a pastoral and agricultural society: material prosperity and security ensured by mutual cooperation.[67] Yet, *šālôm* was also a gift of Yahweh,[68] dependent upon God's good will.[69] Just as *šālôm* could denote the cooperation enjoyed within a community or between peoples (Jos. 9:15; Is. 27:5), so too it could imply a covenant with God.[70] Much like the *pactum* that brought the Romans the *pax deorum*, *šālôm* implied a high level of communion with God, a harmony in God's kingdom[71] dependent both on external ritual (as in Roman and Greek religion) and on the inner disposition of those entering into the covenant.[72]

Yahweh was thus not only the source of peace for the community as a whole, bringing material success, prosperity, safety, and victory, but also the source of peace for those individuals who kept the covenant.[73] Men and women actively cooperated with God in the establishment of his *šālôm* through their own justice and righteousness.[74] Thus, for the first time, the Old Testament concept of peace implied a divine benevolence toward humans[75] that is the summation of all other blessings,[76] a God-given salvation that transcends human success.[77]

## THE PROPHETS

Peace in the above sense was the lesson taught to Israel by the painful history of the divided kingdom—the Assyrian conquest (c. 725 B.C.), the conquest of Jerusalem (586 B.C.), and the Babylonian Captivity (586–538 B.C.)—and reiterated in the prophetic literature.[78] The prophets taught that God's blessing was not granted by material success, the defeat of enemies, or the establishment of a strong and orderly political state, but by the repression of sin.[79] God's covenant with Israel was not with the state but with the people who survived the downfall of the state.[80] This was the central and profound wisdom latent in Jewish teaching from the time of Moses and fully realized by the prophets of the New Covenant.[81] This insight raised the religious consciousness of the Jewish people far higher than that of the Romans or the Greeks.[82]

The interpretation of peace as an inner disposition toward the world characterizes the writings of Isaiah,[83] Jeremiah,[84] and Ezechiel.[85] It is epitomized by Jeremiah's condemnation of the false prophets and their vision of peace as institutional or military strength devoid of justice. "They would repair, as though it were naught, the injury to my people: 'Peace, peace,' they say, though there is no peace" (Jer. 6:14). True peace is salvation, eternal life.[86] For Isaiah, Emmanuel the Messiah is the future "prince of peace," the bringer of salvation, a peace without end (Is. 7:14, 8:23, 9:6; see also Dn. 7:13, 18, 22; Mi. 5:1–4). Peace is the essence of the future messianic kingdom (Is. 54:10; Ez. 34:25, 37:26), a state of material well-being transformed into spiritual salvation.[87]

## ESCHATOLOGICAL PEACE

*Šālôm* thus came to mean the gift the future Messiah would give to those who remained faithful to the covenant until Israel's deliverance from Babylon.[88] It took on an eschatological meaning as the future time of fulfillment without end (Ps. 71:7; Is. 9:6), a time of restoration (Is. 11:1, 29:17–24, 32: 15–20, 61: 4–11; Hos. 2:17–25; Jl. 3:18; Am. 9:13–15), of the renewal of heaven and earth (Is. 65:17–19), of salvation and glory (Is. 62:1–2), of healing (Is. 57:19), of harmony among individuals (Is. 11:9, 54: 13–14, 65:25; Jer. 31:31–34), nations (Is. 2:2–4, 19:23–25; Mi. 4:1–4; Zec. 8:23, 9:9), and even among the wild beasts.[89] Ultimately the prophets taught that peace is the completely free gift of God[90] made possible by his changing the hearts of individuals[91] who themselves fulfill the covenant and share in the future kingdom in this world. These individuals make peace both a goal in seeking salvation and a process by living the life of justice that fulfills the covenant.

## PEACE AND JUSTICE

The promise to those who live according to the covenant and in opposition to wickedness is clear.[92]

Watch the wholehearted man and mark the upright; for there is a future for the man of peace (Ps. 37:37).
Justice will bring about peace; right will produce calm and security (Is. 32:17).
The humble will possess the land and will taste the delights of an unfathomable peace (Ps. 37:11; see Prv. 3:2 and Léon-Dufour, 412–13).

Peace, the sum of all the benefits of the covenant, then, is granted to those who fulfill the covenant by living in justice (Lv. 26:1–13). Peace and justice are thus inextricably bound: cause and effect, journey and goal.

The Jewish rabbinical tradition bridges the gap between the prophets and the New Testament and makes clear the connection between peace and justice. Though the peace promised by the prophets is God's alone to give, strife and discord hold up the coming of the Messiah. *Šālôm* therefore becomes a positive process of ending strife between individuals and between nations. Those who truly seek to keep the covenant must therefore become positive peacemakers.[93] The individual's role in salvation and salvation itself consequently become clear in the Old Testament. Peace is the end and the means.

Originally a term used to designate well-being, *šālôm* rises above similar Greek and Roman conceptions and defines peace as a positive condition and a creative process. Peace is active in the world, inspired by God, and based on love to end conflict and to remake the world according to the justice and goodness promised in the New Covenant. It operates not by force or material prosperity but by the creative power of individuals living the covenant: by peace itself.

The peacemaker becomes the true fulfiller of the covenant and of God's creation: one who seeks God's justice in the world. Peace becomes an active power that realizes the promise of Israel, whose people are God's children. The disciple who brings the wholeness of God is perfect as only *šālôm* means perfect. "The peacemakers are the true Israel and acknowledged by God as his children."[94] So it is that the peacemakers can truly be called the children of God.

## CONCLUSIONS

We have assembled the basic elements of a definition of peace and peacemaking. Peace is an active force in the world based on love of God and of other people. Built on justice, it seeks positive reconciliation between people and between people and God. Far from being a passive principle, peacemaking is an active principle that seeks to liberate all people; yet because it is both the end and the means of salvation it neither imposes order from above nor silences through force or through the institutions of power. It converts the hearts of individuals to work for peace and to convert society from below. An examination of the New Testament will reveal the full implications of this peace.

# CHAPTER 2

# THE CONTEXT AND MESSAGE OF PEACE IN THE NEW TESTAMENT

Before defining what peace in the New Testament means for us, we must first outline what it meant for Jesus and his audience. We must delineate the predominant values of his age and the social and political world that received—or rejected—Jesus' message. Jesus speaks to our age both in faith and in historical appreciation, but he also spoke in his own time and way. We will, therefore, touch briefly on the situation in Palestine and in the Mediterranean world of the Roman Empire in which Christ lived and in which the New Testament was written, and then outline the ethical ideal of the Jewish and Roman worlds that set the context for the Christian message.

## THE PAX ROMANA

We have examined the Roman meaning of *pax* and found it to be essentially an order based on the rule of conquest. The Roman peace did have positive effects, bringing order, the suppression of violence and civil disturbance, unity of rule, prosperity, local autonomy and harmony, and a patronage of cultural and religious life that was the impetus for Roman civilization for three centuries.

Augustus' achievement in ending the Roman Republic's civil war and in uniting the Mediterranean under one ruler (27 B.C. – A.D. 14) set the tone for the concept of the Pax Romana as we understand it today. Velleius Petreculus wrote between 19 B.C. and A.D. 32 that "the *pax augusta,* which has spread to the regions of the east and of the west and to the bounds of the north and of the south, preserves every corner of the world safe from fear of brigandage."[1]

In his *Discourses* Epictetus sounds a theme that was to become a standard motif in the following centuries:

> You see that the emperor appears to provide us with a profound peace, that there are no longer wars, nor battles, nor extensive brigandage, nor piracy, but at any hour we may travel the roads or sail from the rising of the sun to its setting.[2]

Seneca and the Stoics provided emperors with an ideology of rule that rationalized order in the interest of the *pax animi.*[3] In his *De providentia* (IV.14) he asserts that Rome was invested with a mission to impose law and culture on the world.

*15*

Yet there were drawbacks to the order: autocracy and the death of democracy as it had existed in the ancient world, the continuing presence of poverty and ill health, the stagnation of invention and of cultural and spiritual life, and the rigid control and systematic exploitation of the majority in the interests of political stability.[4] All these combined to bring about instability and socioeconomic maladjustment.[5]

Tacitus records the complaints of English rebels who saw the Romans as the brigands of the world, impoverishing their subjects through their lust for power: "Robbery, butchery, rapine the liars call Empire; they create a desolation and call it peace."[6] Their indictment echoes Jeremiah's condemnation of false peace. Zampaglione noted that

> it was implicit in the reasoning [of the Romans] that the nonsubject peoples could not enjoy conditions of peace and tranquility. This feeling was an aspect of the conviction among the Romans that they were the sole artificers of history and were free to ignore completely the reactions of the nations over which their dominion was exercised. None took the trouble to question the subject peoples, of whose views very little is now known, mainly because, even when expressed, nobody thought them worth writing down.[7]

## ROMAN VIRTUE

It would not have occurred to typical Roman aristocrats, the imperialists of the day, to look beyond their own personal deeds and glory, the very definition of virtue for the Roman.[8] While the highest ideal for the Roman, as for the Greek citizen, remained loyalty to the *polis* or city-state, and the classical human being was above all else a political being,[9] political loyalty was expressed in a language of service and preeminence summed up in the term *virtus*:[10] manliness, courage, excellence. *Laus* (praise) and *gloria* (glory) were the fitting recognition of this *virtus* and as such were avidly pursued by the Roman aristocrat,[11] first because they acknowledged a preeminence in service through good deeds, and second because these virtues distinguished the aristocrat from the rest of society.[12] The most natural field of preeminence for the aristocrat in the Greek and Roman periods, as throughout the Middle Ages to the end of the ancien régime, was war.[13] It can be argued that, parallel with concrete economic and political motivations, this aristocratic ethos set the stage for the series of Roman wars and the imperialist expansion that resulted in the Pax Romana.[14] This ethos seems to have extended to all levels of society. Opposition to war from either patrician or plebeian was unheard of until late in the Republican period.[15]

Just as war expressed the nature of Roman excellence so the status of victim expressed the nature of the subject peoples: the inferior, the slave, the barbarian, the outsider. The relationship between the victors and the victims in Greek and Roman society was characterized by "rigid differences between higher and lower levels."[16] The differences derived from the natures and relationships of the gods and extended to every aspect of classical life,[17] from the high and low styles of language,[18] drama, and literature,[19] to noble and common styles in the visual arts,[20] to manners and dress, and to political and personal ideologies. Far more telling than the Greek economic distinction between the *plousioi* (rich) and the *penetes* (poor) was the ontological distinction between master and slave.[21] It denoted a difference of level between lord—citizen and ruler—and victim—the subhuman and the moral inferior.

The distinction is a commonplace in ancient literature. It was formulated by Aristotle in the *Politics*[22] as the basis for the ethos of exploitation. For the Greeks, as for the

Romans, subject peoples were the natural victims of repression. Roman attitudes to slaves in this period, despite widespread manumission and fair treatment,[23] showed contempt for the conquered and equated the enemy and the outsider with the slave and the subhuman.[24] Jews, Syrians, and other Asiatics in particular were looked on as barbarians, "born to slavery."[25]

Nor was the poor citizen looked upon as possessing dignity or moral value.[26] Even the Greek notion of neighbor *(pleision)* denoted not a relationship of affection, but a relationship of position, the physical proximity of one person to another.[27] On a broader level the Roman concept of *societas generis humani,* human society, meant only the bond of citizenship in the city-state, not love of neighbor or equality based on a shared human nature.[28]

But perhaps I have painted too bleak a picture of ancient social relations.[29] Greek and Roman civilization attained some of the highest levels of community and social life in human history. Aristotle's aim in writing the *Politics* was to demonstrate the essentially human quality of society, the moral as well as the economic and political underpinnings of a human community. Later Greek and Roman thought, especially among the Stoics, amplified the idea of the moral nature of society and of the state, and this influenced Christian thought.[30]

Indeed the Stoics, especially Seneca and Epictetus, present a concept of community that transcends mere political considerations to include good relations with the neighbor, and even at times with the outsider and the inferior class. Seneca, in *De Otio* (I.4) and *De Beneficiis* (VII.30.2, 5), recommends an attitude of toleration even in the face of injury, and restraint from anger and revenge. Epictetus, in his *Discourses* (I.25.29; II.13.11), calls upon his readers to rise above hatred in the face of injury and to refrain from revenge. Neither writer shows any of the violence and individual glorification, the will to power and to subjugation that characterized the Pax Romana. Paradoxically the Stoic call to restraint is only the reverse of the coin of *virtus*. For fundamental to Stoic restraint is not a sense of community with the enemy who injures but a sense of the enemy's inferiority and foolishness. Seneca explains that the "great soul" or the "noble man" displays mastery over inferiors.[31] The enemy committing a personal injury is seen to act out of foolishness, out of a mistaken view typical of the uninformed and the inferior.[32] Epictetus agrees that wrongdoing committed against the Stoic is based on ignorance.[33] To seek revenge would be to mingle one's passions improperly with those of one's inferiors. Besides, Epictetus argues, a person's best revenge for injury is the impassivity of the stone, the ability to rise above injury,[34] to retain inner tranquility and so to visibly demonstrate one's natural superiority and one's scorn for inferiors. Thus, for the Stoic, to demonstrate tolerance is to assert one's self-righteousness, and this is an act of moral aggression.[35]

Subtle revenge aside, the Stoic's purpose in demonstrating any forbearance was to cultivate an inner "moral purpose,"[36] an internalized glory that manifested *virtus* no less surely than valor in physical battle. Implicit in this idea is the clear distinction between inner attitude and external behavior—both interdependent certainly, but only because a distinction between the inner soul and the outer body is believed to exist. Inner peace, *pax animi,* aptly parallels the peace of the empire, the Pax Romana. Both are secured through the subjugation of internal discord and the exclusion of the outside world, be it the passions within or the barbarians all around.[37] Stoic personal ethics are therefore nothing more than the ethics of the ancient *polis* toward the outsider written small. Thus for the classical world virtue implied domination in every sense of the word, external subjugation of foes as well as inner domination of passions. This, in brief, was the prevailing social ethic of the Pax Romana at the time of the New Testament. We must now examine Roman relations with the Jews of Palestine before we examine what peace meant for Christ and his disciples.

## GENTILE AND JEW

Rome's relations with the Jews had many of the same features as Roman administration elsewhere in the empire but they were complicated by the nature of Judaism and the special history of Israel. Although Judaism was a *religio licita,* a religion tolerated by the Roman state, the separateness of the Jewish kingdom and its tradition of messianic prophesy proclaiming a revived kingdom made the Romans uneasy. The Romans had, after all, removed the kingdom of the Maccabees and replaced its leaders with their own puppets, the Idumaean dynasty under Herod the Great. Jewish hostility to the Romans was met by Roman prejudice, contempt, and repression.[38] Internally the hatred of the conquered was complicated by the class and political divisions between Sadducees and Pharisees, Zealots and Quietists, hellenized Jews of the diaspora and the Jews of Palestine who maintained their cultural identity.[39] The Greco-Roman *polis* and contempt for the outsider expressed in the social, religious, and political forms of citizenship were met by Israel's own concept of political autonomy expressed by the Covenant.

Within the Covenant, Jewish culture had developed a concept of community that went beyond the political limits of Greco-Roman citizenry. While Greek and Roman society implied an external *virtus* and a formal, political link of citizens, Jewish community was expressed in a view of the "neighbor" that meant a "companion in the Covenant," one united simultaneously in external devotion to the Law and in the internal devotion of the individual heart to God expressed by the term "Israel."[40] This attitude is spelled out clearly in Leviticus: "You shall love your neighbor as yourself: I am the Lord" (Lv 19:18). Indeed, in contrast to the Stoic's external impassivity and inner calm born of contempt for the world, the people of Israel were told: "You shall not bear hatred for your brother in your heart, Though you may have to reprove your fellow man, do not incur sin because of him. Take no grudge against your fellow countryman" (Lv 19:17–18). This law applied not only to Jews but also to sojourners in Israel, that is, the non-Israelites who became members of Israel: "Have the same love for him as for yourself; for you too were once aliens in the land of Egypt" (Lv 19:34). The Jew is to "befriend the alien" (Dt 10:19) living in the land.[41]

For all this the Jews showed love only toward their neighbors and drew a sharp distinction between neighbors and enemies (Ex 23:22, 27). They were to aid their enemies (Ex 23: 4–5), not to exult in their enemies' misfortunes (Prv 24:17), and to feed and give them drink (Prv 25:21), but by so doing they insured God's enmity to these outsiders (Prv 24:18–20). In the very act of aiding them they heaped burning coals on their enemies' heads (Prv 26:22) because by obeying the laws Israel kept the Covenant, and God, who maintained the Covenant, would fulfill his promise and protect his own.

In stark contrast to Stoic and to later Neo-Platonic ideas, which separated spirit from the external world, Jewish tradition saw no distinction between the outer, political and the inner, religious person. An attitude of heart must accompany an external attitude: one implies the other in devotion to the Covenant. External amity can therefore not conceal hatred in one's heart. Inner love must imply an external attitude of love and vice versa. The quietism of the Stoic that can accept inner hate and external calm cannot exist in Jewish life and in Jewish concepts of love and peace.[42] Though the opposite has often been argued,[43] it remained for the New Testament to confound existing Greco-

Roman attitudes and to make explicit the Judaic connection between inner peace and change of heart and the external and active seeking of justice that accompanies it.

## THE MEANING OF PEACE IN THE NEW TESTAMENT

We would do well here to pause and examine the meaning of the word "peace" in the New Testament. We can then go on to recount the message of peace spoken by Christ and the apostles and to see what their words meant to those who heard them.

As we have already seen,[44] *eirene* is the Greek word used in the New Testament for peace. It was derived from the Septuagint Greek translation of *šālŏm*.[45] *Eirene* in the New Testament means far more than it did for the ancient Greeks, but it has essentially the same meaning it did in the Greek Septuagint or as the Hebrew *šālŏm* in the Old Testament and the rabbinical tradition.[46] Its primary meaning is "wholeness";[47] but this "wholeness" took on an incomparable richness. *Eirene* in the New Testament denotes not only the opposite of war,[48] security,[49] order,[50] harmony;[51] a greeting or farewell,[52] health, and healing;[53] but also the restoration and healing inherent in the forgiveness of sins[54] and in fulfillment. In this last sense it also takes on the connotations of messianic salvation,[55] both fulfillment of the world and of individuals and preparation for that salvation that exerts an active influence on the whole world. Thus, while it includes all the prior meanings of peace in the Old Testament, in the New Testament *eirene* also defines salvation in a deeper sense.[56]

The various meanings of *eirene* can be divided into four groups.[57] First, the Acts of the Apostles (9:31) describes the flourishing condition of the church as one of peace. The well-being of the people and the church also takes on the meaning of salvation as expressed by Saint Paul.[58] Second, *eirene* means peace among all: linked with justice in the Holy Spirit,[59] *eirene* is the harmony and justice that brings people together in the kingdom of God.[60] Third, it means the kingdom of God itself. Yet as we saw in our examination of peace in the Old Testament,[61] "kingdom" does not mean the external human power of institutions and states, but the inner disposition of those who keep the Covenant, a community joined by love *(agape)* and grace *(charis)*.[62]

In the New Testament this inner disposition is deepened. Through his suffering and death on the cross, Christ, who is himself peace (Eph 2:14–18), brings about forgiveness of human sins and union with God's grace through a renewal of the Covenant.[63] The fourth meaning given to *eirene* is thus a reconciliation with God[64] that is both a free gift of God and the fruit of that gift (Gal 5:22–25), both union with the grace of God and the effect of that grace: theologians call this justification.[65] By reconciling humanity with God, Christ brings unity, the healing of division, the end of the Old Law, and the creation of the new person (Eph 2:14–22). He replaces the unity and order of the Pax Romana with the new peace of salvation.

Peace is a free gift that heals and overcomes evil.[66] It pervades the whole person,[67] who thus shares in the assurance of inner peace and in the hope of the future eschatological kingdom.[68] In turn, the hope of this heavenly kingdom, the *visio pacis* (vision of peace) described in the Apocalypse (21:2) prompts the pursuit of the kingdom,[69] the new community, here on earth.[70] Peace is both a goal that is fully reached only when the new creation is complete and a sign of the new creation already begun.[71] It is the end and the means.

As both an inner disposition of reconciliation (Rom 15:13) and an external participation in the new community, peace in the New Testament becomes more than a mystic rapture or a Stoic withdrawal to cold indifference.[72] It is the external commitment of those saved by the free gift of the Spirit. So Luke's recounting of the angels' message at the Nativity—"Peace to men of good will" (Lk 2:14)—is not a lame wish but an announcement of fact,[73] a call to salvation and an external sign of it. Peace brings the commitment and the path to the kingdom of God that shines forth in the Christian's relations with others.[74] "The fruit of justice is sown by those who make peace" (Jas 3:18).[75]

Peace extends to all persons of good will who pursue peace.[76] Christ's peace is a pure gift to those who accept it. With the gift comes the obligation to be committed to spreading peace. Jesus says to his disciples, "My peace I leave you; my peace I give unto you" (Jn 14:27).[77] Peace is then both a gift and an obligation to retain Christ's gift by constantly seeking it.[78] This is what the theologians mean by salvation as both the gift of justification and its product, as both the future community to be sought and its present reality among men and women. In this peace the Christian finds not the "peace and quiet" or "law and order" that the Pax Romana offers the world,[79] not the buying and selling of daily life (Lk 17:26–36), but a break with accepted norms of security (Lk 12:51), an inversion of earthly values,[80] and active conflict with evil.[81]

The concrete manifestation of this new community is the unity of its members in the Mystical Body.[82] Saint Paul explains this theological and political idea when he writes: "For as in one body we have many members, and all the members do not have the same function, so we, though many, are one body in Christ, and individually members one of another" (Rom 12:4–5). Just as a body has a head and various parts, so in the Mystical Body Christ is the head and Christians are the body bound not by force but by love. Thus Christians live "forbearing one another in love, eager to maintain the unity of the Spirit in the bond of peace. There is one body and one Spirit . . . one Lord, one faith, one baptism, one God and Father of us all, who is above all and through all and in all" (Eph 4:2–6 [RSV]). In this unity of the Mystical Body a new world order is created. "As many of you as were baptized into Christ have put on Christ. There is neither Jew nor Greek, there is neither slave nor free, there is neither male nor female; for you are all one in Christ Jesus" (Gal 3:27–28). Paul explicitly emphasizes the political nature of this new community. "Here there is not 'Gentile and Jew,' 'circumcised and uncircumcised,' 'Barbarian and Scythian,' 'slave and freeman,' but Christ is all things in all" (Col 3:11). Christ's peace and unity thus stands in stark contrast to the peace and unity of Rome and clearly challenges it.

## THE NEW TESTAMENT MESSAGE OF PEACE

I have presented the historical context and have discussed the meaning of peace in the New Testament. To understand the New Testament basis of peacemaking we must now examine the concrete message of peace spoken by Christ and made manifest in his life. As Jean Lassere has noted,[83] Christ and the apostles lived in a world no less cruel, one founded no less on pursuit of power and position than our own. Their message was spoken not in a vacuum but in the context of values and power relations. Their words were aimed at concrete problems and concrete solutions, and they were meant to save not only the soul but also the world.

Yet we must be careful in discussing Christ's words. Biblical texts, perhaps more than others, are prone to unintentional misinterpretation and to deliberate exploitation in the service of various causes and programs. They can be quoted out of context to justify the most extreme positions; the same words have supported both pacifism and wars of aggression. Scholars who have devoted an entire lifetime of study to biblical texts still hesitate to interpret isolated texts on their merits alone. Biblical critics and scholars agree that if specific passages are obscure, doubtful, corrupt, or open to divergent interpretations, determining the *context,* the overall meaning of the work, is the only valid means of beginning to understand them. Let us therefore look at the message of the New Testament as a whole before examining specific passages in it.

The New Testament is first and foremost the "gospel of peace."[84] God is the God of peace,[85] and love itself (1 Jn 4:7–21). Christ is the peaceful king,[86] the way to peace,[87] and peace itself (Eph 2:14). The cumulative message of the New Testament is a message of peace,[88] of the reconciliation of humanity, with God and with itself, of forgiveness, and of love. Christ makes it clear that his kingdom is not of this world,[89] that his weapons are spiritual and not physical.[90] His life and death are the fulfillment of the prophesies of the Son of Man,[91] of the suffering servant,[92] of Emmanuel,[93] the Prince of Peace.[94] He comes not to bring destruction but to save lives.[95] He heals,[96] teaches,[97] forgives,[98] nourishes,[99] and restores life.[100] His final entry into Jerusalem[101] is not like the entry of a conqueror, a Pompey; it is humble and peacemaking in fulfillment of the prophecy of the Messiah.[102] His death was a free gift producing not destruction but life.[103] New Testament style and language is a fitting vehicle for this message; in stark contrast to classical heroic style, it is humble, speaking of common people and everyday events and demonstrating their essential nobility.[104]

Never in the gospels is there any evidence that Christ or the disciples ever fought their enemies, despite the classical texts that are marshalled to assert the contrary. Until the time came to manifest his kingship Christ counseled and resorted to escape[105] or to some form of concealment.[106] He was adamant in his message that violence was never to be used.[107] The apostles and disciples followed his model and avoided violence by flight[108] or nonresistance.[109] Their response implies neither cowardice nor passive quietism. Christ's purpose was clear. When the time was right to announce the truth about the way things are he offered himself to the violence of his enemies (Mt 26:47–50) as a confutation of violence (Lk 23:33–34) as did the apostles later.[110] After his resurrection his first words to the asembled apostles were "Peace be unto you" (Lk 24:36). Only once in the gospels is violence explicitly considered: in the controversial passages involving Christ's command to his apostles to buy swords at the time of his arrest in the garden of Gethsemane.[111] The arms used in the New Testament struggle are not physical (2 Cor 10:3–4); they are light (Rom 13:12) and justice (2 Cor 6:7), the fruits of the Spirit, which are essential to peacemaking.[112]

What then of the specific texts that embody the Christian life of peacemaking? The entire message of the New Testament can be summed up in the Beatitudes[113] and in the New Law (Mt 5:38–48) preached by Christ in the Sermon on the Mount in Matthew and the Sermon of the Plain in Luke.[114] Both contain essentially the same message although the Sermon of the Plain is more particular and concrete.[115] These passages convey the essence of Christian peacemaking from which all other texts and interpretations, indeed all Christian lives and works of peace, have come.

These two texts have been the object of two thousand years of criticism and interpretation. To unravel all that is neither my purpose nor my province. I will, however, summarize certain general principles that are commonly taken as the basis of Christian peacemaking.[116] First, these texts are plainly addressed to Christ's followers as commands to imitate and not as exaggeration for the sake of exaggeration, advice for excellence meant only for particular individuals, or counsels to perfection aimed at a select few. Second, Christ directly and openly contradicts the law of the Old Testament, condemns the ethos of the Gentiles—the Greco-Roman world—and replaces both with a new law. Third, the new law is not a temporary ethic, an ad hoc solution, or an intermediate guide, but a sign of membership in the present and future kingdom of God. As such Christ's message is not simply personal and internal in its implications but social and political. Finally, its means and its essence are love: of neighbor, of God for all, and of Christ as shown through his life and suffering.

Having stated these principles in the abstract, I will now examine the texts more closely for their meaning. In the Beatitudes Christ defines the nature of the new people of God and the reward that awaits them. The text bears quoting in full:

> Blessed are the poor in spirit, for theirs is the kingdom of heaven.
> Blessed are those who mourn, for they shall be comforted.
> Blessed are the meek, for they shall inherit the earth.
> Blessed are those who hunger and thirst for righteousness, for they shall be satisfied.
> Blessed are the merciful, for they shall obtain mercy.
> Blessed are the pure in heart, for they shall see God.
> Blessed are the peacemakers, for they shall be called sons of God.
> Blessed are those who are persecuted for righteousness' sake, for theirs is the kingdom of heaven.
> Blessed are you when men revile you and persecute you and utter all kinds of evil against you falsely on my account. Rejoice and be glad, for your reward is great in heaven, for so men persecuted the prophets who were before you [Mt 5:3–12 (RSV)].

The meek, those who mourn, those who hunger and thirst for justice, the merciful, the peacemakers, those who suffer persecution, in short, the lowly, the powerless, all those considered outcasts in the ancient *polis*: these are the people of the new kingdom. Luke (6:20–22) makes the connection even clearer: the poor, the hungry, those who weep, the hated, and the excluded are members of the kingdom.

> But woe to you that are rich! for you have received your consolation.
> Woe to you that are full now, for you shall hunger.
> Woe to you that laugh now, for you shall mourn and weep.
> Woe to you when all men speak well of you [Lk 6:24–26 (RSV)].

But what is the connection between the Beatitudes and the work of peace? While the outcasts of the present order who are praised here clearly are not the rich and the dominant in the world, there seems nothing inherently peacelike in their mourning or their meekness that would warrant our reading this as a peace text. In fact, one could argue that the inclusion of the peacemaker among the humble and the suffering seems to emphasize the passive aspect of peace.

*Eirenopoios,* peacemaker, is used only once in the New Testament, in Matthew 5:9.[117] The New Testament uses a second term for peace that will help clarify the function of the peacemaker in the Beatitudes: *epiekeia.* Originally used to denote the opposite of *hubris,* the pride of those who rigorously insist on their rights, *epiekeia* meant in the Septuagint (Dn 4:24, 27) the virtue of moderation, of reasonableness, and of equity, the attribute of the judge or of someone else in authority.[118] Although in the Old Testament the word could mean God's mercy (Bar 2:27; Dn 3:42 JB), in the New Testament it contained the nuance of the meekness *(prautetos)* and gentleness *(epiekeia)* of Christ[119] found also in those who imitate him.[120] The term was not used to imply weakness, as Lasserre would read "non-violence,"[121] but forbearance: the ability to transcend one's rights in selflessness (as in 1 Cor 6:1–11).

"Meekness" here implies a humility in terms of a basic trust in other people, not a tameness, but a refusal to despair. It also implies an avoidance of a self-righteousness that is the moral equivalent of aggression. Thomas Merton pinpointed this essentially hostile attitude of the self-righteous who flaunt their moral superiority.[122] He called it a form of psychic aggression, just as violent as physical force. Gandhi also recognized it as the opposite of *satyagraha*. Piper notes that on textual grounds

> nowhere does the [gospel] tradition suggest that the imitation of God or Christ could be a justification of abusing or injuring someone. While the early Church knew God as judge of his enemies, it was precisely this divine prerogative of which imitation was explicitly forbidden [see Rom 12:19].[123]

But while Christians thus imitate only the gentleness of Christ the judge and his forbearance in exercising power,[124] they also share in the splendor of Christ the glorified judge.[125] Thus the connection between peace and meekness toward the world made in the New Testament not only closely identifies the sufferer in the Beatitudes with Christ as sufferer but also equates Christ's glory with the Christian's future glory.

This message would not have comforted the Roman Stoic. While Christ's value system is clearly not of this world; it was actively opposed to the prevailing values of Greece and Rome. He makes this clear in his admonition to the apostles to avoid making self-righteous judgments:

> "You know that those who are regarded as rulers among the Gentiles lord it over them, and their great men exercise authority over them. But it is not so among you. On the contrary, whoever wishes to become great shall be your servant, and whoever wishes to be first among you shall be the slave of all; for the Son of Man also has not come to be served but to serve, and to give his life as a ransom for many" [Mk 10:42–45].[126]

Being the outcast in Roman society has meaning and great value: it distinguishes the new people. Christ tells his new people to "rejoice and exult, because your reward is great in heaven, for so did they persecute the prophets who were before you" (Mt 5:12). If reward awaits those who live up to the Beatitudes, surely the Beatitudes are the basis of salvation. As such they cannot be optional choices but are the necessary precondition for the new community to exist.[127]

## THE POLITICS OF THE GOSPELS

Although Jesus may have been actively contrasting the new people and the virtues of the kingdom of God with those of his own world, did he thereby mean to give these an explicit political content? To answer this we must first examine his New Law, the constitution of the new kingdom. Jesus outlines it in the Sermon on the Mount.

> "You have heard that it was said, 'An eye for an eye and a tooth for a tooth.' But I say to you, Do not resist one who is evil. But if any one strikes you on the right cheek, turn to him the other also; and if any one would sue you and take

your coat, let him have your cloak as well; and if any one forces you to go one mile, go with him two miles. Give to him who begs from you, and do not refuse him who would borrow from you.

"You have heard that it was said, 'You shall love your neighbor and shalt hate your enemy.' But I say to you, Love your enemies and pray for those who persecute you, so that you may be sons of your Father who is in heaven; for he makes his sun rise on the evil and on the good, and sends rain on the just and on the unjust. For if you love those who love you, what reward have you? Do not even the tax collectors do the same? And if you salute only your brethren, what more are you doing than others? Do not even the Gentiles do the same? You, therefore, must be perfect, as your heavenly Father is perfect" [Mt 5:38–48 (RSV)].

Immediately clear is Christ's rejection of the Old Testament ethic of revenge, the *lex talionis,* the law of retaliation—"An eye for an eye," and "a tooth for a tooth" (Ex 21:24)—and its replacement with a new code: "do not resist the evildoer"(Mt 5:39).

Far from taking revenge, the true Christian will seek to aid the enemy. In addition, tyrannical domination is to be met without violence. Being sued (the symbol of the Roman system) and being forced to go two miles (the duty of forced labor imposed by the Romans) are not to be resisted (see Mt 5:40–41).

Jesus does not even stop here. Neither his morality nor the response of the Christian is to be passive, nonresistant. This is not the indifference of the Stoic. "You have heard that it was said, 'Thou shalt love thy neighbor, and shalt hate thy enemy.' But I say to you, love your enemies, do good to those who hate you" (Mt 5:43–44). The Torah (the Law) and the Prophets, that is, the Old Testament, had established love as the bond between neighbors in the Covenant, and this principle was enshrined in the Golden Rule: "Therefore all that you wish men to do to you, even so do you also to them; for this is the Law and the Prophets" (Mt 7:12).[128] But here Christ establishes a New Law; he builds upon the old in a moral progression. Not only is one not to resist one's enemies, but one is to love them.[129] This love applies not only to one's personal enemies but to public enemies and potential foes in battle. *Ecthros,* the Greek word for enemy, is used in the New Testament for both.[130]

Peace then is not acquiescent or passive; it is not restricted.[131] It is an active force in the world. Christ's appeal to love recognizes the humanity even of the enemy, the oppressor, and teaches the fellowship of all people as brothers and sisters. "Love your enemies, do good to those who hate you, and pray for those who persecute and calumniate you" (Mt 5:44). The humanity of the evildoer is plain; God does not exclude them; he "makes his sun rise on the good and the evil, and sends rain on the just and the unjust" (Mt 5:45).[132] His ethic is starkly and explicitly a rejection of both pagan and Jewish ethics.

We have noted above that the Torah commands that one aid one's enemy. Textual criticism shows, however, that nowhere before in the Old Testament, in popular wisdom, or in the scribal and rabbinical traditions, is this new element of loving one's enemy found.[133] Anyone can love a neighbor, one bound in community: do not even the publicans (Rome's Jewish tax collectors) and the Gentiles do that?[134]

Love of one's enemy thus clearly distinguishes the members of the new kingdom and sets the new law apart from the old.[135] "You therefore are to be perfect, even as your heavenly father is perfect" (Mt 5:48). The message is not a conditional counsel to perfection: "If you want to be perfect," or "To be even better, do this," but a statement of fact: those who follow Christ will be perfect in the new kingdom that is to come; and those who seek the kingdom are to live the new law, so that they may be children of their Father in heaven.[136] If this is the essence of salvation it cannot, then, be taken as a mere recommendation. Christ has offered the goal; he has also provided the means.[137] The external love and forgiveness of enemies (Mt 18:21–22; Mk 11:25) becomes a sign, not of inner remoteness such as the Stoics preached, but of a complete change of heart, a conversion of individuals to love that gradually inaugurates[138] the kingdom as Jeremiah[139] and Ezechiel[140] said it would. John the Baptist made this connection clear when he cried: "Repent, for the kingdom of heaven is at hand" (Mt 3:2).[141] *Metanoeite,* repent, literally means to change one's mind or purpose;[142] thus inner conversion of individuals is the change that signals that the outer kingdom has arrived.

But can we say that this outer kingdom has any real and direct political significance? It is, after all, the result of inner change and spiritual commitment, not of political action per se. To answer this question it would help to sum up some of what we have said above about the context of the New Testament.

Jesus lived in a definite cultural and political setting summed up in the word "Israel." Like Western societies up until the Industrial Revolution and like many Third World societies today, Israel was at the same time a religious, a cultural, and a political entity that knew no modern division between church and state. Although the Jewish concept of kingdom underwent an internalization during the time of the Prophets, it never lost its external identity. The Covenant was the sign of both an internal devotion to God and an external devotion and concrete community of those who kept it. While living under the domination of various foreign powers—the Gentiles—Israel retained its laws, its religion, and its definite national aspirations for *šālôm* to be brought by the Messiah in the time of fulfillment.

Israel's exclusiveness—its distinction from the Gentiles as God's chosen people—and the promise of messianic salvation continued to dominate Israel's political and religious thinking into the time of Christ. Israel at that time was full of expectation and speculation as to the time of the Messiah's arrival and the nature of his political victory over Israel's foes. No one doubted that the Messiah would overthrow foreign domination, and that this overthrow would be more than an internal, personal change. The spirit of rebellion that this expectation produced was everywhere.

Jesus himself fully shared this outlook. That he conceived of himself as the Messiah, savior not only of the souls of believers but of the kingdom of Israel, is beyond doubt. His outlook shows itself in his fulfillment of the prophecies, in his powers to heal and restore, in his words about himself. As leader of Israel he constantly contrasts the behavior of the new people with that of the Gentiles, rejecting Gentile domination and actively seeking to overthrow Gentile rule. The clear-cut distinction of his words "Render to Caesar the things that are Caesar's and to God the things that are God's" (Mt 22:21; see Appendix, p. 28). is not a twentieth-century separation of church and state. That distinction would not have occurred to anyone at the time. The statement is more than a clever retort to the Pharisees' attempts to compromise Jesus. It is a statement of Christ's own conception of his messianic mission and is therefore a call to others to choose between the domination of the Gentile and the life of Israel.

Christ's resistance of Satan's temptations shows that his means of achieving liberation were fully in keeping with that end.[143] He rejected outright the use of physical force to fulfill his messianic role. Returning from the desert, Jesus entered the synagogue in Nazareth and announced his mission:

> "The Spirit of the Lord is upon me, because he has anointed me to preach
> good news to the poor.

He has sent me to proclaim release to the captives and recovering of sight
to the blind,
to set at liberty those who are oppressed,
to proclaim the acceptable year of the Lord'' [Lk 4:18–19 (RSV)].

The consequences of Jesus' choice to reject physical force were immediately apparent. He was abandoned first by his large following and finally by his closest associates. Jesus saw his repudiation of physical force lead inevitably to his passion and humiliating death on the cross. His refusal to inflict suffering and to take revenge made it certain that he would endure both. Nevertheless he accepted this outcome in order to bring salvation and to present a model to his followers. By not repaying hate with hate one overcomes hate and liberates the people and the kingdom from the oppressor.

## PEACEMAKING IN PAUL'S WRITINGS

Saint Paul makes the politics of the gospels even more explicit. Although his letters appear after the gospels in our Bibles, they were actually written before the other parts of the New Testament, about twenty years after Christ's life. They truly reflect the spirit of the gospels and the primitive church.[144] In the Epistle to the Romans[145] Paul lays out the principles of active peacemaking:

Let love be genuine; hate what is evil, hold fast to what is good; be patient in tribulation, be constant in prayer. Contribute to the needs of the saints, practice hospitality.

Bless those who persecute you; bless and do not curse them. . . . Repay no one evil for evil, but take thought for what is noble in the sight of all.

If possible, so far as it depends upon you, live peaceably with all. Beloved, never avenge yourselves, but leave it to the wrath of God; for it is written, "Vengeance is mine. I will repay, says the Lord." No, "if your enemy is hungry, feed him; if he is thirsty, give him drink; for by so doing you will heap fuming coals upon his head." Do not be overcome by evil, but overcome evil with good (Rom. 12:9, 12–14, 17–21 [RSV] ).

Paul's message is plain and realistic. Unlike the Platonic or Stoic traditions, which held that evil is mere error and should be ignored, Paul affirms that evil does exist. Love is not to be self-deceptive or flattering to evil; one can neither ignore one's hatreds and act out of feigned love nor pretend friendliness to the evildoer. Evil makes enemies, and Christians must abhor it. But they must love the people who commit evil and "live peaceably with all" (Rom 12:18). Paul's words, "bless . . . and do not curse," echo Christ's.[146] Do not seek vengeance—that is God's prerogative—but provide for the enemy's well-being. Do not meet evil with evil, but do not let evil win. Do not be overcome but "overcome evil with good."[147] Peace is an active force. Though it is "patient in tribulation" (Rom 12:12), it does not abdicate to evil.[148] It recognizes evil, and far more importantly, it seeks to overcome it,[149] not with evil means, by violence, deceit, or lies, "evil for evil" (Rom 12:17),[150] but with good.

Paul's remarks on nonviolence in his Letter to the Romans introduce his well-known appeal for obedience to higher authorities (Rom 13:1–7). The two passages do not spell out a twentieth-century distinction between personal and public morality; rather they share a single theme. Paul's juxtaposition is deliberate. Far from recommending acquiescence to political power, Paul here lays out the framework for obedience to legitimate authority. Two extremes are to be avoided. One the one hand, armed resistance will end only in terror and condemnation; but on the other, when domination is evil, one is not to be overcome by evil, but is to overcome that evil with good. The method, explained in Romans 12:17–21, is to imitate Christ through the new law of love established by him.

The means are once again identified with the end. The peacemaker attains the kingdom of God by sharing in it: by doing good in imitation of Christ. The weapons are not physical but moral and spiritual.[151] Peacemaking confronts the world and sets it in an uproar (Acts 17:6–7) by contradicting its cherished ethics.[152] The life of the gospel is thus one of "perpetual tension, a continual strife."[153]

## CONCLUSIONS

How can suffering personal injury, not overcoming evil with its own weapons, and not eliminating evil by eliminating evildoers be effective or have any true merit? Although suffering educates the Stoic and helps the Christian avoid doing harm, by itself it seems senseless. Indeed, taken on its own terms, it is. But suffering for the Christian, as for Christ, has not only a personal but also a public, a social, and a political context.[154] Christ himself, after all, chose to flee or to hide from danger until his time had come, that is, until his suffering and death could receive public recognition and meaning in fulfillment of his messianic role.[155]

By adopting and sharing Christ's suffering, Christian peacemakers fully imitate Christ. In their perfect imitation they approach the true meaning of *šālôm,* that is, perfection. Peacemakers share in God's perfect ethical personality and are perfect as the Father is perfect.[156] "These God calls his children because they are like him."[157]

The emphasis in the New Testament, then, falls not on the suffering but on the love and the witness to the truth that motivates it.[158] Christians recognize evil but are not so preoccupied with it that it can drag them into its vortex. The pursuit of the good redirects the life of the Christian and converts life from reaction, bitterness, and frustration over the effects of evil. It rechannels energies and hopes to the creation of good. In seeking to live the kingdom of God one thus overcomes, transforms, and liberates the human kingdom, first from its hold on the heart, and then from its grasp on the world outside. The life of the early church and its imitation of Christ set these principles into action.

# APPENDIX

Although the New Testament basis of peacemaking appears to be beyond question, throughout Christian history many have attempted to interpret the words of Christ, the evangelists, and Paul in another way. Peter Brock has analyzed the basic nonpacifist responses and classified them into groups that believe: first, the Beatitudes and the New Law to love one's enemies is a temporary ethic spoken in expectation of the final days; second, the Beatitudes and the New Law are merely counsels to perfection, and those who would be perfect, for example the clergy, are clearly distinguished from the normal run of Christian (a view popular in the Catholic tradition); third, the message of the Beatitudes and the New Law is personal and individual, directed to specific persons literally and the inner person generally (a view voiced by Luther and revived in our own day by Niebuhr); fourth, even though we love our enemies we can still kill them, provided the cause is just (the view of Augustine, which underlies the just-war tradition).

Critics argue that much of the imagery in the New Testament is violent or contains references to the military (Zampaglione, 213–15). Further, many key texts can be seen as supporting both personal and institutional violence in the defense and the pursuit of justice.

Peter Brock's work addresses each of the four groups named above. Zampaglione (213–17) analyzes the imagery of violence in the New Testament and finds that in all cases it is used either allegorically or in parable form. Lasserre notes (57) that violence in the parables is always extraneous to the main point of the story. Zampaglione argues that it is difficult to justify even the so-called just, defensive war if one takes seriously the message of the Sermon on the Mount, which is the heart of the gospel. MacGregor discusses the major theological objections to pacifism, often in the context of debates that are now passé. McSorley (4–21) highlights five principles that summarize the New Testament's message. He argues against both individual texts and broad generalizations used to support killing or war. MacGregor (16–28) also deals with specific texts.

Lasserre (31–35) analyzes at some length the distinction between the two orders based on the counsels to perfection and relies on the scriptural evidence of the doctrine of the Mystical Body to refute it. Both Lasserre (25–31) and McSorley (7–8) address the notion of violence done in the spirit of love and both reject it on scriptural grounds. Lasserre (180–96) and McSorley (3, 10) examine the distinction between the indiscriminate violence of war and the legitimate function of the police who seek to contain violence and uphold the law. They establish criteria to use in distinguishing the two. Lasserre (79–127, 128–44) and MacGregor (79–105), writing from the Protestant tradition, take pains to examine the role of the state and its legitimate use of force.

It is not our purpose here to examine in detail the specific texts in the New Testament used to support militarism. We can, however, briefly survey them by book and refer the reader to various peace analyses.

1. Matthew 8:5–13 (Luke 7:1–10, John 4:46–53). This is the story of the centurion at Capharnaum who asks Jesus to heal his servant saying "only say the word, and my servant will be healed." Christ marvels and praises the soldier's faith. The passage is sometimes interpreted as Christ's praising the military profession (see MacGregor, 18–20; McSorley, 28–29; Lasserre, 53–55; Cadoux, *Attitude*, 32–34). Christ is clearly praising the faith of the Gentile, not his profession. McSorley asks whether Christ's praising Mary Magdalene's faith was also an endorsement of prostitution. (See Luke 3:14 for John the Baptist's advice to soldiers, to which similar analysis applies.)

2. Matthew 10:34. Christ foretells opposition to his mission and warns, "Do not think that I have come to bring peace on earth; I have not come to bring peace, but a sword." The text is taken by militarists as a Christian call to war (see MacGregor, 20–22; McSorley, 27; Ferguson, *Politics*, 30; Lasserre, 43; Cadoux, *Attitude*, 38–39). The passage must be related to the following text, Mt 10:35–42. The word "sword" used here means "division" elsewhere in the New Testament. Christ's New Law is to bring division within families, communities, and nations, as indeed it has done.

3. Matthew 21:12–13. See John 2:13–17 (no. 16 below).

4. Matthew 22:7 (Luke 19:27, 20:16). The parable of the king destroying his enemies (see Lasserre, 17, 57). The point of these parables is not the action of the characters, but the specific moral. Otherwise Christ would approve of unjust judges, misers, and so on.

5. Matthew 22:15–22 (Mark 12:13–17). Is it lawful to render tribute to Caesar? Christ's answer is: "Render therefore to Caesar the things that are Caesar's, and to God the things that are God's." The text is taken by militarists and by many mainline Protestants to imply the duty of obedience to the state during wartime (see McSorley, 35–38; MacGregor, 79–94; Ferguson, *Politics*, 34–35; Lasserre, 86–97; Cadoux, *Attitude*, 40–42). Christ was not here advocating the separation of church and state. On one level he was escaping a trap set by his enemies that would force him to choose between treason and collaboration. On another level he was delineating the New Law from that of the Gentiles. The confrontation lies at the heart of Christ's claims to be the Messiah and king. McSorley (38) quotes Dorothy Day who notes: "If we give God what is God's, there is nothing left for Caesar." On the historical context see Grant, "Taxation and Exemption," in *Early Christianity and Society*, 46–47; and Sherwin-White, *Roman Society*, 126–27.

6. Matthew 26:52. Jesus is arrested in Gethsemane. Peter cut off the ear of the high priest's servant. Jesus tells him, "Put back thy sword into its place; for all those who take the sword will perish by the sword." Militarists quote only the second half of this text in support of defensive

war (see MacGregor, 25; McSorley, 26; Lasserre, 37–42). In verse 53 Jesus clearly rejects recourse to armed force. The only violence here is that done to the text in clear ignorance of the central point. Christ is rejecting the use of force.

7. Mark 12:13–17. See Matthew 22:15–22 above (no. 5).

8. Mark 13:7–13. The prophecy of the destruction of Jerusalem and the end of the world. "And when you hear of wars and rumors of wars, do not be alarmed; this must take place" (see Ferguson, *Politics,* 40–41; Cadoux, *Attitude,* 35–38). Prophecy does not imply approval. The emphasis in the text appears in verses 9–13; it is not on war, but on the suffering of Christians.

9. Luke 7:1–10. See Matthew 8:5–13 above (no. 1).

10. Luke 11:21–22. "When the strong man, fully armed, guards his courtyard, his property is undisturbed." The text is used as justification for the defense of one's person and property and for the existence of the military establishment (see MacGregor, 25; Ferguson, *Politics,* 38–39; Lasserre, 55–56; McSorley, 30). The rest of the passage reads: "But if a stronger than he attacks and overwhelms him, he will take away all his weapons that he relied upon, and will divide his spoils." The strong man here is Satan, who possesses men and women. Christ is the stronger one.

11. Luke 14:31–32. A king prepares for battle (see MacGregor, 26; Lasserre, 57). The point of the parable is the prudence of those who renounce the ways of the world to become Christ's disciples. For Christ's other allusions to war see Cadoux. *Attitude,* 38–40.

12. Luke 19:27. See Mathew 22:7 (no. 4 above).

13. Luke 19:45–48. See John 2:13–17 (no. 16 below).

14. Luke 20:16. See Mt. 22:7 (no. 4 above).

15. Luke 22:36–38. Christ's predictions of future tribulations for his followers.

> "But now, let him who has a purse take it, and likewise a bag. And let him who has no sword sell his mantle and buy one. For I tell you that this scripture must be fulfilled in me. 'And he was reckoned with transgressors'; for what is written about me has its fulfillment." And they said, "Look Lord, here are two swords." And he said to them, "It's enough" (RSV).

This difficult text is used as a call to use violence to protect the church in the days ahead (see MacGregor, 22–24; McSorley, 34; Ferguson, *Politics,* 31; Lasserre, 37–44). Literal interpretation causes difficulties. Was Christ confused just before his arrest in Gethsemane, where he commanded Peter to lay up his sword? Was he play-acting to fulfill the prophecies? Why are two swords enough for twelve apostles? Christ's words must be taken figuratively, but the apostles misunderstand his predictions of future troubles couched in concrete terms. Christ realizes their misunderstanding and commands "Enough."

16. John 2:13–17 (Mt 21:12–13; Lk 19:45–48). Christ cleanses the Temple and makes "a kind of whip of cords" to drive out the moneychangers and the animals. The text is used in support of war by the righteous (see MacGregor, 17–18; McSorley, 24; Ferguson, *Politics,* 28–30; Lasserre, 46–48; Cadoux, *Attitude,* 34–35). Though Jesus is clearly angry, there is no evidence of violence done to people or, according to Matthew and Luke, even of a whip. John's gospel is generally regarded as the least literal. Even if literally true, Christ's action does not show the force of war; rather the scourge is used to show his messianic role.

17. John 4:46–53. See Matthew 8:5–13 above (no. 1).

18. John 15:13. "Greater love than this no one has, that one lay down his life for his friends." Commonly used as a prayer over those killed in war to compare the soldier's sacrifice to Christ's (see MacGregor, 27–28; McSorley, 30–32; Ferguson, *Politics,* 36). The text itself is extracted from a call to love. The purpose of the soldier in war is not to lay down his life, but to make the enemy lay down his. McSorley (32) comments, "It is near blasphemy to appeal to the cross as the motive for war."

19. 1 Corinthians 9:7; Ephesians 6:10–17; 2 Timothy 2:4. The "soldiers of Christ" (see MacGregor, 26–27: Lasserre, 56; Ferguson, *Politics,* 41; Zampaglione, 213–15). The spiritual context and figurative sense of these texts is obvious; they were so understood by the early church. See chapter 3 below.

20. Romans 13:1–7. The text begins: "Let everyone be subject to higher authorities" (cf. 1 Pt 2:13–17). The state has a right to require its citizens to kill in war (see Ferguson, *Politics,* 11; MacGregor, 83–87; Lasserre, 165–218). Police power is the legitimate realm of civil government, if it is just. This is the point of the passage. But civil law does not annul the Christian's duty to "obey God rather than men" (Acts 5:29). (See chapter 3.)

21. Revelation 12:7–9. Michael overcomes the dragon: "And there was a battle in heaven." The text is used by militarists as the basis of crusades against the forces of evil in the world (see Ferguson, *Politics*, 43–44). The context is clear. The war is in heaven and is a spiritual one waged against a spiritual enemy. God does not use human beings but angels as fighters.

CHAPTER 3

# PEACEMAKING IN THE EARLY CHURCH: FROM PAUL TO CONSTANTINE (33–300)

## THE HISTORICAL PROBLEM

The study of the peace tradition in the early church derives from a common and wide range of sources, but it is marked by radically differing concerns and approaches on the part of both Catholics and Protestants. Many Catholic historians try to read a Christian loyalty to the Constantinian state into all the church's dealings with the Roman Empire, and simultaneously find nonpacifist causes for early Christian opposition to war and militarism.[1] The Protestant pacifist tradition seeks assurance in the view that only in a small, elite form of Christianity does the truth abide. They must attempt to prove that the early church was a sect, a group unified in outlook, in purpose, in the personalities of its members, and in their clear understanding of the gospel message.[2] They maintain that the purity of the message and the sectarian nature of the church were lost, tragically and almost irrevocably, when Christianity was accepted by the Roman Empire under Constantine.

A third tradition, which includes mainline Protestant scholarship, follows the Lutheran lead in distinguishing between the private morality and spirituality of the individual Christian and the very different, often immoral, norms of society and the state.[3] This distinction results in an emphasis on the quietist and otherworldly message of early Christianity, the precedence supposedly given by the Fathers to the "things that are Caesar's" and their "joyous irresponsibility" and "certain quietistic indifference" to social and political concerns, including war and peace.[4] Like the sectarian school, the mainline Protestant tradition sees the Catholic Middle Ages as a time of decline following the reign of Constantine. True understanding of any aspect of the gospel message thus became possible only with the Protestant reformers of the sixteenth century.[5] Historical interpretations seem by and large to reflect a particular writer's disposition to pacifism, to the avowal of just wars, or to outright Christian alliance with the aims of the state.[6]

The issue of Christian peacemaking in the early church has unfortunately been dominated by too narrow definitions, generally revolving around the anachronistic ideas of "conscientious objection" and "pacifism."[7] Although neither term is ever adequately defined, one can assume that the negative connotations of both terms in recent times dominate the thought of the scholars who use them. "Conscientious objection"[8] often implies the legalistic, rigid, selfish, and arrogant aloofness assumed by the self-righteous "pacifist."[9] The "pacifist" is the individualist who dismisses social responsibility and leads a passive life of nonresistance, too concerned with his or her own salvation or private morality to care about community or political issues. These negative connotations have put the study of early Christian peacemaking in a negative light and have imposed on the historian of whatever outlook the impossible task of attempting to prove or disprove a negative thesis. The debate over the question "Was there a selfish individualist refusal to participate in social responsibilities by the early Christians?" is bound to be fruitless.

I will, therefore, attempt to redefine the problem by posing a different set of questions more conducive to inquiry, discussion, and proof. Did the Christians of the church from the time of the apostles to the time of Constantine understand Christ's message of peacemaking? In what context did they understand it? What methods did they formulate in order to live it? What was the intellectual tradition behind their formulation? How was it expressed in their lives and actions?

## THE BACKGROUND

We have already discussed the nature of the Pax Romana and the social ethos that supported it. The real benefits of this peace brought by the Roman Empire were apparent in the early church. Through the reigns of the Julian-Claudian, Flavian, Nervo-Trajanic, Antonine and Severan dynasties (27B.C.–A.D. 235) the entire Mediterranean world enjoyed order, tranquility, prosperity, and freedom of travel and communication.[10] Except for local revolts and border warfare, the empire was undisturbed. It expanded its natural borders and made them secure enough to keep the barbarian world at bay. The grafting of Greek art, literature, and philosophy onto Roman traditions produced an international, imperial culture that spread out from the center and was superimposed on the diverse cultures and peoples of the empire. The unity of civilization was apparent in a common style of urban life, universal law, and imperial religion.[11]

The spread of Christianity during this period has been recounted many times and need not be repeated here. We should note, however, that up to the fourth century Christianity remained a minority religion, sometimes persecuted but largely ignored, restricted to the trading centers of the Mediterranean and a few cities in Gaul and Britain.[12] Throughout this period Christians belonged to the lower and middle urban classes: they were shopkeepers, tradespeople, merchants, and craftspeople.[13] Their culture was neither that of the slave nor that of the Hellenic aristocracy; it has been described as half-educated and "middlebrow."[14] Christians were predominantly Greek-speaking; they formed a rootless, mobile coalition of small communities throughout the empire, sharing a common language, custom, organization, and tradition, an international and catholic (universal) nation within a nation.[15] By A.D. 250, as the result of internal disputes and needs, the church had developed a recognizable hierarchy of function and ministry and had formed a canon of Scripture from its diverse oral and written traditions.[16] It had begun to move away from its Judaic roots and to attract a fair number of aristocratic Hellenic converts.

This trend was on a small scale, however, and Christianity was to be a minority religion well into the fourth century. During the reign of Constantine (306–337) and the Christian emperors who followed the church began to attract the aristocracy in considerable numbers. Constantine's reorganization of the empire and his elevation of the lower and middle classes into senatorial rank brought many Christians into the forefront of power.[17] Despite these gains Christianity failed to penetrate the conservatism of the pagan aristocracy until the sixth century. It only began to reach the peasantry with the mass conversions that followed Constantine's reign.[18]

## CHRISTIANITY AND ROME

The Christian religion came on the heels of a variety of oriental cults and mystery religions and like them had much personal and individual appeal in a world growing tired and skeptical of rigid official cults.[19] While much of Christianity's appeal was in its new concept of God and the relation of the human to the divine, the ethics of the new religion also was attractive to many. It broke down the ancient social ethos by changing individual loyalties, voiding the distinctions between slave and free, man and woman, citizen and barbarian.[20] Its emphasis on personal responsibility reversed the ancient emphasis on the priority of the state and community as the agent of salvation and thus set the scene for the social and religious struggles of the late Roman world.[21]

Although generally Christians accepted and approved of the Roman Empire,[22] the call to "render to Caesar what is Caesar's and to God what is God's" was spoken and heard in the context of God's new kingdom that claimed all the world. Peter's call in Acts to "obey God rather than men" (5:29) is inherent in the juxtaposition of Paul's command to "overcome evil with good" (Rom 12:21) to his exhortation to obey the "higher authorities" (see chap. 2). The call to "render to Caesar" becomes a test of loyalty to Christ's command to love one's enemy. The Christian recognizes the position of the oppressor and realizes that loyalty to God cannot be considered on the same plane.[23]

Paul accepts suffering and obedience to the empire because he expects the new kingdom and Christ's promised return. His critique of the Pax Romana is never far below the surface and is accompanied by a strong apocalyptic sense.[24] His realization that suffering and persecution are an essential element of his discipleship to Christ forms a major theme of his letters.[25] This apocalyptic tradition is most clearly revealed in Revelation.[26]

The apocalyptic tradition has taken forms and interpretations often tied to violent upheaval and sectarian struggle,[27] but in the early church it was never used as a call to the sword. While the elect are on the side of the Messiah on Zion, heavenly forces, not human forces, overthrow the beast of Rome. However, the apocalyptic tradition is not passive.[28] It conveys two positive values: it consoles those who are persecuted and calls them to resist evil,[29] even that of authority and of earthly powers. The apocalyptic tradition is thus fully consonant with the gospel call to love one's enemies and to resist nonviolently. It recognizes the evils of the world and calls upon Christians to overcome them through their witness to truth.

The emergence of this Christian apocalyptic tradition from Jewish political roots[30] and popular prophecy can probably be explained by the rise of the imperial cult (A.D. 70–80).[31] The Book of Revelation and the Shepherd of Hermas (A.D. 100–130) both make explicit the opposition of Jerusalem and Babylon, of the Christian and Roman worlds.[32] A continuing Christian apocalyptic, expressing the same clear but nonviolent opposition to Rome, stretches unbroken through the works of the Christian Sibylline tradition, Irenaeus, Justin Martyr, Theophilus of Antioch, Clement of Alexandria, Tertullian, Hippolytus, and Victorinus of Pettau to Lactantius in the fourth century.[33] In the West the apocalyptic tradition long outlived the peace made between Christianity and Rome through the time of Augustine and beyond.[34]

Thus the divergent strains represented in Romans 13 and Apocalypse 13 can be shown to have coexisted within the church throughout this period. Actually the two strains are only facets of the same New Testament message: real political power and institutions cannot be ignored, and the Christian form of political action is to work nonviolently to overcome tyranny and oppression until the New Jerusalem, the new community of Christ, is founded. The process is not individualistic or mystical in the broad sense but takes place amid political context and real suffering, and works from below to transform the world.

The early church established itself from the start as an active opponent of pagan society.[35] From the time of Paul, Christians identified themselves as a separate political people (Philem 3:20), a *polites*,[36] a state,[37] a kingdom,[38] the true Israel,[39] and, as Basil noted by stealing the very name of the empire, a new world community, the *oikumene*.[40] The Christian movement aimed to liberate the victims of oppression and thus had deep social and political potential.[41] The apocalyptic tradition was not alone in its juxtaposition of Jerusalem and Babylon. Irenaeus, Hippolytus of Rome, Tertullian, Gregory Nazianzen, Basil of Caesarea, Ossius of Cordova, John Chrysostom, and Ambrose all stressed the Christian duty to obey God above human beings and to resist the unjust laws and actions of tyrants.[42] The Christians ''set out to harass their foes with the intransigence peculiar to reformers convinced of being inspired by a supernatural will.''[43] Their challenge was not to destroy but to convert.

The process of conversion worked on two planes.[44] The first plane was that of the intellectual tradition of the Apologists. They attempted to persuade the Greco-Roman intelligentsia by explaining Christian doctrine and life. This tradition is easily studied and analyzed because of its literary texts. The second plane was that of the Christian tradition of nonviolent action exemplified by the lives of the confessors and martyrs. This tradition, more than any text, sets the context for the study of peacemaking in the period: first, because these confessors and martyrs represent the concrete, undeniable application of the commandment to love one's enemies; and second, because they are evidence of the attitudes and understanding of most of the early Christians attempting to apply the gospel teaching of peacemaking. A study of texts alone could stalemate on points of interpretation and intent and critics could justly observe that literary texts are the product of a small elite, but the history of the martyrs provides us with a firm and undeniable witness to peacemaking that both supplements and supports the literary tradition.

## THE APOLOGISTS: THE THEORY OF CHRISTIAN PEACEMAKING

The early church understood the meaning of peace in the New Testament as a positive and creative force—the fruit of love.[45] Its peacemaking was not based on a specifically political opposition to an unjust state, on the abhorrence of idolatry, or on apocalyptic expectations, but on the gospel command to make peace that was the basis for all these attitudes.[46] From the early second century, when the New Testament was being completed, to the end of the Constantinian period the tradition of specific opposition to war is continuous.

Ignatius of Antioch (d.c. 107), for example, wrote that ''nothing is better than peace, by which all war of those in heaven and those on earth is abolished.''[47] He instructed his listeners in behavior toward their enemies: ''toward their anger be gentle, toward their boasting be meek . . . against their savageness be mild, not being eager to imitate them . . . and let us be eager to be imitators of the Lord."[48]

Justin Martyr (c. 100–c. 165), who died during persecutions under the Stoic emperor Marcus Aurelius, makes the same point clearly in his *Apology* to Emperor Antonius Pius[49] and in his *Dialogue with Trypho:*[50] the Christians, converted from war and violence, have turned swords into plowshares and "cultivate piety, justice, and love of mankind." Rather than deny this faith under persecution they "prefer to die acknowledging it."[51]

Tatian, a Syrian convert of Justin, asserts the same principles in his *Discourse to the Greeks*[52] (c. 160). Political power, wealth, and military office are all rejected; war is equated with murder. In his *Embassy Regarding the Christians,* written to Marcus Aurelius (c. 177) at the time of the emperor's persecutions and the massacre of Christians at Lyons, Athenagoras explains that Christians refuse to kill, even with just cause, and that watching the capital punishment of criminals condemned to be killed in the gladiatorial shows would be the same as taking part in murder.[53]

The middle of the third century was a period of material and economic crisis: plagues, famines, economic collapse, political instability, and barbarian invasion nearly brought the empire to an end. A series of soldier-emperors from the Danubian border restored order.[54] They renewed the intellectual and physical attacks on the Christian church. Christian Apologists, however, continued to stress the theme of peacemaking. In *Octavius,* the earliest known work of Latin Christian literature, Municius Felix starkly contrasts the ethic of the Romans with that of the Christians. "All the Romans hold, occupy, and possess is the spoil of outrage. Their temples are full of loot, drawn from the ruin of cities, the plunder of gods, and the slaughter of priests."[55] As for the Christians, "It is not right for us even to see or hear of a man being killed" (30.6).

Clement of Alexandria (c. 150–c. 210), like Justin Martyr, attempted to win over the Hellenic world through a synthesis of philosophy and revelation and accepted the Roman world for the benefits it offered.[56] Nevertheless his message in *Exhortation to the Gentiles* (chap. 11), *Miscellanies* (4.6, 4.8.61), and *Christ the Educator* (I.12) is plain and consistent: Christians are educated not for war, but for peace. They are soldiers of peace and handle the arms of peace, justice, faith, and salvation. Justice and peace need no arms except the word of God, and "nowhere will they inflict wounds."

Perhaps the most controversial Christian of this era is the North African Apologist, Tertullian (c. 160–c. 220).[57] A lawyer converted by the example of martyrdom, Tertullian composed increasingly critical rhetorical polemics against Roman values. He finally embraced the radical millennarianism of the Montanists, eventually going even beyond their rejection of contemporary society and church teachings. Because of his swing into heresy Tertullian has often been dismissed in his entirety by later Christians, most strongly by fervent Catholic writers of the Counter Reformation. Yet Tertullian's influence on orthodox Christian thought was strong and long-lasting.[58] Antimilitarism runs through the writing of both his "orthodox" and his "heterodox" periods.[59] Furthermore, his thoughts on peacemaking have never been questioned despite his brush with heresy.

Tertullian has long been considered a master of the phrase, and for just reason: many of his rhetorical statements captured the early church's positions in several areas. "What has Athens to do with Jerusalem?"[60] epitomizes the "Christ against Culture"[61] position of the early Christians in their dealings with pagan society. Tertullian condemned militarism in the phrase "The Lord in disarming Peter ungirded every soldier,"[62] and it became a motto for peacemakers.

The consistency of Tertullian's writings on peace has been demonstrated in both his later works and in the *Apology* and other works of the orthodox period, including *On Patience* (chap. 3), *Against Marcion* (3.14), and *Against the Nations*.[63] These texts demonstrate a clear unity of theme: the Lord has cursed the sword forever, the duty of the Christian is to suffer death rather than inflict it, and the sword can never produce truth, gentleness, or justice.[64]

Nor was opposition to violence restricted to radical circles in this period. The *Apostolic Tradition,* a series of canons for the conduct of the Roman church attributed to Hippolytus (c. 160–c. 236) and widely used in the East,[65] offers a contemporary's confirmation of Tertullian's thought.[66] Several general principles emerge from the *Apostolic Tradition*'s list of forbidden professions:[67] Christians are not to hold military governorships or magistracies because of the role these offices play in executing capital punishment; Christians who join the army are to be excommunicated, "for they have despised God"; gladiators and their trainers must resign their posts or be rejected from the church; and finally, "a soldier of the civil authority must be taught not to kill men and to refuse to do so if he is commanded, and to refuse to take an oath; if he is unwilling to comply, he must be rejected." This text implies the presence of Christians or potential converts to Christianity in the Roman army, but its wider meaning is far more important: Christians are forbidden to enter or to remain in occupations that employ violence.

Origen of Alexandria (c. 185–c. 254) is the most important figure of the next generation.[68] Origen shared the Apologists' desire to promote Christianity to the Greco-Roman intellectual. Generally favorable to Rome and the benefits of the Pax Romana,[69] he wrote in a world threatened by barbarians from without, a world increasingly hostile to what it saw as the Christian lack of patriotism. Origen's best known apologetic is *Against Celsus,* a reply to a Greek intellectual's treatise against the Christians. Written around A.D. 178, the treatise has been lost except for the portions quoted by Origen and others. In his reply Origen spells out the Christian response of peacemaking in a violent world. He argues that even if Christians support Rome, they must still be prepared to die for their beliefs.[70] In answer to Celsus' compelling call to defend the empire and its benefits, Origen replies that Christians who have beaten swords into plowshares cannot take up the sword, "having become children of peace for the sake of Jesus, who is our leader."[71]

Christians do aid the empire, however, through their prayers, which are greater than weapons, but only if its aims are just.[72] Although this condition has been interpreted as an embryonic form of the just-war theory,[73] Origen did consider war to be the realm of the pagan world, not that of Christians, who cannot use violence. That he did not forsee a Christian empire and its use of war is clear in his reply to Celsus' plea "What if the whole world were Christian?"—that is, what if a pacifist empire had to defend itself against barbarians. Origen's reply is not that Christians would fight the just war, but that the barbarians would become Christian (VIII.68). Instead of envisioning the unlikely possibility that those who have suffered persecution without offering violence would now fight wars, Origen envisions the more likely outcome that God would protect his people and that Christians would convert the barbarians (VIII.69–70).

In the middle of the third century Christians underwent a period of persecution. Nevertheless the early church continued its active attempt to convert the Roman world. Gregory Thaumaturgus (the Wonderworker, c. 213–c. 270)[74] was a student of Origen who set out (c. 242) to convert the citizens who lived in the interior of Pontus in Asia Minor. He accepted the Greco-Roman world as he found it and sought to use it as a stepping-stone to a higher good, to convert it to a new life. His career was the precedent for the nonviolent Christian mission of overcoming Roman opposition. Amid war, persecution, plague, and popular hostility, Gregory confronted pagan priests and discredited their cults, replacing pagan temples with Christian churches and pagan feasts with equivalent Christian celebrations (a policy that was later to prove so successful in Gregory the Great's conversion of the Western barbarians).

About the same time, Cyprian, bishop of Carthage (c. 200–258),[75] wrote in the same spirit of activist peacemaking. In his treatises *On the Value of Patience* (chap. 14), *To Donatus* (VI.10), *On the Dress of Virgins* (chap. 11), and in his *Letters* (1.6; 56.3) Cyprian consistently reminds his congregation that killing is a mortal sin. God made iron for cultivating fields and not for killing, taking a life ranked with adultery and deceit as mortal sins, and the bloodied hand is unfit to receive the sacrament, that is, the one who kills is excommunicated. Cyprian's injunctions did not apply simply to private morality. He notes with scorn that although society views the murder of one person as a heinous crime, it considers the murder of thousands on a general's order during war a great virtue (*Letter* I.6). Rather than inflict injury, Cyprian urged Christians to suffer martyrdom as a witness to peace. Forced to flee during the persecution of Decius (A.D. 249), he returned to Carthage in 251 and was one of the first to be arrested under Valerian's persecution in 258. He was exiled for refusing to disclose the names of his priests and continued his organizing until he was brought to Carthage for trial, convicted of treason, and executed. Another African, Arnobius, composed *Against the Nations* between 290 and 300. The book condemns Rome's tyranny, greed, and violence. Contrasting the way of God to that of the empire, Arnobius concludes that God cannot possibly accept militarism; it is against the very nature of his being.[76]

The last part of the third century saw the Great Persecution under Diocletian, renewed civil war, the accession of Constantine,[77] and finally the so-called Peace of the Church[78] with the empire. The acceptance of Rome in a Christian context brought the rise of a new Christian patriotism exemplified by Eusebius and Lactantius.[79] Some assert that from that point on the gospel message of peace was lost amid approbation of the just war by a church all too eager to celebrate the victory of Christianity. Although this is true to an extent (and will be discussed at greater length in chapter 4), Christian acceptance of the Roman Empire dates back to New Testament times and is not really new in this period. Neither should we ignore the continuing tradition of Christian peacemaking and active resistance to political tyranny that survived the Constantinian settlement with the church.

Among the framers of the Peace of the Church was Lactantius,[80] a member of the inner circle of the emperor Diocletian (284–305), who was known for his brilliant attempt to renew ancient Roman forms of social, political, and religious life. Lactantius was forced from the emperor's court in 303 at the beginning of the Great Persecution. He remained in Asia Minor until 305, when he went to Gaul. In 317 he was called to Trier in northern Gaul to tutor Constantine's son Crispus. Although he was a supporter of the Christian empire, his *Divine Institutes,* written between 303 and 311, demonstrates that the shift in Christian attitudes during the age of Constantine must not be oversimplified. The views of Lactantius on violence and peacemaking are fully consistent with the tradition of the early church:

God prohibits killing . . . and so it will not be lawful for a just man to serve as a soldier— for justice itself is his military service— not to accuse anyone of capital offense, because it makes no difference whether you kill with a sword or

with a word, since killing itself is forbidden. And so . . . no exceptions ought
to be made to the rule that it is always wrong to kill a man, whom God has
wished to be a sacrosanct creature.[81]

Lactantius extends the prohibition to violence even to the act of attending capital
punishment, a view already expressed by Athenagoras and Municius Felix.[82] The *Divine
Institutes* is a fundamental work of Christian social and political criticism. In its apocalyptic vision of the late Roman Empire, it was to influence Christian thought for centuries.[83] Lactantius' condemnation of Roman "riches, honors, powers, and kingdoms"[84]
was fundamental. His portrait of Roman history as evil was a prelude to his vision of
the empire's division and collapse amid political chaos and natural disaster.[85] As with
all apocalyptics, Lactantius' vision contained a social, political, and religious criticism
of his age and a call for Christians to "seek after justice" in order to "attain the reward
of virtue promised by the Lord."[86]

Thus a continuous tradition of peacemaking stretches from the New Testament to the
foundation of the Christian empire and the era of the barbarian invasions. This tradition
combines a strong and active opposition to the values of Roman society with a commitment to their nonviolent overthrow. To better understand the nature of this commitment
we must now examine the Roman view of the Christian tradition of peacemaking.

## ROMAN RELIGIOUS REACTION

The Christian attack on Roman values was not political in the modern sense of the
word, but for the ancients no fine distinction could ever be drawn between the realms
of politics, culture, and religion. For the Romans, as for the Greeks before them, religion brought the *pax deorum* upon the community as a whole.[87] The state prospered
only because of the strict, contractual observance of sacrifices and other rituals that
together defined Roman religion. Thus Rome identified itself by and was identified with
its gods and their cults. Other nations were likewise identified with their own gods. It
followed naturally that when Rome conquered its neighbors it granted recognition and
toleration of the conquered peoples by recognizing their gods, provided that the conquered peoples recognized the Roman pantheon and gave it due honor. The relationship
between all these gods expressed in religious terms the political realities of power of the
Pax Romana. Not that the ancients dealt in pious allegories: Roman peace *was* the peace
of its gods extended over the gods of its subjects.

Rome's imperial domination over a diversity of cultures and religions was expressed
by the imperial cult, which was superimposed over and synthesized with local cults to
form a standard of worship and political allegiance to the center.[88] From the time of
Julius Caesar imperial leadership was expressed in the cult of the emperor. This also
was natural: the divinization of an emperor, a notion borrowed from Hellenistic concepts, made manifest for the whole empire the special role of Rome in bringing the *pax*
and *providentia deorum*.[89] To worship the emperor was to visibly express one's patriotism; it showed the participation of all citizens in supporting the state by imploring the
aid of the gods. Every cult that aided citizens in supporting the state was a *religio licita;*
every foreign religion following the ancient traditions of a conquered people that aided
the imperial cause was a *religio externa* and thus *licita* for that people.[90] Both were
tolerated because they were both part of the life of an empire that was an all-inclusive
religious, social, and political body.[91]

Rome learned how dangerous the loosening of these cultural loyalties could be in the bloody Jewish revolt of A.D. 66 that led to the destruction of Jerusalem (A.D. 70). Tolerated as a *religio licita,* Judaism had made an accommodation to Rome by offering sacrifice to the emperor. The first act of Jewish revolt—a manifestation of political defiance—was appropriately therefore the refusal to offer these prayers and sacrifices.

Christianity, with its emphasis on an internal change of allegiance, gave rise to a new problem: "for innumerable humble men and women it subtly loosened the molding power of classical culture and the habitual sanctions of behavior."[92] From the time of Paul to the time of Constantine the popular and intellectual charges against the Christian cult were remarkably consistent and indicate fundamentally political perceptions of this revolutionary force.[93] Christians came from the dregs of society, from classes of natural outcasts of the *polis.* They indulged in bizarre rites; they were antisocial and strange, a third race, a state within a state.[94] By turning away both from the national religion of Judaism and the imperial cult of Rome, the Christians had neither gods nor political allegiance: they were, therefore, atheists and subversives. Unlike the Gnostics, who were indifferent to the demands of the imperial religion, the Christians actively opposed it; the more the Christians became known, the more the pagan world reacted with fear and suspicion.

Pliny,[95] who wrote as governor of Bithynia to the emperor Trajan (c. 115) concerning the Christians, revealed the Roman fear of the political threat posed by the clandestine organization and secret loyalties of the new religion. The test of loyalty was thus to be an external act: sacrifice to the imperial cult. This was only the test for Christianity: everyone knew that a true Christian would never abandon loyalty to Christ. The real issue for Roman and Christian alike was the very fact of being a Christian, which refusal to sacrifice betrayed. No conspiracy was proven, but Pliny concluded that the Christian crime was the *nomen,* the "name" or the fact of being a Christian, and not any *scelera,* individual crimes, that Christians had committed. For the Romans the very fact of Christianity evoked a set of attitudes that struck at the heart of the empire.[96]

Celsus,[97] writing around 178, provides some insight into how Roman attitudes toward Christians had developed. Christians formed an illegal organization, were intolerant of and attacked the imperial cult, and therefore formed a revolutionary movement. They refused to defend the empire, they were arrogant and self-indulgent in their refusal to take on their duties as citizens. Their proselytizing destroyed the unity of families and homes, incited a rebellion that especially affected the poor and women and threatened the fabric of society. A similar list was drawn up by Porphyry in *Against the Christians* (c. 270).[98]

The charges were repeated again and again. Pliny's charge of Christian "obstinacy" was repeated by Marcus Aurelius in his condemnation of the Christians' "tragic show,"[99] that is, their activist approach. The legal charge always involved refusal to sacrifice either to the emperor's image, as under Trajan, or to the gods of Rome, as under Decius,[100] but the real cause for bringing Christians to trial was the threat to public safety that they posed. The charges brought against Cyprian of Carthage after his refusal to sacrifice on September 13, 258 are typical:

> You have long lived an irreligious life, and have drawn together a number of men bound by an unlawful association, and professed yourself an open enemy to the gods and the religion of Rome; and the pious, most sacred and august Emperors.[101]

The source of conflict was not the Christians' refusal to sacrifice, as many would contend, but the nature of Christianity itself.

This pagan appreciation of the new religion confirms the message of the Christian intellectuals. The early church was activist and sought to overturn the very fabric of Roman society.[102] Conflict was inevitable. Rome recognized the danger and brought its power to bear, but it was not prepared for the Christian response.

## THE MARTYRS: CHRISTIAN PEACEMAKING IN ACTION

"Love your enemy" and "overcome evil with good" were not idle sayings, the pious speculation of ineffective intellectuals. Christianity grew out of the living Jewish tradition of Daniel and the Maccabees—a tradition in which the kingdom was defended through persecution, heroic suffering, and death.[103] The apocalyptic tradition we have examined is witness to this and so is the history of Christian martyrdom.

Early Christianity had none of the outward evidences of religious life that the Romans expected—no temples, outdoor ceremonies, or distinctive priestly garb. Christianity's only public record was the virtue of its members and their witness to the truth:[104] the very name "martyr" derives from the Greek *martus,* witness. From the time of the Acts of the Apostles this witness to the truth found its expression in martyrdom.[105] As early as 107 or 108 Ignatius of Antioch had worked out a Christian theology of martyrdom.[106] In imitation of Christ and the apostles the Christian seeks confrontation with the pagan world, not out of explicit political hostility but as a means of ushering in the new kingdom. The suffering of the martyrs became an exhortation to the kingdom: today we would call this nonviolence a political and a public act designed to win over the opposition. Quite the opposite of the Cynic, who was indifferent to political conditions, the Christian martyr was actively opposed to the Roman gods.

The story of Polycarp,[107] bishop of Smyrna, who was martyred around 165, is a vivid example of the actions of thousands of Christians under the empire. The narrator of the bishop's last days makes it perfectly clear that Polycarp lived and died in imitation of Christ, the Son of Man, who had suffered and died to save the world. Attempting at first to escape persecution, Polycarp retired to a country estate. Finally convinced that he must suffer martyrdom, he was betrayed and handed over to the authorities. He refused to say "Caesar is Lord," and he was hurried off to the stadium at Smyrna. Before the assembled populace the proconsul attempted to persuade the aged bishop to save his life. Refusing to denounce Christ or to plead for his life, Polycarp faced the threat of the lions and death by fire "full of confidence and joy." Amazed, the proconsul proclaimed that "Polycarp had confessed himself to be a Christian." The people's response revealed their fear and hatred: "This is the teacher of Asia, the father of the Christians, the destroyer of our Gods, who teaches many not to sacrifice or worship."

The fire was prepared with the stake and nails; Polycarp eagerly accepted his suffering in imitation of Christ. Finally run through by an executioner, the martyr caused th crowd to marvel "that there should be so great a difference between the unbelievers an the elect." Then, fearing that the Christians would worship the crucified, the Roman burned the body. The author of the account interjects that this would be impossible "for Him, the Son of God, we adore, but the martyrs we love as disciples and imitator of the Lord." The narrator concludes by recounting the praise given to Polycarp:

> Not only a famous teacher, but also an illustrious martyr, whose martyrdom all desire to imitate, as being after the pattern of the gospel of Christ. Having vanquished by his patience the unjust ruler, and thus received the crown of immortality, he rejoices greatly with the apostles and with all the just.

Christian martyrs thus confront pagan society and accept the conflict of the amphitheater. In imitation of Christ they vanquish the unjust ruler. We need not go into the entire history of martyrdom. While many of the most vivid accounts concern the lives of Christian leaders like Polycarp, martyrdom was a popular opposition movement. It complemented the treatises of the intellectuals, who often paid for their attacks on Rome with their own blood. The ideal of nonviolence was early enshrined in the cult of the martyrs. Rome based its Christian preeminence on the grace of the martyrs, especially Peter and Paul, who gave their lives and whose bones were buried there.[108]

The total number of martyrs is uncertain, but estimates run into the thousands.[109] The exact number is not important however. What matters is that so many Christians were willing to suffer death rather than to inflict it and that their suffering had an important effect on the Roman world. Pagan society had long been prepared to appreciate this drama.[110] The lives of the philosophers and their witness to the truth—Socrates was the most famous example—served as precedents. The Stoics accepted death, often self-imposed, in political opposition to tyranny, as Seneca had done under Nero. Greek and Roman literature of the empire also provided many stories of voluntary suffering of young men and women in pursuit of love and freedom. Thus Christians' willingness to die for their creed and their "uncompromising opposition to the obvious evils of a materialist and uncreative society won support. The church strengthened its role as focus for much of the latent discontent in the provinces."[111]

That the blood of the martyrs was the seed of the church has almost become a pious and lifeless cliché.[112] Yet it is essential to make the point in an account of Christian peacemaking. Only by appreciating the blood of the martyrs can any discussion of Christian nonviolence proceed fruitfully. The nonviolent resistance offered by thousands of Christians to Roman society not only showed faithfulness to Christ's command to love one's enemies, it also achieved the fulfillment of the promise behind the command: after three centuries of persecution, nonviolence succeeded. Pagan society left the field exhausted, bewildered, and defeated.[113] The "story of the successful Christian revolution against the Roman Empire"[114] thus was the single most important factor in the transformation of the Roman world.[115] This is the premise upon which all the theories of early Christian peacemaking must stand or fall.

## CHRISTIANS AND THE ROMAN ARMY

The historical problem of the service of Christians (of whatever numbers) in the Roman army during the first three centuries, its meaning then for nonviolence, and its implications for the later history of peacemaking must be approached in the context of the above discussion. Evidence of Christians serving as Roman soldiers is undeniable; yet the dates, extent, and significance of such service have been much debated and opposing interpretations exist. Catholics have tended to stress Christian loyalty to the state and have taken the traditional view of medieval Christendom as normative, that is, that idolatry was the main issue involved in Christians' refusal to serve in the military. Not opposed to fighting per se, they were loyal subjects of the empire and refused service because of the oath and sacrifices soldiers made to the emperor.[116]

The evidence for Christian military service is easily summarized. Before 172 there was none.[117] For that year, however, an account was later written of Christians serving under Marcus Aurelius in the Twelfth, or Thundering, Legion on the Danube frontier, whose prayers were responsible for a deluge, escape from danger, and ultimate Roman victory. The story derives from the account in Eusebius' *Ecclesiastical History* (V.5.1-7), written about a hundred and fifty years after the event, and cites Tertullian as its source. The responsibility for the events, according to pagan sources however, lies either with an Egyptian sorceress or with Jupiter Pluvius, the bringer of rain.[118] The purposes of Eusebius' history for Christian apologetics are obvious; the idea that he would read Christian intervention for the empire into the pre-Constantinian era is not too far-fetched. Eusebius notes one pagan source and advises his readers to make up their own mind.

Evidence of Christians serving in the Roman army before the third century is suspect for other reasons, however. Until the militarization of society under the Severans and the extension of citizenship to all residents of the empire by Caracalla's *Constitutio Antoniniana* in 212, Christians were not called on to serve; service was voluntary until then.[119] After 212 until the fourth century military service attracted mainly the rural peasantry of Asia Minor or of the Danube frontier. This peasantry remained pagan well into the fourth century, after which recruits were drawn mainly from the Franks and Alemanni. They were pagan even after the time of the Christian emperors.[120] City folk, who included the vast majority of Christians, were considered poor material for army duty.[121] All this, combined with the fact that army service became hereditary in the late fourth century, points to an army that excluded most Christians. The army was a rural, barbarian, and hereditary group.[122]

A study of tombstone inscriptions reveals that only 7 Christians out of 4,700 extant inscriptions were members of the military.[123] Yet, such inscriptions do indicate that Christians who served were accepted by the church.[124] Whether these Christian soldiers converted once they were in the service or entered it as Christians is impossible to know. Tertullian's arguments against Christians serving in the military has been taken as evidence that only a handful of extremists were pacifist.[125] Yet Tertullian's *Apology, On Idolatry,* and *Military Crown* seem only to prove the existence of some Christians in the army and to record his urgent call that they abandon that service.[126]

Some early Christians were undoubtedly soldiers. Some early Christians also murdered, stole, lied, and lapsed into idolatry under persecution. Catholic theology has always admitted the existence of sin and has always tried to reincorporate sinners into the body of the church. The issue of Christians in the army should be put into perspective. It implies neither wholesale treachery against the gospels on the part of some Christians nor proof of their unwavering loyalty to the state. That a minority of Christians served as soldiers does not change the early church's unfaltering devotion to Christian peacemaking.

The martyrs and the Apologists offer far more compelling evidence of Christian peacemaking. It clearly reflected official Roman papal teaching into the fourth century. The *Apostolic Tradition* of Hippolytus has already been discussed above.[127] Pope Damasus' praise of soldier martyrs who refused to obey[128] and Innocent I's opposition to ordaining former soldiers as priests should be noted.[129] Not until Athanasius, who wrote in the Eastern Imperial Church after Constantine, is there any evidence of specific approval of Christians serving in the army, praise for Christian warriors, or formulations of a Christian theology of war.[130]

## SOLDIER SAINTS

One topic that has been used as evidence of early Christian militarism sets the tone for the analysis of later Catholic history in the West: the soldier saint. We must distinguish between two types here: warrior saints and soldier saints. A number of accounts tell of the semimythological warrior heros, who include George, Mercury, Theodore, Dasius, Procopius, and others. Many of these accounts are hagiographical fictions based on stereotyped genre, pagan legends, and mistaken transmission.[131] A full discussion of these really belongs to the hagiographer and the literary historian.[132] However, even accounts that do have historical basis extol the heroes not for their military deeds but for their refusal to serve when called on to do so.[133] But what of those Christian martyrs who did serve in the army? From the early centuries we know only of those who refused active service; the epigraphical evidence provides few clues;[134] the literary texts are also ambiguous. Tertullian's writing must be taken again as the norm.

In his *Apology* (c. 197), Tertullian uses the word *militare* to describe Christian service in the army (I *Apology* 42.3). Yet *militare* was used at the time to designate the public service of any bureaucrat.[135] *Bellare* more accurately defined service in war *(bellum)*. Service in the Roman army through most of the history of the early church was in fact more likely to be peaceful police work:

> The Roman (garrison) life with its routines was peaceful in the extreme. Many a recruit need never have struck a blow in anger outside a tavern. His unit . . . remained fixed in the same camp over a period of centuries. In the conventional sense, he was a soldier only very occasionally. [The military needs of the provinces] were in this peaceful age restricted to such problems as an occasional bandit in the hills, a drunken riot in the streets, or housebreakers and other criminals found even in the most prosperous scene.[136]

Although they did not always refrain from inflicting violence,[137] those who functioned as police for the Roman army[138] may well have explained the small number of Christians found in its ranks. Tertullian, Clement of Alexandria, Pseudo-Melito, Cyprian of Carthage, and Eusebius seem to have admitted the possibility of such service.[139] We also know that the third canon of the Council of Arles, held in 314 after the church's peace with Constantine, stated "that those who cast down their arms in peacetime are to be excommunicated." This makes sense only if we accept the validity of peaceful service in the empire.[140]

We cannot survey here all the types of Christians in the Roman army who were martyred. We can observe, however, that we have knowledge of them because Christians refused to fight even in times of active military crisis. A few examples must suffice. In 260, when the Persian frontier burst into flames with the defeat of Rome and the capture of Emperor Valerian,[141] Marinus,[142] a Roman centurion stationed at Caesarea in Palestine near the front, was denounced by a fellow officer as a Christian. Refusing to recant, he was summarily executed. Eusebius, who records the story, notes that Marinus was executed because of his Christianity: the test had been his refusal to sacrifice.

In 296 war was declared against Persia and a large-scale conscription was ordered.[143] Christians were among the draftees. Maximilian is the best known.[144] The son of a veteran soldier who brought him forward for enlistment at Theveste in Numidia, Maximilian revealed that he was a Christian and that he could not serve. Entreated by his father and the civilian governor, he replied, "My army is the army of God, and I cannot fight for this world, I have already said it, I am a Christian." For his declaration of loyalty he was condemned and executed.

In 298, during the war with Persia, Marcellus,[145] a centurion stationed in Tangier, refused to continue service. His opposition was active and public. Throwing down his military belt during a celebration of the Emperor Maximian's birthday, he declared, "I serve only the eternal king, Jesus Christ." Brought to trial before the deputy prefect at Tangier, he argued that he could not inflict wounds and pleaded guilty to the Roman charges against him, defying the emperor. He was executed.

To object that such instances centered around the Christian horror of idolatry[146] and the refusal to perform the military duty of sacrifice, or that these soldiers were punished only for a breach of military discipline is to beg or to miss the point. Even today conscientious objectors who declare themselves once they are in the army and do not receive the appropriate discharge are punished not for "pacifism" but for specific breaches of army regulations. The evasion of the larger issue by the military code is the military response to issues of morality. Yet this should not blind us to the real issue involved: the defiance of authority on the grounds of Christian belief.[147] This was true even during the Great Persecution.[148]

At the end of the Persian War (298), Diocletian decided to purge his army of Christian troublemakers. The campaign lasted from 298 to 302 and numbers of Christians were found in the ranks.[149] Had they enlisted years previously in the time of peace or been recently drafted? Had they fought in the Persian Wars? Maximilian's trial indicates that some Christians might have.[150] The evidence focuses only on those who refused to serve.

In 291 Diocletian elevated the cult of the emperor to include worship of his own person.[151] He was attempting to revive the fortunes of the political empire by reviving ancient religious piety.[152] Just as he saw himself as the reimbodiment of Augustan leadership, Diocletian saw the cult of his person as the embodiment of a new political loyalty among Roman citizens. He blamed Manicheans, Christians, and other cults for causing Rome to lose the protection of the gods, a protection insured through adherence to the rites of the Roman religion. The Christian refusal to participate in this religion was tantamount to treason. Christians were to comply even if they had to be dragged to the altars and forced to go through the motions. In a religion of external act and formula this would have been enough to satisfy the gods. But to the Christian who believed in an inner spirituality the implications of the act went far beyond the question of loyalty; they evoked the conflict between Christ and Caesar, between the forces of compulsion and those of love.

The examples of the soldier martyrs point to the active Christian defiance not of the cult per se but of its religious and political implications. These soldiers suffered because they voluntarily renounced violence in obedience to their Christian faith.[153] Had the issue been anything but a commitment to peacemaking, what could have prevented these Christian soldiers from rising up and using their weapons to overthrow the idols in defense of Christ? If they did not adhere to nonviolence as the way of the new kingdom, why did they suffer martyrdom?[154] Acting out of obedience to military discipline cannot explain the nonviolence of those who actively defied military obedience to begin with. But we have gone far afield. Christians certainly served in the army; but their numbers were small, their service peaceful, and their testimony one of peace and not of violence.

## CONCLUSIONS

We have tried to show that the early church was active in affirming Christian love, nonviolent in its means, and that its activity was not restricted to an intellectual elite, but involved all levels of Christian life. Through the positive role given to nonviolence the Christian ethic aimed to overthrow Roman society by converting its heart and soul.

Thus the history of the early church demonstrates the principles of active peacemaking. It recounts a nonviolent revolution that attacked the roots of Roman social and ethical life by breaking down all the human relationships within it and setting them up again in a new way, mirroring the new relationship with God and humanity. Christianity refilled the old bottle of Roman civilization with the new Christian wine; it did not destroy the vessel, but it changed its spirit. Institutional change followed individual conversion. Change began at the heart and worked outward to external life.

Questions remain. To what extent did the church succeed in this revolution? How real and how deep was the conversion of the Roman world? On what levels was it converted? Was there a perceptible change in the attitudes of Roman institutions and individuals when the empire accepted the church? Was the message of peacemaking changed or lost in the centuries immediately following Constantine? The next chapter will deal with these questions.

# CHAPTER 4

# CHRISTIAN PEACE AND THE BARBARIANS: FROM CONSTANTINE TO CHARLEMAGNE (300–800)

## CHRISTIAN EMPIRE AND IMPERIAL CHURCH

With the conversion of Constantine and the beginning of the Christian Roman Empire the early church faced a new problem. Born out of opposition to the prevailing value structure and nurtured in persecution, the church of the martyrs now suddenly became an accepted, favored, religion and would soon be an official religion of the state. The alliance of Christian church and Roman empire produced changes in both. The Christian victory over imperial power resulted in a new intellectual apologetic (especially in the East) aimed not at defending Christianity to the pagan world but at explaining its sudden power and new status.

Constantine typified the changes of his age. Baptized on his deathbed and tolerant throughout his life of orthodox Christian, Arian heretic, and pagan cult alike, the emperor transferred the powers of the pagan sun-god and of Jupiter to the Christian God and transformed the dignities of the Roman *pontifex maximus* to his own role in the church. Just as his predecessors had used the imperial cult of pagan Rome in order to unite and protect the empire,[1] Constantine assumed the title of the thirteenth apostle and directed the inner life of the Christian church through leadership of such things as the Council of Nicaea (325). Constantine's acceptance of Christianity and his administrative reorganization of the empire brought into the new structures of Christian power a large number of superficial converts.[2] Conversion now proceeded from above, leaving Roman administrative machinery and institutions largely untouched by Christian ideals.[3] Pagan aristocracy soon became Christian aristocracy; those who found no outlet for their ambitions in the increasingly autocratic and stultified political sphere found ample outlet in the church.[4]

This romanization at the upper levels of the church was expressed in many ways. The law code of Theodosius II (416) specified that only Christians could serve in the army.[5] Christians had come to be synonymous with the Roman citizens just as the church had come to represent *Romanitas*. The empire put on the robes of Christianity and the protection of the Christian God as a means of preserving its rule, and the church began to borrow more and more of the trappings of the empire.[6] Christian bishops of the large cities and towns became increasingly involved in the civil lives of their congregations and in the administration of the empire as a whole. Their talents were recognized by the central government *de jure* as well as *de facto*. The early history of the Roman bishops, the popes, as imperial governors of the city is one example of this recognition. The bureaucratic manners of official Roman dress and ceremony and the Roman imperial diocese became the basis for the church's own organization. The Roman administrative building, the basilica, became the model Christian church, and the Roman *cursus honorum* of graduated steps of civic duties and posts became that of the church hierarchy. The empire as *oikumene*[7] became the model of the universal, or catholic, church. Because Rome had been the capital of the empire the bishop of Rome rose in power and gradually came to replace the Roman emperor in the West and to take on his attributes.

Even the vocabulary of peace used by the church took on distinctly Roman accents. In the alliance of emperor and church the external order of the *Pax Romana* fused with Christian peace to create the *pax ecclesiae*. It represented both the final settlement between church and empire and a new order of Christian hierarchy and authority that insured external harmony and internal salvation.[8] Early Christian thought, influenced by Stoicism and Neoplatonism, had prepared the way for this by distinguishing between inner peace, Greek *hesychia* or Latin *tranquillitas,* and the external condition of peace.[9] On the highest official levels Christian *pax* became bound more and more to the ideas of *ordo* (order) and *concordia* (harmony), or the Greek *homonoia*. Divine justice gave each person his or her just due according to his or her place in an ordered hierarchy.[10] The holy emperor and the Christian clergy became the instruments of this justice.

Barbarian notions soon merged with the new definition of peace and added the element of the special protection given by a king or chief to his followers, his special *pax*.[11] Thus the *pax ecclesiae* meant both the salvation and protection granted to Christians by the hierarchy[12] and the treaty privileges *(feoda)* and protections granted to the hierarchy through its *pax* with the Roman Empire.[13]

## PEACEMAKING IN THE ROMAN WEST: AMBROSE AND AUGUSTINE

Despite these changes Christian thinkers retained the gospel meaning of peace. Peace for them remained a goal and a process of the spirit working within the world.[14] Ambrose of Milan (c. 330–c. 397) played a fundamental role in forging this new Christian spirituality of the Latin West.[15] An imperial governor based in Milan, his leadership ability thrust him into the episcopate even before he was baptized. Once a bishop, he became a loyal defender of the Christian empire;[16] he saw its wars as a legitimate means of attaining peace.[17] Ambrose recognized peace as the higher goal of war and placed the "peace-loving inclination" beyond criticism. His condemnation and excommunication of the Emperor Theodosius I for massacring six thousand rebels at Thessalonika in 390,[18] his imposition of a severe public penance, and the emperor's humiliation in fulfilling it are landmarks in the history of Christian checks upon the violence of the state. Ambrose showed the same abhorrence for violence in his dealings with heretics, forbidding any recourse to it during the dispute with the Arians in Gaul.[19]

His *Sermon against Auxentius* (386), written during his conflict with the Arians, is an important treatise on ecclesiastical freedom and on nonviolent action and Christian martyrdom.[20] In it Ambrose tells his congregation of his defense of the church of Milan amid threats of assassination or execution by a heretical emperor. He declares that nonviolence is his weapon

against arms, against soldiers, against the Goths. These are the means by which
a priest defends himself. I ought not or could not resist in any other manner. But
neither am I accustomed to leave or abandon the church, so let no one interpret
my action as fear of a more severe punishment. You yourselves, know well, also,
that I usually defer to the requests of the emperors, but I do not yield to their
threats, or fear those prepared for me, but willingly mock their tortures.[21]

Fearing neither weapons nor the barbarian foe, Ambrose tells his congregation that
"when one is the servant of God, it is not a human army, but the providence of the
Lord which will protect you."[22] Both Old and New Testaments abound in examples of
nonviolent resistance and martyrdom, he explains.[23] Ambrose recounts that his congregation risked death to protect him from imperial troops in a mass nonviolent protest
outside the cathedral.[24] Ambrose's defense ultimately was as successful as it was nonviolent; the Catholics won the dispute, and imperial legislation against them was rescinded.[25]

In his *Commentary on Psalm 118*,[26] Ambrose notes that peace is the virtue of the
humble, who refuse involvement in dissension, cruelty, debauchery, and wealth and
who follow justice. Quoting Christ's message of peace, "Peace I leave with you; my
peace I give to you" (Jn 14:27), Ambrose stresses that Christian peace is not a possession passively hoarded but a process vigorously pursued. It is granted not to the passive,
but to those who actively dominate life's problems.[27]

These ideas find their fullest expression in the thought of Ambrose's protégé, Augustine of Hippo (354–430).[28] Fountainhead of so much of the moral and theological thought
of the Western world, Augustine is responsible for helping to define two traditions that
have had immense bearing on the peace tradition within the Catholic Church. The first
is the tradition of peace as *ordo;* the second, the theory of the just war. In both areas
Augustine reflects the converted pagan intellectual of the late Roman world with all the
contradictions inherent in that position. Once a Manichaean, Augustine carried over first
to his Neoplatonism and then to his Christianity Manichaeism's irreconcilable split between evil and good, matter and spirit, outer material person and inner spiritual person.
Augustine was a member of the Roman ruling class and a loyal citizen of the late
empire. He accepted the Stoic concepts of peace and organic order of the empire, which
also became part of Christian political thought once Christianity made its peace with the
empire.[29]

Augustine shared Eusebius' admiration for Rome as the agent of peace and fellowship[30]
and maintained that its wars and emperors were aided by God.[31] In response to Volu-
sian's charges after the sack of Rome by the Visigoths (410) that a still active Christian
pacifism had ruined the empire, Augustine set out to write the *City of God,*[32] which he
composed between 413 and 426. In it (and in other works) he developed ideas (not
really a consistent theory) on the just war. Augustine's ideas on war are based on Cicero
and other Roman thinkers, but they also owe much to Manichaean and Neoplatonic
influences.[33] Thus he distinguished between inner disposition and external act, subordi-
nating externals to inner attitudes—in effect returning to the ethics of the Stoics.

The dichotomy has influenced Western thought on war into our century. Augustine
postulates that it is possible to love an enemy internally and still to kill him, just as the
Christian bishop can love the heretic and still exercise this love through punishment or
coercion.[34] The distinction parallels Augustine's general idea of peace as a dichotomy
between the inner tranquility of the individual Christian and the temporal needs of society, including the need to wage war.[35] Thus he contrasts true peace, the ascetic,

perfect tranquility of God's servants in the perfect vision of God,[36] which is not to be experienced in this life, with the false, imperfect, and external peace of the world attained through *ordo* and directed by Christian love or *amor*. Augustine's description of *tranquillitas* fit well into late Roman ideas of the Christian state. It allowed an inner peace to be insured by external order based on force, as long as that force was motivated by love, the *ordo amoris*.[37]

Yet Augustine's *City of God* also laid the framework for a Christian vision of peace in the world that derives from the gospels and was destined to act as a check upon the claims of the state. Rejecting the synthesis of pagan empire and Christian church established in the East, Augustine developed the theory, central to early Christian thought, of two societies, two cities—one of God, the other of the world—that would coexist in the world until the end of time. He admits that Rome brought a certain "peace of its own, which is not to be rejected," and that "it is important for us also that this people should possess this peace in this life, since so long as the two cities are intermingled, we also make use of the peace of Babylon."[38] Even the ultimate aim of Roman war was peace. Examined closely, however, Augustine's praise for the empire and its wars is really a critique of violence and exploitation and this critique finds a place in the mainstream of the Christian tradition of peacemaking.

Augustine sees the Roman state as "alienated" from God (19.26). While it possesses a certain peace, "it will not possess it in the end, because it does not make good use of it before the end" (19.26). The very extent of the empire has given rise to wars of a worse kind (worse than just wars against external enemies, that is, civil wars)—even just wars, if considered by the wise man, seem lamentable, "and consequently there would be no wars for a wise man" (19.9). Roman peace, he asserts, is built on tyranny and the domination of others. It is a peace among thieves, the peace of a thief over the thief's own household, maintained by "savage measures" (19.12). The monster Cacus, who sought his own peace through savagery to his victims, is a prime example of the absurdity of waging war to secure peace (19.12). Augustine defines the peace of the just war as a perverted imitation of God, which "seeks to impose its own domination of fellow men in place of God's rule" (19.12). Although it hates God's peace and chooses instead the peace of injustice, it does maintain some semblance of peace, just as the body hung upside-down resembles true posture (19.12), or as the body preserved in embalming fluids resembles a living person (19.12, 19.13). Augustine's analogies are hard to misunderstand; in case we miss his point about political order he notes that kingdoms without justice are nothing but "gangs of criminals on a large scale" (4.4). Generals on a small scale are called pirates, and on a large scale, emperors (4.4).

True peace is the love of God and the love of all people (19.14). It is an active quality of the virtuous life (19.11) resulting not from "lust for domination, but from a dutiful concern with the interests of others" (19.14). Augustine defines peace in many ways: an inner "condition of being" even for an evil life (19.13); harmony or "tranquility of order . . . which assigns each its proper position" (19.13). His definitions are intrinsically bound up with his notion of the City of God as the Christian community set in opposition to the material state.[39] Peace must be seen in the context of the true city of God, the mystic Jerusalem, which itself means "vision of peace."[40] In this sense Augustine's *City of God* can be read as a Christian peace tract[41] and represents a break with Roman notions of *pax*.[42] The theme of the *City of God* is that individual reform is the sole remedy against the ills of history; that individual, not institutional, change alone can lead to perfection.[43] Shocked by the sack of Rome (410), Augustine placed his hopes not in the empire but in his God. He faced the barbarian invasion of North Africa in the spirit of the martyrs, urging his followers to nonviolence, to flight, or if necessary to death in order to witness to Christ's truth.

Other intellectuals of the empire offered a Christian critique of imperial power and violence.[44] In the East, Athanasius, Basil, Gregory of Nyassa, Gregory Nazianzen, and Dionysius the Areopagite[45] emphasized Christian differences with the empire, the necessity of peace as a positive force, and a rejection of war that was to remain a strong tradition throughout later Byzantine history.[46] In the West, the brutality of the barbarian invasions set the context for a Christian response but did not change its consistent message. Lactantius' tradition of political criticism and praise of peacemaking remained strong. Marius Victorinus (c. 280–c. 363), for example, quotes Ephesians 6:23–24 to remind his readers that peace is the natural law of the universe and war its negation.[47] Hilary of Poitiers (c. 315–367),[48] a convert to Christianity and bishop of Poitiers in southern Gaul, was exiled to Asia Minor for his opposition to the Arian heresy of the emperors. A "mischief-maker" even when he was under close imperial scrutiny, he was sent back to Gaul in 360. Hilary defined peace not as the cessation of conflict but as seeking perfection,[49] a definition of peace as active peacemaking. "Learning peace," he declares, "is the characteristic of those who listen to their will."[50]

Jerome (342–420), loyal citizen of Rome, was truly shocked at the fall of the city in 410.[51] Yet he contrasts the *militia Christi*, the soldiers of Christ, and the *militia mundi*, the military.[52] He notes that the goal of individual peace can only be attained by possessing the peace of God, and that, conversely, inner peace can only lead to love and peace on a societal level.[53] The truly peaceful person, he says, is the one who "first in his own heart and then among his brothers, out of raging discord shows his determination to make peace.[54]

## THE MONASTIC REVOLT

Although there is ample evidence of the attitudes of the great thinkers after the founding of the Christian empire, little literary evidence exists of popular attitudes. What evidence of popular attitudes does exist is associated with the new monastic movement.[55] It is no coincidence that the appearance of the first monks comes within a few years of the reign of Constantine and the victory of the church.[56] With the new romance between the empire and the church, many Christian bishops, intellectuals, and aristocrats embraced the despotism, violent coercion, and wars of the empire as somehow divinely sanctioned. Christian laypersons by the thousands, however, began to abandon urban civilization and settled agricultural communities to flee to the purity of the desert.[57] The monastic movement was both a prophetic revolt against society[58] and an active spiritual attack on the invisible demons that beset late antiquity.[59] As such it was a constructive as well as a critical force.[60] The monks, both men and women, fled for many reasons: to escape imperial injustice and heavy taxation, to imitate Christ and the martyrs in their lives of sacrifice, and to carry on the struggle against a still active paganism.

The revolt started among the lower classes of the provinces: in Egypt first, then Palestine, Syria, and Mesopotamia, and it soon spread west. Anthony the Hermit (c. 251–356),[61] the founder of monasticism, and Pachomius (c. 290–346)[62] were the prototypes.

The son of a wealthy family, Anthony abandoned his inheritance to embrace a Christianity that was nondoctrinal, nonhierarchical, and nonintellectual, based strictly on the literal observance of the Beatitudes. He fled the city for a life of constant spiritual strife lived in absolute poverty, both material and cultural. Anthony's struggles and temptations became famous throughout the Christian world and set the tone for the monastic movement. As a member of the new *militia Christi*,[63] in the vanguard against evil, the monk became an active alternative to the soldier. By focusing on the inner struggle, Anthony replaced the appeal of physical violence with the heroism of ethical conflict. By refocusing on Christ's spiritual kingdom and his community of peace, the monk offered a stark contrast to the Christian empire of Constantine and Eusebius and once again affirmed Christ's message of peacemaking as an active alternative to the temptations of political power.

Pachomius exemplifies the process that Anthony set in motion.[64] A Roman soldier who had been drafted into the army, he abandoned his profession to become a Christian. First a hermit for many years, he later established a new communal form of monasticism in upper Egypt that by the end of his life had attracted thousands of Egyptian peasants. Many were fleeing political oppression, taxes, and poverty; others were escaping the comforts of the Christian empire.[65] The monks formed a new society characterized by political and economic self-government, bound together by a willing adherence to abbots and rules, and based on Christian love and peace.[66] The success of the new community was telling; nonviolence and organization based on mutual trust could have substantial impact on the world. The Pachomian settlements attracted tens of thousands of Christians and had become so large by the fifth century that collectively they represented one of the largest economic organizations of the ancient world.[67]

From the outset the movement represented a nonviolent protest against the injustice and violence of imperial society.[68] But the monks represented more than an alternative. The holy woman and man were among the very few who could actively oppose the powerful aristocracy of the late Roman world and who could stand in the way of its autocratic justice. The intervention of Syrian monks, which saved Antioch from imperial vengeance and destruction in 387, demonstrates the kind of check monks could provide.[69] The lives and sayings of these Christians represent a new prophetic voice of the simple folk who took the commands of Christ literally.[70] Certain themes are repeated endlessly: the imitation of the suffering of Christ and the martyrs,[71] the use of miracles instead of physical violence to explain to a popular audience the effect of peacemaking,[72] and the prophetic call to justice and right living.

The monastic revolt against imperial church and Christian empire mainly affected the largely Christian, urban, and Hellenistic East. Though it also spread to the West,[73] there the provinces long remained virtually untouched by Christianity, a condition exascerbated by the barbarian invasions. Nevertheless the monastic movement in the West produced men and women whose lives displayed both the inner tranquility and the outer peacemaking of the *militia Christi*. The fact that knowledge of their lives have come down to us at all is evidence of a living tradition that prized the peacemaker.

The life of Martin of Tours is archetypal.[74] Martin was born in Sabaria in Pannonia in what is now Hungary (c. 316), the son of a military tribune. As the pagan son of a pagan soldier, at age fifteen he was required by imperial law to enter military service. When he tried to avoid it, he was turned in by his father and enrolled into the imperial guard of Emperor Constantius, taking the military oath bound in chains.[75] He is often portrayed as a soldier, especially in the famous scene of his cutting in two his military cloak to share it with a beggar.[76]

Converted at age twenty-two soon after meeting the beggar, he stayed in the service at the request of his military tribune.[77] Yet this was no longer an age of peaceful police service.[78] Gaul was being overrun by the barbarians, and Martin was called into active duty. Refusing to accept his bonus pay, even for a just, defensive war, he applied for a discharge, telling the Caesar in command, "I have been your soldier up to now. Let me now be God's. Let someone who is going to fight have your bonus. I am Christ's soldier. I am not allowed to fight."[79] Martin's biographer, Sulpicius Severus, notes that his refusal to fight was not based on cowardice, on the fear of being killed, but on his refusal to kill. To prove his courage he offered to lead the battle line the next day unarmed, protected only by his faith; that night the barbarians miraculously withdrew.[80]

After his discharge Martin became a disciple of Hilary of Poitiers, traveled through Illyria and Italy, and finally returned to Gaul to live as a hermit.[81] He was soon called out of seclusion to become bishop of Tours. As bishop he put the principles of Christian peacemaking into action, preaching and converting the pagan Aedui around Autun. Attacked while destroying a pagan temple, Matin offered his bare neck to the sword. Confounded by his example, the pagans destroyed their own temple and converted.[82] Martin combined this missionary peacemaking with a prophetic criticism of the brutality of the new ruling class in Gaul[83] and resisted both violence against heretics[84] and capital punishment.[85]

While rhetorical and full of miraculous causality, Sulpicius' writings do reflect the reality of Martin's life and the ideas of the author and his circle.[86] Martin and his followers were typical. Despite criticism that Sulpicius was embarrassed by Martin's military past, his biography portrays the saint's life as a movement of protest against militarism.[87] "The ascetic *militia Christi* of that age represented not a refinement, but a flat repudiation of militarism. Martin adopted monasticism partly at least in order to affirm the nonviolent way of life."[88] Nonviolence would be an essential element of the monastic revolt against militarism for the next thousand years.

Among Martin's circle Paulinus of Nola[89] and Victricius of Rouen[90] attempted to imitate Martin by rejecting their military oaths.[91] Victricius (c. 330–c. 407) converted while still in the army. Nearly killed as punishment, he was discharged from service and led the life of an itinerant preacher until he was named bishop of Rouen around 385.[92] A bishop in a remote frontier town with a small Christian community, Victricius did not enjoy the power that his eastern Roman colleagues did. He lived as an active missionary, attempting to convert the people of the countryside by establishing monasteries, Christian communities of men and women designed to win over the pagans by their exemplary lives.[93] He brought peace to the troubled province of Belgica Secunda (modern Normandy), converting "to a peaceful way of life both the barbarians outside the frontier and the oppressed classes within it."[94]

## CHRISTIAN PEACEMAKING AND THE BARBARIANS

The fifth century saw the further disintegration of imperial authority and administration in the West, the sack of Rome (410), the migration of the Germanic peoples into the empire (the Barbarian Invasions), and the establishment of the shadow-Roman successor-kingdoms carved out of the carcass of the empire. The history of Rome after 400 is, in fact, the history of its response to new peoples.[95] The Eastern Empire reacted to the barbarians with bloody defense and reconquest, the West opted for relatively peaceful assimilation.[96] The reasons for this difference are complex. The East was more populous, richer, stronger, better administered, and provided with shrewder diplomats and more energetic generals than the West. The West had generals but lacked the will to fight. In any case, confrontation was not on a large scale in the West.

The barbarians numbered no more than five percent of the population of the conquered provinces,[97] their ruling classes certainly no more than two percent.[98] Into the fifth century the Christians were a minority in the West, restricted to the Rhone valley and to such centers as Trier, southern Spain near Cordova, and the cities of Italy and North Africa.[99] We cannot therefore speak of mass movements to postulate either a barbarization of Christianity or a wholesale conversion of "barbarian Europe." The invaders replaced only the ruling classes at the center and in the western provinces. The rest of the population remained unchanged and untouched except for the effects of aristocratic violence on their daily lives. The new ruling class brought with it a Germanic warrior ethic, similar to the Roman ethic in its identification of virtue with heroism in war but different in that it replaced Roman civic virtue with personal loyalty to a war leader and was contemptuous of the comfortable urban life of the empire.[100] The Germanic dissociation of personal ethics from religious ritual, a dissociation the Christians had ended for Roman society, now complicated the process of conversion.[101]

Even after their acceptance by the empire, Christians had remained wary of civic life and indifferent to the protection of the Pax Romana,[102] as Augustine's ambiguity reveals. The Christian church did not share the pagans' horror and contempt of the outsider or the barbarian and was quite willing to accept them.[103] *On the Governance of God* by Salvian of Marseille (c. 450) typifies Christian attitudes.[104] Salvian believed the barbarians to be less blameworthy than Christian Romans who returned to the evils of Roman paganism—games, theater, and vice—and certainly less blameworthy than the Romans themselves. He was outspoken in his criticism of growing social exploitation in the empire, including the growth of serfdom. He equated the imperial official with corruption and the imperial soldier with rapine, and wondered whether life under the barbarians might not be preferable.[105] His views are echoed by Paulus Orosius, a Spanish priest and disciple of Augustine, who notes that the barbarians treat their fellow Christians equally and do not oppress or plunder them.[106] In the Alps around Turin, the bishop of that city, Maximus (fl. 450–465), who had witnessed a massacre of missionary bishops by the barbarians, pressed for the nonviolent conversion of the pagans and the barbarians. He warned, "What should be said of us, who are forced to live piously, not by devotion but by terror?"[107]

The Christian response to the invasions was clear. Rather than being weakened by the barbarian ideal, the church's message became even stronger: "It is hardly surprising that the church took a more unfavorable view of warfare than before and set itself up in resolute opposition to the barbarian ethos."[108] In fact, "the invasions far from interrupting the preaching of the Gospel, made it even more necessary."[109] On the upper levels of the church "Christian statesmen and administrators maintained what order could be saved from the Roman past (and) instilled what Christian principles they could into their people."[110] They did so, however, in the image of the Roman Empire—hierarchical and despotic—concentrating their efforts on the barbarian leadership.[111] Modern scholarship has concentrated on the upper levels, noting the merging of Christian and barbarian, but it has ignored the process of peaceful conversion and nonviolence on the lower levels that took place from the time of the collapse of Rome in the fifth century to the foundation of Charlemagne's Christian Republic in the ninth.

Christian communities in the West were isolated and small. Their bishops were most often missionary leaders and pastors. Monasticism, which had begun to penetrate the western part of the empire and the countryside, represented not a withdrawal from established society but an active campaign of Christian peacemaking in the rural population. It offered an opportunity for spiritual leadership and development of resources where none had existed before.

Despite the barbarism of the age, the record of Christian peacemaking is impressive. A few examples must serve to illustrate this point; many more could be used to reinforce it. The chief source is the lives of the saints. These popular accounts offered immediate and simple examples of behavior to their readers over many centuries. The status given the saints shows that they were officially recognized by Catholics as exemplary models for imitation.

Christian suffering under the Vandals is well attested. Nominally Christian, the Arian Vandals swept through Spain between 409 and 429 leaving destruction behind them. An inscription commemorating the Christians slain during the period gives some indication of the Christian response to the violence of the barbarians. "May our peace glorify those the enemy despised," it reads, "and honored be (the martyrs) rather than the shock of destruction."[112] In North Africa the Vandals set out to persecute the orthodox Catholics and produced a new strain of martyrs. Victor of Vita's *History of the Persecution of the African Province* (c. 485),[113] recounts in detail Christians' solidarity and nonviolent defiance of their oppressors amid the most horrible conditions of imprisonment and persecution.[114]

In Gaul, Paulinus of Nola (353–431),[115] a follower of Martin of Tours, who, like him, had abandoned military life, sang the praises of nonviolence in the midst of the invasions.[116] Honoratus of Arles (c. 350–429) followed a similar pattern.[117] The son of a Gallo-Roman family of consular rank and privilege, he scandalized his family by converting to Christianity soon after the sack of Rome.[118] After making a pilgrimage to Greece and Italy he returned to southern Gaul to establish a hermitage off the coast. It became the monastic house of Lérins. According to his eulogist, Hilary of Arles, Honoratus lived as a constant witness to, and martyr for, peace.[119] "Peace, like persecution," Hilary notes, "has its martyrs, and you, so long as you dwelt in the body, were a constant witness for Christ." The community of Lérins shared this ideal of peacemaking. Lupus of Troyes (c. 383–479) was a monk there by 426 and reputedly saved his province from Attila and the Huns by peaceful means.[120] His example was repeated by others of the Lérins community.

The story of Niceta of Remesiana[121] (c. 370–c. 414)[122] comes to us through a poem written by Paulinus of Nola.[123] A missionary in Illyria during the invasions, Niceta brought peace to the area by converting both the barbarian tribes and the Bessian brigands, who were in armed rebellion against Roman rule and were actively aiding the barbarians. The conversion of the Bessians had significant results. Once converted to Christianity the brigands became monks. Their conversion illustrates the transformation of violent rebellion into nonviolent social protest that we have already seen take place in monasticism. Niceta went on to restore peace as well as "and perhaps better than, any contemporary general could have done."[124]

The story of Severinus of Noricum (d. 482)[125] complements that of Niceta. Severinus lived on the northern Danube frontier in what is modern Austria and Bavaria. Freed from the menace of the Huns in 453, the Heruli, Rugians, Alemanni, Thuringi, Suevi, and Goths poured into the province, destroying the Roman cities (which had been abandoned by the army) and massacring or enslaving the inhabitants. An unknown wanderer arrived upon the scene. Little else is known of Severinus's social background or origin except that he had spent some time in the East. He began to rebuild civil life for the Romans of the province, stressing nonviolent resistance to the barbarian, and Christian forms of social organization: almsgiving, the ransoming of prisoners, and a life of good works based partly on the rules of Saint Basil. Hunger strikes against the barbarian occupation (as at Comagenis) and the nonviolent expropriation and redistribution of food supplies were among his methods.[126]

Yet even as he ordered his followers to flee from city after city and to offer no resistance, his fame among the barbarians spread. They came to fear and respect him, accepting him as arbiter of their own disputes. Late in life he confronted King Feletheus of the Rugians and prevented the capture of the last Roman stronghold at Lauriacum. He warned the king that Christian methods of leadership and not military control best suited the people. Through such nonviolent means Severinus worked throughout his life to insure the safety of the province.

Germanus of Auxerre offers a similar example.[127] Born around 378 in Auxerre in northern Gaul of aristocratic Christian parents, he became a lawyer in Rome, married, and then returned to Gaul where he was appointed a *dux,* or military commander. He was soon elected bishop and thereupon abandoned his old life.[128] Germanus' episcopate coincided with the barbarian invasion of Gaul and Britain. He made two trips across the Channel, one reportedly with Lupus of Troyes. At the time of his first voyage he converted the British army and brought about their nonviolent, if not miraculous, defeat of the Saxons and Picts.[129] Like Salvian of Marseille and Severinus of Noricum, he combined peacemaking with the active pursuit of social justice, protecting the poor from the oppression of taxes,[130] blaming poverty for crime,[131] and seeking to remedy the exploitation of the people within his diocese.[132]

Returning from one of his trips to Britain, Germanus was greeted by a delegation from Armorica (western Brittany) seeking his protection from the savage King Goar of the Alans. Goar had been sent against the Britons by the Roman general Aetius "the Magnificant" as punishment for their rebellion against the tattered remains of the empire. "The movement of tribes had already begun and their iron-armed cavalry were filling the roads."[133] Alone and unarmed, the aging bishop went out to confront Goar. "The march was already in progress when the meeting took place, the priest was opposed to a war-lord clad in armor and surrounded by his bodyguard."[134] At first Germanus requested a meeting through an interpreter. He was ignored until he rebuked the King, seized his horse's bridle, and halted him along with his whole army. The bishop's firmness impressed the barbarian. "Shaken by the strength of such insistent authority" the king turned from his mission. "The mediation of the Bishop, and his holiness, had restrained a king, recalled an army and delivered a province from devastation."[135]

But the affair was not yet settled. Germanus needed imperial approval of the agreement, and so he traveled across the Alps to the exarch's court at Ravenna.[136] While at the imperial palace he intervened in the case of several prisoners who had been condemned to die at the whim, it seems, of the palace officials "the night before," and caused them to be released. His biographer notes, "For once the jail was harmless, because empty."[137]

The story of Germanus' life, written about 480 by Constantius of Lyons, is a tribute not only to any individual peacemaker but also to the peace tradition active in Gaul at the end of the fifth century. At the insistence of Censurius, bishop of Lyons around 470, the account was widely circulated and influenced thought and action well into the Merovingian period.[138]

Germanus' most famous disciple was Saint Patrick (c. 385–461).[139] The son of a Romano-British civil servant and Christian deacon, Patrick went to Ireland as a missionary in 432, confronting the pagan Druids and silencing them with his spiritual authority. He soon established a thriving Christian community around him. In his *Letter to Coroticus* (c. 450),[140] Patrick rebukes the nominally Christian king whose followers, the Picts, had massacred a group of recently baptized Christians. Patrick condemns the work of the soldier, calling Coroticus' men "gangsters," "ravenous wolves," and "fellow citizens of demons," who have "cruelly butchered and slaughtered with the sword."[141]

Without fear for himself, he called on Coroticus and his followers to abandon their ways. That the letter survives (it is one of three surviving works by the saint) is evidence of its impact.

Genevieve of Paris (c. 420–c. 500), another disciple of Germanus, became a nun because of his influence and moved to Paris, where in 451 she is said to have saved the city from Attila the Hun without violence.[142] Later she ran the blockade of the Franks to provide food for the besieged. In the midst of barbarian domination she requested and obtained both the release of prisoners of war and mercy for condemned criminals. The stories of Germanus and Genevieve find an echo in the story of Pope Leo the Great (d. 461).[143] He confronted Attila the Hun, preventing the sack of Rome (452). Later he prevented a massacre by the Vandals under Genseric in the captured city (455).[144] Although the account of Pope Leo's achievements by Prosper of Aquitaine is not detailed and seems to have the same general characteristics as other stories, it is nonetheless evidence that Christians of the late fifth century believed that nonviolence was a viable response despite the worst realities of barbarism and the end of traditional civilization.[145]

## THE SIXTH CENTURY

The barbarians settled into kingdoms by the sixth century: Vandals in North Africa; Ostrogoths in Italy; Merovingian Franks in Gaul; Visigoths in Spain; Anglo-Saxons in Britain; Frisians in the Low Countries; and Saxons, Thuringians, Bavarians, Lombards, and others ranging from north to south beyond the Rhine. The forms taken by Christian peacemaking reflect this new consolidation of political power in the hands of the barbarian kings. The Christian hierarchy sought to tame the barbarians by converting them from the top down, as is illustrated by the baptism of King Clovis of the Franks (503).[146] The monastery, however, continued to be a power, to act as a fortress of the *militia Christi*, and was called on time and again to deny the power of the sword and to confront the violence of the barbarians.

Caesarius of Arles (470–543) was a monk at Lérins before becoming bishop of Arles in 503, the year of Clovis' baptism.[147] He acted as arbiter among the warring tribes, saving Arles from destruction during the changeover from the rule of the Visigoths to that of the Ostrogoths (508) and from Ostrogoths to Franks (536). He used church funds to ransom prisoners of war and once confronted the Ostrogoth King Theodoric at Ravenna over the king's charges that Caesarius had aided the Visigoth defenders against him. He turned over to the poor the gift Theodoric gave him as a peace offering. He was a staunch promoter of the religious life for women and founded the first convent for women in Gaul, insisting that every nun be taught to read and write. A popular preacher, he urged his congregation to "match your behaviour to the words you sing."[148] He realized the need for basic laws that could free subjects from the whims of local warlords and so published an adaptation of the Roman *Theodosian Code* that became the *Breviarium Alarici,* the civil code for Gaul.

Nicetius of Trier (d. 566) was another monk who was called to be bishop of his frontier city.[149] Like Caesarius, he used his position to protect his city and his people from the depredations of the Frankish nobility. He criticized King Chlotar I for his excesses, and was banished as a result (560). Germanus of Paris (c. 496–576) was abbot of St. Symphorian near Paris until he became bishop of the city (c. 556).[150] He was unswerving in his attempts to end civil strife and to curb the viciousness of the Frankish kings. Gregory of Tours (538–594) was bishop of his city and counselor to four Merovingian kings.[151] His *History of the Franks*[152] corroborates other accounts of the efforts of the Christian clergy to make peace and to end the constant feuding of the barbarian kings. Gregory was responsible for the peace treaty agreed to by Childebert II and Guthram I (587).[153]

Martin of Braga (c. 515–580) introduced communal monasticism to Spain about 550.[154] Monks there, as in Gaul, were in the vanguard of Christian penetration of the pagan hinterland. Appointed archbishop of Braga before 572, Martin led a successful mission to convert the Arian Suevi. His sermon, *On the Correction of Rustics*, spells out the process of their conversion, accomplished not through violence or compulsion but persuasion.[155] This work was the basis for other missionary and teaching tracts: one by Pirminus in Germany (c. 753) and Aelfric's Anglo-Saxon *Homilies* (c. 1000).[156]

The career of Pope Gregory I, the Great (c. 540–604)[157] is the ultimate example of the promotion of the monk into Christian leadership. Born of a patrician family, Gregory served as a civil magistrate who endowed several monasteries and then became a monk himself (c. 575). From 579 to 585 he served as Roman ambassador to Constantinople and in 590 was elected pope. In the face of the Lombard invasion and the conquest of Italy by the Byzantines, Gregory used the wealth of the church to ransom prisoners and to relieve the sufferers of war, disease, and famine. He worked to preserve peace with the barbarians.

For Gregory peace was the beginning of all other virtues, including charity.[158] Believing that only peaceful means could truly convert the barbarians, he rejected coercion. He closely supervised the mission sent to Anglo-Saxon England under Augustine of Canterbury.[159] The example of the missionaries' Christian lives and their willingness to die for their faith attracted the pagans.[160] Bede notes that conversion was "accepted freely and not under compulsion."[161] Gregory's instructions to Augustine and to his legate Mellitus are specific and include the injunction not to destroy pagan shrines but to remove their idols and convert the shrines and rituals peacefully to Christian usage.[162]

The life of Patrick's successor Comgall (517–603) demonstrates the process of conversion from barbarian warrior to *militia Christi* sought by the missionaries in Ireland.[163] A soldier as a young man, he converted to Christianity. By the age of forty he was a priest at Bangor and taught the young Columba (521–597).[164] Columba founded the monasteries of Derry and Durrow before 563, when he was forced to leave Ireland as a penance for his role in encouraging the bloody battle of Cuil Dremne (561). He went to Iona, where he established a base for the conversion of the Scottish Picts, and converted their king, Brude. Columba's life exemplifies two important strains in Irish Christianity: its pursuit of missionary work to convert the barbarians and its emphasis on penance and strict discipline as a sign of inner conversion. The *Rule*[165] is falsely attributed to him, but it faithfully reflects his spirituality. It stresses the imitation of Christ and the gospels, poverty and communal life, forgiveness and prayers for enemies, and a desire for martyrdom: the "red" for the witness to Christian truth and the "white" of ascetic discipline. Sometimes carried to extremes, ascetic discipline was viewed as a true sign of inner conversion.

## EDUCATING THE BARBARIANS FOR PEACE: PENITENTIALS AND CANON LAW

Given the emphasis on the inner spiritual life, it was natural that Ireland would develop a system for regulating the life of its monks in monasteries and the life of the semibarbarian communities around them, which they administered like bishoprics.[166] They did so with a series of manuals for confessors that specified certain penances for certain categories of sins. A penance could mean fasting on bread and water for weeks, seasons, or years; giving compensation to victims in money, goods, or property; exile or pilgrimage; and excommunication. Readmission to the Christian community was possible only after the completion of the penance and only with the permission of the abbot/bishop. To remain outside this communion was to court eternal damnation. The "penitentials,"[167] sets of church rules, grew from early Christian councils and disciplinary canons (such as those of Hippolytus) and from monastic rules such as Columba's and its antecedents, the rules of John Cassian, Basil, and the Eastern ascetics.[168] The penitentials flourished from the fifth to the eleventh century, when they became part of canon law. They found their fullest expression in Celtic monasticism and were exported by it to the rest of Western Europe.[169] The penitentials touched every aspect of the spiritual and physical lives of the monks and their dependents and thus provide an index to the morality and attitudes of the early medieval church in many areas, including violence.

The violent conditions of the barbarian West are acknowledged: murder, homicide, blood feuds, parricide, infanticide—each has its place in the catalogues of sins and punishments. Even war is not excluded. Although punishments for clerics were more severe (depending on ecclesiastical grade), laymen were also required to do severe penances. The canons of the fifth century attributed to Saint Patrick imposed a one-year penance on any Christian who killed another person.[170] The Canons of the Welsh Synods (500–525)[171] and the *Penitential of Finnian* (c. 525–550) repeat the prohibition against killing. *The Penitential of Finnian* imposed penalties on the clergy[172] of up to ten years of exile.[173] The *Penitential of Columban* (c. 600)[174] was applied widely and refined the distinction between monks, clergy, and laity; its chapter 13 prescribes severe punishment for laypersons who kill: three years of exile, unarmed, living only on bread and water.[175] This penance of disarming the killer is also found in chapter 5 of the *Penitential of Cummean*.[176] The *Irish Canons* (c. 675)[177] and the *Penitential of Theodore* (668–690)[178] both prescribe harsh punishments for murder: ten years of fasting in the first[179] and seven in the second.[180] The *Irish Collection* (700–725) continues this tradition.[181]

The penitentials do not stop at punishing individual violence and murder. Chapter 6 of the *Penitential of Theodore*[182] ranks even killing in war under the legitimate command of one's lord along with murder, although it prescribes only forty days of penance and exclusion from the church and its life-giving sacraments. As late as 800 the *Old Irish Penitential*[183] categorizes killing in battle with homicide, revenge in a blood feud, and murder of offspring, and imposes a penance of one and a half years, provided that the soldier "does not pursue the slaughter after the battle is over."[184] Penances on those who kill, even in a just war, were also imposed by Saint Egbert (750)[185] and by the penitential attributed to Bede (c. 800).[186]

The penitential system as it developed on the European continent during the ninth century continued to affect attitudes and behavior.[187] Most penitentials restricted the punishment for killing in war to forty days of penance, but the act was considered a sin and a defilement for which penance was due. This attitude prevailed well into the eleventh century. In most cases, after the penance was imposed the penitent was expected to lay down his arms and never again to take part in war.[188]

The penitentials also affected secular legislation. The *Welsh Canons* (c. 550–650), for example, required a substantial payment in slaves as recompense for homicide[189] and imposed fines for bearing arms in church.[190] The *Laws of Edmund* (c. 942–946) prohibited anyone who had shed the blood of a Christian from coming near the king until that person had done penance.[191] While the refined phrases of Tertullian, the apocalyptic indignation of Lactantius were no longer used, the penitentials spoke their opposition to violence in a language of concrete crime and punishment that an unsophisticated people and age understood.

The penitentials stemmed from and paralleled the development of the movement for clerics to completely refrain from violence. We cannot trace here the gradual separation of the clergy from the laity and its arrangement into hierarchical orders, but we can outline the trend to clerical nonviolence. Prohibitions keeping former soldiers or those guilty of killing from entering the clergy are found as early as the third century in the *Canons of Hippolytus*.[192] The *Didascalia* and the *Constitutions* of the fourth century expressly forbade bishops from doing violence.[193] The prohibition was reinforced in 378 by the Council of Sirmium's rule keeping former soldiers or civil magistrates from entering holy orders.[194] Innocent I repeated this prohibition in his letters to Victrucius of Rouen (404) and to Felix of Nuceri and other bishops gathered in Toledo (Spain).[195] Saint Ambrose repeated the same theme.

The restriction was repeated in the councils of Chalcedon (451), Angers (453), Agda (453), Lerida (524), Macon (583), Toledo (633 and 675), Bordeaux and St. Jean of Losne (after 650), Ratisbon (742), the Frankish General Council of 747 and that of Mainz (813), when it became official Carolingian policy.[196] This movement was bolstered by the penitentials' specific regulations for both layperson and cleric. In the ancient, hierarchical world that the church had inherited it seemed natural to all that those closer to divine nature should live a life close to the divine model.[197] Early medieval men and women expected high clerical standards and saw them as a confirmation of the value of peacemaking.

## MEROVINGIAN EUROPE: THE CONTINUING TRADITION OF PEACE

The seventh and eighth centuries saw major changes in Europe. North Africa and Spain succumbed to the rise of Islam, the Avars threatened from central Asia, the Christian conversion of the successor kingdoms was consolidated, and the process spread into northern Europe.[198] Christian peacemaking during this period took two forms, both active responses to the conditions of the times: first a prophetic criticism of contemporary rulers and the protection of the oppressed; and second, the nonviolent spread of the Christian religion in the face of pagan hostility and the violence of the Christian kings.

Columban (c. 540–615) combined the characteristics of both forms.[199] A monk, scholar, and poet at Bangor, at age forty-five he left with twelve companions for the continent where he founded monasteries and converted the barbarians. He fell afoul of the Burgundian queen Brunhild for his condemnation—"like a second John the Baptist,"—of her grandson King Thierry II.[200] Rather than make a martyr of the abbot, Thierry chose to exile him to Besançon.[201] There Columban heard of a prison full of condemned persons awaiting the death penalty. They promised to amend their lives, so Columban arranged their escape and was then himself hunted—unsuccessfully—by the king's troops.[202] He finally surrendered to the king's knights so that they would not be executed for not capturing him.[203] Columban and his Irish companions were deported to Ireland in 610. During the journey a guard struck one of the missionaries. Columban's reply was firm and echoes the Sermon on the Mount:

Why, cruel man, do you add to my grief? Is not the guilt of the crime which you have committed sufficient for your destruction? Why do you appear merciless against the merciful? Why do you strike a wearied member of Christ? Why do you vent your wrath on the gentle? Remember that you will be punished by God in this place, where in your rage you have struck a member of Christ.[204]

The group managed to escape their captors. Given refuge at the court of Chlotar, king of Neustria in western France, Columban set out to call on the king and ask that he reform several abuses at his court.[205] Eventually Columban and his companions founded the monastery of Bobbio, where he died.[206]

There are many other examples from the sixth and seventh centuries. Sulpice, who died bishop of Bourges (c. 647), combined a pattern of protection of the people with prophetic resistance to Merovingian tyranny.[207] Amand of Maastricht (584–679) lived as a hermit near Bourges until the age of forty-five, when he began missionary work in Flanders and around Antwerp, among the Slavs along the Danube, and in Gascony.[208] Although he was himself opposed by the pagans, he reproved King Dagobert I for using force to convert them. Lambert of Maastricht (635–c. 705) was a missionary exiled to Stavelot for his criticism of a Frankish magnate.[209] He was later killed for his criticism of Pepin of Herstal. Paulinus of Aquilea (c. 726–802) spoke out against Carolingian attempts to effect the conversion of the Avars by force.[210] Philibert of Nourmoutier (d. 684) was a monastic leader exiled for his denunciation of the Frankish mayor of the palace, Erobin, for his crimes.[211]

Queen Bathild was born in England.[212] Taken by pirates in 641 and sold as a slave to the mayor of the Frankish king Clovis II, she moved to abolish the slave trade and continued to foster justice for her subjects until deposed and exiled to a convent in 665. Adamnan (628–704), the ninth bishop of Iona, was widely known as a peace-loving man.[213] *Adamnan's Law* (c. 697) is a set of regulations for the Christian life designed to protect women, children, and the clergy, especially during wartime.[214] It anticipates the provisions of the Peace of God.[215]

Contemporaneous with these prophets were many missionaries and martyrs. The two Hewalds, born in Northumberland, were killed (695) attempting to convert the Saxons of Westphalia.[216] Ludger was born near Utrecht (c. 744) and studied under Alcuin of York.[217] In 755 he was sent to revive missionary work in Friesland, was driven out, but returned there in 785. In the 790s he was sent to Saxony by Charlemagne where he succeeded through nonviolent methods in converting a people whom Charlemagne's massacres had failed to move. He eventually became bishop of Munster and died on a preaching tour in 809.

Perhaps the best known missionary of this period is Boniface of Crediton.[218] Born about 675, he became a monk and taught and preached in Wessex until 718 when he went to the Continent to spread Christianity in Hesse, Bavaria, Westphalia, Thuringia, and Wurtenberg. He traveled to Rome three times to report on his progress and was named bishop of Mainz on his second trip. He had a tremendous reforming influence over the Frankish church and did not hesitate to criticize the Frankish kings for their injustices. He resigned his see in 754 to resume a missionary life. He worked in Friesland and there was attacked by a band of pagans (c. 754). As his followers prepared to defend themselves he rebuked them saying, "Sons, cease fighting. Lay down your arms, for we are told in Scripture not to render evil for good, but to overcome evil by good."[219] He and his followers were martyred.

Boniface's methods have been well recorded. He used pagan beliefs as a springboard for dialogue, offering Christian civilization as an incentive to conversion,[220] founded strict monastic houses as centers of Christian life among the barbarians,[221] and established clear-cut administrative and penitential systems to maintain his work.[222] The life of Boniface marks a new period when the preacher and martyr were once again closely linked with the hierarchical church. By the end of the eighth century Europe had entered a new age—the age of the empire of Charlemagne, the Carolingian renaissance of arts, letters, and religious life, and the expectation that a revived Christian empire could support a new Christian citizenship for laypersons and clerics alike.

Many historians call the intervening centuries a dark age of violence and ignorance. If they are right it may be because our sources for the period are so scant and our view so dim. Barbarism did overwhelm the ancient civilization of the empire, extinguishing many great lights, but the Christian life of peace was not interrupted. It survived the conversion of Constantine and his marriage to the church in intellectual discourse and in monastic revolt. In the slow and steady process of conversion and prophetic critique the Christian life of peace gradually won over most of the pagan and barbarian West to the point where it began to prize the creative Christian values of love and peace.

# CHAPTER 5

# FROM CAROLINGIAN PEACE TO PEOPLE'S PEACE (800–1100)

## INTRODUCTION

The years 800 and 1100 outline a distinct period in the history of Catholic peacemaking. The year 800 marks the rise of the Carolingian Empire. The year 1100 marks the early Crusade movement (begun in 1095), its symbolic sanctification of violence, and the export of the new European order by force to the Moslem and pagan worlds. Two elements emerged during the Carolingian period that would alter Christian concepts of peace and peacemaking for centuries to come. The first was the political rise of the new Carolingian dynasty in the renewed Roman Empire of the West. The second was the beginning of fresh barbarian invasions from the north and east and the rise of Islam. Internal efforts to legislate the life of the Christian Republic were matched by its external defense against Viking, Magyar, and Saracen invasion. The Carolingian Empire thus brought about a renewed militarization of society, seeking to protect Christendom from external threat. It used the hierarchical bonds of feudal oath and vassalage to bring the new class of mobile horse warriors, the *milites,* under a central authority.

At the same time European intellectual and political elites were formulating new theories of the relationship between political and spiritual leadership in a unified Christian society. Their problems and conditions were in many ways similar to those of Christian thinkers under the late Roman Empire when the state was identified with Christian society and its leadership was accepted as the legitimate interpreter of the gospels. These conditions and ideas were to shape the forms of Christian peacemaking into a new image emphasizing hierarchy, order, and compulsion as legitimate means to Christian perfection. These formulations, in turn, evoked strong responses and new interpretations of the gospel of peace that would reaffirm the life of Christ and seek to apply it to this new world.

## CAROLINGIAN PEACE

Charlemagne's achievements and his impact on history have been much debated by modern historians. We are concerned here, however, with how Charlemagne and his successors, their advisors, and their subjects viewed the renewed Christian empire and how their theory and practice affected the ideas and practice of peace.

The Carolingian Empire inherited the ideology of the Christian Roman Empire and determined the forms that official peacemaking would take.[1] First, the empire was hierarchical: all authority flowed down from heaven's own hierarchies through the emperor, the representative of Christ acting as intermediary between the earth and the heavens.[2] All grace, authority, and order was diffused through the emperor to all levels of Christian society.[3] Peace was therefore something imposed from above, a state of order, tranquility, and unity within the empire guaranteed by force.[4] Like the Germanic king's peace, Carolingian peace was a special protection granted to subjects as a privilege,[5] a possession of the powerful dispersed like wealth or favors.[6]

Second, the *foedus pacis*,[7] the close political alliance of the Carolingians with the papacy and with the ecclesiastical hierarchy, found its practical application in the Gelasian theory of the two swords.[8] This theory established two separate spheres of authority within Christian society—ecclesiastical and secular, one to lead the body and one the spirit. From the eighth century on, Christian peace would therefore entail two things:[9] the external protection of the social order by force[10] and imperial legislation,[11] and a distinct internal peace of the heart, based on gospel ethics but restricted to monks and clerics.[12] The Carolingians insured that each sphere kept to its own business. Monastic life was supported, encouraged, and carefully directed, and late Roman prohibitions against clerical participation in the army were repeated again and again,[13] despite the tendency of the church[14] to become enmeshed in the net of feudal obligations.[15]

Third, the identification of the Carolingian Empire with Western Christianity served to revive the late Roman associations of *Christianitas* (Christendom) with the *orbis Romanus* or *oikoumeme* (the Roman world).[16] Only membership within this empire guaranteed salvation;[17] all those beyond the frontiers of Christendom, or even those within it who did not recognize the supremacy of the Christian emperor, were enemies of the Christian faith, the *pax* of the emperor, and, therefore, of the church. Thus on the official level Christian peace implied the need for a defense against the attacks of external enemies, their conquest, and forced conversion.[18] Popes and Frankish clergy cooperated to refine a theory of divine kingship and holy war based on Old Testament models.[19] The brutal subjugation of the East Saxons, their forced conversion, and Charlemagne's policy of genocide against those who refused to convert or who returned to paganism are examples of the outcome of this theory.[20]

According to official Carolingian thought the peacemaker was the person charged with imposing peace from above. "May there be peace in the realm," swore the emperor on his coronation day.[21] Charlemagne's title *Imperator Pacificus*[22] meant that he was to bring glory and prosperity, peace and life to the realm; the imperial lawman was called the *paciarius*, the peace man;[23] and the *pax* of a village or a place became the area of jurisdiction of the *paciarius*.[24] Official Carolingian notions of peace followed this hierarchical and external pattern, a pattern more in keeping with Roman ideas of order than with the gospel idea of peace.[25] Charlemagne's heirs maintained these notions of peace through legislation until the dissolution of the empire.[26]

## CAROLINGIAN THEORIES OF PEACEMAKING

The peace of the gospels was officially exiled to the monasteries and restricted to the clergy, but intellectual and religious leaders continued to ponder the application of the New Testament to contemporary society. Alcuin of York (735–804) is the thinker of the period most closely associated with the intellectual, cultural, and religious life of the Carolingian court. His role in formulating the ideology of Charlemagne's Christian empire was fundamental.[27] Alcuin accepted the distinction between clerical and lay as essential and conceded that the lay arm held the authority to protect the good and to punish the bad,[28] but he devoted his life to peace and justice and criticized Charlemagne's brutal methods in Saxony.[29] Alcuin's thinking on peace goes far beyond the Carolingian definitions that we have noted above.[30] Peace is born from charity and among those who love their neighbors.[31] Only through love of neighbor can one become the child of God.[32] The mission of the priest, therefore, is not simply to contemplate Christ and the vision of peace but to actively preach peace.[33] For Alcuin peace is both the end and the means of social life.[34]

These views are echoed by Smaragdus (d. 830), an Irish monk and abbot of Saint-Mihiel. Only by living peace, by being the children of God, can Christians find peace, he writes.[35] Christ's gift of peace (John 14) is an inheritance and a challenge. It is a gift freely given, but also a duty to be undertaken, an inheritance that will be attained only if Christians are truly children of God and make peace.[36] Although Smaragdus' audience was primarily monastic, peace for him was not merely an internal state or a monastic virtue. The peace of those possessing serenity of mind, tranquility of soul, and simplicity of heart transforms society by stopping war, restraining anger, humbling the proud, loving the humble, calming discord, and reconciling enemies.[37]

Druthmar, a monk of Corbie (d. 850), distinguished two types of peace: the false peace known to the world at Christ's birth, that is, the political order of the Pax Romana,[38] and true peace, which is the product of just action. Paschasius Radbertus (786–865), abbot of Corbie, expands on the distinction between true and false peace. The peace of the world, of the political order, cannot truly exist without real peace, which derives from God's grace and is lived by people of good will who pursue peace.[39] The life of peace is therefore the truest sign of the children of God. Walafrid Strabo (c. 809–849) refers to a decree of Pope Innocent I (401–417) that elucidates the same truth through the liturgy of the sacrament.[40]

In his encyclopedic definitions of peace, Rabanus Maurus (c. 780–856), abbot of Fulda, stresses the same themes of true and false peace and of peace as Christ's heritage and charge to his disciples. Only by living the life of peace can Christians become children of God, and only by performing the good works of the Beatitudes can they live this life. The duty of the priest is to lead the people to peace; the duty of the laity is to heed the priest's call.[41] Those who refuse peace have no place in Christ's body, nor can they find eternal peace.[42] Hincmar, archbishop of Reims (c. 860), devoted an entire work—*On Restraining the Rapine of Soldiers*—to condemning the military,[43] as did Rather of Liège (c. 975).[44] Atto of Vercelli[45] and Agobard of Lyon[46] offer similar testimony to the unity between inner peace and the external actions of peacemakers.

Pope Nicholas I (c. 825–867) showed by his life that the peace tradition could be lived at the highest level of Christian society.[47] Famous for his aid to the poor and the pursuit of social justice, Nicholas also vigorously pursued missionary expansion on the borders of Christendom. Against the backdrop of Carolingian conquest Nicholas penned what is both a "classic summary of Christian faith and discipline" in dealing with the outside world and a harsh condemnation of war.[48] In his *Reply to the Inquiry of the Bulgars* (866),[49] Nicholas attempted to answer a series of questions from the newly converted Khan Boris on the Christian ethic a kingdom should follow. The pope condemned conversion by force, branding war as a diabolical fraud. He conceded that war may be permissible in cases of inescapable necessity, in self-defense, but he warned that "in itself it is the devil's work." He advised that deserters be treated leniently and gave Boris many examples of martyrs who fled in the face of violence.[50] The pope further noted that the clergy, "the soldiers of the church," are to take no part in the affairs of the world that "involves them inevitably in the spilling of blood."[51] His condemnation was not intended merely as a further restriction on clerical nonviolence but was a reversal of the official Carolingian acceptance of war as a Christian duty in the spread of the Christian republic.

In response to Boris' question as to how Christians are to prepare for war, Nicholas answers ironically:

> Go to the churches, say prayers, forgive sinners, attend solemn masses, offer oblations, make confessions of sins to priests, effect reconciliations and communion, open the prisons, dissolve the chains of slaves, and especially [those of] the broken and the crippled, give freedom to captives, and give alms to the poor.[52]

In short, he advises Boris to employ all the Christian works of mercy that make peace, affirm life, and negate the motives for and works of war.

This intellectual tradition was not without its effects. Nicholas I, Alcuin, Rabanus Maurus, Paschasius, and others who were prominent at the courts of Charlemagne and his successors, influenced the ideology and administration of the Carolingians. The capitularies of Louis the Pious (who ruled from 814 to 840) contain several references to the duty of the Christian king not only to insure peace through order but also to instill peace through justice and charity.[53]

When the central authority collapsed new structures emerged to support peacemaking. A series of laws, secular and ecclesiastical, were produced by the Frankish clergy in the late ninth century that tried to instill the ideas and practice of gospel peacemaking into a society in chaos. The *False Capitularies,* a collection of genuine legal texts merged with forgeries sometime between 847 and 857,[54] placed the pursuit of peace in the context of Carolingian law and the functions of the Christian king.

Although the *Capitularies* maintained that it was still the role of the secular arm to insure peace in the Carolingian tradition—by force—its emphasis was really on the function of laity and clergy in bringing Christian peace to human hearts. Peace is based on the gospel blessing of the peacemakers, who bring the kingdom of heaven to earth. The function of government is to insure that peace and justice penetrate every level of society, "both the high and the low," and to heed the pleas of the poor, of widows, pilgrims, clerics, and the weak.[55] In order to insure this the *Capitularies* prohibited feuds and the bearing of arms and set aside Sundays and certain feast days on which warfare was forbidden, thus anticipating the Peace and the Truce of God.[56] The code clearly condemns violence: "Whoever sheds human blood," it warns, "spills the blood of Christ"[57] and is thus thrust outside the body of Christ, which unites those who live in peace.[58]

The *False Capitularies* had sought sanctions in royal power; the *False Decretals,* a similar collection written in northern France (c. 850),[59] sought to protect episcopal power and influence in the midst of the growing anarchy of the Carolingian collapse. The foundations of the *False Decretals* were papal and episcopal legislation, canon and secular law, and patristic sources. This collection developed a theory of ecclesiastical independence and superiority. The *False Decretals* acknowledged the role of the emperor and nobility to maintain unity and peace according to the rule of law,[60] but broke with Carolingian ideas of peace in placing the responsibility for peacemaking directly on individual Christians. Peace must first start in the heart before it can penetrate society. Even hatred of a neighbor was considered homicide. Only the good will of Christians, that is, their constant pursuit of Christ, who is the word of peace and justice, can bring peace to the world. Peace is spread not by the sword, then, but by love and by preaching the gospels. Only then can it be enforced by the clergy and the emperor. Thus both the *Capitularies* and the *Decretals* joined with the theory of Christian writers to establish important principles: first, peace is the work of love and of justice, not of force and of order alone; and second, it is the duty of every Christian to actively pursue peace and justice through love of neighbor and adherence to the gospel message.

Conciliar decrees and penitential regulations were incorporated into the Catholic Church's canon law that continued the official condemnation of war.[61] The penitential of Rabanus Maurus (841)[62] explicitly demanded penances of those who killed in a war declared by their princes. This tone of condemnation was picked up by Regino of Prum (c. 906)[63] and by Ivo of Chartres (c. 1040–1116).[64] Rabanus further condemned killing in war as the work of avarice and invoked the use of spiritual, not material, weapons.[65] The *Roman Penitential* of Halitgar of Cambrai (c. 830) grouped killing in war with other forms of homicide, worthy of twenty-one weeks penance,[66] only a little less than the twenty-eight weeks imposed for homicide in time of peace.[67] The *Penitential of Pseudo-Theodore* (835) imposed a penance on anyone who participated in public war, even on the order of one's lord. The lord incurred a ten-year penance.[68] The English *Arundel Penitential* of the late ninth century imposed a penance of one year for killing in a royal battle, two years in a war of doubtful justice waged by a prince, and one year in a just war.[69] Regino of Prum's *Ecclesiastical Discipline* (c. 906) groups killing in war with murder and parricide but reduces its penance to forty days.[70]

Burchard of Worms (d. 1025) picked up Rabanus Maurus' condemnation of war in his *Decretum* (c. 1008–1012),[71] which was a prime source of Catholic canon law.[72] Burchard condemned killing, even in a just war commanded by a prince, on the assumption that the soldier participates in order to obtain favor from his lord.[73] In his *Corrector or Physician* he groups killing in war along with voluntary homicide.[74] Elsewhere he distinguished penances for killing on the order of a legitimate prince in a war to reestablish peace or in tyrannicide committed under orders as worthy of three Lents' penance.[75] If not done under orders both acts were considered equivalent to homicide.[76]

*On Mortal Sins* by Fulbert of Chartres (c. 1029)[77] imposed a one-year penance for killing in war.[78] Fulbert also rejected the idea of the just war and condemned bishops who helped promulgate it, restricting the use of the secular sword to the suppression of the wicked, that is, the police function of government outlined by Paul in Romans 13.[79] Finally, the anonymous *On True and False Penitence*[80] of the eleventh century not only imposed penances for participation in war but condemned the military itself.[81]

These penitentials were active influences throughout the period. Two well-known examples are the penances imposed on the participants in two of the rare pitched battles of the period, that of Soissons (923) and that of Hastings (1066). Those who participated in Soissons were required to perform penance for three successive Lents, the first year in excommunication from the church, and three days a week on bread, water, and salt.[82]

The Battle of Hastings raises even more interesting evidence. After William the Conqueror's defeat of the Anglo-Saxons, the Norman council of Westminster drew up the *Establishment of Penance* (1070) for the victors.[83] Substantial penances were imposed on William's soldiers according to their actions before and after the battle: one year for each man killed (art. 1), forty days for each wounded (art. 2), three years for any participation in the battle (art. 7), and seven years if they fought "for profit" (art. 6). Penances were imposed even on those who never struck an enemy (three days, art. 4) or who never saw their enemies struck. The archers, for example, who fought at long range and who did not know whether they had hit anyone, were to perform penance for three successive Lents (art. 8). Penances also applied to soldiers' actions after the battle and during the military occupation—killing while taking booty (art. 9), rape and willing sexual relations (art. 12), violation of churches (art. 13), and killing a civilian (art. 10) or a resister (art. 11). The penitential decree was signed by Ermenfrid, the papal legate.[84] William himself did not escape without blame. The reason for his founding Battle Abbey may have been to commute his own penance into almsgiving,[85] a common feature of the penitential system.[86] William and his successors seem to have taken prohibitions against killing seriously. The "Laws of William the Conqueror" prohibited capital punishment in any case,[87] and English common law prohibited private wars, trial by battle, and murder in war.[88] The Laws of Henry I imposed penances for killing in war into the twelfth century.[89]

## CAROLINGIAN MONASTICISM AND ANTIMILITARISM

In practice the traditional forms of Christian peacemaking were never abandoned; monastic life maintained its role as an agent for peace in the midst of barbarian invasion and anarchy.[90] "All in all, before the rise of the university, the monasteries were the principal cultural agency leading Europe toward a pacific and progressive civilization."[91] The feudalization of society gained momentum in the ninth and tenth centuries and the monastery took on increasing importance as the "great interrogation point thrust against the castle."[92]

The lives of monastic leaders and saints who abandoned the career of the knight for that of the monk demonstrate the revolt against militarism. Odo of Beauvais (801–880) left the military to become a Benedictine.[93] He eventually became tutor to Charles Martel's sons, and in 861 he was elected bishop of Beauvais. In the tenth century Guibert (892–962)[94] and Gerard of Brogne (c. 895–959),[95] both well-known military and political leaders, embraced the monastery as an alternative to violence. In the eleventh century Romuald (c. 950–1027),[96] the founder of the ascetic Camaldolese monks and teacher of Peter Damian,[97] became a monk in response to his father's murder of a relative in a dispute over property. Theobald of Provins (1017–1066),[98] the son of the count of Champagne, rejected the military profession for which his father was preparing him and became an itinerant hermit who supported himself through manual labor. By assuming a life of nonviolence and by identifying with the poor and the workers, Theobald repudiated the violence and the exploitation of the feudal class and anticipated the popular poverty movements of the next century.

The most important monastic movement of this period is that of the Cluniacs. Although Cluny was a rich and powerful order, its reputation for encouraging the violence of the Spanish *reconquista* has been exaggerated.[99] Cluny's original concern was with the spiritual struggle of the Christian and the conversion of the feudal aristocracy to the peaceful service of Christian society.[100] Odo (879–942), the second abbot of Cluny, who was responsible for its first great expansion, had been reared in the household of Duke William of Aquitaine, the monastery's founder. Odo's *Life* by John of Salerno recounts the young man's resistance to the military training imposed on him by his father. After three years of depression, accompanied by exhaustion, headaches, and nightmares, at the age of nineteen Odo left for Tours where he entered the monastic life after taking vows to Saint Martin, the patron of nonviolence.[101] He became abbot of Cluny and took an active role in converting the feudal aristocracy to peace. He expressed his ideas in a poem on the *Life of St. Count Gerard of Aurillac* (c. 920).[102] In the poem Odo tells the story of Gerard's turning his arms inward in order to defend the church without violence. Odo's abhorrence of war and rejection of feudal values is clear. The *miles* (knight) is the worst form of human life, he wrote; *patientia,* nonviolence, is the highest of all the virtues.

Hugh of Cluny (1024–1109)[103] is known for his efforts at peacemaking between Pope Gregory VII and Emperor Henry IV. He was the eldest son of a Burgundian magnate and thus was expected to enter military life. His choice of the monastic profession therefore represented a rebellion against his class. Hugh's *Life of Hildebert* gives us some insight into his own revolt and into the Cluniac support of peacemaking.[104] The son of a nobleman, Hildebert was trained as a knight against his will and was prevented from entering a monastery. In the military he was forced to witness scenes of spoil and ravage that he "profoundly loathed." Ordered to seize a poor man's property, he refused, made restitution to the man, and fled to Cluny. By the time his father arrived at the monastery, Hildebert had already become a monk.

Odilo, the fifth abbot of Cluny (c. 962–1048),[105] was known both for his relief work with famine victims and the poor—for which he sold church lands—and for his support of the peace movements behind the Peace and the Truce of God, which he helped spread throughout southern France and Italy. In the next century Peter the Venerable (abbot from 1122) would offer conversion as a viable alternative to the Crusades.[106]

## THE PROPHETIC TRADITION

Christian witness lived on not only in the monastic confrontation of militarism but also in nonviolent missionary work, in prophetic protest against the political tyrannies of the day, and in martyrdom suffered as a witness to the gospels. We have already seen the peacemaking tradition at work during the barbarian invasions.[107] In the context of official Carolingian theory the tradition takes on even greater importance and asserts the positive values of peacemaking to the outside world. A few examples of the missionary alternative will make the point clear.

Frederick of Utrecht (d. 838) was the son of King Radbon of the Frisians.[108] Ordained a priest, Frederick gained a reputation for holiness and learning that brought him the bishopric of Utrecht (825). He was successful in launching missions of conversion to the northern Low Countries but earned the hatred of the Carolingian court for reproaching Empress Judith for her immorality. According to eleventh-century sources, he was assassinated at Maastricht by the queen's agents.[109]

Boniface (Bruno) of Querfurt (c. 974–1009) was one of Romuald's followers at Ravenna.[110] Outraged by imperial wars against fellow Christians, he sought an alternative to violence. He went as a missionary first to the Magyars and Pechenegs and then to the Prussians around Masovia. There he and eighteen of his companions were martyred.

At the end of the period, Stanislaus of Cracow (1030–1079) symbolized Polish nationhood in his nonviolent confrontation of political tyranny, injustice, and cruelty.[111] Born of noble parents near Cracow, he was educated at Gnesen before being ordained a priest. A popular preacher and spiritual leader, he was named bishop of Cracow in 1072. He soon incurred the enmity of Boleslaus the Bold, however, for his prophetic criticism of the king's injustice and immorality. When the king refused to change his policies Stanislaus excommunicated Boleslaus. He even halted services when the king forced his way into the cathedral. Shortly after this Boleslaus slew Stanislaus with his own hands while the bishop was saying Mass in a chapel outside the city. Like Thomas à Beckett in the next century and Oscar Romero in our own,[112] the bishop's martyrdom brought ultimate victory as public opinion rose to condemn the king.

## THE MARTYRS OF CORDOVA

Perhaps the most important, though least known, movement of nonviolent protest during the early Carolingian period was the ninth-century martyr movement of Cordova.[113] At the outset of the movement most of the Iberian peninsula had been Moslem for about a century. From their capital of Cordova the emirs of the Umayyad dynasty ruled over a brilliant civilization that excelled anything in Christian Europe and that threatened the southern flank of the Carolingian Empire. Religious toleration in the modern sense was unknown in the medieval as in the ancient world, but the Moslems did tolerate Christianity so long as Christians refrained from attacks on Mohammed, his religion, and his law, and as long as no Moslem converted or returned to Christianity. Moslem officials controlled the church hierarchy and imposed heavy taxes for, and humiliating restrictions on, the practice of their faith. Those who converted to Islam, the *mawali*, often gained high office and status in Moslem society. It is not surprising then, given the inferior status of the Christians, the cultural and social incentives that Islam offered, and the Islamic religious revival of the ninth century, that many Spanish Christians did convert to Islam at this time, abandoning their Christian faith and its cultural inheritance.[114]

In the middle of the ninth century, however, a group of Christian intellectuals in Cordova, both cleric and lay, initiated a movement of cultural and religious revival. Speraindio of Cordova is considered the father of the group.[115] A lecturer in Scripture at the Christian school, he composed the *Memoriale sanctorum* (Memorial of the Saints), an anti-Islamic literary tract. His pupils, the priest Eulogius[116] and the layman Paulus Alvarus (Albar), carried on his work. Both well educated, they sought to revive Christian life in Cordova through an intellectual and religious renewal and opposed the Christian hierarchy, who accepted or sought accommodation to Moslem control of the church.[117] However their program was neither negative nor violent.

Eulogius first devoted himself to reviving a Latin literary culture that had almost completely disappeared from Spain. Traveling north he gathered over 300 manuscripts of the classics from the Latin Christian past, ranging from Virgil's *Aeneid*, the symbol of *Romanitas*, to Augustine's *City of God*. His plan was to provide the basis for a new Christian sense of identity.[118] Alvarus devoted himself to a defense of Christian orthodoxy and to a literary attack on heresy, whether the Christian or, as medieval people thought, the Islamic variety.[119] Together the two men stressed the ascetic and penitential aspects of Christian spirituality as a counterbalance to Sufi spirituality, and they founded quasimonastic communities of penitents that served to accentuate the boundaries of the two faiths.[120]

By 850 the Christian revival in Cordova spurred a Moslem pogrom that initially met little Christian resistance. In April 850, however, a mob arrested a Christian cleric named Perfectus, accused him of openly attacking Mohammed, and executed him. Eulogius and other Christian leaders were arrested.[121] In 851 John, a Christian merchant, and Isaac, a former Moslem official who had become a monk, came before the *qadi*, or Moslem magistrate, and condemned Islam outright. Isaac called on the magistrate to convert to Christianity. Struck by the *qadi* in response to this, Isaac said, "Blessed are they who are persecuted for righteousness' sake, for theirs is the kingdom of heaven." Both Isaac and John were executed.

The Moslem persecution unleashed an "unprecedented nonviolent fury."[122] Within a week of Isaac's execution seven more Christians openly proclaimed their Christianity and denounced Islam; in a few weeks three more joined them. Despite continued arrests, the nonviolent protests continued for more than a year as married couples, monks, Moslem converts, and repentent apostates, men and women, defied the Islamic authorities.[123]

In late 852 Emir Abd al-Rahman died. His successor, Emir Mohammed I (852–856), faced with an uncontrollable nonviolent revolt in Cordova and a violent rebellion in Toledo, persuaded church leaders to call a council at Cordova to seek an end to the confrontation. In December 852 a compliant council honored those fallen but called on Christians to refrain from seeking martyrdom. The Christian community, however, heeded other leadership. Eulogius composed his *Memoriale sanctorum* and Alvarus the first part of the *Indiculus luminosus* (The Remarkable List); both writings explained the martyrdom of the Christians not as acts of suicide but as positive assertions of Christianity and witnesses to the truth.

In June 853 five more Christians came forward to proclaim their faith. After backing down from a threat to massacre all Christian men and to sell Christian women to prostitution,[124] Mohammed began a purge of Christians from the government, imposed severe taxes, destroyed church buildings, and pressed for forced conversions to Islam. For nearly two years there were no new martyrs. In 854, however, Alvarus published the second part of the *Indiculus,* in which he equated Mohammed with the Antichrist of the Apocalypse.[125] By 855 Christians were again appearing before the magistrates,[126] pressing them to convert to Christianity, and meeting their deaths.

Many of the more that fifty martyrs are included in the Acts of the Saints.[127] They include Flora and Mary, who were sold into prostitution as a punishment for confronting the *qadi.* Encouraged by Eulogius' *Exhortation to Martyrdom,* they were beheaded in 851.[128] Regilo of Elvira and Sirvo-a-Dios of Syria entered a mosque and denounced Islam;[129] the nuns Columba and Pomposa openly defied the magistrates;[130] Aurelius and Natalia[131] and Felix and Liliosa, two married couples, openly challenged the magistrates by announcing their Christianity. The two women further defied Islamic restrictions by taking off their veils and appearing in public. All four, along with the monk George, were beheaded in 852.

The martyrdoms continued throughout the 850s.[132] Finally in 859 Eulogius himself, who had been chosen bishop of Toledo one year before but prevented from taking the post, was arrested for sheltering Leocritia, a Moslem woman who had converted to Christianity. Accused of harboring a Moslem apostate (a capital offense) Eulogius told the magistrate, "Had you asked me, I would have gladly done as much for you." Refusing to renounce his faith, he was executed.[133] With him ended the martyrdoms. In 884 the remains of Eulogius and his protegee were brought to Oviedo in northern Spain along with a manuscript of his writings. From there knowledge of the events in Spain reached a wide audience.[134] Usuard, a Frankish monk who had visited Cordova in 858, included over thirty of the Cordovan martyrs in his martyrology and helped spread their influence throughout Europe.[135]

Although the significance of these events is controversial,[136] the Cordovan movement represents an excellent example of Christian action based on the gospels, a movement clear in its adherence to Christian means and in its vision of Christian ends. The movement was a nonviolent confrontation of political, cultural, and religious oppression. It sought not only to protest injustice, but also to assert Christian identity and to win over the enemy by example. The parallels with the situation of early Christians in Rome are instructive; so too are the differences. Beset by a superior and alien culture, confronted with a faith that was as certain and unyielding as their own, and lacking both solidarity with other Christian centers and the active support of Christian leaders in Western Europe who could have understood the nature and possibilities of their struggle, the martyrs of Cordova were unable to achieve a victory any greater than their own personal witness and the recognition of posterity. Yet the fact that such a clear pursuit of the gospel message was possible on the farthest frontiers of Christian Europe indicates the extent of understanding of Christian peacemaking in the Carolingian period.

## THE PEOPLE'S PEACE: THE PEACE OF GOD

The most important outcome of Carolingian forms of peacemaking was the medieval peace movements: the Peace of God and the Truce of God.[137] The Peace of God was the protection from military violence won by special groups in medieval society. These included the clergy and their possessions; the poor; women; peasants and their tools, animals, mills, vineyards, and labor; and later pilgrims and merchants—in short, most of the medieval population, who neither bore arms nor were entitled to bear them.[138] The Truce of God, often confused and later merged with the Peace, protected certain times of the week and year from the violence of the feudal class: no private or public wars were to be waged from Wednesday evening until Monday morning, on certain saints' days, during Advent, Lent, and Rogations. At certain times and places it, like the Peace, extended protection to persons and property.[139]

The Peace and the Truce of God have provoked much debate over the past century, and this book cannot do justice to all the research that has appeared on the topic. It can, however, at least discuss the origins, motives, and nature of the movement, briefly surveying its progress and attempting to shed light on its role in the history of Catholic peacemaking. Opinions differ on every aspect of the movement, from its origins, composition, and content to its methods and effectiveness. Only its rapid spread and wide influence are commonly acknowledged.[140]

The Peace of God originated in the assemblies of the Frankish and Carolingian periods. Frankish bishops traditionally (from the sixth to the ninth century) met to legislate on social justice issues according to the gospel precepts.[141] By their legislation they attempted to alleviate the conditions of the poor and to protect them from exploitation, to establish basic health care, to protect the rights of prisoners, Jews, slaves, and refugees seeking asylum, and to guarantee some measure of due process. This was a "corporate function" of the Catholic bishops, "who saturated this society with Christian elements" and who directly touched the daily lives of the rural population.[142] Their decrees, promulgated in parish and town churches, accustomed the laity to the legislative benefits of the assembly on their daily lives.

The laity also played an active role, in theory at least, in the imperial assemblies of the Carolingian period, especially under Louis the Pious. Louis held from two to three open assemblies every year between 814 and 840 at which the common people were often present[143] to hear decisions be promulgated or to themselves be formally, if only ritually, called on to agree to these decisions by acclamation.[144] Nor was this Carolingian legislation an empty formality. Both Louis the Pious and Lothair called public assemblies to balance the power of the lords.[145] Legislation was passed protecting the poor and their means of livelihood from the thievery of the nobles.[146]

As Carolingian authority began to decline, especially on the outskirts of the empire, as in southern Gaul, the bishops took steps to protect their congregations and their holdings against the encroachments of local nobles.[147] The clergy also moved into the power vacuum in order to protect their own positions. Canon law was rapidly assembled, for example, to insure clerical immunities.[148] Yet the clergy were also seeking to restore peace and justice. Their *restauracio pacis* broke with Carolingian ideas in crossing the line between sacred and secular forms of peace.[149] Yet the bishops chose spiritual and nonviolent methods to bring about peace, and in this they were actively supported by the laity,[150] the *rustici* and *pauperes* (peasants and poor people), the victims of feudal exploitation and violence.

From the start the new peace movement attracted both men and women and included peasants of the lowest social orders. Under the leadership of the bishops the people came together in a series of church councils that legislated for each diocese. The councils were also the scenes of mass demonstrations for peace and justice. Moved by eloquent sermons on the need for reconciliation, thousands joined together amid chants of "Peace, Peace, Peace!" and swore on the relics of the saints to do penance and to work for peace, equality, and the love of their brothers and sisters.[151] The councils legislated on the methods to be used within the diocese to protect the peasants' labor, property, and basic rights from exploitation.[152] The participants of the councils broke the bonds of the medieval hierarchical order by swearing pacts of peace to one another as free equals.[153] The methods used, at least in the first or "sanctified" phase,[154] were almost wholly nonviolent: spiritual sanctions of excommunication and interdict against knights who refused to obey the call to peace.[155]

Adhemar of Chabannes (d. 1034) gives us a vivid account of the Peace council of Limoges (1031).[156] By that time the clergy of Aquitaine had long been in the habit of holding biannual legislative meetings in the Carolingian tradition.[157] According to Adhemar, the Limoges councils drew large numbers of princes, nobles, and common folk.[158] The council of November 1031 was particularly memorable.[159] The clergy were determined to bring the "unity of peace" and the establishment of social justice to the diocese. In a series of stirring speeches to the assembly, Bishop Jordan of Limoges condemned the nobles who broke the Peace, profaned churches, afflicted the poor and the clergy, and refused to heed the warnings of the councils. Citing the gospels, Jordan and the other bishops sought to reconcile the nobles with the rest of the Christian community. The clergy backed Jordan's demands for the cessation of feudal warfare and for an end to the oppression of the poor. They declared that whoever tormented any of the faithful tormented Christ himself. Those who refused to change their ways were to be excommunicated, their arms and horses forfeited. The clergy solemnized their intent with dramatic ceremony. Lowering their lit tapers, they extinguished them in the dirt, declaring, "May the Lord extinguish as well the joy of those who refuse to accept peace and justice."

These spiritual weapons effectively limited feudal violence.[160] Wielded by the ecclesiastical hierarchy but made effective by the nonviolent participation of the Christian people, they kept the violent from participating in the Christian community: no Eucharist, no forgiveness of sins, no engagements or marriages, no attendance at Mass, no Christian burial. Nor were these empty threats. Excommunications were pronounced, the violent who "refuse to accept peace and justice" were excluded from the church, the body of Christ that they had tormented, and their own bodies were exposed without Christian burial.[161] In an age when salvation was the goal of life, such measures were of incalculable power. The oath that bound together medieval men and women was strong;[162] just as strong was the curse that cast them into the shadows. The means used by the civil government to implement the more institutional and official Truce of God were also largely nonviolent: financial reparations or banishment were imposed along with excommunication.[163]

Even then those within the Peace movement were accused of arrogance, intransigence, hostility toward the nobility, and of not keeping their proper place.[164] In fact, many historians note that the Peace movement represented a real shift in the consciousness and the status of the majority of the European population. In a world where weapons gave status, to be unarmed was to be poor, a member of the *vulgus,* the mob, and thus powerless.[165] The Peace movement, however, transformed the unarmed from poor victims in need of protection into active peacemakers.[166] The Peace movement was truly revolutionary—not in its occasional violence, but in its nonviolent assertion of the dignity of the humble, in its sworn oaths between equals that disrupted the rigid hierarchies of society,[167] and in its call on the aristocracy to reject barbarism.

The Peace movement can be viewed as a consensus[168] between groups—the higher clergy and the lower laity—that eventually converted the nobility.[169] The Peace assemblies became occasions of high emotion and solidarity between classes, in which masses were moved to penitence and conversion, to abandon arms and seek peace and justice.[170] The ideas of absolution, forgiveness of sins, reconciliation, communion, and the admission of the penitent to communion were inherent in the medieval idea of *pax*.[171] The influence of the penitential system within the Peace movement always remained strong.[172] The Peace of God was also a sociopolitical movement, born of ecclesiastical concerns but powered by a popular movement of a religious, even a mystical, nature.[173]

The rapid spread of the Peace movement is an indication of its impact.[174] Begun at Charroux in eastern Aquitaine (c. 989), it immediately gained the support of both ecclesiastical and secular leadership. Councils of peace soon followed in Le Puy and Narbonne (990) and in Limoges (994). A council was held at Poitiers in 1000;[175] by 1010 or 1011 the Peace had spread north to Orleans and to Burgundy by 1025.[176] The Peace had traveled up the Rhone via Lyons and had reached northern France[177] by 1030 and Flanders by 1043 or 1044.

Assemblies were called over and over again in all these areas from the 1020s to the 1040s.[178] By 1041 the Peace had spread throughout France.[179] The bishop of Arles and Abbot Odilo of Cluny exported the Peace to Italy, where councils were held in Aosta, Turin, Ivrea, Milan, and Pavia by 1050.[180] From the council at Vich (c. 1018) and the council at Elne (c. 1027) in southern Aquitaine the Peace was extended to Catalonia,[181] Barcelona, Gerona, and Urgel. Assemblies were held into the 1060s.[182]

In Spain at least until this time the Peace served to protect church lands, the rights of asylum, and the poor. After that, however, it became increasingly institutionalized as a tool of the territorial lords to maintain the lord's peace.[183] It served to protect roads, bridges, and the safety of all subjects, and was insured not by spiritual sanctions but by force. This tendency had been present at the origins of the Peace but was always secondary. Military expeditions were launched against nobles who failed to cooperate with the Peace, but these were isolated and rare. The disastrous military expedition launched against recalcitrant nobles by Bishop Aymon of Beauvais (1038), which has often been cited as typical of the movement,[184] was condemned by contemporaries as inappropriate, a "peace war," a contradiction in itself.[185]

## THE PEACE CO-OPTED: THE TRUCE OF GOD

The Peace movement reached its peak at the council in Narbonne (1054) when an injunction was brought against all violence by Christians against other Christians. "He who kills a Christian spills the blood of Christ''[186]: the injunction repeated the words of the *False Decretals*.[187] In the second half of the eleventh century, however, the Peace was merged with the Truce of God and thereby co-opted, "institutionalized," by the lay lords in the interests of political centralization and unification. Peace militias were formed to enforce the decrees of the councils, hostages were taken to insure obedience to oaths, and the castles and lands of resisting lords were destroyed. Local lords levied "peace taxes" to maintain the militias and they dubbed themselves "peacemakers."[188]

The institutionalized Peace and the Truce were sometimes used to the advantage of the local prince. Situations in Barcelona and Aragon provide two examples.[189] By the fourteenth century the Peace and the Truce were defined by Catalonian jurists in purely secular terms, as "a certain protection of all persons and things living within the principality of Catalonia."[190] The movements retained many of their original elements: swearing of oaths, truce days, restitution by offenders. However these were centered not on popular assemblies but on the prince and were enforced through his agents, the *paciarii*, and his peace courts.[191] The pattern was the same throughout France, in the Empire, and in the English possessions in France.[192]

This institutionalizing process was well under way throughout Europe in the eleventh and twelfth centuries. The process culminated in the shift from the Peace of God, the popular assemblies and mutual oaths to the Truce of God, which from its beginnings was inspired by the aristocracy, sworn by knights as their individual duty, and enforced with the bishops' blessings by territorial lords using force.[193] Any discussion of the Truce is confused because of the many terms used to describe it by both medieval writers and modern historians.[194] Like the Peace, the origins of the Truce are disputed; the milestones in its development are frequently confused or actually coincide with those of the Peace.[195] Like the institutional Peace, the Truce came to be used as a weapon of territorial lords to establish their control by force or to maintain order while they fought foreign wars. At the Council of Clermont (1095) Pope Urban II extended the Truce to all of Christendom in preparation for the First Crusade.[196]

What had started, then, in the late tenth century as a popular movement of the laity and clergy in nonviolent pursuit of peace and justice had become by the twelfth century a violent tool of the feudal aristocracy and great monarchies. The benefits of centralized measures to end feudal anarchy and other lawlessness cannot be denied. Still this centralization had serious consequences for the peace movement in Europe. It gave ecclesiastical support to the idea of elevating the warrior as a Christian type associated with chivalry and the Crusades. It also robbed the people of their active and positive role in Christian peacemaking. We have little idea of the people's perspective on this shift or their motives for cooperating with it, but we do have ample evidence of the motives of the feudal and clerical aristocracy in bringing it about.

Georges Duby, in his brilliant essay *The Three Orders,* analyzed the forms and significance of this shift as revealed in the writings (1024–1031) of two bishops: Gerard of Cambrai and Adalbero of Laon. The power of the Peace movement in northern France, spread by popular preachers,[197] soon began to appear to many as a social revolution. Its practice of mutual oaths, sworn among equals to maintain the Peace, seemed "a violation of paternal institutions," a movement of *novitates* or innovators.[198] Gerard, a descendant of the Carolingians and a cousin of both the king of France and the German emperor,[199] epitomized this aristocratic reaction. As a counter both to the popular Peace movement and to feudal attempts to co-opt it Gerard linked the theory of the just war with an older hierarchical model: the three orders of society.[200]

To counter the sworn, popular, and egalitarian Peace movement and its implicit threat to the Carolingian hierarchies Gerard revived the Carolingian ideal of the king who joined with the clergy to curb the violence of the *bellatores,* the knights, to bring about order and to protect the *agricultures,* the poor peasants (who were thus reduced again to passivity). The people, Gerard argued, do not have the competence to judge the weighty matter of war and peace; it is the province of the king and the bishops alone to judge and to dictate to the people. Gerard's theory is a restatement of Carolingian definitions of peace as order. For the people's Peace the bishop substitutes the king's peace, the Truce of God, sworn and maintained by the nobility and enforced by violence.

Gerard's views were reinforced by Adalbero, bishop of Laon.[201] The Peace of God, he wrote, disrupts the hierarchical order of things in its exaltation of serfs as brothers and sisters. Bishops who participate humiliate themselves not only by encouraging the serfs, but also by shedding their wealth and preaching equality. The world had become topsy-turvy. To counter this dangerous trend Adalbero explicitly redefined *pax* as *ordo,* an order based not on the unity of the Mystical Body of Christ, but on the image of Christ the King. True peace for Adalbero was thus not the peace of justice and Christian equality but the order of the perfect city, an order based on rigid social divisions and maintained if necessary by military force. Peace was a function of law and order enforced by the king; it was not a function of the fraternity of the peasants swearing mutual love. Peace was based first on the *rex* (the king), then on his *lex* (law), which brought about *pax* through force. According to this order, reestablished by Adalbero and in line with his model of heaven, the serfs are again relegated to their proper function: *labor, dolor, et sudor,* work, sorrow, and sweat. For both Gerard and Adalbero the just war—the ruling class's right to violence—thus became once more what it had been under the Roman Empire, a means of maintaining order as a substitute for true peace.

## CONCLUSIONS

Europe's aristocracy of the eleventh-century thus closed the door on popular, nonviolent peacemaking by co-opting the Peace into the Truce of God and by turning both into a pretext for their own wars. Urban II's preaching of the Truce of God at Clermont in the same breath with his launching of the First Crusade was a logical outcome. The aristocracy, at least for a time, mobilized their own definition of Christian peace and launched it against the outside world. Although the communal movement of the towns inherited and kept alive some of the elements of the sworn peace associations of the Peace of God,[202] the *pauperes* and the clergy who preached Christ's peace were silent. Yet even as the Crusades stormed against the earthly Jerusalem, the *pauperes,* their dialogue with the upper classes silenced, began to seek the vision of the Heavenly Jerusalem and to speak with a new voice of peace that struck both at existing violence and at new forms of domination and exploitation. We will examine their response in the following chapters.

# CHAPTER 6

# THE ERA OF THE CRUSADES: PEACEMAKING IN EUROPE (1100–1400)

## HISTORICAL BACKGROUND

The Peace movement of the eleventh century spurred an aristocratic and conservative reaction that worked on three levels. On the first level, that of theory, conservative intellectuals, such as Gerard of Cambrai and Adalbero of Laon, formulated a concept of hierarchy that would once more return the world to the rigid order of Carolingian society and mute the voices of the popular Peace movement. On the second level, that of political power, the newly emerging states and principalities of the period used the mass appeal and the structural innovations of the Peace of God as a tool for their own consolidation of power. Their efforts are reflected both in the institutionalized Peace and in the Truce of God. On the third level, that of social and religious thought, religious thinkers and secular writers attempted to incorporate the controls of the Peace and the Truce of God into the existing warrior ethic by christianizing it into the cult of chivalry.[1] No less a figure than Bernard of Clairvaux (1090–1153) lent his prestige and religious insight to this sanctification of the warrior.[2]

Thus by the end of the eleventh century peace had once again come to be defined by those who wielded political power, a power maintained by violence. The tendencies toward power and violence were embodied in two movements of the eleventh and twelfth centuries that were to have fundamental importance for the development of Western society: the Investiture Conflict and the Crusades.

## THE INVESTITURE CONFLICT

The Investiture Conflict between the papacy and the emperors[3] revolved around several issues: the spiritual and institutional renewal of the church (the Gregorian Reform), the papacy's campaign to assert its leadership of the Western church, and the attempts of the papacy and the ecclesiastical hierarchy to rid themselves of the interference of the secular powers—especially the German emperors—in their affairs.[4] This last issue was the most far-reaching, since it posed the core questions of the nature of Christian society and its proper leadership. If Christendom were one society, a fusion of secular

*76*

and sacred functions, who then was to exercise ultimate leadership?

In the Carolingian Empire, as in the late Roman Empire, this question was easily answered: the emperor as representative of Christ on earth was entrusted with the rule of the Christian people. But at the same time, the clergy, those higher in the hierarchy of Christian life by virtue of their higher responsibilities, put forward their claim to lead and instruct all aspects of Christian society. The alliance of the Carolingian dynasty and the papacy beginning in the eighth century provided the model and the precedent for these claims of the clergy, which were preserved and expanded during the collapse of the Carolingian Empire. By the late eleventh century these claims were finally put forward in concrete terms by a group of intellectuals and reformers surrounding the papacy. As embodied in the life and thought of Pope Gregory VII (1073–1085) they came into direct conflict with the claims of a revived Christian Empire under the Salian kings of Germany.

The struggle for the leadership of Christendom began under Pope Leo IX (1049–1054) and continued until the Concordat of Worms in 1122. It brought a civil war to the Holy Roman Empire and a propaganda war to Europe. The struggle was over two things: control of church properties and imperial fiefs, and ideological supremacy. It resulted in both material destruction and spiritual disasters. The pope excommunicated and deposed the emperor, the emperor attacked and deposed the pope; entire regions, kingdoms, and the empire itself were placed under interdict, making impossible the celebration of the Mass and the dispensation of the sacraments in many parts of Christendom. The struggle created the first propaganda war in Western history. Each side wrote treatise after treatise to justify its own claims for leadership and to demolish the position of the opposition. The effects of this propaganda war were, perhaps, even more far-reaching than the issues involved: for the first time in Europe, the Christian people were being asked to decide which of the claims of rival factions was valid.

In the war of words and ideas being waged at the highest clerical level many voices on both sides of the struggle emerged to condemn the violence and bloodshed. In contrast to the Gregorian ideology of a holy war to overthrow the emperor, an entire pamphlet literature arose—often inspired by pro-imperial loyalties—that condemned Gregory VII and his party for "killing Christians for Christ."[5] Huzmannn of Speyer, an enemy of the papal party, wrote that he looked forward to the election of a new pope who would bring peace to the church, not dissension and war; the antipope Guibert (Clement III) in a pamphlet written about 1085 declared that Gregory VII had deposed himself because he had stained the papacy with murder and was guilty of bringing about the German civil war. Guibert strikes at the just-war theory by quoting the injunction against even litigation for the sake of justice in Paul's letter to the Corinthians. He cites gospel, patristic, and papal sources prohibiting the use of the sword to Peter, finally declaring:

It is Christian to teach, not to make war, to endure injustice with patience, not to avenge it. Christ did nothing of the kind, and neither did any of his saints.[6]

While one might be tempted to dismiss such sentiments as the self-serving ploys of partisans engaged in war, the words were intended for a Christian audience; they had force only to the extent that they appealed to genuine sympathy for Christian peace. Peter Crassus, a Ravenna jurist writing in 1084, claimed that Gregory VII had no right to bear the sword for the sake of God. On the contrary, he wrote, God wants peace, and Gregory offends God by making war. Crassus proposed that a canonical tribunal settle the dispute by legal arbitration.

The life of Peter Damian (1001–1072), a Doctor of the Church, the cardinal bishop of Ostia, and one of the chief architects of the papal reform, provides further evidence of the genuine desire for peace on both sides of the struggle. Born into poverty near Ravenna, he tended pigs until he was sent to school at Faenza. He later became a disciple of Saint Romuald and devoted his life to the reform of monastic life with a steadfast, often harsh, asceticism.[7] As a leading monastic reformer he won the attention of Pope Stephen IX and was made a cardinal.

Peter Damian held violence in horror throughout his life and was an exemplar of the inner, monastic peace of the Carolingian age.[8] Yet he strongly pursued an active life of peace and justice. He declared that force was never permissible and criticized the excesses of the reform papacy that he had helped to create. In his *Letter to Bishop Olderic*[9] he condemned war as an "evil spirit" and looked to the Sermon on the Mount as the basis of Christian life, calling on the clergy and the hierarchy to lead the way. In his *Letter to Pope Alexander*[10] Peter condemns the warrior for attacking the poor and unarmed and robbing them of their possessions, declaring that the sword created more widows and orphans than it protected.[11]

The major impetus of the age, however, came from the laity. Appealed to by both emperor and pope, they saw each side hurl excommunication, curse, and derision at the other. Deprived of the traditional moorings of Christendom—the order imposed by the emperor and the spiritual hierarchies of grace and salvation supplied by the church—the people were called on to judge the conduct of their superiors, to expel corrupt priests and bishops, and to disregard the curses of excommunication and anathema hurled by rival pope or bishop. They were caught in a psychic revolution of their own. In the end, when a final political concord was reached between pope and emperor, the people had a new voice and a new set of criteria by which they would judge the behavior and ideas of their superiors. They emerged on the European stage to confront the institutions and individuals that centuries of Carolingian theory had taught them to obey and accept. This was to have a profound effect on the history of Christian peacemaking in the era of the Crusades.

## THE CRUSADES

Pope Urban II brought together the clergy, nobility, and people of much of Europe at the Council of Clermont (1095) and launched the First Crusade. Here Urban co-opted a Peace council and the apparatus of the Peace of God. Mutual oaths, the backing of a church council, the depiction of the Moslems as the disturbers of Christian peace, the appeal of a penitential pilgrimage, even the cross, the symbol of the Peace movement, were all co-opted for the Crusade.[12] A series of seven major military expeditions followed. First the Holy Land was captured. Then the Crusaders attempted to hold, expand, and recapture the Crusader States, which stretched from Antioch in Syria to Gaza in southern Palestine. By the time the last Christian citadel at Acre fell to the Moslems in 1291 the Crusades had involved Europe's kings, queens, and emperors, its popes, bishops, monastic leaders, and laity of every class in wars of aggression against Moslems in the East, pagans in the North, Orthodox Christians in Constantinople, and Christian dissidents and heretics in southern France.[13]

We cannot possibly enter here into a history or discussion of the Crusade movement. We must, however, deal with the effects of this movement on Europe in the high Middle

Ages and on later interpretations of medieval Catholic ideas of peace. These questions are interrelated. Our understanding of the nature and significance of the Crusades is bound closely to historical interpretations. Before examining the Christian response to the Crusades, we must, therefore, begin with a brief examination of the historiography of the Crusades, especially from the nineteenth century on.

The Crusades have dominated historical thinking about both the forms of spirituality in the West of that time and the peace tradition in the Catholic Church. The Crusades in fact have come to represent for Catholics and non-Catholics alike the form taken by the spiritual life of the Catholic Middle Ages. As early as 1793, in Condorcet's *Outline of a Historical Survey of the Human Mind,*[14] the Crusades were considered a turning point in the history of Western civilization, a sign of the rebirth of knowledge, trade, science, individuality, and religious life.[15] The Crusades were generally condemned during the Enlightenment as anti-Christian and fanatical;[16] but in the nineteenth century several movements in European cultural and political life thrust the Crusades into the position of symbolic precursor of expansionism, cultural aggression, subjugation, and the "defense" of Western values against an ignorant and backward world. Political nationalism glorified the deeds of European princes, monarchies, and national armies; Romanticism saw in the Crusades a great epic of chivalry, nobility, and self-sacrifice; bourgeois individualism united with Romanticism and nationalism to glorify epic battles, heroic confrontations, and the deeds of great warriors. European imperialism and colonialism of the nineteenth century launched expedition after expedition into the Third World convinced of the superiority of the European race and the evil and inferiority of its enemies and victims. The Crusades were studied as a model. Louis Brehier's *L'Eglise et l'Orient au Moyen Age: Les Croisades* (1907),[17] is typical. Brehier, writing in the context of the Western struggle against the Ottoman Turks and economic and colonial expansion on the eve of World War I, declared that:

> It would be unjust to condemn out of hand these five centuries of heroism which had such fertile results for the history of Europe and which left behind in the consciences of modern peoples a certain ideal of generosity and a taste for sacrifice in behalf of noble causes which the harshest lessons of reality will never erase completely.[18]

Such sentiments fit all too well into the style of writing history during this period and have affected all later thought and writing on the Crusades. The story of the hero, the great man, the battle, invasion, kingdom, and treaty—so popular in the nineteenth century—was admirably suited to the new imperialism and nationalist thought. Even the Suez Canal project was hailed as a continuation of the Crusade movement. "Crusade" became the catchword of the nineteenth-century social vocabulary: the "crusade" in Europe, the "crusade" for charity, the "crusade" against the Ottoman Empire, against slavery, against the papacy in Risorgimento Italy—all stirred deep emotion.[19] British troops entering Jerusalem after capturing it from the Turks in World War I even saw themselves as new Crusaders avenging the Christian defeat by Saladin in the twelfth century. The United States undertook "crusades" against alcohol, socialism, anarchy, atheism, communism, even the gold standard. Using the word "crusade" not only sanctified a cause but also helped to give the original movement an aura of holiness and myth.

Twentieth-century studies, however, have abandoned the nineteenth-century myth that the Crusades were responsible for the rebirth of trade in the Mediterranean or for the introduction of luxuries, of new ideas, and of new forms of art and thought from the East. Historians have now properly placed these influences at earlier times and places, and, in fact, see many of them as factors contributing to the Crusade movement. The Crusades were embraced by a large number of Europeans of every social class, but to maintain that they were the norm for the Catholic Middle Ages is to ignore a substantial body of evidence that demonstrates both widespread criticism of the Crusades and an active movement to provide alternatives to their violence. Christian response to the Crusades took two forms. The first was a criticism of the ideal of the Christian knight and of the association of power and violence with Christian goals in Europe. This response emerged from the new poverty and peace movements of the high Middle Ages and will be discussed below. The second response was the peaceful alternative to the Crusades expressed by the movements for nonviolent conversion. This will be examined in chapter 7.

## THE NEW POVERTY MOVEMENTS

The criticism of violence and injustice in European society during the Crusade era took several forms: the poverty movements of the eleventh to the fourteenth centuries, the mendicant orders and their lay third orders, and the intermittent but widespread peace movements that affected both town and country throughout the period. These movements were largely the result of factors we have already discussed: the Investiture Conflict and the repression of the Peace movement of the tenth and eleventh centuries. Using the early church as model, the Gregorian Reform had attacked the basis of contemporary society in its call for the purification of Christian individuals and institutions. The reform was a profound and far-reaching challenge to Christians to assume personal responsibility for their spiritual well-being and a critical attitude toward Christian leadership.

Recent studies of the high Middle Ages[20] indicate that the popular sense of the time was that the traditional forms of Christian leadership had become bankrupt.[21] This consciousness united with the emergence of new forms of power in the West—the urban, capitalist money economy and the crusader ideal—to produce original forms of prophetic protest and of positive peacemaking. That the new form of peacemaking linked its criticism of the urban money economy with the violence of the feudal classes was natural, first because capitalism was seen as a strange new form of exploitation, and second because the power of the feudal classes had always been linked to violence and to the exploitation of the poor.

As we have seen in chapter 5, to be poor in the Carolingian period meant to be unarmed, that is, to be unable to provide the resources needed to be a member of the feudal class. The *laborator* (the worker, the peasant) was therefore the natural inferior of the *bellator* (the warrior) and was considered the passive victim of social exploitation and physical violence. With the Peace of God the poor assumed a position of Christian leadership but they were eventually repressed by the aristocratic reaction. In the aftermath of the Gregorian Reform, however, poverty became a potent means of reform, and once again brought the poor and the powerless into a position of dignity and leadership. Many factors contributed to the rise of the new poverty movement.[22] The discontent in the wake of the Gregorian Reform was a prime spur to the call to imitate the primitive church among individuals and small groups. The appearance of large numbers of hermits reflected a reaction to the laxity and wealth of traditional monasticism.[23] The hermits' stress on simplicity of life and then separation from church institutions as a means of penance and purification became a strong model for others in this period.[24]

The reform movement was both a theoretical quest for apostolic perfection and a concrete reaction to the personal poverty of the mass of the new urban dwellers.[25] Although too much can be made of the class origins of the new poverty movement, it seems fair to say that the real humiliation of poverty combined with the gospel ideal of poverty of spirit to create a new ideal and a new confrontation of power. *Pauper* became synonymous with *humilis* in describing this new poverty of spirit.[26]

Poverty became the equivalent of the sufferings of the early martyrs, a suffering willingly accepted in witness to the truth of the gospels that the humble and the poor of spirit will inherit the earth.[27] The meaning of poverty shifted radically from a passive state to an active imitation of the evangelical life of Christ, the apostles, and the primitive church. Poverty ennobled those who practiced it[28] and changed the thinking of theologians[29] and legislators.[30] It gave new meaning to the sufferings of the poor and of those who cared for them.[31]

Until the era of the Crusades the poor had been considered criminals, vagabonds, and troublemakers;[32] but the new ideal began to equate the *pauperes* and *laboratores* with the highest ideal of the Christian life.[33] Voluntary poverty became a means to an inner, spiritual poverty, the sign of a conversion of the "inner person," and thus of the worthiness of its preachers.[34] At the same time nonviolence, the official status of the poor, gained new dignity as a positive imitation of the gospel life.[35] From the late eleventh century an unending succession of preachers, prophets, and groups appeared all over the West dedicated to the twin ideals of poverty and peace. These ideals were an indictment of the violence of the time and offered a new model of living. We will briefly examine these movements and explain their impact on peacemaking in the Catholic tradition.

As the Peace of God declined in the middle of the eleventh century, a succession of wandering preachers in northern France announced the call to repentance and to the imitation of the gospels. Robert of Arbissel, Norbert of Xanten, Vitalis of Savigny, and Bernard of Tiron are among the best known of these.[36] These preachers and their movements were essentially orthodox,[37] but alongside them developed a startlingly large number of heterodox movements[38] including the Arnaldists and the Patarines of Italy,[39] the Waldensians of southern France and northern Italy,[40] and the Cathars of Italy, southern France and Spain. They all appealed to the desire for purification and reform;[41] they all spread a criticism of the clergy and the hierarchical church that soon spurred official reaction and condemnation. This reaction was to culminate in the bloody Albigensian Crusade in southern France (1208),[42] the spread of the Inquisition, and the fall into heresy of the Waldensians and other reform groups. Throughout this period the orthodox movements of protest maintained their allegiance to the Roman Church, embraced the poverty that symbolized penance and the refutation of power relationships, and steadfastly pursued the gospel ideal of peace.[43] Chief among these groups were the Humiliati, or the Humble People, the Poor Lombards, and the Poor Catholics.

## THE HUMILIATI, POOR LOMBARDS, AND POOR CATHOLICS

Little is known of the early history of the Humiliati. They apparently had most of the characteristics of the other voluntary poverty movements: they were laypersons gathered together for a life of simplicity and peace, renouncing wealth, devoting themselves to performing the works of mercy, all in imitation of the gospel life. The Humiliati shared one characteristic in common with some of the most radical poverty movements: they refused to bear arms or to take oaths. In medieval society to refuse to take oaths was particularly dangerous. It meant that the Humiliati could not and would not submit to the feudal oath of homage, not to a manorial or feudal lord, to a town council, or to a king or prince. The refusal to swear oaths reinforced the prohibition against bearing arms, for it implied the refusal to render the other element of feudal vassalage, the duty of military service.[44]

For this and other reasons involving their refusal to obey ecclesiastical authority, in 1179 Pope Alexander III excommunicated the Humiliati. Lucius III repeated the ban in 1184. By 1198 a delegation of Humiliati came to Rome to plead their case for orthodoxy before Pope Innocent III. In 1201 a papal commission recommended the acceptance of the Humiliati as a recognized lay order, granting them a *propositum* or unofficial rule that enshrined their principles of Christian activism, poverty, nonviolence, and a common identity and religious practice.[45] The rule[46] guarantees the Humiliati practice of nonviolence and protects their right not to swear oaths, except in necessity. The first three chapters of the rule set forth the gospel life of Christian peacemaking. The Sermon on the Mount and Romans 12 formed the basis of their life. The Golden Rule was their guide:

> It is said of old, "an eye for an eye, a tooth for a tooth," but I say to you: do not resist evil, if someone strikes you on the right cheek, offer him also the left. . . . Do not defend yourselves, beloved, but give way to anger. . . . Love your neighbor as yourself." You should also show love to enemies . . . "bless those who hate you and pray for those who calumniate you, so that you might be children of your father, who is in heaven, who makes his sun rise on the good and the bad, and causes rain to fall on the just and the unjust."[47]

The exact number and influence of the Humiliati are not known. It is known that they came from all social classes[48] and made their living predominantly by working in the Lombard textile industry. The women cared for the sick, the poor, and the lepers, the outcasts of medieval society; the men participated in social and civic work, in organizing trade associations, aiding the indigent, and performing services for the unemployed.[49] By 1216 they had organized 150 houses in the archbishopric of Milan alone, and this did not count households of the members who did not live communally. By 1279 the Humiliati had 220 convents in Milan.[50]

The Poor Lombards were granted official recognition by the papacy in June of 1210 for a similar rule.[51] The Poor Catholics were a group of Waldensians who, under the leadership of Durando of Huesca,[52] returned to the obedience of the church and were officially recognized by a papal bull (December 1208), which became their rule.[53] They and the Penitents directed by them devoted themselves to imitating Christ and the apostles,[54] living by the evangelical counsels of love and peace, practicing poverty, restoring goods obtained unjustly, and converting the rich and the powerful to a Christian life.[55]

By the beginning of the thirteenth century this "surge of new orders"[56] had reached such proportions that the papacy decided to forbid the establishment of new groups. But just at this time there appeared at the papal court another preacher of penitence, of love, and of the imitation of Christ and the gospels. He had been setting central Italy astir and had gathered around him a devoted following. With hesitation Innocent III admitted yet one more order and thus opened the way to a new chapter of Christian peacemaking. Francis of Assisi and his Little Brothers were to change the meaning of the imitation of Christ and the gospels as no one had done before or since.[57]

## SAINT FRANCIS AND THE FRANCISCANS

Francis typified the direction of the age and of Christian protest against violence and hate. Francesco Bernardone was born in Assisi in 1181, the son of a wealthy capitalist in the cloth trade. The young man led a carefree and pleasure-seeking life until, like Martin of Tours, whom he revered, he experienced a conversion while serving as a soldier.[58] He renounced both war and wealth and set out to lead a life of apostolic poverty, reconciliation, and peace. His decision earned him the ridicule of his towns-people and the hatred of his father. Francis's biographers relate the dramatic scene in which he boldly confronted his father before the bishop and the assembled town, denounced his worldly family and life, and vowed to devote himself to the gospel life.[59]

Having become the "new soldier of Christ,"[60] Francis set out to demonstrate by his life and preaching the intimate connection between poverty and peace in medieval society. He converted the forms and conventions of chivalry and courtly love to the service of peace, courting "Lady Poverty,"[61] becoming the "troubadour of Our Lady,"[62] and referring to his own order as Christ's "three-fold army."[63] He once told the bishop of Assisi, when asked why the Franciscans had no property, "If we had property, we should have need of arms to defend it."[64] Francis's life was a continual message of peace.

Francis may not have been a pacifist, but "he lived as if he were";[65] he came closer to living a life of total pacifism than any other medieval figure.[66] He went from village to village "announcing the kingdom of God, preaching peace, teaching salvation and penance and the remission of sins."[67] He courageously confronted the knights who harassed him while he was preaching outside Perugia and condemned the military;[68] he made peace between the mayor and the bishop of Assisi;[69] he brought about the reconciliation of warring factions in Bologna;[70] and he performed many other acts of peacemaking.[71] He brought peace wherever he traveled and moved with a spirit of charity and compassion for all,[72] especially for the disenfranchised and the outcasts of medieval society—the poor, the sick, and the lepers.[73] His love of nature is legendary.

Francis soon gathered around him a substantial following. The group won the approval of Pope Innocent III in 1210 and evolved into the Franciscan Order. Francis's *Rule of 1221*,[74] *Rule of 1223*,[75] *Letter to All Superiors*,[76] *Letter to All the Faithful*,[77] *Letter to the Rulers of the People*,[78] *Admonitions*,[79] *Canticle of the Sun*,[80] and final *Testament*[81] are filled with references to the need for peace, the reconciliation of enemies, forgiveness, and to suffering evil rather than inflicting it. He identified his brothers as those who preach, pray, and work *(laboratores)*[82] and he prohibited their riding on horseback.[83] He was thus directly contradicting the three orders of feudal society—those who pray, those who work, and those who fight[84]—and replacing the knight with the preacher, the true "soldier of Christ."[85] The Franciscans became peacemakers, calling society to reconciliation through their own lives of repentance and nonviolence.[86] They brought peace with them as they spread throughout the land.[87]

The Dominican Order was closely related to the Franciscan and addressed many of the same popular needs for a life of gospel simplicity. It was founded by Dominic of Guzman a few years after the Franciscans had been founded. The method and inspiration of the two orders were originally the same: poverty and a life of wandering preaching, the attempt to confront and win over heretics by nonviolence through reason and ethical persuasion.[88] We will look at their efforts for peace and justice below.[89]

## THE THIRD ORDERS

The greatest effect of Franciscan and Dominican peacemaking on medieval society can be observed in the history of the third orders of these two groups. Third orders, or tertiaries, are the lay affiliates of religious orders. They are composed of men and women, married and single, living in the world, pursuing their professions and crafts, but organized around basic principles inspired by the sponsoring order. Laypersons may either live in their own households or share a common house. They remain laypeople, however, and thus are an index of the effects of Franciscan and other mendicant forms of gospel imitation during the age of the Crusades.

The Franciscan Third Order was the direct result of Francis's preaching throughout the countryside of Italy. Married persons, those with professions and trades, responded to his call for repentance, reconciliation, and simplicity.[90] The implications of this new order were revolutionary.[91] The tertiaries were devoted to the life of poverty and reconciliation that marked the Franciscan Order, but unlike the first Franciscan Order, which made peace and peacemaking the implicit form of Franciscan life, they explicitly included in their rule the prohibitions against bearing arms and swearing oaths that were common in earlier voluntary poverty movements.

Francis's *Letter to All the Faithful* set out the basic principles of the Third Order of Penitents.[92] The first appearance of a formal rule, however, comes to us in two versions, a rule of 1215[93] and the so-called Venice Rule of 1221.[94] After calling for simplicity of life and dress and regulating days of fast and abstinence, the rule went on to specify the forms of peacemaking that the Penitents were to follow:

> They are to be reconciled with their neighbors and [are] to restore what belongs to others . . . [5,15].They are not to take up lethal weapons, or bear them about, against anybody . . . [5,16].They are to refrain from formal oaths except in the cases exempted by the pope, that is, for peace, for the Faith, under calumny, and in bearing witness [5,17].

They were to perform the acts of mercy; visiting and caring for the sick, burying the dead, and caring for the poor (6–7,24). The reconciling of enemies, both among their own members and among nonmembers, was specifically written into the rule (7,26).

The rule for the Penitents foresaw that peacemaking by an organized body would threaten the established order and invite repression.[95] As early as 1221[96] a crisis arose in Faenza as the Ghibellines (the imperial faction) called on their vassals to take up arms in one of the endless civil wars of the Italian city-states. In compliance with their rule, the Penitents refused either to take up arms or to swear the oaths of loyalty.[97] Shocked, the grandees attempted to force them to obey but were finally compelled to appeal to Pope Gregory IX, himself a Franciscan. The papal response (March 1227) in its various versions[98] confirmed the right of the Penitents to live lives of nonviolence and set a precedent for the next century. The ruling was reiterated many times by papal letters, legal interpretations, and Franciscan commentaries[99] when local governments attempted to force military and civil service on the Penitents.[100]

The Third Order spread rapidly throughout Italy and Europe, appealing to all classes of lay society.[101] In 1251 Pope Innocent IV ordered that membership rosters of all Penitent houses be made. These documents reveal the movement's wide social appeal. Its members included scribes, notaries, bakers, cobblers, potters, barbers, tradespeople of all types, professionals in every occupation, nobles, and a few kings and queens.[102] It is estimated that by the end of the fourteenth century the tertiaries had over fifteen hundred congregations throughout Europe.[103] Most towns of any size had a house, either of the common life or of laypersons living their own family life. In Italy alone the numbers of Penitents are startling. By 1450 John of Capistrano estimated 600,000 members there.[104] The numbers in northern Europe were not as high.

Among the Penitents were some of the most important women of the age: Elizabeth of Hungary (1207–1231),[105] Elizabeth of Portugal (1271–1336),[106] and Bridget of Sweden (c. 1303–1373).[107] Bridget of Sweden is particularly interesting for her part in the history of Catholic peacemaking. A noblewoman with close ties to the court of Sweden, she entered the Third Order after her husband's death in 1344 and became an outspoken critic of corruption in the Swedish court. She was an active peacemaker and condemned King Magnus's crusade against the pagan Letts and Estonians as nothing more than an excuse for looting and conquest. Her criticisms soon earned her the hatred of the king and his courtiers, so in 1349 Bridget left Sweden for Rome, where she devoted the rest of her life to monastic reform, aiding the poor, attacking corruption, and encouraging the papacy to mediate peace between France and England.

Other orders also had tertiaries. The Dominicans set up a Third Order of Penance of Saint Dominic, which received official guidance and regulation from the Dominican Order.[108] Other orders of laypersons, such as the Norbertines, drew large followings in northern Europe as early as 1125.[109]

## POPULAR PEACE MOVEMENTS

One of the outgrowths of the mendicant orders and their tertiaries was the peace movement of the mid-thirteenth century known as the Great Alleluia.[110] Several factors contributed to its formation: the struggle between Emperor Frederick II and Pope Gregory IX, the revolt against the emperor throughout Italy and consequent imperial repression, the papal crusade against the excommunicated Frederick, and the war and civil discord in northern Italy's city-states.[111] Those with apocalyptic expectations saw Frederick as the Antichrist and awaited the new age.[112] Spontaneously, thousands of people throughout northern Italy began to search for alternatives to the violence around them. Urged on by wandering preachers, including the Dominican John of Vicenza, they began to make peace.

The Franciscan chronicler Salimbene wrote: "This Alleluia . . . was a time of peace and quiet, wherein all weapons of war were laid aside, a time of merriment and gladness."[113] Preached by both laypersons and mendicants, the peace movement recalled the days of Saint Francis's wanderings through the Italian countryside. Through sermons, processions, devotions, and other demonstrations the peace spread rapidly through northeastern Italy, into Tuscany and the Romagna around Bologna. At Verona on August 28, 1233, on the Plain of Pasquara, four hundred thousand people of all classes and from all parts of northern Italy reportedly assembled to demonstrate for the end of war, for peace, and for reconciliation.[114] The demonstration moved many to abandon violence and embrace their enemies. Even the emperor and the pope agreed to make peace.[115] The Great Alleluia was not an isolated instance.

Similar movements of reconciliation emerged in the 1250s and 1260s. That involving the Disciplinati, or the Flagellants, sought to bring reconciliation and peace through dramatic, self-imposed penance. Often naked, chanting "Mercy and Peace!", beating themselves and one another to relive Christ's sufferings and to atone for the hatred and violence of their neighbors, these "missionaries of peace" staged processions throughout the towns of northern and central Italy and, like St. Francis and the Great Alleluia, brought many to make peace with their enemies.[116] The peacemaking efforts of Philip Benizi (1233–1285)[117] throughout central Italy, of the pilgrims attending the jubilee of Boniface VIII in 1300, and of the followers of Venturino da Bergamo on their "peace crusade" to Rome in 1335 testify to the continued strength of the popular peace movements.[118]

Such efforts at peacemaking continued to the end of the Middle Ages. One of the better known was the Bianchi movement of northern Italy (1399), named after the white *(bianco)* dress its members wore. This peace movement emerged during the wars of the early Italian Renaissance. By 1399 Duke Gian Galeazzo Visconti of Milan was tightening his grip on Tuscany. He took Pisa, Perugia, and Siena, and encircled Florence. To the south, dynastic war over the crown of Naples had just ended.[119] The movement began in a series of visions to peasants along the Genoese Riviera and perhaps as far afield as Piedmont.[120] The people of the countryside were moved to reconciliation and peacemaking and began a series of penitential processions proclaiming peace. The movement spread rapidly along the Italian coast and to the major cities: to Genoa, northeast to Milan and Bergamo, and into Tuscany, south toward Rome and to the industrial and commercial cities of Lucca, Prato, Pistoia, and eventually Florence.

The Bianchi demonstrated their commitment to peace in long, nine-day processions, in the purity of their dress and behavior, in their lives of poverty and simplicity, some even in their vegetarianism. "Everywhere the Bianchi went, peace-making was their major function."[121] Moving from city to city in groups of thousands, their arrival was always marked by high emotion, the reconciliation of enemies, forgiveness, repentance, and a return to peace. The movement brought together *paesani* with *huomini grandi* and *mercanti,* peasants with wealthy townspeople and merchants. Like the Peace of God, the Bianchi cut across class and occupational lines, breaking down the hierarchical structures of medieval society.

The numbers of Bianchi swelled the population of the major cities. In Florence Bianchi poured in from the city's *contado,* or area of control: two thousand from San Miniato and Empoli, another thousand from Volterra, and more from the towns of the Colle di Val d'Elsa and San Gimignano. Coluccio Salutati, the Renaissance humanist and chancellor of Florence, counted three thousand from Lucca, "not rustics, but the leaders of that city and notable merchants."[122] In Milan the numbers in the peace movement were so large that the duke had to give orders to end the processions by early September so that the wheat harvest could proceed. Yet "the orderliness and beneficent effects of the *bianchi* were almost universally acknowledged."[123] By the time the processions reached Rome in September 1399, their number reached 200,000, according to one chronicler.[124]

## CONCLUSIONS

It is a historical irony that these documented peace movements have been passed over as extremist, disruptive, and misguided, while the disastrous history of the Crusade movement, which consistently attracted fewer, more disreputable, and more destructive forces, has received the awed respect and solemn judgments of historians. Juggling medieval numbers is a hazardous enterprise; chroniclers' estimates of crowd sizes and army strengths are relative. They most often give attention only to the significant components of medieval groups: high ecclesiastics, barons and knights, noble families.

However, a general comparison of the relative numbers involved in the Crusades and the peace movements may prove instructive.

The First Crusade left Constantinople with between 25,000 and 30,000 combatants;[125] approximately 10,000 were left to defend the Kingdom of Jerusalem in 1100. At no time did the permanent garrison of barons and knights of the kingdom exceed 1,000; the sergeants numbered about 5,000.[126] On the disastrous Second Crusade (1146) Emperor Conrad of Germany led the largest army ever assembled in Europe. It was estimated at one million but probably numbered about 20,000, including unarmed pilgrims and other noncombatants.[127] The "wild overestimate"[128] made by medieval chroniclers of Emperor Frederick Barbarossa's army for the Third Crusade, the largest army of the time, was between 100,000 and 150,000.[129] King Philip Augustus left Genoa with a fighting force of about 2,000.[130] In 1192 Richard the Lionhearted took Jaffa with 2,500 men, admittedly an emergency muster.[131] The Fourth Crusade left Venice in 1202 with approximately 35,000 combatants;[132] the Fifth Crusade fought outside Damietta in Egypt with a force estimated by contemporaries at about 50,000, including a large contingent of unarmed pilgrims.[133] Saint Louis's Crusade left Cyprus with about 20,000 soldiers. When Acre fell to the Moslems in 1291 the combined Christian garrison of refugees who had left the conquered Holy Land, of Italian marines, and of Crusaders totaled about 15,000.[134]

How can we judge these figures? What comparisons can we make? Communal houses of the Humiliati in Milan alone in 1279 were estimated at 220. The Franciscan Third Order had 1,500 communal houses in Europe by 1400. John of Capistrano estimated that the order had 600,000 members in Italy in 1450. Peace demonstrators at the Plain of Pasquara on one day (August 1233) reportedly totaled 400,000. In 1399, the Bianchi were demonstrating in every region of Italy from the Piedmont to Lombardy to Tuscany, and more than 7,000 converged on Florence alone. A penitential army estimated at 200,000 thronged Rome, and Milan lost most of its workers for the wheat harvest. The councils of the Peace of God, which convened every year throughout Europe, attracted thousands of laypersons to each meeting.

Medieval numbers are not exact statistics. Used without proper controls and critical criteria they prove nothing. They are not used here as conclusive evidence. Yet they do give an idea of the impact of both the Crusades and the peace movements of the later Middle Ages. A balanced history of the period could not be written without discussing both, and the effects and contributions of the popular peace movements must be admitted into the equation.

# CHAPTER 7

# ALTERNATIVES TO THE CRUSADES: PEACEMAKING IN THE NON-CHRISTIAN WORLD (1100–1400)

## CONVERSION

Just as the apostolic poverty movements confronted the violence of the feudal order of Europe, so Christian missionary work countered the violence of the Crusades overseas. Both imitated the life of Christ and the apostles in preaching the gospels to all nations. From as early as the ninth-century martyr movement in Cordova[1] Christians had attempted to confront the Moslem world in the way prescribed in the gospels, actively preaching the word, meeting persecution with patience and love in the hope that the witness of suffering and perhaps even martyrdom would win the enemy over.

We have little evidence of active missions to the Islamic world during the Carolingian period,[2] but in the eleventh century the Cluniacs went as missionaries to Spain. Other attempts followed there.[3] Recent opinion is that the anonymous Monk of France, who wrote to Caliph al-Mugtadir bin Hūd of Saragossa (1049–1081) attempting to introduce him to Christian doctrine and to win his conversion and that of Islamic Spain,[4] was none other than Abbot Hugh of Cluny.[5]

The opposition to the Crusades voiced by Peter the Venerable, abbot of Cluny in 1122, has long been a subject of controversy. He did cooperate with the Second and Third Crusades, but his efforts appear to have been halfhearted.[6] While his opposition to a military solution was not overt, it was fundamental to his thought.[7] In his *Book Against the Sect or Heresy of the Saracens* Peter declared that Christians must approach the Moslems

> not as the Latins were wont to do—with weapons—but with words; not with force—but reason; not with hatred—but love, the kind of love that should exist between Christians and non-Christians, the same love with which the Apostles approached the Gentiles, the love that God Himself had for those who did not serve Him.[8]

Peter's efforts at peacemaking, the arbitration and reconciliation of warring groups in Europe, were unfailing.[9] He once wrote to King Louis VII of France protesting Christian pogroms against Jews, reminding him that "God does not will cold-blooded murder or outright slaughter."[10] His attitude toward the Saracens was similar. Writing to Bernard of Clairvaux, known for his support of the Crusades, Peter reminded the Cistercian that

> the Church has no sword. Christ took it away when he said to Peter, "Put back thy sword into the scabbard; for all those who take the sword will perish by the sword" [Mt 26:52]. This is true, true indeed. The Church does not have the sword of a king, but the staff of a shepherd, of which the Apostle [Rom 11:13] has this to say: "What is your wish? Shall I come to you with a staff, or in love and in the spirit of meekness?" [I Cor 4:21] . . . Yet it may also be said to have a sword, according to him, "And take unto you the helmet of salvation and the sword of the Spirit, which is the Word of God." [Eph 6:17].[11]

Peter's alternative to the physical sword was the gospels. He felt as strongly as the most ardent Crusader that the Holy Land must be won for Christendom, but he contended that preaching and conversion were more effective Christian means to this goal.[12] As early as his trip to Spain in 1142 Peter seems to have planned a major project for the study of the Moslem religion in order to strengthen Christian resistance and to refute peacefully what he considered Islam's false elements.[13] His *Book Against the Sect or Heresy of the Saracens* was an outcome of this project.[14] Although Peter's criticism of the Crusades was muted, the alternative he put forward flew in the face of Carolingian attitudes and set the tone for future centuries of peaceful conversion.

By the thirteenth century the idea of peaceful conversion as an alternative to the Crusades had become widespread in Europe.[15] The most explicit and influential voice of protest came from the mendicant orders, who linked the evangelical imitation of Christ with the peacemaking of the apostles and their mission to the Gentiles.[16] Francis of Assisi took the lead in showing the West a nonviolent path to Jerusalem.[17] Francis, throughout his life, sought the perfect imitation of Christ in all things, most especially in Christ's suffering. The crucified Christ became his model, and Francis was seen to be the perfect imitation of Christ, bearing the sign of Christ's passion, the stigmata.[18] Francis made this imitation explicit in his Rules[19] and combined it with an acute sense of the apocalyptic last days in which the whole world must be converted before Christ's second coming and the founding of the New Jerusalem.[20]

Francis made three expeditions to convert the Moslems,[21] two unsuccessful attempts to North Africa and to "Syria," and a third, successful, voyage to Egypt (1219–1221) in the wake of the Fifth Crusade. At Damietta, where the Christians had been surrounded and cut off from their supplies and reinforcements, Francis preached to the army "forbidding the war, denouncing the reason for it."[22] Ignored by the Crusaders (who went on to defeat) Francis approached the sultan himself. At first beaten and repulsed, he was finally admitted to see the ruler, who received the missionary of peace, listened attentively to his sermon, but refused to be converted. Francis and his companions were well treated when they preached the gospel in Egypt, but when they began to denounce Mohammed, as with their predecessors in Cordova, they earned the wrath of the Moslems and were expelled.[23]

Francis explicitly included the mission to the Saracens in his Rules of 1221[24] and 1223.[25] Winning the New Jerusalem through martyrdom was a recognized goal for the members of the Franciscan Order.[26] Mobile, vocal, often fanatical in their desire to convert the Moslems or die in the attempt, the Franciscans chose a method of public and active nonviolence designed to confront Islam at the heart of its power. They preached inside mosques, calling on Moslem officials to renounce Mohammed and embrace Christianity; they entered bazaars to preach the gospels. "Outrageous, consciously ineffective, yet designed to engage the forces of heaven at some mystical level, [this method] seized the imagination of contemporary Christendom."[27] Creative nonviolence had its effects; the Franciscans were able to persuade both persecutors and public in East and West that the imitation of Christ was real and strong, and that victory through conversion was a real possibility.[28]

The recapture of the Holy Land, especially in the wake of military failure there, was the Franciscans' first priority. This was most important since the imitation of Christ argued in this literal age for the physical retracing of Christ's steps. The Crusaders had been unable to penetrate the Holy Land after the fall of the Kingdom of Jerusalem in 1187, but Franciscans had established missions there by 1215. By 1221 they had established houses in Antioch; and by 1229, following Emperor Frederick II's negotiated treaty with the Moslems, they had houses in Jerusalem, Nazareth, and along the coast, giving Christian pilgrims access that military measures had not won. These missions lasted until the military adventures of the remaining Crusader States led to the final destruction of Western power with the fall of Tripoli (1289) and Acre (1291), during which the friars were special targets of the Moslems.[29]

Franciscan missions were active in North Africa beginning in 1219 and in Moslem Spain by 1228, where friars were executed for publicly preaching in Valencia.[30] Missions were established all over North Africa in the 1220s, despite harassment and massacres, and continued to exist into the fourteenth century.[31] They had the support and direction of the papacy.[32] To the East, Franciscan missionaries penetrated the Mongol Empire of Genghis Khan in the 1240s and reached as far as Beijing, where they established a long-lived mission.[33] By the end of the thirteenth century they had traveled to Armenia, Persia, and India.[34] To the north, Franciscan missions to Lithuania were peaceful, a stark contrast to the genocide committed by the Teutonic Knights in their "crusade" against the pagan peoples of the Baltic.[35]

The actions of the Franciscans, like those of the martyrs of Cordova and of the early church, were not the result of a suicide wish. Franciscan theory was aware of the dangers of such an attitude and explicitly emphasized that the aim of these missions was not death, but the spreading of the gospels through nonviolent means. This could end in suffering and death, and Franciscan writers stressed that this was, after all, the heart of the imitation of Christ.[36] Franciscan thinkers brought the message of nonviolence to the highest levels of European discourse. Roger Bacon, the great Franciscan philosopher, was typical.

Roger Bacon composed his *Compendium of the Study of Philosophy* in response to the election of Pope Gregory X (1271). Chapters 13 and 14, "On the Study of Languages,"[37] spell out the intellectual alternative to the Crusades. Bacon, a keen student of ancient and Eastern languages, offers a positive alternative to the violence of the Crusades.[38] Bacon's principles are clear: "Oh, how many tyrants and evil men have been confounded at the words of power and convicted [overcome] rather than through wars. . . . The histories give us definite information in regard to them."[39] Bacon is just as explicit regarding the policy of the Crusades. War does not succeed against the infidels, in fact it hardens the hearts of the living with hatred for Christianity; it only sends the souls of those killed to hell.[40] Instead of killing and destruction, Bacon urges toleration for minority groups, such as the Jews in Europe, and the conversion of the Jews, the Saracens, and the pagans of the north.[41]

Bacon has a special criticism for the Teutonic Knights and their northern crusade:

> For there is no doubt that all nations of unbelievers beyond Germany would have been converted long since but for the violence of the Teutonic Knights, because the race of pagans was frequently ready to receive the faith in peace after preaching.[42]

Further, he says, the Teutonic Order does not want peace, but wants to subject these people to slavery.[43] Regarding the Holy Land, Bacon reminds his reader that "the faith did not enter into this world by force of arms, but through the simplicity of preaching, as is clear."[44]

About the same time another Franciscan, the lay tertiary Ramón Lull (c. 1232–1315), formulated a detailed approach to the conversion process.[45] Once a courtly poet, Lull experienced a conversion around 1265. In 1276 he set up a school at Miramar (Majorca) to teach languages to missionaries.[46] For many years he lobbied at church councils and with prelates and princes for support of his missionary plans. Between 1277 and 1282 he traveled throughout Europe, the Levant, and North Africa;[47] he went to Tunis in 1292 where he began preaching, was arrested, and deported. In 1300 he journeyed to Cyprus in the hope of converting the Tartars but was prevented from sailing to Syria and returned to Europe to further develop his ideas.[48] Lull sailed to Bugia (Algeria) in 1307, where he denounced Mohammed. Saved from death by the local *qadi,* he was imprisoned and finally deported.[49] In 1314/5 he returned to Tunis and was well received by the local Moslems, who gave him permission to preach in the countryside where he became a revered figure. Finding this too easy, he returned to Bugia, where he began preaching, was recognized and killed.[50]

Lull's views on the Crusades and conversion are complex and appear contradictory. Some consider him a pacifist;[51] others point out his proposals for the Crusade[52] and attempt to trace some process of conversion in one direction or the other.[53] Throughout his life, however, Lull seems to have combined support and plans for military campaigns with the hope of nonviolent conversion.[54] It is therefore difficult to discover Lull's true intent. He did however state that military conquest without conversion was fruitless and that conversion could not succeed through force. Despite his grandiose military schemes he longed for and finally took the path of martyrdom. His contemporaries paid more attention to his words of peace than to his plans for war.[55]

Lull knew Arabic and translated many of his own works into that language. He was convinced, as was Bacon, that resolving problems of communication was a real alternative to wars and sectarian division, and so he actively lobbied the pope to support the teaching of biblical and Eastern languages. At the Council of Vienne (1311) his influence was decisive in enacting legislation to set up chairs at the major European universities to teach Arabic, Hebrew, and Chaldean.[56]

In his *Book of Contemplation on God,* written between 1272 and 1277, he wrote that only nonviolence can win the Holy Land:

> The conquest of that sacred land will not be achieved save by love and prayer and the shedding of tears as well as blood. . . . We must put an end to the material war between Christians and Saracens because so long as it lasts neither

side can begin those peaceful discussions which will certainly result in the triumph of the cross.[57]

This theme is developed further in chapter 80 of Lull's novel *Libre d'Evast e d'Aloma e de Blanquerna* begun in 1283.[58] A Saracen messenger arrives at the papal court from the sultan of Babylon. In his letter the sultan marvels that the Christians imitate the Moslems in trying to take the Holy Land by the sword:

> He marveled that the pope and the Christians worked not after the manner of Jesus Christ and of the apostles, who through preaching and through martyrdom converted the world, and they followed not in the manner of those who preceded them in conquering other countries; for this cause, he said, God willed not that they should possess the Holy Land beyond the seas.[59]

So moved by the letter were the pope and the cardinals (in the story) that they decided to establish schools of languages, modeled on Miramar, to promote missionary work throughout the world. The military orders were also commanded to provide training in intellectual struggle as well as physical conquest and to soon begin winning over the infidels by their expositions of the faith. Tartars, Saracens, and Jews all began learning Christian truths and converting. In chapter 81, And on Earth Peace to Men of Good Will,[60] the papacy sets up a special office of mediation under a cardinal and establishes itself as a peacemaker within Christendom.

The Franciscans were not alone in the pursuit of the nonviolent conversion. The Dominicans placed a special emphasis on language and learning. They established language centers all over Spain for the study of Arabic and other languages, including the Hebrew of the Talmud.[61] They produced such activists as Theodore of Celles, Ramon Martí, and Ramon of Peñafort. Through never formally a Dominican, Theodore of Celles was a knight whose experience of the brutality of the Third Crusade led him to abandon warfare for a life of nonviolent missionary work. He joined Saint Dominic in southern France, where he was preaching to the Cathars, and later founded the house of Seyl (Celles) on the Meuse in Belgium.[62] The minister general of the Dominican Order, Ramon of Peñafort resigned his post to devote himself to missionary work in Tunisia, Murcia, and Valencia. He wrote specifically of the need to replace force with language study, education, and preaching, and warned that anyone seeking Christian perfection must abstain from violence.[63] Thomas Aquinas's *On the Truth of the Catholic Faith*[64] was written at the instigation of Ramon of Peñafort and stemmed in large part from the Dominican policy of conversion by convincing Moslem theologians "of the truth of the Catholic faith."[65]

The voices of European laity, missionaries, and philosophers were echoed in the Holy Land. The views of William of Tripoli, a Dominican, were typical of the large body of public opinion among the Christians there at the time.[66] William's *On the Condition of the Saracens* (c. 1273), addressed to Pope Gregory X, stressed that arms would not succeed in keeping the Holy Land, only peaceful conversion preceded by cultural and religious understanding of the Moslems could win them over.[67]

## THE HEAVENLY JERUSALEM AND THE VISION OF PEACE

The movement for nonviolent conversion, strong on its own merits, went hand in hand with another medieval movement that stirred even more hearts and represented an even stronger critique of the Crusaders' campaign to take and keep the earthly Jerusalem by force of arms. This was the continuing Christian tradition of Jerusalem as the *visio pacis*, the apocalyptic image of Jerusalem as the symbol of peace and justice on earth.[68]

Closely associated in medieval thought with the apocalyptic city, the earthly Jerusalem had long been the focus of both the idealized dreams of medieval society for peace and justice and, since at least the fourth century, the goal of peaceful pilgrims who wanted to retrace the steps of Christ and relive the gospel.[69] By the eighth century, under the influence of the penitential system, exile and pilgrimage to Jerusalem were considered ways of assuring the forgiveness of sins. By the eleventh century the city had become the destination for pilgrimages by all classes of European society seeking reconciliation.[70] Many literally believed that they were headed for the Heavenly Jerusalem of the Apocalypse.[71] Travelers on this pilgrimage to Jerusalem, as on all journeys of penitence, went unarmed. So did the 12,000 pilgrims attacked by Moslems (c. 1064) on their way to the city.[72]

For medieval people, the Crusades were a form of pious pilgrimage to Jerusalem. The term for pilgrimage, *peregrinatio*, was in fact used to describe the Crusade movement until the eighteenth century.[73] Urban II's preaching of the First Crusade combined the mystical idea of Jerusalem, the apocalyptic city and traditional goal of pilgrimage, with a new call for military action.[74] Penitence, millennial fervor,[75] pilgrimage, and conquest motivated all Crusaders to some extent, but military exploits seem to have been the realm of the feudal aristocracy. Europe's poor, raised to new consciousness by decades of the Investiture Conflict and by the appeal of the new poverty movements, saw a special place for themselves in this new pilgrimage to Jerusalem,[76] an opportunity that would allow them to physically retrace the steps of Christ and imitate the early church.[77]

The poor, women, clergy, and noncombatants of all types made up most of the First Crusade, despite repeated attempts by the pope and the feudal leaders to exclude them.[78] From the beginning this "crusade" of the people was nonviolent. Despite the rigors of the journey, attacks by Moslems, and the lack of food to the point of starvation, most of the unarmed pilgrims remained nonviolent. There were exceptions: Peter the Hermit's People's Crusade and the incident of the cannibal Tafurs are the best known.[79] Only one-sixth of the expedition was armed when it reached Asia Minor, and by the time it reached the Holy Land, only 20,000 persons were actually combatants.[80] Later Crusades carefully and strictly limited the number of noncombatants allowed and thus failed to evoke the popular enthusiasm enjoyed by the First Crusade. These facts are significant and alter the traditional view of the popularity of the military adventure of the Crusades.

The Heavenly Jerusalem appealed to another, powerful European tradition that saw the events described in the Apocalypse as a nonviolent alternative to the Crusades. One of the most influential apocalyptic interpreters of the Middle Ages was Abbot Joachim of Fiore, whose works have sparked centuries of debate, interpretation, and anxiety in the West.[81] Joachim saw all history as the material record of the divine plan for salvation. History was a gradual process of revelation plotted out in a series of three ages or stages of growth: the age of the Father, corresponding to the Old Testament, the age of the Son and the New Testament, and the age of the Holy Spirit, a time yet to come in which the church would be purified and its elect members granted new insight and spiritual understanding. Joachim's writings were mystic interpretation of Scripture; they were not intended as prophesies.[82] Nevertheless, because he based his interpretations on a series of historical concordances between the Old and New Testament and sought to explain the mysteries of the Apocalypse, his words were taken as prophesies concerning the age of the millennium about to dawn.

Joachim initially supported the Crusade movement and fitted it into his schema of historical parallels to Scripture.[83] He was therefore consulted as a prophetic seer by Richard I of England on the king's way to the Third Crusade.[84] Appalled by the terrible waste of life of that expedition, however, Joachim abandoned his support of the Crusades in favor of a solution that he found in the words of Scripture.[85] Joachim came to realize that the Christians' faith in arms was not bringing about victory in the East. It was furthermore blinding Christians to God's historical plan. In the last days only the patience, faith, and understanding of God's will by true Christians could give them strength to endure the persecutions of the Moslems and to reach the mystic Jerusalem. Only the *viri spirituales,* the spiritual people of the third millennial age, could accomplish through their patient suffering and understanding what the violence of the Crusaders had not. In the dawning third age they would convert the infidels and the Jews, reunite the Greek with the Latin church, and unite all people in peace, freedom, and enlightenment.

Joachim's nonviolent eschatology was forceful, and influenced intellectual and popular audience alike. His most important impact, however, came in the fusion of prophecy with the poverty of the mendicant orders, especially the Franciscans.[86] Francis had spoken in apocalyptic terms himself,[87] and his order was soon seen as the group of elect foretold by Joachim to bear the persecutions of the Antichrist and to usher in the new age of the Heavenly Jerusalem. Thus within the Franciscan Order Joachite mood combined with the already strong Franciscan tradition of nonviolent conversion to produce a new movement for apocalyptic conversion as an alternative to the Crusades.[88]

The Franciscan Spiritual wing, which included such figures as Peter John Olivi,[89] Ubertino da Casale,[90] and Angelo Clareno,[91] gave the nonviolent alternative to the Crusades explicit formulation: it was vain to attempt to conquer Jerusalem, the symbol of earthly as well as heavenly peace, by force. Peace was gained not through war, but through the agents of peace, the new spiritual people, whose sufferings for Christ must precede the millennium. The papacy should therefore abandon its vain efforts to raise armies and concentrate on the efforts of conversion.[92] Angelo Clareno, for example, spent many years in missionary work in Asia Minor during the Mongol invasion. In Greece he devoted much labor to translating the works of the Greek Fathers in order to help reform the Latin church.[93] The chronicler Salimbene de Adam[94] shared the Joachite views and recorded their widespread appeal.[95] He recounts a strong tradition of anti-Crusade prophecies, even in the Dominican Order,[96] and the testimony of many returning missionaries, who predicted peaceful conversion in the East in the near future.[97]

## THE POETRY OF PROTEST

Many looked expectantly for the New Jerusalem, the vision of peace; others in the increasingly lay world of the late Middle Ages looked critically at the world around them and transformed their criticisms into poetry. The most important of these were the troubadours' *sirventes,* protest songs with frank propaganda and political purpose, and wide popular appeal.[98] The wandering troubadours of Languedoc (southern France) protested the whole Crusade movement but took special aim at the Albigensian Crusade.[99] This was fought at the beginning of the thirteenth century to stamp out the Catharist, or Albigensian, sect in southern France; but the brilliant culture of the region was also wiped out amid the pitched battles, sacks, and massacres by both sides, but especially by the Crusaders.[100]

Guillem Daspols, Guilhem de Tudela, Guillaume le Clerc, and Étienne de Fougères were a few of the troubadours who condemned the Crusades as anti-Christian and called for toleration and peaceful conversion. In *Tenzone,* for example, Guillem Daspols called the Crusade wasteful carnage; if God were truly on the side of the Christians, he would convert the Saracens and thus stop the war.[101] In the *Chanson de la Croisade des Albigeois,* attributed to Guilhem de Tudela, the tone suddenly shifts[102] away from support of the Albigensian Crusaders to bitter condemnation of their atrocities in the taking of Toulouse. Mocking a proposal to have the slain leader of the Crusade canonized, Guilhem notes:

If by killing men, by shedding blood, by destroying souls, by consenting to murders, . . . by killing women and destroying children, one can overcome Jesus Christ in this world, one should wear a crown and shine in heaven![103]

Guillaume le Clerc[104] and Étienne de Fougères[105] not only decried the violence of the Crusades, they also wrote against the injustices of a social system based on the exploitation of the poor and the violence of the feudal aristocracy.

Criticisms of the Crusade movement were not confined to Languedoc; it also appeared in England in the fourteenth century. In the words of one critic, "the greatest of all the alliterative poems of social protest is *Piers Plowman,*"[106] written between 1362 and 1387 by the English poet William Langland, a contemporary of Chaucer. The poem presents in an allegorical dream-vision a scathing review of all the vices of English society of the time and recommends the means to remedy them.[107] In his criticism Langland expresses the thought of the English middle class in clear form[108] and reflects contemporary popular preaching style.[109]

Speaking through the mouth of Conscience, Langland prophesies the apocalyptic age to come in which the weapons of war will be outlawed and turned into instruments of peace: swords into plowshares and spears into pruning hooks; priests will once again care for souls, and kings will rule with justice for all.[110] Later, in his enumeration of the virtues,[111] Langland considers Islam and calls for its peaceful conversion, noting the examples of the apostles' mission and the peaceful conversion of England and Wales. He exhorts the clergy, beginning with the pope, to take up their proper duty of preaching the gospels.

A more explicit condemnation of war is found in the work of John Gower, a contemporary of Chaucer and Langland, whose *Confessio Amantis* (Lover's Confession) written around 1390 became a medieval best seller[112] and was one of the first books published in print.[113] Like *Piers Plowman,* Gower's work is an essay on public and private virtues but is told in the form of popular moral tales. In Book 3[114] Gower discusses war and violence, condemning them in some detail. Despite the possibility of just wars, he notes, all war is the result of greed and the cause of destruction, an offense against nature, the virtues, God's law, and Christ's commands.[115] Gower allows that the king might wield the sword of police power to constrain evil and to do justice, and the individual might have the right to protect home and family, but he questions whether killing in war can be similarly justified.[116] We know that God forbids murder, he says, and that Christ was sent to bring peace and the rule of charity. War offends this rule and also sins against nature. In place of peace, the most precious jewel among Adam's treasures, war brings poverty, pestilence, woe, famine, and all other pains; it destroys the gifts of God's creation,[117] and violates churches, priests, women, and the law.[118]

What then, are the motives for war? Gower's answer is clear: greed, the personal advantage of the warlords, economic gain, land, spoil, and pay. He recounts the story of Alexander the Great and the pirate chief (already familiar through Augustine's writings), the one distinguished from the other only by the degree of his barbarity.[119] If war is so sinful and love and peace are clearly God's will, what of the Crusades? Once again the answer is plain: Christ never said "slay"; instead he gave his own life. He sent the apostles to preach the gospels to the world; they all died in the effort to spread the gospels. Never did they set an example to kill. All slaying then is evil.[120]

## CONCLUSIONS

The troubadours wrote popular literature that reflected the feelings and attitudes of the lay audience of the age of the Crusades. "Although a few of the clergy joined in this chorus of discontent, the greater part of the criticism came from laymen. . . . Not only were these critics from all walks of life, they were from many different parts of Europe."[121] So widespread had opposition to the Crusades become by the late thirteenth century that the Crusade movement was practically dead. At the Second Council of Lyons (1272) Pope Gregory X requested briefings from all over Europe concerning the popular opposition to war. His aim was not to extol the peacemakers, but, like a modern politician concerned with adverse public opinion, to find methods of getting around or overcoming the opposition.[122] Gregory entrusted the task of coordinating the collection and summation of this material to Humbert of Romans (c. 1200–1277), minister general of the Dominican Order.[123] The result was Humbert's *Opus tripartitum* (Work in Three Parts).[124]

In typical scholastic fashion the Dominican listed all the categories and forms of opposition, from outright pacifism, which he notes was widespread and dangerous (based as it was on the gospels, Paul, church councils, and even papal pronouncements)[125] to cynicism about the Crusades' aims and uses by the church to the vocal opposition of women and poets and serious reservations about the justness of these wars.[126] All classes of European society are represented, all its major groups and occupations, all the reasons that have brought other military adventures to a halt—from the highest ideals to the deepest indifference toward the slogans of the masters of war. Humbert dutifully recorded and attempted to counter them all. His work unintentionally became a monument to peacemaking in the era of the Crusades.

# CHAPTER 8

# THE PAPACY AS PEACEMAKER: ARBITRATION, CANON LAW, AND THE RIGHTS OF CONSCIENCE (1100–1500)

## INTRODUCTION

We have considered the papacy only in passing, examining instead Christian thought as a whole or the actions of individual peacemakers and mass movements for peace. We will now examine several areas in which the papacy consistently set standards and definitions for the rest of the church and specifically contributed to the history of Catholic peacemaking. The first area is that of papal arbitration of international disputes. The second is canon law and theology, both officially sanctioned by the authority of the papacy in the Middle Ages and both contributing to an essential element of Catholic peacemaking: the right of the individual to refuse service in war according to the dictates of conscience, in short the Catholic origins of conscientious objection.

Certain characteristics of papal thought and action should first be made clear. Papal formulations of problems and their solutions are institutional; that is, problems are posed and answered not in the personal terms of the individual Christian, but in forms most relevant to the position of the pope as head of a religious body with a specific set of beliefs, a specific corporate identity, and a specific set of norms for action that reflect the norms and behavior of other corporate bodies. Popes thus carry out diplomacy as political figures in a setting that includes other political figures. They formulate laws and regulations that reflect human knowledge and experience as well as divine wisdom. If we accept the notion of an institutional church, not a sect of true believers, we will therefore not be surprised to find that the institution, grounded in the world of its time, makes concessions to that world and attempts to make peace using the institutional means at its disposal. This is not said to excuse the papal institution from its responsibility of making positive peace but by way of explaining the forms of peacemaking that it could and did pursue.

## PAPAL ARBITRATION

Since the dawn of the Middle Ages the peaceful resolution of conflicts has been acknowledged to be one of the prime duties and prerogatives of the papacy. The papacy, in fact, originated many of the basic elements of modern diplomacy and international law: the protection and safe conduct of ambassadors, the secrecy of diplomatic negotiations, the insistence that treaties, once made, are to be strictly adhered to, the condemnation of violations, provisions for the release of prisoners and hostages and their humane treatment while in detention, the protection of exiles, aliens, and racial minorities, and the condemnation of unjust wars and piracy. All these derive from the dual papal position as the leader of Christian society and as a force for international unity among secular states.[1]

A comprehensive modern history of papal diplomacy and arbitration has yet to be written,[2] but we can still trace the development of papal theory and practice in international arbitration clearly. We should first, however, examine the limitations of the papal view of peace and of the scope of papal diplomacy. Papal diplomacy has been largely restricted to Christendom. There is evidence of papal dealings with the northern barbarians in the early Middle Ages and of negotiations with the Moslem and Tartar worlds at the end of the age, but peace was what it had always been in official Carolingian thought: a gift and a responsibility restricted to Christians.

The nature of papal diplomacy changed profoundly during the Middle Ages. The changes can be divided into three phases. During the first period of development, from Gregory I (590) to the Investiture Conflict, papal diplomacy grew hand in hand with the developing theory of papal monarchy over Christendom.[3] The second period, from Gregory VII (1073) and the Investiture Conflict to Boniface VIII (1294–1303) and the Avignon Papacy, coincided with the era of the Crusades and the emergence of the pope as the supreme judge and leader of Europe.[4] During this period papal diplomacy enjoyed unchallenged power and prestige, as popes intervened in the affairs of Western kings and princes to impose arbitrations, treaties, and other judgments. These were carried out by their pope's fully empowered legates and backed by church councils and canon law.[5] The third phase began with the Avignon papacy in the fourteenth century. It was characterized by the growing theory and practice of national sovereignty, a general decline in papal prestige, and a decreased regard for papal judgments and threats of excommunication and interdict.[6] Papal diplomacy came closest to modern norms during this period as papal arbitration was accepted on the merit and offices of individual popes and not on the power of the office. Papal diplomacy was carried out less frequently by fully empowered papal legates who passed judgments and more often by nuncios and other intermediaries who carried limited commissions, acted as real ambassadors, and attempted true diplomacy.[7]

It is worth remembering that we are dealing here solely with papal diplomacy, not with the efforts of other ecclesiastics—bishops, abbots, and friars.[8] We will also restrict ourselves to those efforts of papal diplomacy intended for the benefit of third parties and general Christian peace, not with political or feudal treaties in which the papacy participated as a secular power. Papal diplomacy often tried to unite Christians in order to launch a Crusade, but we will exclude negotiations or treaties used by the popes in order to build military alliances to combat heretics or infidels.[9] Avoiding the extremes of praise[10] or blame[11] of papal peacemaking and admitting the limitations of papal diplomacy, we can judge the popes' efforts to bring peace to their world to have been continuous, consistent, and impressive.

The first medieval pope, Gregory I, was the first true papal diplomat. Although he owed allegiance to the Byzantine Empire, administering Rome and its territory as a Byzantine governor, even raising troops for its defense, Gregory took the daring step of dealing independently with the Lombard invaders of Italy. In a series of direct contacts with Agilulf, the Lombard king, Gregory secured treaties of peace that guaranteed the safety of Rome and its people from the invaders and opened the way to the conversion of the Lombards. He thus ignored the authority of the Eastern Roman Empire to conclude foreign policy and opened the way for the papacy to deal directly, for the first time, with nations beyond the empire.[12]

For the next three centuries papal diplomacy was intimately linked to missionary activities and to the conversion of the barbarian successor kingdoms. It consisted largely of instructions, first to missionaries, such as Boniface, and then to the rulers and prelates of the new kingdoms.[13] With the rise of the Carolingians and the subordination of the papacy to the power of Charlemagne and his successors, papal diplomacy was confined to the theoretical partnership between the secular and sacred authorities.[14] With the collapse of Carolingian power and the onslaught of fresh waves of invasion, however, the political and diplomatic map of Europe again became fluid. By the ninth century the papacy once again emerged with a strong theory of papal government[15] and an active theory of the role of the popes in maintaining Christian peace through international arbitration.

Nicholas I, the Great (858–867), already noted for his condemnation of war,[16] held opinions just as strong on the waging of peace. More than any other medieval pope he refined the theory of papal arbitration and international diplomacy.[17] Nicholas began with the standard Christian association of Christ as *pax nostra,* the peace of Christians and of the church, and the body of Christ as the manifestation of this peace. As the vicar of Christ, the pope then has been entrusted with the jurisdiction over this peace of the Body of Christ and thus has the responsibility for promoting peace and concord within it, that is, within the realm of Christendom. This is accomplished, according to Nicholas, through papal jurisdiction over treaties of peace, that is, over international diplomacy.[18]

Nicholas's immediate successor, Adrian II (867–872), demonstrated the same strong inclination toward peacemaking. Adrian called peace the highest of all virtues, the one to be followed by Christians more than any other;[19] peacemaking is also the pope's prime duty and goes hand in hand with his role as chief dispenser of justice. As such the pope is the supreme arbiter of Christendom and is thus charged with the duty of preserving peace among Christians. This duty is based on the gospel message proclaimed by the angels at the Nativity, who in declaring "peace on earth to people of good will" (LK 2:14) declared that peace must be brought to Christians in the temporal as well as the spiritual world.[20]

By the twelfth century papal legal and ideological leadership in the West enabled it to exercise enormous influence over secular lords. Papal influence was reinforced by the threat of excommunication and interdict and by the fresh memories of the anarchy and ruin that such papal attacks could bring to a kingdom.[21] By this time the development of the Western monarchies into something resembling nation-states had made the process of international diplomacy run more smoothly. Urban II (1088–1099) and Paschal II (1099–1118) actively pursued the establishment of peace among Christians, even though it was often in the interests of uniting Christians to join the Crusades.[22] Papal endorsement of both the Peace and Truce of God from the time of Sylvester II (999–1003) to Urban II helped bring about their application throughout Europe and their inclusion into the official canon law of the church.[23] Innocent II (1130–1143) intervened between England and Scotland in the wake of the battle of Allerton to arrange an armistice, to provide for the freeing of female prisoners, and to guarantee special protection for children, the old, and women.[24] Adrian IV (1154–1159) used a papal legate to bring peace to Scandinavia,[25] and Clement III (1187–1191) negotiated a treaty between Pisa and Genoa (1188).[26]

Twelfth- and thirteenth-century popes launched several peace initiatives as the conflict developed between the English and French monarchies over Angevin and Capetian claims to sovereignty and territory in western France. Adrian IV attempted to arbitrate a peace between Henry II of England and Louis VII of France (1158/9).[27] Alexander III (1159–1181) arranged the Peace of Nonancourt between the two kings (1177).[28] Clement III tried unsuccessfully to negotiate between Henry II and Louis's son, Philip Augustus of France (1188/9).[29] Celestine III (1191–1198) continued the policy of arbitration[30] as did Innocent III (1198–1216) between Henry's son, Richard I, and Philip Augustus. Threatening both monarchs with interdict and excommunication, Innocent succeeded in arranging a five-year truce in hostilities (1199).[31] Later in the year he continued negotiations between King John, Richard's successor, and Philip, offering to bring the dispute to the impartial judgment of an assembly of bishops and nobles. Innocent wrote to Philip (June 8, 1203) of his papal duty to search for and to make peace and reminded the king that war destroys churches, ruins riches, and oppresses the poor. In another letter (November 3) the pope repeated his plea, threatening spiritual sanctions for noncompliance.[32] Innocent III used his position as supreme judge of Christendom to impose treaties between Sweden, Denmark, and Norway; Portugal and Aragon; Castile and Navarre; and Leon and Castile.[33]

Papal attempts at peacemaking continued through the thirteenth century under other popes. Honorius III (1216–1227) arbitrated a peace treaty between Pavia and Milan and prevented a French invasion of England (1216).[34] Gregory IX (1227–1241) arbitrated a treaty of alliance between Genoa and Venice (1235)[35] and from 1230 to 1238 repeatedly attempted to make peace between England and France.[36] Celestine V (1294) continued the effort to make peace between the two countries.[37]

Boniface VIII (1294–1303) represented the high point of papal claims to temporal power in the late Middle Ages. He was an active arbiter, intervening repeatedly from 1294 to 1298 to bring peace between France and England, Scotland and England, and Charles of France and Prince Robert of Sicily.[38] With his humiliating capture by agents of King Philip IV of France, however, great changes, already in the making for some time, came about that showed the weakness of the papacy and of its claims to universal monarchy in Europe. In 1298 Philip IV and Edward I had allowed Boniface to arbitrate between them only "as a private person, as Lord Benedict Gaetani."[39] Henceforth, although the papacy maintained its claims to arbitrate the destinies of kings and princes, its commands would fall on ever more deaf ears. The correlative of this, however, was that in order to make their influence felt popes came to rely more on the tools of diplomacy and persuasion and less on the threat of spiritual sanctions, and to act more often as individuals and as a force for peace within Christendom.[40]

By the fourteenth century three factors contributed to the change: the removal of the papacy from Rome to Avignon in southern France (1305–1378);[41] the Great Schism, between the rival Roman, Avignon, and Conciliar popes (1378–1417);[42] and the Hundred Years War between England and France (1337–1453).[43] The popes at Avignon embraced a foreign policy with a three-fold aim: to secure general peace in Europe, to recapture the Holy Land,[44] and to return the papacy to Rome.[45] To accomplish these aims required that the papacy have active diplomatic ties with Europe's emerging states and that peace be established throughout Christendom. This was the time of the bloody conflict between the English and the French with its accompanying large-scale destruction. Throughout the conflict papal diplomacy was active, both in order to alleviate the widespread suffering of noncombatants and to minimize the destruction of church holdings and in order to pursue a Crusade against the rising power of the Turks.[46]

Ironically, the scandals of the Great Schism—with rival popes casting excommunication and interdict on their opponents and their political followings, and a series of papal crusades launched against each pope's enemies—brought both the Crusade movement and the papal claim to universal monarchy into widespread disrepute. Since all of Europe at one time or another fell under interdict or was excommunicated by one or the other rival pope, Christians on all levels began to take a skeptical view of such papal weapons and pretensions. Their resulting unwillingness to heed the political dictates of the papacy aided the process toward true diplomacy.

The first pope at Avignon, Clement V (1304–1314),[47] had served as a papal diplomat before his elevation.[48] As pope he devoted himself to bringing peace between rulers and subjects.[49] In England he negotiated a settlement between Edward II and his rebellious barons. In Hungary he arbitrated the issue of the royal inheritance in favor of Carobert, thus ending fifteen years of civil war.[50] In Italy Clement attempted to establish peace between the rival political factions of Tuscany and between the cities of Lucca, Florence, and Pistoia, finally arranging a truce in 1305 and persuading King Robert of Naples, the "protector" of Florence, to withdraw his forces. When diplomacy failed, however, Clement's chief ambassador to Florence, Napoleone Orsini, was not above using force as a means of persuasion.[51] Clement himself did not hesitate to excommunicate, and he called for a Crusade against his Italian foes.[52] Elsewhere, even though papal power was not as immediate, Clement was able to arbitrate a calm in the growing storm between England and France and arranged a temporary peace in 1307.[53]

John XXII (1316–1334)[54] was a strong-willed man who pressed the traditional claims of the papacy to impose truces upon Christian princes.[55] He also conducted an active diplomacy. In 1317 John intervened in the war between Edward III of England and Robert Bruce of Scotland, pressuring Bruce to accept a two-year truce (which the Scottish king later ignored). In November 1318, the pope excommunicated Bruce and maintained the ban until he sued for peace. In 1322 the Scottish leader renewed the war but by October of that year he was persuaded to offer a thirteen-year truce, which Edward accepted.[56] John stood firmly behind the Treaty of Paris of 1259 and intervened repeatedly from 1317 to 1325 and again in 1330 to preserve peace between England and France.[57] In 1317 he settled a conflict between Philip the Long and Robert of Flanders. Here again his arbitration was accepted not as that of a judge but as that of a private person.[58] In the same year John arranged a six-month truce between Robert of Naples and Amadeo of Savoy over disputes in southern France.[59] In France he arranged two truces in 1318 in the long feud between the forces of the counts of d'Armagnac and Foix.[60]

Throughout the Hundred Years War a succession of popes set themselves to restoring peace between the English and the French, sending legates to both sides, arranging truces and armistices, and hosting peace conferences at Avignon.[61] Benedict XII (1334–1342) was elected as a peace candidate. This pontificate was intended to bring to an end the conflict begun between Pope John XXII and Emperor Lewis of Bavaria.[62] As Bishop Jacques Fournier, Benedict had been an active inquisitor and never an absolute pacifist.[63] At his first consistory, however, he declared that he intended never to make war, even to defend the patrimony of the church. All papal wars, he noted, had resulted in disaster. Instead he resolved to defend the church through spiritual means, echoing Saint Ambrose's words[64] that he had more confidence in prayers and tears of repentance than in arms.[65]

At first Benedict shared his predecessors' disdain for secular diplomacy, considering international arbitration a papal prerogative.[66] Early in his pontificate he intervened in the struggle between England and Scotland; in November 1335 he negotiated a truce between Edward II and David Bruce.[67] Between 1337 and 1341 he attempted to dissolve the Anglo-Imperial alliance, actively prevented Philip IV of France from forging an imperial alliance against Edward III, requested him to revoke his confiscation of the Duchy of Guienne, which Edward III held as a fief from him, and acted through papal nuncios to postpone Philip's military offensive against the English.[68] In 1337, as war seemed imminent, he ordered the clergy of England and France to aid the peace process.[69]

Although French historians[70] condemned all Avignon attempts at peacemaking as "appeasement" and undue interference in their country's affairs, the papal efforts can be viewed in another light today.[71] Benedict seems to have changed his position over time; by 1339 he acted impartially and vigorously to persuade Edward to reopen peace negotiations, warning him that his claims to the French throne were shaky and the war ill-advised and destined to embitter Philip.[72] Edward was determined to fight, however. After the battle of Sluys (June 1340) a treaty was signed at Esplechin (September 1340), without papal participation.[73] Although he was rebuffed at Esplechin, Benedict was later invited by Edward and Philip to mediate as a private individual and friend, not as a judge or arbiter.[74] Benedict's accomplishments were equally mixed elsewhere in Europe. Although he was conciliatory toward Italy's princes and city-states, who had once been enemies of the papacy, he did not hesitate to authorize Crusades against those who refused to make peace.[75] Yet he successfully negotiated a treaty between Aragon and Castile (1336) and arranged truces between Portugal and Castile and Aragon and Majorca (1338).[76]

Papal efforts, though vigorous and sincere, were hampered by the dynastic ambitions of the Western kingdoms. Clement VI (1342–1352)[77] attempted several times to arbitrate between England and France.[78] As Pierre Roger, cardinal of Rouen, Clement had previously attempted to mediate. In January 1343 he brought about the Truce of Malestroit during the English campaign in Brittany; from October to December 1344 he hosted a peace conference at Avignon to try to bring the two sides to agreement.[79] After the English capture of Calais in 1347 Clement devoted much of his energies until his death in 1352 to concluding a peace treaty.[80]

Innocent VI (1352–1362)[81] seems to have had more success than Clement. In 1354 his legates negotiated the Treaty of Mantes between Charles of Navarre and King John the Good of France.[82] At Maupertius (September 1356), papal legates persuaded the French and English armies to accept a truce just before the battle of Poitiers;[83] and in January 1358, in the wake of the battle, papal legates concluded the Treaty of London, arranging for the release of the French king and for a general peace. Edward III later repudiated the treaty.[84] Finally in Brétigny, southwest of Paris, papal legates managed to bring together all the actors in the struggle and agree on a general peace. The Treaty of Calais between England and France, the French king and Charles of Navarre, and Edward III and the count of Flanders, ended the first phase of the Hundred Years War.[85]

Urban V (1362–1370)[86] continued mediation efforts as the fighting was renewed. The Peace of Brétigny was kept through most of Urban's pontificate. He devoted special attention to the plight of the peasants caught in the struggle.[87] Gregory XI (1370–1378), the last Avignon pope,[88] summed up papal efforts for peace in the late Middle Ages. Gregory pursued policies that were both a continuation of previous papal initiatives and a preliminary for the papacy's return to Rome. Gregory's diplomatic skill and energy were instrumental in bringing peace to much of Christendom. He sent legates all over Europe to help mediate wars and conflicts, reminding the belligerents that "the constant conflicts involve huge expenditures which are necessarily shifted upon the people. The turmoil [of these wars] impedes the work of salvation."[89]

Between 1371 and 1373 Gregory concluded peace agreements between Castile and Portugal, between Henry of Trastamare and Charles of Navarre, between Queen Joanna and Frederick of Aragon, between Emperor Charles IV of Germany and King Louis of Hungary, and between the duke of Bavaria and the count of Savoy.[90] Despite suspicions from both sides of the Hundred Years War,[91] Gregory worked tirelessly for peace.[92] His legates went all over the West—to Toulouse and Bordeaux, to London and Paris— before finally choosing Calais as their major diplomatic post. Throughout 1372 and 1373 in a series of peace conferences at Calais and later at Bruges papal agents brought together the chief ambassadors of England and France. After initial failures the Bruges conference finally produced a truce in March 1375 that would last until 1377.[93] Between 1373 and 1376 papal negotiators also arranged a peace between the warring factions of d'Armagnac and Foix.[94]

In the fifteenth century papal arbitration did much to bring to an end the war between England and France. In the wake of the English victory at Agincourt in 1415, Martin V (1417–1431) used legates and diplomatic correspondence to arrange a preliminary, secret consistory in Rome in 1419. A conference sponsored in Florence between the English and French ambassadors finally brought England, France, and Burgundy to conclude a peace treaty at Troyes in May 1420.[95] Martin's efforts to secure a lasting peace continued throughout the 1420s. In Italy he continued the work of Boniface IX (1389–1404)[96] and arranged a treaty between Milan and Genoa (1419)[97] and two settlements (1426 and 1428) in the spreading conflict between Milan and Venice, Florence, and their allies.[98] Martin's successor, Eugenius IV (1431–1447), used both legates and ambassadors to help negotiate the Treaty of Arras between England, France, and Burgundy in 1435.[99] He negotiated a settlement between Alfonso of Aragon and René of Anjou, who were struggling for the crown of Naples,[100] and used legates to restore peace in Hungary, Moldavia, Lithuania, and Albania.[101]

Nicholas V (1447–1455) continued his predecessors' policies to the end of the Hundred Years War (October 1453).[102] He pressed for a Crusade against the Turks, a major concern after the fall of Constantinople in 1453, and issued a bull to all Christians, pleading for unity and peace within Christendom and for all Christian leaders to consent to armistices under pain of excommunication and interdict.[103] As with all of his successors in Renaissance Italy, however, Nicholas' main concern was with the politics of the peninsula, the emerging delicate balance of power between its cities and territorial states, including the Papal States.[104] During the war between Milan, Florence, and Venice in the 1450s, Nicholas remained deliberately neutral and used his powers to provide a diplomatic link between the rivals, thus turning Rome into a center of diplomacy.[105] Finally, in April 1454 he arranged the Peace of Lodi between the Italian powers, which eventually led to the Treaty of Venice in August 1454 and to twenty-five years of peace and a balance of power in Italian, and European, relations. Nicholas's subsequent adherence to the Most Holy League of the major Italian powers did much to guarantee the peace and to make diplomacy a permanent feature of first Italian, and then European, relations. For the next three centuries the papal court was to remain a center of international diplomacy.[106]

Nicholas's successors, Calixtus III (1455–1458), Pius II (1458–1464), Paul II (1464–1471), Sixtus IV (1471–1484), and Innocent VIII (1484–1492) made arbitration an accepted function of the papacy.[107] The papacy played a pivotal role in ending the dispute between Spain and Portugal over the spheres of influence of their colonial empires at the beginning of the sixteenth century. In May 1493, after lengthy negotiations, Alexander VI (1492–1503) issued the bulls *Inter caetera* and *Eximiae devotionis,* now called collectively the Bull of Demarcation. They were followed in June 1494 by the carefully nurtured Treaty of Tordesillas between the two powers.[108] Then began a new age of discovery and a new phase of international competition and relations.

## FROM THE JUST WAR TO THE RIGHTS OF CONSCIENCE

The pope's association of peace with justice that motivated the arbitration of the papacy in international relations also promoted papal interest in another area associated with justice, that of *jus* or law. In the international sphere, the papacy adopted the ancient Roman theories of the *jus gentium,* a body of custom and agreements among peoples and sovereign princes, linked from the tenth century on with the revival of Roman law in Italy.[109] Closely associated with Roman law and custom was the notion of the just war, which was christianized by Augustine and handed on to the Middle Ages through Isidore of Seville.

While we cannot here enter into the history of the just-war theory,[110] we will outline its major features and survey their interpretation in the canon law of the church. We will then examine one aspect of the medieval just-war theory: the right of the combatant to examine the justness of the conflict. This principle helped lay the groundwork for modern notions of conscientious objection.

The theory of the just war is not Christian in any proper sense of the word: it has no biblical, theological, or canonical foundation; it is the product of secular and ecclesiastical pressures during the Middle Ages.[111] Nor is the classic just-war theory, which stipulates both the causes and the conduct for such a war, to be found in medieval thought.[112] As we have already seen,[113] Augustine did not present a developed theory but only a series of observations on the conduct of just war inherited from Roman theory, in turn derived from Cicero and ancient practice.[114]

By the time of the Crusades, however, medieval lawyers had generally agreed that for any war to be just it must meet three prime requirements: it must be waged by legitimate authority, its cause must be just—generally the defense of the realm or the redress of some loss—and it must be fought with the right intent: the restoration of peace. It thus could not be an aggressive war or one waged for vengeance or to acquire territory or wealth. These requirements were termed the *jus ad bellum,* the right to war, as opposed to the *jus in bello,* the proper waging of that war, which concerned lawful weapons, the rights of noncombatants, proportionality of the means used, and proper discrimination in the use of force.[115] The *jus in bello,* however, rarely concerned medieval thinkers or practitioners.[116] Medieval theory concentrated instead on the justness of the war and the restoration of peace through mercy and justice that the war was supposed to achieve.[117]

Medieval theory of just war emerged from four sources: canon law, the scholastic philosophy of the clergy, the notions of chivalry espoused by the feudal classes and their poets, and Roman concepts of just war revived by the towns.[118] By 1140, with Gratian's collection of canon law known as the *Decretum,* the criteria for the just war had been narrowed to two: it should be waged by proper authority and there should be a clear legal wrong or injustice and the intention to correct it.[119] Thomas Aquinas (1225–1274) defined the criteria as just cause, the legitimacy of the authority commanding the war,[120] and the right intention.[121] Later definitions, such as that of Ramon of Peñafort, were nothing more than elaborations of this position, specifying the just causes and the intentions of those who waged the just war.[122]

Within this fairly straightforward definition, however, there was much room for comment and debate: What constituted proper authority? What was just cause? What was proper intent? In addition to the motives of the prince commanding the war, however, canon lawyers and theologians debated another issue that had serious consequences for the individual Christian bound to fight in that war. What, they asked, were the consequences for the individual if the prince waging the war lacked proper authority, if he were a heretic or a schismatic? What if the war were being waged by legitimate authority but without just cause—against other Christians or merely for territorial gain? What if the intent of those waging or commanding the war were unjust—greed for booty or vengeance? What, then, was the duty of individual Christians and how were they to determine it?

As canon law developed, legal interpretation sided increasingly with the rights of conscience. Gratian, for example, held that subjects were bound to obey their princes, even if they were unjust or fighting an unjust cause. In fulfilling their duty they therefore put the burden of the sin on the prince, who alone must bear it.[123] Later commentators on Gratian's *Decretum,* who were called the Decretists,[124] expanded and modified this definition. Individual commentators, such as Simon of Bisignano, and collections of commentators, such as the *Summa Monacensis* and the *Summa Parisiensis* (all from the mid- to late-twelfth century) recommended obedience but allowed for exceptions. Simon of Bisignano and Huguccio specified that a subject was not bound to obey a heretical, schismatic, or excommunicated lord;[125] the *Summa Monacensis* enjoined full obedience in a just war, but not in an unjust one; the *Summa Parisiensis* recommended obedience unless the prince's orders clearly contradicted divine law, which must always be obeyed above human law.[126]

Other Decretists specified the classes of individuals who could refuse to serve, even in a just war. Rufinus (c. 1157) interpreted canon law as strictly forbidding clerics and penitents from bearing arms,[127] a far-reaching exemption considering the vast numbers in medieval society of sacramental penitents and those in third orders who were legally defined as penitents.[128] Rolando Bandinelli, later Pope Alexander III (1159–1181),[129] and Ramon of Peñafort[130] repeated Rufinus' prohibition against clerics, actually a long-standing church tradition,[131] and added all those in minor orders and those who wished to follow the path of evangelical perfection—again,[132] a large group in the late Middle Ages.

Later interpreters of canon law, who were called the Decretalists after the collection completed in 1234 by Ramon of Peñafort under a commission by Pope Gregory IX (the *Decretales*),[133] further refined this definition, specifying that the subject could disobey the lord when the orders contradicted divine or canon law or when the cause was unjust. The subject could refuse to obey commands to commit atrocities, to attack one's own country, or if participation in the war would lead the soldier into sin.[134] In general, however, all the compilers and commentators on canon law, with the possible exception of Pope Innocent IV (1243–1254),[135] were remarkably vague as to how the individual was to determine the justness or unjustness of the authorities, causes, and actions.

Although theologians of the twelfth and thirteenth centuries saw much to commend the waging of just wars,[136] they tended to follow the lead of Peter Lombard and the penitential tradition and considered military service itself as sinful. More concerned with the salvation of the individual soul than the outer workings of human justice, they placed less emphasis on authority and obedience than on the Christian pursuit of perfection guided by the Sermon on the Mount. The injunction to obey God's law above human law guided their thoughts on war and set the general criteria for obedience to commands or even to participation in war.

Robert of Courson, a master at the University of Paris and a cardinal legate in 1215,[137] wrote that subjects have the right to debate the justice of wars commanded by their lords and even to refuse to serve in them. If a knight considers a war unjust, Robert wrote, he is under no obligation to serve; when he knows it to be unjust, he is positively bound to disobey. He may then take a Crusader's vows in order to avoid fighting against fellow Christians. Thomas of Chobham (c. 1230) wrote that in any unjust war, that is, any war against other Christians, knights may refuse to obey commands and choose instead to obey divine law. Prelates, for their part, must actively warn Christians against shedding blood in unjust wars; and the justice of the war in question must be discussed publicly by those in the realm.

Roland of Cremona, a Dominican writing about 1230, expanded this line of legal argument even further. In general, he wrote, subjects should not fight in a war that is contrary to their conscience. Nor can an unjust war be considered just because of the enemy's supposed wickedness or by the argument that the soldier in an unjust war somehow fulfills a divine mission of vengeance against the wicked. But what of the person's judgment concerning the injustice of a conflict? Roland interprets canon law to mean that when individuals are in doubt over the justice of a war, they may follow the general consensus in favor of a war and obey commands. They may, however, lend less than their full support to the war effort. If, however, the consensus says that the war is unjust, individuals are bound to disobey commands, even on pain of death.

Roland is unclear about how this consensus is reached or ascertained. Yet in the context of the Italian, urban, and newly democratic republics in which he wrote, he must have had some idea of public discussion and debate that would determine consensus. This is further indicated in his discussion of the process by which individuals make up their minds. If the prince and his council have approved a war, and individuals are lacking the pertinent facts on which to base a decision, they may then obey commands to participate in the war without incurring sin. If, however, after taking expert counsel, presumably from those informed as to the facts or the ethics of the case, they then oppose the war, they are bound by divine command to refuse to serve; nor can the prince rightly compel obedience from such doubting subjects. Roland's ultimate conclusion was that the prince's ability to wage war was limited by his subjects' right to heed the dictates of their own consciences without incurring sin, in short their right of conscientious objection.

Roland's influence was limited,[138] but the thought of both canonist and theologian on participation in war rested firmly on the rights of the individual conscience to pursue Christian perfection.[139] But what did conscience mean in the Middle Ages? What were its limitations and rights? What was the ultimate relationship between the individual and authority? Each of these questions has demanded and received ample attention from scholars. Here we can indicate only the main lines of medieval thought. We will conclude with a specific example of the development of a theory of obedience born from conflicts within the church hierarchy.

## LIBERTY OF CONSCIENCE IN MEDIEVAL THOUGHT

Christian thinking on conscience derives from Paul's Epistle to the Romans[140] and was passed on through Jerome[141] and Augustine[142] to medieval thinkers, such as Peter

Abelard (1079–1142)[143] and university philosophers and theologians called the scholastics. This tradition held that conscience (*syneidesis* in Greek or *conscientia* in Latin) is an intellectual ability, a form of action and a capacity of reason that can distinguish good from evil and keep the individual from doing evil. Peter Abelard reasoned that since conscience is a form of action, a decision toward the good or bad, and not an innate knowledge or inclination to the good,[144] we must be bound by Saint Paul's injunction to "let every one be fully convinced in his own mind" (Rom 14:5). For if a person chooses what he or she subjectively perceives to be good, but which may be objectively bad, that person is judged not by the objective standard but by his or her beliefs, as Saint Paul indicates. Thus the individual has an absolute obligation to follow his or her conscience, even if in error.[145]

With the development of high scholastic thought, new elements were introduced into the argument. Peter Lombard (d. 1160),[146] in his *Book of Judgments,* wrote of conscience in terms of *synteresis,* an innate capacity, a natural power of the soul that always seeks the good, but which can be overruled by acts of the will.[147] While the will is free to choose good over evil, the innate call of the conscience always retains some capacity for discerning the good. Thirteenth-century philosophers would develop this notion to limit the total freedom of the conscience to the moral authority of God's will.[148] For the philosopher Peter the Chancellor of Paris (d. 1236) conscience was bound to the ability of the human soul to perceive divine truth. The soul could be blinded, he thought, by a lack of faith, as in the case of heretics who follow their subjective consciences against the promptings of *synteresis,* which is never completely extinguished, and who are thus objectively in sin and therefore responsible for their sins.[149]

Thomas Aquinas, whose work is considered by many to be the summation of medieval thought, gave the problem of the mistaken conscience clear and careful analysis.[150] While conscience as a form of action can indeed be objectively mistaken, either in its content or in its application, it still binds the individual to its dictates as long as the individual perceives those dictates to be God's law. Yet this misinformed conscience binds only relatively and accidentally: if, for example, it demands what is clearly bad, such as adultery, setting aside its dictates clearly involves no sin; while if it commands what is good, following it also entails no sin.[151] Since the human soul has the capacity of *synteresis,* an innate moral capacity,[152] all acts of conscience can be informed by basic moral principles and can therefore be informed by objective truth. Conversely, the individual is responsible for ascertaining these truths.

Aquinas's views seem to contradict and limit the freedom of the conscience set forth by Abelard by requiring the individual to determine the objective truth and good of a situation. Aquinas did in fact increase both the authority and the freedom of conscience.[153] For if men and women have it in their power to dispel errors and inform their consciences through an innate power of their souls, ignorance is voluntary and enlightenment a duty of every free person. Thus Aquinas confirms the sovereignty of the individual conscience, even if in error,[154] broadens its powers of discretionary action,[155] and makes the obligation to follow the precepts of the Sermon on the Mount even more binding.[156]

The problem remaining in all scholastic discussions of conscience—how the conscience is to be informed—was addressed by the English Franciscan philosopher William of Ockham (c. 1285–c. 1349). Differing sharply with many of his predecessors over the relative merit of human reason in ascertaining the truth,[157] Ockham denied that the human soul possesses the faculty of *synteresis,* of innate appreciation of good and evil,[158] and argued instead that right reason, which informs the conscience, is available through divine revelation, that is, through the Scriptures.[159] Thus Ockham returned to the tradition of Abelard, reemphasized the ability of the conscience to choose good or bad, and reaffirmed its complete freedom. With no innate sense of the good or the bad, the dictates of the conscience must always be heeded. If an individual is in error unavoidably (invincibly), he or she cannot be held responsible for any sin; in fact if the person acts according to what he or she mistakenly believes to be God's will and thus acts out of love of God, the act "is virtuous and meritorious."[160] If, however, the error is correctable, then the individual has an obligation to be informed.[161] Thus, while Ockham postulates that it is never virtuous to act against the dictates of conscience,[162] he also argues that the individual must clear the conscience "through an investigation of the truth," that is, through an examination of Scripture.[163]

Ockham built on previous scholastic thought to establish two important principles concerning individual action: first, the conscience is always supreme even if invincibly in error, and second, the individual is obligated to investigate the truth, mainly through an informed study of Scripture. Ockham furthered the consensus of medieval thought, which held that conscience has an independent authority, that to act against its dictates is always evil, even if acting in accordance with it is not always objectively good. Whether or not philosophers agreed that humans had an innate appreciation of the divine moral order, they all held that the individual was obligated to discover and to act according to divine law.[164] The individual, disturbed by qualms of conscience, must therefore make a reasonable effort to investigate the truth and to act accordingly.[165]

## CONCLUSIONS: CONSCIENCE AND DISSENT
## IN LATE MEDIEVAL THOUGHT

We have devoted a good deal of discussion to the abstract ideas of medieval schoolmen on conscience in order to answer the questions posed by the canon lawyers and theologians: What are the limits of obedience to commands and how does one determine the justness of a war? What is the prince's authority to command that war or the individual's right to refuse to participate in it or to follow specific orders? The preceding discussion on conscience would lead us to conclude that medieval men and women had an intellectual and moral tradition that reinforced the theories of individual rights to refuse orders, a tradition that placed heavy emphasis on the obligation of the individual to be informed both as to the facts and the morality of the situation and to act accordingly.

Such rights were clearly recognized by the papacy as demonstrated in its repeated protections of pacifist groups (such as the Third Order of St. Francis) who steadfastly refused to bear arms, even when pressed by their civilian and justly constituted governments.[166] A clear example of the medieval right to disobedience based on the dictates of conscience can be found within the structure of the church itself. This example is in the conflict between Pope John XXII and the Franciscan Order over the pope's authority to alter the Rule of the order, and the right of individual friars to disobey because of a higher law.[167]

The Franciscans contended that since Francis had received divine inspiration for the Rule and Christ's own command not to alter it, and since later popes had confirmed this Rule, it was against both divine law and papal legislation to alter it. As the papal position became more rigid, the Spiritual party within the Franciscan Order moved from the position of reformers and partisans within the church and were declared heretics for their disobedience of papal commands to conform.[168] In response William of Ockham[169] and earlier Spiritual leaders, including Peter John Olivi (c. 1248–1298)[170] and Angelo Clareno (c. 1250–1337),[171] wrote vigorously in defense of the Spiritual right to retain their Rule and of the pope's own heresy in altering it.

As Ockham put it, "When the pope falls into heresy he is understood to be not superior but inferior to any Catholic."[172] Further, as Clareno maintained, it is not the pope, but the church as a whole that is infallible—the church not in its hierarchy or head alone but in the totality of its members brought together in their faith and imitation of Christ.[173] In this sense the faith of the church never fails, because even if the head falls into error the truth continues to abide, even among its lowliest members, even in only one member, as with Mary at the foot of the cross.[174]

This true church remains constant even when the head exceeds the limits of its authority.[175] These limits, according to Clareno, are those of the Christian virtues. He condemned overt acts of rebellion, such as that of the antipope Pietro da Corbara in 1328,[176] but he warned that those who act against the dictates of conscience in upholding Christian virtue are likewise damned.[177] When those in authority act against virtue, one is bound by the injunction of Saint Peter to obey God above the human.[178] The only recourse of the faithful is to flee, if possible,[179] or to remain silent in nonviolent disobedience, suffering unjust persecution for the sake of justice.[180] The resister has a model, the true exemplar of those who, accused of heresy, follow truth. This is Christ himself, condemned by the synagogue as an apostate.[181] As with Christ, the ultimate test of resistance is the willingness to die for one's witness to the truth.[182] Although he was hunted and excommunicated repeatedly by the church hierarchy during his life, a cult to honor Clareno sprang up soon after his death among the peasants of southern Italy who found more truth in his Christian witness than in the dictates of the popes. He has since been beatified.[183]

In the last analysis, when all the powers of authority command a course of action that runs contrary to God's law, truth resides in the totality of the Mystical Body. But the individuals who make up that body must still decide according to the truth, like Christ and the early martyrs, risking even persecution and death.

# CHAPTER 9

# HUMANIST PEACEMAKERS: THE SIXTEENTH CENTURY

## INTRODUCTION

In the sixteenth century Europe entered an age of political and social organization that set new challenges to the Catholic peacemaker. The emergence of the nation-states of Western Europe brought about profound changes in relationships between peoples and between people and their governments. Centralization and other administrative improvements slowly developing during the Middle Ages now enabled the monarchs of England, France, the Empire, Spain, and many smaller states to accumulate substantially greater power than their predecessors had enjoyed and to raise greater revenues than ever before. Civil wars, invasion, and conquests under aggressive dynasties weakened the medieval tradition of constitutional restraints on monarchs, and the revived use of Roman law helped to establish theories of monarchical absolutism.[1]

Vast revenues, efficient governments, clearly defined national identities, and aggressive monarchies eager to expand their rule resulted in a new age of European wars that were to spell the death of medieval Christendom. By the time of the wars of the 1520s papal arbitration was cynically ignored and completely ineffective as the secular states became their own masters.[2] Monarchs now had at their disposal the means to raise, maintain, and pay vast standing armies, unrestricted by the limits of feudal service, bound more or less tightly to the central government, and aided in their destructiveness by new weaponry and tactics—artillery, explosives, massed infantry combat, and stricter leadership and discipline.[3] The imaginations of the monarchs and their feudal aristocracies, however, did not progress with the new destructiveness at their disposal. Personal glory and the dream-visions of a dead chivalry continued to stir their imaginations and their desire for war.[4] However, the sixteenth century was no longer the age of one-to-one combat or ineffective cavalry encounters between knights. Now the grandiose plans of monarchs were carried out by large levies of foot soldiers, often professionals—the mercenaries so hated by Machiavelli[5]—who, either under orders from their governments or to supplement their wages, systematically ravaged entire regions, destroyed cities, massacred civilian populations, and left economic ruin behind them.

All forms of life and thought, in fact, were permeated with a new glorification of the warrior, a new militarization of society.[6] Even the printing press was put to work in favor of the new war propaganda. Pamphlets aided enlistment, spread stories of atrocities by the enemy, promoted jingoism, and molded public opinion to the policies of the monarchs. By the end of the century officially sponsored textbooks fed children a constant diet of wars, battles, and military heroes. The pulpit, the theater, and public oratory were all tightly controlled, and all sang the praises of bloodshed and destruction, stressing the just war, unquestioned obedience to rulers, the biblical supports of war, and the treason of pacifists.

The names of the great monarchs are enough to remind us of the times and their events. Henry VIII of England (1509–1547), Francis I of France (1515–1547), Maximilian I (1493–1519) and Charles V of the Holy Roman Empire (1519–1558), and Pope Julius II (1503–1513) conjure up a history of ever-changing alliances, broken treaties, and invasions. The French invasion of 1494 and the subsequent Italian Wars brought an end to the Italian Renaissance, the English invaded France during the reign of Henry VIII, the Valois of France and the Imperial Hapsburgs of Germany and Spain continued their struggle, as the pope rode in full battle armor leading his troops through the devastated lands of central Italy.

## NEW FORMS OF CATHOLIC PEACEMAKING

This new age of mass destruction and war propaganda produced an equally new and vigorous form of Catholic peacemaking. Its roots were multiple. The popular spirituality of the high and late Middle Ages, the poverty movements, the Third Orders, and the secular literature of peace retained their strength into the Renaissance and Reformation periods.[7] In the late fifteenth century a new reform movement, the *Devotio Moderna* (Modern Devotion), developed in the Low Countries and the Rhine Valley. It drew on the popular spirituality of an earlier age, applying it to new conditions. The movement was largely the work of an order of tertiaries and their monastic counterparts named the Brethren and Sisters of the Common Life.[8]

The best-known proponent of the Modern Devotion, Thomas à Kempis (1379 or 1380–1471), wrote *The Imitation of Christ* between 1425 and 1441,[9] which summed up the spirituality of the movement. The *Imitation* set out the principles of the gospel life, the overcoming of vices, and the learning and application of virtues. It emphasized the humility, patience, and suffering of Christ as goals for imitation,[10] and the superiority of the peaceful, tolerant, and charitable person to the learned and powerful.[11] For Thomas true peace was not a state of contentment, of living undisturbed, or of holding mastery, but of true humility.[12] The Christian God was "not of dissension but of peace, which peace consists rather in true humility than self-exaltation."[13] The grace of God leads true Christians to love their enemies[14] and to see Christ as the true peacemaker and source of peace.[15]

## THE HUMANISTS

Another strain of major reform, the Humanist movement, developed in Italy in the late fourteenth century, flourished in Florence and other Italian centers in the fifteenth century, and in the early sixteenth century was beginning to have an impact on the rest of Europe. Humanism stressed a return to the literatures and philosophies of both Christian and pagan antiquity in order to bring about reform, first in letters and then in life.[16]

The Humanists, like the Franciscans and other evangelical reformers, concentrated on ethics and the moral life rather than on the academic abstractions of the medieval schoolmen. They focused on the life of the individual acting in community, whether this was the political community of the Italian city-state or the religious community of Christendom. This citizen was above all an ethical creature who could be educated to live honorably, intelligently, and virtuously according to the moral principles of the gospels and of the ancient philosophers who reflected Christian truths.

Not all Humanists shared a common philosophy, however, and not all Humanists questioned the current political system or the role of violence and war within that system. Yet the Humanists were prominent among those who did attempt to combat war and to make peace during this time.[17] Using their considerable literary skills, their familiarity with ancient satire and invective, their command of the new technology of print and mass communication, and their privileged position as popular personalities and valued counselors of princes, these "unarmed prophets" were in a unique position to make their ethical views known and their influence felt. Their attacks on war and their efforts to make peace and to offer alternatives to a Europe bent on destruction set the tone for Christian peacemaking for centuries after. Their thought forms the core of our modern literature of peace.

John Colet, Thomas More, Juan Luis Vives, Guillaume Budé, Josse van Clichtove, and especially Desiderius Erasmus, are not only among the most brilliant Humanist scholars and writers of the age but were also "committed men,"[18] steadfastly devoted to the goals of Christian peacemaking. The Humanists' program, if it can be called that, combined several elements, all stemming from the Humanists' role as Christian reformers and educators. They sought first to end war because it was a sin against the Mystical Body and an affront to the gospels. Second, they hoped to restore justice to the victims of war: the poor farmers whose lands, crops, and livelihoods were devastated or taxed away; the middle classes whose wealth and urban civilization were collapsing under the onslaughts of violence and the extortion of war taxes; the nobility, whose true role in society—enlightened service—was perverted by a steady diet of misplaced values and poor education; and women, whose chief role in the romances was that of uneducated, passive victim, sexual object, and adultress. Hand in hand with the Humanists' attack on war and aristocratic values was their conscious, if often understated, struggle against political tyranny.[19]

There were tensions in the Humanists' position. Humanists were not pacifists in the strict sense of theoretically opposing all wars universally. They all agreed that the just war—if properly motivated, led, and conducted—was a possibility; yet they used the criteria of the just war so scrupulously and wrote against unjust wars so effectively that for the Humanists no known war in the past, present, or future was or could ever be just.[20] Their position was exactly that of the conscientious objector today, whose claim must demonstrate opposition not to all wars as they might exist, but to wars as they have existed and are likely to exist given a realistic view of human nature and affairs. The Humanist position between the ideal and the practical is reflected in their sometimes ambiguous relationship to power. The Humanists were both prophets of Christian morality and reform and counselors to those in power at whose courts "there was no place for a prophet."[21]

## THE PROGRESS OF HUMANISM: JOHN COLET

The sixteenth century began in an optimistic mood. Learning had made great advances throughout Europe, men of letters had risen to positions of great influence and respect, and finally, with the accession of three young, well-educated, and intelligent princes—Henry VIII, Francis I, and Charles V—it seemed, as Erasmus said,[22] that a new age of peace and enlightenment, a true renaissance, was about to dawn on Europe. In the early years of the century, Christian peacemaking seemed eminently possible.

The earliest stirrings of the new spirit emerged from the group of English and international Humanists called the London Reformers. On Michaelmas 1496, in his Oxford lectures on Saint Paul, John Colet (1467–1519), dean of St. Paul's Cathedral from 1504 to 1519 and one of England's greatest Humanists,[23] delivered an interpretation of two essential pacifist texts—Matthew 22:15–22, "Render to Caesar," and Romans 13, "Let every person be subject to the governing authorities." This interpretation was to be "a landmark in literary and social criticism."[24]

Colet broke new ground in his examination of the biblical texts by applying historical criticism to his subjects. He said that only by understanding the social conditions of the Roman Empire in the first century could one really appreciate the message of Christ and Saint Paul.[25] Both texts, Colet claimed, show that the scholastic teaching of the just war is unfounded; for true Christians violence is always futile. Only humility and love can overcome evil; for

> it is not by war that war is conquered, but by peace, and forbearance, and reliance in God. And in truth by this virtue we see that the apostles overcame the entire world. . . . This [peaceful kind of contending with evil persons] was alone used by those first soldiers of the Church, who fought under the banner of Christ, and conquered gloriously.[26]

Colet went on to say that far from requiring Christians to obey royal commands in all things, Romans 13 is actually an admonition for those living under tyrannies not to invite violent repression by rebellion but to meet oppression and to overcome it with Christian charity.[27]

Colet's opposition to war was not academic. Henry VIII was becoming more interested in foreign conquest and dreams of chivalric glory than in the ideals that the Humanists cherished. After 1510 court style and rhetoric began to reflect an emphasis on martial vigor and the just-war theory became a pretext for adventures in France.[28] Henry began to appear more the absolute tyrant than the ideal prince, and many at court feared to express their views against the king's war policies openly. On Good Friday 1513, after Colet had become dean of St. Paul's and a major figure in the English hierarchy, Henry VIII invited him to preach a sermon to his army, which was preparing to invade France. In the presence of the king, the court, and the army, Colet condemned the war. After exhorting his fellow Christians to fight under Christ's banner, that is, by gospel love, Colet went on to note that most soldiers fight under the devil's. Although the war might seem to have a just cause, few who fight are untouched by hatred or love of gain. Colet again exhorted his listeners to follow Christ and not the bloody path of Julius Caesar or Alexander the Great.

When the sermon was over, the king quickly rose and left, visibly shaken and clearly apprehensive over the effect of Colet's words on his soldiers. A few minutes later the dean was summoned to the king's chambers. The two remained alone together for nearly an hour. When they emerged Henry embraced Colet, announced that "this is the doctor for me," and exhorted him to further clarify his condemnation of the war so that "the rough soldiers" would not misunderstand Henry's purpose. According to Erasmus, who is the source for the incident, Colet's friends praised him for standing up against the insane tide of war.[29]

John Colet was not alone in the peace party of Henry's court. Other prominent members, who included Humanists and their patrons, were William Warham, Archbishop of Canterbury (1450–1532);[30] Richard Fox (1446 or 1447–1525), the bishop of Winchester, a patron of the new learning, later founder of Corpus Christi College at Oxford, and the leader of the peace party;[31] Cuthbert Tunstall (1474–1559), the English ambassador to Brussels and the imperial court and a close friend of Erasmus;[32] and, most important, Thomas More.

## THOMAS MORE

Satirist, Humanist, lawyer and politician, lord chancellor of England, and Catholic martyr, Thomas More epitomized the hopes and possibilities of Humanist peacemaking.[33] He was born in London in 1478 of middle-class parents, received a Humanist education, became a lawyer, entered Parliament in 1503, and in 1518 was named one of Henry VIII's privy counselors. More was of two minds about this service. He had earlier distinguished himself as a Humanist writer, critic of royal excesses, and the author of *Utopia,* which had taken Europe by storm. He finally accepted the post hoping that his service would further Henry's supposed peace policy. Erasmus publicly worried that by entering the king's service More would lose his voice as a critic and free intellectual.[34]

This conflict had already been examined in More's *Utopia.* In the fictionalized account More was in Antwerp on a royal embassy when he was introduced to a noted intellectual and explorer, Raphael Hythloday. The traveler's expertise on the geography and nations of the New World and on the proper ways of governing a kingdom so impressed More that he wondered why the explorer did not enter royal service to use his knowledge and gifts of persuasion to bring about the common good and peace. Hythloday replied that such subordination of the free intellectual to political power would be a form of servitude and a waste of talent and effort. The idealist, the social critic, the intellectual, and the peacemaker must always stand as prophets, away from power, in order best to criticize and reform it. More, however, felt differently:

> You must try to use subtle and indirect means, insofar as it lies in your power. And what you cannot turn to good, you must make as little evil as possible. To have everything turn out well assumes that all men are good, and this is a situation that I do not expect to come about for many years.[35]

Hythloday's reply reflected More's fears: "The only trouble with this approach is that while I would tend to save others from insanity, I would myself become mad."[36]

The fears of Erasmus and Hythloday soon began to prove true. By the 1520s Henry's and Wolsey's secret war dreams and Henry's absolutist tendencies were becoming apparent. The king tolerated little dissent, and More wrote that it was becoming dangerous to be too open on "peace and war, upon morality, marriage, the clergy, the people."[37] In 1521 More was knighted and in 1523 he was chosen Speaker of the House of Commons. In this post he was obligated to spend much of his energy lobbying for Cardinal Wolsey's huge war tax of 1523 and to take part in collecting it. In 1524, as part of the royal service, he was also implicated in the vicious English invasion of France, for which Wolsey issued orders that Henry's troops were to destroy everything in their path and make civilian populations special targets.[38] In August 1524 More wrote to a friend in Louvain in despair that war had become synonymous with public life.[39]

More could take just pride for his key role in arranging the Treaty of Cambrai (1529) between England, France, the Empire, and the pope.[40] By then Henry's divorce had become the chief concern of the realm. Cardinal Wolsey was toppled from power for his failure to please the king. When offered the chancellorship, the ultimate position of power, from which he felt he could finally achieve some reform, More accepted.[41] Once in power More began to attack Wolsey, seeing him as the prime mover behind both the divorce and Henry's war policy.[42]

The new chancellor quickly ran aground on the issue of Henry's usurpation of powers over the church and his divorce. In 1534 More's refusal to swear the oath of obedience to Henry brought his arrest, trial before Parliament for treason, and condemnation. On July 6, 1535, on Tower Hill in London, Thomas More mounted the scaffold, joked politely with his executioner, and summed up his entire life: "I die the king's good servant, but God's first."[43]

### More as a Catholic Peacemaker

Can we call Thomas More a Catholic peacemaker? As a member of the Privy Council and a royal ambassador he was closely involved with the waging of war, and as lord chancellor he was charged with executing royal policy, including the forceful suppression of heretics. In this capacity he wrote the controversial *Dialogue Concerning Heresies* (1529).[44] The book called for the forceful repression of Protestants; but the work's intent, the context of the age, and More's actual record on heresy are debated. Yet we know that More considered his role in negotiating the Treaty of Cambrai his most worthy achievement, that his record on heresy is ambiguous, and that he died as a martyr in defense of the rights of conscience against tyranny and for the unity of the Mystical Body against violence and division. Finally, More's works, most especially his *Utopia*, present vivid and effective condemnations of war, violence, and repression, and some of the most far-reaching recommendations for reform that the West has ever produced.

The debate over the meaning and nature of *Utopia* is as old as the work and comprises a body of literature in itself.[45] More's vision is expressed in two parts, the first a criticism of contemporary European society with its mockery of Christian values, and the second a description of a society guided by human reason but open to divine grace.[46] Utopia is not an anti-Christian or an un-Christian state but an ideal pre-Christian society capable of greater perfection through Christianity. It is thus the political extension of Thomas Aquinas's synthesis of Christian revelation and human reason.[47] As such Utopia is infinitely superior to the false Christianity and barbarous conduct of Europe's greedy rulers and warring states.

Despite the nature of his Utopia, however, More's outlook is neither rationalist nor impersonal, nor is it "utopian" in the modern sense of otherworldly fantasy. It is profoundly Christian and fundamentally realistic. More's society was based more on Christian monastic ideals than on Plato's *Republic*,[48] and its appeal to individual conscience was altruistic in the best Christian sense; but his society was also bound by the rule of law and offered practical advice for reforming European government and for ending the vicious cycle of war, destruction, impoverishment, and greed for conquest and profit.[49]

Perhaps more than any of his contemporaries, More was deeply conscious of the economic and social causes of war and violence. Yet, like his Humanist colleagues, he held that the individual possessed freedom of will and moral responsibility and thus could be educated for good or bad. Like most Renaissance Humanists, More believed that nurture was more responsible than nature for much of human suffering and evil, and that education, values, perceptions, and visions of heroism and nobility had great influence on war and peace. His attacks on war therefore focused on the ruling classes, on their values, forms of social behavior, pastimes, educations, titles, symbols, even their language and literature.[50] More took special aim at such popular "noble" pastimes as the hunt, which as Hythloday says, merely brutalizes hunters and insensitizes them to violence and death.[51]

More also turned his gifts of satire and historical narrative against the medieval courtly tradition. His *History of King Richard III* helped demythologize the chivalrous histories of England's rulers.[52] He loathed the brutal love triangles of the chivalrous tradition and saw courtly love as the ritualized subjugation of women to the barbarian norms of a warrior society. He made sure that his own daughters received the same Humanist education as would men of the time.[53]

## More and Social Justice

More's *Utopia* deals with three problems of importance to Catholic peacemakers; social violence and injustice, war, and political tyranny. Book I describes and condemns abuses in European society through Hythloday's and More's dialogue. Book II's description of Utopian society offers the positive alternatives available to human reason, before Christian principles are applied.

More's treatment of violence and social justice is classic in Western literature. During his conversation with More on the effects of war, Hythloday recounts a discussion he once had at the table of Archbishop John Morton of Canterbury with a prominent lawyer about the steady rise in England's crime rate and efforts to curb the chief crime, theft.[54] The lawyer's solution to the problem was that of Henry's government: deterrence, that is, the death penalty. Only when the criminal element realizes that stiff penalties, widely applied, are the law of the land will the crime rate drop. He approves of the ever-mounting number of executions but wonders why crime still keeps increasing. Hythloday gives More's answer. Capital punishment, he counters, "is neither just in itself nor is it beneficial to the public."[55] It is first too severe, and second not a deterrent. In fact, as everyone can observe, the crime rate increases as the number of executions increases. Criminals faced with capital punishment for lesser crimes, in fact, are encouraged to murder to eliminate witnesses.

Besides, Hythloday argues, getting to the heart of More's point, crime is not caused by evil men who will be deterred by drastic punishments, but by poverty. All around England, he goes on, one sees an increasingly impoverished, hopeless new class of poor, who are thrust off their farms by the greed of large landowners. They are deprived of their livelihoods, which also would benefit the entire nation, by entrepreneurs who maximize their profits by cutting back on their labor forces.[56] These "monopolistic practices of the rich"[57] lead to the closing of home industries, unemployment, and the creation of an entire class of people born into hopeless poverty—a new generation of thieves. This class is constantly supplemented by the recently unemployed who are given no opportunity to learn new trades and by an ever-increasing legion of disabled or impoverished veterans who are ignored by the government and eventually forced into crime in order to survive.

There are alternatives both in history and in contemporary society, Hythloday reminds the lawyer. The Romans, known for their brilliance in law, sentenced those convicted "of major crimes" to life imprisonment at hard labor and to restitution and compensation for smaller crimes. Such a system, supplemented by paroles and pardons, would give criminals the opportunity and the obligation to make amends to their victims.[58] In

Utopia there is no capital punishment for either "vicious crimes" or "some atrocity," but rather the punishments of enslavement and labor.[59] More's ultimate argument, however, is moral:

> God has not given man the right to deprive another, or even himself, of life. Would it not be placing human laws above God's law if men agreed by mutual consent to free themselves from the divine law forbidding homicide?[60]

Divine law, then, must in the end always take precedence over human statute. So argues Hythloday in the book and so argued More on the scaffold.

## War and Peace in Utopia

More begins his discussion of war and peace in Book I of *Utopia* by attacking the war lusts of Europe's rulers. Asked why he does not put his talents at the service of princes, Hythloday tells More:

> In the first place, most princes are more interested in warfare . . . the acquisition of more territory by fair or foul means occupies them more than the wise administration of those they already possess.[61]

Further, they are dominated by the lust for power and fed on the false myths of chivalrous romance and conquest.[62] War is the work of thieves, who are indistinguishable from soldiers, "for the two professions are so closely related that thieves sometimes play the role of brave soldiers and soldiers the role of industrious thieves."[63] The history of French aggression shows that kings do not want peacemakers in their councils.[64] Hythloday anticipates a later period's criticism of uncontrollable war machines. The very structures of government administration and policy, he says, are geared for a state of continuous war:

> The so-called wise men insist that public safety requires that a strong army, preferably of veterans, be in constant readiness. Since they feel that inexperienced troops are unreliable, they sometimes even provoke wars in order to keep their soldiers and cutthroats in shape.[65]

Such policies bring ruin to all civilized life.[66] They throw nations into confusion, impoverish kingdoms and peoples, placing the hateful burdens of war taxes on those least able to pay, and throw the fortunes of peoples into the uncertain arena of war. Eventually constant war and desolation have an effect even at home among noncombatants. Lack of peace or of any hope for it ultimately brings moral breakdown and a lust for plunder and violence until all creative, constructive, and peaceful pursuits come to be considered effeminate.[67] This brutalization of society is only matched by the brutal excesses of the governments that wage war.

In Utopia, on the other hand,

> War is considered utterly detestable and plainly beastlike—although there are no animals so diligent in practicing it as are men. Nothing is considered as inglorious as is the glory gained from war.[68]

Although considered more civilized than war, butchery, hunting, and all violent sports are also considered brutal, and Utopians are trained rather in the arts of peace and creative production.[69] Yet all Utopian citizens, following the dictates of natural reason, are trained for defense, and—only as a last resort and with as little bloodshed as possible—Utopians do fight wars of defense.[70]

More saw these Utopian wars as another aspect of living under the laws of natural reason, unaided by revelation. Yet the Utopians, when exposed to Christian truth through missionaries, immediately appreciate the truth of Christian revelation and ethics.[71] More thus makes the point that on human terms alone, given the proper function of natural reason, humans can behave admirably according to the minimum standards of virtue achieved by the best of the ancients and can exceed the norms of the decadent Christian society of his time. The implication is that given a rational society, proper education in Christian virtues will create a truly Christian state, one in keeping with the Sermon on the Mount and the gospel life. Wars then, even the most just wars, are not acceptable to Christians as Christians but are an aspect of a society following right reason alone and without Christian revelation.

### More and Tyranny

If wars between Christians are immoral, what of defensive wars fought for the clear-cut preservation of Christian life against the barbarity and tyranny of foreign invaders and evil empires, such as the Turks? One of More's last works gives compelling and consistent answers to this question. It was composed after he was sentenced for treason while he was awaiting execution. The *Dialogue of Comfort Against Tribulation*,[72] written in the Tower in 1534, is an extended meditation on the Christian virtues of faith, hope, and charity, More's attempt to alleviate his fears of death and an exhortation to patience for anyone who endures suffering under persecution. Significantly More's meditation is in the form of a dialogue between an uncle and nephew living in Hungary after the Turkish victory over the Christians at Mohacs (1526) and before Sultan Suleiman's second invasion and conquest (1529).[73] The discussion turns to their fears of living under the persecution and tyranny of the infidels and, ultimately, to their determination to follow the example of Christ in defending the truth of the faith even to giving up their lives.

More's subject was actually the tyranny of Henry VIII and the duty of the Christian to resist through nonviolence,[74] but the Turkish threat was also real both for him and for his readers, who may or may not have understood his oblique references to the English king. As in his *Dialogue Against Heresies*, however, More also identified the Turks with the Protestants, since both, in his eyes, persecuted the faithful and destroyed the unity of the Mystical Body. More well knew the alternative to the suffering he described: accede to the wishes of the tyrant, abandon the faith. Yet the desire to imitate Christ and the knowledge that this must inevitably lead to the scaffold permeates the work. One must resist evil, but without violence. As he concludes, "the Turk is but a shadow"[75] of the evil that all Christians must face: the powers of violent tyranny. More died because of his nonviolent resistance. His refusal to violate his conscience was a threat to Henry's tyranny greater than any revolt or violent opposition could ever have been.

### JUAN LUIS VIVES

Among the Humanists of international career and reputation associated with More in his opposition to Henry VIII was Juan Luis Vives (1492–1540).[76] A friend of Erasmus,

More, Linacre, and other English Humanists,[77] Vives gained a reputation that eclipsed even that of Erasmus for a time. His works ran to many editions and were translated into six languages within fifty years of his death.[78] Vives was born in Valencia to a family of low nobility. After an ultraconservative, scholastic education he went on to study under the Humanists.[79] By 1522 Vives was established as a popular Humanist lecturer and tutor at Louvain.

In 1523, with More's influence, Vives became a lecturer in Latin, Greek, and rhetoric at Cardinal College, Oxford. Among his students and auditors were many of the most influential of the English nobility, including Reginald Pole, King Henry, and Queen Catherine, his compatriot, who soon became his patroness.[80] When Wolsey's cold war against Spain and the question of Henry's divorce became political debates Vives was fired from his lecturership, which Wolsey then abolished. Vives was eventually forced out of the kingdom because of his loyal support of Queen Catherine.[81] The next ten years were the most fruitful of Vives's writing career. Although reduced to poverty and often ill, he traveled through the Low Countries and France, writing to kings and prelates, urging peace, reconciliation, and the pursuit of the new learning. When Erasmus died in 1536, Vives was recognized as the leader of the Humanists' struggle for reform. He died in May 1540.[82]

Vives combined a deep desire for Christian renewal with sharp learning, a skillful pen, and keen analysis. His efforts for peace among Christians began in 1514, when he published *Jesus Christ Triumphant*. The work contrasts the glory and triumph won by Christ in his suffering and death with that of Caesar, whose career inflicted suffering and death on countless victims.[83] Vives's edition and commentary on Augustine's *City of God*, commissioned by Erasmus for Froben's Basel press in 1520, is one of the great Humanist texts. Vives saw Augustine's work as a basic commentary on Christian peacemaking amid the fall of empires and warring kingdoms.

Augustine, Vives wrote, "makes fighting as far from Christian piety as religious humanity is from barbarous humanity."[84] Empires built on war, he comments, are as brittle as glass. When one man commits murder, it is a crime; when many commit it, it is seen as a virtue. The "greatness of the fact," he remarks, "sets it free from penalty." Vives highlights Augustine's reported exchange between the admiral and the pirate captain, the one distinguished from the other only by the extent of his thievery. Although Vives agrees with Augustine's view of "all things to consist by peace and concord" and that war creates a hell on earth, he breaks with the church doctor by considering all war to be evil and all its results to be bad.[85]

By the 1520s Vives was known throughout Europe, and he used his fame to persuade Europe's rulers to make peace. *On the State of Europe and Its Upheavals* (1522),[86] addressed to Pope Adrian VI (1522–1523), and letters from Vives to Charles V and to Henry VIII (1525) call on the princes to heed the suffering of the people, to exercise restraint, and to deal honorably with one another. Vives's letter to Henry VIII of October 8, 1525, stressing the need for a peace policy, was probably the immediate cause of his being fired from the Oxford faculty in early 1526.[87]

Francis I's repudiation of the Treaty of Madrid (made with Charles V) and the Turkish victory at Mohacs (both in 1526) completely changed the political mood of Europe. At Bruges Vives published his *On Europe Divided and the Turkish War* late in 1526.[88] As the Turks press ever deeper into Christendom, Vive warned, Christian princes and the pope himself are caught in hatreds and rivalries. Europeans, he wrote, are not really Christians but raving wolves. No war between them can be considered just, all wars are *latrocinium*, theft. He recognized the oppression that the Turks might bring, but Vives warned that there are worse oppressors than the Turks: those European princes who use force, conquest, and domination as instruments of rule. Only Christian unity and Christian principles of government can create the spiritual and material strength needed to overcome the Turks.

In two works, *On Pacification*[89] and *On Concord and Discord in Mankind*,[90] both of 1529, Vives summed up the Humanist criticism of war and social injustice. *On Concord and Discord* was addressed to Emperor Charles V and called on him to look beyond narrow nationalistic boundaries and exert his power and leadership for true peace in Europe,[91] not the false peace of armed security.[92] In this age of discoveries, of the study of languages, and of renewed capacities for human unity, only imbeciles could want war. Unless Charles acts decisively, Vives warned, even the renewal of the pure forms of the Christian life will be imperiled. Christendom has witnessed too many of war's evils—

> fields destroyed and unpeopled, buildings razed, cities equally desert or wholly plundered and abandoned, food scarce and dear, scholarly work sluggish and almost abandoned, manners depraved, justice almost wholly corrupted, and evil received as though it were good.[93]

Yet all these trends could be reversed; all that is needed is the will and the power. Those with one usually lack the other, but Charles, as emperor, has both the inclination and the capacity to restore Christian institutions. He could bring unity and peace through a general assembly that would root out violence and war through applying the principles of the gospels.

Vives's concern for peace between states was matched by his commitment to social justice in Christian societies. In response to the misery caused by the English-French wars, the enormous war taxes, and the revolts of peasants in Germany and England,[94] Vives wrote *On Aid to the Poor*,[95] which was published in January 1526 and dedicated to the senators of Bruges. In it he echoes More's social and economic analysis in the *Utopia*, calling poverty a human-made evil caused by the twin oppressions of war and wealth. Unrelieved poverty will eventually cause more war and crime within society. Yet all humans possess an essential dignity and all Christians are obligated to aid their brothers and sisters. To solve the problem of poverty Vives recommends several steps: a program of public work projects for those capable of work, charity for those who cannot, and humanitarian aid to refugees and victims of catastrophe, including war.[96]

Vives blamed the educational system for much of the evil and violence in society. The steady diet of chivalrous romances glorified the warrior, stressed the violence of masculine nature, and made passive victims of women. In his *Education of a Christian Woman*, which was commissioned by Queen Catherine of Aragon in 1523 for the instruction of Princess Mary, Vives attacked the medieval romances and their Arthurian heroes as a pack of lies about human nature, physiology, psychology, and the true nature of war. Tales of heroic combat and manly feats, he argued, were hilariously funny when looked at objectively but extremely dangerous in their essentially pagan glorification of violence.[97]

Women are particularly victimized by this propaganda. Because the romances portray them as passive victims of blind and adulterous passions they further the brutalization of women as sex objects. Women are made to participate vicariously in violence through their supposed pleasure at the tournaments of male warriors. Vives's alternative is to provide women with the same Humanist education given males, teaching them independence, judgment, and active morality. His *Livery or Emblems (Satellitum sive symbola)*[98] and *On Education*[99] of 1531 continued these themes.

Vives's most influential work on eduation, a classic Humanist textbook, was his *Introduction to Wisdom* (1524). The work conveys a remarkably gentle tone in an increasingly polarized Europe. This probably explains its wide appeal and many editions.[100] The *Introduction* surveys a vast field of ethical principles and reflections for a popular audience: wisdom, beauty and strength, the body and soul, learning, the vices and virtues, true and false honor, food, sleep, social life, love, religion, and Christ. The book leaves the reader with a complete statement of Humanist principles of positive Christian life and a sense of the necessity to make peace in the world. Humans are by nature capable of the greatest peace and love, but they are also capable of violence and war-making that reduces them to a level below that of beasts. Only conciliation, compromise, and mutual agreement can remove violence, and Vives pleads for these.[101]

The chapter "On Charity" contains most of Vives's thought on violence and peacemaking.[102] The Golden Rule has been proclaimed by nature and confirmed by Christ, who orders us to love those who hate us, just as he loved those who persecuted him.[103] Christ's life, moreover, is the model for ours. Christ's nonviolence, in fact, is a compelling model for imitation.[104] No true Christian can hate; the love of one's brothers and sisters goes beyond love of nation, city, kindred, profession, state of life, or level of intelligence.[105]

War, brawls, contentions, dissensions, factions and parties, and private profit are the inventions of the devil and are worse even than the ferocity of animals. Nature, Vives reminds his readers, abhors war and created humanity unarmed. God ordered mutual love, and people cannot therefore wage war without serious offense against both nature and religion.[106] The contrast is clear:

> They who study to bring peace among men, and to preserve tranquility safe and sound, shall be called the children of God, as Christ testifies. These are the true peacemakers of whom he spoke. Contrarily, those who sow discord and destroy charity among men are the sons of the devil.[107]

## THE PARIS HUMANISTS

A number of Humanists in Paris during these years joined in the English Humanists' attack on war and their call for peacemaking. Josse van Clichtove (d. 1543), a leading French Humanist,[108] published his *Short Work On War and Peace* in 1523.[109] The gods of the ancients brought the peace of Vergil's *Aeneid:* war, conquest, and warrior virtue, but the Christian God is the "god of peace," for whom the bloodless victory is the best. Despite the interpretations of many schoolmen, war is not the law of the Old Testament and certainly not that of the New Testament, in which Christ both counsels and commands love. Indeed, "the whole law of Christ consists of love."[110] Even human reason shows the world's interdependence. Peace brings education, travel, commerce, agriculture, and prosperity; war, especially as practiced by modern "Christians," negates all of these and betrays Christ's holy law.

Guillaume Budé (1467–1540), another Paris Humanist, ranked with Erasmus among the greatest thinkers and scholars of the age.[111] In his *On the As and its Denominations*[112] Budé digressed at length to attack the abuses of power by Europe's monarchs. War, he contended, springs from the egotism of these tyrants and dilutes the energies of the state by going beyond its borders and natural concerns.

Budé's *On the Institution of the Prince* (1519)[113] sought to replace the lust for power found in chivalric literature gradually with a new lust for learning and service. Budé employed both biblical and classical sources, especially Plutarch's *Lives*, to demythologize the warrior heroes of the past. His Alexander the Great, for example, is a violent-tempered adolescent bent on cruelty and revenge, hardly a worthy model for Christian princes, whose glory should lie in good government, not military adventure.

Robert Ceneau, bishop of Vence and almoner to the queen regent of France, Louise of Savoy, brought the Humanist strategy for peace to the highest levels of European leadership. In 1529 he delivered his *Peace Oration*[114] in honor of Queen Louise and her role in the Peace of Cambrai. Using the Sermon on the Mount's "blessed are the peacemakers" (Mt 5:9) as his text, Ceneau went on to praise the royal women for bringing peace to Europe, to their own countries, and to countless widows and orphans. Like the woman who found the lost coin (Lk 15:8–10), these women found peace and made their princes meek and peaceful once again.

Peace is, in fact, the most glorious achievement, for it is better to protect one citizen by peace than to kill one thousand in war. Thus the peace that saves a hundred thousand lives is a hundred thousand times better than any victory in war. The peacemakers are called blessed because they will receive the reward of being the children of God. This is the legacy promised by Christ when he said, "My peace I give you, my peace I leave to you," which is both an inheritance and a duty.[115]

## DESIDERIUS ERASMUS

Desiderius Erasmus epitomizes Renaissance Humanism and the revival of ancient learning. He was born in Rotterdam about 1466.[116] At the age of nine he was sent to Deventer to study under the Brethren of the Common Life. In 1487 he entered the Canons Regular of St. Augustine at Steyn, but he soon left monastic life and took a degree in theology at the University of Paris. The scholastic abstraction and academic disputation of the university proved sterile for Erasmus, and by 1499 he had joined the circle of the new Humanists. In that year he made his first trip to England and there became friends with John Colet and Thomas More. Colet especially helped move Erasmus to "a coherent and purposeful form of social criticism against the developing war and repressive social policies of Henry VII and other monarchs"[117] and to the Fathers and Scripture as a source for this criticism. In 1501 Erasmus went back to Paris to study the Bible, Jerome, and Augustine—the sources of Latin Christianity.

Erasmus mastered the study of Greek at Louvain and visited England a second time. In 1506 or 1507 he traveled to Italy, still the prime source of the new learning. His stay was marred, however, by the warlike atmosphere created by Pope Julius II (1503–1513). Erasmus was in Bologna in November 1506, when Julius, who had just conquered the city, entered its gates at the head of a triumphal procession, sword in hand, in full armor. This event and Julius's later career profoundly affected Erasmus's ideas on war and peace.

In 1509 or 1510 Erasmus returned to England as the acknowledged leader of the Humanist movement. He was attached to the court of Henry VIII until 1514. While there he joined in the work of the London Reformers. Henry's war plans changed the mood in England, however, bringing talk of war, high war taxes and consequent inflation, and a sense of hostility and isolation.[118] Disgusted with England's war fever, in 1514 Erasmus returned to his homeland, where he remained until 1521, writing and editing, mostly at Louvain.[119] In 1517 he was named councilor to Prince Charles, the future Holy Roman Emperor. It seemed that the Humanist would finally have some influence over the policies of Christendom's future leader. However, the storm of the Reformation was already on the horizon.[120] In 1521 suspicions over Erasmus's sympathies with the reformers forced him to leave Louvain for Basel. Nevertheless, Christian unity and the reform of learning and religion remained his chief goals, and he continued his efforts to mediate between Rome and Luther.[121]

In 1529 the success of the Reformation in Basel forced him to leave the city for Freiburg-im-Breisgau. In 1535, as the Reform began to dominate that city too, he returned to Basel. That same year he declined Pope Paul III's invitation to take up the Catholic standard at a long-awaited reform council and his offer of the cardinal's hat. On July 12, 1536, he died at Basel.[122]

Erasmus was condemned during his lifetime by the Protestants on the one side for his reluctance to aid the Reform and by the University of Paris on the other for his alleged support of the Protestants. After his death he was still criticized for his moderation and attempts to reconcile enemies. In 1559 the works of the man who had enlightened all of Europe, who had worked diligently to retrieve the sources of Christian wisdom, and who had once been offered the cardinalate were placed on the Roman Index of Prohibited Books. His former friend, Pope Paul IV, condemned all of Erasmus's commentaries, annotations, translations, and colloquies, forbidding Catholics to read them. The Council of Trent later allowed censored versions to circulate.[123] Yet Erasmus's popularity, his influence, and his ability to stir controversy have continued to grow since his death.

By his focus on individual motivation and the effects of education and environment for good or bad, Erasmus contributed significantly to the modern debate on war and peace.[124] Contemporary analyses must still contend with his questions: Are violence and war innate to human nature? Or are they socialized? Can they be prevented by changing individual hearts or by changing institutions and governments? Is the appeal of peace due to self-interest and utility, or is peace fundamentally a moral and religious issue of justice and love? Where does the power to effect change lie, with those in politics or with the intellectual, who can both influence politics and change hearts?

Erasmus answered these questions in three major categories of works: those that deal generally with the Christian attitude to war and peace, those that deal specifically with the Christian soldier, and those that deal with the responsibilities and abuses of Christian leadership. Many of his works are overlapping, touching on more than one of these categories. We will survey several works illustrating each of these aspects of Erasmus's approach to peacemaking, and then discuss his ideas on the just war and the Turkish threat.

## War and Peace

Between 1488 and 1509 Erasmus wrote several works that focus on war and peace, including *On the Contempt of the World* (1488)[125] and the *Handbook of the Militant Christian* (1501).[126] His best-known work from this period (still a popular book today) is his *Praise of Folly* (1509).[127] This gentle but penetrating satire[128] explores the whole moral, political, and social scene of the time and casts a mocking eye on abuses of every sort. Folly takes on an allegorical life to describe the prevailing value system and to speak for its opposite, the *folia Christi,* Christ's disruption of earthly values and the gospel imitation of his life that is considered folly by the world.

The wise person has no place in war, but the fool finds full employment there. War is "fought by parasites, panderers, robbers, murderers, yokels, drunks, debtors, and the other scum of this type."[129] War's leaders are the worst bandits, and it opens the door to every transgression of Christian morals and to every vice. The church was founded and built on the blood of the martyrs, so Folly is delighted that warrior popes and priests defile their sacred duty[130] and sycophants echo Augustine and the just-war theorists. These pen-pushers

> refer to this obvious madness as zeal, piety, or fortitude, thus making it legal for a man to draw his sword, kill his brother with it, and still be considered to be of the greatest charity—charity, which according to Christ, is due every man by his neighbor.[131]

True Christians, those who follow Christ's example, are the minority, Erasmus says.[132] Those who follow Christ's folly, his command to spread the gospels nonviolently, are judged mad by the majority of people, princes and subjects alike, who call themselves Christians. Yet, Erasmus remarks, to be a "fool for Christ's sake"[133] is in the spirit of the gospels. It is the secret hidden from the wise and powerful of the world. This is the folly embraced by the early Christians and the ultimate folly of salvation.[134]

If the *Praise of Folly* mirrors a light-hearted optimism on human affairs, the *Complaint of Peace* (1517)[135] reflects the growing pessimism of Europe, its obsession with war among Christians, the advance of the Turks, and the toughened Humanist approach to war and peace.[136] The *Complaint* appealed to the power of the press and to public opinion and quickly became a best seller.[137]

The book is a blend of Hellenic and Roman views on war and peace informed by the Sermon on the Mount.[138] Its theme is announced in the opening epigraph: "The whole purpose of our religion is peace and unanimity."[139] It deals with all aspects of war and peace, beginning with an examination of the solar system and the laws of physics, vegetable, and animal life. Unlike the world of nineteenth-century social Darwinists, Erasmus's universe mirrors medieval cosmology[140] and is built on love: harmonies, mutual attractions, and concord, symbioses that cooperate to guarantee life and peace within bodies and species. Even human nature was created with love, compassion, and cooperation as its key elements. Humans are born peaceable and defenseless; their lives depend on bonds of kin and society; their talents create cities and civilizations, the works of cooperation and love.[141]

Yet Christian society is a mockery of peace and concord. Peace is only a sham that hides the corruption and violence of all institutions and professions. Greed, lust, anger, and ambition vie with Christian piety and true peace. Erasmus looks at what commonly passes for peace and exposes it for the lie that it is. Monastic withdrawal into self-centered contemplation, domestic tranquility, and inner calm are insufficient forms of Christian peace, even if properly followed. Peace is not a withdrawal or a calmness but "a work of justice." Peace is the highest virtue, and the Christian God is the God of peace. Scripture reinforces this. Only in an allegorical sense can the wars of the Old Testament be acceptable to Christians, as Christ's life and sacrifice make clear. At his Last Supper Christ could have asked for anything; he asked for peace. The sign of his followers is thus not the military uniform but that "you love one another as I have loved you."[142] Christians are thus linked together in one body, as in a vine, through love and nonviolence.

Yet today Christians fight and kill one another "with all the weapons of hell."[143]

Ordinary citizens may have some excuse, since ignorance and corrupt leadership tax them bare, lead them into war, and destroy their works of peace:

> The common people construct excellent cities, rule them peacefully, and enrich them. Governors and rulers, like wasps and drones, creep into those cities and secretly steal that which was provided by other men's industry. What many have gathered is wasted by a few, what was well constructed is ruined. If you will not remember things long past, remember the battles and the wars fought during the past ten years. You will find that they were fought for causes that did not concern the common man.[144]

Erasmus's condemnation of the clergy and its support for war is blunt:

> What do mitres and helmets have in common? What has a crosier to do with a sword? What has a Bible to do with a shield? How can one reconcile a salutation of peace with an exhortation to war; peace in one's mouth and war in one's deeds? Do you praise war with the same mouth that you preach peace and Christ? Do you herald with the same trumpet both God and Satan? . . . What filth is the tongue of a priest who exhorts war, evil, and murder![145]

The Humanist recommends positive steps for Christian peacemakers. On the international level he warns that peace is not found in leagues and defensive alliances but in checking the true causes of war: personal ambitions and evil. At root war and peace are personal decisions. Individual Christians must first disassociate themselves from the warmongers and reject propaganda that sets citizens of one nation against those of another, faction against faction, ideology against ideology. Peace has a price—the loss of disputed territory, perhaps, and loss of prestige. But even a war fought for a just cause involves so much destruction, so many costs, that the advantages of victory, so dearly won, are far outweighed by the disasters involved—the eruption of personal vices onto a higher scale; the disruption of trade, commerce and urban life; graft, corruption, and the waste of lives and resources all planned, led, and waged by the true criminals of society.[146] Erasmus concludes with an appeal to individual Christian conscience and an attack on tyranny:

> Most people detest war and piously pray for peace. A few, whose wicked happiness thrives on public chaos, loathfully wish for war. Conscientiously judge whether it is right or wrong that their dishonesty should so heavily outweigh the earnest will of all good men.[147]

Throughout his career Erasmus produced a continuous stream of short, popular works, *The Adages,* covering a variety of subjects, including war and peace.[148] Among the most popular and influential works in this collection was his *Dulce Bellum Inexpertis* (War is Sweet to Those Who Do Not Know It), also called the *Bellum Erasmi* (Erasmus Against War).[149]

*Erasmus Against War* is an open letter to Europe's leaders, a plea for peace and an analysis of the nature of violence and war and individual responsibility for them.[150] The work grew out of Erasmus's chief question of the 1510s: What is it to be a Christian? Erasmus states that most of the answers of the time miss the mark. Aristotelian philosophy and Roman law have so corrupted the pure Christian message that most Christians believe that their religion condones meeting force with force, accumulating wealth and honors, and living a religion of externals. The ultimate corruption of this approach is war, and war fought in the name of Christ. The true answer is accessible neither in learned discourse nor in intellectual assent to a creed, but in living in imitation of Christ. The scholar can help by using learning to free the gospels from the corruption of academics and lawyers.[151]

Drawing on a variety of Christian and Stoic sources, Erasmus presents a series of arguments against war. These fall into several categories. Natural reason and law illustrate peaceful cooperation in nature and among beasts. The medical argument compares war to a blight that spreads across morality. The practical and legal argument pinpoints the injustice of war, its cost in lives, economic development, and money. Finally revelation shows the anti-Christian nature of war and its effects. Erasmus sketches what is to become a classic Humanist anthropology of violence.[152] The original pacific nature of humanity and its early inventive talents were perverted by the first violence as revenge against animals for their preying on people for food. This led to the perversion of meat-eating and hunting—a bestial sport that eventually insensitizes and dehumanizes human beings—and then to war as an occupation of groups, tribes, and nations. A gradual degeneration from a first Golden Age follows,[153] until finally the worst thefts, murders, plunder, and other obscenities are considered the greatest virtues.

Today war ruins all the works of civilization and human creativity:

What a tidal wave of misfortune rushes in, flooding and overwhelming everything! Flocks are driven away, crops trampled underfoot, peasants slaughtered, farms burnt, flourishing cities which took centuries to build are overturned by a single squall.[154]

War crushes the people beneath huge defense costs and exploits and humiliates the soldier.[155]

The worst crime of all is the conflict between Christian and Christian, which mocks the name of Christ and his ministers:

Under that heavenly banner, symbolizing the perfect and ineffable union of all Christians, there is a rush to butcher each other, and we make Christ the witness and authority for so criminal a thing! For where is the kingdom of the devil if not in war? Why do we drag Christ into it?[156]

War between Christians is worse than fratricide. It destroys the Christian religion, the City of God, and tears apart the members of the Mystical Body.[157]

Christ has defined what Christian life is: charity, humility, poverty, and nonviolence. The life of Christ, the apostles, and the early church are models for imitation. The Sermon on the Mount provides the basic rules:

One commandment Christ called his own—the commandment of love. What could be more opposed to this than war? He greets his friends with the blessed salutation of peace. He gave his disciples nothing but peace, only peace he left with them [Jn 16:21]. . . . When Christ was born, the angels sang not of wars or triumphs, but of peace. Before his birth, the poet of prophesy had sung of him: his place was made in peace [Ps 75:3]. Examine the whole of his teaching: you will find nothing anywhere which does not breathe the spirit of peace, which does not savour of love.[158]

In Gethsemane Christ ordered Peter to put up his sword. Christ's entire life was a lesson in nonviolence. The martyrs and all the popes and doctors who lived and preached peace are more compelling than any theories of Bernard of Clairvaux or Thomas Aquinas on the justness of Christian wars. No excuse—the wars of the Old Testament, the arguments of the schoolmen and lawyers, a few papal letters, war as a punishment for evil-doers, territorial integrity and sovereign rights, the defense of the church and religion, even defense against the Turks—can justify war.[159] Nations' real motives for war are plain:

> Some are urged into war by a secret hate, others by ambition, others by the fierceness of their character. Our *Iliad* contains nothing, indeed, but the heated folly of stupid kings and peoples.[160]

The choice for the Christian is clear:

> If Christ is a figment, why do we not frankly reject him? Why do we glory in his name? . . . If we acknowledge Christ as our authority, Christ who is Love, and who taught nothing, handed down nothing that is not love and peace, come, let us follow him, not only in name, not by wearing his badge, but in our actions, in our lives.[161]

### Onward Christian Soldiers

Erasmus turned his satiric eye with deadly aim and seriousness on what he considered the crime and plight of the individual soldier. Almost without exception in his writings, he condemned the soldier as the epitome of evil, avoiding the pious sentimentality and glorification of the warrior heroes of myth and history.[162] He sympathized with the plight of the common footsoldier,[163] but he had seen firsthand the destruction caused by both "just" wars and the atrocities of mercenaries.[164]

In *Against War* Erasmus repeats a theme first heard in Augustine: what passes for crime among civilians becomes a virtue for the soldier. Such crime

> would be an atrocity *[infamis]* if done stealthily without a uniform, but when it is part of military service, they acquit themselves and return, after having despoiled many innocents, into the number of honest citizens. Those soldiers who have behaved with the greatest cruelty are considered worthy to become commanders in the next war.[165]

Military service is a "busy sort of time wasting and it is by far the most destructive, for from it results the complete cessation of everything worthwhile and the source of all things evil."[166] Soldiers are "that barbaric flux of men in the last stages of depravity" and mercenaries "the most abject and execrable type of human being."[167]

Erasmus realized that the awed respect and aura of nobility that the soldier enjoyed were the result of several factors, among them the heroic mythology given combat and the glorification of violence on the highest levels of the church. The highest abomination in Christian Europe was the figure of the warrior pope, Julius II, the summation of clerical hypocrisy, corruption, and lust for power. Erasmus wrote his *Julius Exclusus* (Julius Excluded From Heaven) in 1513 or 1514 and published it in 1517.[168] The work is written as a dialogue between the pope and Saint Peter. The pope, recently dead and swaggering like a drunkard, arrives with his legion of dead soldiers to knock on heaven's door. Showing Peter his papal key, triple crown, and glorious robes, he demands that the Fisherman open the heavenly gates, but the saint recognizes the pope for a barbarian tyrant and asks what claim Julius and his mercenary brigands have to heaven.[169] Julius boasts of all his conquests, his additions to the papal treasury, treaties confirmed and broken, the satisfaction of his lusts for land and power. These have left dead the thousands that he brings behind him, to whom he has promised eternal salvation for fighting in his holy wars.[170] Peter replies that the gates of heaven open for those who have performed the works of mercy, not of power, that the pope never used his bloody sword rightly, and that Julius was corrupt and devoid of all Christian virtue. Francis and Benedict were the true Christians, in their poverty and simplicity.

Julius counters that his methods have long been used by Catholic popes, and that he has only improved on them.[171] After stressing his absolute power within the church,[172] he goes on to brag of all his "gimmicks," the schisms and wars that he inspired.[173] Peter interrupts the "madman" with a discourse on the simplicity, humility, poverty, and nonviolence of Christ, the apostles, and the early church. In a frenzied climax Julius replies with a vicious mockery of the poverty, toil, and danger of the early church, countering Peter's exposition of Christian morals with the worldly power, military triumphs, palaces, incomes, and building projects of his pontificate.[174]

Peter stops Julius's rantings with a final comment:

> I ask you, when you were the supreme shepherd of the Church, didn't you ever reflect privately on how the Church was born, how it grew, how it became established? It wasn't by wars, by wealth, by horses, was it? No, it was by suffering, by the blood of the martyrs and by ours, by dungeons, by lashes.[175]

By now, however, Peter (and Erasmus with him) has had enough. Julius and his legion are dispatched to go and build their own paradise in hell.[176]

By 1517 Erasmus was reaching a wide and popular audience with specific attacks on war in his *Colloquies,* which he had started writing around 1497 as Latin exercises for his tutorials. These dialogues between fictional characters, often thinly disguised real-life personalities, were widely used as school texts and were part of the reading of Rabelais, Shakespeare, and Walter Scott.[177] Among Erasmus's most popular pieces were *Military Affairs,*[178] *The Soldier and the Carthusian,*[179] *The Funeral,*[180] *Cyclops,*[181] *Charon,*[182] and *The Ignoble Knight,* all published between 1522 and 1529 and all dealing with war and the life of the soldier.

*The Ignoble Knight* or *Faked Nobility*[183] appeared in 1529 and is typical of the style and antimilitarism of the *Colloquies.* It pits Harpalus ("grasping," "greedy"), the braggart soldier, against Nestor, the urban swindler. Harpalus seeks Nestor's advice on how to buy a noble title and life. Nestor outlines the requirements for his brand of nobility: the company of high society, expensive clothes, empty conversation, absurd coats of arms, armor, and predigree. Such a noble reputation, he advises, is bolstered by writers and publishers who prostitute themselves for quick money, and is honored by fools.[184] Worthless military men, Nestor adds, "are indulged in our society."[185]

The basics established, Nestor instructs Harpalus on the true nature of knighthood:

Now the fundamental principle of knighthood must always be maintained: that for a knight to relieve a common traveler of his money is just and right. What's more outrageous than for a vulgar trader to be rich while a knight hasn't enough to spend on whores and dice? . . . Drum up some excuse for quarreling with those who are well off. . . . Through your ambassador declare irreconcilable war on them. Scatter dire threats of execution, destruction, total war. Terrified, they'll issue for peace. . . . Above all, bear in mind that insolence has never passed more readily for wisdom than it does today. . . . But above all, beware of that irritable and ill-humored breed of men, the poets. They spill their malice on paper, and whatever they put down is quickly scattered throughout the world.[186]

### The Scourge, and Tutor, of Princes

The responsibility of Europe's rulers for war and peace and the intellectual's duty to expose them are themes that run throughout Erasmus's works. International peace is first an individual moral concern, but it is also the product of political stability and thus of the proper governing of kingdoms, principalities, and the church.[187] Monarchs are in a unique position to shoulder praise and blame for war and peace. Erasmus shared the view of his time that monarchy was a God-given form of government and he was suspicious of popular movements. Yet he had been raised in the free urban and democratic atmosphere of the Low Countries, where the consensus of the governed was essential to good government. His classical education had also afforded him many examples and theories of just rule.[188] His *Panegyric* to Archduke Philip the Fair of Burgundy[189] and his *Adages,* including *The Grub Pursues the Eagle,*[190] *Kings and Fools Are Born, Not Made,*[191] *Sparta Is Yours, Now Make the Best of It!*[192] and *Sileni Alcibiades,*[193] all take up the themes of tyranny, the connection between war abroad and oppression at home, and the need for good government.[194]

Although Erasmus preferred to follow Hythloday's example and avoid direct involvement in politics, in the course of his life he wrote over one hundred letters to statesmen. This is a small percentage of the over three thousand letters we know he wrote, but it is still an impressive number considering that many were full treatises on good government, meant not only for their recipient but for the whole reading public. In these letters to leaders (as well as in many dedicatory prefaces to his other works and in his paraphrases of the Gospels) Erasmus advised and admonished all the great princes of the time: Emperor Charles V of Germany and Spain, Archduke Ferdinand of Austria, Francis I of France, Margaret of Angoulême, Henry VIII of England, James V of Scotland, Sigismund I of Poland, John III of Portugal, and Leo X, Adrian VI, Clement VII,[195] and Paul III.[196] In each letter his themes are the same: princes have the duty to further Christian peace, and through war they betray their trust and despoil the people, no matter how just the cause may appear. The peaceful settlement of disputes, arbitration, compromise, and reconciliation are the proper activities for Christian princes and prelates.

It is no accident that Erasmus and Machiavelli are contrasted in discussions of Renaissance political theory. To many historians they represent the opposing poles of political thought: Machiavelli, the cold *raison d'etat* of power politics, the use of war and peace as instruments of state and means to an end; Erasmus, the thoroughgoing Christian to whom the state and its power serve only as means to the Christian ends of peace and unity. Machiavelli wrote *The Prince* in 1513, but until its publication in 1532 it was not known to most Europeans, including Erasmus, who in May 1515 composed his own "Prince," *The Education of the Christian Prince,* dedicated to the young Prince Charles, the future emperor.[197] The book was an immediate success and had great influence on the Continent and in England.[198]

The *Christian Prince* repeats the themes of the *Panegyric,* the *Complaint of Peace,* and the *Adages,* but it focuses more closely on the interdependence of Christian leadership and peace. Erasmus and Machiavelli had the same talent for a clear-sighted and hard-hitting style. Peace, liberty, restraint of tyranny, and social justice are his major themes, but Erasmus avoids the flattery and innocuous clichés of other similar treatises.[199] He flatly regrets the loss of electoral rights and popular consensus and the growth of princely tyranny. The liberty of the individual Christian is more than spiritual, and the inconsistency between this liberty and unlimited monarchy is obvious. Since God has given humans free will, rulers who deprive their subjects of choice reduce them to animal slavery. When Christ said "render to Caesar," he was speaking in a pre-Christian world of slaves and masters, as was Saint Paul;[200] but Christian rule is not the same. "But it shall not be so among you," Christ said.[201] In the Christian world "principate is administration, not imperial power, and kingly authority is service, not tyranny."[202] Christian princes should thus rule differently, by consensus and with restraint and respect for the governed.[203] Ultimately, it is better for a prince to resign his throne voluntarily than to defend it against the consensus of the people with loss of blood.[204]

If the prince is to reject pagan forms of rule, he must first reject pagan models. In this regard Erasmus's Humanist program blends perfectly with his pleas for peace and individual liberty, since the proper education of the prince can sweep away the false dreams of military glory and the models of egotistical tyrants. Achilles, Alexander the Great, Xerxes, Julius Caesar, Arthur, and Lancelot were all robbers, tyrants drunk with ambition, and poor examples for the contemporary prince.[205] Erasmus sets out to demythologize militarism, imperial glory, and the entire aristocratic world of sham. The *Christian Prince* takes special aim at the nobility, a useless class who live on the labor of others, softened by luxury, lacking any useful skills, their imaginations glutted by the foolish fantasies of heraldry, lineage, and honor. "Why," Erasmus asks, "should this class of persons be placed on a higher level than the shoemaker or the farmer?"[206]

All this is a necessary preface to the Humanist's chief concern in the prince's education: peace and justice, for only by stripping away the lies of violence can true Christian principles be taught. Most medieval treatises give equal emphasis to the arts of war and peace, but the *Christian Prince* is almost solely devoted to peace and good government. Only in the final chapter (eleven), "On Beginning War," is the possibility of war ever considered. This chapter, however, highlights the evils of war, its few benefits, and the greater benefits of peace.

While canon law, Augustine, and Bernard of Clairvaux may approve of war "in one or two places," "the whole philosophy of Christ teaches against it."[207] As Erasmus stresses in many other works, war is far more expensive than peace. So many arguments exist against the prince waging war that the Humanist cannot see how he could possibly decide to begin one, but, he concludes, "if the whole teachings of Christ do not everywhere inveigh against war, if a single instance of specific commendation of war can be brought forth in its favor, let us Christians fight."[208] The imitation of Christ should hold sway finally. Erasmus tells Charles, "He rejoices to be called the Prince of Peace; may you do the same."[209]

*Erasmus on the Just War*

"On Beginning War," chapter 11 of the *Christian Prince*, raises a problem in Erasmus's thought. Although the Humanist offers every reason for the prince not to wage war unless it is impossible to avoid, he still concedes the possibility of fighting just wars, warning that such wars should be fought with as little bloodshed as possible.[210] He thus appears to admit two of the prime requirements of the classic just-war theory: proper cause (inescapable necessity) and proper conduct in the waging of the war.[211] At the same time, he questions whether "there really is any war which can be called 'just' "[212] and states outright that "we will not attempt to discuss whether war is ever just."[213]

In his *Letter to Anthony Bergen* (March 1514)[214] and in the *Sileni Alcibiades* (1515)[215] Erasmus attacked the just war as a mockery, a pretext of princes to rob the people. He uses the just-war notion of proportionality of means to disqualify every known war, repeating a theme of all his works on the subject: the evils that stem from war are far greater than the benefits that accrue.[216] The history of the Roman Empire, with all its pretexts of legal grievance and just war and all its conquest in the name of peace, is a case in point.[217] In the final analysis the wars of kings are fought on flimsy pretext, and the welfare of their people has nothing to do with war:

If you look narrowly into the case, you will find that they are, chiefly, the private, sinister, and selfish motives of princes which operate as the real causes of war.[218]

Erasmus amplified this criticism of the just war in *Against War* (1515) and the *Complaint of Peace* (1517). Even the theories of war as a punishment for wrongdoers and of the prince's right to defend national sovereignty are shams. In a court of law, Erasmus reminds his readers in *Against War*, a wrongdoer is convicted in front of judges before he is punished. In war each side prosecutes the other, and the only ones punished are old people, wives, orphans, and young women.[219] Using the notion of proportionality, Erasmus states that it is better to allow a few wrongdoers to go unpunished than to have thousands of innocents die as a result of war.

As for the prince's right to defend his sovereignty, Erasmus reminds his readers that princes' rights stem from the people and that rulers therefore have no right to endanger the people in pursuit of trivial grievances.[220] Even in the clearly recognized danger of Turkish aggression (which we will examine below), Erasmus rejects recourse to arms as counterproductive and anti-Christian.[221] Erasmus concludes that all just-war claims are nonsense. " 'Just', indeed—this means any war declared in any way against anybody by any prince."[222]

Men fight, the *Complaint of Peace* declares, because they love it.[223] "All pretense aside," Erasmus asserts, "ambitions, anger, and the desire for plunder are at the base of Christian wars. . . . The most criminal of all causes of war is, of course, the desire for power."[224] He also attacks the notion of necessity, of unwilling defense:

The excuses that are made to explain warfare are well known to me. They protest that their action is not the least voluntary. It is time they threw aside the mask and dropped their pretenses. If they examined their consciences, they would find that the real reasons are anger, ambition, and stupidity. If these constitute necessity, you ought to reevaluate them.[225]

Erasmus repeats his doubts over the just war in the popular *Paraphrase of Matthew* (1522).[226] His opposition to war, based on his thorough study of Scripture, only intensified over time.[227] In his colloquy *Charon* (1529) he mocks those friars and other clerics who preach the false doctrine of just wars:

> To the French they preach that God is on the French side: he who has God to
> protect him cannot be conquered! To the English and Spanish they declare this
> war is not the emperor's but God's: only let them show themselves valiant men
> and victory is certain! But if anyone *does* get killed, he doesn't perish utterly but
> flies straight up to heaven, armed just as he was.[228]

As early as 1518 Erasmus came under attack for his pacifism. He defended himself by asserting that he had never said that he absolutely rejected war, a claim he repeated in 1522.[229] In his letter to Francis I in 1523, Erasmus asserted that when he said that Christ had ordered Peter to put up his sword he never intended this prohibition to apply to the prince, but only to Peter as the cleric. Nevertheless, Erasmus adds, the sword mentioned by Paul in Romans 13 is to protect the public peace, and not for the prince's own ambitions.[230] He says in his commentary on Romans 13 that not all princes are ordained by God, although all authority ultimately derives from God with the consensus of the governed.[231] In the 1526 edition of *Against War,* Erasmus notes that a Christian doctor should never approve of war, but that he may be forced to "think it permissible, but with reluctance and sorrow."[232]

How are we to interpret these ambiguities and apparent contradictions? Erasmus complained more than once that he had been misinterpreted. In his *Letter to Paul Volz,*[233] the preface to the 1518 edition of the *Handbook of the Militant Christian,* he complains that:

> If anyone should deter men from the wars . . . he is marked out by the tricksters
> as if he holds with those who deny that Christians should wage any war. For we
> have made heretics out of the authors of this opinion because some pope seems
> to approve of war. He is not censured, however, who, contrary to the teaching
> of Christ and the Apostles, blows the trumpet to summon men to war for any and
> every cause.[234]

In the 1526 edition of *Against War* Erasmus complains of those "great doctors" who condemn opposition to war as heresy and then interpret the Scriptures to satisfy their own princes' lust for power.[235]

Perhaps the best explanation for this misunderstanding was Erasmus's tendency, shared by many of the Humanists, to examine war both in the abstract and in its real context. Thus while Erasmus might admit of the possibility of the just war in the ideal, just as More was willing to admit it in *Utopia,* in reality no war that he knew in history, in the present, or in the foreseeable future was just.[236] He thus ironically used the notion of the just war to condemn all wars, for while admitting its possibility in accord with the stringent requirements of the theory, he simultaneously rejected all of Europe's wars of the time as unjust. Like the Utopians, he could admit just war in the abstract, but remained a "determined and passionate" pacifist in the real world.[237]

## The Turkish Threat

One problem haunted Erasmus, as it did the other Humanist pacifists. The just-war restrictions of Christians fighting against Christians did not seem to apply in one case. This one case was Turkish aggression and the Christian response to it. It is key both for understanding Erasmus and for Catholic peacemaking in our world, which is faced with the real threat of aggression and oppression. It leads to the classic question posed to pacifists: "What would you have done about Adolf Hitler?"—a question again raised today in regard to other "evil empires." Erasmus asks many of the same questions we do and his analysis may provide us with some relevant answers.

In his *Letter to Anthony Bergen* (1514) Erasmus dealt with the issue of the Crusade against the Turks but reminded his reader that the apostles and the early church had always opposed war, even when faced with barbarian invasions.[238] When Leo X's bull calling for a Crusade against the Turks was promulgated (1516),[239] Erasmus commented that a war against Christian vice was certainly called for, but a Crusade against the Turks was dubious.[240] In letters to Thomas More and John Colet (1518) the Humanist mocked the preparations for the Crusade, denouncing it as a cynical ploy of papal power politics.[241] In his *Letter to Paul Volz* Erasmus notes the preparations in progress for a war against the Turks. Sarcastically commenting that at least a few Turks will survive the war, he goes on to remark that the disunity among Christian theologians and the ambitions, tyranny, debauchery, avarice, and lust of Christian rulers and people will dissuade even these Turks from converting, which should, after all, be the function of any Crusade. "And although . . . it will happen," Erasmus concludes, "that the pope or his cardinals perhaps may rule more widely, but not Christ, whose kingdom flourishes at last only if piety, charity, peace, and chastity thrive."[242] Erasmus suggests a pamphlet and propaganda campaign against the Turks coupled with the example of simple Christian virtues in an effort to convert them before Christians resort to arms.[243] The *Christian Prince*[244] and the *Complaint of Peace*[245] repeat the same message.

Even in the 1520s, when the Turkish threat was growing more real every day, Erasmus's position changed very little. In the third edition of *Erasmus Against War* (1523), after the fall of Belgrade and during the siege of Rhodes, and in the edition published the year of the Turkish victory at Mohacs (1526), Erasmus continued to insist that Christians follow the example of the primitive church in dealing with the barbarians. If Christians put away the Christian cross of nonviolence, they themselves become Turks.[246] Even if the Turks launch the first strike, Christian war against them must be waged "in the name of Christ, with Christian means and with Christ's own weapons."[247] Erasmus states what these weapons are:

> If we wish to conquer for Christ, let us gird on the sword of the word of the Gospel, let us put on the helmet of salvation and take the shield of faith, and the rest of the truly Apostolic panoply.[248]

Drawing a parallel to the unholy wars of Pope Julius II, he implies that plans for a Crusade are a farce and a pretext.[249] His *Paraphrase of Luke* (1523) repeats the call for martyrdom in the face of aggression.[250]

Nowhere are Erasmus's views on the Turkish war more clear than in his controversial *Most Timely Consultation on the War Against the Turks*,[251] a letter to John Rinck published in 1530.[252] The University of Paris had recently condemned pacifism as Lutheran.[253] Erasmus aims, therefore, to refute the Lutheran claim that the Turkish invasion is a divine punishment and a plot among Catholic leaders[254] and to agree with the general principle of the just war. He admits that the Turks are rapacious, tyrannical, impious, and degenerate[255] and scoffs at those, including the Lutherans, who would prefer life under the Turks to life under Christian tyrants.[256] A Christian war against the Turks, led by the emperor, who would be joined by the great princes of a united Europe, if inevitable and if waged in a strictly Christian way, with as little bloodshed as possible and with a true attempt to convert the Turks,[257] is acceptable to Erasmus. He asserts that he has never embraced total pacifism and, in fact, that such a charge against him is "so absurd that one hardly needs to refute it."[258] Toward the end of the treatise he addresses the question directly:

> Hereupon someone will accuse me, asking, "What are you getting at with this wordy sermon? Blurt it out, do you support fighting, or not?" If the Lord had spoken to me, I would announce it freely: but what I desire is dangerous to say now; it may be different in the future. . . . Nor do I advise against war, but I plead for my part that it be undertaken and waged auspiciously.[259]

From the *Handbook of the Militant Christian* through all the editions of *Against War*, waging Christian war auspiciously had meant only one thing to Erasmus: nonviolent struggle with the spiritual weapons named by Saint Paul. Rejecting Luther's call for passive nonresistance, Erasmus reminds his readers that Christians must resist evil.[260] Admitting the possibility of a just war, he also moves toward a theory of Christian nonviolent resistance to aggression.

Throughout the *Consultation* Erasmus repeats the themes that he stressed all his life: Christians must reform their own spiritual and political lives before embarking on any crusade to spread Christianity;[261] Christians should follow the example of the apostles so that their Christian lives will persuade the Turks to convert willingly; and the Christians' failure to behave as Christians will insure their defeat by the enemy.[262] By thinking they can lead a Christian life by slitting Turkish throats Christians mock Christ and degenerate into Turks themselves.[263]

Thus when an unquestioned evil threatens Christendom—the modern problem of Hitler—Erasmus focuses not on the evil outside but on the Turk within. Like More he might have said "the Turk is but a shadow" of our own capacity for tyranny, oppression, greed, and violence.[264] Certainly he acknowledged the evils of the Turks, but he emphasized just as strongly that if Christians do not live as Christians there will be no difference between them and Turks.[265] Just as the Israelites under the tyranny of the Egyptians and Babylonians, just as Lot in Sodom and Daniel in the lion's den, it is possible for Christians to retain their faith under oppression, without need for violent resistance.[266] Although he does try to silence his critics by this treatise and he does bend to the fanatical pressures of the times, Erasmus remains true to the message of peacemaking and emphasizes the issues of social justice, unity, and true peace. The example of Christ, the apostles, and the martyrs is more valid for him, even in his treatise against the Turks, than any crusade.

## CONCLUSIONS

The Renaissance Humanists stand between the popular peace movements of the Middle Ages and the modern intellectual analysis of the war-state. Colet, More, Vives, the

Paris Humanists, and Erasmus drew their strength from the simple reform piety of the late Middle Ages, the revived learning of Humanism, and their clear understanding of the Scriptures. They used their considerable literary talents and a command of the printing press to confront the power lusts and warmongering of Europe's rulers before a wide and receptive audience. Each combined in himself the best Catholic ideals of the times—vigorous and progressive learning placed in the service of justice and peace. Their words were not empty. Many paid for their prophecy with death, exile, or condemnation, and each left an enduring legacy for the world. This legacy is not only a historical treasure but also a challenge—to intellectuals to confront the issues of war and morality, to governments to fulfill their functions of service and peace, and to individuals to delve into their consciences and to answer for themselves whether war and injustice are truly compatible with the philosophy of Christ.

# CHAPTER 10

# MISSIONARY PEACEMAKING: THE STRUGGLE FOR PEACE AND JUSTICE IN THE NEW WORLD (1500–1800)

## INTRODUCTION

Every student of American history is familiar with the story of the Portuguese and Spanish voyages of discovery and conquest beginning in the fifteenth century and continuing into the colonial era.[1] The Castilians first reached the Canary Islands in 1344; in 1425 the Portuguese began their conquests there. The Portuguese arrived in the Azores by 1439 and soon established trading and missionary posts southward along the coast of Africa. Bartholomew Diaz was the first European to round the Cape of Good Hope (1488). In 1492 Columbus's voyage opened up a whole new world to the Spanish. On his voyage between 1497 and 1499, Vasco da Gama rounded the southern tip of Africa and brought Europe into contact with India and the Spice Islands. In 1521 Magellan's fleet reached the Philippines and the Spice Islands, only to find the Portuguese already there. Competition for new paths to the Orient soon changed into rivalry for possession of new lands.

Pope Eugenius IV (1431–1447) intervened in the Portuguese conquest of the Canaries and ordered that steps be taken for the spiritual and material instruction of the native converts. He also ordered a halt to all further conquest of pagan and Christian alike. By so doing he was drawing on a tradition of papal thought that went back to Innocent IV (1243–1254).[2] Nicholas V, in the bull *Romanus Pontifex* (1454), granted the Portuguese the right of the peaceful occupation of the West African coast in pursuit of peaceful conversion.[3] Finally in 1493, after Columbus's discoveries of a new western world, Alexander VI issued the three bulls known as *Inter caetera*. They were designed not so much to divide up the world politically between Spain and Portugal as to state principles for the peaceful conversion of the non-Christian peoples and to reiterate the papal duty to protect and convert these peoples. The bulls set a precedent for future church involvement in the non-European world.[4]

Catholic missions were sent everywhere in the Third World.[5] Catholic missionaries went wherever the Portuguese and Spanish traveled—to Africa,[6] Brazil,[7] India,[8] Indonesia and Indochina,[9] the Philippines,[10] Japan,[11] and China.[12] The efforts of the new Jesuit Order in these missions was especially noteworthy. We have only to think of Francis Xavier (1506–1552),[13] Robert de Nobili (1577–1656),[14] and Juan de Britto (1647–1693)[15] to recall the activity of the early missionaries. Their works were in the medieval tradition of nonviolent conversion. From the start the missionaries realized the need to learn the languages and cultures of the peoples with whom they were involved, to understand their religions, and to use all this as a basis for Christian practices and beliefs, as Boniface and Augustine of Canterbury had done long ago in converting Europe's barbarians,[16] and as a means of meeting the new peoples intellectually and winning them over to Christianity. These methods had already been embraced by Bacon, Lull, and the mendicant missionaries.[17]

In Canada the Jesuits adapted their mission to the culture and language of the native Americans.[18] Thoroughly educated in Christian doctrine, the Jesuits appreciated the elements of native religion that could be used to communicate the Christian message. Long before the Enlightenment, with its social message, these missionaries brought back to Europe careful descriptions of Indian culture. They formulated a theory of the relativism of European and other cultural forms, and argued in the best Humanist tradition for the nobility and equality of the Indians. The North American mission, they believed, offered the European the opportunity to view poverty and simplicity like that of the church's first, uncorrupted, age.[19]

The missions also offered the Jesuits the opportunity to imitate the virtues of the primitive church, to live in poverty and simplicity, to spread the gospels, and if necessary, to suffer martyrdom in imitation of Christ.[20] The first Jesuits arrived in Canada in 1632 and soon numbered fifty missionaries and lay assistants. In 1639 they were joined by the Ursuline Sisters who established a mission in Montreal.[21] The story of Jesuit efforts among the Hurons and other tribes has been told many times, as have the stories of Jesuit martyrdoms at the hands of the Iroquois.[22] The North American Martyrs—Jean de Brébeuf (1593–1649),[23] Antony Daniel (1600–1648),[24] Isaac Jogues (1607–1646),[25] René Goupil (c. 1607–1642) and John Lalande (d. 1646),[26] Gabriel Lalemant (1610–1649),[27] and Charles Garnier (1606–1649)[28]—are all part of the history of the region and are models of nonviolent activism.

## SPANISH AMERICA

The Spanish conquest of Central and South America is probably the most controversial topic in Latin American history[29] because it focuses the debate among conservatives, liberals, and Marxists on the Spanish role in the destruction of the region's pre-Columbian cultures and because of the role of the Catholic Church in this process. There is no need here to recount the story of the conquistadors. The Spanish society that effected the conquest was essentially medieval. The prime duty of Spain's rulers in the conquest was to spread Christendom in both its secular and spiritual arms; the methods sanctioned for the conquest, at least at the outset, were those of the Carolingians: expansion by the sword and the spirit of the Crusades.[30] The conquerors brought on the rapid extermination of the native population through war atrocities, the brutalities of slave labor, and the waves of epidemics. The quasifeudal *encomienda* aided the process of extermination by delegating to conquistadors royal rights to exact tribute and labor from the Indians in exchange for protecting and converting them to Christianity.[31]

It is unnecessary to debate the validity of the "Black Legend" of Spanish cruelty.

The figures speak for themselves. Between 1532 (when the indigenous population of the major Caribbean islands had already been nearly obliterated) and 1608 the Amerindian population under Spanish control had dropped from 16.87 million to 1.06 million.[32] The 120,000 Spanish who accomplished this also managed to obliterate the political, educational, social, cultural, and religious life of the pre-Columbian peoples and to leave them spiritually adrift and culturally and physically impoverished.[33] On this *tabula rasa* the conquistadors were fully content to impose a Christian domination in the worst tradition of Charlemagne and his successors.

If the spread of Spanish arms was identified with the expansion of Christendom, did contemporaries view the excesses of that process as a necessary price to pay for spreading the gospels? Did contemporaries perceive this conquest to be fundamentally Christian? Did the extermination of the Indians and the conquest of their lands have the blessing, or even the tacit consent, of the church? What measure of consciousness can we expect of the Spanish of that time, and what forms of Catholic peacemaking should we expect to find during the period? Given that the native population, superficially converted, was barely educated in Christian doctrine and ethics and that the Spanish population consisted mainly of conquistadors and their beneficiaries, what classes and groups of Catholic peacemakers can we expect to find in the New World?

Catholic peacemakers no longer had the dubious comfort of being a strong countercultural minority as under the Roman Empire, the vanguard of a new faith as during the barbarian invasions, or the guiding conscience of society as in the high Middle Ages. The church in early modern Europe was well on the way to becoming simply another department of state and was soon to become so officially under the Protestant Reformation in England, Gallicanism in France, and the *patronato* system in Spain and Portugal.[34] Given its status as an intrinsic, but now subordinate, part of society, how could the church even distinguish itself enough to raise a voice of protest? Finally, given the increasing absolutism of the Spanish crown and the ruthlessness of much of the colonial administration, what effects could nonviolence or individual voices of protest have against the violence and oppression of the conquest?

These questions are important, for in Latin America the problems raised by the conquest have still not been resolved: the disparity between ruling European elites and impoverished native populations, the resort to authoritarianism and force as a means of maintaining rule, and the alienation of vast numbers of the population from the mainstream of material and spiritual culture. Were the origins of these problems essentially linked to the role of the church or to the acquiescence of individual Christians, and did their solutions lie with Christian forms of action? In what follows we will address a few of these questions.

## A VOICE CRYING IN THE WILDERNESS

In 1510 the first three Dominicans arrived on the island of Hispaniola in the West Indies from Salamanca, led by Pedro de Córdoba.[35] In December 1511, on the Sunday before Christmas, one of the group, Antonio de Montesinos, rose before an audience of Spanish grandees and conquistadors to deliver a sermon on the text of John 1:23, "I am the voice of one crying in the wilderness." His congregation had expected to hear a comforting sermon on the season of Advent, on John the Baptist promising the coming of Christ. Instead they heard the voice of the prophet rising to condemn their barbarism and violence against the Indians, their brutality as landlords, and the evils of the *encomienda* system on which the entire economy of the colonies depended:

Tell me, Montesinos asked his startled audience, by what right or justice do you keep these Indians in such cruel and horrible servitude? . . . Why do you keep them so oppressed and weary, not giving them enough to eat, not taking care of them in their illness? For with the excessive work that you demand of them, they fall ill and die, or rather you kill them with your desire to extract and acquire gold every day. . . . Are these not men? Have they not rational souls? Are you not bound to love them as you love yourselves? Be certain that in such a state as this, you can no more be saved than the Moors or Turks.[36]

Montesinos condemned the economic oppression of the Indian and questioned the right of the Spanish to wage "a detestable war" against Indians living peacefully on their own lands.[37]

Shocked, the congregation stormed out of the church to lodge a complaint against the monk with his order and with the civil authorities. Yet both his superiors and the Spanish system of government under Isabella, Ferdinand, and Charles V allowed wide scope for dissent.[38] Montesinos was backed by his Dominican companions; Pedro de Córdoba commissioned him to sail for Spain to personally inform the king of the injustices being committed in the New World and to seek remedies. Ferdinand was stunned to hear Montesinos' accounts of the atrocities and injustices against the Indian population. He denied his own guilt in the matter[39] but ordered legal reforms of the *encomienda* system. Montesinos delayed the sailing of an expedition to the Caribbean in 1513 until further reforms urged by Pedro de Córdoba were enacted. Finally, in the Laws of Burgos (1513) the crown commanded humane treatment and the provision of food, health care, and shelter for the Indian population.[40]

Montesinos and the Dominicans in Hispaniola thus began the prophetic tradition of peace and justice in Latin America that continues to the present.[41] They were not alone in their protest. Forces had long been at work in Renaissance Spain that were to have a major impact on Spanish policy throughout the sixteenth century and that were to establish the tradition of protest in the missionary church. Two of the most important among these forces were the Humanism derived from Italian and Erasmian sources and the strong reform tradition of the Franciscan Order. They combined to produce a reform movement based on the imitation of Christ and the simple ideals of the early church. Erasmus's influence[42] was felt through his personal contacts with many Spanish Humanists, through editions of his works in Latin and Spanish translation, and through a circle of younger Spanish Humanists.

Both Erasmus[43] and Vives[44] condemned the Spanish conquest in the New World. This influence was strong in the Franciscan reformer, Humanist, university founder, and chief ecclesiastic of the realm, Cardinal Ximénez de Cisneros (1436–1517). Ximénez combined the ideals of the Spiritual Franciscans and the *Imitation of Christ* with the educational methods and scholarly approach of the Erasmian Humanists.[45] At the universities of Salamanca, Valladolid, and at the university he founded, Alcalá de Henares, Ximénez fostered the development of a highly educated, reform-oriented, and activist missionary clergy that was ready to bring the message of the gospels and the early church to the New World.

Thus a committed and powerful circle with great influence at the Spanish court was ready to lend Montesinos support. In 1510 Tomás de San Martin, a Franciscan, wrote his *Opinion on Whether the Property of Conquerors, Settlers, and Overlords Was Properly Acquired.*[46] He concluded that it was not. In 1512 *Of the Ocean Isles* by Juan Lopez de Palacios Rubios and *Concerning the Rule of the King of Spain over the Indies* by Matias de Paz both condemned the wars against the Indians, called the enslavement of the native populations illegal, and argued for restitution of their property and lands.[47] Charles V (Charles I of Spain) was crowned Holy Roman emperor in 1516. In him they saw a young Christian prince who had been made sensitive to his duties by Erasmus and the northern Humanists and who was conscious of the need to heed reformers' criticisms.[48]

## BARTOLOMÉ DE LAS CASAS AND THE THEOLOGY OF LIBERATION

Pedro de Córdoba went from Hispaniola to Venezuela, where he attempted to put the words of the Dominicans into deeds through nonviolent settlement and conversion. He was martyred soon after his arrival there in 1518.[49] Before he left Hispaniola, however, he planted the seeds of a fertile vine of social justice and peace. Once he had heard the confession of a young cleric who was living as an *encomendero* and exploiting the slave labor of his Indian clients. Citing the text from Ecclesiasticus (Sirach) 34:22, "A man murders his neighbor if he robs him of his livelihood, sheds blood if he withholds an employee's wages," Pedro had refused him absolution. This rich young man, Bartolomé de Las Casas, was to dwell on these words until they produced his conversion and the beginnings of a new Catholic theology of peace and justice.[50]

For his strong defense of Indian rights, his advocacy of peaceful conversion, and his role in the development of the "Black Legend" of Spanish cruelty in the conquest of America, Bartolomé de Las Casas is one of the most controversial figures in Latin American history.[51] His legacy in these fields is not unique, but Las Casas typifies the forms of peacemaking in his age, and in his life we can see woven many important strands of events and ideas in the early struggle for liberation in Latin America.

Las Casas was born in Seville in August 1474[52] and witnessed Columbus's return from his discovery of America. After taking part in a military expedition against the Morisco uprising (1497), he completed his university studies, and was ordained a priest. In April 1502 he arrived in Santo Domingo. He enjoyed the life of the colonial gentry as an *encomendero,* ignoring the spiritual care of the Indians charged to him. After several years, he returned to Europe and was scandalized by life in Rome under Julius II.[53] He then went to Cuba. There, in 1514, after reading the same text that Pedro de Córdoba had once quoted to him, he experienced a conversion, gave up his *encomienda,* and began speaking out against the Spaniards' exploitation of the Indians.[54] In 1515, with Pedro's support, he went to Spain to plead the Indians' cause to the crown.

In Spain Las Casas soon won the support of Cardinal Ximénez, of Cardinal Adrian of Utrecht (later Pope Adrian VI [1522–1523]), and of the Flemish reformers and Humanists in the court of Charles V.[55] At Las Casas' urging Cardinal Ximénez ordered the formation of a commission of Hieronymite friars to investigate the allegations and to take control of the colonies.[56] The Hieronymites gathered enough evidence of abuses to support the reform party and to win over Charles. Las Casas then added the treatise *The Indians Are Free Men and Must Be Treated as Such.* Its fourteen recommendations included the elimination of forced labor, the abolition of the *encomienda,* the replacement of conquest with peaceful settlement by farmers, and ecclesiastical protection of the native population. In addition it allowed for the provision of agricultural land, animals, health care, basic education, food supplies, and legal representation to the natives.[57] Las Casas suggested that black slaves be imported to replace Indian labor, but he eventually also repudiated this slavery "and for the same reasons."[58]

Charles was eventually persuaded to begin the Indians' emancipation and their establishment as self-sufficient farmers.[59] Ximénez named Las Casas as his delegate, called him "Protector of the Indians," and charged him with implementing the reforms in the New World.[60] Essential to Las Casas' plan was the establishment of a series of conversion centers on the South American mainland that would win over the native population by peaceful means, as he said, "because one friar is worth more than two hundred armed men."[61] His plan would import farmers and skills to the New World to introduce silk, spice, wine, wheat, and sugar production. Peaceful settlers would receive free passage, lands, animals, seeds, and tax abatements and would work alongside free Indians.[62] In September 1518 he won the king's approval for settlements in the Cumana of Venezuela. He had the privilege of making the announcement of Indian emancipation in the New World. In 1520 the experiment was begun, but opposition from colonial authorities and the armed intervention of conquistadors against the Indian population caused the downfall of the community by 1521.[63]

Las Casas' first attempt at peaceful conversion had been approved by the royal court but had failed in action. In 1522, he retired to a Dominican monastery. In the late 1520s Las Casas began work on his monumental *History of the Indies*, the story of the Spanish discovery, recounting the atrocities of the conquest. In the early 1530s he again became active, defending Indian rights and campaigning against the slave trade.[64] In 1535 and 1536 his antiwar activities in Nicaragua prevented its military conquest and resulted in a royal grant permitting Las Casas to attempt peaceful conversion in the area.

Las Casas maintained a clear ideological commitment to peaceful conversion as the aim of the Spanish settlement, a goal shared by his Dominican colleagues.[65] He wrote:

> The aim which Christ and the Pope seek and ought to seek in the Indies and which the Christian Kings of Castile should likewise strive for—is that the natives of those regions shall hear the faith preached in order that they may be saved. And the means to effect this end are not to rob, to scandalize, to capture or destroy them, or to lay waste their lands, for this would cause the infidels to abominate our faith.[66]

In this spirit he wrote *The Only Method of Attracting All People to the True Faith* (1537). The work describes the natural rights of all peoples and the goals and means of peaceful conversion based on the Bible, the Fathers, doctors, and papal pronouncements. It denounces war, pleads for Christian peace, and establishes the basis of modern Catholic missionary work on the same principles later affirmed by the Second Vatican Council.[67]

In response to Las Casas' words, on June 2, 1537, Pope Paul III, the same reform pope who had offered Erasmus the cardinal's hat, issued the bull *Sublimis Deus*, a document of fundamental importance in the Catholic struggle for justice. The pope condemned all theories that argued the inferiority of the Indians and forbade all attempts at violent conversion. All theories that seek to justify wars against non-Christian peoples on the basis of their alleged inferiority are only designed to ease their enslavement and exploitation, he wrote. Indians and other peoples are the full equals of Europeans and as such have full rights to the Christian faith and Christian education. Further, Indians

> are by no means to be deprived of their liberty or the possession of their property, even though they be outside the faith of Jesus Christ . . . nor should they be in any way enslaved; should the contrary happen, it shall be null and of no effect.

. . . The said Indians and other peoples shall be converted to the faith of Jesus
Christ by preaching the word of God and by example of good and holy living.[68]

The significance of the bull is enormous. In an instant Paul III had overturned two
notions, both legacies of the just-war tradition: the notion that Christianity was restricted
to the kingdoms of Europe; and a corollary, the notion that war is legitimate as a means
of converting the infidel. The bull established basic principles of Catholic action for the
future: the right of all peoples to liberty and economic justice, and the duty of the church
to further these.

Las Casas backed up his words by actions. In 1537 he obtained permission to establish a peaceful settlement in Guatemala's Tuzutlan province. The area had been so
impenetrable to Spanish attempts at armed conquest that it had earned the name *Tierra
del Guerra,* Land of War. Las Casas' proposal to convert it through nonviolence therefore brought the derision of the conquistador population of Central America. Yet the
Dominican soon proved himself both more idealistic and more intelligent than the military. He carefully prepared a delegation of merchants who penetrated the hinterland,
sought out the Indian leader, and whetted the natives' appetite for European goods and
their curiosity about the Christian religion. He was soon able to enter the province,
preach the gospels, and lead the Indians to accept conversion. The news of the mission
fell like a bombshell in military circles. By 1544 his success had earned him royal
support and the hatred of the colonial aristocracy. The region was renamed Tierra del
Vera Paz, Land of True Peace. Despite constant harassment by conquistadors, the region remained in peace until Las Casas departed for Spain.[69]

The last years of Las Casas' career were of great significance for the future of peacemaking in Latin America. In 1540 the Dominican returned to Spain to seek further
remedies against injustice in America. His lobbying efforts with Charles V resulted in
the promulgation of the New Laws (November 1542) for the reform of the colonial
government, the protection of Indian rights, and the eventual elimination of the *encomienda* system. We will return to the effects of these laws below. We should note now
that by the 1530s the crown already saw the dangers of the feudalization of the colonies
under the *encomienda* system, as conquistador families sought to create a hereditary
aristocracy that threatened royal power and exploited the native Americans. Charles V
therefore moved into alliance with the friars and other reformers, establishing the Council of the Indies in 1524 and a series of *audiencias,* or royal courts, throughout the
colonies.[70] Las Casas' efforts therefore fit well with royal policy.

Las Casas provided the king and his court with more than enough material on which
to base their decisions. His *Remedies for the Existing Evils* and *Very Brief Account of
the Destruction of the Indies* (1542 and 1543)[71] moved the Supreme Council of the
Indies to revoke the licenses of all expeditions of the conquistadors, at least temporarily;
in 1549 the Council openly questioned the justice of any war against the Indians.[72] In
1544 Las Casas was named bishop of Chiapas in southern Mexico. Thirteen other reformers where named to bishoprics in Spanish America. Shocked on his arrival in Mexico by the failure of the colonials to obey the New Laws, he forbade his priests to give
absolution to any *encomendero* and soon aroused such hatred among the ruling class
that he was expelled from the province.[73] In 1546 he returned from Spain with new
powers and at the first synod of bishops of Latin America won their approval of the
*Declaration of the Rights of the Indians.*

The *Declaration* is a major document in the struggle for liberation in Latin America. It states in part:

> All unbelievers, whatever their sect or religion and whatever their state of sin, by Natural and Divine Law and by the birthright of all peoples, properly possess and hold domain over the things they have acquired without detriment to others, and with equal right they are entitled to their principalities, realms, states, honors, jurisdictions, and dominions. War against unbelievers for the purpose of subjecting them to Christian control, and to compel them by this means to accept the Christian faith and religion, or to remove obstacles to this end that may exist, is reckless, unjust, perverse, and tyrannical. The sole and definitive reason of the Papacy for granting the supreme rule and imperial sovereignty of the Indies to the monarchs of Castile and Léon was to preach the Gospel, spread the Faith, and convert the inhabitants; it was not to make these monarchs richer princes or greater lords than they already were.[74]

The document recalls the words of Erasmus, Vives, and Paul III, and undercuts the entire economy of exploitation and the doctrine of the medieval crusade and just war.

Las Casas remained in Mexico working for reform for several years. When he sailed from Veracruz for Spain for the last time (1547), the elderly bishop had become the most hated man in the New World, among the military oligarchy at least.[75] He faced an even greater challenge in Spain. Since the late 1540s Juan Gines de Sepulveda, an opponent of Erasmus,[76] had been writing for both learned and popular audiences on the justness of the wars against the Indians. He based his theory on Aristotle's notion that some peoples, the barbarians, are naturally inferior and thus natural slaves of others.[77] The theory had not been applied in the Middle Ages, but Spain's conquests of the fifteenth century revived it.[78] Las Casas threw himself into the controversy. Finally at Valladolid, the royal capital, a series of debates was arranged between the two men before King Charles and a royal commission (1550–1551).

The Valladolid debates are a landmark in the history of human rights and of international law.[79] Several important theories and practical results emerged from the series of meetings. Las Casas turned Sepulveda's Aristotelianism on its head by using Aristotle to show many instances of the Indians' superiority over the Greeks and Romans. He modified his earlier opinion of Aristotle as "a gentile burning in hell,"[80] and went beyond the ancient philosopher to an empirical observation of the native Americans, thus developing the foundations for the Enlightenment theory of the "noble savage."[81] The judges gave no immediate decision,[82] but the winner was obvious. The crown forbade Sepulveda to publish his views either in Spain or in the colonies and showed Las Casas even more favor than before.[83] Charles V moved closer to Las Casas' policy of persuasion and nonviolent conversion and placed increasing restrictions on the military in the New World. The Supreme Council resisted a substantial bribe offered by the colonists to make the *encomienda* hereditary (1554–1555).[84]

Las Casas died in 1566. By then major changes had taken place in Spanish royal policy on human rights and the justness of wars of conquest in America. But the legacy of Las Casas was to prove more long lasting and widespread. He was to become a hero of the Protestant Reformation for his condemnations of Spanish despotism, a hero of the Enlightenment and of the age of revolution for his theories of the rights of all to liberty and self-determination.[85] He has been seen as a prophet of liberation theology[86] and of the spirit of the Second Vatican Council.[87]

## THE EFFECTS OF PEACEMAKING

Las Casas' works and words were neither isolated nor without effect. From the New Laws to the work of the reform bishops in Latin America, the spirit of peace, justice, and liberation lived on into the seventeenth and eighteenth centuries. The New Laws[88] effectively kept the *encomienda* system from being maintained in perpetuity by stipulating that the Indians granted to Spanish colonists must be freed and the *encomiendas* must revert to the crown after one generation. The New Laws also banned the Indian carrying duty, a service similar to that imposed on medieval serfs. The legislation provided for the good treatment, education, and health care of the Indians.[89] The enactment of the New Laws sparked protest all over the New World from the military aristocracy and even from many of the missionary friars. The viceroy and colonists of New Spain refused to comply and the New Laws spurred active revolt in Peru.[90] Although a major provision, the elimination of the *encomienda* (Law 35),[91] was later rescinded, the principles and general tendencies of the legislation had a fundamental and lasting effect on the activities of the conquistadors and on Indian rights.[92]

One of the most important results of the New Laws was the appointment by Charles V of fourteen reform-minded bishops, including Las Casas in Chiapas, to implement their provisions.[93] The bishops were almost all Dominicans from Salamanca, all committed to nonviolent action and basic human rights for the native population. In defying the military the bishops risked exile, prison, physical attack, and even death for the defense of the Indians, mestizos, peasants and workers, the poor and uneducated.[94]

One of the most important of these bishops was Antonio de Valdivieso, bishop of Nicaragua, who arrived at his see in 1544. He immediately began a campaign to expose abuses against the Indians and soon came in direct conflict with Governor Contreras, his own brother, who controlled one-third of the land in Nicaragua. Valdivieso's letters to the king show his increasing struggle for justice and his concern for his own safety, while his sermons continued to infuriate the conquistadors and the colonial administration. Finally, in February 1550, one of Francesco Pizarro's henchmen, on leave from Peru, entered the bishop's home and assassinated him.

Cristobal de Pedraza, bishop of Honduras from 1545 to 1583, defied the opposition of the conquistadors and ministered to the local tribes. He soon won over the Indians despite the soldiers' threats that they would kill them if they cooperated with the bishop. He was able to collect much testimony on Spanish abuses against the natives and brought this evidence into open accusations.

Pablo de Torres became bishop of Panama in 1547. He immediately clashed with the *encomenderos* over the enforcement of the New Laws, excommunicating those who refused to obey. His decisions were so radical that both the colonial governor and later the Supreme Council of the Indies nullified them. After his return to Spain in 1554 the bishop was accused of treason for his actions and forbidden to return to Central America.

When Juan del Valle was made bishop of Popayán in Colombia he was a professor of arts at Salamanca University. He arrived in Colombia in 1548 and immediately began exposing the atrocities committed against the Indians there and taking steps to protect them. In two church synods (1555 and 1558) he defined the theological basis for the liberation and defense of the Indians. He quickly earned the military's hatred and in 1559 was finally forced out of Cali and Popayán. When he reached the royal *audiencia* at Bogotá armed with evidence against the conquistadors, he was denied a hearing and decided to sail for Spain. There even the Supreme Council of the Indies received him coldly, so the bishop decided to travel to the Council of Trent, then in session, but he died in southern France on the way. Agustín de la Coruña, who arrived in Popayán in 1565 as del Valle's successor, took up the struggle. In 1570 colonial pressures on the king brought Coruña's suspension, but by 1575 the bishop was back at Popayán, "the only one who protests." Coruña's work became so effective against the conquistadors that a band of soldiers kidnapped him from the cathedral in 1582 and held him in Quito until 1587.

Luis Cancer de Barbastro, another Dominican, attempted to use Las Casas's nonviolent methods in Florida and was martyred near Tampa in 1549.[95] The Humanist playwright Cristobal de Llerena, a layman, was expelled from Santo Domingo around 1548 because of the Erasmian skits he wrote criticizing social abuses and injustices.[96]

The reformers' campaign continued to the end of the sixteenth century, but the effects lasted beyond the seventeenth century.[97] In 1573 King Philip II enacted the *Ordenanzas sobre Descubrimientos* (Ordinances on Discoveries). They became the models for enlightened legislation on human rights in the New World. Not only did they abolish the legal fiction of the *Requirimiento,* the declaration of just war against the Indians that underpinned the early conquests,[98] but they also required peaceful relations with the native peoples, their freedom from servitude and carrying services, and the abolition of all licenses to enslave the Indians.[99] The bishops continued their work as well. At the third episcopal council of Lima (Peru, 1582–1583), for example, Archbishop Toribio enacted far-reaching reform legislation for the education of the Indians in their own languages and for their protection from exploitation. At the council the assembled bishops reaffirmed their role as "protectors of the Indians." The decrees of the council were approved by Pope Sixtus V in 1588.[100]

The reform efforts extended to all parts of the Spanish empire. From the beginning of their mission to the Philippines the Franciscans had taken an active interest in the health, education, and economic well-being of the Filipino population, introducing new crops and skills to make the people self-sufficient. They waged a constant campaign to expose the abuses of the conquistadors and to oppose their exploitation of the Filipinos. Others joined in the struggle. In 1573 Diego de Herrara, an Augustinian, traveled to Spain to protest the soldiers' extortions, and in 1574 Martin de Rada, the leader of the Augustinian mission to the Philippines, denounced the Spanish conquest of the islands as unjust and condemned the oppression of the Filipinos.[101]

As a missionary in Mexico, Domingo de Salazar (b. 1513) was a strong defender of the Indians against Spanish oppression. In 1573 he received a royal commission to travel to Manila with orders freeing Filipinos enslaved by the conquistadors. Once there he worked for human rights and set the Spanish missions on a new footing by forbidding soldiers to accompany the expeditions. He thus made it clear that Christianity was not to be associated with force. Throughout the 1570s Spanish rights by conquest were openly debated in the Philippines.[102] In 1579 Philip II named Salazar bishop of Manila in recognition of his efforts. By the time of his death in 1594 Salazar had gone far toward establishing a permanent legacy of liberty in the Philippines. In 1591 Pope Gregory XIV ordered the emancipation of all Filipinio slaves and the restitution of all their goods and lands, illegally taken by the Spanish.[103]

## THE MENDICANTS IN MEXICO

Peacemaking in Latin America took several forms. Bartolomé de Las Casas and other reform bishops imitated the gospel life of nonviolence and promoted social justice through royally decreed institutional reform. However, the mendicant orders in Mexico—the Franciscans, Dominicans, and Augustinians—imitated the simplicity and poverty of the primitive church and emphasized direct involvement with native American communities. The friars' emphasis differed from order to order, but their methods and goals were essentially the same.[104] The mendicants combined an evangelical radicalism built on the imitation of Christ and the apostles with strains of Spanish Erasmian Humanism. They had the full support of the Spanish crown for their missionary efforts.[105] They went out barefoot and unarmed to meet the Indians and saw them as the ideal flock for the gospel message, a people uncorrupted by the decadence of the European society that More and Erasmus had so strongly condemned.[106] Although the friars generally accepted the feudal aspects of the *encomienda*,[107] they tried to protect the Indians from its violence, corruption, and exploitation and to fill the spiritual void left by the Spanish conquest as best they could:[108]

> To them America offered a larger and more challenging stage than Europe. The non-Christian peoples were not simply to be converted. They were to be civilized, taught, humanized, purified, and reformed. To the humanist friars America appeared as a Christian obligation writ large. Its vast populations were to be set on new paths of Christian virtue and godliness. The Erasmian Philosophia Christi was to be applied. Utopia was to be realized.[109]

As the Indians themselves explained, they loved the Franciscans,

> because they go about poor and barefoot, like us; because they eat the same food as we do; because they establish themselves among us; because they live peacefully with us.[110]

Two mendicant friars, Bartolomé de Olmedo and Juan Diaz, arrived with Cortés and prevented him from using violence to impose conversion on the Indians. Because of their influence the crown forbade Cortés to establish the *encomienda* and *repartimiento* systems, though apparently this made little difference.[111] The friars' thoughts about the conquest, however, stayed with Cortés and, after many years of debate, he sought forgiveness for his violence and injustice.[112]

In 1524 the first twelve Franciscan "apostles" arrived in Mexico and were greeted by a kneeling Cortés. In 1526 twelve Dominicans joined them, and in 1533 seven Augustinians. By 1559 there were nearly eight hundred friars in over a hundred and fifty houses throughout Mexico.[113] They were soon in conflict with the conquistadors and the *encomenderos* over questions of exploitation and violence. The work of the friars was prophetic, and it was also an attempt to fulfill the call of the Sermon on the Mount. The friars learned Nahuatl, the native Aztec language, and produced dictionaries, catechisms, confessionals, and sermons in that language.[114] They collected and recorded local customs, myths, and ways of life and thought in order to better understand the native Americans and to be able to demonstrate their intrinsic worth to the Europeans.[115] The friars assimilated Indian arts, festivals, music, and dance consciously into Christian liturgy and drama;[116] even after the Council of Trent insisted on a strict Roman liturgy for all Catholics, they retained Indian practices in paraliturgies.[117] They founded schools on every level from trade to university in an attempt to create an autonomous, self-sufficient population with its own leaders, who could deal effectively with the new conditions.[118] They founded hospitals both as places of healing and as asylums of Christian love and virtue in a world suddenly turned hostile to the Indian.[119] With rare exceptions their work was peaceful and promoted the nonviolent way of the gospels.

A few examples must illustrate these trends, although many could be cited. The Franciscan Pedro de Gante (Peter of Ghent), founded San Francesco College early in the sixteenth century as a missionary school for Franciscans and Dominicans. The college soon became an active center for an arts and crafts revival, instructing the natives in sculpture, painting, and singing.[120]

Toribio de Benavente clashed with Las Casas over methods of conversion and even advocated the *encomienda* and limited coercion,[121] but his Franciscan devotion to poverty and simplicity was a hallmark of his attitude to the Indians. When he learned that one of the most commonly heard Indian words, *motolinea,* meant "poor," he immediately changed his name to Motolinia and bore it proudly in his struggle against the cruelty and oppression of the conquistadors.[122] His *History of the Indians of New Spain* did much to preserve Indian history and culture and demonstrated the mendicants' full absorption into the life of the Indians.[123]

One of the best-known friars in Mexico is the Franciscan Juan de Zumárraga.[124] Educated in the Erasmian Humanist tradition, Zumárraga became the first bishop of Mexico (1528). After the Contador Rodrigo de Albornoz[125] approached Charles V in 1525 for permission to found a college to train an Indian leadership, Zumárraga established the College of Santa Cruz de Tlatelolco in Mexico City, as a center for rhetoric, logic, music, philosophy, and languages. Fully in the tradition of Erasmus and Ximénez, Zumárraga supported the translation of the Scriptures into the native languages. He considered the native population fully the equals of the Europeans. He also founded a school for Indian girls in Mexico City, established the first printing press on the American continent, and supported the writing and publishing of books for the Indian population.[126] Both his *Doctrina Breve* and *Doctrina Christiana* were prepared for Indians to use as introductions to Christian doctrine; they show the influence of Erasmus's spirituality.[127]

Zumárraga acted energetically to preserve Indian traditions, history, and rights. He supported and developed plans to establish home industries for the Indians in order to make them self-sufficient, commissioned books of instruction on silk production, and arranged for the means of production and transport—all in a conscious effort to prevent the Indians from becoming a passive proletariat.[128] He was the chief ecclesiastic organizer of opposition to the aristocrats' exploitation of the Indians and devoted much time to combating the *audiencias,* largely because of their confiscation of Indian lands. On the Indians' behalf he wrote to the king against both the courts and the royal governor, Nuño de Guzman.[129]

Zumárraga's letter to Charles V of August 27, 1529,[130] recounts his efforts to defend the Indians, despite assassination threats from the conquistadors. He actively sought out Indian testimony of mistreatment, exploitation, and injustice. In the face of the conquistadors' threats to kill anyone who testified to the bishop, many Indians bravely made their way to him secretly to provide evidence, which Zumárraga used to expose the military's "Diocletian cruelties" to the king. The soldiers' threats were not empty. They had even dared attack the bishop of Tlaxcala in his pulpit for speaking out for Indian rights. Nevertheless, Zumárraga accepted his duty to report abuses as a "cross and a martyrdom" and spared no effort to relate the truth.

Vasco de Quiroga, a judge of the second *Audiencia* in Mexico, was a close associate of Zumárraga and was later made bishop of Michoacán.[131] Quiroga had been influenced both by the evangelical ideal of the primitive church and by the Humanists. The bishop read Thomas More's *Utopia*[132] and set out to apply the Christian ideals of More's state to Mexico. He founded several Utopian communities for the Indian population that included collective farms, hospitals, asylums, public granaries and warehouses. Taking his cue from More's *Utopia,* from Christian monasticism, and from the Indians' own need for schedules of work, celebration, and religious observance, Quiroga established a week of labor mixed with exercise, recreation, and instruction in handicrafts. Having founded a native crafts industry, he then sought to create an interdependent regional economy, encouraging specialized trades—woodworking, shoemaking, the production of lacquer ware and the like—in various communities to guarantee commerce and communication between them.

Perhaps the most remarkable spokesperson for this movement was the Franciscan Geronimo de Mendieta (1525–1604), who combined a fervent patriotism for the Spanish imperial crown with a medieval Joachite interpretation of history. In his *Ecclesiastical History of the Indies* Mendieta viewed Mexican history from conquest of Cortés to his own time as an apocalyptic period, the Spanish kingdom as the Joachite millennial kingdom of the last days, its conquest of the Indians a liberation from the bondage of paganism, and the years of the conversion a golden age akin to the era of the early church.[133] Mendieta supported the conquest and certain aspects of the *encomienda* system, but his historical and missionary work contained elements of a fresh and forward-looking analysis of the relation between Christianity and the indigenous culture of America.

In the face of centuries of European history and Spanish theory that equated the political realm with the Christian republic, Mendieta stressed that the hispanization of America was not equivalent to its christianization and that, in fact, the two processes were opposites. Turning the native Americans into grotesque mimics of their conquerors, he wrote, destroys the possibility of making them true Christians. Anticipating modern cultural anthropology, Mendieta noted the destructive impact of Spanish culture and customs on the Indians, the cultural shock and demoralization that followed the conquest, and the destruction of all positive native cultural and social structures.[134] Converting the native Americans to a Christianity freed from its Hispanic overlays was more than enough for the missions to accomplish. The native Americans, in fact, already possessed most of the virtues stressed by Christ in the Sermon on the Mount: meekness, gentleness, purity of heart, humility, obedience, patience, and simplicity of life. These virtues made them pure humans and children of God both in their simplicity, which is needed to attain heaven, and in their need for the friars to instruct and protect them from European decadence.[135]

To accomplish this process of conversion and purification Mendieta envisioned an Indian commonwealth organized, like Utopia, on the model of the monastery. He saw no need for Indian ordination because of the natives' almost direct access to grace, but he defended the College of Tlatelolco, advocated the establishment of the Indians' own courts to handle all but the rarest violent crimes,[136] and denounced the labor services imposed on the Indians under the *repartimiento* system of Philip II's reign, which had replaced the *encomienda* under the New Laws.[137] A product of his still-feudal age, Mendieta opposed the *repartimiento* not because of the patron-client relationship that it established over the Indians (which he believed helped the Franciscans to better serve and save them), but because of the economic exploitation that it allowed under the guise of just sovereignty.[138] He wrote to Philip II:

> The purpose of the sovereignty that Your Majesty has over the Indians is to endeavor by every means to have the Christian law preached and taught with such gentleness that the Indians may be invited and persuaded to embrace it voluntarily. To teach Christianity only by words and to commit contrary actions obviously will give the Indians occasion to abhor it, not to embrace it.[139]

Mendieta called for the peaceful conversion of the Indians. Countering Sepulveda's Aristotelianism, he argued that the pagan philosopher had no relevance in the Christian age in which no differences existed between Gentile and Jew, free and slave.[140] Far from subjecting them to the Spaniards, the conversion of the Indians had guaranteed their human and religious freedom,[141] the natural right of their "evangelical liberty."[142] Theories such as Mendieta's often opened the way to abuse by substituting the clergy for the Indians' secular masters, but his notion of the freedom of the Christian and the need to create a new form of Christianity independent of the structures of Spanish culture helped pave the way for a genuine theology of liberation. Mendieta's Utopia was to be a fiction in New Spain, but his belief in the equality of the Indian laid the foundation for future Catholic peacemakers and anticipated the efforts of others, including the Jesuits in South America.

We have examined the social teachings of the first two generations of missionaries in the New World in some detail here because they provide concrete evidence of the groups involved in active peacemaking and because they show that the essential gospel connection between peace and social justice was not lost in the age of discovery. We do not intend, however, to trace the entire history of the missions in America and elsewhere around the world. We will instead focus on a few individuals and trends in the colonial history of Latin America that will help us draw some conclusions on the forms of peacemaking that emerged in the New World and on the strengths and limitations of these forms.

## THE PROMISE OF MISSIONARY PEACEMAKING

By the seventeenth century the legacy of the first two generations of missionary peacemakers had been permanently fixed in the consciousness of Latin Americans. An entire popular literature of "saints of action"[143] had developed combining official hagiography with stories of adventure in the wilds by heroic missionaries and martyrs. Many of these adventurers rivaled the conquistadors in the popular imagination and were venerated side by side with the social reformers and prophets of the New World. Among these we can mention only a few. They include the Franciscans and Jesuits who penetrated California and the American Southwest;[144] Louis Bertrand or Luis Betran (1526–1581), who traveled throughout Peru, Colombia, and the Lesser Antilles converting thousands to Christianity and defending them against the exploitation of the conquistadors;[145] Felipe de Jesus, who left Mexico for a life of adventure in Asia preaching the gospels;[146] and Francisco Falcon and Polo de Ondegardo, who wrote and spoke in defense of Indian rights.[147] Francisco Solano (1549–1610) worked extensively among the Indians, learned their languages and customs, and converted many in northern Argentina to peace. He set Lima (Peru) into a panic in 1604 when he preached against Spanish corruption until he was silenced by the civil authorities.[148] Alfonso de Sandoval and Peter Claver[149] were Jesuits whose work among the black slaves in Cartagena (Colombia) has become legendary.

The Jesuits came to Latin America after the mendicants;[150] their members were soon distinquished as peacemakers. They were activists in the tradition of Padre Angulo, Diego de Torres, and Ruiz de Montoya, who spoke out against the *encomienda* and managed to win royal emancipation of enslaved Indians;[151] they were settlers of Paraguay (we will discuss this below); and they were Humanists of the Jesuit tradition, who in the eighteenth century provided a bridge between the ideals of the first generations of missionary peacemakers and the world of the Enlightenment and of revolution.[152]

The Jesuit Humanists blended the social and political ideals of the Philosopher with the older tradition of Christian Humanism to attack political and economic abuses, racism, the caste system, and the educational discrimination of the Latin America of their time. Like their mendicant predecessors, the Jesuits composed treatises on Indian culture and history, languages, and social organization to demonstrate the Indians' high cultural achievements and their right to equal treatment. Given the autocratic mood of the times, however, the Jesuits did all this from a safe distance, in self-imposed exile in Europe. Their numbers included Francisco Xavier Clavijero (1731–1787),[153] Andres Cavo (1739–1802), Andres de Guevera y Basoazabal (1748–1801), Francesco Xavier Alegre (1729–1788),[154] and Pedro Jose Marquez (1741–1820).[155]

Xavier Alegre's *Theological Institutions* and *Memoires for the History of the Jesuits in New Spain* developed a Christian theory of popular sovereignty that based society on a social contract and defied the claims of contemporary absolutism. He condemned the Spanish conquest as unjust and called its violence in the name of Christianity a cruel and needless mistake, the slave trade a disgrace to life, and Bishop Quiroga's Utopian experiments in Mexico[156] a precedent that should have been continued.[157] Jose Marquez's Christian philosophy reached to the roots of the Humanist tradition to announce the full equality of all races and cultures.[158]

## THE LIMITATIONS OF PEACEMAKING IN LATIN AMERICA

The missionaries who brought Christianity to the New World embraced peace and simplicity as the highest virtues, fought the violence and exploitation of the conquistadors, and did much to preserve the culture and independence of the native Americans; yet they did this in the context of medieval Christendom. Geronimo de Mendieta understood the dangers of hispanization, yet most of his contemporaries were men of their times and accepted the link between political domination and religious belief. Their notion of Christianity was bound to the notion of Christendom as a political unit, not the spiritual kingdom of the Mystical Body. While we cannot blame them for this, we can note that they often ignored the real nature of Amerindian religion—its "ethico-mythical nucleus"[159]—and the spiritual needs of their missionary audience. Misunderstanding the nature of the indigenous religion and exaggerating its similarities to Christian doctrines and practices, they often failed to confront its key elements and to win the hearts of the Indians to true Christian ethics or belief.[160] Besides this, they accepted the hierarchical worldview of their times, its monarchism and its class structure. The radical evangelism of the mendicants often challenged the foundations of wealth, power, and violence, but it rarely advocated social revolution. Not even Erasmus's radical Christian piety could condone this. Thus while the aims of the first two generations of missionaries matched the Humanist and reform ideals of the court of Charles V, the world of the Counter Reformation and the age of absolutism had a drastic effect on the nature of the Christian message in Latin America.

We cannot possibly examine here the nature and progress of these changes.[161] We can note, however, that by the reign of Philip II changes were already in progress that would put the friars and the Jesuits outside the circles of power and make their work all the more difficult. In 1550, for example, Philip II ordered the hispanization of the native Americans; their instruction was to be in Spanish.[162] In 1555 the Council of Mexico denied ordination to anyone of "Moorish," that is, mestizo background.[163] Following the Counter-Reformation reforms of the Council of Trent, qualifications for ordination and prescriptions for liturgy became stricter; orthodoxy in belief and practice were enforced even more tightly by the Inquisition;[164] and although the Council of Lima (1585) declared that race was not a prerequisite for ordination, no Indians and few mestizos were judged equal to Trent's high moral standards. It was not until 1774, after these restrictions had been removed by the Third Council of Lima (1772) that the first three Indian priests were ordained in Peru.[165]

Thus during the seventeenth and eighteenth centuries the gulf widened between the culture of a small elite, the descendants of the conquistadors and *encomenderos,* and the culture of the native population, whose education in both secular knowledge and Christian wisdom matched the poverty of their material conditions.[166] This background should be kept in mind in analyzing the success or failure of peacemaking and nonviolent change in Latin America. The failure of the missions to penetrate to the core of the native soul and to create a truly educated Christian class among the majority of the people held grave consequences for the future and contain lessons for us today.

The failure of the missionary pacifists to create a broad-based and lasting legacy of peace and justice was due as much to their attempt to bring reform from the top down as to the lack of a Christian mass movement among the native population. A movement that could have understood and implemented this message had been impossible under the conditions of the barbarian invasions and the Carolingian period and became the hallmark of the era of the Crusades only after long centuries of Christian education. In the same way peacemaking on a mass scale in Latin America has had to await the education of a Christian population. The reason for its failure to develop in Latin America until relatively recently lies not with the native peoples, then, but with the outlook of the missionaries and their political world.

One example will help illustrate this point. Between 1606 and 1767 the Jesuits succeeded in establishing a social utopia in the jungles of Paraguay similar in many ways to that begun by Quiroga and dreamed of by Mendieta in Mexico.[167] In the early sixteenth century the Society managed to obtain royal grants to evangelize the Guarani and other tribes by bringing them together into dozens of self-sufficient communities. They were instructed in the Catholic religion, given health care, education, and housing, taught arts, crafts, and agricultural skills. They were set up under the administration of the Jesuit missionaries to conduct trade and they lived a peaceful life protected from slavery and economic exploitation. By 1767 it is estimated that 150,000 Indians lived this settled, Christian life in 38 *reducciones,* as the communities were called.

Yet there were profound obstacles in the way of this experiment. In 1629 the first large-scale raid by the *Memelucos,* Portuguese slave traders from the São Paulo coast, carried away 15,000 Indians.[168] Despite efforts by the Jesuits to seek them out in Brazil and return them to freedom, the raids continued, and Indians began to abandon the settlements. In desperation the Jesuits asked the royal viceroy in Lima for permission to arm the villagers and after a series of battles finally were able to protect their Utopia.[169] Although the Jesuits had trained the Indians to form militias and to defend themselves, following the paternalistic and elitist theories of the age they did not allow an Indian leadership or an Indian population sophisticated in Christian principles of action to develop. Thus when the Jesuit Order was dissolved and the Jesuits were expelled from South America in 1767, their republic dissolved overnight as others grabbed the land and the Indian populations melted away.[170]

## CONCLUSIONS

The Jesuit Republic provides an admirable model of Christian organization of one type, but it cannot really be considered an example of Christian peacemaking. Its peace was that of the gun, and its justice that of paternalism. Our point, however, is not to pass judgment on the past but to show the limitations of true Christian peacemaking in the age and under its conditions of cultural alienation and caste division. We cannot demand from such social experiments what they were not intended to produce, but we can learn from them about the future of nonviolent action.

We have answered positively many of the questions posed above. The official church policy declared by councils, popes, bishops, missionaries, intellectuals, and, at times, enlightened Catholic rulers actively and continuously condemned the conquest of Latin America and the conquistadors' exploitation of the Amerindians. Catholic teaching also sought to protect, educate, and liberate the Indians as equals and Christians.

Yet for the hopes of a Las Casas, a Zumárraga, or a Quiroga to succeed, influence in high places, the conviction of the elite, and enlightened leadership over the masses were not enough. To succeed nonviolent action must be broad-based, it must build on a foundation of education for leadership and ethical action that touches the people whom this action will affect, and the people must be trusted to know and to act on the convictions of their hearts and their consciences. This was the hope of Erasmus, the belief of Las Casas, and the promise of the theology of liberation.

# CHAPTER 11

# THE EBB TIDE OF CATHOLIC PEACEMAKING (1550–1850)

## INTRODUCTION: THE AGE OF ABSOLUTISM

The Middle Ages and the Renaissance were periods of vigorous and often truly popular peace movements among Catholics.[1] Between the Council of Trent (1545–1563) and the First Vatican Council (1869–1870), however, gospel peacemaking in the Catholic tradition diminished. Both church and state during this time put strong obstacles in the way of Catholic peacemakers: the rise of absolutism, the Counter Reformation, and a decline in the religious life and spiritual care of many Catholics.[2] To examine the forms of Catholic peacemaking during these years, we must examine the avenues that were open for dissent and for the pursuit of the gospel ideals of peace and justice. These include Humanist pacifism, the emphasis on individual conscience that sometimes led to theories of conscientious objection, and the growing Catholic tradition of international law and peaceful world order.

Early modern Europe was the age of kings and autocrats.[3] Between the Protestant Reformation and the French Revolution, the political tendencies condemned by More, Colet, Erasmus, and Vives[4] had grown to maturity: autocracy, the relentless pursuit of centralized power and external expansion, the militarization of society, and the pursuit of war on an unparalleled scale sharply divided the ways of medieval Christendom from those of the modern nation-state. Despotic control over all the organs of political life were matched in both Protestant and Catholic countries by an ever-tightening control over the religious life of individuals. The Peace of Westphalia (1648), ending the Thirty Years War, turned the motto of the political reformation, *cujus regio, eius religio* (whose territory, his religion), from a formula for international toleration to a license for princes to control the spiritual life of their subjects.[5]

In Catholic countries this control worked internally, co-opting all efforts of reform into agencies of state control, as in Richelieu's France,[6] the Hapsburg empire of Maria Theresa, Joseph II, and Leopold of Tuscany, and the Spain and Portugal of the Inquisition. It also effectively isolated the national churches from papal control and thus from any sense of unity as Christendom or the Mystical Body. In Spain and Portugal, for example, the *patronatus* system gave Iberian monarchs full control over their subjects' relations with Rome;[7] in France Gallicanism precluded papal interference with royal control of the episcopacy and with its internal regulation of spiritual matters.[8] Theoretically and effectively charged with the direction of their churches, the new autocrats paralleled full political control with suppression of opposition or dissent in the areas of religious practice and discipline.[9] Thus religious zeal increasingly became an object of scorn among the intellectuals of the Enlightenment, and popular sentiment for justice and peace were suspect and tightly controlled by political structures until the end of the ancien régime.

It would be a mistake to portray the Counter Reformation solely as a reaction to Luther and Protestantism. The Council of Trent had several major effects on Catholic life and infused the church with a spirit of reform.[10] Yet the Council also embraced a narrowness of doctrinal definition unknown in the Middle Ages.[11] Doctrinal dissent among intellectuals was tightly regulated by the Inquisition (revived in 1542), by episcopal controls, and by strict censorship through the *Index of Prohibited Books.*[12] Trent also imposed control over the spiritual lives of individual Catholics unheard of in the Middle Ages. Trent prescribed proper education and religious instruction for Catholics, but it left no room for the participation of the laity in the activities of the church and gave bishops the power to stamp out any signs of deviation or dissent, any "challenge to orthodoxy or uniformity."[13] In this "state of siege" mentality, the Counter Reformation church established itself as highly centralized, rigoristic, and authoritarian.[14]

One tragic result of this defensive stance was the condemnation of any work that seemed to encourage the Protestants or was tainted by their "heresy." Thus much of the Humanist program for reform, including Humanist writings on peace, became suspect even during the lifetimes of these writers.[15] Erasmus's works were put on the Index in 1559, only a few years after he had been offered the cardinal's hat. The Protestant Reformation spread and the traditional Protestant peace churches—the Anabaptists, the Mennonites, and later the Quakers[16]—gained influence, but the position of Catholic pacifists became increasingly untenable. During Erasmus's lifetime comparisons were already being drawn between the Protestant peace churches and the heretical groups of the Middle Ages—Cathars, Waldensians, and others who had advocated nonviolence. Quickly forgotten were the orthodox Humiliati, Poor Catholics, and mendicants who had preached peace.[17] Like the brand "communist" in the 1950s, it was enough for a dissenter to be labeled "Waldensian" or, after Luther's condemnation, "Lutheran."[18] One might speculate that many Catholic pacifists were forced into the Protestant peace churches during this period, thus leaving orthodox Catholicism even more rigidly militarist.

Once the impetus of Trent had passed, the hierarchy showed signs of increasing absolutism and isolation from the social and political concerns that had marked the great epoch of the medieval church. Although several brilliant and reform-minded popes reigned during the Counter Reformation,[19] the partisan tone of the era of religious wars, culminating in the atrocities of the Thirty Years War (1618–1648), compromised the religious leadership of Rome and cast it into international isolation. By the time of the Peace of Westphalia (1648) the pope's influence for reconciliation and peace was at an all-time low.[20] By the eighteenth century the pope had become little more than a puppet of the Hapsburgs and then of the Bourbons. These rulers took pains to secure the election to Peter's throne of compliant and mediocre personalities lacking moral leadership and religious zeal.[21] During the first half of the nineteenth century, therefore, the papacy was firmly on the side of authoritarianism and favored the repression of popular aspirations throughout Catholic Europe.[22] In 1864 Pius IX's *Syllabus of Errors* condemned most of the liberal and democratic tendencies of the nineteenth century.[23] The pronouncement of the doctrine of papal infallibility at the First Vatican Council (1869–

1870) marked the final defeat of liberal Catholicism and summarized the autocratic tendencies that had been in place since Trent.[24]

The episcopacy, once a champion of popular aspirations for peace and justice, also mirrored the autocracy of the age. Especially in France,[25] and to a lesser degree in Italy,[26] Spain,[27] and Portugal,[28] the bishops were aristocratic, alienated from the people, and identified with the interests and values of their autocratic governments, the last a trait they shared with their Protestant counterparts. The lower clergy, though they gradually became better educated through the new diocesan seminaries, were overworked, underpayed, and often frustrated in their attempts to stem the falling religious level of their communities.[29] Under attack from both Humanists and Reformers, who shared the conviction of the age that "monasticism is not holiness,"[30] the monks lost the respect of the European people as they lapsed into secular pursuits and easy living divorced from the ancient and medieval ideals of social protest and peacemaking.[31]

The effects of these changes on popular spirituality[32] were dramatic. The old Third Orders and confraternities, which had been powerful tools for nonviolent peacemaking all over Europe, began to decline in appeal and effect, especially toward the end of the period.[33] At the same time popular spirituality fell under the control of the church hierarchy and was directed away from external demonstration, processions, and marches[34] and toward internal and sacramental devotions, including devotions to the rosary, the Sacred Heart, and the Stations of the Cross.[35] The devout Catholic laity found itself shut off from concerns of justice and active peacemaking and directed to the "inner" peace of Carolingian monasticism.

With few channels for either dissent or for positive acts of peacemaking, Catholic spirituality became increasingly passive and internal,[36] trends typified by the popularity in the seventeenth and eighteenth centuries of Jansenism and Quietism, both of which stressed inner peace and frowned on religious activism. By the eighteenth century, therefore, rigidity, implacable suppression of dissent, inflexible control over popular devotion, the failure to produce a truly educated Christian populace, and skepticism among Europe's ruling elite combined to have a devastating effect on the religious life of the people. As much as fifty percent of the population of many regions experienced "dechristianization."[37]

Many of these trends had also been characteristic of the Middle Ages,[38] but conditions in early modern Europe were starkly different. The medieval church had always stood as a bulwark of opposition to the claims of the state, as a real alternative to the secular arm for the affections and loyalties of the people. In the wake of the Reformation and religious wars all opposition to the state collapsed, leaving the laity at the mercy of the prince. Medieval secular and religious leadership shared a common devotion to the ideals of the gospels that allowed dissent and appeals to Christian conscience, but the early modern state effectively closed off this channel of dissent. Thus by the eighteenth century the spiritual void left by the collapse of popular religion opened the way to the complete supremacy of the state and the religion of nationalism. Nowhere was this impact on the life of the people more striking than in the replacement of Christian values by those of forced militarism:

> Obligatory military service broke entirely the Christian traditions of the young man. The eighteenth century army represented a rejection of Christian morality; rape, bloodshed, blasphemous utterances, a masculinity defined by holding one's drink and laying the girls.[39]

The antimilitarism of a Jean-Baptiste Vianney (1786–1859) reflected the pacifist revolt of many medieval saints,[40] but little in the popular imagination or in church and political structures existed to support or to idealize such dissent. The saint's contemporary and subsequent fame rested rather on the ideals of the Counter Reformation—skills as a country parson of unusual spiritual zeal, as a confessor and spiritual guide—and not in his opposition to war.

## FORMS OF CATHOLIC PEACEMAKING: THE FRENCH INTELLECTUAL TRADITION

Catholic peacemaking took many of the forms of the Carolingian age: literary pleas for peace and plans for world order formulated by the intellectual elite and intended to be imposed by Europe's rulers. Thus as time passed the approach of the Humanists, who aimed to bring about real change, appealed only to the cultured elite among whom the Christian passion of an Erasmus soon cooled to the Stoic detachment of a Montaigne. The transformation was a gradual one, and the basic appeal to the gospel message of love and peace never died out completely. The spread of printing and the growth of the literate class, in fact, helped promulgate the original message of the Humanists, which became part of the standard education of the elite into the twentieth century. It is significant to note, however, that the works of most of the French Humanists discussed below were listed on the Index until its abolition by Paul VI in 1965.[41]

### RABELAIS

The influence of Erasmus in the period immediately following his death was strong, even in Spain[42] and in France.[43] In the sixteenth century five works on peace appeared in France alone paraphrasing Erasmus's *On War* and *Complaint of Peace.*[44] Perhaps the best known of the French Erasmians was François Rabelais, whose *Gargantua and Pantagruel*[45] is a masterpiece of satire in the best tradition of the *Praise of Folly.* His attacks on the warrior and the just-war tradition are worthy of comparison to *Julius Exclusus* or the *Colloquies.*[46] Born near Chinon sometime around 1490 of a professional family, Rabelais entered the Franciscans but was soon drawn to the Humanist circle and began corresponding with Erasmus. He eventually earned a doctorate in medicine and became the personal physician of Cardinal Du Bellay and a personal counselor to Francis I.[47] *Pantagruel* (1532 or 1533) and *Gargantua* (1535) were immediately popular. The novel saw several editions; all its five books were finally published (1564) after Rabelais's death (1553).[48]

Rabelais's satire is broad, often heavy-handed, and earthy; but his appeals for peace and Christian conduct permeate the work as a whole and ennoble the words of his chief characters, Gargantua, his father Grandgousier, and his son Pantagruel. Book I[49] relates the folly of an invasion launched against Grandgousier's kingdom by his neighbor Picrochole. Caused by a quarrel over a few cakes,[50] the war satirizes the flimsy just-war excuses used by Europe's kings. Though absurd, the war is led by corrupt clergy and evil counselors who feed the king's mad lust for conquest by comparing him to Alexander the Great and Augustus.[51] It causes great destruction, particularly among the common people. Like a true Christian prince, however, Grandgousier takes every measure to prevent war, even to the return of the cakes,[52] not from cowardice but from a sense of humanity.[53] His ambassador tells Picrochole:

What fury is it, then, that stirs you now to break all alliances, tread all friendship underfoot, transgress all right, and make hostile incursions on these lands, without having been in any way injured, annoyed, or provoked by him or his? Where is faith? Where is law? Where is reason? Where is humanity? Where is fear of God? Do you think that these wrongs are concealed from the external spirits and from Almighty God, who is the just rewarder of all our undertakings?[54]

Gargantua's comically absurd rescue of his father's realm does not diminish the seriousness of Rabelais's points about war, reconciliation of enemies, and good government.[55] Grandgousier tells his noble prisoner Touchspigot:

He who grasps at too much grips almost nothing. The time is past for the conquering of kingdoms, to the hurt of his Christian neighbor and brother. This emulation of the ancient Herculeses, Alexanders, Hannibals, Scipios, Caesars, and such like, is contrary to Gospel teaching, by which we are enjoined each to guard, protect, rule, and administer his own lands and territories, and not to make hostile attacks on those of others. What the Saracens and Barbarians of old called deeds of prowess we now call robbery and wickedness.[56]

Book II satirizes More's Utopian just conquests and, one must suppose, the real Spanish conquests in the New World. Pantagruel, Gargantua's son, leaves on a mission of mercy and defeats the Dispodes amid scenes of absurdly heroic adventure.[57] Pantagruel then sets out, on More's best advice, to colonize the country of the Dispodes with Utopian citizens. Despite the satiric tone, Rabelais's comments are sober and earnest:

So here, my dear boozers, please take note, that the way of preserving and retaining newly conquered countries is not—as has been the erroneous opinion of certain tyrannical spirits, to their own hurt and dishonor—to pillage, distress, torment, ruin, and persecute the people, ruling them with a rod of iron; in fact to devour and consume them.[58]

Pantagruel's methods, Rabelais notes, are in stark contrast to Charlemagne's brutal mass resettlements of Saxons and Flemings, which ended in total failure.[59]

Book III offers a remarkably modern observation on the link between sexual aggression and the destructive capabilities unleashed in war. Panurge's brief philosophical treatise[60] on the proposition "For the codpiece is the first piece of harness in the arming of a warrior"[61] highlights the absurdity of the soldier but contains a grim reminder of the true nature of war and military glory.

## MONTAIGNE

As the French Renaissance approached the Enlightenment, much of the religious fervor apparent in Erasmus and Rabelais faded into the background. Thus while Michel de Montaigne "presents a chastened restatement of Erasmus's Renaissance humanism, stripped of all its bright optimism and Christian idealism,"[62] he carries on the Erasmian tradition of peace literature.[63] Although their sober tone and classical inspiration owe more to Aristotle, Plato, and the Stoics than to the gospels, Montaigne's *Essays* retain much of the Christian teaching on war and peace.

Born in 1533, Montaigne received an excellent Humanist education and saw distinguished public service as a judge, mayor of Bordeaux, military commander, mediator between the rival factions in the French wars of religion, and adviser to Henry IV.[64] Tired of war and harassed by both sides for his tolerance of religious differences,[65] Montaigne retired to his family estate where he began writing and publishing his *Essays* in 1571.[66] He died in 1592.

Montaigne wrote so often of the valor of the ancient Romans and Greeks, of the need for prudence and honesty on the battlefield,[67] and of soldiering as a matter of honor[68] that his place in a history of Catholic peacemaking would be hard to justify were it not for his most famous essay, the *Defense of Raymond Sebond,*[69] written between 1575 and 1580. The treatise is a lengthy defense of faith and good works, of conscience and the ethical life, of simple Christian spirituality and humility, even of religious skepticism as opposed to reason. Montaigne writes of many topics, using classical authors to bolster the truths of Christian revelation.

Many of Montaigne's arguments on war and peace are familiar to readers of Erasmus; the animal ferocity of men, which exceeds even that of the beasts,[70] the absurdity of the great wars and the blood lust and lechery of the heroes of the past,[71] the condemnation of the just war as merely "an ornament and a covering" for greed, the misuses of religion as an excuse for its exact opposite,[72] and the absurdity of wars of religion and compulsion against heretics and dissenters.[73] Montaigne's condemnations of war match those of Erasmus in their passion and commitment:

> As for war, which is the greatest and most pompous of human actions, I should be glad to know whether we want to use it as an argument for some preeminence, or, on the contrary, as testimony of our imbecillity and imperfection. . . . This frightful array of so many thousands of armed men, so much fury, ardor, and courage—it is comical to consider by what inane causes it is stirred up and by what trivial causes extinguished.[74]

The motives of individual soldiers are no better:

> Let us confess the truth: if anyone should sift out of the army, even the average loyalist army, those who march in it from the pure zeal of affection for religion, and also those who consider only the protection of the laws of their country or the service of their prince, he would not make up one complete company of men-at-arms out of them.[75]

At the opposite end of the scale are the motives of kings and princes who command wars:

> The souls of emperors and cobblers are cast in the same mold. Considering the importance of the actions of princes and their weightiness, we persuade ourselves that they are produced by some causes equally weighty and important: we are wrong. They are led to and fro in their movements by the same springs that we are in ours. The same reason that makes us bicker with a neighbor creates a war between princes; the same reason that makes us whip a lackey, when it happens in a king makes him ruin a province. Their will is as frivolous as ours, but their power is greater. Like appetites move a mite and an elephant.[76]

Like Erasmus[77] and Rabelais, Montaigne sees an essential unity between the morality of individuals and governments. He condemns the Caesars and Alexanders of the past for their lust for power and glory that leaves thousands dead in their wake.[78]

## PASCAL AND BEYOND

The intellectual opposition to war continued into the seventeenth and eighteenth centuries. Blaise Pascal (1623–1662) devoted several essays in *Pensées*[79] to the absurdity of war,[80] the killing of a fellow human simply because "he lives on the other side of the water."[81] Echoing More's *Utopia*,[82] Pascal asserts that truth is not defined by national boundaries, nor is any law or war just that holds that right rests with one nation or people.[83]

François Fénelon (1651–1715), a leader of the French church during the time of Louis XIV,[84] used his influence to promote peace abroad and justice at home. *The Law of Nations Grounded in Social Charity* stressed the general good over the advantage of any one king or state and the fundamental right of all peoples to peace.[85] He condemned Louis XIV's wars of aggression, reminding the king that his campaigns were only impoverishing his own people,[86] that all war is really civil war, and that the king was fighting only for his own glory and the subjugation of others. In his *Adventures of Telemachus* Fénelon used Homeric myth to satirize the king's wars, naming even preventive wars for what they are: lame excuses for aggression. The work so incensed the king that Fénelon lost favor and influence at court.

The eighteenth century produced several critics of European aggression in the New World, including Claude Fleury (1640–1723), whose *Ecclesiastical History* advocated a missionary pacifism along the lines of Las Casas;[87] and Guillaume Raynal (1713–1796), a priest and a philosophe, whose work on the *Philosophical and Political History of the Colonies and of the Commerce of the Europeans in the Two Indies* (1770) was publically burned (1781). Excepting the Jesuits in Paraguay, Raynal condemned the Spanish for their conquest of the Americas and their mistreatment of the Indians. Not only was this conquest an atrocity against the natives, but colonialism and its violence dehumanized the colonizers themselves and robbed them of true peace.[88]

We can thus trace a continuing intellectual tradition of peace among Catholics from the Reformation to the French Revolution. This tradition, though vital, was often divorced from any real peacemaking among Catholic clergy and laity. Yet it was not the sole avenue open to the age. In one major area of concrete action, the development of internationalism and world government, Catholics took an active lead in achieving substantial gains toward world peace.

## CATHOLIC INTERNATIONALISM: ORIGINS AND
## EARLY TRADITION

The idea of the essential unity of all peoples and of mechanisms to regulate the relationships between states is deeply engrained in the Catholic consciousness. Long before the League of Nations and the United Nations, the idea of the Mystical Body uniting all its members regardless of class, race, and nation provided the basic framework of Catholic political thought. In the Middle Ages the notion of Christendom as the true unit of political and religious life surpassed all national boundaries and loyalties as the prime motivating force in international politics. It determined much of the policy of the medieval papacy in its attempts to mediate peace among Christian states[89] and permeated the thought of Erasmus, More, Vives, and other Humanists.[90] Before examining Catholic internationalism we should, therefore, briefly review the medieval forms of world government.

## The Millennial Tradition

The Catholic millennial tradition was strongly supranationalist throughout the Middle Ages. Joachite prophesies[91] of a last world emperor who would unite all peoples and religions of the world in the Last Days[92] affected medieval political thought from the thirteenth century and played a major role in forming the policies of the Hapsburg and Valois rulers. Dreams of an angelic pope, who would accomplish the same pacification on a spiritual plane through the new spiritual people, inspired friars to look forward to a bright new age of unity, peace, and love among all peoples and nations.[93]

These influences continued into the early modern period[94] and appear in several treatises that attempted to fit Joachim's prophesies into concrete political schemes. Typical of these is the *Commentary on the Apocalypse* by Giovanni Annio of Viterbo (c. 1480).[95] Annio saw Christ's millennial triumph as a tangible world government, a New Jerusalem under a universal emperor and an angelic pope, who would divide the world into twelve regions, each corresponding to one of the gates of the Heavenly Jerusalem. In the sixteenth century Serafino da Fermo's *On the Apocalypse*[96] looked forward to a millennial age in which the schism caused by the Reformation would be healed, the church reformed, the New World converted, and all peoples of the world brought together in a true City of God.[97] Most of these treatises are vague about the agency of such change—whether unity would come through human conquest, through divine struggle, or through a combination of the two. Their real importance lies in the impact they produced on the Catholic psyche to look forward to some form of world government, some promised age of unity among all peoples.

## Medieval Universalism

The idea of one world also had a long tradition in secular terms during the Middle Ages. We have already examined the Franciscan tradition of nonviolent conversion[98] and the work of Ramon Lull.[99] Lull's thought is also important in the history of internationalism. His *Blanquerna* describes the mechanisms by which a reformed church would form a world government under the pope, employing the converted military classes to maintain justice.[100]

Lull's contemporary, Dante Alighieri (1265–1321), considered the same problem of war and peace and found a similar solution, though he put it in more secular terms. *On World Government,*[101] written between 1310 and 1313,[102] was a fitting prologue to the condemnations of corruption and violence of the *Divine Comedy*. Dante looked at the anarchic struggles between the Guelphs and Ghibellines and concluded that the only way that humanity could be guaranteed unity, civilization, and peace was through some form of universal monarchy.[103] Drawing on contemporary theology and natural law, Dante concluded that a unified government under one head was the best way to preserve both individual freedom and local autonomy.[104] He therefore looked to the rule of the Holy Roman Emperor as Christendom's only salvation, drawing on historical material to show how papal and clerical attempts to usurp secular power had only brought disaster.[105] This same call to free the secular state from the divisiveness of papal political claims marks Marsiglio of Padua's (1275–1342) *The Defender of Peace,* which was written in 1324 and immediately condemned by the pope.[106]

### Pierre Dubois

The most discussed medieval treatise on internationalism is *On the Recovery of the Holy Land*[107] by Pierre Dubois (c. 1250–c. 1320). Dubois was a legal advisor to the kings of France, a member of the Estates General in 1308, and an active propagandist in French royal struggles against the papacy and the Templars.[108] Dubois wrote the *Recovery* around 1306; it is divided into two parts. The first is a public letter to Edward I of England on the need for a new Crusade and on the methods of planning it. These include the reform of the church and of education and the establishment of peace within Europe. The second part is a private letter to King Philip IV of France on internal government.[109] Although the work's immediate influence was limited, it accurately reflects accepted Catholic opinion of the late Middle Ages and the Renaissance.[110]

Dubois's ostensible topic was the Crusade, but his real purpose was reform and peace within Christendom.[111] He draws on many traditions, including scholastic philosophy and theology, canon and civil law, Roger Bacon and Ramon Lull, Aristotle's *Nicodemian Ethics* and *Politics,* and the Gospels.[112] Dubois offers little new in his proposals aside from specific plans for educational reform, which included the establishment of language schools and the complete education of women from grammar school to schools of medicine and surgery—all in an attempt to convert the Moslems.[113] His originality lies in his plan for bringing about Christian unity. His general principle on war and peace is clear: no Christian should spill the blood of another Christian.[114] As Aristotle says, "all war is in itself wicked and unlawful; so much so that he who seeks war for its own sake has reached the extreme of wickedness."[115] Further, all wars fought to avenge wrongs are evil.[116]

Although he seems to call for a Crusade, Dubois's ideas on recovering the Holy Land often stress nonviolence. In order to take the Holy Land, he reminds his readers, a change of heart is first needed in the homeland,

> in accordance with the saying of the Prophet, "turn away from evil and do good; seek after peace and pursue it." Then when they have attained true peace in their hearts, all Catholic prelates, together with the whole clergy and people entrusted to their care, will in a spiritual sense form one body politic.[117]

The conclusions Dubois draws from this proposition are clear:

> We ought therefore to seek universal peace. . . . Your minds, which are souls endowed with reason, are generally destroyed rather than protected by wars and discord and by incessant wranglings in the courts, which is just as bad as war. Therefore every good man ought as far as possible to shun and avoid these evils.[118]

Dubois repeats his central theme: "Now the goal we seek, which is our chief objective, is universal peace."[119]

How is this peace to be achieved? Dubois rejects the conclusion of the millennialists and of Dante, Lull, and Marsiglio for some sort of universal monarchy[120] and calls instead for a forum of equal and independent nations assembled in a general council of the church to bring peace to the Christian commonwealth.[121] All disputes between states, including illegal aggression, are to be arbitrated by carefully chosen judges,[122] with final appeal to the pope. Should the pope's judgment not be obeyed, the council of nations then has the right and power to impose economic sanctions, including boycotts, against recalcitrant parties or nations who fail to live up to their international commitments. As a last resort the concerted military action of the council can be used against the offending nation.[123] Generally, however, the agency of the international council and the threat of economic sanctions will prevent aggression, and the monies thus saved on war and defense can be devoted to education.[124] In all these international peace efforts the pope should play the chief role in striving to "wipe out each and every war, rebellion, and controversy"[125] and is duty-bound to establish peace for all Christiáns.[126]

## CATHOLIC INTERNATIONALISM IN EARLY MODERN EUROPE

The sixteenth century brought new ideas about an international organization that could guarantee peace. Because of the decline of papal prestige and the religious wars that divided Christendom, appeal to religious authority no longer provided adequate theoretical support. Its place was taken by two new realities: the revived classical tradition of the law of nations *( jus gentium)* and the supremacy of the nation-state as the unit of international life. Together these created a new approach to internationalism that, though conceived by Catholics, was often not explicitly Catholic or even Christian[127] and appealed more to the force of governments than to individual conscience. This internationalist tradition took two main forms: the legal and scholastic revival of Spain (sixteenth and seventeenth centuries) and the continuing Humanist tradition in France (from the sixteenth to the eighteenth century).

### VITORIA AND THE SPANISH SCHOOL

In sixteenth-century Spain a revived scholasticism combined with Humanist classicism and the medieval legal tradition[128] to produce a new approach to war and peace.[129] This approach was expressed in a revived theory of the just war and in the development of the law of nations and of international law. The Spanish contribution to the just-war theory has been discussed thoroughly by many scholars[130] and need not detain us here. Scholarly literature on the Spanish origins of international law, especially of the school of Salamanca, is also extensive.[131] We are here concerned with those aspects of the law of nations that tended to restrict recourse to war and to define the rights of all peoples to peace and liberty. Chief among the Spanish theologians concerned with the legal basis of international peace is Francisco de Vitoria (1492/3–1546).[132]

Vitoria entered the Dominican Order and began lecturing at Valladolid, the royal capital, in 1523. He was elected to the Prime Chair of Theology at Salamanca University in 1526. Since the time of Cardinal Ximénez de Cisneros,[133] Salamanca had been a center of reform; it was involved closely with missionary efforts to curb the abuses of the conquistadors in the New World. In his post at Salamanca Vitoria was thus close to the Supreme Council of the Indies and used his theological and legal skills to complement the historical and ethical approach used by Las Casas to defend the Indians.[134] In November 1534 Vitoria wrote to the emperor condemning the atrocities committed in the Spanish conquest of Peru. At Charles V's urging he selected twelve Dominicans to go to Mexico to aid Archbishop Zumárraga's efforts for peace and justice.[135] In 1541 he was consulted by Charles V over the validity of Las Casas' complaints against the conquistadors[136] and with Domingo de Soto (1494–1560)[137] and other theologians urged the reforms contained in the New Laws.[138] Vitoria subsequently played a key role in the debate over Indian rights and was instrumental in the condemnation of the views of Juan Gines de Sepulveda, which held that the Indians and other non-Europeans were inherently inferior and thus justly conquered.[139]

Vitoria's chief works were never intended to be published in their present form: *De Indis et de iure belli* (On the Indies and On the Law of War) were first given as lectures (1539) and only later published at Lyons (1557) as part of *Relectiones theologicae*.[140] Calling on the system of natural law that governs all peoples regardless of race or religion, Vitoria asserted that the Indians were the legitimate rulers of the New World by their natural right and the human nature that they shared with all people. Despite the Aristotelian arguments of the Sepulveda school, Vitoria claimed that no humans were born to be slaves of any others.[141] Further, since Christianity gave no prior or more legitimate claim to sovereignty over another, neither the pope nor the emperor could claim the New World. Even the Indians' refusal to accept the overlordship of Jesus Christ offered no basis for conquest or for just war against them. The only right possessed by the Spanish was that common to all human societies: that of peaceful settlement and colonization, of communication and nonviolent conversion.[142] While the Spanish might have the right to defend peaceful colonists and missionaries and to protect the victims of cannibals and human sacrifice, wars under such pretexts could not be justified. In fact,

> war is not an argument for the truth of Christianity; the Indians cannot be made to believe by war, only to pretend to believe and to receive the Christian faith, which would be horrible and sacrilegious.[143]

Yet there are several carefully delineated Spanish claims to sovereignty in the New World, based not on the rights of conquest or religious orthodoxy, but on natural law that governs the peaceful relations between equal peoples.[144] These Spanish rights can be defended by a just war. Vitoria further justified Spanish trusteeship over the Indians in what was to become a classic theory of European colonialism.[145] But his chief concern and his lasting influence lay in spelling out the legal relationships between the different peoples. Abandoning the universalism of the ancient Stoics and of Dante's universal monarchy,[146] Vitoria used natural law to defend the natural rights of all people and their right to live in independent states. He thus built his universalism on a pluralist structure, which since has formed the basis of international law and human rights.[147]

In Vitoria's system Aristotle's and the Stoics' teaching of the basic unity of all humanity is underscored by the biblical injunction to "love your neighbor as yourself."[148] Thus, although states form the natural and basic units of international life, the same natural law that supports that political society also guarantees the essential human right to participate in it and imposes the moral duty of mutual aid to one's fellow citizens.[149] In relations between states, therefore, certain general rights must be acknowledged: the inviolability of ambassadors, the rights of nations to live in peace, the right of free communication and commerce.[150] Among Christian states this natural duty to peace underscores a moral duty to preserve the unity of the Christian republic; thus any war between Christian states is unjust by any standard.[151]

Vitoria divides the law of nations into sanctions of natural and of positive law to maintain peace and justice between states. Among the sanctions of positive law, war may sometimes be waged in the service of justice, as a last, unfortunate resort by some form of coercive agent. This coercion cannot be used by princes on their own behalf except imperfectly; it must therefore be exercised by some supranational force that Vitoria never defines.[152]

Among the sanctions of natural law is the ethical and moral right of the people to exercise their conscience to maintain peace and justice and to condemn the despotism and immorality of rulers.[153] This right even extends to the individual's participation in war. In words that repeat many of the medieval arguments on individual conscience and war,[154] Vitoria postulates two situations for the individual confronted with the possibility of fighting. In one of them, soldiers or citizens

who have no place or entry into the prince's council of state are not bound to investigate the causes of a war, but may rely on their superiors and fight. The proof of this is that it is impossible and undesirable to explain every act of state to the whole commonality, and secondly, even if the common people saw that a war was unjust, they would not be able to stop it, for no one would listen to them; so that it would be useless for them to investigate the causes of a war. Then, again, the fact that the war is being waged after public counsel and by public authority is enough proof of its justice for men of this sort unless the contrary is quite certain; therefore they are not bound to enquire further. However, the proofs and signs of the war's injustice may be so strong that even such subjects could not plead ignorance and fight in it.[155]

Even though Vitoria wrote in an age of increasing despotism, when the opinion of the "commonality" was held in contempt, he still admitted that ordinary people could object to war and that, although their opinions might be systematically ignored by those in power, a process of consensus could gradually turn public opinion against wars waged by even legitimate governments. Should this happen, the individual is thus not only relieved of the duty to fight in such an unjust war but is bound to refuse such service and cannot plead ignorance of the issues involved. Further, Vitoria gives special consideration to the individual conscience. If an individual subject is thus convinced that a war is wrong, he ought not to fight even if ordered to do so: "the corollary of this is that whether a war is just or unjust, if a subject's conscience tells him that it is wrong, he must not fight in it."[156]

Vitoria's pioneering work in international law linked the maintenance of peace among nations with inalienable human rights, placing individual right on the same natural-law footing as the state's rights but further bolstering the individual with the moral rights of conscience set firmly within the Catholic tradition. Vitoria's influence was immense; thousands of students heard his lectures and helped spread his ideas on international peace and justice throughout the Catholic world.

## THE INTERNATIONAL TRADITION IN FRANCE

Much of the significant peace literature in France reflected a more Humanist influence than was the case in Spain. Its appeal lay both in its recalling the tradition of Erasmus and in its admitting the new developments of the law of nations. In 1585 the anonymous *Apologie de la paix*[157] drew on biblical, patristic, classical, and contemporary scientific insights to echo Erasmus's call for peace between states. True peace, according to the *Apologie,* should be more than a passive peace of the heart. It should be active in its opposition to war, which is a corruption of human nature. True peace, on the contrary, is the unity, the heart, and the life of states by which justice and piety flourish. The law of nations may allow defensive wars, but war has been the cause of so many evils and soldiers the cause of so much ruin and desolation that war must be abolished. Yet, the anonymous author maintains, war will never be abolished so long as the nation-state continues to act like a dark forest, providing a haven for brigands and other criminals who venture forth to destroy the peace.

### Emeric Crucé

The *Apologie* failed to offer any substantive alternative to the state, but its criticisms pointed the direction for most of the thinking on peace during the next two centuries. In 1623, in the midst of the Thirty Years War, Emeric Crucé (c. 1590–1648)[158] published *The New Cyneas, or Discourse of the Means to Establish a General Peace.*[159] Little is known of Crucé's life, but it seems certain that he was a monk, educated in the classical tradition of the Humanists, who shared the pacifist outlook of Erasmus and Rabelais.[160]

Crucé divided his *New Cyneas* into five parts, the first dealing with the causes of war, the second, the international foundations for peace, the third, the principles of internal government of states, the fourth, freedom of commerce and standardization of weights and measures, and the fifth, the means to realize the plan for international peace.[161] Crucé finds five major causes for war, which are consistent with Erasmus's analysis; the honor of princes, profit, the avenging of wrongs, "just for the exercise," and differences of human character and religion. Dismissing those wars caused by the whims of princes and for other worthless reasons, Crucé attacks the very notion of the just war, calling it a pretext for aggression.[162] Not one in five wars is just, he contends; even just wars involve the possibility of far greater damage than whatever originally caused them could do. Since God will always guide the affairs of the just, nonviolent resistance to evil is always preferable to violence, and princes have no excuse to resort to violence. War, in fact, has had its day.[163]

Crucé argues that all men are brothers and that only the traditional emnity between nation-states causes hatred and war. Even religious differences offer little excuse, since all religions share a common love of God and seek a reign of peace and justice that far excels the inhumanity of war. Crucé further breaks with the just-war tradition of Augustine by arguing that no amount of religious compulsion can truly alter a person's mind and that God alone can judge a person's conscience,[164] a point already established for international law by Vitoria.[165] Differences of Persian and Turk, of French and Spaniard, of Chinese and Tartar, of Christian, Jew, and Moslem are only political distinctions. Echoing Pascal, Crucé says that "geography cannot weaken the ties of blood."[166]

Peace, however, is essential to civilization.[167] Its benefits far exceed the triumphs of Alexander, Hannibal, Caesar, and Sertorius. "Their glory," he writes,[168] "was founded on murder and plunder, in which they should have found instead perpetual regrets and shame." The honor and glory of peace,

> is not to be acquired by pillage, slaughter, and hostile actions, but by consistent government, by lawful and regulated power, in contradistinction to the kingdom of tyranny, uneasiness and short duration.[169]

Establishing this "consistent government" is the heart of Crucé's appeal. In contrast to the internal tyranny and external anarchy that then ravaged Europe, Crucé calls for two major reforms; the first, external peace, is based on the second, internal justice.

Within states peace must be preserved not by force and compulsion but by good government, justice, provision for the poor, the creation of a civil service based on merit, just taxation, and economic reform.[170] Externally the world can preserve this peace only by abandoning the anarchy and vicious self-interest of nation-states locked in deadly competition and by embracing a world confederation of states.

Cruce's plans for this world confederation are explicit. All the states of the known world, including those of Europe, the papacy, the Turkish Sultan and the Holy Roman Emperor, of Islam, India and the Great Mogul, Africa, Japan, and China, are to come together in a World Council of Representatives headquartered in a convenient and appropriate world capital: Venice would be ideal because of its commercial preeminence, ease of communication and travel, and long history of republican government.[171] Each nation is to maintain permanent diplomatic representation at the Council headquarters; voluntary membership in the world body will by no means entail any diminishing of the individual sovereignty of any member state. The Council is to maintain world peace through the public forum of its assembly. It will listen to the cases pleaded by the ambassadors of contending nations and then arbitrate their disputes. Should any one nation fail to abide by the decision of the Council, the ambassadors of the other major nations are to apply diplomatic pressure and persuasion to reach a settlement.[172]

Although the World Council may use force as a last resort to bring aggressors into line, to maintain peace, and to intervene in the internal affairs of a member state in order to reestablish stability and justice,[173] such a military solution would be rare. Far more important is the outlawing of war between individual states and the development of peaceful relations between members. This is to be accomplished through the development of international commerce and economic interdependence, through tax benefits to merchants, export incentives, and the elimination of tariff and other trade barriers.[174]

Cruce's new peacemaker is thus the merchant, whose continuous work of exchange and international contact peacefully breaks down barriers and unites all peoples. His work thus reflects the changing outlook of his age. While his outlook is inspired by Christian ethics and Humanist approaches, the religious universalism expressed by Erasmus and the nobility of the martyr and the missionary have been replaced by the smiling merchant, the mercantilist saint who spreads a new gospel to a new world.

### Saint-Pierre

Cruce's Humanist internationalism was translated for the Enlightenment in *Project for Perpetual Peace*[175] by Charles Irenée Castel de Saint-Pierre (1658–1743).[176] Educated by the Jesuits and an intimate of the Enlightenment's salon-and-café society, Saint-Pierre was abbot of Tiron, a member of the French Academy, and the almoner of King Louis XIV's sister.[177] He was a passionate devotee of the new secular learning and a harsh critic of Catholic abuses.[178] Saint-Pierre attacked the absolutism of Louis XIV in his *Discours sur la polysynodie* of 1718, which resulted in his ouster from the French Academy.[179] When he was in royal favor Saint-Pierre served as secretary to the future Cardinal Melchior de Polignac, one of the three French plenipotentiaries to the Utrecht Peace Conference (1713) that helped end the War of the Spanish Succession.[180] Saint-Pierre's frustration and disillusionment over the conduct of the negotiations led him to write the *Project,* which became an immediate best-seller.[181]

Saint-Pierre's work is an open letter to Europe's rulers that condemns the wars of Louis XIV as unjust, waged only for personal and dynastic glory.[182] As an alternative to Europe's legalized anarchy Saint-Pierre called for a permanent league of European union, a federation of the states of Europe modeled on the Swiss Confederation and the United Provinces.[183] The abbot provided a detailed list of articles for the confederation.[184] The union was to include both Christian and non-Christian states, which would be represented at the confederation headquarters, the "City of Peace," by resident ambassadors. They would form the federation's Assembly. While all forms of government and constitution were to be accepted, the federation would "renounce and renounce for ever, for themselves and for their successors, resort to arms as an instrument of national policy."[185] All disputes between states were to be settled by the arbitration of the federation's commissioners in the City of Peace, with the final decision of disputes subject to the binding vote of the federation Senate. As in Crucé's world government, the federation could resort to force against monarchs who refused to abide by its peaceful decisions and could intervene in the affairs of member nations on behalf of legitimate governments and in defense of the status quo.[186] Like Crucé's union, the assembly was to encourage world peace through international trade.

Saint-Pierre's influence on later thinkers was great. Rousseau read the *Project* and wrote a commentary; Gustave de Molinari used the *Project* in *L'Abbé de Saint-Pierre* (1857) to call for a union of nations and for universal disarmament.[187] The intellectual appeal of the Humanists would continue to motivate Europe's elite toward peace throughout the nineteenth century.

## CONCLUSIONS

Late nineteenth-century and early twentieth-century internationalist literature summarizes peacemaking efforts since Trent and offers some surprising lessons for contemporary peacemakers. In contrast to the direct moral appeal to individual conscience by the Humanists of the sixteenth to eighteenth centuries and the popular peace movements of the Middle Ages, the nineteenth century offered an elitist appeal to the *Pax Romana*[188] and to enlightened political leadership. In place of Christian peace, this genteel movement offered the absence of war. The "pacifism" of the nineteenth century left a legacy of enlightened elites, of international agreement between governments, and of a sentimental appeal to "Christian" virtues that went hand in hand with an idolization of the nation-state, with "love of fatherland, the cult of the fatherland, the honor of the noble and holy traditions of the fatherland."[189] The elitist approach that could naively discuss the "pacifism" of the French military genius Vauban[190] would eventually place all its hopes for peace on the diplomatic efforts and military balances of Europe's governments and ignore the true wishes of the people. Devoid of any popular resistance to militarism, of any appeal to the individual Christian conscience, this "pacifism" was powerless to prevent Europe's juggernaut into the holocausts of the twentieth century.

# CHAPTER 12

# THE LESSONS OF THE TWENTIETH CENTURY

## INTRODUCTION

In 1970 a symposium convened at Boston College entitled "The Vatican and World Peace." Michael P. Walsh, S.J., soon to become president of Fordham University, addressed the audience of Catholic intellectuals and clergy on the role of the papacy as peacemaker in the twentieth century. Walsh summed up papal efforts in this way:

It is largely a question of fulcrums and levers, is it not? Stalin asking the question, "The Pope—how many divisions has he?" was missing the point.[1]

Gathering at the height of the Vietnam War, when thousands of young Americans, many of them Catholic, faced brutal death or the bleak prospect of killing or refusing to kill, Fr. Walsh and his fellow conferees ignored their nation's involvement in an unjust war and spoke in self-congratulatory phrases of "world peace" and "international cooperation," of a world "order" imposed by civilized agreement, enlightened essay, and subtle "leverage." Though written after the holocausts of the twentieth century, Fr. Walsh's remarks were more in keeping with the internationalism of the nineteenth century, when clergy and laity gathered to issue similar optimistic assurances of peace through trust in states, treaties, and like-minded men of power.

Stalin might well have scoffed at the "leverage" of the Vatican, for without the pope's "divisions," that is, a Catholic laity educated for and committed to active peacemaking, all the pope's words of influence and exhortations to peace were doomed to impotence. The Boston College Symposium showed that many Catholics had not learned the lessons that the catastrophes of the twentieth century had taught.

This chapter will outline the nature of those lessons, this education for peace. It will follow the evolution of papal thinking on war and peace in the modern world, the actions of the church hierarchy in implementing or failing to implement these thoughts and words, the responsibility of the Catholic laity in the disasters of the century, and the witness of individual Catholic martyrs and prophets who gave their lives for peace and justice, and in whom the spirit of Christ renewed the Mystical Body for a new age of Catholic peacemaking.

*168*

## PAPAL PEACEMAKING IN THE MODERN WORLD

The century between the First and the Second Vatican Councils was one of virtual revolution in papal thought and action. By 1870 the papacy under Pius IX had helped repress the democratic revolutions of the nineteenth century and had imprisoned itself in Vatican City, locking the Catholic Church behind the even stronger walls of medieval philosophical and ethical systems.[2] It had condemned modern social, economic, political, and theological trends and had declared itself and itself alone the authoritarian focus of all Catholic theological and ethical life, brooking no opposition from councils, bishops, clergy, or laity. By 1970, after the pontificate of John XXIII and the Second Vatican Council, the papacy had aligned itself with many of the liberal and revolutionary doctrines of the modern world. It had embraced the modern Catholic world and had extended its open hands to Christians of all denominations, to all religious opinions, and to all humanity. It had declared that the external universalism of the church was to be matched by a new universalism of the spirit within the church, a sharing of the church's pastoral, teaching, and prophetic role by all levels of the hierarchy and by the laity in all walks of life. In 1870 the pope was associated with European monarchy and established order, with the powers of the world. By 1970 he had once again embraced the poor and the simple, the suffering and the persecuted, and had opened the path to the true imitation of the gospel life.

If papal authoritarianism and its fears of the non-Catholic world were largely responsible for the repression of most Catholic dissent and individual peacemaking in the era after Trent,[3] the changing attitudes of popes from Leo XIII to John XXIII toward the role of Catholics as peacemakers can indeed be seen as the fountainhead of Catholic efforts for peace in the twentieth century. The progress of papal thought on peace was certainly not simplistic—a move from a theology of authoritarianism to a theology of liberation. During this hundred years the popes rediscovered the essence of the Mystical Body: truth resides not only in the head, but also in the members and spiritual strength resides throughout its physical and spiritual being.

The papacy's virtual isolation from the major trends of the nineteenth century may, paradoxically, have been beneficial for its involvement in the twentieth century. By the turn of the twentieth century the popes had developed a consistent policy toward the modern world. Their policy was to be refined over the course of the century and was eventually to offer a haven for those discontented with many of the trends of modern civilization. Papal thought became characterized by its increasingly sharp critique of capitalism and its systems of exploitation, by a doctrine that the rights of private property were limited by social function, by a rededication to problems of poverty, social repression, and exploitation, by a concern for workers, and by a belief that government must intervene on behalf of the disenfranchised, the poor, and the exploited. The twentieth century saw a steady stream of papal words and works on behalf of Catholic social action, international cooperation and world order, human rights in the face of totalitarian systems of whatever label, democracy, and the sovereignty of truth, justice, love, and peace.[4] Most importantly for the church as an organization, papal thought began to declare its independence from any particular social order or system for the first time since Constantine.[5]

There is no need here to review the long tradition of papal efforts on behalf of international peace.[6] By the mid-nineteenth century the papacy had once again shown itself ready to act as an impartial arbiter. In 1861 Pius IX offered papal offices to the Catholic countries of the Latin American Union. Although his offer to mediate in the Franco-Prussian war was rejected because his political loyalties were suspect and because claims of papal sovereignity had long been rejected,[7] by the time of the pontificate of Leo XIII the Vatican was well on the way to reestablishing its role as an international peacemaker.

## Leo XIII

Leo XIII (1878–1903) was not a liberal. He stood firmly with Pius IX in his theological attitudes toward the modern world.[8] Yet he was aware of the need to remove the church from the reactionary social, economic, and political trends of the century. He weaned French Catholicism from its love affair with monarchism, revived the prestige of biblical and historical research, and faced the problems of industrial society directly.[9] His encyclical *Rerum Novarum* (1891) has been called the Magna Carta of social Catholicism in its identification with the rights of workers and its belief in the role of the church in promoting social justice. Leo XIII was also a well-traveled diplomat and extended his role as peacemaker into every aspect of modern life.[10]

Leo's letters and encyclicals repeated many post-Tridentine themes: respect for church, authority, and public harmony.[11] He identified peace with the tranquility of order. Yet this order was not the lockstep of repression, but the fruit of justice.[12] Although Christians must fulfill their duties as citizens, "no man can serve two masters" (Mt 6:24), and in the case of conflicting loyalties, Christians must follow Peter's call to obey God above humans.[13] In his allocution *Nostis Errorem,* addressed to the college of cardinals (Feb. 11, 1889), Leo expressed an attitude to peace that was to become a hallmark of papal thought in the twentieth century.

Stating that "there is . . . nothing of more importance than to remove from Europe the danger of war," Leo realized that sentiment was not enough:

> The wish does not do much to render peace assured, and the mere desire for peace is not a sufficient guarantee. A vast number of soldiers and stupendous armaments may for a while prevent an enemy attacking, but they can never secure a sure and lasting peace. Moreover, armaments which are a menace are more likely to hasten than to retard a conflict; they fill the mind with disquietude for the future, and among other drawbacks, impose such burdens upon nations that it is doubtful if war would not be more bearable. Wherefore we must seek for peace some basis more sound and more in accord with nature; for if nature does not forbid one to defend one's rights by force, she does not permit that force should become the efficient cause of right. Since peace is based upon good order, it follows that, for empires as well as for individuals, concord should have her principle foundation in justice and charity.[14]

Peace is the daughter of justice, Leo wrote in *Molti e Segnalati,*[15] and in pursuit of this justice he called for a renewal of the internationalism of the medieval papacy, a renewal not of monarchical powers, but of conciliation and arbitration,

> to defend the weak against the unjust oppression of the strong, to prevent war, and to save Christian civilization . . . to fill the mind of people with the Christian idea of justice and love, to recall nations to reciprocal obligations of broth-

erhood . . . to oppose to the law of might the might of the law in conformity with the principles of the Gospel.[16]

Leo used every means available to press for international peace. He supported an international forum that would guarantee peace without diminishing the rights of sovereign states (a position fully within the Catholic tradition),[17] encouraged Catholic and other international peace conferences,[18] and arbitrated between nations. In 1885 he settled the dispute between Germany and Spain over the Caroline Islands,[19] in 1891 between Portugal and Belgium,[20] and throughout the 1880s he appealed for a nonviolent solution to the religious and political turmoil in Ireland.[21]

The need for a new international order based on justice, the false peace of military defense, the crushing burden on the peoples of the world of sustaining a military defense, the need to reevaluate the justice of even defensive wars in a technological world, the convergence of private and public morality, and the foundation of peace on justice and love—Leo XIII's central concerns echoed the best of the Catholic peace tradition and were to be the major themes of the Catholic peace movement in the twentieth century.

### Benedict XV and World War I

Pius X during his relatively short reign (1903–1914) continued the peace policies of Leo XIII into the twentieth century.[22] He aligned himself with all the peace movements of Europe and the United States,[23] encouraged the Carnegie Endowment for International Peace,[24] and arbitrated an international agreement between Brazil, Peru, and Bolivia.[25] His successor, Benedict XV (1914–1922), however, was faced with the full impact of world war and its aftermath of hatred and destruction, as he fully implemented the principles of Leo XIII.[26]

Benedict truly earned his title "Pontiff of Peace." Elected as Europe plunged into the First World War, he was admirably suited to meet drastic new conditions with a clear vision of the role of the Christian peacemaker. As close to an absolute pacifist as any pope since Benedict XII during the Hundred Years War,[27] Benedict set out to reconcile the major conflicts of the day. He began by resolving the debate over Modernist theology within the church, ending the repression of new thought and scholarship.[28] He lifted the ban on Catholic ties with the Italian state, in effect since Pius IX's flight from the Risorgimento, and openly embraced Catholic political groups, including Don Luigi Sturzo's liberal Popular Party.[29]

A former papal diplomat, Benedict opposed war in any form and rejected the theory of the just war as historically outmoded and theologically inadequate. Echoing Erasmus, he saw the theory as only a lame excuse designed to prolong wars.[30] In the best tradition of Catholic peacemaking he rejected the Machiavellian distinction between private and public morality, arguing that "the Gospel has not one law of charity for individuals and another for states and nations, for these are but collections of individuals."[31] Benedict's debt to the Humanist peace tradition is clear. His encyclical *Ad Beatissimum*, issued at the outbreak of World War I (Nov. 1, 1914), outlines the causes of war and the methods for attaining peace. His words could well have come from the pen of Erasmus:

The dread image of war overshadows the world, and absorbs nearly every thought. The strongest and wealthiest nations are in conflict. What wonder, then, that, furnished as they are with the latest weapons devised by military science, their struggle is causing enormous slaughter. . . . Who would think that the nations, thus armed against each other, are all descended from one ancestor, share the same nature, belong to the same human family? Who would realize that they are brethren, children of the same Father in heaven? And while the mighty hosts are contending in the fury of combat, cities, families, individuals are being oppressed by those evils and miseries which follow at the heels of war; day by day the numbers increase of widows and orphans; the paths of commerce are blocked; the fields are left untilled; the arts are at a standstill; the rich are made poor, the poor are made destitute, all are made to mourn.[32]

Benedict proceeds to list the causes of war—lack of mutual love, disregard for authority, class war, gross materialism—and to outline the path to peace: the Beatitudes and Christ's command that "you love one another as I have loved you."[33]

Throughout the war Benedict condemned its barbarities and futility, calling for a peace without victory, offering peace plans to both sides.[34] He remained strictly neutral during the war, earning the enmity and distrust of both sides[35] for his efforts, an enmity that recalls the distrust that met papal efforts to end the Hundred Years War.[36] During the war years Benedict issued over one hundred encyclicals and letters of instruction and exhortation to bishops, Catholic leaders, and laity on the rights of prisoners, the wounded, and noncombatants, on organizing relief work, on arranging truces, on reducing unnecessary violence. He protested conditions in Poland and Belgium, warned against U.S. and Italian entry into the war, condemned aerial bombing, the sinking of the *Lusitania,* attacks upon any civilian targets, forced deportation of civilians, and the taking of hostages. He personally rebuked Kaiser Wilhelm II for the use of poison gas and pressed for a nonviolent solution to the Irish rebellion.[37] He diverted huge amounts of church funds for the relief of war victims both during and after the war, emptying the Vatican treasury so that on his death there was barely enough money left to hold the conclave that elected his successor.[38] He spent much of his personal family fortune in this work. Working with the Red Cross, he made the Vatican a clearinghouse for missing persons, for the exchange of prisoners, the reunion of families, the rescue of children and refugees, and he prevented the execution of many prisoners of war.[39]

At the height of the war Benedict appealed directly to all the belligerent peoples and their leaders,[40] calling for an end to hostilities and prophetically reminding them that nations do not die if defeated but only harbor revenge and hatred for their conquerors. True Christians, he declared, must make the first offer of peace. True peace, he stressed, depends upon "mutual benevolence and respect for the rights and dignities of others, much more than upon hosts of armed men and a ring of formidable fortresses."[41] Benedict called on all Catholics, on both sides of the conflict, to do all they could for the restoration of peace.[42]

At the end of war Benedict pressed for an equitable and just peace treaty that would not be in the spirit of revenge but would promote active reconciliation and forgiveness.[43] He called on all Catholics to lay aside nationalist enmities, to lend their support to international organizations, and to aid the victims of famine in Central Europe and Russia, as the Vatican itself was doing.[44] The pope's peacemaking efforts and his aid to the conquered Central Powers were resented by the Allies, especially by France, which felt betrayed by his pacifism.[45] He was specifically excluded from the Versailles Peace Conference by France, Great Britain, Russia, and Italy.[46]

Before Woodrow Wilson's Fourteen Points, which became the focus of peace negotiations after World War I, Benedict had proposed his own series of "points, which seem to offer the basis for a just and lasting peace.''[47] Among these were the principles that moral force must always be preferred to the force of arms, that disarmament must proceed reciprocally and with guarantees and rules, that arbitration is always preferable to armies, that international law must safeguard commerce and the rights of all peoples, and that the belligerent nations and peoples must extend total pardon to each other. A letter (Sept. 28, 1917) from Cardinal Gaspari, the papal Secretary of State, to British Prime Minister Lloyd George, explains Benedict's ideas on disarmament proposals, including the "simultaneous and reciprocal suppression of all compulsory military service," and "imposition of a general boycott in sanction against any nation that might attempt to reestablish obligatory military service.''[48] The pope's condemnation of the draft is as clear as it is categorical and is a strong precedent for later Catholic peacemaking.

### Pius XI and the Dictators

Pius XI's reign (1922–1939) coincided with the rise of Fascism, Nazism, and Communism, witnessed the destruction of democracy through most of Europe, and ended with the outbreak of World War II. The problem of the relationship of papacy and dictatorships has been studied in detail elsewhere.[49] Here we must try to measure Pius's words on peace against their real effect on the course of peace and justice in the era between the wars.

Pius XI's ideas on peace were neither of passive acquiescence nor of rigid order. He introduced the term "social justice" to the Catholic vocabulary[50] and considered justice synonymous with peace. From the beginning of his reign he argued against the repressive peace terms imposed on Germany and its allies, stressing that "the best guarantee of peace is not a forest of bayonets, but mutual confidence and friendship.''[51] On the one hand he opposed heavy war reparations and the Allied occupation of the territories of the Central Powers,[52] and on the other he continued church relief work in the Soviet Union, arguing that the church has an obligation to aid people, whatever their political system.[53]

Pius expressed his ideas on peace in the modern world in the encyclical *Ubi Arcano Dei*.[54] While he makes the point that the papacy looks fondly on the religious unity of medieval Christendom as an ideal[55] and stresses that the church is the custodian of international law,[56] Pius's real aim was to pinpoint the dangers of war and the true nature of Christian peace. He wrote that since the end of the Great War peace has existed only on paper and that

> the nations of today live in a state of armed peace which is scarcely better than war itself, a condition that tends to exhaust national finances, to waste the flower of youth, to muddy and poison the very fountainheads of life, physical, intellectual, religious and moral.[57]

True peace, he argued, is not external and formal convention between nations, nor can it be found in the refuge of exaggerated patriotism.[58] "The Peace of Christ can only be the peace of justice according to the words of the prophet, 'the work of justice shall be peace.' ''[59] Justice itself, he stresses, is not the end, but only the means to remove obstacles to the true practice of Christian love. Justice and love become synonymous with peace in all of Pius XI's writings on war and peace, political systems, and the structure of society.[60]

While Pius's words helped lay the foundation for a modern theology of social justice and liberation, he still thought in terms of Humanist and Enlightenment Europe, where political rhetoric reflected political conviction and supported the commitment to abide by spoken principles. Yet he lived in the era of Hitler, Mussolini, and Stalin, the era of modern propaganda and intellectual cynicism, of great lies that masked brutal realities and lust for power. In that age, spoken words of peace, as Thomas Merton observed,[61] served as little more than external smokescreens for naked power, bearing little or no relation to true motives and actions.

Pius's political universe was that of the European elite, who made decisions for the masses and gave little heed to the aspirations or the power of the people. He feared the growing disorder of European life and was convinced of the need for firm law and order, which could help reinstall the virtues of Christian love and justice. He therefore attempted to deal with the new dictators as legitimate agents of political authority, and sought political concordats between the Vatican and the Fascist and Nazi regimes. In general he gave the dictators a free hand with the political destinies of their own citizens, as long as the formal rights of the church as a political and social institution were respected and protected.

As early as the 1922 election in Italy the pope began withdrawing his support of Catholic political parties in order to facilitate a broad political consensus and remove the threat of socialist or communist infiltration.[62] With the Lateran Treaty and Concordat with Mussolini in 1929, Pius seemed explicitly to give approval to the Fascist state.[63] He thus set precedents for the rest of the century: a willingness to break with the state and to raise a voice of protest only in matters that concerned church-state relations and church activities within its own sphere of action,[64] and an almost unquestioning respect for the state within its own, supposedly proper, sphere of activity—politics, war, and peace.

Pius's reaction to the Italian invasion of Abyssinia (Ethiopia) is a case in point. He never actively supported the war effort,[65] but he never condemned Mussolini's aggression and in July 1935 he opposed the League of Nations' attempt to apply sanctions as undue interference in Italian affairs. The Italian hierarchy took their cue from Pius's relative silence and spoke out in enthusiastic support of Italian arms and the restoration of the Pax Romana. They openly opposed League sanctions and even collected money for the war effort. Embarrassed by the bishops' support for the crusade Pius softened some of their rhetoric. Thus, although Pius's thought on peace was clearly in the direction of a theory of social justice and liberation, his political action showed that he maintained the definition of peace as order imposed from above and arranged by political agreement among a ruling elite.

Nowhere is this more clear than in Pius's relations with Nazi Germany. Through his dealings with Hitler, Pius came to realize the emptiness of a peace based on such order. The Vatican had tried to reach a political understanding with every German government and individual state since the time of Bismarck.[66] In July 1933 the newly elected Nazi government offered a Concordat to the pope.[67] The treaty provided the legal basis for the maintenance of church rights within Germany and guaranteed the German government autonomy within the political sphere of secular activities.[68] The pope soon found that Hitler's Germany, like Mussolini's Italy, mocked the distinction between what is Caesar's and what is God's and claimed all for Caesar, including what had presumably been set aside for the church by international law and formal treaty. Conflict soon arose over the autonomy of Catholic religious services, processions, festivals, lay organizations, youth groups, the exemption of the clergy from military service, the independence of Catholic schools, the use of crucifixes in them, the rights and livelihoods of Catholic schoolteachers and civil servants, and such moral issues as Nazi programs of euthanasia and forced sterilization.[69]

As papal and episcopal resistance mounted and church leaders began using the Concordat as a legal basis for protest, the Nazi state struck back with vicious propaganda campaigns citing the supposed sexual abuses of Catholic clergy and alleged financial misconduct by the church in breaking Germany's currency laws. The government also arrested and persecuted individual priests, nuns, and bishops.[70] The Nazis feared organized church opposition and overt papal hostility.[71] For a time the legal foundation of the Concordat carried some weight, but Pius gradually realized the indifference of the Nazis to its terms and the party's hostility to Christianity.

When Pius's response came it was almost too late, but it showed that the pope had learned one of the most important lessons of the Catholic peacemaker in the twentieth century: that a Constantinian alliance—the practical identity of the church with secular authority—provided only a false peace, that the modern state was at best indifferent to Christian goals and at worst nakedly hostile to them, and that to continue cooperation with it was to ignore Paul's injunction not to acquiesce to evil.[72]

On March 14, 1937, the pope issued *Mit brennender Sorge* (With Burning Sorrow)[73] to the people and clergy of Germany. The letter is a burning indictment of Nazism, an exposé of the German government's violation of the terms of the Concordat, and a declaration of the unbridgeable gap between its paganism of race, blood, and soil, of might makes right, and the Christian ethic. "You are often told," Pius tells German Catholics, "about heroic greatness, in lying opposition to evangelical humility and patience. Why conceal the fact that there are heroisms in moral life?"[74] What Hitler feared had finally happened: the pope was beginning to use the strength of his moral leadership, not to promulgate lofty words, but to call on German Catholics to the "heroisms in moral life." The Nazis ordered the encyclical confiscated and its circulation restricted. However it had been distributed secretly all over Germany before it had reached Nazi censors and it continued to circulate underground and to be read from pulpits.[75]

Pius was now convinced that he must speak out. Five days after *Mit brennender Sorge* he issued *Divini Redemptoris*,[76] a condemnation of "atheistic communism." The encyclical expressed strong opposition to the totalitarian state, emphasizing the alternatives of individual human dignity, of Catholic action, of Catholic workers and Catholic priests ministering among the workers. On December 24, 1937, Pius promulgated *Il Santo Padre ha Incominciato*,[77] in which he condemned the persecution that he saw in Nazi Germany. He addressed *Voilà une Audience* (Sept. 18, 1938)[78] to French labor unionists and condemned the totalitarian state in all its forms. Pius's progress from abstract principle to concrete political stance was cut short by his death on February 10, 1939, just as he was preparing an "explosive encyclical" denouncing Nazi and Fascist persecution of the church and their racial policies against the Jews and other minorities.[79]

## Pius XII and World War II

When the college of cardinals gathered in February 1939 to elect a new pope, its members felt that only a skillful and experienced diplomat, one familiar with the new dictators, could steer the church through the coming turmoil. Their choice naturally fell on Eugenio Pacelli, who as Pius XII was to fully embrace the diplomatic, internationalist approach of his predecessors. In so doing he would preserve the structure of the church and become one of the most controversial figures of the twentieth century.[80]

The debate over the silence of Pius XII—his refusal to condemn the Nazis and Fascists outright, especially for their genocide against the Jews and other minorities—has raged ever since World War II and received new impetus with the appearance in 1963 of Rolf Hochhuth's play, *The Deputy.*[81] I do not propose to enter this debate here. The issues involved, the literature covering them,[82] and the passions stirred on both sides of the debate are all beyond the scope of this study.

There seems little doubt that Pius XII's personal and official reserve aided the Nazis in their program of extermination and appeared to lend them at least the tacit support of the Roman Catholic Church. Yet the record of his accomplishments and the Catholic Church's work in saving Jews, Slavs, and other displaced and persecuted peoples through diplomatic and quiet methods is also clear. More than 800,000 Jews were saved through the pope's offices.[83] But what did Pius's silence mean in real terms for the history of Catholic peacemaking? Was the pope's silence the only or the best form of nonviolent confrontation of the Nazis? Why did his resistance take this form? Pius argued that his silence spared many from even greater persecution and kept open the Vatican's information networks.[84] But did his diplomatic maneuver and appeal to international law really serve justice and peace in the best possible way given the circumstances of the times? We will address these questions first by examining Pius's concept of peace and then by analyzing the effects of his policy among the hierarchy and laity of Nazi Germany.

On August 24, 1939, Pius XII issued a radio appeal for peace amid mounting certainty of another war. *Un'Ora Grave* spells out the major themes of Pius's pontificate: the nature of peace as justice, the role of government in implementing justice, and the futility of war:

> All humanity seeks justice, bread, and freedom; not steel, which kills and destroys. . . . It is by force of reason, and not by force of arms, that justice makes progress, and empires which are not founded on justice are not blessed by God. Statesmanship emancipated from morality betrays those very ones who would have it so. The danger is imminent, but there is yet time. Nothing is lost with peace; all may be lost with war.[85]

With the outbreak of war in September 1939, however, Pius could do little but acknowledge his powerlessness.[86] His first encyclical, *Summi Pontificatus* (Oct. 20, 1939),[87] summarizes his approach to war and peace. He condemns Nazi and Soviet aggression plainly and denounces the evils of the totalitarian state,[88] but it is clear that the state is the framework for all Pius's thinking. Undue patriotism should be avoided if it hinders love of all humans; however, the state is worthy of obedience. The Christian must "render to Caesar."[89] The rights of the state are limited by international law, by treaties, and by the unity of supranational society in the tradition of Vitoria, but the pope maintains the paramount position of the state and of international agreement as the best way to peace.

Throughout the war Pius continued to appeal for disarmament, arbitration by international bodies,[90] respect for international law,[91] and for a "new order" in international relations that consciously recalled Benedict XV's Five Points.[92] Pius's 1941 Christmas message, *Nell'Alba,*[93] stressed the rights of minorities, economic equality and justice, and freedom of religion, but it did so "within the limits of a new order"[94] based on the primacy of the nation-state and the recognition of treaty rights, international agreement, and ruling elites.

Only toward the end of the war, when the Western democracies were clearly reaching victory, did the pope acknowledge the will of the people and their role in bringing about peace.[95] In his Christmas broadcast of December 24, 1944, Pius observed that the war had awakened a "new attitude" in people, "one that questions, criticizes, distrusts," and a dawning feeling "that had there been the possibility of censuring and correcting the actions of public authority, the world would not have been dragged into the vortex of a disastrous war."[96] Pius concluded that the duty is "imposed on all . . . to do everything to ban once and for all wars of aggression as a legitimate solution of international disputes and as a means towards realizing national aspirations."[97] For the full implications of Pius's shift in emphasis from the head to the members we must examine the effects of official church teaching on popular Catholic peacemaking before and during World War II.

## THE REBIRTH OF POPULAR CATHOLIC PEACEMAKING

To gain some understanding of the history of Catholic peacemaking in the first half of the twentieth century, we will briefly survey here its characteristics, examine the forms of European Catholic resistance to Hitler and his wars, and then concentrate on the role of German Catholics in the Nazi war effort. Our study will touch on only a few salient trends and major examples, focusing in the end on one of the few known conscientious objectors to Hitler's wars, the Austrian farmer Franz Jaegerstaetter.

The papacy was looked on with suspicion by most liberal Europeans in the nineteenth century, including European peacemakers.[98] Many individual Catholics, however, did begin to participate in European peace societies from about 1848, especially in Italy, France, and England.[99] Catholic mass movements among trade unionists, Catholic worker organizations and democratic political parties began in the 1870s in Germany, Belgium, Holland, France, and Italy to fight for social justice, decent working and living standards, decentralization, and reconciliation of labor and capital.[100]

With the endorsement of the international peace movement by Leo XIII[101] and Pius X,[102] European Catholics eagerly responded to the challenge of peacemaking. In 1899 French Catholics formed the Gatry Society, and by 1910 the International Catholic Peace League had branches in France, Spain, Switzerland, and Belgium.[103] Yet by the outbreak of World War I the pacifist substitution of international harmony for personal nonviolence had failed to excite even lukewarm interest or to hold any but the most committed members.[104] In Italy even committed pacifists embraced the war out of nationalistic fervor.[105] While "White Cross Societies" survived in France and Germany throughout World War I to work for peace,[106] far more significant were the eighty thousand priests from the belligerent nations who served in the war, including the five thousand to six thousand French priests who were killed in action.[107]

## CATHOLIC PEACE GROUPS IN NAZI GERMANY

Since the Reformation German Catholics had been on the defensive, closely associated with the papacy and thus with a foreign power.[108] Living mostly in rural and poor areas, Catholics were regarded as a problem class until the nineteenth century, when they became increasingly articulate and socially and politically active with their own press and lay organizations.[109] The *Kulturkampf* brought about the first test of Catholic power. This *Kulturkampf* was the struggle between Chancellor Bismarck and the Catholic Church over the autonomy of Catholic schools and the Catholic defense against anticlerical and anti-Catholic liberals.[110] Both sides eventually backed off, but the conflict put German Catholics in an unpatriotic light for some time, pressuring them to prove their Germanness even after they had won some political power.

To this problem was added the fear of many Germans of the rise of Bolshevism in Russia and its attacks on Christian values and interests. Then came the 1933 Reich Concordat between the Vatican and the Hitler government.[111] To these factors one must add the nature of the Catholic church as it was understood by the bishops, clergy, and laypeople who participated in Germany's peace movement. The church existed not as a sect but as an *ecclesia*, a corporate body, a clearly recognizable institution that accommodated society at large within its universal mission. It was an institution whose survival as a corporate body was considered one of the chief functions of its hierarchy and members.[112] Given all these factors, when the time came, the church in Germany was all too willing to give the injunction to "render to Caesar what is Caesar's" as broad an interpretation as possible.[113]

After the *Kulturkampf*, eager to show their patriotism to the German state, Catholics were notably absent from the International Catholic Peace League. They did not join the German Peace Society founded in 1892 or the World Alliance of Churches for Promoting International Friendship.[114] Immediately after World War I several Germans (including Franziskus Stratmann, O.P.), founded the *Friedensbund deutscher Katholiken* (German Catholic Peace Union). The movement spread quickly throughout the country and at its height included about forty thousand members.[115] Among its patrons were Cardinal Bertram of Breslau, Cardinal Faulhaber of Munich, Bishop Schreiber of Berlin, Bishop Spröll of Rothenburg, and Bishop Gröber of Meissen—most of the top level of the Germany hierarchy.

The movement's patrons spoke eloquently of the need for disarmament. In February 1932 Cardinal Faulhaber told the Geneva Disarmament Conference:

> Moral disarmament must precede the military disarmament. The nimbus surrounding the uniform and the military parade has faded. The old songs of war can now be quietly laid to rest in the war museums. The heroism of the sword is not the only form of the heroic life.[116]

Faulhaber repudiated the ancient adage, "If you want peace, prepare for war," with "a new principle: If you want peace, prepare for peace!"[117] Similarly, Bishop Gröber exhorted the German Catholic Peace Union (November 1931) that true international peace is founded "on the universal and open intention to block a new murderous war at any price."[118] Gröber condemned "devoting billions to armaments while millions of people in virtually every country on earth suffer from unemployment and physical as well as spiritual hunger."[119] War must be viewed as a scandal to civilization, as mass fratricide. Nothing must be allowed to block general disarmament.

After the Nazis came to power in 1933, the German Catholic Peace Union became one of the first targets for repression. The organization was dissolved, its offices and records destroyed, and its membership scattered. Two members were put on a showcase trial, and the rest of the leadership either went into hiding, as did Fr. Stratmann, or disassociated themselves from the group. So feared was the union that during the Nazi era no one who had once been a member could be employed as a civil servant.[120] Despite Nazi fears, however, only seven members of the Union were known to have

## Jesus Is Arrested in Gethsemani

"And behold, one of those who were with Jesus reached out his hand, drew his sword, and struck the servant of the high priest, cutting off his ear. Then Jesus said to him, "Put back your sword into its place; for all those who take the sword will perish by the sword." [Mt. 26:51-53. See Chapter 2, pp. 21 and 28-29, n. 6.]

**Giotto, *The Kiss of Judas***
**Padua, Arena Chapel**

*Pacifism in the Roman Empire:*
*Martin of Tours (c. 316–397)*

"So [Martin] said to the Caesar, 'I have been your soldier up to now. Let me now be God's. Let someone else who is going to fight have your bonus. I am Christ's soldier. I am not allowed to fight.' " [Sulpicius Severus, *Life of St. Martin* IV. See Chapter 4, pp. 51–52.]

**Simone Martini,** *St. Martin Renouncing the Sword*
**Assisi, San Francesco, Lower Church, Montefiore Chapel**

*Poverty and Peacemaking*
*Francis of Assisi (1181–1226)*

With all Assisi gathered around, Francis confronts his father's rage, gives him back all his worldly goods, and sets out to live a new life of poverty and peacemaking. [See Chapter 6, p. 83.]

**Attributed to Giotto, *Francis Renounces His Worldly Goods***
**Assisi, San Francesco, Upper Church**

## Papal Peacemaking:
## Benedict XII (1334–42)

Benedict's work for arbitration and peaceful settlement of wars between states was typical of papal efforts during the Middle Ages. The church itself, he declared, must be defended by prayers and suffering, not arms. [See Chapter 8, pp. 101–2.]

**Paolo da Siena, *Benedict XII*
Rome, St. Peter's Crypt**

*Humanist Peacemaking:*
*Desiderius Erasmus (1466–1536)*

"If Christ is a figment, why do we not frankly reject him? Why do we glory in his name? . . . If we acknowledge Christ as our authority, Christ who is Love, and who taught nothing, handed down nothing that is not love and peace, come, let us follow him, not only in name, not by wearing his badge, but in our actions, in our lives." [*Against War.* See Chapter 9, p. 127.]

**Quentin Metsys, *Erasmus at Fifty***
**Rome, Corsini Palace**

*Peacemaking in the New World:*
*Bartolomé de las Casas (1474–1566)*

"War against unbelievers for the purpose of subjecting them to Christian control, and to compel them by this means to accept the Christian faith and religion, or to remove obstacles to this end that may exist, is reckless, unjust, perverse, and tyrannical." [From *Declaration of the Rights of the Indians*, as approved by the bishops of Latin America, 1546. See Chapter 10, pp. 142–43.]

**Diego Rivera, *Las Casas and Cortes***
**Mexico City, National Palace**

## Catholic Internationalism: Charles Castel de Saint-Pierre (1658–1743)

Saint-Pierre proposed a plan for European Confederation, whose Assembly would meet regularly in a "City of Peace" to "renounce and renounce for ever, for themselves and for their successors, resort to arms as an instrument of national policy." [From his *Project for Perpetual Peace*. See Chapter 11, pp. 166–67.]

**French School, 18th Century**
**Versailles Museum**

Cliché des Musées Nationaux, Paris

## Pope Benedict XV (1914–1922)

On the outbreak of World War I Benedict warned, "The dread image of war overshadows the world and absorbs nearly every thought. . . . And while the mighty hosts are contending in the fury of combat, cities, families, individuals are being oppressed by those evils . . . day by day the numbers increase of widows and orphans; the paths of commerce are blocked; the fields are left untilled; the arts are at a standstill; the rich are made poor; the poor are made destitute, all are made to mourn." [*Ad Beatissimum*, 1914. See Chapter 12, pp. 171–73.]

Felici

## Pacifist Opposition to Hitler: Franz Jaegerstaetter (1907–1943)

When ordered to swear obedience to Hitler or face death, this Austrian farmer wrote: "Christ too demands a public confession of our faith. . . . The commandments of God teach us, of course, that we must also render obedience to secular rulers, even when they are not Christian. But only to the extent that they do not order us to do anything evil, for we must obey God rather than man." [From his *Nine Commentaries*. See Chapter 12, pp. 182–84.]

From Gordan Zahn, *In Solitary Witness: The Life and Death of Franz Jaegerstaetter.* Used by permission of Professor Zahn.

## Pope John XXIII (1958–1963): A New Theology of Peace

"Therefore in an age such as ours which prides itself on its atomic energy it is contrary to reason to hold that war is now a suitable way to restore rights which have been violated." [*Pacem in Terris*. See Chapter 13, pp. 189–90.]

**John XXIII Announces Second Vatican Council**

### The Irish Peace People: Betty Williams and Mairead Corrigan in 1976

For their leadership in helping both Catholic and Protestant "live and love and build a just and peaceful society" and their commitment to "reject the use of the bomb and the bullet and all the techniques of violence" they were awarded the Nobel Peace Prize in 1977. [See Chapter 13, pp. 201–4.]

AP/Wide World Photos

### Jaime Cardinal Sin of Manila

Sin's transformation from "critical collaboration" with Ferdinand Marcos to his outright condemnation of his regime and call for nonviolent revolution was instrumental in deposing the dictator and bringing President Aquino to power. [See Chapter 14, pp. 214–19.]

Religious News Service Photo

**Cardinal Sin (left) addresses an anti-Marcos meeting in 1984**

## The "Voice" of the Third World: Bishop Helder Camara

John Padula

In the late 1960s, in the midst of the martial-law state, Camara declared, "The injustices within Brazilian society constitute Violence Number One, and terrorism is Violence Number Two. It is easy for the government to fight the secondary violence. Why don't they have the courage to fight the primary violence?" [See Chapter 14, pp. 224–28.]

## Argentina: The Mothers of the Plaza de Mayo

Rex Gowar

Despite harrassment and physical violence, the mothers, sisters, and daughters of the "disappeared" gave witness to the truth that justice must prevail in Argentina. They based their actions on the gospels and offered their own nonviolence against the injustice and brutality of the generals. [See Chapter 14, pp. 228–31.]

### Archbishop and Martyr:
### Oscar Romero of San Salvador
### (1917–1980)

In March 1980, the day before he was assassinated, Romero called on the Salvadoran army to lay down its arms: "Brothers, you are part of our people. You kill your own campesino brothers and sisters. And before an order to kill that a man may give, the law of God must prevail that says 'Thou shalt not kill!' " [See Chapter 14, pp. 233–37.]

Octavio Duran

## *Dorothy Day (1897–1980) during a UFW Protest in 1973*

Religious News Service Photo

The founder of the Catholic Worker movement and newspaper, Day combined an evangelical pacifism with a life of simplicity dedicated to helping the poor and outcasts of American society. She showed that living the Beatitudes was a real option in the twentieth century. [See Chapter 15, pp. 241–43, 259–60.]

## Thomas Merton (1915-1968): Monastic Protest

"I make monastic silence a protest against the lies of politicians, propagandists and agitators, and when I speak it is to deny that my faith and my Church can ever seriously be aligned with these forces of injustice and destruction." [From Japanese edition of *No Man Is an Island*. See Chapter 15, pp. 249–52.]

from *The Geography of Lograire.*
Used by permission of New Directions.


## Daniel and Philip Berrigan: Voices of the Prophets

"When at what point will you say no to this war?/ We have chosen to say/ with the gift of our liberty/if necessary our lives:/the violence stops here." [From Daniel Berrigan, *The Trial of the Catonsville Nine*. See Chapter 15, pp. 257–59.]

**The Berrigans with a U.S. Marshall in 1971**

Religious News Service Photo

resisted Hitler's wars as conscientious objectors. Six were executed and one was confined to a mental institution for the rest of the war.[121] No other protest, either by mass demonstration, as did occur over church rights, or by small groups, ever emerged from the Peace Union. Many of the Peace Union's original supporters, including Archbishop Gröber and Cardinal Faulhaber, later became some of the strongest supporters of the Nazi war effort.[122]

## THE CATHOLIC CHURCH AND THE NAZIS

After the collapse of Nazi Germany in 1945, German historians and churchpeople, aided by the Western Allies, who were eager to rehabilitate the defeated nation, collectively manufactured what has since been called the postwar myth of the German church resistance to Hitler.[123] Despite some revisionist work since the Adenauer period in Germany, the picture of religious opposition to the Nazis has remained unchanged, and with good reason. Although German Christians, including German Catholics, share in the guilt for World War II, the Holocaust, and the other injustices of the Nazi era, all the evidence leads us to conclude that no institution—the courts, the press, the unions, the universities, the army, or the political parties—offered any effective resistance. Whatever opposition did exist came from the churches alone.[124]

The Catholic Church was not only active in this opposition but, according to Nazi sources and later historians, offered the most serious and important challenge to the Hitler government, both because of its stronger hierarchical structure and because of its international character and appeal.[125] That its bishops and clergy often spoke out against Nazi abuses and injustices is certain, that it offered many hundreds of martyrs to Nazi persecution and concentration camps is also without doubt.[126] Yet this resistance was limited. The Nazis grew stronger despite church protests, and when war came few bishops or clergy actually opposed it, and the number of known Catholic conscientious objectors can be counted on two hands.

Two factors have been proposed to explain the failure of any organized peace movement against the Nazi onslaught. The first was the total and completely novel form of Nazi repression, a totalitarianism that brooked no dissent and had the means to implement its will. The second and perhaps more important factor was the fundamental weakness within the German Catholic resistance to Hitler, a weakness common to all other groups except the Protestant pacifist sects. This weakness was the conflict within Catholics between their Catholicism and their patriotism. German Catholics protested many Nazi social and religious policies vehemently in the pulpit and in mass demonstrations[127] but rarely protested the nationalism of the church as an institution and the patriotism of its individual members. Gordon Zahn calls this the "patriotism-and-protest" dynamic.[128]

Catholic criticism of Nazi policy began as early as 1923 and was condemned as undue church interference with politics.[129] In the March 1933 elections that gave the Nazis power the Catholic vote was largely with the Catholic Center Party.[130] The German Catholic Church spoke out against the SS, the storm troopers, and the Brown Shirts,[131] and the Austrian bishops condemned Nazism in a pastoral letter (Jan. 15, 1934).[132] By 1934 official church resistance to the Nazis was underway in Germany. It was led by the Fulda Bishops' Conference and expressed in pastoral letters read from pulpits all over the country.[133] In its first attack the bishops' conference warned Catholics that, although they owed obedience to the state, this obedience was not absolute and was tempered by their duty to obey God before human beings.[134]

Before the war began, resistance took several forms. It protested the Nazis' "unnatural nationalism," their attempts to control Catholic education and school groups, the neopaganism of the Nazi regime, government restrictions on church organizations and services, its attacks on priests, nuns, and monks. Catholics resisted Nazi government demands that they refrain from political activities and that the churches keep silent on such issues.[135] Over the protests of Nazi officials, churchpeople co-opted many Nazi symbols and displays for church use to rob them of their power, a tradition going back to Boniface's missionary work in Germany.[136] Catholic laity for their part rallied to the call with increased attendance at services, processions, and pilgrimages and with boycotts of Hitler's birthday celebrations.

Yet for all its fervor and appeal, Catholic resistance was passive and ad hoc, aimed at specific abuses of the Nazi regime and at certain legal transgressions of the Concordat.[137] The resistance never attacked the Führer as the legitimate head of government, never attacked the Nazi government per se, and blamed most abuses on Hitler's lieutenants. Such passive resistance allowed the Nazis to choose the issues and terms of the debate. The resistance was thus doomed to fail, given the supernationalism of all elements of German society—especially when Hitler launched World War II.[138]

## GERMAN CATHOLICS AND WORLD WAR II

With the coming of war several elements of the "patriotism-and-protest" dynamic began to work against the church. First, the bishops were caught up in the nationalistic mood of the times. Their emphasis on patriotism and pride in the nation, if not in the Nazi regime, gave most German Catholics the implicit message that to fight in Hitler's wars was just and right. In addition, most of the church hierarchy, even those like Archbishop von Galen, who risked his life to protest Nazi euthanasia programs, and Cardinal Faulhaber, who was outspoken against Nazi attempts to discredit the validity of the Old Testament, became avid supporters of the Fatherland, Homeland, German Folk, and Reich.[139]

From the pulpits, in pastoral letters, and in whatever Catholic press still functioned under Nazi censorship,[140] the message was pressed home to the Catholic laity that "good Catholics will never be on the side of the revolutionaries, no matter how bad things may get."[141] Good Catholics were Good Germans, the Catholic soldier was the "soldier of Christ," called on to defend the Homeland—a Christian duty since the birth of Germany—and to continue the fight against godless Bolshevism.[142]

Catholics who might still wonder about the morality of fighting in Hitler's wars were further assured by the authoritarian tradition of German Catholic thought on the just war. This tradition believed in the strongest "presumption of justice" on the part of the government, in its superior claim to decide the justness of its wars, and in the individual Catholic's incompetence to judge on such matters,[143] an attitude criticized by Vitoria in the sixteenth century and clearly not consistent with the full tradition of canonical thought on the just war.[144]

Finally, and probably most importantly, after the war it became evident that "the German hierarchy had come to the conclusion that they could not count on the loyalty of their 'troops' in the event of an open and all-out church-state confrontation."[145] Catholic tradition since Trent and the radical split between orthodox piety and secular political life had caused most Catholics to consider their religious life as quite distinct from their life in the secular world of business and politics. Not that they ever felt any acute conflict between rendering to Caesar and rendering to God. Modern orthodoxy had taught them that religion was confined to one small corner of their total life, an escape and refuge from the "real world," which demanded most of their attention and loyalties.

Thus being a good Catholic was not in conflict with being a good German. Catholicism was fully consistent with nationalism, the demands of the nation-state, and its wars. It would have been the rare German—as the rare French person, Italian, or American in World War II—who would have defined Catholicism as anything else but loyalty to nation and government and the surrender of individual conscience to the collective wisdom of all citizens and church and political leaders. Coupled with this indifference to any but the most superficial forms of religious observance, the active association of the church with secular society and the state served to eliminate all forms of questioning and dissent.[146] Thus Stalin's observation "How many divisions does the pope have?" showed an insight into the religious consciousness of the secular citizen of the twentieth century that Catholics are only now beginning to understand and change.

## CATHOLIC PROPHETS AND MARTYRS

The Catholic Church is the Mystical Body, and to concentrate on any one part of this body, head or members, at any one time is to misunderstand its nature and the working of the Spirit within it. Popes trusted in diplomacy, bishops in good intentions and patriotism, and laity in the enlightened leadership of their pope and bishops; but many individual Catholics risked their lives to speak out, and many others died for their witness to the truth. Their resistance, in the long run, probably "had more tangible effect than all the protests issued from chancery offices or, for that matter, from Rome."[147]

These Catholic martyrs were often left to their own devices and thus differed from earlier witnesses such as the ninth-century martyrs of Cordova,[148] who acted with the full support of their church leadership. They have nevertheless left a clear record of Catholic peacemaking. While we cannot do full justice to this record, we can give a few examples of Catholic resistance to Hitler in Germany and in the rest of Nazi-dominated Europe.

The Dutch bishops warned of the growing danger of Nazism as early as January 1934. In 1936 Catholics in Holland were forbidden to support the Nazis under pain of excommunication. Even during the Nazi occupation of Holland the bishops issued a strongly worded pastoral condemning Nazism and the occupation, ordering Catholic journals not to submit to Nazi censorship. Catholic radio stations and trade unions were disbanded when the bishops refused to cooperate with Nazi demands, and the Catholic University at Nijmegen was closed after the hierarchy ordered students not to swear the oath of allegiance to Hitler. In May 1943, after the Dutch bishops issued a pastoral condemning the deportation and persecution of the Jews, the Germans turned on the Dutch Catholics themselves.[149]

In Belgium Catholics were forbidden to support the candidacy of Leon Degrelle, a Rexist ally of the Nazis, and in 1941 Cardinal van Roey condemned the Rexist Party. In 1943 Degrelle was excluded from Holy Communion and Rexists were forbidden to enter Catholic churches in uniform. In April 1944 Cardinal van Roey condemned Nazi racial policies against the Jews and others.[150] In Limburg Bishop Antonius Hilfrich encouraged political dissent against the Nazis and made his diocese a center of resistance.[151]

In France under the Vichy and German regimes, bishops were also outspoken.[152] Cardinal Gerlier, the archbishop of Lyons and primate of France, at first welcomed the

Vichy government. After his return from Rome in January 1941, however, he became closely associated with the resistance. His protest to Pétain's deportation of the Jews was read from every pulpit and broadcast throughout France. He declared a split between the French state and the church and refused to bless volunteers in the Vichy army or to celebrate masses for those killed in war. Archbishop Saliège of Toulouse joined in this protest, as did Bishop Pierre-Marie Théas of Lourdes. Bishop Théas was arrested and imprisoned by the Nazis as a result; after the war as a sign of forgiveness he founded Pax Christi.[153] Nor was protest restricted to the hierarchy. Thomas Merton has written about the work of Ignace Lepp and Emmanuel Mournier against the injustices of Vichy and the Nazis.[154]

In Germany protest took many forms. We have already mentioned the protest of the Fulda Conference; of Archbishop von Galen against Nazi euthanasia programs, restrictions on church activities, and Nazi confiscation of monastic and other clerical property for the war effort;[155] and of Cardinal Faulhaber against the anti-Semitic–inspired attempts to vilify the Old Testament. Johann Spröll, bishop of Rothenburg, received physical threats and was finally removed from his see by the Nazis and forced into exile for speaking out against the German annexation of Austria in 1938.[156]

Bernhard Lichtenberg was dean of the Cathedral of St. Hedwig in Berlin, under the very nose of Nazi power. He had had a long career of protest, refuting claims that the church blessed arms in war in its liturgy, protesting conditions in Nazi concentration camps to Hermann Göring, and condemning the Nazi euthanasia program. He was turned over to the Gestapo (although not by his own congregation) for including prayers for the Jews in his daily services. It was later revealed that he also prayed for Bolsheviks, displaced persons, and soldiers on both sides of the war. The record of his hearing details a stirring condemnation of Nazi policies and an appeal to the unassailable claims of Christian conscience. In answer to the claim that Christians must do their duty to the state, Lichtenberg proclaims the Christian duty to obey God and Christian ethics above human beings. Sentenced to a concentration camp after a harsh imprisonment, he died in transit in November 1943.[157]

Max Josef Metzger was a Catholic priest and founder of *Una Sancta,* a pacifist group. Arrested by the Gestapo for his attempts to organize a peaceful settlement to the war through Scandinavian intermediaries, he was executed in 1944. Two of his followers were also executed for refusing to bear arms in Hitler's wars.[158] Franz Reinisch, a Pallotine priest, was beheaded for his refusal to take the military oath of unconditional obedience to Adolf Hitler.[159] Many other examples could be cited.[160]

## FRANZ JAEGERSTAETTER

The story of the Austrian farmer Franz Jaegerstaetter (1907–1943),[161] who refused to fight in Hitler's wars, makes one recall that when all else in the church may seem to fail, truth still endures, even if in the heart of the most simple and powerless.[162] Born and raised in the Austrian village of St. Radegund, Jaegerstaetter had an elementary school education and was brought up in the conventional spirituality of the time. Around 1936 he experienced some form of conversion to a more ascetic and devout spirituality. His conversion went hand in hand with a clear political opposition to the Nazis. As his opposition headed toward open confrontation, he began writing short works, influenced by simple devotional tracts and the lives of the saints. His writing drew on the traditions of the prophets and martyrs and both explained and further motivated his own witness.

His first rebellion came with the German annexation of Austria, a move welcomed or accepted by the majority of Austrians and by the country's Catholic clergy. As Jaegerstaetter later wrote, he dreamed that the entire nation was like a "beautiful shining railroad train" headed at high speed to some unknown destination. As he prepared to climb aboard, a voice warned him, "This train is going to hell," and someone took him by the hand. "Now," the voice said, "we will go to purgatory."[163] Jaegerstaetter was the only person in his village to vote against the annexation. He removed himself from the Nazi social system, refusing Nazi charity collections and social benefits, resigning from the farmers guild and, as sexton of St. Radegund Church, refusing all cooperation with Nazi social works.[164]

Social pressures immediately were brought to bear on the farmer, husband, and father. Friends, relatives, clergy, and local officials all warned him against his outspokenness; they called him selfish and self-centered for not thinking of his nation, his community, his farm, his wife, and his children. Even when the war was long over the villagers remembered his witness only as self-righteousness and an act of vanity at a time when everyone else from the highest political leaders and clergy to the simple soldier and worker had all agreed to support their country in its time of trouble.[165] Nevertheless, Jaegerstaetter refused to cooperate with the Nazis, and he made his refusal public, rejecting entreaties to hide or to flee.[166]

On March 1, 1943, Jaegerstaetter took the final step and refused induction into the German army. Relatives and friends reminded him of the punishment for conscientious objection: death. His friends and neighbors saw his refusal to fight as a criticism of them as fools and his protest as purely political and in no way religious. While most thought the Nazis wrong, they were committed to service and obedience to "legitimate authority" and held Jaegerstaetter incompetent to judge the situation. Even after the war the Linz diocese and the chaplain who had visited Jaegerstaetter in the Linz prison dismissed him as a simple, isolated, uneducated peasant in no position to judge the justice of wars.[167] Instead, the diocese praised those Germans who had died fighting the war "firm in the conviction that they were fulfilling the will of God at their post, just as the Christian soldiers in the armies of the heathen emperor had done."[168]

Imprisoned at Linz until June 1943, Jaegerstaetter was transferred to Berlin for trial before a military tribunal. Despite entreaties to take the military oath out of love for his wife and family, or at least to accept noncombatant service, Jaegerstaetter refused. His sincerity and courage touched everyone who came in contact with him. Asked by his court-appointed lawyer if he were holier than the Catholic Church that approved Hitler's wars, Jaegerstaetter appealed to the sovereignty of the individual conscience, which even wife and children could not violate. Begged to change his mind by high army officers who were deeply moved by his courageous protest, he remained firm, condemning Hitler and the Nazis and affirming the power of the spirit, the weapons of Saint Paul, over material weapons.[169] Having forgiven his enemies, he was condemned to death and beheaded in prison on August 9, 1943.

In the writings he left behind, his letters to his wife and pastor, his prison statement smuggled out of jail, his *Nine Commentaries,* and his letter to his godson, all written between 1938 and 1943, Jaegerstaetter reveals a clear understanding of the issues and of his place as a Christian. Ordered to render the oath of obedience to Hitler, the farmer writes:

Christ, too, demands a public confession of our faith. . . . The commandments of God teach us, of course, that we must also render obedience to secular rulers, even when they are not Christian. But only to the extent that they do not order us to do anything evil, for we must obey God rather than man.[170]

Called on to defend Christianity against Bolshevism, Jaegerstaetter ponders whether "Christians today are perhaps wiser than Christ himself."[171] Christ and the apostles, Christians believe, went out against the heathens unarmed. Germans must face up to the immorality of their war. They cannot escape their guilt by placing "the whole dirty business on one person alone."[172]

Franz Jaegerstaetter's life was summed up in his last words:

> The true Christian is to be recognized more in his works and deeds than in his speech. The surest mark of all is found in deeds showing love of neighbor. To do unto one's neighbor what one would desire for oneself is more than merely not doing to others what one would not have done to himself. Let us love our enemies, bless those who curse us, pray for those who persecute us. For love will conquer and will endure for all eternity. And happy are they who live and die in God's love.[173]

We know of Franz Jaegerstaetter only by accident. An American sociologist chanced upon his story and pieced it together by patient research into personal reminiscences and scattered writings that had once been smuggled out of prison to relatives and then half-forgotten by them. The Nazis kept few public records of their conscientious objectors, and with good reason. Much else of the record was destroyed by World War II. We will, therefore, never know the true extent of the nonviolent resistance to Hitler and the Nazis. Yet one thing is clear: despite the bright record of the few prophets and martyrs whom we do know, most Germans—like most Italians, French, Americans, and Catholics of all the countries who fought in World War II—obeyed their government and defined their Christianity as service to Caesar, not as service to God. Thomas Merton observed:

> The real question raised by the Jaegerstaetter story is not merely that of the individual Catholic's right of conscientious objection . . . but the question of the church's own mission of protest and prophecy in the gravest spiritual crisis man has ever known.[174]

This question was to have a profound impact on Catholic peacemaking for the rest of the century.

## THE LESSONS OF WORLD WAR II

Had World War II, then, taught the church a new lesson?—that true peace can only be made and preserved by individuals acting as Christians who "question, criticize, and distrust" authority. When World War II was over, did Pope Pius XII come to acknowledge that an approach to political tyranny that ignored the strength of individual Christians was doomed to failure, and that the active encouragement of *dis*obedience and dissent would have saved the world from war? The answer to both questions seems to be Yes. The pope's late Christmas broadcasts clearly show a shift in emphasis.[175] Gone was the nineteenth-century optimism, the trust in the rational capabilities of governments and of international law as checks to war.

A new spirit, however tentative, seems to have emerged in the pope's words acknowledging, for the first time since the Middle Ages, the role of the Catholic laity in making peace. This spirit survived into the Cold War. In his radio address (Nov. 10, 1956) on the plight of Hungary following the Soviet invasion, the pope made an open and forthright appeal, not to governments, but to the people, to resist tyranny and to reunite the nations of East and West:

> Their own peoples will be the first to find it impossible to remain oblivious of the need for returning to form a part of the human family. . . . Then all of you will be united in liberty and peace, beloved peoples of the East and the West, as members of a common human family. Peace and liberty! Nowadays these tremendous words leave no room for an ambiguous position.[176]

Pius's words of peace and liberation contained a clear and renewed call to individual Christian conscience:

> May God arouse you from your lethargy, keep you free from all complicity with tyrants and warmongers, enlighten your consciences, and strengthen your wills in the work of reconstruction.[177]

For the rest of his pontificate Pius XII continued to stress that peace "is not a kind of silence which resembles death, but rather a power and a vital dynamism."[178] Such dynamic peacemaking depends on the broad-based ability of individuals to distinguish "justice from injustice, right from wrong."[179]

Yet going beyond the limitations of the past was to be the work of another generation. Pius XII was still a product of his age and he continued to believe to the end in the virtue of an international system. This was not the old internationalism of ruling elites, but one that the common consent of newly awakened laity could invest with supreme power.[180] At the end of World War II the pope welcomed the creation of the United Nations but stressed that it must have the coercive powers that the League of Nations lacked, as well as legislative and judicial powers.[181] His position was in keeping with the tradition of Catholic internationalism beginning in the fourteenth century.[182]

Pius emphasized the duty of individuals to dissent, to question, and to prod their governments to new international cooperation. At the same time he seems to have been grappling with the logical conclusions of his new direction: the rights of nations and of individuals to self-defense in a new world and the rights of individual Christians to exercise their consciences in making peace. Pius's thought was often contradictory, but he recognized the basic problems facing the peacemaker in the late twentieth century and helped toward some solutions.

Much of his thought was within traditional Tridentine limits. His Christmas broadcast of December 24, 1954,[183] indirectly associated "pacifist" efforts or propaganda with Communism. For nations faced with unjust attack, self-defense "could not be considered unlawful,"[184] and in a democratic country that decides on such a defensive war through the normal process of consensus, "a Catholic citizen cannot invoke his own conscience in order to refuse to serve and fulfill those duties [of combat that] the law imposes."[185] Yet, Pius concedes, there are times in which only recourse to higher principles can bring peace to consciences. "It is therefore consoling," the pope concludes, "that in some countries, amid today's debates, men are talking about conscience and its demands."[186]

Pius XII showed similar ambiguity in his attitude to defensive wars. He allowed that states may have the right of self-defense, but the pope welcomed new international efforts for peace.

> No one could hail this development with greater joy than he who has long upheld the principle that the idea of war as an apt and proportionate means of solving international conflicts is now out of date. . . . No one could wish [more] success to this common effort . . . than he who has conscientiously striven to make the Christian and religious mentality reject modern war with its monstrous means of conducting hostilities.[187]

War can no longer be considered the simple instrument of foreign policy, but must be seen as the evil that it is.[188]

Not only wars of aggression, but even the old moral categories of defense have been outmoded by the new weapons—atomic, bacterial, and chemical—of the modern age.[189] So serious is the threat of the new warfare that the old criteria of the just war—defense, avenging evil, and restoring violated rights—have now been reduced to only one excuse: legitimate defense "forced upon one by an obvious, extremely serious and otherwise unavoidable injustice."[190] Without such an excuse all use of these modern "ABC" weapons "must be rejected as immoral."[191] Pius sounds like Erasmus when he concludes that even a just war of defense

> must be waged at the risk of giving a free hand in international affairs to brute violence and lack of conscience. It is not enough, therefore, to have to defend oneself against just any injustice in order to justify resorting to the violent means of war. When the damages caused by war are not comparable to those of "tolerated injustice," one may have a duty to "suffer the injustice."[192]

As the horrors of World War II proved, modern warfare has become so destructive, so out of proportion to the supposed justice of waging even defensive wars, that it may be better to suffer the injustice rather than resort to war. By the end of his pontificate Pius had come to realize the emptiness of new defensive systems and the hollowness of even the most just war fought in the modern world. Despite the promises of "peaceful atoms," he said:

> Still, everyone is aware that other uses more suited to destruction and death are being sought and found. And what a death! Every day there is another sad step along that tragic road, another rush to arrive there alone, first, best. And the human race almost loses hope of the possibility of stopping this homicidal and suicidal madness.[193]

Modern nuclear war can bring no defense because it can bring no victory:

> There will be no song of victory, only the inconsolable weeping of humanity, which in desolation will gaze upon the catastrophe brought on by its own folly.[194]

The horrors of modern war and its nightmare peace of death had finally begun to change the Catholic hierarchy's attitudes to war. Pius XII had come to recognize the problem and was groping toward its solution. It was the achievement and revolution of his successor, John XXIII, to acknowledge this change and to begin to provide new answers for a new age.

# CHAPTER 13

# A CATHOLIC THEOLOGY OF PEACE: EUROPEAN PEACEMAKING FROM VATICAN II TO SOLIDARITY

## JOHN XXIII

Elected by a deadlocked conclave as a transitional figure, John XXIII, ironically, brought a revolution to the life of the Catholic Church.[1] His pontificate marked the church's final break with the Constantinian era and with European Christendom. *Mater et Magistra,* the Second Vatican Council, and *Pacem in Terris* signaled a new direction in Catholic thought on war and peace. A moral theology concerned with defining and limiting war moved to a theology of peace aimed at implementing the Sermon on the Mount. John XXIII shared Pius XII's hierarchical outlook on the nature of the church, but his life and works put a new emphasis on the role of the laity within the church and on the individual as the starting point and frame of reference for all human institutions.[2] The laity was no longer passively to obey the commands of the hierarchy, to remain politically subservient and morally quietist, but to "observe, judge, act."[3]

In his *Ad Petri Cathedram* of June 29, 1959, John returned to an Erasmian, Christian Humanist tradition. God, he wrote, has created all humans as brothers and sisters and has given them the positive fruits of creation as a common trust to be shared by all. Yet, in the modern age humans have degenerated to a level worse than that of beasts, filling the cemeteries with thousands of young persons killed in war. Now, peace can be restored only if people become eager for peace. Only then will it be possible for states to return to harmonious relations.[4]

This unity of all humans is explored in John's first, great encyclical, *Mater et Magistra* (May 15, 1961).[5] Social justice now replaces international order as the key to peace. While much of the encyclical builds upon the teaching of Leo XIII and Pius XI in *Rerum Novarum* and *Quadragesimo Anno,* John's tone sets the burden of implementing justice firmly on individual Christians "who find a most notable motive in the fact that we are all members of Christ's Mystical Body."[6]

Thus the work of the church infuses every aspect of society through the efforts of individuals to produce justice. True justice must insure that all the peoples of the world, rich and poor alike, have access to the world's common resources; that the principles of justice and humanity guide one's actions on property, wages, living conditions, means of production, and economic relations between individuals, classes, and states. In this light the luxury and abundance of the few in the midst of the poverty and suffering of the many is an offense against both justice and humanity.[7]

In the face of such inequalities and human needs the arms race becomes one of the world's chief injustices. It affects both "developing" and "developed" countries, who devote greater and greater portions of their national wealth to armaments in an effort to bolster a misguided national prestige.[8] As armament levels rise, mutual trust falls. Each nation fears that the other harbors plans of conquest and awaits only the right moment to launch its attack. Each arms itself, supposedly, not to attack but "to deter other countries from aggression." Vast human energies and resources are funneled into destructive purposes. "Meanwhile, in the minds of individual human beings and among peoples there arises and grows a sense of uneasiness and reluctance which lessens the spirit of initiative for works on a broad scale."[9] John's words describing the effects of militarism on the individual and society recall those of More or Erasmus.[10]

John XXIII deepened this understanding of international peace in his *Address to World Leaders*.[11] Quoting Pius XII, who said that "whereas everything is lost, and lost to everyone, through war, nothing will be lost through peace," the pope reminds politicians that the Christian fights only with the spiritual weapons recommended by Saint Paul: loins girded with truth, heart fitted with the breastplate of justice, feet shod in the readiness to spread the gospel of peace, protected by the shield of faith. Such weapons, he insists, "ought to be the attitude of a good Christian in the face of any event, in any time and under any circumstances."

## PACEM IN TERRIS

Pope John was moving gradually to a total repudiation of war in the modern world, toward a revolution of Catholic thinking on peace and justice. The revolution is made explicit in *Pacem in Terris* (Peace on Earth),[12] published on April 11, 1963, between the two sessions of the Second Vatican Council. While the encyclical repeated many of Pius XII's radio messages and made popular many of that pope's little-known views on peace,[13] *Peace on Earth* marks a shift in the meaning of Catholic peacemaking. One commentary noted that "the incredibly tortured language of papal monarchy was gone, replaced by a language of fraternity, shared concern, and mutual responsibility."[14]

Four major themes are treated in the papal letter: the rights of the individual, the relation of individual conscience to authority, the immediate need for disarmament and the obsolescence of war in the modern age, and the development of international bodies aimed at protecting the common good and based on the common consent of individuals.[15] Two principles underlie these four themes: the freedom of the individual and the validity of natural law. These principles, seen as major departures for the church even by Catholic writers,[16] are intrinsic to John's profoundly Humanist approach. His emphasis on ethical action and the common moral foundations of all human behavior goes back to Erasmus and to the natural-law tradition of Vitoria.[17] What is new, however, is the open and optimistic embrace of the entire world, not just of the Catholic Church. Gone forever is Trent's hostility to the world and its defensive and authoritarian insistence on the church as the sole source of salvation. The encyclical is addressed to all people of good will, not only to Christians or to believers, and appeals to the reason and good will of all to end hatred and war.

The encyclical is divided into five parts. Part 1 (pars. 1–45), following an argument traditional since Erasmus, notes that the universe and everything in it is held together in the harmony and order of peace (pars. 1–3). This is not the order of coercion but of the freedom of each of its elements. It is an order not imposed from above but springing forth from each individual:

> But the Creator of the world has imprinted in man's heart an order which his conscience reveals to him and enjoins him to obey: "This shows that the obligations of the law are written in their hearts; their conscience utters its own testimony." [Rom 2:15]. And how could it be otherwise? [par. 5].

All human society thus rests on the individual personality of each human being (par. 9), and all order in the world and in society is based upon this moral foundation (par. 37). All societal rights and obligations flow from this essential consciousness of universal law imprinted on each heart and imposes on individuals the duty "to claim those rights as marks of [their] dignity, while others have the obligation to acknowledge those rights and respect them" (par. 44).

*Peace on Earth* thus sides decisively with the rights of individual conscience, even over and against the rights of political authority. Part 2 (pars. 46–79) defines this even more clearly in discussing the relationship between authority and the individual. Although John follows the Catholic tradition based on Saint Paul, regarding all authority as ultimately derived from God, he breaks with authoritarian and quietist traditions and reaffirms Catholic teaching that not all leaders deserve unquestioning obedience (par. 46). Authority is not without any controls and "must derive its obligatory force from the moral law" (par. 47). Consequently, "it follows that civil authority must appeal primarily to the conscience of individual citizens, that is to each one's duty to collaborate readily for the common good of all" (par. 48).

The direction of John's thought is clear. Since all authority is based on moral law, and all moral law is ultimately based on God,

> it follows that, if civil authorities pass laws or command anything opposed to the moral order and consequently contrary to the will of God, neither the laws made nor the authorizations granted can be binding on the consciences of the citizens, since "God has more right to be obeyed than man" [Acts 5:29; par. 51].

The apostles, apologists, and martyrs have given witness to this truth (par. 14).

After having established the priority of the individual conscience and the duty to obey God above human beings, in Part 3 of the encyclical, John defines the proper role of government in securing peace: to win and keep truth, justice, and solidarity (pars. 80–129). Truth will eliminate the evils of racism and extreme nationalism and will remind human beings that they are all members of the same human family. Justice guards the equal access of people to the means of development and protects minorities. Solidarity, that is, mutual cooperation and Christian love, protects the work of justice.

Essential to accomplishing the work of justice is dealing with the problem of war in the modern age. John's condemnation is unequivocal. Repeating a theme voiced by the Humanists, by Pius XII, and in his own *Mater et Magistra,* John contrasts the needs of people in developing countries for economic and social progress with the "vast outlay of intellectual and economic resources" (par. 109) squandered on the development of armaments:

> Justice, then, right reason and consideration for human dignity and life urgently demand that the arms race should cease, that the stockpiles which exist in various

countries should be reduced equally and simultaneously by the parties concerned, that nuclear weapons should be banned, and finally that all come to an agreement on a fitting program of disarmament, employing mutual and effective controls [par. 112].

True peace, he declares, "consists not in equality of arms but in mutual trust alone" (par. 113).

John XXIII does not stop even with this call for the banning of nuclear weapons and for general disarmament. He goes on to attack the notion of war, even of just war, in the modern age:

Therefore, in an age such as ours which prides itself on its atomic energy it is contrary to reason to hold that war is now a suitable way to restore rights which have been violated [par. 127].

Two points should be stressed. The first is that Pope John is not condemning nuclear war alone, but all war waged in the nuclear age. The second is that in rejecting the suitability of war as a means of restoring violated rights he explicitly rejects the theory of the just war.

Yet the pope was a realist. Like Erasmus, he knew that every warlike posture, every penny spent by governments on war preparation is presented as an act of defense, "not for aggression they affirm—and there is no reason for not believing them—but to dissuade others from aggression" (par. 128). Modern states as constituted are thus incapable of even distinguishing the true path to peace, much less following it. In Part 4 of the encyclical the pope therefore sets the foundation for a new order: an internationalism based on a functional United Nations (pars. 130–45). But this is not a return to the old internationalism of the nineteenth century, as some have seen it.[18] Pope John's new world order is built, not on force imposed on the peoples of the world by their ruling elites, but on consensus and consent of the world's peoples acting together to bring peace. *Peace on Earth* thus comes full circle back to the primacy of the individual right and duty to make peace, which ultimately informs and judges all actions by governments and organizations.

John returns to this theme clearly in Part 5 with the Pastoral Exhortations (pars. 146–73). The Christian's duty in the modern world is to act, "to take an active part in public life, and to contribute towards the attainment of the common good of the entire human family" (par. 146). The Christian faith must be reintegrated both externally, with action, and internally, within the individual human psyche (par. 152). The old walls between the inner spirituality of the pious and the demands of the active world that allowed Catholics to acquiesce to the atrocities of World War II must fall just as surely as the "inconsistency in their minds between religious belief and their action in the temporal sphere" (par. 152).

John's challenge to Catholics in the modern world is clear and uncompromising. War can no longer be considered a valid form of policy and must be outlawed. Yet Christians live in a world "but slightly affected by Christian motivation or inspiration" (par. 151), a world that we have come to call "post-Christian." As Pius XII and the Catholics who lived through the traumas of two world wars had learned, governments can no longer be trusted to seek peace and justice. This, then, is the work of the individual Christian. Informed by the authority of natural reason and God's law, the individual must "observe, judge, act" according to the dictates of his or her own conscience and, if necessary, confront the authority of the state and "obey God rather than man." This is an "immense task" (par. 163), but only thus can freedom and justice be served and true peace be acheived, a peace "founded on truth, built according to justice, vivified and integrated by charity, and put into practice in freedom" (par. 167). This is the gift and the promise of peace that Christ left with his diciples: "Peace I leave with you, my peace I give to you, not as the world gives do I give to you" (Jn 14:27; see par. 170).

## VATICAN II

Pope John XXIII died on June 3, 1963, between the first and second sessions of the Second Vatican Council.[19] He had left *Pacem in Terris* as a kind of final testament, and the encyclical influenced the outcome of the Council. After lengthy debate and various drafts,[20] the final version of *Gaudium et Spes,* the Pastoral Constitution on the Church in the Modern World, was promulgated and incorporated into the formal teaching of the Catholic Church.

On December 7, 1965, *Gaudium et Spes* became an official statement of Vatican II.[21] It covers every aspect of the Christian's relationship with the world from conjugal love, marriage and the family, culture, education, and social life, to economic relations, politics, relations between nations, and the building of world community. Part 2, chapter 5, "The Fostering of Peace and the Promotion of a Community of Nations,"[22] follows the path already taken by John XXIII in *Pacem in Terris* and is truly the constitution for modern Catholic peacemakers. Though it builds firmly on the mainstream Catholic tradition on war and peace, it broke decisively with many of the authoritarian and reactionary tendencies that had crept into the church since Trent. *Gaudium et Spes* presents "an evaluation of war with an entirely new attitude."[23] It appeals to individual conscience, and it presents not the worn-out moral theology of war in the just-war tradition but a new pastoral theology of peace. It does not aim to form a conscience for the proper waging of war but one for the waging of peace.[24] After Vatican II Catholics can no longer view war as a normal condition of human life and international relations, but as a "disruption, indeed a negation of human life."[25]

*Gaudium et Spes* treats the subject of peace in three parts: a theology of peace (arts. 77–78), restrictions on war (arts. 79–82), and the conclusion of the theology of peace (arts. 83–90).[26] After an introduction declaring that "artisans of peace are blessed, 'for they shall be called children of God' " (art. 77), the document sets out to define what peace means for Catholics in the modern world:

Peace is not merely the absence of war. Nor can it be reduced solely to the maintenance of a balance of power between enemies. Nor is it brought about by dictatorship. Instead, it is rightly and appropriately called "an enterprise of justice (Is. 32:7)." Peace results from that harmony built into human society by its divine Founder, and actualized by men as they thirst after even greater justice [art. 78].[27]

Peace is not the order imposed by governments, dictators, and elites, but an inner force motivating individuals to "thirst after justice."[28] Peace is not a concrete goal that can be won once and for all; it is instead a process, a constant effort to master passions and to heal wounds. It goes beyond justice and is the fruit of love (art. 78).[29] Human peace is the reflection of heavenly peace, taught to us by Christ and the cross. In imitation of Christ all Christians are urgently summoned to make peace. Yet because this peace is a process and an imitation of Christ's sacrifice, individual Christians can achieve peace only through peace. The Council, therefore, "cannot fail to praise those who renounce the use of violence in the vindication of their rights," resorting to the methods of defense available to the weaker party (art. 78). The message is clear: only by actively seeking a dynamic peace, by individually renouncing violence, can Christians hope to "beat their swords into plowshares, and their spears into pruning hooks" (Is 2:4; art. 78).[30]

After declaring that war is the product of human sin, *Gaudium et Spes* recommends specific actions to curb the savagery of war (art. 79),[31] including the general application of conventions for the wounded, prisoners, and racial and ethnic minorities. The thrust of this section, however, is in the statement of the two chief curbs to warfare: natural law and individual conscience, including the condemnation of blind obedience to unjust orders and the championing of the right of conscientious objection. Although we have seen many examples of the legitimacy of conscientious objection in the Catholic tradition, from its definition in canon law in the twelfth century[32] to the theory of Vitoria,[33] Vatican II was the first time that the Catholic Church had ever officially said anything about conscientious objection.[34] The church's approval is clear:

> Moreover, it seems right that laws make humane provisions for the case of those who for reasons of conscience refuse to bear arms, provided, however, that they accept some other form of service to the human community.[35]

The Council balances the right to nonviolent service to the community with an admission that governments must still defend themselves. Yet it goes on to severely limit the traditional doctrine of the just war (art. 79).[36] Defense of society can be justified, but not all methods used are just and "the mere fact that war has unhappily begun does not mean that all is fair between the warring parties."[37] In the modern age of total war, in fact, scientific weapons cause destruction "far exceeding the bounds of legitimate defense." The Council must heed the words of *Pacem in Terris* "to undertake an evaluation of war with an entirely new attitude" (art. 80). Vatican II does not condemn the weapons themselves, and thus avoids any technological discussion; but it does address the use to which they are put: the total destruction of cities and their populations "is a crime against God and man himself. It merits unequivocal and unhesitating condemnation."[38]

The Council followed the Catholic tradition of a strictly limited just war, but it rejected one of the main doctrines of defensive war in the modern age: deterrence.[39] The balance of terror is clearly not peace, and the arms race that produces it "is an utterly treacherous trap for humanity, and one which injures the poor to an intolerable degree" (art. 81). The only solution for the world and "our clear duty, then, [is] to strain every muscle as we work for the time when all war can be completely outlawed by international consent" (art. 82). Lacking a supranational authority that can implement this, Catholics must still work for peace between nations, for disarmament, and for international community.[40] The most effective measure to take was that learned in the holocausts of the world wars: the peoples of the world must be educated for peace, and each and every person must undergo a "change of heart," a conversion to peacemaking.[41]

After discussing the means of limiting and outlawing war, *Gaudium et Spes* returns to its definition of a theology of peace (arts. 83–93). The council expands its definition of peace as "an enterprise of justice," and as the active participation of Christians in the "building up of the world" in cooperation with God's own creation. Thus Vatican

II calls for a massive effort to aid the Third World in the integral development of all aspects of its life (art. 86).[42] It seeks a community of nations; it encourages economic, social, and political cooperation; and it invites the active participation of Christians to redistribute the world's wealth (art. 88) and to support all efforts for a "universal solidarity" that will supercede nationalism (art. 90). Catholics must also act on the local level in dialogue with all their neighbors (art. 93).

Vatican II and its Pastoral Constitution *Gaudium et Spes* set off a revolution in the church that has not yet ended or even fully been felt in much of the world. By opening itself to all the peoples of the world, believers and nonbelievers, by addressing the problems of the entire world as the province of the church, it placed the church back into the history of the world, not outside or above it. At the same time it divorced itself from any one social, political, or economic system. Vatican II thus ended the church's alliance with European civilization, an alliance that had existed since the age of Constantine and that had produced a complete theory of Christendom. The council thus marked the end of the church's ambition to secular power and reaffirmed its biblical mission to the poor and the oppressed.[43]

These factors had a tremendous impact on the church's notions of peace. The scriptural tradition replaced the un-Christian traditions of Roman law, natural law, or Aristotelian logic. This change opened the door for a gradual discarding of the just-war tradition.[44] Its evangelical outlook and concern for individual conscience also put Vatican II firmly behind the rediscovered tradition of biblical pacifism.[45] The council's emphasis on the shared apostolate of all members of the Mystical Body[46] was a reaffirmation that the church was not only the pope or even the bishops but all the "people of God." The Council legitimized direct action by individual Catholics as a valid form of Christian life.[47] Finally, the church's declaration of independence from any one cultural, political, or economic system served to reaffirm its traditional supranationalism and universalism. The church again became a haven for dissent and a source of protest against social injustice and violence.[48]

## PAUL VI

When John XXIII died (1963) it was a foregone conclusion that the college of cardinals would elect his chosen successor, Cardinal Giovanni Battista Montini.[49] Yet no one within or outside the Catholic Church realized how energetically Paul VI would pursue John XXIII's program of reform and further his work for peace. Paul encouraged the progressives in the council. In December 1965 he addressed the United Nations with an impassioned call for peace.[50] In December 1966 he called for a negotiated settlement to the Vietnam War and in May 1968 he offered the Vatican as a site for peace talks.[51] He established the Justice and Peace Commission in Rome in 1967.[52] His Day of Peace messages condemned the arms race as a "scandal."[53] In remarks prepared for testimony before the United Nations in 1978 the pope questioned not only the use, but also the possession of modern armaments as "an act of aggression which constitutes a crime, for *even when they are not used,* by their cost alone *armaments kill the poor by causing them to starve*" (italics in original).[54] Paul had once dismissed pacifism as a flight from Christian responsibility,[55] but by his support for nonviolent methods of social change he moved the church toward a new approach to peacemaking.[56]

In *Populorum Progressio* (*On the Development of Peoples,* 1967) Paul approved conscientious objection and alternative service (par. 74). In that document Paul VI spelled out the connection between the arms race, the poverty of the Third World, and the need for Catholics to redefine their concepts of peace along the dynamic lines set out by Vatican II.[57] In the tradition of papal social encyclicals from Leo XIII to John XXIII (pars. 1–4), the pope's letter reflects his experience of the poverty of the developing world.[58]

Instead of helping the Third World, the past decade of capitalist "development" has only widened the gap between rich and poor (pars. 6–10). It is therefore the church's duty, in line with the words of Vatican II, to scrutinize the "signs of the times" with a critical and prophetic attitude, to call attention to injustices, and to teach the ways of justice and peace that can set these right (pars. 12–13). No one can ignore certain social situations—the lack of material necessities and the oppressive and dehumanizing social structures (pars. 14–21) "whose injustice cries to heaven" (par. 30). In such situations real peace is impossible. In fact, when all opportunities for cultural, social, and political participation are denied the people, "recourse to violence, as a means of righting these wrongs to human dignity, is a grave temptation" (par. 30).

Yet the pope does not recommend violent revolution as a solution:

> We know, however, that a revolutionary uprising—save where there is manifest, long-standing tyranny which would do great damage to fundamental personal rights and dangerous harm to the common good of the country—produces new injustices, throws more elements out of balance and brings on new disasters. A real evil should not be fought at the cost of greater misery (par. 31).

The pope seems to admit the possibility of a just revolution, using the same criteria as for a just war. However he qualifies the admission with the notion of proportionality: that the evil fought must not be met by even greater evil, either in the actual struggle or in the regime that will follow. Though they are often taken as the fountainhead of a modern theory of "just revolution,"[59] the pope's words are actually a recognition of injustice and a warning against recourse to arms. What, then, is his solution to oppression and injustice?

"Development Is the New Name for Peace" is both a chapter heading in Part 2 of the encyclical and the major solution offered for the problems of the Third World.[60] By "development," however, the pope does not mean a one-sided emphasis (as with some technocrats and capitalists) on GNP, imports and exports, and other statistics of "growth," but rather an integral development of cultural, social, political, and economic aspects of life that rejects many of the fundamental characteristics of both capitalism and communism. The pope rejects the atheism, materialism, and collectivism of Marxism, but he also condemns the unrestricted right of private property, the profit motive, and capitalist reliance on free trade, insisting on the people's right of expropriation for a greater social good (par. 24). He calls for a new humanism, a development of human potential in both individual and social values.[61]

True peace, he contends, can only be achieved when the rich nations voluntarily sacrifice their excess wealth for the poor, produce more and better goods, stop using aid as a form of neocolonialism, and devote their monies, now being used for the arms race, to a World Fund to benefit the developing countries (pars. 43–52). In words that recall Catholic peacemakers since the Middle Ages, the pope sums up the message of his letter:

> When so many people are hungry, when so many families suffer from destitution, when so many are steeped in ignorance, when so many schools, hospitals and

homes worthy of the name remain to be built, all public or private squandering of wealth, all expenditure prompted by motives of national or personal ostentation, every exhausting armaments race, becomes an intolerable scandal. We are conscious of Our duty to denouce it [par. 53].

The church's role is not only to denounce but also to teach and to encourage Catholics working for peace. Echoing Vatican II and the entire Catholic peace tradition, Paul stresses that

peace cannot be limited to a mere absence of war, the result of an ever precarious balance of forces. No, peace is something that is built up day after day, in the pursuit of an order intended by God, which implies a more perfect form of justice among men [par. 76].

In this work "the peoples themselves have the prime responsiblity to work for their own development" (par. 77), and in this work, "in countries undergoing development no less than in others, the laymen should take up as their own the proper task of renewing the temporal order" (par. 81).

The pope's words clearly reflect the lesson of the twentieth century: that true peace can only be the work of individual Christians working together to make a new society from the grassroots. Peace cannot be imposed from above or arranged among enlightened minds for the benefit of their followers:

If the role of the Hierarchy is to teach and to interpret authentically the norms of morality to be followed in this matter, it belongs to the layman, without waiting passively for orders and directives, to take the initiative freely and to infuse a Christian spirit into the mentality, customs, laws, and structures of the community in which they live [par. 81].

A revolution in Catholic peacemaking has taken place. The disasters brought on by passive obedience, reliance on authority, the glorification of war, and the wedding of the church to the temporal world had affected the head of the Mystical Body and shown the way to true peace. This radical realization taught by the head was now to be taken up and applied to the world by the members of the body.

## THE IMPACT OF VATICAN II: CONSCIENTIOUS OBJECTION IN EUROPE

Even before the Second Vatican Council had ended, European Catholics began applying the teachings of John XXIII. In Italy, France, Spain, Portugal, Belgium, and Germany the struggle of Catholic peacemakers influenced church teaching on peace and was in turn strengthened by that teaching. The case of the Italian Giuseppe Gozzini[62] is representative of the many Catholic conscientious objectors all over the world who have witnessed to the truth that the Christian must obey God's laws above human laws.

In January 1963, three months before the publication of John XXIII's *Pacem in Terris,* Gozzini refused military service, a universal obligation under Italian law, citing his duty to obey the law of God first. Conscientious objection was rare in Italy. By 1961 only two cases, both Jehovah's Witnesses, had been reported. Both objectors had been sentenced to long prison terms by a military court. In 1962 a French film in praise of conscientious objection, *Thou Shalt Not Kill,* was banned in Italy for condoning actions and attitudes contrary to Italian law. In defiance of the ban Florence's Mayor La Pira held a not-so-private screening of the film that immediately resulted in police action and prompted the Vatican's *Osservatore Romano* to write that "the principle of conscientious objection make[s] no sense to the Catholic."[63]

By 1963 the situation had changed very little. Gozzini was condemned by a right-wing, former military chaplain writing in the respected *La Nazione.* The priest wrote that Gozzini, by his refusal, disobeyed not only Italian law but also "the moral laws imposed by Christ and his church." The attack seemed to have the approval of the Italian church until an article in Florence's *Il Mattino* came to Gozzini's defense. Its author, Fr. Ernesto Balducci, a noted Catholic philosopher and scholar, told an interviewer that in an age of atomic weapons the Catholic "has not only the right but the duty to desert" from the military.

Balducci soon found himself under arrest for inciting soldiers to disobey the law and for holding authority in contempt. The director of *Il Mattino* was also prosecuted. Balducci's trial became known worldwide. The philosopher based his defense on the immorality of total war and the condemnation by Pius XII and the moralists of the post-Hiroshima age of such war. Balducci was acquitted in November 1963; but the Italian government appealed the case, and Balducci and his fellow conscientious objectors were finally sentenced to eight months in prison. *Pacem in Terris* appeared soon after the sentencing, however, and Fr. Balducci's position was vindicated by the official church and supported all over Europe.

When the second session of Vatican II convened, many of the council fathers openly declared their disapproval of the appellate court's decision and spoke openly in solidarity with Balducci. The Balducci case became a symbol to the Council of individual rights and of Christian opposition to militarism. The Italian state refused to reconsider the verdict, but the number of Italian conscientious objectors grew rapidly. By February 1965 thirty-one had been jailed. The situation seemed to be getting out of hand. An Italian military chaplain condemned the pacifists and all those who supported them. In a letter circulated privately, Don Lorenzo Milani defended the objectors. When his letter was published in the Communist paper *Rinascità,* both Milani and the paper's publisher were jailed under Italy's harsh conscription law.

The Milani trial opened in October 1965. The priest, too ill to attend, sent a lengthy letter defending the rights of conscience that had been written into the Italian Constitution after the Fascist era. He condemned modern warfare as aimed indiscriminately at civilians and therefore unjust. Milani demonstrated to the court that the Catholic's right to obey God above human beings can be found in the Cathechism of the Council of Trent[64] and challenged church authorities to contradict him if he misconstrued his Catholic rights of conscience and his duty to disobey war orders. The church was silent, and on February 16, 1966, the court acquitted both Milani and the editor of *Rinascità.*

Even though it remained difficult into the 1970s for an Italian to earn the legal classification of conscientious objector, by 1982 over twelve thousand Italians had obtained that status.[65] In 1984 Italian conscientious objectors were heartened by Pope John Paul II's endorsement and were also successfully resisting war taxes on "grounds of particular moral and social value."[66] The Italian example was to be repeated throughout the Catholic world.

In 1964, when a conscientious-objection law was passed in predominantly Catholic Belgium,[67] only 134 young men claimed CO status. By 1980, however, that number had grown to 2,317, or 7.5 percent of all conscripts, and 51 percent of draft-age Belgians polled opposed compulsory military service.[68] After the 1974 coup and the April

1976 Constitution the Portuguese government recognized the right of conscientious objection. It declared an amnesty for all resisters between 1974 and 1976.[69]

In May 1971 José Luis Buenza was sentenced to fifteen months in prison by a military court in Valencia (Spain) for refusing military service. It was the first time that a Spanish Catholic had ever refused military service on religious grounds. Until then the only conscientious objectors had been Jehovah's Witnesses.[70] Buenza based his claim on the teachings of Vatican II and the declaration of *Gaudium et Spes* that governments should make provision for those who refuse to bear arms on the grounds of religious conscience. Buenza's conviction resulted in small but unprecedented demonstrations of solidarity throughout Spain and in several other countries. In 1970 a law covering conscientious objectors had been proposed to the Spanish Cortes but it had been rejected.

In February 1975 Jesus Vinas Cirera became the first of seven Spanish conscientious objectors to be convicted for refusing to bear arms. All were members of GOCE, a Catholic organization doing basic education and performing social services in a marginal community near Barcelona. One of the group's organizers was the now freed Buenza. The pacifists and over a thousand other petitioners asked the government to convert their military service to alternate service such as that of GOCE. They were joined in their request by the Spanish Catholic Commission for Peace and Justice, by the Catholic international peace group Pax Christi,[71] by the ecumenical Fellowship of Reconciliation, and by War Resisters International.[72]

Since the succession of King Juan Carlos to the Spanish throne and the 1978 Spanish Constitution, conscientious objection has been recognized as valid grounds for exemption from military service. COs must perform alternate service for one year more than the military term of service, usually in environmental or firefighting units. Spanish law also recognizes conscientious objection for those already in the army; by 1983 no Spanish conscientious objectors were imprisoned.[73]

In France conscientious objection flew in the face of a long tradition of French militarism that associated the armed forces with the glory of the nation. Before 1958 the maximum sentence for conscientious objection was ten years in prison. By 1962, however, when this had been reduced to three years in the midst of the Algerian revolt, a hundred and fifty French pacifists were in French jails as external pressures from both Catholic and non-Catholic peace groups intensified.[74] Although President de Gaulle admitted that it was "absurd and indignant to treat conscientious objectors as delinquents,"[75] he refused to take any action until the war was over. What finally moved the government to act, however, was the hunger strike waged by the seventy-four-year-old anarchist and pacifist Louis Lecoin, a respected figure in French politics. In the summer of 1962 the president promised the release of all conscientious objectors and the provision for an alternate service clause in French law. By 1963 a French conscientious objection law had been passed.[76]

Into the 1970s, however, it was still difficult for French Catholics to win the classification entitled them by the law. The CO law was harsh. It required COs to serve twice as long as military conscripts, denied them many of their constitutional rights to organize and speak, and forbade all dissemination of literature or other information on CO status. Between 1964 and 1971, therefore, there were few French objectors. When the law was incorporated into the National Service Code on June 10, 1971, however, the number of French COs swelled. In reaction, the Decree of Bregancon forbade all meetings of conscientious objectors, CO unions, or CO strikes and dealt harshly with resisters.[77] After socialist President Mitterand was elected (May 1983) the CO law was reformed. The number of French COs approached seven thousand at that time.[78]

A different situation applied in West Germany since World War II. The right to refuse to bear arms is explicitly written into the *Grundgesetz*, or Constitution.[79] In August 1977 German law was further liberalized, allowing Germans to declare their pacifism without having to substantiate or explain their religious or philosophical beliefs. Within five months between forty and fifty thousand Germans applied for conscientious objector status. Most did eighteen months of low-paid, social-service work instead of fifteen months with full pay in the army.[80] The Catholic Church became one of the major supporters of this alternative service. Its *Caritas* organization immediately hired about two thousand pacifists for work in youth hostels, meals-on-wheels, and programs for the elderly, homeless, and other marginal groups.[81] Within months the image of the conscientious objector had changed from that of the "loafer" to that of the "social fire brigade" performing socially essential works that others avoided.[82]

These are only a few examples from the Western industrial nations. What had been an isolated and fearful witness a generation ago now has the full support of the highest levels of the Catholic Church. Individual Catholic laypersons now began to find new solidarity with their hierarchy in their struggle against militarism and new meaning in the dialogue between head and members of the Mystical Body. This dialogue also took place on issues other than anti-militarism. In nonviolent action throughout Europe Catholics were showing the connection between peace and social justice defined by Vatican II.

## DANILO DOLCI

Danilo Dolci was born in 1924 near Trieste of a comfortable middle-class family. He had a conventional Catholic upbringing and read widely in the philosophy and religion of many cultures. Involved in nonviolent resistance to the Fascists after Mussolini's establishment of the Salò government in the north in 1943, Dolci fled to Rome, carrying with him Giuseppe Mazzini's *Rights and Duties of Men* and Thomas à Kempis's *Imitation of Christ*.[83] In 1947 he completed his architectural studies. He had intended to pursue a comfortable practice designing homes for the rich, when he experienced a conversion. He decided to devote himself to work for the poor and joined the staff of the orphanage at Nomadelphia under the eccentric Dom Zeno. His decision scandalized his family and so shocked his fiancée that she broke their engagement.[84] While at Nomadelphia Dolci was drafted into the Italian army,[85] but he refused conscription on the grounds of conscientious objection, a claim that was allowed to stand.

By 1952 he was finding the orphanage's social work too conventionally pious and he began searching for the kind of work that he felt could truly aid the poor. He remembered the small, impoverished village of Trapetto in Sicily, where his father had worked as a stationmaster, so he set off for the south. In Trapetto he found a society dominated by poverty, ignorance, and indifference, reduced to passivity by its own alienation and by the oppression of the Mafia, which controlled entire areas in a patronage system reminiscent of medieval feudalism.[86] Dolci soon began to organize small community self-help groups that aimed both to improve living conditions and to raise the people's consciousness of their oppression. In an effort to bring promised government services to the area he began a series of hunger strikes and publicity campaigns calling Europe's attention to the plight of the Sicilians.[87] By 1953 he had begun to step on the Mafia's toes, interfering with their control of the heroin traffic to the United States and revealing the widespread political corruption that protected it. At the same time, his consciousness-raising efforts were beginning to build a popular movement dedicated to gaining the rights of the farmers, the fisherfolk, the poor, and the unemployed of the area. By consensus the movement decided that the only way to combat the Mafia, corrupt land-owners, and politicans was through concerted, patient, and nonviolent action.[88]

One of the earliest and best-known triumphs of the movement came in January 1956 at Partinico, a poor agricultural area where the Mafia controlled the water supply and where high unemployment and inhuman proverty were taken as facts of life. Training in Gandhian nonviolence was followed by group action and individual commitment and a well-planned publicity campaign. After a hunger strike by nearly twelve hundred un-employed persons, Dolci took action. Taking advantage of a clause in the Italian Con-stitution that guarantees employment to every citizen, Dolci and his group staged a "strike-in-reverse" and repaired a stretch of road that had been ignored by the local government for years.

The twelve hundred activists converged on the road at Partinico to begin repairs and were met by scores of police armed with machine guns. They ordered the workers to disperse. When the people refused, on the grounds that the police orders were unjust, Dolci and over two hundred of his companions were arrested. The action was the first successful instance of mass civil disobedience in modern Western Europe, and Dolci's trial was one of the most famous of the day.[89] In his trial statement Dolci declared that the movement was not violent or subversive, as had been alleged, but sought only to give hope, health, and work to the poor:

> May I repeat that we took no weapons with us, not even a knife to cut the bread, and that this was meant to be a symbol of a new spirit. The people understood this—that the days of the machine gun were finished and that true revolutions were born from within. There was to be an end of shooting.[90]

The court found the defendents guilty, but noted "the high moral value of Dolci's action" and imposed only a light sentence.

Palermo's Cardinal Ruffini[91] accused Dolci of being a Communist and a subversive. But the Partinico action showed that Mafia control could be broken and that nonviolence was effective. By 1958 Dolci had established a series of schools, Centers for Study and Action, all over Sicily.[92] By 1960 he had defeated Mafia attempts to gain control of the Iato Dam project through a series of fasts, public demonstrations, and the establishment of a farmer consortium.[93] By 1962 Danilo Dolci defense committees had sprung up all over Europe.[94] In 1963 Dolci and his associates held open hearings against leading Mafiosi and their protectors in high political circles, and by 1966 they were leading demonstrations against the Mafia all over Sicily. In Rome in November 1971 Dolci led a mass demonstration of over 300,000 protesting the resurgence of Fascism in Sicily.[95]

Dolci is not specifically Christian in his orientation. He has been called a Christian Communist by some and an apostate by others. He is admittedly religious and quotes the Bible easily, but the historical indifference of the Sicilian clergy to the suffering of the people of south Italy led Dolci to break with the institutional church. This gained him the rebuke of the Sicilian hierarchy and the disdain of the Vatican.[96] Yet his meth-ods are fully consistent with the teachings of Vatican II. They seek first to raise the consciousness of individuals, to awaken them to their human dignity, and to break down the alienation that helps to keep them oppressed. By the intelligent use of hunger strikes and by attracting the attention of the media Dolci's groups have magnified the impact of their actions. In a land that well knows revenge, vendetta, and violence, Dolci's nonviolence broke the cycle of oppression. It liberated individuals and communities for constructive work, and convinced Sicilians that honor lies not in the silence of complicity with the gangsters who oppress them but in the freedom to speak out and to rebuild their world. Dolci does not seek to convert the enemy but contends that to turn individual Sicilians away from violence is enough for the time being.[97]

Dolci sees his role primarily as that of teacher and prophet, not as an organizer or leader of the masses.[98] He sees the people as the agents of their own salvation in this world, and thus rejects both the individualistic piety of the pre-Vatican II church and the collectivism and elitism of the Marxists. He rejects passivity and considers nonviolence to be revolutionary.[99] Many agree with him. He has received several death threats from the Mafia and there has been at least one attempt on his life. In Latin America his work is taken as an example of the process of liberation and is an inspiration for Catholic nonviolence there.[100]

## LANZO DEL VASTO

Danilo Dolci represents the secular activism of Europe's cultural Catholics whose efforts merge with the new spirit of Vatican II. Lanzo del Vasto represents the Catholic whose religious culture was reinforced, purified, and augmented by contacts outside Catholicism. Del Vasto emphasizes, in a sense, a monastic retreat from the world in order to create a utopian society based on peace and justice. Like all the monastic movements of antiquity[101] and of the Middle Ages,[102] like the prophetic witness of Thomas Merton,[103] this monasticism contains the seeds of protest against injustice and violence and has blossomed more than once into activism.

Lanzo del Vasto's life follows the pattern of the medieval nobleman who renounces privilege and adopts a life of voluntary poverty.[104] Born of noble parents near Brindisi (Italy) in 1901, del Vasto was raised as a Catholic. The rich young man, who studied at a Paris lycée, also studied poetry and painting in Florence and philosophy in Pisa, where his dissertation was on syncretism in the world's religions. He experienced a religious conversion upon reading a passage from Thomas Aquinas and then began a life of wandering. In Ceylon in 1936 he began to rediscover his Christianity. As a disciple of Gandhi at Wardha, del Vasto relearned the Christian virtues of simplicity, voluntary poverty, and nonviolence. He took the name Gandhi had given him: *Shantidas*, "Servant of Peace."[105]

From Gandhi, del Vasto learned true peacemaking, a nonviolence more active than violence because it presupposes both the courage to die and to do violence, a nonviolence that is not passive but that seeks to fight and to win. Gandhi gave his nonviolence a new name: *satyagraha*, the nonviolent struggle. The victory to be won is not against the enemy but against the enemy's evil. The struggle seeks not to humiliate the aggressors but to elevate and free them. As a Christian, del Vasto found nothing new or unique in all this. Gandhi's nonviolence owed much to Christianity, especially to the Sermon on the Mount.

Del Vasto returned to France in 1939; by 1945 he had established a small community on Gandhian principles in Paris. The assassination of the Indian leader in 1948 profoundly shocked Shantidas and moved him to form the Community of the Ark at Tournier. His experiment in communal living was a failure, however, and in the early 1960s del Vasto and his wife, Chantarelle, made a new beginning, establishing their utopian society along more ordered lines, which included a three-year novitiate. The society's members, male and female, took seven vows: service, obedience, responsibility and coresponsibility, purification, poverty, honesty, and nonviolence.[106] Their practice of nonviolence influenced everything, from their way of raising livestock and of practicing agriculture to their system of administration of justice and of authority.[107] Shantidas believes that nonviolence can work only in small groups who are trained in its use and whose lifestyle is completely nonviolent. He insists on not being political, but he also emphasizes that the goal of nonviolence is to change the enemy and to be engaged in the world. The life of his predominantly Catholic congregation is therefore one of nonviolent action.[108] In 1953 he took part in social actions in India with Gandhi's successor, Vinoba Bhave. In 1956 he joined Danilo Dolci in Sicily; in 1957 he and his followers began a nonviolent protest against the French use of torture in Algeria. In 1958 they planned and executed the nonviolent occupation of a French atomic bomb plant. In 1960 the Community of the Ark took actions against the French concentration camps set up for Algerian prisoners and started a campaign for the legal recognition of French conscientious objectors.[109] This campaign lasted until the passage of legislation covering CO status in 1963.

What had started as the eccentric action of an isolated, Eastern-style mystic was by the 1960s accepted by the Catholic Church as genuine witness to the gospels. In 1963 del Vasto was presented with a prepublication copy of John XXIII's *Pacem in Terris*, a direct tribute from the pope to del Vasto for his Christian peacemaking. In 1965 del Vasto's wife, Chanterelle, had joined many Catholic peacemakers (including Dorothy Day from New York's Catholic Worker) in a fast for nonviolence that influenced the writing of the sections on peace in *Gaudium et Spes*.[110] Del Vasto has not hesitated to prod the hierarchy to his witness for peace, but like Francis of Assisi he has always remained faithful to the church's hierarchy and teachings.[111]

In the 1970s the Community of the Ark engaged in a campaign against the French military's plans to expropriate over forty thousand acres of land in the Larzac region of southern France for an expanded army training ground. Mobilizing farmers, shepherds, the Roquefort cheesemakers, and local artists, the Ark began a series of hunger strikes, nonviolent demonstrations, blockades of military vehicles, land expropriations, and letter and publicity campaigns. Farmer committees and support groups were formed all over France, and the Ark won the support of the Catholic bishops of Rodez and Montpellier. Nonviolent actions were staged all over France. The active cooperation of all religious and political groups was welcomed so long as the movement remained nonviolent. The struggle continued into 1976, eventually questioning NATO policy, the support of foreign dictatorships, and nuclear testing and weapons, all without losing its original commitment to basic human issues, local concerns and grassroots organization.[112]

## THE PEACE PEOPLE IN NORTHERN IRELAND

The Peace People of Northern Ireland represent yet another facet of modern Catholic peacemaking: that of reconciliation of enemies and the repudiation of violence. The Community of the Peace People was born on August 11, 1976, in Belfast at a demonstration against the accidental death of three children in an IRA (Irish Republican Army) incident.[113] Mairead Corrigan, an aunt of the three children, Betty Williams, a witness to their deaths, and Ciaran McKeown, a journalist attracted to the women's protest, came together to form the group.

Theirs was not the first peace movement in Ulster's bloody history. The Women Together and the Derry Peace Movement helped pave the way,[114] as did the Northern Ireland Civil Rights Association (1968). The Witness for Peace led by Protestant minister Joseph Parker had emerged briefly in 1972 to call for an end to the violence.[115] Like many other voices of protest it had soon faded amid the assassinations, bombings, riots, and deep-seated religious and economic tensions between Northern Ireland's Protestant majority and its Catholic minority. Like the Sicilian Mafia, the paramilitary fighters from each side held their own people hostage to terror and intimidation and refused offers at reconciliation and peace as betrayals of their devotion to "Christian" traditions and fierce nationalism. Yet the three leaders turned the Peace People into a powerful movement in Northern Ireland and a focus of world attention and hopes.

Mairead Corrigan[116] came from a Catholic working-class section of Belfast and received a conventional Catholic education. As a young woman she engaged in traditional Catholic social activities, including the Legion of Mary. In that organization she did some community organizing and counseling of Catholic prisoners. Like many other Belfast Catholics she had herself experienced discrimination and disadvantage from both the Protestant majority and the British. She found herself dissatisfied with traditional Catholic quietism and admired the courage of the IRA "provos" who were willing to sacrifice their lives for the cause of justice and peace. She had even been tempted to join the provisional IRA. Yet she was also aware that a decade of violence had not solved anything, and her familiarity with the gospels confronted her with Christ's own nonviolence. She therefore attempted to combine her social-work approach with gospel Christianity and made some early, unsuccessful, attempts to convert individual IRA members to nonviolence.

Betty Williams[117] came from a middle-class background and married a Protestant, a rare enough feat in Northern Ireland. She too had a Catholic education and a conventional spirituality, but she was impatient over the hierarchy's conservatism, their resistance to change, and their failure to speak out on Northern Ireland's needs for peace and justice. She participated in the 1972 Witness for Peace movement, but she described herself as passive toward issues of peace and justice. She shared the Catholics' sense of oppression and injustice and had actually supported the IRA provisionals. She had been tempted to take up the gun until she once found herself praying over the body of a British soldier killed before her eyes. The rebukes of her Catholic neighbors for her mercy seem to have changed her outlook.

Ciaran McKeown[118] was a well-known Catholic journalist for the *Irish Press,* university-educated with a background in philosophy. His deeply religious opposition to violence was based on the Gospels, Gandhi, and Martin Luther King. He abandoned academics for a more active life and began covering the conflict in Northern Ireland and meeting the leaders on both sides. Feeling that his journalism was not doing enough to bring peace to Ulster, he began work on a philosophy of nonviolence. At this point Corrigan and Williams launched their peace protest (August 1976). The women's leadership, their strong personalities, and their articulate presentation of nonviolence combined with McKeown's organizing skills and theoretical expertise to make the Peace People a major force in Northern Ireland.

At first the call of the Peace People for peace and reconciliation was dismissed by all sides as a passive attempt to gain "peace at any cost," a pale reflection of the IRA's "peace with justice," which translates as the violent integration of Ulster with the rest of Ireland. Nevertheless, the women's courage, their organizing, and their commitment to challenge both the IRA and the Ulster Defense Association on their own turf soon won them a large following. Through a series of dramatic demonstrations and community events they reunited the Catholic and Protestant working-class districts first of Belfast and then of every major Northern Irish city. They refused police or paramilitary protection for their marches, crossed forbidden no man's lands, and risked retaliation from the IRA and the UDA, rock-throwing youths, death threats to individual members, and public denunciations, especially from Catholics in the IRA.[119]

The marches resembled medieval peace rallies.[120] There were emotional scenes of reconciliation, forgiveness of former enemies, and reunions of Protestant and Catholics who embraced, sang hymns, and participated in ecumenical services at rally after rally between August and December 1976. Catholics walked for the first time in Protestant districts of Belfast, Londonderry, and Armagh; Protestants gave up their fear of Catholics and accepted invitations to their homes and communities.[121]

The success of the movement was rapid and impressive. Ten thousand participated in the first march in Andersontown, Belfast.[122] Successive marches attracted large numbers: thirty-five thousand at Shanskill, twenty thousand in Londonderry, from five to eight thousand in Falls Park, Belfast. At the Peace Bridge at Drogheda, the site of the battle that divided Ireland into Catholic and Protestant in 1690, northern and southern Irish and the primates of the Catholic, Anglican, and Presbyterian Churches met and embraced in an emotional reconciliation.[123] The first phase of the movement climaxed in a demonstration of approximately fifty thousand people in London's Trafalgar Square, where the Peace People were joined by peace activists from Great Britain, Europe, and the United States, the archbishop of Canterbury, and the Catholic archbishop of Westminster in celebrating a newfound peace for Ireland.[124] Petitions supporting the movement were signed by six million Germans. In October 1977 Mairead Corrigan and Betty Williams received the Nobel Peace Prize.[125]

The peace movement in Northern Ireland went beyond mass demonstrations and emotional reconciliations, however. From the start its organizers realized that true peace could only come through the commitment of individuals to live peace. Their real work lay in identifying the problems of violence and hatred, calling attention to them through demonstrations and marches, and then beginning the long, slow process of educating for peace. All three leaders saw this as a process of consciousness-raising among the working classes, of teaching the skills of community organizing, self-help, and community control that go beyond mere political organizing. Their aim was to overcome apathy in the face of injustice and indifference to violence.[126] They consciously worked from the people's level, for they believed that only through the slow, steady conversion of individuals, and then communities, to nonviolent action can the peacemaker avoid the dilemma of replacing one violent oppressor with another potential oppressor, creating power structures and bureaucracies that impose new injustices.[127] Only by overcoming the old myths of the soldier-hero and the nation can the divided peoples of Northern Ireland come together to build a just society.[128]

The Peace People's approach was consciously Catholic. John XXIII and Vatican II clearly lay behind their theoretical and organizing statements, the *Declaration of the Peace People,*[129] *The Strategy for Peace,* and their *Model Constitution.*[130] Yet the movement was often critical of the Catholic hierarchy in Ireland, accusing them of actually avoiding the issues of peace and reconciliation, although they spoke eloquently of the need for peace at Vatican II,[131] and of lacking the moral courage to denounce injustice.[132] Instead of seeking the common ground that would unite Ulster's warring factions and special interests, the Peace People pursued what was controversial and attempted to resolve what was divisive.[133]

By March 1977, a hundred thousand Northern Irish, both Catholic and Protestant, had signed the Peace People's *Declaration* ''to live and love and build a just and peaceful society'' and had committed themselves to ''reject the use of the bomb and the bullet and all the techniques of violence."[134] Over a hundred peace committees had formed throughout Northern Ireland.[135] Yet the movement had its flaws. Its sudden rise resembled that of many medieval movements: it seemed broad rather than deep. The founders did not intend to continue the mass demonstrations, a fact that lost them the favor and attention of the press. They admitted that only seven thousand of their members were active and of these only seven hundred were steadily engaged in the community and intercommunity organizing essential to the movement's goals.[136] They also faced organizational, financial, and ideological problems.[137] The movement alienated many church leaders, politicians, and even its own associates by its denunciations of official inaction.[138]

The announcement by the three founders that they were stepping down to allow room for new leadership was taken by many as a sign of the organization's demise. In late 1977 Peter McLanchlin, a Protestant politician, was invited to head the group. By March 1980, however, Betty Williams and Mairead Corrigan had split over policy and personality issues, McKeown had denounced McLachlin publicly and caused him and Williams to resign from the group, and McKeown and Corrigan had taken over the formal leadership. By late 1984, however, the Peace People continued to bring Catholic and Protestant youth together in athletic activities and camps, thus laying the groundwork for a new generation.[139] Several smaller organizations uniting Catholics and Protestants have since been formed on local levels.[140] Meanwhile Northern Ireland continues its sad history of assassination, reprisal, and riot.

Despite their troubles and their disappearance from the public eye, the Peace People demonstrated that Catholic nonviolence can have an impact. The movement brought about a crisis of conscience for members of both the IRA and UDA, prompting many of the commandos in both groups to escape from the violence.[141] As Danilo Dolci had, the movement proved that communities organized for nonviolence can fight off threats of violence and intimidation and can begin to build a just society. It also showed that the Catholic laity, properly informed and motivated, can act as a vital force for change within society and can lead a reluctant hierarchy toward peace by their prophetic denunciations and their example of peacemaking.

## SOLIDARITY IN POLAND

We have been talking about Catholic movements in Western Europe, within societies that, at least in official language, accept Christianity as an essential part of their cultural life or, at the very least, tolerate it as one of the formative experiences of their cultural development. This acceptance has posed its own problems: a superficial acquiescence to Christian principles, for example, as part of the national scene, as part of a people's own cultural genetics. For many Christians in the West their religion is little more than a formal cult, essentially a post-Christian[142] ritualism resembling official Roman paganism,[143] maintained by pious myths and official church membership. Much of the struggle of a del Vasto, a Dolci, or of the Peace People has therefore been to overcome the assumption of most of their compatriots that Christianity is limited to formal cultic routines and to the comforts of an inner spirituality that has little or nothing to do with the worlds of politics and economics.

If the Catholicism of many Western Europeans can be compared to the formal cults of the Roman Empire, the faith of Catholics in Poland has, paradoxically, come to resemble that of the early Christians within the pagan empire. "Paradoxically" because of all nations that emerged from medieval Christendom, Poland has most retained its fervent identification with the Catholic Church. The church preserved the seeds of the Polish nation when the nation ceased to exist as a political reality. The church preserved Poland's sense of integrity through World War II and has come to symbolize and define its spirit under communist rule.

Poles look to the church, not to the Polish government or the Communist Party, as the champion of Polish nationalism. In a nation where eighty percent of the young people attend Mass regularly, Poles of every class and profession maintain a loyalty to the church that the Party could never hope to match.[144] Poland's most sacred and popular site, the shrine of the Black Madonna at Częstochowa, is more than a cultic center of miraculous spiritual power; it is a sacrament of Poland's nationhood. The Madonna has been credited with saving Poland from foreign invasion, once against the Swedes in 1655, and most recently against the Soviets in 1920.[145]

This does not mean that the Poles are anticommunist or that they view the church as a means of salvation to a Western capitalist system. Although Poles have rallied against overt attacks on the church by hostile communist regimes—for example, Cardinal Stefan Wyszynski's defiance during the Stalinist period of the 1950s—Poles see themselves as Marxists, or at least socialists, and their society is a unique blend of Marxist and Christian principles. This blend of outlooks is evident in the political analyses that have emerged during the Solidarity period.[146] Polish opposition to the current system stems from what they perceive as the betrayal of socialist ideals, the abuse of power by a small ruling elite, the alienation of the people from political participation, and behind all this the role of the Soviet Union in maintaining the present regime and in dominating the Polish nation. The election of a Polish national, Cardinal Karol Wojtyla of Krakow, as Pope John Paul II only cemented the Polish alliance of church and nationalism.[147]

Solidarity, which began in August 1980, was not the first popular movement to arise in Poland since World War II. The 1956 uprising, the 1968 Polish revolt of students and intellectuals, the 1970 Gdansk workers' movement (which was bloodily repressed), and the 1976 alliance of workers and intellectuals and the foundation of KOR (the Committee for the Defense of the Workers)—all are strong memories for the Polish people.[148] Each movement built on memories of past movements and each fueled hopes for the future. In Poland the past is seen as the key to the future and the commemoration of the past is a rehearsal of things to come.[149]

The events that took place in the Lenin Shipyard in August 1980, the foundation of Solidarity, Lech Walesa's rise to national prominence, the rise in union membership to ten million in the space of one year, the union conventions of September and December 1981, the coup of December 13, the proclamation of martial law, the outlawing of Solidarity in October 1982, the "state of war" and the emergence of the Solidarity underground, and the second visit of John Paul II in June 1983 have all been analyzed many times.[150] The events of these four years in Poland are of great importance; but here we shall focus on just one question: What place does the Solidarity movement have in the history of Catholic peacemaking?

From the start Solidarity acted—and was seen by the Poles themselves—as a Catholic movement. The Lenin Shipyard actions were set against a backdrop in which crucifixes and photos of John Paul II were prominent. The form for the monument to the workers slain in the 1970 Gdansk strike that the strikers felt most appropriate was that of three huge crucifixes.[151] Every Solidarity office throughout the country displayed a portrait of John Paul II and a crucifix.[152] Lech Walesa from the beginning of actions at the Yard wore a large medal of the Black Madonna, his personal patroness.[153] One of the basic demands and governing principles of Solidarity was religious access to the media and the broadcast of Sunday Masses throughout the country.[154]

All this does not, however, imply a simplistic, or superficial, allegiance of the workers' movement to the institutional church as in pre–World War II Catholic Action, or an attempt to infuse church influence into society through the type of "lay apostolate" that dominated church thinking during the 1950s. The union admitted the formative influence of Catholicism on Polish history and culture,[155] but declared that the union

> identifies itself with no ideology and no religion. It is true that among the union symbols those of the Catholic religion are of great consequence. . . . But the union itself, as a social movement, is secular. . . . nor does it consider the Catholic social doctrine to be its programme.[156]

To find the true link between Catholicism and the Solidarity movement one must go back to Vatican II, to the notion that Catholics and the church exist within the world, not above or outside it, and that their progress toward salvation takes place within the world through love of others and the creation of God's kingdom on this earth as a society of peace and justice. According to John XXIII this will be achieved through devotion to truth, human justice, and active solidarity of all parts of human society.[157]

Adam Michnik, a Jewish Solidarity theorist, outlined the role of the church as a force for justice and freedom and against totalitarianism. He noted that "the Polish bishops in their pastoral letters defended the right to the truth, to liberty, and to human dignity."[158] He sees the church as the guiding force behind the move to worker freedom.[159] In a lecture in Warsaw in November 1980 Michnik linked the church and the need for an individual conversion within each Pole as the prerequisites for the transformation of Polish society. Only through nonviolence, he noted, can this change occur within each person, and only its application to society in general will bring about the needed changes.[160] Michnik, in fact, saw the post-Vatican II church as a good model for Solidarity in its coexistence with the state, a parallel and open institution seeking to avoid authoritarianism, accepting a pluralistic society, and avoiding the temptation to ally itself with power. The church also provided a model of an organization constantly prodding the power structure toward justice.[161]

Solidarity's official program includes these religious principles.[162] In the spirit of Vatican II, the union states that it seeks not just bread, but justice, solidarity, and national renewal, and calls itself "a movement for the moral rebirth of the people." It fulfills both a critical and positive role, denouncing as well as building. Pope John Paul II, his encyclical on labor, *Laborem Exercens,* and Christian principles are the union's chief inspirations. The Catholic intelligentsia within Solidarity note that the movement is based on both socialist and Christian principles of equality, justice, and freedom.[163] They stress that only nonviolent opposition and commitment to the truth can bring success.

It would be a mistake to take Lech Walesa as the spokesperson for all Solidarity members. However from the start of the movement Poles have taken him as the symbol of their nonviolent resistance and their attempts to build a just society.[164] He is widely viewed as the spiritual son of John Paul II.[165] He personifies the wedding of socialist principles with devout Catholic spirituality and sees no conflict between the two.[166] Like Dolci and like the Peace People, he sees his role as one of consciousness-raising among the people, not as one of politics. He seeks justice for both sides and refuses to accept any of the labels that the press has attempted to give him: he is neither capitalist tool nor Catholic reactionary. Like most members of Solidarity[167] he explicitly rejects Western democratic forms and capitalism, and seeks to eliminate the differences between rich and poor within Polish society and to continue the dialogue between the people and the government. His work toward these goals won him the Nobel Peace Prize in December 1983.[168]

Solidarity's commitment to nonviolence has become ever clearer since the December 1981 coup and the imposition of martial law. With the arrest of Solidarity leaders and members the movement was forced underground, but in its resistance it always heeded the Polish hierarchy's call to nonviolence.[169] It has used a variety of methods to fight the military regime: strikes, demonstrations, deliberate incompetence on the job, secret broadcasting from radio stations, and printing on over 250 presses[170]—all the while reminding the Polish people that "you must turn the numerical advantage . . . into an overwhelming moral advantage that will render billy sticks, gas, and tanks useless."[171] Adam Michnik spoke for Solidarity's leadership when he wished his fellow Poles strength for the days ahead, "lying between despair and hope, and also much patience, so that they may learn the difficult art of forgiving."[172]

The role of the official Catholic Church is the most controversial aspect of the Solidarity struggle in Poland. Jozef Cardinal Glemp was John Paul II's chosen successor as primate of Poland and seems to mirror the wishes of the Vatican in Polish affairs. His role, therefore, has been unsettling because of his ambiguous position toward Solidarity and the Polish people's struggle. On November 8, 1982, the cardinal cut a deal with General Jaruzelski. The pope was to be allowed in June 1983 to visit the country apparently in exchange for a call by the official church for "maintaining and consolidating calm, social harmony, and work,"[173] in effect discouraging the general strike called by Solidarity for November 10, 1982. The strike failed.

Cardinal Glemp's role as a "conciliator" seems to imitate the ways of the church in the 1920s and 1930s, when it initiated diplomatic agreements and concordats with governments in order to insure the "liberties" of the institutional church at the expense of the laity's concerns.[174] Acting from a position of hierarchical authority and in obedience to political power, Glemp has avoided all overt criticisms of the government on "economic" and "political" issues.[175] He has moved to silence priests who were outspoken in their support of Solidarity.[176] At the same time, however, his high-level contacts with the government have provided a shield for the local churches to continue their work of aiding the Solidarity network, of recording arrests and instances of violence, and of making the church the focus of resistance to the government.[177]

Cardinal Glemp's approach is in strong contrast to that of many other high church leaders, including Bishop Ignacy Tokarczuk. In a sermon at the shrine of the Black Madonna in September 1982 the bishop preached open defiance of martial law, recalling that the church has a duty to speak the truth, to defend the oppressed, and to *be* the truth. He called on the army and the secret police to reject "blind and brutal force" and to disobey orders.[178]

The two bishops' views reflect the changing attitudes toward peace within the official church hierarchy since World War II. Glemp, following the model of a Pius XI or Pius XII, makes high-level arrangements with governments to preserve peace; Tokarczuk, adhering to the principles of John XXIII, Paul VI, and Vatican II, calls the church to its duty to speak the truth no matter what the consequences, to side with the oppressed in their struggle for justice, and to urge the agents of violence, even the agents of the government, to lay down their arms in the interests of true peace.

The visit of Pope John Paul II to Poland (June 1983) brought home to the country and to the world the full dimensions of the situation. The pope's return to his homeland is credited with having broken Poland's season of despair. Before crowds of up to two million, in city after city, at Mass after Mass, the pope spoke openly and honestly of government abuses, of political prisoners, of social and economic injustices, and of the demands of the people for justice.[179] He confronted General Jaruzelski and the country's political leaders, openly criticizing their rule, as millions watched the general tremble before the cameras.[180] Yet the visit was disturbing and disappointing to many. The long-awaited reunion of the pope and Lech Walesa took place in seclusion; no great symbols of struggle or alliance emerged. The pope met twice with General Jaruzelski in a way that seemed to exclude Walesa, Solidarity, and the Catholic people of Poland from any say in the final settlement of the Polish problem. The pope thus appeared to revert to a pre-Vatican II form of peacemaking, to the Constantinian alliance of church and state, pope and emperor.[181]

The pope's statements at Krakow, at Jasna Gora, and later in Vienna (to Polish Catholics) seemed to many commentators to reinforce the Constantinian image.[182] At Krakow the pope appeared to ignore the social and political struggle of Solidarity and to call for an inner, pietist form of struggle, "to call these weaknesses, these sins, these vices, these situations, by name, and to fight against them constantly—not to allow yourselves to be swallowed up by the wave of immorality and indifference."[183] At Jasna Gora the pope offered a lengthy meditation on the monastery's motto, "I Watch":

> What does it mean "I watch"? It means that I make an effort to be a person with a conscience. I do not stifle this conscience and I do not deform it; I call good and evil by name. And I do not blur them. I develop in myself what is good, and I seek to correct what is evil by overcoming it in myself. "I watch" also means "I see another." I do not close in on myself, in a narrow search for my own interests or my own judgments. "I watch" means: love for one's neighbor. It means fundamental human solidarity.[184]

Some see this statement as a commendation of justice and freedom in the abstract; others as an inner, individualist piety, a turning away from revolution to private salvation; still others as a call on the tired Poles for "national reconciliation," for respite from struggle, and for a passive resignation within the bosom of the church.[185] These assessments seem to have been confirmed by the pope's comments several weeks later in Vienna. "The only road that leads to victory and the regaining of lost freedom," he said, "is through internal conversion."[186] For the peace of justice, the peace of Vatican II and of popes John and Paul, John Paul II seemed to substitute the peace of inaction. Yet after the pope had left Poland, Zbigniew Bujak, a leader of the Solidarity underground's TKK, called the pope's teachings the "basic inspiration for our life, for our work and struggle. We shall spread them and we shall always go back to them."[187]

How could such an inactive concept of peace be the major inspiration for one of the most important Catholic peace movements of the century? For the answer to this we must look not to Poland or to Vienna but to other continents and other emerging movements, movements and places that despite their distance and differences remain vital and integral parts of the same church, contribute to the same doctrine, and form part of the teaching of the same pope. We do not have to look long for papal statements that are remarkably similar to those made by John Paul II during his June 1983 visit to Poland. In February 1979, on his return to Rome from the Latin American bishops' conference at Puebla (Mexico),[188] John Paul endorsed the theology of liberation that had been defended and expanded there. He told his audience that "the theology of liberation is often connected, sometimes too exclusively, with Latin America," when in fact there is "reason for a theology of liberation on a universal scale." Emphasizing the close links between Christ's message of liberation and "knowledge of the truth," the Pope said that "it is necessary to call by name every social injustice, discrimination, and violence inflicted on man against his body, his spirit, his conscience, and his convictions." . . . He also praised the basic tenet of liberation theology, or "conscientization," that awakens the poor to their dignity and rights as human beings; and he deplored the ways whereby social, political, and economic injustices suppress that dignity.[189]

For John Paul II and the Polish people, then, the Black Madonna and her motto, "I watch," were symbols of liberation, of a struggle for freedom and justice that begins first with individual conversion to peace, with the individual's conscience and convictions, and then flows to the world in "love of one's neighbor and fundamental human solidarity." Far from being a call to acquiescence, then, the pope's words matched those of Solidarity theorists like Adam Michnik.[190] They called for nonviolent revolution, for the struggle that liberates and brings "fundamental human solidarity."

The struggle of Polish Catholics for their revolution has not ended, although the spectacular threat of violence that drew media notice has subsided. On May Day 1984 Lech Walesa and tens of thousands of Solidarity supporters emerged from the underground to take part in mass nonviolent actions.[191] In November 1984, following the murder of pro-Solidarity priest Jerzy Popieluszko by government security police, 400,000 Poles turned out for funeral ceremonies to hear Lech Walesa sum up Poland's nonviolent struggle and its meaning:

> They wanted to kill, and they wanted not only a man, not only a Pole, not only a priest. They wanted to kill the hope that it is possible in Poland to avoid violence in political life.[192]

Polish commitment to nonviolence, like the Polish struggle, is, indeed, "to be continued."[193] The pope's words at Jasna Gora, far from isolating the Poles in individual passive obedience, brought them together in solidarity with the struggle for liberation that is going on throughout the Third World and joins them with the majority of the world's Catholics. We will examine the struggle of the Third World in the next chapter.

# CHAPTER 14

# THE THIRD WORLD: CATHOLIC PEACEMAKING AND LIBERATION

*There are only two invincible forces in the twentieth century—the atom bomb, and nonviolence.*

—Bishop Leonidas Proaño

## INTRODUCTION

When John XXIII, Paul VI, and the council fathers at Vatican II spoke of peace as the work of justice, declared "development as the new name for peace," and linked the vicious arms race to the poverty of the majority of the world's peoples, they brought world attention to the role of the Catholic Church in the Third World. It came as a shock then and still comes as a surprise to many Catholics in Europe and North America that most Catholics live in the Third World: in Central and South America primarily, but also in Africa and on the rim of Asia—India, Vietnam, Korea, and the Philippines. Catholicism in the Third World was the product of European expansion and colonialism.[1] The Catholicism brought by the European colonists was a marriage of European culture with Christian religion as concretized in the medieval and early-modern periods. We have already shown the problems and the legacy of this identification of European culture and Christian religion, especially in the intermingling of hispanization with christianization in Latin America.[2]

Over the centuries the former colonies of Europe have undergone their own religious development, and in the late twentieth century the separateness of these traditions impressed the church with the need to define new forms of Catholic life. This process fortunately coincided with the era of Vatican II, when the church finally ended its Constantinian era. The development of new forms of Catholicism in the Third World also coincided with the devastating effects of three decades of Western-style "development." National economies were drastically redirected toward rapid industrialization, exploitation of natural resources, and participation in the world economic system of free trade and international finance. More often than not this development left Third World countries better off only on paper. Theoretically these nations saw yearly increases in GNP, in per capita GNP, in industrial production, in miles of paved roads, in the capacities of their ports and airports, and in the prevalence of Western consumer products. Yet,

*210*

despite official statistics, the living conditions of the vast majority of peoples of the Third World have deteriorated.

The disparity between the educated, westernized, and affluent international elites and the rest of the peoples has grown more glaring by the year as greater and greater proportions of a nation's wealth flow into fewer and fewer hands. We need cite only a few development statistics to illustrate the point. The 1980 per capita GNP in the United States was $10,517.[3] In West Germany it was $13,590.[4] In the Philippines it was $720[5] and in Brazil, $2,050.[6] Half of the people in Latin America earned only 14 percent of the continent's total income, and 207 million people in its most populated countries earned less than $75 a year in 1979.[7] In 1979 fourteen families in El Salvador controlled 90 percent of the wealth, 2 percent owned 58 percent of the arable land, 90 percent of the peasants had no land at all, and the average monthly income of 50 percent of the population was $12.[8] Even these figures do not really show how much better the rich in Latin America live than their counterparts in the United States. They have an almost feudal grip on the lives and "services" of the vast majority of the people.[9]

The gap between poverty and wealth continued to grow, and simultaneously most of the nations of the Third World fell under the iron glove of the National Security State.[10] This system protects the process of economic modernization through a highly centralized, authoritarian, militarized, and brutal political state calculated to destroy all dissent in the name of "development." As poverty increases, arms budgets to support ever larger armies, security forces, and police grow out of all proportion to human needs, such as health care, literacy and education, proper housing, land reform, employment and fair wages, well-functioning systems of justice, and popular rule.

Thus by 1960 and the time of Vatican II several trends had come together to create a new situation for Catholic peacemakers. Freed from its bondage to European traditions of power, the church was able to return to the gospel and its message of peace and justice. It proclaimed once more that true peace was the "work of justice," that the kingdom of God was both the gift and the challenge of Christ to be created here on earth, and that the process of creating Christ's peace was a dynamic one. It was both the goal and the means. Peace is ongoing, it is in the present and it has many forms. We cannot survey all the forms of Catholic peacemaking in the Third World, but we will examine several examples from around the world: from South Africa, the Philippines, and Latin America.

## SOUTH AFRICA

Between 1911 and 1960 the Catholic Church in South Africa grew from an insignificant minority of fifty thousand to a major force numbering nearly two million members out of a total population of 30 million.[11] It is especially significant that three-quarters of South Africa's Catholics are black. This is largely because of the linguistic and anthropological approach of the Catholic missionaries and the church's creation of an indigenous black leadership. The Catholic Church has been far more serious in these respects than many other religious groups in South Africa.[12]

The Catholic Church is, however, a minority church in South Africa. Its early immigrant base left politics to the Protestant majority,[13] especially the Dutch Reformed Church. This church claimed biblical roots for white minority racist rule and played a large role in developing South Africa's apartheid system.[14] By the end of World War II the Catholic Church found itself committed to the religious life of its black majority but outside the structures of white power. It was one of the first churches in South Africa to denounce the country's system of apartheid (1948). In 1952 and again in 1957 the pastorals of Catholic bishops repeated the church's denunciation of oppressive racial policies. In 1960 the bishops reiterated this opposition by calling on Catholics to obey God's law over human law.[15]

The attitude of the church at large was slower to change.[16] The prejudice of the Catholic white laity initially matched that of their white neighbors. Little by little the lead of the bishops seems to be meeting positive responses among the white elite and is bringing at least a beginning of solidarity with the black majority.[17] When the Bantu Education Act (1953) in effect created a segregated system of schools throughout South Africa,[18] the Catholic schools, however, remained steadfastly integrated, even after their noncooperation with the law brought cuts in federal funds. The Group Areas Act (1960) then decreed separate residential areas for white and black populations, thus insuring the segregation of neighborhood schools and making integration virtually impossible unless parents and communities were to undertake widespread civil disobedience.[19]

In the 1970s—given the influence of Vatican II, of Paul VI's *Populorum Progressio,*[20] and of the developing theology of liberation—the church moved to a new level of struggle. In 1972 the Catholic Bishops Conference unanimously adopted its *Call to Conscience,* which condemned detention without trial, banning, and the exploitation of black labor.[21] In 1976 the bishops announced their intention of breaking South African law by integrating two Catholic schools. The government ignored the action. In 1977 the church integrated thirty schools in the Transvaal. The central government in Pretoria looked on, and the regional Transvaal administration threatened legal sanctions. Despite the danger of repression, the church stood firm, and Pretoria's opposition crumbled. The intransigent Transvaal administration was replaced. The victory proved to be a model of peaceful change. Not only did 85 percent of the Catholics surveyed approve of the move, but the church's determination actually enabled the Pretoria government to make changes that many South Africans favor privately but fear to support as public policy.[22] A basic tenet of nonviolence was thus proved: through peaceful commitment to justice the peacemaker frees not only the oppressed, but also the oppressors from their own injustices.

The influence of Vatican II was also felt in other areas. By the 1970s the Catholic Church was entering into ecumenical cooperation with the other South African churches. Through its membership in the Christian Institute the church put itself firmly behind the black theology and liberation theology movements.[23] Black theology

> is a theology of black liberation. It serves to plumb the black condition in the light of God's revelation in Jesus Christ, so that the black community can see that the Gospel is commensurate with the achievement of black humanity. Black Theology is a theology of "blackness." It is the affirmation of black humanity that emancipates black people from white racism, thus providing authentic freedom for both white and black people. It affirms the humanity of white people in that it says No to the encroachment of white oppression.[24]

Only through raising the consciousness of the black majority to their human dignity and their rights can the gospel be fulfilled and Christ's kingdom appear on earth. Change must come from the poor and the weak, from those on the margins of society. Black theology seeks neither white patronizing nor limited reform but rather a total change in African society. Yet black aspirations have met only further white oppression and violence. Revolutionary counter-violence has therefore emerged,[25] forcing theologians to forge a theory of nonviolent resistance to evil and to injustice, even if this involves suffering and martyrdom for one's witness.[26]

South African Catholics have actively pursued this theology of nonviolence. In a country where communities are kept divided and at odds through physical segregation, press censorship, arrests and imprisonment, banning and exile, the church's information service, *Diakonia,* has became a major source of resistance. By providing news and education on such topics as interracial relations and oppressive conditions of the black "homelands," it invites state oppression while it actively attempts to transform the Catholic Church into a true force of the poor and the oppressed.[27] In its 1977 *Declaration of Commitment* the Catholic Bishops Conference vowed to promote more blacks to all levels of the hierarchy, to give them equal pay, and to integrate all Catholic institutions—all in open defiance of South African apartheid laws.[28]

By the late 1970s government repression by naked force was the chief means of defending apartheid against an increasingly active black majority. The brutal repression of the Soweto demonstrations (June 1976), in which the police and the army killed over one hundred seventy-five persons and injured over a thousand, has become a symbol of the people's oppression.[29] The role of the military and the police has become crucial to any attempt to establish a just society. The Catholic Church therefore joined the South African Council of Churches in advocating the right of conscientious objection. Under South African law conscientious objectors are subject to arrest and to harsh military punishment.[30] The Catholic bishops endorsed both general conscientious objection on the basis of a universal opposition to war and selective conscientious objection on the grounds of the individual's right and duty to object to specific unjust wars.[31] Their call strikes at the heart of the South African state: to declare, on the one hand, that the system of apartheid is immoral and unjust and, on the other, that such injustice can be the basis for a citizen's refusal to defend the system is to call for unarmed rebellion.

Many have critized the church's approach for being too slow and too closely tied to the dominant white elite. The church, they say, is being outpaced by the people's impatient urge for violent revolution.[32] In South Africa today the term "nonviolent" has fallen into disrepute. It has come to mean only pious sentiments for false reconciliation, peace through order. Catholic work for nonviolent change continues, however. Through its Justice and Reconciliation Commission, the Bishops Conference attempts to raise the consciousness of youth, worker, and student groups to the need for liberation and justice.[33] Prominent leaders, such as Archbishop Denis Hurley of Durban,[34] have embraced nonviolent action in all its forms: marches, demonstrations, consumer boycotts, strikes, and stay-aways. Hurley has called on South Africa's Catholics

to join the revolution. Not the revolution of violence, but the revolution of ideas and attitudes, the revolution of minds and hearts, the revolution that makes man our chief concern, and not any formula or policy or prejudice.[35]

Despite criticisms from conservative Catholics,[36] the church has also pressed its conscientious objector drive vigorously and continues to urge noncooperation with the state.[37]

In the 1980s the Catholic attack on apartheid became even more pronounced. In 1981 the Bishops Conference announced a boycott of all apartheid sports and followed this with a boycott of Republic Day, the most official form of symbolic noncooperation with the state possible. The church continued its policy of integration and defiance of the country's national-security regulations by naming Swangaliso Mkhatshwa, a banned priest, as secretary of the South African Catholic Bishops Conference.[38]

The Catholic Church in South Africa thus clearly demonstrates an emerging Catholic commitment to peace through justice. While its transformation is not yet complete, over the last generation the church has changed from a silent and inward-looking minority to a vocal and prophetic force within South African society. It has demonstrated the impact of Vatican II in its break with prevailing political authority, in its alliance with the poor and the oppressed, in its role as educator, and in its nonviolent pursuit of fundamental change from the grass-roots level.

## ASIA

Since World War II Asian Catholicism has emerged as one of the most vital test cases of the post-Constantinian church. The church came to the Asian continent and to its eastern island rim through European expansion and colonialism.[39] Catholicism was attached to the cities and the westernized elites and therefore grew and stagnated along with the authoritarian, dependent cultures that the Europeans imposed. By the twentieth century it encountered the growing hostility of Asian societies, who were in the midst of liberating themselves, often through Marxist revolutions against Western, capitalist, and imperialist pasts. As Marxism spread the westernized nations of the region responded by embracing the "national security" doctrine.[40] Often the Christian churches found themselves aligned through their cultural affinities to the national-security regimes and their ruling elites. Furthermore, in Asia Christians represent only five percent of the Asian population and only ten percent of Christians worldwide. Asian Christianity was and remains, therefore, a marginal religion.[41]

By the 1960s, however, the many factors of the Asian Catholic scene—marginality, the increasing poverty of the continent, the pressing need for social change caught between Marxist revolution and national-security reaction, and the church's tradition of criticism—combined to make necessary a new pastoral mission. The church, already on the fringes in most of Asia, began to adapt the message of Vatican II and to accept its proper place with the poor and oppressed, the marginal in Asian society. By the late 1960s and early 1970s two organizations, PISA (Priests Institute for Social Action) and FABC (Federation of Asian Bishops Conferences), began directing the Asian church toward the pressing issues of justice and nonviolent change.[42]

In a series of meetings, in Manila in 1970 and 1977 and in Taipei in 1974, the FABC reaffirmed the Catholic Church's "preference for the poor," the young, and the oppressed. In so doing it combined the historical experiences of the Asian church with the lessons of Vatican II and the liberation theology of Latin America.[43] Most noteworthy in this new alignment was the attempt by the Asian hierarchy to forge a new synthesis between the gospel message and the methods of Marxist social and economic analysis.[44] To this synthesis have also been added the examples of Gandhi, Martin Luther King, and Mao.[45]

## THE PHILIPPINES

The problems and possibilities of Catholic peacemaking in Asia are best illustrated in the Philippines. The majority of Asia's Catholics live in the Philippines. The country has a crosscurrent of theological and ideological trends from Maoism to liberation theology, a highly literate and christianized population, and a society brought to the brink of crisis by the poverty of "development," twelve years of martial law under Ferdinand Marcos's national security state, and Maoist rebellion. Its sheer size and the rapid unfolding of its Christian witness make the Filipino church the major influence in Asian Catholicism.[46]

Until the 1970s the Philippine church was content with the passive and institutional approach of the colonial churches. Because Catholicism claims the vast majority of the people,[47] the church had thus come over four hundred years to be closely associated with the social and political directions of the nation at large; it fit perfectly into the Constantinian model. Protest, therefore, came not from the center but from the periphery of the church. Because of the church's alliance with the powerful elites and its traditional clerical understaffing on the local level, the church's pastoral mission came to depend on the people, on the marginal and the oppressed.[48] The directions of the local church therefore began to follow the needs of the people—education to social justice and human dignity, to having a voice in their own destinies—and to use the critical and analytical tools available to it. Often this involved a Marxist socioeconomic analysis linked to the pastorals of Vatican II and the papal encyclicals from *Pacem in Terris* to *Populorum Progressio.*[49]

Meanwhile development widened the distance between the westernized elite and the majority of the population, reducing them to even greater poverty as wealth shifted upward. Literally millions have been displaced from their homes and deprived of their livelihoods by large-scale capital development and infra-structure projects—dams, irrigation systems, new docks and airports, international-class hotels—that benefit only a small sector of the population. Such "progress" requires the coercion of the national security state, "greater and greater militarization, the perpetration of the law of the gun, the facile naming of any opposition as subversive, in one word, violence, institutional, protracted."[50]

This institutionalized violence has tempted many in the Philippines to the counter-violence of revolution in the hope of toppling the capitalists. The Catholic Church found itself caught between two forms of violence: that of the Marxists and that of the martial-law state. Its choices were harrowing: accommodation with its old ally, the oppressive elite, or accommodation to Marxist pressures to pick up the gun and to join in the violent liberation of the people.

The church's pastoral mission—the educational work of raising people's consciousness through basic Christian communities, Bible study and action groups in parishes, and through organizing farmers, workers, students, and young people to move toward a just society—has been caught between the two forms of violence as well. Marxists have sought to co-opt church programs for their own ends,[51] while reactionaries in the ruling elite, including many church leaders, disapprove of such programs as active subversion. Those who disapprove of the programs have been supported by official church statements that condemned the subversive violence of the oppressed but ignored the institutional and oppressive violence of the ruling elite.[52] Many Catholics of the basic Christian communities, and some clergy, have joined in revolutionary activity, concluding that the church's option for the poor can only be realized by accommodation to the revolutionary forces committed to creating a more just society. Many have suffered persecution, arrest, torture, deportation, and death for their pastoral activities.[53]

Slowly the church began to emerge as the leading force for nonviolent change in the Philippines. From the early labor-union and cooperative organizing of the 1960s to its concerns with more general political and economic concerns in the 1970s the church steadily pursued its goal of empowering the poor and the oppressed.[54] President Marcos's declaration of martial law on September 21, 1972, may, in fact, have only hastened this process[55] by causing the hierarchy to realize the true conditions of oppression that the church of the people had long been suffering. The Philippine Bishops Conference at first called for calm and acceptance of the state of emergency, but by September 28 seventeen bishops and seventeen superiors of religious orders had signed a public letter calling for the restoration of media freedoms curtailed by martial law. By 1973 the Bishops Conference showed greater unity in criticizing various aspects of the martial law regime. In 1974 they wrote a private letter urging the curtailment of the emergency regime.

The changing attitude of the institutional church encouraged the members of the church in their own defiance. An example was the 1975 bishops' pastoral statement on the upcoming referendum on martial law. The Marcos government claimed that previous referenda had been legitimate democratic endorsements of the regime. Voting is compulsory, and failure to cast one's ballot is a crime punishable by imprisonment. Despite this the bishops layed down specific conditions that could justify Filipino participation in the voting. In effect the letter left it to the conscience of the individual whether to obey the voting law. The impact of the bishops' statement was stupendous. Eight million of the twenty-seven million eligible Filipinos refused to vote, despite the government's threat of severe penalties. Not a single person was ever arrested for civil disobedience.

In 1977 the bishops were jolted into unified action by the intentional leak through the papal nuncio of a list of a hundred and fifty subversives slated for arrest. Many clerics, including four activist bishops, were on the list. The leak was intended to cow the clergy into submission; instead the bishops issued a strongly worded pastoral condemning government policies on birth control and ethnic minorities, military abuses under martial law, and the harassment and deportation of foreign missionaries. The government rescinded many of the warrants.

By 1979 the church had finally found a voice and a unified position in Jaime Cardinal Sin, archbishop of Manila and president of the Bishops Conference. The archbishop is typical of a new breed of church prelates. At first Sin opted for a policy of "critical collaboration," attempting to remain personally friendly with Marcos while rebuking his "parishioner" for isolated human-rights abuses. He refused to support any mass protests against the regime.[56] He soon began calling for an end to martial law, however, condemning the abuses of the military government. He reminded the people that subversive violence only brings retaliation on the suffering poor it is intended to liberate.[57] At the same time the Bishops Conference issued a pastoral condemning violence on the right and left and calling for nonviolent change.[58]

By the early 1980s this message was being accepted on the diocesan level, as both clergy and people began to adopt the practice of "total vulnerability," a nonviolent commitment to peace and justice. In so doing Filipino Catholics recognized that they were opening themselves up to the criticism of, and putting themselves at the mercy of, the violent on both the left and right.[59] Nevertheless they began to conclude that to opt for either the violence of oppression through an alliance with the powers-that-be or for the violence of revolution with the powers-that-will-be is an accommodation to power that replaces Christian faith with political craft.[60]

The events of the 1980s have begun to show the real impact of these choices. In February 1981 Pope John Paul II visited the country, publicly rebuked President Marcos for human-rights abuses, and stressed the laity's unique role in bringing about nonviolent change, reminding the clergy to restrict their leadership to magisterial functions.[61] Marcos's health was said to be failing; and the dictator made plans for an autocratic transfer of power to his appointed heir. In February 1983 the church hierarchy stepped up its criticisms of martial law.[62] In March 1983 Cardinal Sin condemned the excesses of the military. Charging that the Filipino people were being "slaughtered and massacred" by weapons provided by the United States and other allies, he called on these nations to stop arms shipments and to replace them with educational funds. He then called on the business community to join with the church in creating a more just political and economic system.[63] In Marcos's national security state such statements were implicit treason. In August 1983 the Bishops Conference was about to issue a pastoral condemning the president's powers to imprison without trial or other due process when Marcos unilaterally repealed the Public Order Act and the National Security Code empowering such actions.[64]

The assassination of political opposition leader Benigno Simeon Aquino on August 21, 1983, brought the Catholic struggle for nonviolent revolution in the Philippines to the attention of the world.[65] Popular reaction to the assassination was overwhelming. In late August almost two million Filipinos took part in nonviolent demonstrations, and Cardinal Sin became the most vocal leader of the Catholic opposition.[66] Throughout the fall the Filipino people kept up their nonviolent pressure against Marcos with mass demonstrations, strikes, protest jogs, motorcades of honking drivers, and daily bell ringings in all Catholic churches to protest the Aquino murder and demand justice.[67] The business and middle-class communities joined in the demonstrations, despite Marcos's threats of retaliation.[68] Marcos testified to the Catholic nature of the opposition by also threatening Catholic priests and nuns, who, he alleged, were preaching hatred and subversion in the schools.[69]

Cardinal Sin compared Marcos's national security state tactics to those of Nazi Germany[70] and called for a Council of National Reconciliation to restore democratic government and ease the transition from Marcos to the new government.[71] The umbrella opposition coalition, JAJA,[72] declared its

> overriding objective of restoring free democratic process and ultimate establishment of a free government with nonviolent confrontation or civil disobedience as the immediate means.[73]

By January 1984 the opposition had drawn up a complete agenda of political reforms, and the Catholic bishops once again freed Catholics to follow their own consciences in choosing whether to disobey laws requiring them to vote in the May 1984 legislative elections.[74] Culminating with the stunning victories of the opposition in those elections, the nonviolent campaign of nine months had done more to cripple the Marcos dictatorship than twelve years of violent insurrection. The opposition forced extensive modifications of the martial-law regulations on arrest, trial, and habeas corpus; it forced the restoration of the office of the vice-presidency and thus set up the process for normal succession; it forced Imelda Marcos out of the government and broke the family's dynastic dreams; it crippled the regime's image of stability that allowed foreign governments to pour in economic and military aid in the name of development; and it even persuaded the U.S. Congress to halt military aid.[75] Mass demonstrations on the first anniversary of Aquino's death proved the strength of nonviolence. While real changes in social and economic structures are yet to come, the Catholics of the Philippines are showing that millions can join in an effective nonviolent campaign aimed at creating a society of peace and justice.

## POSTSCRIPT ON THE PHILIPPINES, MARCH 5, 1986

Under increasing pressure from the nonviolent opposition, from growing Communist insurgency, economic collapse, and the U.S. government, in November 1984 Ferdinand Marcos suddenly declared that he would hold presidential elections the following February. Thrown off guard, the political opposition was divided and hesitant. Two candidates, Benigno Aquino's widow, Corazon, and Salvador Laurel, long a reform leader, announced plans to seek the presidency. It appeared that Marcos would thus have an easy time defeating a divided opposition until Cardinal Sin intervened to bring it together. On December 11, 1985 Aquino announced that she would run as president on a united ticket, with Laurel as her vice-president.

The campaign that followed was the most dramatic in Philippine history and was watched closely throughout the world. Despite a virtual media blackout against Aquino managed by the Marcos cronies who controlled the networks and newspapers, her campaign gradually began to gain both organization and widespread support. The contrast between her appearances and those of Marcos was striking: there an aging dictator mumbling set speeches before relatively small and unenthusiastic crowds, rallies well orchestrated with professional ward stewards and entertainers, advance men paying attractive bribes to attract support; here massive demonstrations of hundreds of thousands—one of nearly a million—people of all classes dressed in yellow, waving yellow banners, the symbol of the nonviolent opposition, calling for change amid the simple lyrics of Filipino folk and resistance songs, and the Lord's Prayer. Aquino's rallies were compared to a hundred Woodstocks; their dynamics were certainly like those of medieval peace assemblies.

As the balloting drew nearer, reports of political assassinations by Marcos supporters in the military and among local political machines, widespread plans for ballot tampering, and voter intimidation began to emerge. NAMFREL, the citizens group established to monitor the election, drew thousands of volunteers from all walks of life, including Catholic clergy, both men and women. They volunteered to protect ballot boxes against armed soldiers and hired goons assigned by Marcos forces to steal them away. Three days before the election Cardinal Sin publically endorsed Aquino. The following day Marcos placed the armed forces on full alert, claiming that his opponent was calling for civil war.

After the voting on February 7, 1986 two things became apparent: Corazon Aquino had won overwhelmingly, by at least 5.3 million to Marcos' 4.5 million votes, and Ferdinand Marcos was determined to use everything in his power, from ballot tampering to military force, to prevent the outcome from becoming official. As tensions grew, both sides claimed victory, and the *Batasan,* the National Assembly controlled by Marcos, began to rubber-stamp his claims. Demonstrations continued uninterrupted, and on February 14 the Catholic bishops declared Marcos' electoral victory fraudulent and urged a campaign of "nonviolent struggle" and resistance. On February 23 both Marcos' defense minister and a leading general revolted and announced their support for Aquino; and it looked as if Marcos was preparing for civil war. At that point however, the years of nonviolent confrontation and grass-roots organizing suddenly had their effect.

As Marcos' troops moved on the rebels' barracks, Cardinal Sin came over Radio Veritas to urge Filipinos to head off a confrontation. The scene recalled Germanus of Auxerre before the horsemen of King Goar or Francis of Assisi before the Crusaders in Egypt: thousands of unarmed Filipinos, bearing flowers, banners and crucifixes, halting tanks and heavily armed troops, protecting each side from the other, celebrating masses, urging both sides to lay down their arms, to join in the nonviolent revolt. The scene was repeated time and again: unarmed civilians bodily throwing themselves between armed soldiers to avert bloodshed. The "people protecting the soldiers," became a symbol of the Philippines. On February 25 both Aquino and Marcos held separate inaugurations. On February 26 Ferdinand Marcos, his wife, family, and closest military and political allies "limped into exile." On March 2 in Manila Cardinal Sin and President Aquino presided over an outdoor mass of thanksgiving and a celebration of nonviolence attended by over one million Filipinos, the country's largest assembly ever. Nonviolent revolution, the Filipinos' "People Power," had done what nearly fifteen years of armed rebellion had not. The Catholic Philippines had become a symbol of Christian nonviolence for the world.*

## LATIN AMERICA

The history of Catholic peacemaking in Latin America began in the sixteenth century with Montesinos, Las Casas, and the other missionary prophets of nonviolence;[76] their tradition of liberation has been reborn in the era after Vatican II. Like the rest of the Third World, Latin America passed through its stages of colonialism only to enter a new age of dependency on Western, especially U.S., economic interests and "development" plans.[77]

During the late 1960s and the 1970s the massive scale of many development projects and the desire to protect the wealth of the oligarchs against the needs of an increasingly impoverished majority led to the creation of the National Security State in one Latin American republic after another.[78] Authoritarian regimes kept power by military force and widespread violation of human rights, including imprisonment without trial, torture, disappearances, and murder. In country after country, from Brazil in 1964 to Argentina in 1983, the military juntas or lifetime dictators defended their actions against scores of Catholic laypeople, priests, monks, nuns, and bishops[79] in remarkably similar words: the defense of "Western Christian Civilization."[80]

Meanwhile, however, the church in Latin America had undergone fundamental changes that were to give the lie forever to the generals' hollow pieties. By the late nineteenth century the colonial alliance of church and state had changed radically. Liberal governments and popular and official anticlericalism stripped the churches of their privileged positions of power and expropriated most of their monastic and episcopal lands. The Latin American church, impoverished and deprived of official political power, felt itself ignored by Europe and became increasingly understaffed and incapable of maintaining its pastoral and evangelizing missions to large segments of the Latin American population. Indigenous forms of belief and practice commingled with the official cult and teaching of the Catholic Church. By the twentieth century a form of Catholicism particular to Latin America had developed.[81]

The Catholic Church that faced the era of development was thus truly marginal—deprived of wealth, political power, and connection to Europe.[82] On its upper, official

*. For further background see Robert F. Drinan, S. J. "Passiontide for the Philippine Church," *America* 152 (March 16, 1985): 209–12; Francisco Claver, S. J., "Revolution, the Church and Nonviolence," *Fellowship* 51, 6 (June 1985): 9–11; Richard Baggett Deats, "The Philippines: Islands in Ferment," *Fellowship* 51, 6 (June 1985): 3–7. For the most recent events see *NCR* Jan. 24, 1986, 1, 26–28; Feb. 21, 1986, 1, 4, 8; *Time,* Feb. 17, 1986, 34–40; March 10, 1986, 14–37; *New York Times,* March 2, 1986, 4: 1; March 3, 1986, A1, 6.

levels the church may have retained the illusion of being at the center of Latin American developments. The growth of Marxism in Latin America and its appeal to wide segments of the population, especially following the Cuban revolution in 1959 and the reaction of the National Security State, caused the church to be beset by new realities that threatened its official authority and its power among the people.

Despite these realities, many in the church, especially among the hierarchy, maintained their Constantinian alliance with the state. The state, for its part, tolerated an alliance with Christendom as long as it aided its authoritarian purposes and maintained harmony among the ruling elite. At the same time, however, Marxist criticism of development and of increasing poverty combined with the prophetic tradition of protest in Latin American Catholicism to produce a new commitment among large segments of the church. Under the impact of repression the church emerged as the only voice of dissent left.[83] The changes affected especially the lower clergy, theologians, intellectuals, and the laity, and sensitized them to the Christian principles of social and political justice and true peace—to the goals of Christian liberation. The reality of marginality and the insight that Catholicism must truly be a church of the people has only slowly moved into the consciousness of the church leadership in Latin America. These developments grew out of indigenous Latin American experience but found confirmation and new strength in the reform impulses of Vatican II and the popes of the post-World War II era,[84] in John XXIII's *Pacem in Terris* and *Mater et Magistra*, and Paul VI's *Populorum Progressio*.

## LIBERATION THEOLOGY

By the mid-1960s theological and practical elements had combined to produce a theology of liberation in Latin America and a new definition of peacemaking for the majority of the world's Catholics. Liberation theologians and educators such as Gutiérrez,[85] Galilea,[86] Boff,[87] Segundo,[88] and Freire[89] rejected the Platonic dualism of the European medieval tradition with its split between an inner pietistic spirituality and a neutral or hostile attitude toward the world.[90] Following the new directions of papal and conciliar thought, they embraced the integration of the individual and of the world. Individual salvation and the salvation of the world were thus seen as one.[91]

Liberation theologians put less emphasis on traditional doctine, conventional spirituality, and liturgical devotion—orthodoxy—than on the visible imitation of Christ in the world and the life of committed love and justice—or orthopraxis.[92] Like the Renaissance Humanists[93] and the medieval mendicants,[94] their emphasis is not on the intellectual and individualistic aspects of piety and salvation, but on the ethical demands of Christianity: the duty of each Christian to live the Beatitudes and to contribute to making the kingdom of God a reality not only in a spiritual afterlife but in concrete terms in the world, through social justice and peace.[95] The world and its history are one, and the church is neither above nor outside this history.[96] The church is instead the sacrament of the world, that is, the visible manifestation of God's kingdom and plan for the salvation of all creation. As such it cannot act as an institution, protecting a specific and privileged position in the world, but must act as the chief agency of salvation, not only for its immediate members but for all of God's creation.[97] In this respect liberation theology is also profoundly apocalyptic, since it sees the goal of history as God's kingdom emerging into history and looks at the "signs of the times" in hopeful expectation of the New Age.[98]

The mission of the church thus cooperates with and contributes to God's original creation by restoring and renewing the earth by liberating humans from sin. In keeping with its integral approach liberation theology defines sin as recent popes and councils have: as social and economic injustice, as oppression and the will to dominate, as the violence that maintains injustice. The church has both a prophetic and a teaching role: it exposes sin wherever it finds it and condemns it for what it is; it also educates those enslaved and blinded by sin—those oppressed by unjust economic and social systems and those who maintain and extend this oppression—to their human dignity, freedom, and solidarity with all other men and women. Liberation theologians call this process "conscientization."[99] The church seeks not to replace one oppressor with another but to liberate both the oppressed and the oppressors at the same time and to reunite them in the kingdom of God.[100]

In true adherence to the Christian message, liberation theology takes its inspiration from the Bible, from the archetypal story of liberation from oppressive bondage, the story of the exodus,[101] and from Christ's definition of his mission. Luke's Gospel is cited frequently as a model.[102] Christ emerges from the desert after his three temptations: the temptation to turn the dead stones of material development into the bread of life, the temptation to seize the political power of the world in order to save it, and the temptation to cast himself down from the temple, to despair of all human efforts and turn to supernatural interventions, ideologies, or human glory (Lk 4:1–13). Christ then goes to the synagogue at Nazareth and announces the purpose of his mission:

> The Spirit of the Lord is upon me,
> because he has anointed me to preach good news to the poor,
> He has sent me, to proclaim release to the captives
> and recovering of sight to the blind,
> to set at liberty those who are oppressed,
> to proclaim the acceptable year of the Lord [Lk 4:18–19].

The two passages, the temptations and the announcement of the mission, form an essential unit. Having rejected the materialism, power, and despair of the world, the church and its members must embrace hope and preach the good news to the poor, the oppressed, the jailed, and the blind. In short they must bring the gospels not to the rich, the powerful, and the comfortable but to the marginal, the outcasts, and those who neither can nor will see the truth. Liberation theology takes up the call of Vatican II and the recent popes in its "option for the poor." Liberation, however, must be won by the oppressed once they have been conscientized to their own dignity and freedom.[103]

The revolution of liberation theology is based on nonviolence, but clearly the struggle for peace and justice necessitates conflict.[104] This has led some liberation theologians to seek new formulations for Catholic peacemaking in the context of Latin America's revolutionary situation, to speak of "prophetic subversive violence," rather than "nonviolence," as the Christian alternative to the "institutionalized" and "oppressive" violence of the ruling elites and to the "subversive armed violence" of the terrorist or the guerrilla.[105] Others answer the question by using the traditional categories of the just-war theory and embrace the concept of the just revolution[106] or leave nonviolence open to the developing definition of praxis.[107]

Theology thus remains true to its call of defining doctrine in relationship to the developing practice of Catholics and the gradual process of revelation through history. Practice in turn is defined and modified by theology in an unfolding dialogue. We will now examine some of the major theological definitions, events, individuals, and groups who have shaped the practice of Catholic peacemaking in Latin America. We can only illustrate by examples; we cannot examine the entire scope of peacemaking in Latin America today.

## THEOLOGICAL BASIS OF PEACEMAKING: THE MEDELLÍN CONFERENCE

The major theological event for Latin America's struggle for liberation was the conference held in Medellín (Colombia) from August 24 to September 6, 1968.[108] The Medellín conference was the second general meeting of CELAM, the Conference of Latin American Bishops. The thinking expressed at Medellín brought together several strains of the previous decade: the growing sense of unity among Latin America's Catholics, the impact of a developing liberation theology, the influence of Vatican II and of Paul VI's *Populorum Progressio*.[109] The major themes of the conference were the pressing issues of contemporary Latin America and the church's role in the change there: social change and its methods, political reform guaranteeing the people's participation in decisions affecting the common good, and the process of conscientization.[110]

The documents of the Medillín conference deal with two essential topics: Justice[111] and Peace.[112] Both documents follow the same three-part form. Part 1 of the Peace document, The Latin American Situation and Peace, uses Paul VI's definition of peace in *Populorum Progressio*[113] to raise the essential problem of peace and peacemaking in contemporary Latin America:

> If "development is the new name for peace," Latin American underdevelopment with its own characteristics in the different countries is an unjust situation which promotes tensions that conspire against peace [par. 1].

The church can no longer support this situation but must "call attention to those aspects which constitute a menace or negation of peace" (par. 1). These "aspects" include the marginality of most of the people of Latin America, extreme social and economic inequalities, the growing frustration, disintegration, and proletarianization of the people, the oppression and insensitivity of the dominant groups, their unjust exercise of power, and the growing awareness among the oppressed of their state of oppression (pars. 2–7). The reaction of the privileged to the prophetic cries of the church has been consistent: charges of subversion and communism, calls for law and order, and new excuses to retain their privileges and positions (pars. 5–6).

The ruling elites are aided by a new international exploitation and neocolonialism, what Paul VI, [114] quoting Pius XI,[115] called the "international imperialism of money" (par. 9c). They have responded to the extreme poverty and need of their fellow citizens with an aggravated nationalism and an arms race that is a scandal (pars. 12–13). Having denounced the injustices that stand in the way of peace, what else is the Christian to do?

Part 2 of the Peace document, Doctrinal Reflexion, offers several Christian views of peace:

> Peace is, above all, a work of justice. . . . Peace in Latin America, therefore, is not the simple absence of violence and bloodshed. Oppression by the power groups may give the impression of maintaining peace and order, but in truth it is nothing but the "continuous and inevitable seed of rebellion and war" [par. 14a].

The document goes on: "Peace is a permanent task"; it requires "constant change in structures, transformation of attitudes, and conversion of hearts" (par. 14b). The document recalls that Augustine's "tranquility of order" is

neither passivity nor conformity. It is not something that is acquired once and for all. . . . A static and apparent peace may be obtained with the use of force; an authentic peace implies struggle, creative abilities and permanent conquest. Peace is not found, it is built, the Christian man is the artisan of peace [par. 14b].

"Finally," the council declares, "peace is the fruit of love" (par. 14c). It is true kinship, rejecting all inequalities.

Medellín is clear about the role of violence in the social changes that must take place in Latin America:

No one should be surprised if we forcefully reaffirm our faith in the productiveness of peace. This is our Christian ideal. "Violence is neither Christian nor evangelical."[116] The Christian man is peaceful and not ashamed of it. He is not simply a pacifist, for he can fight, but he prefers peace to war [par. 15].

The Christian works for nonviolent revolution, basing it on the awakening of individual conscience and the adequate preparation and effective participation of all people, not the replacement of one ruling elite by another that usually accompanies violent revolution (par. 15). Nevertheless "justice is a prerequisite for peace," and in many Latin American countries a situation of social injustice prevails that is "called institutional violence." It comes as no surprise, therefore, that the " 'temptation to violence' is surfacing in Latin America" (par. 16).

The bishops address their call for nonviolence to all groups. The oppressive elites should "not abuse the patience of a people that for years has borne a situation that would not be acceptable to anyone with any degree of awareness of human rights" (par. 16), nor should they "take advantage of the pacifist position of the church" (par. 17). The poor should not be passive or fearful of the risk involved in the struggle for justice and peace (par. 18). Those committed to violent revolution should note that although their action "frequently finds it ultimate motivation in noble impulses of justice and solidarity" (par. 19), nonviolence is both more practical and right.

Medellín then addresses one of the most controversial and most invoked ideas in contemporary Latin America, one often associated with liberation theology: the idea of just revolution. Though the bishop's words have been misquoted and distorted,[117] they are clear and should be quoted here in full:

If it is true that revolutionary insurrection can be legitimate in the case of evident and prolonged "tyranny that seriously works against the fundamental rights of man, and which damages the common good of the country,"[118] whether it proceeds from one person or from clearly unjust structures, it is also certain that violence or "armed revolution" generally "generates new injustices, introduces new imbalances and causes new disasters; one cannot combat a real evil at the price of a greater evil"[119] [par. 19].

The role of the church is therefore not to condone violence but to change oppression "not into hate and violence, but into the strong and peaceful energy of constructive works" (par. 19).

The methods of this transformation are spelled out in Part 3, Pastoral Conclusions. They include educating the Christian conscience and denouncing injustices, both parts of conscientization; defending the rights of the poor and the oppressed according to the principles of the gospels; forming persons "committed to world peace," that is, educating Catholics for social criticism and service in cooperation with all men and women; forming "grass-roots organizations for the redress and consolidation of their rights and the search for true justice"; pressing for the perfection of the system of justice; and finally urging a halt to the arms race, convincing people that the struggle against misery is the true war that Christians must wage (pars. 20–29). The documents conclude with a Message to the Peoples of Latin America[120] and an urgent call to Catholics not to separate their faith from the real issues of the world and to work for "the dawn of a new era."[121]

## THE PRACTICE OF LIBERATION IN LATIN AMERICA

Medellín provided theological and pastoral reflections on how Christianity builds a new society,[122] and it did so through a dialogue with practice that helped shape its definitions and that in turn has been shaped by it. Examples of individual and group action from the 1960s to the present will help illustrate the nature and practice of Catholic peacemaking in Latin America.

By the late 1960s Latin America had begun to polarize to the twin axes of violence: the institutionalized and oppressive violence of the National Security States against the subversive counterviolence of terrorism and revolution. Catholics and their church were caught between two extremes that called on them to choose to be loyal either to the defense of "Western Christian Civilization"[123] or to the just violence of revolution. The life of Fr. Camilo Torres, who came to embrace the cause of violent revolution as a demonstration of "efficacious love" and the lesser of two evils, was a landmark in Latin American history.[124]

Slowly, however, the church had begun its tranformation to prophecy and conscientization as the hierarchy and the laity became aware of the need for gospel action, for the condemnation of injustice and of "institutionalized violence," and for the creation of a new society.[125] This shift brought the church into conflict with the National Security State. In the 1970s the church underwent a reign of terror, a persecution unparalleled since the time of the martyrs under the Roman Empire. Hundreds of priests, monks, nuns, bishops, and laypersons suffered harassment, imprisonment, torture, and death for their witness to the gospels.[126]

## BRAZIL: DOM HELDER CAMARA

Brazil offers the most frightening, but in many ways one of the most hopeful, situations in Latin America. The largest and richest country on the continent, one of the major economies of the world, Brazil is also a disastrous example of the doctrine of development. It has a foreign debt of $93 billion (1984), the highest of any country of the Third World.[127] Differences in wealth—between a small ruling elite and an impoverished majority—are vast. Between 1960 and 1970, 1.00 percent of the population increased its share of the national wealth from 11.7 percent to 17 percent, while the share of 50 percent of the population dropped from 17 percent to 13.7 percent of the total. The wealth accumulated in 1970 by 1.00 percent of the population was greater than the wealth of 50 percent of the people. In the northeast, one of the poorest, but "developed," parts of the country, per capita income was only $200 a year in 1970; 52 percent of the people earned less than $20 a month. Unemployment in Recife averaged 40 percent.[128] "Development" has caused the dislocation of thousands of small farmers and the conscious extermination of entire Indian tribes in the Amazon valley. Because of "development" the country is deeply in debt to foreign, mostly North American, banks and governments; Brazil's oligarchs have created the largest military establishment in Latin America; and the country is the largest arms exporter of the Third World, the fifth largest in the world.[129]

The pressures and dislocations of development caused political unrest in the early 1960s and threatened the ruling oligarchy. In 1964 the military under General Castelo Branco staged a coup and brought the country under a harsh military dictatorship. With the help of the United States the generals created a dictatorial National Security State that matched Nazi devotion to race and blood with a new myth: the defense of "Western Christian Civilization."[130] In the name of Christian civilization the military suspended all constitutional and human rights and jailed and murdered thousands of political opponents, including many Catholics, lay, religious, and clergy.[131]

In keeping with the Catholic Church's traditional alliance with the state and the ruling elite, at first many of its members supported the military regime.[132] Yet gradually, in small but significant ways, the Catholic Church began to embrace the cause of the poor and the oppressed and to work for their liberation and for the nonviolent overthrow of the generals. The most significant figure in this process has been the archbishop of Recife, "the voice of the Third World" and Nobel Peace Prize nominee, Dom Helder Camara.[133]

Even before the coup Dom Helder was one of Brazil's best-known and most popular churchmen, but he was an intimate of politicians and a friend of the ruling elite. He was born in 1909 in Fortaleza (Brazil) of a middle-class family. He was brought up with a devout but conventional spirituality that led him to the priesthood. In 1931 his Catholic-inspired fear of communism prompted him to join the fascist Integralist movement,[134] but he soon repudiated it. In 1936 he became an adviser to the Brazilian Secretariat of Education and rose quickly through the bureaucracy in an age when educated churchmen mingled easily in the Brazilian government. Consecrated a bishop in 1952, he was named auxiliary bishop of Rio de Janeiro in 1955. By 1951 he had founded the Brazilian National Conference of Bishops with the help of Cardinal Giovanni Battista Montini, his close friend and later, as Paul VI, his loyal protector. During his fourteen years as head of the conference he was instrumental in founding the Latin American Bishops Conference, CELAM.[135]

During the late 1950s and early 1960s Dom Helder was closely involved with Brazil's development schemes and was at various times urged to run for the offices of mayor of Rio de Janeiro and vice-president of the country. By 1960, however, he had begun to pay close attention to the reform ideas of Pope John XXIII and to have serious doubts about the wisdom of capitalist development. The works of the Brazilian educator Paolo Freire on conscientization and the church's role in educating the people added to his doubts. In 1960 Dom Helder negotiated with the government on behalf of the bishops to establish the Movement for Basic Education (MEB). Organized along Freire's theories, the MEB sought to reach out to the oppressed and uneducated to enable them to begin to analyze and criticize, to realize their human potential and dignity, and to act to remove the burdens of their own oppression.[136]

By 1963 Dom Helder had come to repudiate the Alliance for Progress with its emphasis on grand development projects imposed from above. Shortly after he criticized the program to the United States ambassador to Brazil, he lost favor with the ruling elite.[137] Newspapers began to vilify him and in April 1964, immediately after the coup, he was transferred from Rio to the oblivion of Recife in northeast Brazil. His transfer only brought him closer to the problems of Brazil: incredible poverty, ignorance, disease, and social oppression. He called on the military government to make necessary reforms and became such a problem for the generals that in 1967 the neofascist Tradition, Family, Property (TFP) movement demanded that he be purged from "our" church, that is, a church committed to the protection of private property, aristocratic position, and social inequalities taken as divine rights.[138]

Despite the TFP denunciations of all reform attempts as communist subversion, Dom Helder vigorously pursued the new direction of the church, condemning extremes of both capitalism and communism[139] and denouncing the United States and the Soviet Union for their selfishness in the face of world poverty.[140] He has described Brazil's development as a cruel myth that aids only the country's elite, enriching them and their patrons in the United States. International trade only increases the poverty of Brazilians and decreases the number of jobs. Meanwhile multinational corporations accumulate vast wealth through centralizaed, high-technology industries, and maintain their neocolonial hold over the country through their use of technocrats, political contacts, the mass media and, if necessary, military coups.[141] He condemned Brazil's economic and social system in clear terms:

> The *social order?* What social order are people talking about? . . . The one that we see today, that consists in leaving millions of God's children in miserable poverty, should rather be called *social disorder,* systematized injustice.[142]

The archbishop calls this form of violence the M-bomb, the bomb of human misery, worse than the A-bomb.[143]

Dom Helder Camara therefore calls not for reforms or aid, but for a fundamental change in Brazilian society, for justice on a world scale.[144] In October 1968 he united 43 of Brazil's 253 bishops and thousands of Catholic laypersons to launch his Action, Justice, and Peace movement in Brazil, an attempt at nonviolent revolution.[145] Over the past two decades Dom Helder has developed a theology and a practice of this "revolution through peace." His methods have included the witness of religious processions, of human chains to prevent violence between police and protestors (as in Rio de Janeiro in 1968), and his decision to embrace voluntary poverty to live a life in solidarity with the people and to show that the church must align itself with the oppressed and the outcasts of society. He declined to live in the bishop's palace, which he uses only as an office.[146]

Most important to this revolution, however, is Dom Helder's foundation of Operation Hope, a grass-roots organization that coordinates the basic Christian communities.[147] Serving a function similar to that of the medieval Third Orders,[148] the basic Christian communities are small groups within a parish devoted to Bible study and to the application of their study to the problems of society, a fundamental form of conscientization. This effort starts from the premise that change cannot be forced from above or brought about by an elite but must come from the people. These basic Christian communities among the poor therefore aim first to overcome the alienation and fragmentation of urban life, to provide basic vocational training, health care, and literacy education, and then to raise people's consciousness so that they can decide the directions of their own lives and plan their own communities.[149] The efforts of Helder Camara and other bishops to establish basic Christian communities have been a huge success. By 1979 there were 80,000 basic Christian communities throughout Brazil.[150]

Contrary to right-wing accusations,[151] the process of conscientization is not a means to an end, not the building block of a political revolution that will change the ruling class, but the goal itself. For only through the fundamental realization of their own dignity can people create the just and peaceful society that Christianity demands. Dom Helder's approach is consciously humanist[152] and parallels that of Danilo Dolci in Sicily,[153] Lanzo del Vasto in France,[154] and the Peace People in Northern Ireland.[155] Danilo Dolci has in fact been a major inspiration for the Brazilian movement.[156]

Dom Helder's revolution through peace is the natural result and the means of transformation. He respects the sacrifice of revolutionaries like Camilo Torres and Che Guevara, who have been willing to lay down their lives for the cause of justice. These revolutionaries did not use violence cynically nor did they condone it from the safety of academic armchairs.[157] Dom Helder noted that whereas the Cuban revolution brought real changes in Latin America, nonviolence had yet to claim any real victories as it races against time and violence.[158] He therefore refused to condemn subversive terrorist violence amid the injustice of oppression:

> The injustices within Brazilian society constitute Violence Number One, and terrorism is Violence Number Two. It is easy for the government to fight the secondary violence. Why don't they have the courage to fight the primary violence?[159]

Nevertheless, revolutionary counterviolence seems counterproductive and dehumanizing. It pits oppressed against oppressed while intellectuals and other elites sit back comfortably.[160] The archbishop calls instead for creative nonviolence, for Christians to turn the enemy's hate into love. He asks Christians to love even their torturers. In the end this causes the oppressors to doubt their own power and it gives power to the nonviolent. "Only love can build. Hate and violence only destroy."[161] Such a revolution, however, is a long slow process, but it is both the end and the means of Christian change.[162]

The process of nonviolent revolution is a dangerous one. The basic Christian communities faced continual harassment and physical violence from the government. Their members were arrested, tortured, and killed. Foreign missionaires, priests, nuns, and bishops helping the communities were vilified, arrested, tortured, and expelled.[163] The oligarchy continued its attacks in the média against "subversives" and communists. Archbishop Camara was declared a "nonperson" in Brazil; the press and the electronic media could not mention his name or report on his activities. He was denied access to the media, except for a five-minute homily broadcast every morning. His bishop's palace was attacked by the police with machine guns, and his personal assistant, Henrique Neto, was assassinated.[164] Despite the persecution of his followers, threats against his own life, and his offer to enter prison himself to secure the release of his companions, Dom Helder was left untouched.[165] Government tactics recall those used against dissident bishops under the Nazi government in Germany.[166] The rationalization is also the same: the defense of "Western Christian Civilization."

Despite their difficulties the Catholics of Brazil have made changes. By 1973 one-third of the country's 270 bishops had embraced a radical Christianity that did not hesitate to condemn the government.[167] São Paulo's archbishop, Cardinal Paulo Evaristo Arns, began a campaign for human rights in 1970,[168] and the bishops of northeastern

Brazil kept up their prophetic denunciations of the military government, its economic policies, and its torture and assassinations. Their pastoral *I Have Heard the Cries of My People* (1973) denounced church complicity with the power elite.[169] Despite government censorship their letter was circulated underground and by word of mouth, again recalling the situation of Catholics in Nazi Germany.[170] The bishops were joined by many intellectuals and educated laypersons in this process.[171]

Yet the church in Brazil differs greatly from the church of Nazi Germany. The Brazilian church has begun to grasp the lessons of the century and to embrace the world of Vatican II and Medellín. It has begun the solid education of Catholics who must take up the struggle to create a just and peaceful society "without waiting passively for orders and directives."[172]

We cannot predict the outcome or direction of Brazil's nonviolent revolution. During the 1980s mass opposition to the government forced changes in Brazilian life. In January 1984 two hundred thousand people in Sao Paulo and sixty thousand in Dom Helder's Oilinda protested against martial law. These were the largest nonviolent demonstrations in the country's history.[173] In April 1984 over one million Brazilians took part in two demonstrations. By January 1985 pressures on the government finally brought the election of the country's first civilian president in twenty-one years.[174] What will be the ultimate role of Catholics in Brazil's changes? How Christian will the revolution be? And after the revolution, what will be the relationship of the church to the powers-that-will-be in Brazilian society? Will the church once again embrace the state as a means to further its ends? Or will the church retain its witness to prophecy and protest?

## ARGENTINA: ADOLFO PEREZ ESQUIVEL AND THE MOTHERS OF THE PLAZA DE MAYO

In Argentina the overthrow of the junta of General Leopoldo Galtieri (June 1982) and the resignation of the interim president General Antonio Bignone in favor of national elections (October 1983) marked the end of a decade of the most brutal oppression that the Western world has yet seen. We can only list the highlights of Argentina's turbulent recent history: the 1966 military coup that brought an end to Juan Peron's power; the 1969 *Cordobazo,* large-scale civil disturbances by students and workers that shook the military regime; the 1972 internal war against the guerrillas; the ensuing political crisis and the return of Perón in 1973, his death, and the presidency of Isabel Perón (1974); the coup under General Jorge Rafael Videla in 1976 and the beginning of the "Dirty War" against tens of thousands of "subversives."[175]

No one knows how many political opponents and dissidents, Catholic and Protestant clergy, foreign workers, priests, and refugees, were jailed, tortured, and murdered by the army and by secret death squads, nor how many of the kidnapped and officially "disappeared" were murdered without charges or trial.[176] In April 1983 former President Videla, since charged with numerous counts of murder, called the military's final cover-up document on the Dirty War "an act of love."[177]

Argentina is not Brazil. It boasts the second-highest standard of living, the highest per capita income,[178] and the highest literacy rate in Latin America. It has an educated and cultured citizenship. The atmosphere in its cities is often described as European. Its citizens are more politicized and more educated in democratic processes and traditions than are the citizens of Brazil. Argentina's response to dictatorship was therefore different from Brazil's. In Argentina working-class unions, political parties, and middle and professional classes provided a strong base for opposition. In Argentina, as in Brazil, however, this opposition had to be slowly and patiently built. It too involved individual conversions and organized actions, gradual conscientization, and willingness to act on convictions. The life of Adolfo Perez Esquivel, winner of the 1980 Nobel Peace Prize, typifies the process of peaceful change now underway in the country.

Esquivel was born in Buenos Aires in November 1931. Poor as a youth, he received a good, Catholic education and established a successful career as a painter and sculptor.[179] After a trip to Ecuador he was moved to take up the cause of the poor and oppressed. He dreamed one night that he saw Christ on the cross dressed in a poncho. He later painted the scene, Christ crucified in a poncho, goaded by modern riot police, their rifles and bayonets at the ready. Around the cross stand the poor, the peasants, the mothers and children, the tortured and the dead lifting up their arms in prayer.[180] Esquivel says he was influenced by many peacemakers:[181] John the Baptist, Francis of Assisi,[182] Gandhi, Lanzo del Vasto,[183] Thomas Merton,[184] Ernesto Cardenal,[185] Charles de Foucauld, Hildegard Goss-Mayr, Teilhard de Chardin, and Dom Helder Camara. Medellín gave his work even greater meaning and urgency.

Although he is not a prophet like Helder Camara, Adolfo Perez Esquivel has pursued peacemaking as an organizer and as a coordinator, bringing together Latin America's various peace movements,[186] lending them advice and logistical help, cross-fertilizing the many efforts that exist in spite of regimes that use every method to prevent the dissemination of information, curtail travel, and prohibit open meetings and free expression. In the 1970s Esquivel worked as an organizer traveling around Latin America, participating in nonviolent actions and learning different ways of peacemaking. In 1971 in Costa Rica he helped plan for nonviolent liberation, and founded the Servicio de Paz y Justicia. He participated in similar efforts in Colombia in 1974. Later that year he was named general coordinator of Paz y Justicia and participated in meetings in Ecuador, Bolivia, and Argentina. In 1975 he traveled to Paraguay and Brazil. In 1976 he and about forty bishops and religious superiors, including four U.S. bishops, were arrested and expelled from Ecuador for attending a meeting[187] hosted by Bishop Leonidas Proaño of Riobamba.[188] He helped lay the groundwork for the *Latin American Charter of Nonviolence,* which was issued by the bishops gathered at Bogotá in the fall of 1977.[189]

By 1976 he was leading the human rights movement in Argentina and denouncing the government. Later that year the junta ordered the destruction of his Paz y Justicia headquarters. On his return to Argentina in April 1977, when Esquivel went to the local police headquarters to have his passport renewed, he was arrested and held incommunicado without charges. He was saved from "disappearing" only by the quick action of a close friend and his wife, who let the authorities know that she knew of his arrest. Nevertheless, he was held in prison without charges for fourteen months in a cramped cell, repeatedly tortured, denied the Bible or any other religious reading. His torturers tried to force blasphemies from him, all in the name, Esquivel later said, of defending "Western Christian Civilization."[190] An international campaign led by Mairead Corrigan and Betty Williams of the Peace People,[191] Amnesty International, and the U.S. Carter administration finally secured his freedom.[192] After his release he was kept under house arrest for another nine months.

Despite his arrest and torture, Esquivel continues to believe in and to practice nonviolence.[193] He dislikes the word "nonviolence," considering it too passive for the reality, but admits that no better word has been found yet and that liberation theology has not yet developed a complete critique of violence. He rejects armed liberation struggles, believing they only create a new oppressor and a new oppressed. Liberation, he contends, must embrace the entire person, it must avoid do-gooder, social-work solutions, and it must reject both the consumerism and the militarism of development. The chief goals of the liberation process are denouncing injustice and raising the consciousness of local communities. These goals are accomplished in a variety of ways but action must begin from a popular base. The transformation must be nonviolent, must act in truth, and must create solidarity as a deterrent to isolation and despair.

Nonviolence is a method that belongs to the people by its very nature. It is not elitist—it rejects the heroism of a Che Guevera, and it questions the claims of the Sandinistas in Nicaragua of having attained their revolution through violence. While mass violence may have been a justifiable response to Somoza's brutal repression, the victory in Nicaragua, Esquivel maintains, was prepared for, not by counterviolence, but by the mass, nonviolent actions of the Nicaraguan people, who later supported the Sandinistas. Instead of violence Esquivel prefers the boycott and the strike, noncooperation, hunger strikes, and civil disobedience—all means that refuse to grant the field to the enemy by engaging in violence. By its nature, nonviolence involves more people than an elitist armed struggle. Despite the very real dangers of physical harm, which Esquivel has experienced, he contends that nonviolence forces nonviolent reaction, and ultimately fosters respect on both sides as it seeks to change the oppressor as well as the oppressed.

It was a terrible blow to the generals of Argentina, therefore, when in December 1980 Adolfo Perez Esquivel was awarded the Nobel Peace Prize. The Argentine junta, like the Polish generals in 1983 when Lech Walesa won the award,[194] realized the importance of the prize and its meaning for nonviolence in Argentina and immediately condemned it as an "intolerable affront" to their national dignity.[195]

The most dramatic example of Esquivel's work in Argentina has been the phenomenon of the Mothers of the Plaza de Mayo. After the coup in March 1976 led by General Videla, fathers and mothers, brothers and sisters, sons and daughters were taken from homes and workplaces and were never seen again. A group of women came to Esquivel's Paz y Justicia center in Buenos Aires to ask for advice and help. At first the center acted simply as an outlet for their sorrow and despair. One day, however, the center's team suggested that the women bring their grievances to the attention of the government by a silent protest demonstration in the Plaza de Mayo, the main square in Buenos Aires, in the heart of the government district.[196] The weekly protests were at first either ignored or ridiculed; then the women were harassed and sometimes they were driven off violently by police. By 1980 the mothers had become known worldwide as the symbol of Argentina's opposition to the generals, an opposition that stood, peacefully, protesting and giving witness to facts that the generals would have preferred buried.[197]

In July 1980 at the end of a meeting of the Mothers and the Servicio de Paz y Justicia on "The Gospel and the Experience of Human Community," Esquivel issued a statement that summarized their philosophy. The gospel was the guide for their lives. They condemned violence as an attack on the family, on society, and on the body politic. They condemned the institutional violence of injustice and offered nonviolence instead as a means of liberating the poor and the oppressed. They were aware, however, that in this struggle they would face charges of subversion and communism from those who were claiming to protect "Western Christian Civilization" through their "dirty war."[198] Despite these dangers, however, they said they were willing to become martyrs for a more just society, to answer evil and injustice with truth, and hate with love.[199]

The Plaza de Mayo Mothers encouraged other Argentinians to express their protest. Unlike the Northern Irish Peace People's divisive tactics,[200] the July 1980 meeting concluded with a call for unity with the church, international human rights organizations, labor unions, political parties, and student groups.[201] Their call, and Esquivel's efforts for nonviolent change, soon brought results. Argentina's bishops had either ignored Esquivel or disassociated themselves from him after he received the Nobel Prize,[202] but by July 1981 seventy Catholic bishops issued a strong condemnation of the repression and the dirty war.[203] By December 1982, after Argentina's disastrous Falklands/ Malvinas war, the military collapsed under its own incompetence following a series of nonviolent general strikes and demonstrations. In October 1983 Argentina elected a democratic government.[204]

## REFLECTIONS ON THE 1970S: SUCRE, BOGOTÁ, PUEBLA

The spirit of Medellín and the impact of liberation theology brought about strong reactions from the National Security States and the church during the 1970s. Not all church leaders agreed with the new directions toward liberation and nonviolent struggle and maintained pre-Vatican II attitudes concerning accommodation with the state and authoritarianism within the church. This trend manifested itself at the fourteenth ordinary meeting of CELAM held at Sucre (Bolivia) in November 1972.[205] Typical of the reaction to liberation theology was a statement by Bishops Galat and Ordonez, who defended the ruling elites and attacked the church's option for the poor:

Material poverty cannot be confused with spiritual poverty. People may be poor in economic goods without being poor in spirit, or one can deify money and covet wealth one does not possess. Still one can be rich in material goods and be truly *anawin,* or poor in spirit.[206]

Yet the reaction did not sweep all before it. At Bogotá (Colombia) in December 1977, the International Meeting of Latin American Bishops issued a document that has been called Latin America's Charter of Nonviolence.[207] The document repudiated efforts to turn back the tide of liberation and reaffirmed the commitment of the Catholic Church to witness with its blood for "justice, for peace, and for the defense of the weak and oppressed." It also presented a theology of peacemaking for Latin America. The Christian, it declared, must not abide evil, but must defend humanistic Christian values through peaceful means. "Violence," it reminded Latin Americans, "is un-Christian and unevangelical, not to mention inefficacious."

The document condemned the violence of the National Security State, the violence of economic exploitation, and the violence of terrorism and subversion. It warned Catholics to be aware of the "violence done to the Word of God when the very Gospel is used to exculpate and even legitimate violence." Jesus challenged the base of the power structure, but he did so without using violence. Yet violence cannot be ignored. It is used by both extremes, and on both sides it creates faceless, numb masses. It appears to leave Latin Americans with two choices: passivity and conformism or rebellion and violence. The Christian however has a way out of the dilemma, a way demonstrated by Gandhi, Martin Luther King, Danilo Dolci, Cesar Chavez, and Helder Camara. This is the path of nonviolence.

The spirit of nonviolence is not negative. It begins with a radical change of life; it is not instinctual but is slowly developed. Nonviolence is "persevering, clear in its objectives, and methodical in its procedure." It exposes and denounces injustice and violence. Its practice of reconciliation is neither passivity, nor weakness, nor cowardice. It does not tolerate injustice, but it does not seek to dominate. It is open to dialogue with the enemy and realizes that the enemy is not the same as his or her evil deeds. It seeks to implant the same values in the oppressor that it cultivates in the oppressed. Above all, nonviolence is a movement of the people. It is lived first and foremost by the basic Christian communities, in union and peasant organizations, and it respects the initiatives of the people.

The Bogotá meeting stood firmly on Catholic doctrine, recalling Thomas Aquinas[208] and Erasmus[209] in stating the primacy of the people over the state. Should the defense of the state, in fact, call for repressive measures, for violence that would lead to counterviolence and terror, then the state should be sacrificed. The bishops further eroded the basis of the National Security State by dismissing the Soviet threat in the hemisphere as unfounded, as an excuse of dictatorships that attack even the clergy and destroy democratic institutions. By suspending constitutional rule in times of crisis such regimes not only show contempt for democracy but also show that their democracy is irrelevant to real politics, and thus they actually encourage communist influence. Finally the bishops declared that if they must choose between the oppressors and the oppressed, their choice would be clear. A gospel that would hold the same comfort for both the rich and the poor would be a bland message; their good news must be for the poor and the oppressed.[210]

The third meeting of CELAM was held in Puebla (Mexico) in 1979. Since the 1972 appointment of conservative Archbishop Alfonso Lopez Trujillo as secretary general of the Bishops Conference, however, reaction had been growing. The antiliberationist forces in Latin America and in Europe, funded by U.S. and West German conservatives, had been mounting a counterattack to move the church away from the poor and the oppressed and toward Latin America's generals and dictators.[211]

The conservatives' long preparations backfired however. The historic meeting at Puebla was a major media and international event and a landmark in church history.[212] Its Final Document[213] was a triumph for liberation theology. It reconfirmed the positions of Medillín and deepened the church's commitment to the poor and the oppressed, especially after the preceding decade of repression and violence. It rejected the conservatives' attempt to trivialize the church's alliance with the poor with their platitudes about "spiritual poverty" and instead endorsed "evangelical poverty" as the Christian ideal (pars. 1148–52), thus realigning the church with the tradition of the gospels and the social protest of Saint Francis and the medieval mendicants.[214] It rejected capitalism and development as the solution to Latin America's problems and denounced the role the rich nations and multinational corporations play in creating the injustices of Latin America (pars. 1260–69).

Puebla reaffirmed the postconciliar view of the church as the People of God, a church built from the grassroots and not imposed from above (Pt. 2, chaps. 1, 2, pars. 220–303, esp. pars. 261–63). It reconfirmed Vatican II's separation of church and state and highlighted how far the Catholic Church had come since the concordats of the 1930s. The Final Document rarely uses the words "nation" or "state," which had so long dominated church thought on the problems of the world, and replaces them with "the people" as the agency of change. It sides firmly with the Latin American prophetic tradition of Montesinos and Las Casas (par. 8).

The Puebla conference reaffirmed the message of Medellín and of Bogotá on Catholic peacemaking in Latin America. Peace was again identified with justice (for example, par. 1188). Yet justice cannot flourish under the present situation in Latin America, in which violence of all types prevails. The situation includes both the institutionalized violence of repression and the counterviolence of subversion (pars. 508–9, 1259). The conference rejected the violence of the National Security State, "physical and psychological torture, kidnapping, the persecution of political dissidents and suspect persons, and the exclusion of people from public life because of their ideas" (par. 531), and condemned the rationalizations offered in defense of these actions. It also condemned "terrorist and guerrilla violence" and rejected its role in the process of liberation (pars. 532–34).

What means of liberation can the Christian use then? Puebla reaffirms the pacifist position of Vatican II:[215]

> Our responsibility as Christians is to use all possible means to promote the implementation of nonviolent tactics in the effort to reestablish justice in economic and sociopolitical relations. [par. 533].

Finally this struggle must be the work of all people, not just of the church hierarchy or of an ideological elite:

> The sort of liberation we are talking about knows how to use evangelical means, which have their own distinctive efficacy. It does not resort to violence of any sort, or to the dialectics of class struggle. Instead it relies on the vigorous energy and activity of Christians, who are moved by the spirit to respond to the cries of countless millions of their brothers and sisters [par. 486].

The Final Document of Puebla quickly became part of official Catholic teaching around the world. In its nonviolent, and non-Marxist, form it was endorsed by Pope John Paul II,[216] and liberation theology and its nonviolent approach have become an important force everywhere, from Poland[217] to the Philippines.[218] The challenge of peacemaking is as strong as ever for Catholics in the modern world. Its path is not clear-cut and the choices involved in it are dangerous and urgent. Nowhere is this uncertainty and urgency more apparent today than in Central America.

## MARTYRDOM IN EL SALVADOR: OSCAR ROMERO

The life and death of Archbishop Oscar Arnulfo Romero (1917–1980) of San Salvador recalls the sacrifice of the great Catholic prophets and martyrs of history: of Columban and Boniface of Crediton,[219] Thomas à Becket, and Stanislaus of Krakow.[220] Even more significantly, Oscar Romero symbolizes the transformation within the Catholic Church over the past generation from internal piety and political accommodation, from peacemaking as order and alliance with power to prophetic denunciation and social and political activism, to a peace that seeks justice and does not cringe from struggle, that faces persecution and even death.[221] Archbishop Romero came to embrace the poor and the oppressed and to realign the church with its great tradition of criticism, protest, and martyrdom.

Oscar Romero was born in the mountain village of Ciudad Barrios in the southern region of San Miguel in 1917. He was the son of the local postmaster, from a family of small coffee planters. He was brought up according to conventional Catholic piety and was apprenticed to a carpenter when young. In 1937 he entered the seminary and was sent to Rome for theological studies. Ordained there in 1942, he returned to El Salvador in 1943. As a priest he fostered in his people a simple, fervent spirituality centered around the imitation of Christ. Through the 1960s he rose gradually through the hierarchy and in 1970 was ordained a bishop.[222] At first he was attracted to the message of Vatican II and Medellín, but by the 1970s, as editor of *Orientación*, Romero had turned against liberation theology and the activist priests of Central America. He attacked the Jesuits for their Medellín ideas and shifted away from the social implications of the gospel. He generally supported the status quo, the conservatives in the church and the country's ruling elite, the "fourteen families" who are believed to hold 90 percent of the country's wealth. In church matters he retained an authoritarian, preconciliar attitude.[223]

Despite his protests against the government massacres of campesinos in May 1975, Romero trusted in the Constantinian alliance of church and state, preferring to apply subtle "leverage" with the ruling authorities, believing that the government needed only adjustments and reforms, and that the church was most effective for its flock when it maintained its alliance with power. As late as 1976 he continued to attack Jesuit peace and justice activities, conscientization programs, and "Marxist" priests, although he admitted that the military used repressive means and maintained a cruel social system.[224] On August 6, 1976, the Feast of the Transfiguration and El Salvador's National Day, Romero preached a sentimental peace to Salvadoran society. As high government officials and the ruling elite listened, Romero wished for the tranquility of order in the land, "each one in the place where the hand of Providence has put him," led by "the members of the government and the shepherds of the church."[225]

In February 1977 the elderly Archbishop Chavez y Gonzalez of San Salvador stepped down from his post. In his last few years as archbishop, he had energetically mobilized the clergy of the archdiocese, the center of the country's population, around the commitments of Vatican II and Medellín, encouraging the basic Christian communities, worker priests, and the work of peace and justice. The choice of Oscar Romero as the new archbishop was a disappointment to the concerned clergy and laity.[226] Events, however, would soon bring drastic changes to El Salvador and to Archbishop Romero. In February 1977 General Carlos Humberto Romero became El Salvador's president after allegedly fraudulent elections. The elections spurred mass actions ending in the government's "Monday Massacre" of over one hundred protestors in San Salvador's main plaza.[227] Even before his installation Romero consulted with his activist clergy and denounced government repression and violations of human rights, defying the risk of persecution of the church that was commonplace throughout Latin America.[228] By the time of his first formal meeting with the clergy of the archdiocese, Romero had turned against El Salvador's ruling class.[229]

Romero and the Salvadoran church could not reject the ruling class with impunity however. Several days later, Romero's dear friend and mentor, Rutilio Grande, a Jesuit worker priest and organizer in the countryside around Aguilares, was murdered by a death squad. The event pushed the archbishop to fully embrace the cause of the poor and oppressed for whom Grande had died.[230] By March 1977 Romero was speaking out against the violence and oppression of the government. He refused to participate in government events, and declared that the church was being persecuted for its adherence to Vatican II and Medellín. Despite the opposition of the papal nuncio, a close ally of the ruling families, and of conservative colleagues in El Salvador's Bishops Conference, Romero allied himself solidly with the progressive clergy and with the hundreds of thousands of Salvadoran campesinos who attended protest masses, listened to his sermons on YSAX, the diocescan radio, and worked in basic Christian communites. Romero wrote and traveled to Rome repeatedly and received support from Paul VI and John Paul II.[231]

In response to church criticisms the government used many tactics reminiscent of the Nazis in the 1930s:[232] attacks on the orthodoxy of the schools (accusations of Marxist infiltration and the teaching of hate), attacks on individual priests, compesinos, and basic Christian communities, assassinations by death squads, expulsion of foreign missionaries, and the organization of pseudo-Catholic groups like the Association of Catholic Women and the Followers of Christ, which were thinly disguised fronts for government death squads.[233] Threats to kill all the Jesuits in the country and the distribution of handbills urging Salvadorans to "Be a Patriot: Kill a Priest" were common.[234]

Romero kept up his criticisms of the government through a series of nationally broadcast pastoral addresses. In these he condemned violence on both sides, rejected both capitalism and communism as viable choices for Central America, and condemned outmoded forms of quietist spirituality with no connection to social concern as "individualistic piety and disincarnate sacramentalism."[235] He fully adopted the theology of liberation, preaching the mission to save the oppressed, to bear the cross of persecution for one's witness, and urging forgiveness of enemies and persecutors. His understanding of Vatican II and Medellín deepened as he involved himself with the people of El Salvador. He began to describe the church as the sacrament of salvation, the body of Christ in history that, like Christ's living flesh, changes over time. Such a process requires both structural changes within the institutional church and the conversion of individuals.[236]

The government's response to the church's increased campaign for nonviolent change was stupefying. The incident of Aquilares is typical of what is happening all over Central America. On May 17, 1977, the day that the bishops joined Romero in condemning the violence and exploitation in the country, two thousand soldiers, backed by planes, helicopters, and tanks, surrounded the small town just north of the capital in what the government obscenely dubbed "Operation Rutilio" after the slain Jesuit. In a sudden raid troops armed with machine guns slaughtered almost four hundred unarmed peasants and arrested hundreds more over the next eight days. Three foreign Jesuits were arrested, tortured, and expelled from the country for the crime of union organizing. Entering the church, the soldiers shot dead a parishioner trying to ring the church bell in warning and then proceeded to shoot open the tabernacle, scatter the hosts over the church floor, and stamp on them. All photos of Rutilio Grande, whom the people revere as a saint, were confiscated and destroyed. When the archbishop arrived the next day to remove the sacrament, the soldiers were using the church as a barracks and refused him entry. Calling on the president, Romero condemned "these unspeakable outrages on the part of a security force in a country that we call civilized and Christian."[237] From that point on the archbishop's break with government and the ruling class of El Salvador was open.

By the end of 1977 Romero had boycotted the inauguration of General Romero, had publicly called for disobedience to the Law of Public Order (the martial-law statute) and had condemned the country's Supreme Court and judiciary for corruption and cowardice.[238] By 1978 he had brought worldwide attention to El Salvador's torment and had gained international support.[239] He had journeyed to Puebla and there met with Bishops Proaño, Mendez-Arceo, Lorscheider, Camara and other proponents of nonviolent change. In November 1978 he was nominated for the Nobel Peace Prize.[240]

In El Salvador the archbishop continued to condemn violence as "un-Christian and unevangelical,'' both in its repressive and in its terrorist forms. Although he maintained that insurrection could be justified if all other means fail, he insisted that Salvadorans had not exhausted all means possible. Recourse to armed insurrection at this point was, he felt, a "pathological mentality" that divinized violence. He continued to press for the active pursuit of the nonviolent gospel, rejecting the FPL (Popular Liberation Forces, one of the five revolutionary organizations in the FMLN, the Farabundo, Marti National Liberation Front) attempts to use the death of Fr. Ernesto (''Neto'') Barera as an example of a Christian revolutionary, a martyr killed in battle for liberation.[241]

Events were quickly unfolding. On May 23, 1979, the declaration of a state of seige was followed by a massacre of protestors outside the cathedral. The archbishop condemned the government and the acts of terrorism.[242] By now he had been subjected both to physical searches by the government as a publicly accused subversive[243] and to condemnations of accommodation by the underground.[244] The last few months of the archbishop's life saw the bloody repression of a march by a hundred thousand people in commemoration of the 1932 peasant uprising, increased assassinations, and the intensification of the guerrilla campaign. Despite repeated death threats, attacks on his friends, and the bombing of the archdiocesan radio station (YSAX), Romero continued to call for peace and justice.[245]

Finally on March 23, 1980, the archbishop shocked the nation with an impassioned plea for the end of violence. Once a pillar of the established order, he now climaxed his sermon by calling on the enlisted men of El Salvador's army to lay down their arms:

> Brothers, you are part of our people. You kill your own campesino brothers and sisters. And before an order to kill that a man may give, the law of God must prevail that says: "Thou shalt not kill!" No soldier is obliged to obey an order against the law of God . . . In the name of God, and in the name of the suffering people whose laments rise to heaven each day more tumultuous, I beg you, I ask you, I order you in the name of God: Stop the repression![246]

The next day, the archbishop was saying Mass in the chapel of the Carmelite hospital. As he raised the chalice for the consecration, an assassin shot him. In a few minutes Oscar Romero was dead. The next week millions around the world watched on television as government-incited violence disrupted the archbishop's funeral.[247] U.S. government sources and the Salvadoran judge named to investigate the assassination (who has since fled to Costa Rica for his life) blamed Operation Piña, planned and authorized by General José Alberto Medrano and Major Roberto D'Aubuisson (former head of El Salvador's ARENA Party, the Nationlist Republican Alliance).[248] Since then it has been enough to carry a photograph of the slain archbishop or to possess a Bible in El Salvador to be suspected of subversion and to be added to the more than forty thousand persons killed by death squads since 1979.[249]

After his election as president of El Salvador in May 1984 (he narrowly defeated Roberto D'Aubuisson), José Napoleón Duarte went to pray at the tomb of Oscar Romero in the crypt of San Salvador Cathedral. Was he committing himself to the bishop's goals and methods? Or was he merely exploiting the power of the martyr? Will nonviolence have a chance to succeed where violence has failed? Will Christians make it succeed? These are questions for the future. Whatever President Duarte's thoughts at Oscar Romero's tomb, he must have recalled the martyrs final words:

You may say, if they succeed in killing me, that I pardon and bless those who do it. Would that thus they might be convinced that they will waste their time. A bishop will die, but the church of God, which is the people, will never perish.[250]

## CONCLUSIONS

Oscar Romero died a Catholic martyr, a sacrifice to nonviolent change. Yet in El Salvador the struggle for which he died remains unresolved, as uncertain as ever. In Nicaragua many Christians abandoned nonviolence and joined wholeheartedly with the revolution in new alliance with the state in the hopes of creating a new society.[251] That society has begun to be built, but its final nature or success is still not certain. All across Latin America and in the rest of the Third World changes are in the works; the outcome cannot be predicted. In Argentina and in Brazil the mass nonviolence of an educated, conscientized people has brought the collapse of the generals and the beginnings of movement toward democracy and social justice. In the Philippines the conscious nonviolence of the people has brought spectacular successes, but in all these countries fundamental changes in structures are far from won. In Ecuador, Paraguay, Chile, South Africa, and dozens of other countries around the world where Catholics can influence events nonviolence is racing against time, against reactionaries within the Catholic hierarchy,[252] and against violence on both sides.

All around the world Catholics are facing the challenges of peace and justice. Many have opted for the wisdom of the world: for alliance with the powers-that-be or the powers-that-will-be. Many others have opted for faith in the message of the gospels and the Catholic tradition of active peacemaking. There are as yet no clear signs to the future of this tradition. But the struggle continues and the hope remains.

# CHAPTER 15

# CATHOLIC PEACEMAKING IN THE UNITED STATES

## INTRODUCTION

The history of the peace tradition in the United States epitomizes the past two thousand years of Catholic peacemaking. From a marginal, imported church, a small and suspect minority, the Catholic Church in the United States has grown into the largest denomination in the country. Its institutions and individual members have great influence and impact on the nation as a whole. In the first half of the twentieth century the church achieved a position of prominence, of Constantinian alliance with power and authority that characterized the era of the two world wars and their aftermath. By the 1960s, however, the call of Vatican II and the horrors of the Vietnam War had stirred the U.S. church to return to the biblical sources of its mission, to a prophetic criticism of power, to educating its members and the nation at large to the truths of Christian peace, and to a commitment to the liberation of the oppressed both in the United States and in the Third World.

The peace tradition of the U.S. church is a classic model of the dynamic of change and dialogue within the Mystical Body. On the one side stands the hierarchical, authoritarian vision of peace and order handed down by episcopal pronouncements and internationalist organizations. Like the peace of the Carolingian period[1] and of the age of absolutism after Trent,[2] this peace was gained because of the church's close association with power and authority. It was often achieved because of the church's sanctification of "just wars," official church teaching imposed on a laity expected to obey without question. On the other side stands the radical evangelism of such groups as the Catholic Worker and the Catholic Peace Fellowship. This peace is a dynamic process and a personal commitment to the pacifism of the gospels. It starts with individual conscience and conversion and then works to change institutions. This was the peace tradition of the early church,[3] of the medieval Peace of God and of the martyrs of Cordova,[4] of Saint Francis and the mendicants.[5] These movements were born of divergent interests and traditions within the church and often engaged in heated controversy throughout the twentieth century. By the 1980s they had converged to give new strength to the Catholic peace tradition in the United States.

The Catholic peace tradition in the United States has gradually progressed to a full Christian understanding of peace. From the quietism and muted piety of an immigrant

*238*

church, Catholicism emerged into the violence of the great "crusades" of World War I and World War II. During the Vietnam era the American church as a whole clung adamantly to the just-war tradition. This tradition allowed the church to support the U.S. effort at first, then to question both the means and the ends, and finally to condemn the conflict as unjust and immoral. Catholic pacifism first competed with, then cooperated with, and finally supplanted the just-war tradition. It is becoming the major peace tradition within the church today as American Catholics, like their brothers and sisters all over the world, abandon an outmoded theology of war and embrace a renewed theology of peace based on the gospels.

Several characteristics of American society serve to make American Catholic peacemaking unique. First, the predominance of middle-class life in the United States, of a comparatively prosperous, literate, and well-educated Catholic laity. Second, U.S. Catholics, like the Romans of the first century after Christ, are at the focus of power in the world today. They are neither marginalized nor alienated in this respect, and their view of peace therefore shares much of the quality of the Pax Romana.[6] Maintaining their system of life and government, brutally at times, has been, and continues to be, an essential part of the U.S. definition of peace. Third, American Catholics, as perhaps no other Catholic group past or present, have access to power, to communication, and to the protection of their opinions and dissent. Unlike Christians under the Roman Empire or Catholics in Central America or in Poland today, American Catholics are free to formulate and to implement lives and policies of peacemaking without overt or institutionalized threats of persecution or retaliation. Finally Catholics in the United States, unlike their contemporaries in Central America or the Philippines, and unlike the Christians in the Roman Empire or medieval Europe, are living in an essentially post-Christian society.

These conditions combine to make peacemaking in the United States a special challenge. In a materialistic society, which uses over three-quarters of the world's goods and resources though it comprises only five percent of the world's population, American Catholic peacemakers must live lives of justice and solidarity with the poor and the oppressed. Part of a nation that has the capacity to destroy life on the planet and a citizenship that accepts the fact that violence must be used to protect its way of life and that is increasingly insensitive to daily violence of every type, American Catholics must formulate a gospel of nonviolence among their neighbors and around the world. In a society that tolerates every form of expression and absorbs every shock to its sensitivities as easily as it switches a television channel, Catholic peacemakers must dramatize and implement their lives of peace in ways that may have far greater difficulty converting individuals and society than did the obvious and painful witness of the early Christians, of the martyrs of Cordova, of Franz Jaegerstaetter,[7] and Oscar Romero.[8] In a society that accepts neither Christian nor any other religious motivation as an impetus to change, Catholic peacemakers must devise new strategies for peace that rest firmly on their religious faith and the conviction that their religious tradition offers unique paths to peace.

## HISTORICAL BACKGROUND

Catholics first arrived in the United States as a persecuted minority.[9] Through the colonial and early republican periods their growth was slow. They were subject to suspicion and outright prejudice. The Catholic Church's solution was to draw in on itself, to protect itself from hostility and to nurture its traditions and institutions in a society that it often viewed with suspicion and alienation.[10] The great waves of immigration of the late nineteenth and early twentieth centuries brought millions of Catholics to the United States, predominantly from the impoverished classes of southern and eastern Europe. They increased the Catholic presence in the United States but they also reinforced the association of Catholicism with foreign cultures, alien political systems, and suspect allegiances.

Catholics of the immigrant generations were urban, impoverished, and subject to the worst forms of prejudice and discrimination. They viewed mainstream American culture from a safe distance, with suspicion and defensiveness.[11] Since Trent, Catholicism had a Counter-Reformation suspicion of Protestantism and nonconformism and a hostility to much of the Protestant liberal economic, intellectual, and spiritual tradition that had built the United States.[12]

Paradoxically, many of these traits were sources of strength for the Catholic peace movement. Many immigrants had come to America to flee conscription. Many retained emotional, familial, and certainly religious ties to the countries that they had left. Peace in the Catholic tradition always has had a personalistic strain that merged well with the immigrants' suspicion of institutions;[13] Catholic moral teaching retained the medieval exaltation of conscience above human law that many Protestant mainline churches had abandoned in favor of the state's authority; Catholic social thought by the early twentieth century was beginning to be critical of many aspects of capitalist industrial economy and society.[14] The Catholic Church's universality bound Catholics to their coreligionists all over the world; the church's claim of being above society and of being distinct from the mainstream of American culture provided it both institutionally and individually with a reservoir from which later dissent could flow.

With the twentieth century and World War I, however, American Catholics began to emerge from their isolation. The immigrant church, in fact, went out of its way to assert its Americanness and ultra-loyalty[15] in much the same way that German Catholics devoted themselves to the state after the *Kulturkampf* of the Bismarck era.[16] Few Catholics protested against World War I. Of the 3,989 conscientious objectors to the conflict, only four were Catholic.[17] At the end of the war, American bishops wrote a pastoral letter, *Lessons of War*,[18] urging the United States to accept its unique role to "restore peace and order" according to "the principles of reasonable liberty and of Christian civilization," thus condoning the war as a crusade.

## CATHOLIC ASSOCIATION FOR INTERNATIONAL PEACE (CAIP)

Although some Catholics participated in the pacifist World Alliance in the years before and after World War I,[19] in general Catholic peacemaking in the United States until the 1930s shared the traits of the European church since Trent: peacemaking was something done only by the elite and it took the form of international agreement and government action imposed from above. This was the stance taken by the Catholic Association for International Peace (CAIP), which was organized at Catholic University in Washington, D.C., in 1927.[20] From the start CAIP appealed to political pressure and influence, not to individual conscience.

CAIP's founders, John A. Ryan[21] and Raymond McGowan, set elitist goals for the Association. They hoped to remake society by gaining positions of leverage and power, by restricting membership to influential institutional leaders for whom close work with the government and the art of compromise were ways of life. CAIP's educational effort was aimed primarily at the Catholic elite: college students and faculty, with outreach to

Catholic secondary and elementary schools. CAIP was also closely tied to the hierarchical church, as it was a branch of the National Catholic Welfare Conference. Fully within the tradition of the Tridentine church,[22] it supported such internationalist goals as the World Court and the League, and was conservative in its outlook toward the economic and social world order. From the start CAIP rejected pacifism, and came to accept the developing theory of collective military security as the best way to peace.[23]

By the 1930s CAIP's direction was clear: it accepted the growing threat of war, the need for war preparation, and the presence of the Reserve Officer Training Corps (ROTC) on Catholic college campuses as fully consistent with the just-war theory. Instead of attempting to influence, it only followed the directions of the Congress and the Roosevelt administration in their war buildup, and became increasingly hostile to the pacifism emerging in the country.[24] In 1937 it tacitly accepted the official church support of Fascist General Francisco Franco during the Spanish Civil War.[25]

The limitations of CAIP's peacemaking efforts are apparent. During World War II the organization fully supported the U.S. effort according to the lines of the just-war theory. After the war CAIP sought disarmament through international agreement and strongly supported the United Nations and the International Covenant on Human Rights, even holding a UN observer post. It relied on the theory of the just war and collective security more strongly than ever and backed U.S. foreign and military policy without question. Staunchly anticommunist, it opposed the entry of both the People's Republic of China and of North Korea to the United Nations.[26] It proposed moral guidelines for the justifiable use of the atomic bomb.[27] So strongly was CAIP tied to U.S. government interests that most of the members of the CAIP arms control subcommittee that issued the guidelines on the atomic bomb were on the payrolls of either the Defense or State Department.[28] As we will see below, peace through accommodation to U.S. power was CAIP's central policy—even through the war in Vietnam—until its demise in 1967.

## DOROTHY DAY AND THE CATHOLIC WORKER MOVEMENT

Contemporaneously with the CAIP, a peacemaking movement of prophecy and protest was growing from the hearts and consciences of Catholics dedicated to the life of the gospels. In May 1933 in New York City two American Catholics, Dorothy Day and Peter Maurin, founded a Catholic peace group that would embody their ideals of pacifism, commitment to the poor, and the need for fundamental change in American society. The stories of the Catholic Worker[29] and Dorothy Day (1897–1980)[30] are woven inextricably into the fabric of the American church.

Dorothy Day was born in New York of Scot-Irish Calvinist parents.[31] Her father was a journalist. She received a better-than-average education, and joined the campus Socialists at the University of Illinois. In 1916 she returned to New York with her parents. Part of the Greenwich Village bohemian scene, she wrote for the *Call,* the *Masses,* and the *Liberator.* She worked with the Anti-Conscription League in World War I and the women's suffrage movement, for which she was arrested in Washington in 1917.

Returning from jail in 1918, Dorothy Day abandoned her political activism, worked as a nurse and in a variety of clerical jobs, married and divorced, traveled, and began writing novels. In 1923 she married again and had a child. The marriage and its breakup brought about a spiritual crisis and the loss of her friends. She converted to Catholicism in December 1927. Between 1927 and 1933 Day traveled and worked at a variety of jobs, including writing for *Commonweal* and *America* magazines. In December 1932 she met and fell under the spell of Peter Maurin. The next year they founded the Catholic Worker.

Maurin[32] was French, a peasant and a wanderer, a student of the Christian Brothers, and a former member of the liberal Catholic Sillon Movement. He brought with him a "gentle personalism," a Catholic radicalism based on the literal interpretation of the Beatitudes and of the Christian realities of sin, the fall, and the need of redemption, reconciliation, and community. Maurin had read widely in political theory, church history, economics, and law, and he rejected the liberal institutions of capitalism and the modern state and their faith in material progress and technology. He replaced all that with a personal commitment to love and an eschatological vision of the Christian mission. He proposed a radical imitation of the gospel life of voluntary poverty in solidarity with the weak, the poor, the sick, and the alienated.

Day and Maurin complemented each other perfectly. To the pacifism and abstract social concerns of the intellectual and bohemian Day, Maurin added the fundamental realities of human community and commitment, the radical social gospel, and the French peasant's disdain for institutions. Both drew strength and inspiration from the Sermon on the Mount; they combined the commitment to nonviolence with the struggle for social justice that has always characterized true Catholic peacemaking. The result of this combination of talents and spirits was the Catholic Worker movement.

In New York City on May Day 1933, Dorothy Day launched the *Catholic Worker*, the first fruit of her collaboration with Maurin. Between then and 1940 the distribution of the newspaper grew from the 2,500 copies handed out at the Union Square rally to over 185,000.[33] The paper's consistent intellectual position was based on a radical interpretation of the Sermon on the Mount and on papal social encyclicals. The *Catholic Worker* soon became a prophetic voice calling for nonviolent revolution against capitalism and attracted a loose association of reformers and radicals, Catholic intellectuals, scholars, and workers.

Essential to Maurin's Catholic vision was the Christian social ideal: the medieval hospice and the communal farm were models. Dorothy Day's apartment was his first attempt at communal life. In 1933 the Catholic Worker founded its first, St. Joseph's, House of Hospitality. The houses were hospices for Catholic Worker volunteers, soup kitchens and dining halls, meeting rooms, clothing centers, schools, and "revolutionary headquarters" for the movement.[34] By 1941, thirty-two Worker houses were spread all across the United States, from Milwaukee to Chicago to Seattle, centers of radical hope against the backdrop of America's depression.[35] Despite its radicalism, the movement always retained its doctrinal and practical orthodoxy and accepted the supervision of the hierarchy through a chaplain. Unlike CAIP, however, the Catholic Worker was a movement of the people, drawing its strength from them; it was not led or controlled by the hierarchy.[36]

Pacifism was not of immediate concern to the Catholic Worker movement, but the directions of the 1930s soon made it important.[37] In 1935 the *Catholic Worker* came out in opposition to Mussolini's invasion of Ethiopia, alienating many of its Italian readers. In contrast to the U.S. hierarchy, CAIP, and most Catholics,[38] the *Catholic Worker*, along with *Commonweal* and the Catholic *Buffalo Echo*, condemned both left and right in the bloody Spanish Civil War.[39] In her November 1936 editorial, "On the Use of Force," Dorothy Day rejected the claim that Franco and his Fascists were defending Christian civilization. She reminded her readers that those who use force in Christ's name are taunting him to come down from the cross and save himself. All the Spanish were "brothers in Christ—all of them Temples of the Holy Ghost, all of them members or potential members of the Mystical Body of Christ."[40] The *Catholic Worker* urged the United States to be neutral in the conflict and pressed, unsuccessfully, for an arms embargo against the warring factions.[41]

In 1937 a pacifist group called PAX was founded by William Callahan and Joseph Zarella.[42] John T. McNicholas, archbishop of Cincinnati, supported PAX, and in a March 1938 article in the *Catholic Worker* called on Catholics to form a "mighty legion of Catholic objectors."[43] PAX, Day's outspoken opposition to the Spanish Civil War, and the *Catholic Worker's* monthly PAX column urging Catholics to support conscientious objection all raised storms of protest from conservative Catholics, who saw the movement as plainly communistic.[44] By the late 1930s the Catholic Worker movement itself split over the issue of pacifism. Some were more concerned with the Worker's social mission; others, with Day, saw this commitment to pacifism as an essential element of Catholic peacemaking.[45]

By the late 1930s it was plain that the United States was abandoning neutrality and preparing for a war in Europe. The Catholic Worker launched a multi-pronged attack against militarism, the sale of war bonds, and munitions production. It organized a Non-Participation League to press for neutrality and opposed draft registration and conscription. Day, Zarella, and Rev. Barry O'Toole brought this campaign to Congress, testifying on the traditional Catholic opposition to conscription on the basis of individual freedom of conscience and vocation.[46] Day was chastised by the New York chancery because she called for nonregistration.[47]

Three decades before Vatican II, articles in the *Catholic Worker* by Paul Hanley Furfey called for abandoning the "Constantinian compromise" with the warmaking state; Arthur Sheehan urged a return to gospel pacifism and rejected the just war as an impossible position in the modern age of technological weapons and mass destruction.[48] At the same time the Catholic Worker vigorously opposed the blend of isolationism and rabid anti-Semitism espoused by Fr. Charles Coughlin in his popular radio broadcasts.[49]

By 1940 it was clear that the United States would soon be involved in war. The Catholic Worker therefore adopted a new attitude toward the inevitable draft and pressed Selective Service to make provision for conscientious objection. In August 1940 Dorothy Day published an open letter to all Catholic Workers insisting on the pacifist position of the movement. The result was disastrous. Dissidents who believed in the primacy of the social mission of the movement or in the just-war tradition began abandoning the Worker. By 1945 twenty of the thirty-two Catholic Worker Houses had closed and the *Catholic Worker* lost over a hundred thousand subscribers.[50]

World War II was to have profound effects on the Catholic Worker movement and to be of great consequence for the history of peacemaking in the United States.[51] Events around the war demonstrated the fragility of the Catholic peace movement and its inability to affect American policy. Because of Day's insistence on pacifism, the peace issue became the predominant characteristic of the movement after 1940. The remnant of committed Catholic Workers thus became the seed for Catholic peacemaking after the war. By its shift in emphasis to the issue of conscientious objection in the 1940s the Catholic Worker also helped lay the groundwork for Catholic resistance during the war. It thus assured a tradition of conscientious objection within the American Catholic Church that would survive the barren winter of World War II and blossom into a new spring of protest in the 1960s.

## AMERICAN CATHOLICS AND WORLD WAR II

A poll taken by *America*, the Jesuit magazine, in November 1939 asked 54,000 students of both sexes at 141 Catholic colleges and universities if they would become conscientious objectors in the event of war.[52] Of those who responded, 20 percent said that they would volunteer for active service, 44 percent said that they would accept conscription, and a startling 36 percent said that they would claim conscientious objector status. In 1941, before Pearl Harbor, 97 percent of all Catholics polled opposed U.S. entry into World War II, a higher percentage than that of any Protestant denomination.[53] Theoretically and until the attack on Pearl Harbor, opposition to war, including pacifism, had a respectable and widespread appeal among American Catholics.

This opposition took several forms, including CAIP, whose internationalist approach was rapidly moving toward the government's collective-security approach, the Catholic Worker, and the Coughlinites.[54] In general however mainstream Catholic opposition to the war and to conscription followed just-war criteria, resting on the belief that the United States would not be attacked and that to prepare for war would imply aggressive intent.[55] The Catholic hierarchy was almost universally opposed to the Burke-Wadsworth conscription bill of 1940, both because of the priority given to conscience in Catholic teaching and because of institutional concerns: fear that priests and religious would be subject to the draft.

When the Japanese attacked Pearl Harbor on December 7, 1941, Catholic opposition to the war and the draft collapsed. Catholics, like most Americans, became fervent supporters of the war, both out of patriotic duty and from a sense of the justness of the struggle. In their pastoral letter, *The Crisis of Christianity,* the Catholic bishops had already condemned the dangers of Nazism and communism. Telling Catholics that "we support wholeheartedly the adequate defense of our country,"[56] the bishops called on Catholics to "render to Caesar." They reminded them that all authority comes from God, and that therefore, even in democratic countries, citizens must obey their rulers. The following year the bishops declared the war effort just, telling Catholics that although war is a last resort, at times it is a positive duty.[57]

When the war came, the 36 percent of Catholic students who once favored conscientious objection evaporated. The hierarchy neither denied nor supported the Catholic right to pacifism; this lack of policy cut Catholic conscientious objectors adrift.[58] Out of a total of 21 million Catholics only 223 claimed IV-E CO status, objection to military service; 135 were eventually classified, a great change from the time of World War I, when only 4 of the 3,989 COs were Catholic. Catholics were, however, but a miniscule percentage of the 11,887 conscientious objectors to World War II, and a number still small enough for the Catholic hierarchy to safely ignore.[59] Most Catholic objectors chose I-A-O status, noncombatant military service, and generally served as unarmed medics on the front lines.[60] Catholics, Jews, and members of mainline Protestant churches were not allowed CO status in World War I, but the Burke-Wadsworth Act made possible Catholic objection. However the prejudice and skepticism of draft boards and the ignorance of many Catholics (who might have been CO supporters) about the pacifist tradition in their own church made CO status difficult to get.[61] In addition to the 135 Catholic conscientious objectors, 61 Catholics refused induction and were imprisoned— again a small proportion of the 6,068 who were jailed for noncooperation during the war.[62]

Even though conscientious objection was ignored by the institutional church, it became central to the efforts of Dorothy Day and the Catholic Worker.[63] At first Day opposed the conscientious objection provisions as "a form of cooperation with the war and conscription,"[64] but she respected the moral stand of individuals, and by 1939 the Catholic Worker was providing information to potential COs. In 1940 PAX, the pacifist offshoot of the Worker movement, became the Association of Catholic Conscientious

Objectors (ACCO) with the tacit consent of the hierarchy. By April 1941 it had received four hundred Catholic claims.[65] Expecting a ground swell of Catholic COs, ACCO affiliated with the National Service Board for Religious Objectors (NSBRO), a consortium of the traditional Protestant peace churches—the Brethren, the Friends, and the Mennonites.[66]

## THE WORK CAMPS

The 135 Catholics who had sought and obtained draft status IV-E were required to perform civilian alternative service away from home for a period roughly equivalent to that of draftees in military service. After war was declared, this "period" lasted for the duration of the conflict plus six months. Conscientious objectors faced the prospect of unpaid service in isolated work camps, doing forestry and other "labor in the national interest." The alternative service was organized under the Civilian Public Service Camps (CPS). Most objectors were organized by 1946 into 151 camps, which were supported and coordinated by their religious service boards.[67] In order to provide support for the Catholic objectors the ACCO applied for and received permission to set up a camp for Catholic COs in July 1941.[68] The chief source of financial support for the camp was the already impoverished Catholic Worker, and later, when the Catholic program began to founder, the Protestant peace churches. The Catholic hierarchy continued to ignore its own pacifists throughout the war. From 1944 to 1948, *The Catholic Conscientious Objector* took over the peace information services of the *Catholic Worker* and provided some source of solidarity to the scattered Catholics.[69]

In August 1941 sixteen Catholics entered a CPS camp at Stoddard, New Hampshire. They were transferred to a new camp at Warner, New Hampshire, in November 1942. Collectively the two camps were dubbed "Camp Simon," after the biblical Simon, who was pressed into service to bear the cross.[70] Up to 63 Catholics served in these camps until March 1943, when the Catholics COs were disbanded and sent to several Protestant-run camps. About one hundred Catholic COs eventually passed through Swallow Falls Camp in Maryland or served at Rosewood Training School caring for the mentally deficient.[71]

Gordon Zahn, who served in Camp Simon as a young CO, has described the routine and the hardships, the sense of loneliness and futility experienced by most of the Catholics in the camps.[72] Groups of Catholic Worker pacifists, just-war Thomists, Coughlinites, intellectuals, anarchists, and plain misfits,[73] all of whom differed among themselves, gradually realized that the administration of the program was arbitrary, that their civil and constitutional rights had been suspended at the whim of Selective Service and that in the end they performed little work that was useful. Selective Service Director Lewis B. Hershey later revealed the government's true intent with the CO status: "The CO is best handled if no one ever hears of him."[74] Inadequate housing and nutrition, the slave labor and the purposeless activity of the camps eventually brought many Catholics to organize hunger strikes and other acts of Gandhian civil disobedience to protest their conditions. In January 1946 the ACCO objected to NSBRO's complicity in the CPS system as a form of slavery, declared the camp system unconstitutional.[75]

Despite the failings of the system, the Catholic conscientious objectors who emerged from the camps in 1946 included some of the most committed Catholic peacemakers of the period after World War II: Richard Lion, Robert Ludlow, and Gordon Zahn.[76] Many of them continued to bear witness to peace and later formed the nucleus of anti-war activities of years to come. In addition, the recognition of Catholic conscientious objection by the U.S. government and by the American Catholic hierarchy, however grudging, established a precedent for the rest of the century.

## THE JUST LIMITS OF WORLD WAR II

Despite the Catholic bishops' wholehearted endorsement of World War II, the often disproportionate savagery of the means used to fight and win it—obliteration bombing against civilian centers such as Dresden, the call for total war and unconditional surrender, and the atomic bombing of Hiroshima and Nagasaki—caused many Catholics to question the justice of the conflict. The Catholic Worker had always maintained a total opposition to the war and to the means used to fight it and had based its opposition more on evangelical pacifism than on the just-war theory.[77] Now even moderate voices joined the dissenters. Among the most notable of these was John C. Ford, S.J., a moral theologian at Fordham University. Ford supported the Catholic right to conscientious objection[78] and in 1944 wrote an article, "The Morality of Obliteration Bombing,"[79] in which he condemned the practice and concept of total war on the grounds of the just-war immunity of innocent civilians and the notion of proportionality of means.[80] Ford went so far as to imply that in the modern world, with the technologies of destruction available, the entire concept of just war seemed naive and outdated. Other Catholic voices joined Ford in the condemnations.[81]

## CATHOLICS AND THE PAX AMERICANA

At the end of the World War II the American Catholic Church entered into a wholehearted alliance with the U.S. government for the preservation of the world order against international communism. The United States had achieved a power and control over world affairs not matched since the Roman Empire, and the country's church fully accepted the chance to help define this new peace of imposed order.[82] In their 1944 pastoral *International Order*,[83] the U.S. bishops declared, "We have met the challenge of war. Shall we meet the challenge of peace?" Recalling the tradition of Catholic internationalism from Dubois to Vitoria,[84] they echoed papal teaching[85] and called for a new international order based on moral law, the recognition of God, the oneness of humanity, and international community. Blaming "scholars" for unleashing the philosophy that "asserts the right of aggression," they urged the people to press for a strong new international body that could apply force to punish international outlaws and preserve order.

At the same time, however, the bishops began to show a distrust of U.S. interests and actions in the postwar world. In November 1945 they warned the United States against the temptation to make agreements with the Soviets based on simple power considerations, recalling the poverty and helplessness of the world's people as the greatest obstacle to true peace.[86] The next year the bishops condemned the postwar order as no true peace, but an order that imposed settlements on the war-torn and ignored the true calling of peacemakers: care for the imprisoned, the displaced, and all the victims of the conflict. They reminded the victors that

> justice demands that they make promptly a peace in which all men can live as men. . . . How can there be a beginning of even a tolerable peace unless the peacemakers fully realize that human life is sacred and that all men have rights?[87]

The church continued to proclaim this message throughout the 1950s, insisting on the importance of the individual and of personal conscience.[88] Even at the height of Cold War tensions, during the Hungarian Revolt and the Soviet invasion, the bishops declared:

"If you wish peace," said the pagan axiom, "prepare for war." Christianity has revised that saying: "If you wish peace, prepare for peace."[89]

Although the bishops' criticisms had a decidedly anti-Soviet slant, warning the United States against cooperation with communism, they were clearly leveled against U.S. policy as well and showed the bishops' growing willingness to speak out against the government in prophetic form, regardless of political allegiance. This tone dominated the bishops' last pastoral of the 1950s, *Freedom and Peace*.[90] While the letter is clearly a Cold War document and warns of the dangers of atheistic communism, it links this threat to other, equally pressing, dangers. These include an excessive nationalism that blinds Americans to the basic unity of all peoples and the abject "poverty, hunger, disease and bitterness engendered by social injustice" that communist aggression only exploits. Before it can accept the challenge of injustice in the Third World, they said, America must undergo a conversion of its own, abandoning the materialism that characterizes American life and, paradoxically, leaves "the communists to capture the minds of men."[91]

By 1960 the Catholic hierarchy, although it was still firmly allied with American national interests, had begun to prod the government in significant ways and to openly question many of the fundamental assumptions of American life and American power in the world. The Catholic bishops' pastoral, *Personal Responsibility*, (November 1960),[92] repudiated the old Constantinian alliance, noting that too much responsibility for peace had been entrusted to international bodies and not enough to individuals. In this the bishops departed from the model of peace as order imposed from above that had dominated American Catholic thought since World War I. The American church was reflecting the changes in papal thought that John XXIII had introduced[93] and thus prepared the way for the next wave of Catholic peacemaking from the people.

## AFTER THE WAR

At the end of World War II the American peace movement was practically dead.[94] The hydrogen bomb, the Korean War, and the Cold War stilled protest and silenced outrage. CAIP had accepted the role of the United States as international policeman of world order; the hierarchy too seemed to approve of U.S. policy.[95] Among Catholics the Catholic Worker was the sole voice for peace, and even there the postwar period was a low ebb of virtual inactivity.[96]

Still, several continued the Catholic Worker struggle. Chief among these were Robert Ludlow and Ammon Hennacy. Ludlow had served as a CO in the Rosewood Training School and after the war had returned to the *Catholic Worker* to write the PAX column. Ludlow was among the first Catholic intellectuals to absorb and interpret Gandhi's theory of nonviolence. Through the 1940s and the 1950s he developed a Catholic theology of nonviolence.[97] Rejecting the passivity and individualism so often associated with pacifism, he took up the idea of *satyagraha* as "a new *Christian* way of social change."[98] Ludlow urged Catholic pacifists to move from an individual oppositon to violence to a social effort, first to move the church toward a commitment to peace, and then to transform American life.

Ludlow's call was given new impetus with the arrival in the Catholic Worker of Ammon Hennacy, anarchist, socialist, and radical Christian.[99] More than any other single individual, Hennacy was responsible for bringing the Catholic Worker out of the shock of the postwar years and for developing an activist practice of nonviolence and civil disobedience that matched Ludlow's vision. Born of a Quaker and abolitionist family, by 1916 Hennacy was a socialist organizer. In 1917 he was sentenced to five years in federal prison for resisting the draft, and by 1918 he had embraced anarchism. In prison he was put in solitary confinement; there he converted to Christianity. In 1937 he was attracted to the Catholic Worker house in Milwaukee and there met Day and Maurin. After Pearl Harbor, Hennacy wrote to the Internal Revenue Service announcing his refusal to pay war taxes. When Dorothy Day endorsed his action, he wrote to thank her and then began contributing articles to the *Catholic Worker*.[100]

Throughout the 1940s Hennacy maintained his tax protest. He lived as a farm worker in the Southwest and among the Hopi Indians, contributed articles regularly to the *Catholic Worker*, and spread the influence of Gandhi and, later, of Danilo Dolci[101] in the United States. In 1952 he came to the Chrystie Street House in New York and joined the Catholic Worker movement.[102] His arrival breathed a new spirit into the group that lasted even after his departure in 1962. Ammon is best remembered for his resistance to the annual Civil Defense drills that marked life throughout the 1950s. Intended to beef up American resolve and preparedness for atomic war, every year the drills summoned citizens in major cities to underground shelters, basements, and subways, commanded students to cower beneath desks or in darkened hallways as hundreds of air-raid sirens wailed the coming of nuclear destruction. James Forest has described the sense of fear and near hopelessness that the drills inspired, even among the Catholic Workers.[103] Most Americans who are over thirty today recall the silent terror that the sirens inspired. In 1955 the program was made compulsory across the country; in New York the state Defense Emergency Act threatened anyone who refused to go to a shelter with one year in prison and a $500 fine.

In 1953 and 1954 Hennacy picketed against the drills, alone and unnoticed. In 1955, when defying the drills became illegal, he and twenty-eight other people, including ten Catholic Workers, stood outside New York's City Hall and refused to take shelter as the sirens wailed.[104] In 1956 Hennacy, Day, and twenty others were arrested. The protests continued, and the witness to life grew louder amid the cries of coming death. By 1960 a well publicized protest drew a thousand people; the police, unaccustomed to such massive peaceful demonstrations, arrested only twenty-seven and ignored the leaders. In 1961 A. J. Muste's Committee for Nonviolent Action joined the Catholic Workers and twenty-five hundred people demonstrated in New York City. Other groups joined them across the country. Embarrassed by the pacifists' success, in 1962 the Kennedy administration cancelled the drills.

Hennacy continued to plant the seeds of nonviolence throughout the country. In 1957 he joined Muste's CNVA to successfully stop an Atomic Energy Commission hydrogen bomb test near Las Vegas. He was arrested for protests in Washington, D.C., in Florida, and outside Strategic Air Command headquarters in Omaha in 1959. After serving time in federal prison, he returned to the Catholic Worker in New York in 1960, left for Salt Lake City in 1961, and left the Catholic Worker and the Catholic Church in 1962. In Salt Lake City he founded the Joe Hill House of Hospitality and died there in January 1970.[105]

Robert Ludlow and Ammon Hennacy symbolized and largely effected the rebirth of the Catholic Worker and Catholic peacemaking after World War II.[106] They helped create, clarify, and implement a Catholic theology and practice of peace. By the late 1950s and early 1960s Catholic Workers were participating on their own and with other groups like Muste's CNVA in nonviolent actions and civil disobedience across the country that made Catholic activists among the pioneers of the peace movement of the 1960s.[107] By 1960 a new generation of Catholic Workers was taking on the leadership, including Tom Cornell and Martin Corbin, who became editors of the paper in 1962.

The year 1962 was important for Catholic peacemaking in several ways. That year in Chicago a Conference on Christian Conscience and Modern Warfare met to formulate a Catholic position on nuclear arms. Although the conference ended without establishing any clear moral direction, Catholics were at least facing the problem of nuclear war.[108] In New York the Catholic Worker Round Table Group led by Eileen Egan revived PAX as a lobbying and pressure group to attempt to change official church attitudes toward war and peace. The new PAX had more in common with the Catholic Worker than with CAIP and sought to keep its independence from hierarchical control and financial support.[109] Catholics were entering the 1960s with new strength and resolve. The foundation of the Catholic Peace Fellowship in 1964 was the culmination of Catholic efforts of the preceding two decades.

## THOMAS MERTON

With Dorothy Day, Thomas Merton (1915–1968) personified the potential of the Catholic peace tradition in America. Merton stands out as one of the most brilliant peacemakers in the entire Catholic tradition.[110] He was born in Praedes, France, in January 1915, the son of painters. His mother was a Quaker. After studying at Cambridge for a year, he came to the United States and completed an M.A. in English at Columbia University. In the course of his studies, a Hindu monk recommended that he read Augustine and the Early Fathers. His extensive readings in these and in Blake's mystical poetry and his frequent attendance at Catholic services resulted in his conversion to Catholicism in 1938, a process recounted in his popular book, *The Seven Storey Mountain.*[111]

By 1940 Merton had decided on the priesthood. After being rejected by the Franciscans, he applied to the Trappists in 1942 in Gethsemani, Kentucky. World War II was in full swing, and Merton applied for CO status as a "modified pacifist." He was accepted by the monastery, however, before being drafted.[112] His years at Gethsemani fall into three more or less distinct periods.[113] the first, from 1938 to 1949, reflected his ascetic flight from the world, his intransigent and apocalyptic spirituality. The second period, 1949 to 1959, showed Merton's deepening concern to integrate his monastic vocation with the larger concerns of Catholicism and the world. During these years he read widely in psychology, Zen Buddhism, and existentialism. Finally, from 1959 until his death in 1968, Merton confronted the central issues of his time and faith: war and peace, social justice, morality and power, conversion and Christian love.

Merton's monastic journey reflects the historical mission of the monastic life since its origins in the third century: a flight to the desert to purify the individual, a rediscovery of one's ties with God and the world, and a final commitment to confront the injustices and evils of the world from the spiritual citadel of the monastery.[114] Despite his problems with censorship, his temptations to leave the order, and the strict discipline of the Trappist routine,[115] by the 1960s Merton had come to see the monastery as the model of the nonviolent Christian life of community, conscience, and witness. Merton summarized the role of Christian monasticism in clear terms:

> The monastery is not an "escape from the world." On the contrary, by being in the monastery I take my true part in all the struggles and sufferings of the world. To adopt a life that is essentially non-assertive, non-violent, a life of humility and peace is in itself a statement of one's position. . . . It is my intention to make my entire life a rejection of, a protest against the crimes and injustices of war and political tyranny which threaten to destroy the whole race of man and the world with him. By my monastic life and vows I am saying *No* to all the concentration camps, the aerial bombardments, the staged political trials, the judicial murders, the racial injustices, the economic tyrannies, and the whole socio-economic apparatus which seems geared for nothing but global destruction in spite of all its fair words in favor of peace. I make monastic silence a protest against the lies of politicians, propagandists and agitators, and when I speak it is to deny that my faith and my Church can ever seriously be aligned with these forces of injustice and destruction.[116]

Merton came gradually to surpass "rejection" and "protest" with positive building, with an affirmative theology of peace in an eschatological age. His journey took him through several stages, from his first denunciations of nuclear terror in a post-Christian age, to his skepticism of the justice of all wars in the modern age, his rejection of the pacifism of passive retreat, and finally his emergence as the spokesperson for a new nonviolent Catholic activism aimed at rebuilding the world.

Merton never fully embraced pacifism. Like Thomas More[117] and Erasmus,[118] he believed in the theoretical applicability of the just war. Yet, like the Renaissance Humanists, he looked at the horrors of contemporary warfare and concluded that the just-war theory was irrelevant in practice.[119] He was, in fact, one of the first "nuclear pacifists."[120] World War II had made all theories of restraint on war a hollow mockery as victors and vanquished alike were driven to greater and greater excesses of savagery. The atomic bomb finally brought home the full horror of this development. Moralists cling absurdly to the shreds of an obsolete theory, envisioning circumstances in which nuclear war might be justified, but generals and politicians mock them by calmly planning ever new destruction.[121] In "A Devout Meditation in Memory of Adolf Eichman" Merton mocked the sanity of such generals and politicans but warned that it was precisely these "sane" men who bring us the Holocaust.[122]

Instead of offering a true choice between good and evil, the United States and the Soviet Union are actually two aspects of the same apocalyptic reality: Gog and Magog, they threaten to tear the world apart in mass suicide.[123] America is a "sick nation" living on the false myths and illusions of a post-Christian era[124] for which force is the only alternative and power the only basis of human relationships.[125] American power has gone beyond all the bounds of natural law and human rights. It is thus suspect and poses a real threat to individual conscience.[126]

Individual Christians therefore face a dilemma. They can consent to this mass destruction, lost in numbness, or they can choose peace.[127] Yet the alternative is not the inner flight from the world of traditional Catholic piety. The Christian can no longer afford to follow Plato's retreat from concrete reality but must embrace the world and actively make peace and justice,[128] protesting abuses of power and brute force.[129] The Christian must imitate the Old Testament prophets and Christ himself to create a new

Christian peace, not a Pax Romana built on terror and power.[130]

Merton therefore actively rejected the label "pacifist," which he saw as too closely tied to "passiveness" and nonresistance to evil.[131] Nevertheless, pacifism is not to be rejected: it is neither a luxury nor the end of Christian action but an obligation and the beginning point.[132] True peace must begin with a basic change of heart but must go on from there to change the world.[133]

Merton's theology of peace therefore begins with the conversion of the individual heart. For American Catholics this would mean healing the American disease of belligerency and transforming passive ideas of peace into active forces for liberation. American Catholics must demythologize the glory of war and turn back the hopelessness that dominates American opinion, its nihilism, its empty love of "stalemate" and "balance," and its mad rush to destruction preached by its leaders and by a media addicted to violence.[134] Merton called for a new "theology of resistance"[135] that would confront the violence of the state, Augustine's "great band of robbers."[136] He condemned a theology of peace that counsels the poor and the oppressed to accept their lot passively and decries their isolated crime while society at large daily produces more and better technological methods of mass murder and maintains poverty and oppression by force.[137]

Although Merton openly wondered whether the violence of Camilo Torres in Colombia could be justified,[138] he was convinced that only when individuals have undergone an inner conversion can a new age come. Their witness to Christian truth and nonviolent resistance to evil and injustice will earn them nothing but opposition and persecution, but only through the sufferings of true Christians can the new age, the eschaton of God's kingdom, arrive.[139] Merton's revolution thus confirms the appeal of John XXIII in *Pacem in Terris*[140] and continues the long Catholic tradition of nonviolent apocalyptic.[141]

Essential to this Christian revolution is the Christian's willingness to endure suffering rather than to impose it and to end the systems of oppression rather than to take them over. In this and in the methods of nonviolence, Gandhi's inspiration plays an important part.[142] Nonviolence that seeks power either as its end or its means is false. Like Gan-.dhi's *satyagraha,* true "nonviolence is not for power but for truth. It is not pragmatic but prophetic."[143] It is not a disguise for the will to power:

> It does not say "We shall overcome" so much as "This is the day of the Lord, and whatever may happen to us, *He* shall overcome."[144]

More than a pious platitude, this phrase summarizes Merton's attitude to peacemaking. Peace is not so much political revolution as personal conversion; it is not individual human ego and power that is at stake, but God's will to peace that only humans can accomplish on earth, as they are the recipients of God's gift and challenge to peace.[145]

Nonviolence applies to Christian attitudes as well as actions. *Satyagraha* implies the conversion of the enemy and the victory of the peacemaker through nonviolence, but it does not imply the moral superiority of the peacemaker. Again and again Merton warned against an attitude of moral superiority among Catholic peacemakers that he termed "a weak and veiled form of psychological aggression"[146] or of "moral aggression,"[147] fully the equal of physical aggression in its effects and intent. Convinced of their superiority, peacemakers can actually alienate, divide, humiliate, and drive their enemies to violence through wrong intentions or tactics. Even more damaging, they can scandalize their fellow Catholics and prejudice them to the truth of peacemaking:[148]

Christian nonviolence is not built on a presupposed division, but on the basic unity of man. It is not out for the conversion of the wicked to the ideas of the good, but for the healing and reconciliation of man with himself, man the person and man the human family.[149]

The Christian peacemaker, therefore, must be truly meek, not in the world's sense of passive or tame, but as the meek in the Sermon on the Mount, whom Christ had blessed.[150] This meekness seeks not to flatter the enemy or to humiliate but to convince. It does not seek to convince others that the peacemaker is right, but that peace is right—it is truth. This meekness trusts in men and women, refuses to despair, and is ultimately aimed at the conversion of all, including the peacemaker, to peace.

When Merton began writing on peace, he was an isolated prophet condemning modern Catholicism's alliance with the powers of the world. By the time he had developed his theology of peace he had been joined by John XXIII and Vatican II; by the time of his unexpected death in 1968[151] he had become the major impetus in the Catholic struggle against the American war in Vietnam.

The renewed Catholic peace movement of the 1960s coincided with two of the major forces of the century: Vatican II and Vietnam. In the 1960s and the 1970s the dialectic between these two forces would pose new questions and challenges to American Catholics and force the American church to undergo an internal revolution that would alter its outlook on peacemaking for the rest of the century.

## AMERICANS AND VATICAN II

We have already looked at the impact of John XXIII's *Mater et Magistra* and *Pacem in Terris,* of Vatican II, and of the Pastoral Constitution *Gaudium et Spes* on the Catholic peace tradition in Europe and the Third World. Their impact on the United States was just as profound. The political debate that went on between the American bishops and lobbying groups at Vatican II was a microcosm of the dialogue that had been at work within the American church since the 1940s. Chief among the issues debated under Schema XIII,[152] the Pastoral Constitution *Gaudium et Spes,* were the morality of nuclear war and the provisions for conscientious objection.[153]

Many of the progressive bishops at the Council—French, Spanish, and Canadian—sought a complete ban and condemnation of nuclear weapons, believing them to be a clear violation of Christian morality.[154] With the exception of Joseph Cardinal Ritter, who even sought a condemnation of the possession of nuclear weapons,[155] the American delegation, along with the British, opposed any "ban the bomb" movement as "unrealistic."[156] Chief among the opponents were Francis Cardinal Spellman of New York,[157] Lawrence Cardinal Sheehan of Baltimore,[158] and Bishop Patrick O'Boyle of Washington, D.C. These bishops were aided by Harry W. Flannery of CAIP, whose members on the subcommittee on arms vigorously opposed the "European pacifists." They defended nuclear war both on the grounds of the just-war theory and because of their diehard Americanism, the complete association of Catholic Church interests with the interests of the nation, and a commitment to defend the U.S. military position as the best path to world stability.[159]

United States Catholics may well have stood unanimously against the Council's eventual condemnation of war in the nuclear age were it not for the intervention of a delegation of American pacifists sent to Rome by the Catholic Worker and PAX. Among those present were Dorothy Day and James Douglass (a Catholic theologian and critic of the just-war tradition), Philip Scharper (a journalist), Eileen Egan, and Gordon Zahn. They were supported by Thomas Merton, who sent an "open letter" to the Council calling for the explicit condemnation of nuclear war and for clear provisions for conscientious objection. Dorothy Day,[160] Eileen Egan, Chantarelle, and other women from Lanzo del Vasto's Ark undertook dramatic fasts in Rome to dramatize the struggle within the Council.[161] With the help of Bishop John Taylor the pacifists eventually got their opinions to the floor of the Council. They won the support of other American bishops like Fulton J. Sheen, who adopted Cardinal Ottaviani's position outlawing all modern war.[162]

On the issue of conscientious objection the American pacifists were even more successful. Once again the chief opposition to the provision in Schema XIII came from Cardinal Spellman, who was head of the U.S. Military Vicariate. Spellman actually sought to have the church call for obligatory military service for all Catholics, declaring that "individuals cannot refuse their obedience to the state."[163] Here Thomas Merton's moral authority and the intervention of Archbishop Roberts assured the Council's call for conscientious objection as a legitimate and praiseworthy Catholic response to war.[164]

The impact of Vatican II in the United States was decisive. Amid the conflict of Vietnam, Catholics were suddenly awakened to the hard fact that their church had always recognized the call of peace and was now actively challenging Catholics to awaken their consciences to the need for positive peacemaking.

## AMERICAN CATHOLICS AND VIETNAM

The impact of Vatican II on American Catholics was immediate and far-reaching. In 1962 a dozen Catholic Workers proposed founding a Catholic Peace Fellowship as an affiliate of the Fellowship of Reconciliation (FOR).[165] In November 1964 a retreat under Thomas Merton at Gethsemani brought together social activists Daniel and Philip Berrigan,[166] James Forest, and Tom Cornell along with John Heidbrink from FOR and several leading Protestant peace activists, including A. J. Muste, John Yoder, and W. H. Ferry. The result was the founding of the Catholic Peace Fellowship (CPF) with Cornell and Forest as full-time staff and Daniel Berrigan and Thomas Merton as directors.[167]

PAX had had an institutional approach; but the CPF became the chief outlet for individual Catholic radicalism in the 1960s as the Gulf of Tonkin Resolution and increased U.S. involvement in Vietnam shifted Catholic attention away from the nuclear issue and toward resistance to the war.[168] In November 1962 Tom Cornell had already publicly burned his draft card at an anti-Vietnam War rally in Union Square, New York. In May 1964, he again burned a draft card as did Christopher Kearnes, another Catholic Worker. Further draft-card burnings in August 1965 in Washington, in which thirty-two Catholic Workers participated, led to the hasty congressional passage of the Rivers Act, which made draft-card burning a federal offense.[169]

On October 15, therefore, David Miller, a Catholic Worker, publicly burned his draft card before cameras and the FBI. He was promptly arrested, tried, convicted, and imprisoned;[170] Miller's offense became the test case of the Rivers Act. On November 6 at a large demonstration in New York Dorothy Day and A. J. Muste introduced five more card burners, three of whom were Catholic Workers.[171] By 1965 the *Catholic Worker* was again at the center of Catholic peacemaking in America and the paper's circulation rose to 65,000. Members of the Catholic Worker participated in civil rights and anti-Vietnam War coalitions.[172] The Catholic Worker's theology of peace and theory of nonviolent resistance gave form to much of the protest against the war.

Then on November 9, 1965, in front of the United Nations Building in New York, Roger LaPorte, a former Trappist novice and then Catholic Worker, took a cue from the Buddhist opposition in Vietnam and burned himself to death to protest the war.[173] LaPorte's death sent a horrified shock through Catholic peace circles. Thomas Merton immediately wired the Catholic Worker resigning from his directorship of the Catholic Peace Fellowship, affirming his support for nonviolence, but questioning whether the tactics of draft-card burning and suicide were legitimate Christian means.[174] The Catholic Worker was shaken to its roots,[175] and Catholics all across the country were awakened to the agony of Vietnam for the first time. Gradually, however, positive reactions began to build again. The Catholic hierarchy condemned the act of suicide, but did not condemn LaPorte's conscientious objection.[176] Merton eventually rescinded his resignation from the CPF, and the Catholic Workers realized that the "mysterious witness" of LaPorte's death was forcing "a harsh inquiry into why these things are happening among us."[177]

The events of 1965 seriously disturbed the unity of the American Catholic Church. These divisions played before the entire nation when, in December 1965, 126 prominent Catholic priests, intellectuals, and activists ran an "Open Letter to the Authorities of the Archdiocese of New York and the Jesuit Community in New York" in the *New York Times*. It was signed by nearly a thousand supporters and protested the decisions to transfer Daniel Berrigan to Latin America and to silence two other Jesuits for their opposition to the war in Vietnam. College students from the New York area, including students from the Jesuit Fordham University, picketed chancery and archdiocesan offices in support of the priests.[178] A long, slow struggle over war and peace had begun within the Catholic Church. On one side the institutional church sought to maintain its alliance with power and influence and to impose order on an obedient and unquestioning Catholic laity. On the other a new movement for peace had started from the people. The Catholic Worker, CPF, PAX, campus groups, and thousands of Catholic individuals began to respond to the call of Vatican II and awoke to a new awareness of the strength of the Catholic peace tradition. There had been only 4 Catholics among the 3,989 conscientious objectors to World War I, only 135 among the 11,887 COs classified as IV-E during World War II; by 1969, 2,494 Catholics had received CO status among the 34,255 so classified, the single largest percentage of all American religious bodies.[179]

Yet the witness of the Catholic pacifist was still not easy. Not only had he to convince a skeptical draft board of his sincerity, but he had to do so without the sanction of his own church, sometimes in the face of hierarchical condemnation or indifference. Even those Catholics who convinced draft boards of their sincerity had to consciously renounce what many, both Catholic and Protestant, saw as the crusade and just-war heritage of the Catholic Church.[180] Isolated by their tradition and their church, many Catholic pacifists turned to the traditional peace churches for advice and counseling and to find examples of other isolated figures from the Catholic past. Gordon Zahn aptly compares the Catholic's dissent during Vietnam and Franz Jaegerstaetter's solitary witness, a witness condemned, scoffed at, at best ignored by family, neighbors, parish clergy, national hierarchy, and society at large as cowardly, naive, or subversive.[181] In many cases the Catholic pacifist had to accept his own dissent and the truth of his Catholic tradition completely on faith. In other cases Catholics rejected their supposed Catholic militarism for a biblical pacifism.

Catholic support for war, including the Vietnam War, was only too well known. Francis Cardinal Spellman epitomized official Catholic support for the war effort. By his Christmas 1966 visit to Vietnam as the head of the U.S. Military Vicariate and as the most influential American Catholic prelate, Spellman comforted conservatives and outraged liberals. He consciously discarded the Catholic moral tradition by proclaiming his unswerving support of "my country right or wrong."[182] He toured the front, blessed the army's cannons and called for victory,[183] describing the U.S. intervention "a war for the defense of Civilization," claiming that "any solution other than victory was inconceivable." The United States, he declared, was "the Good Samaritan of all nations."[184] American soldiers fighting in Vietnam were "Soldiers of Christ,"[185] defending the "cause of civilization and the cause of God."[186]

The U.S. Bishops Conference largely agreed with Spellman. Despite the CPF's public call for the bishops to condemn the war,[187] in November 1966 the bishops issued their pastoral *Peace and Vietnam,* in which they used Vatican II to support the conclusion that "it is reasonable to argue that our presence in Vietnam is justified."[188] Yet few were willing to go to the same extremes as Cardinal Spellman. In June 1966 Lawrence Cardinal Sheehan of Baltimore issued a pastoral letter instructing Catholics that Vatican II had legitimized both just defense *and* conscientious objection. Conscience, in fact, was the key to deciding the legitimacy of the war and to limiting its violence.[189] Sheehan's position was reflected in the bishops' next pastoral, the *Resolution on Peace* (Nov. 16, 1967), which criticized the extremism of both left and right but acknowledged that the antiwar protestors represented "responsible segments of our society." The bishops refused to repeat their 1966 endorsement of the war as just.[190]

Throughout 1967 and 1968 events in Vietnam and the pressures of the Catholic left brought changes in the thinking of the hierarchy. Despite tremendous pressures brought on him to suppress the Catholic Worker, Cardinal Spellman refused, perhaps because he realized that Dorothy Day was as close to a living saint as the United States had yet produced, perhaps because he realized the value of the movement's evangelical purity.[191] Most of the Catholic bishops had moved toward neutrality on the war, and the number of dissenting bishops steadily grew.[192] Finally in November 1968 the bishops issued a pastoral, *Human Life in Our Day,*[193] the American reply to Paul VI's *Humanae Vitae.* The letter tackled two divisive issues in the America of 1968. First the bishops discussed the church's position on birth control; then they addressed themselves to Vietnam.[194]

Recalling the declarations of Vatican II to "evaluate war with an entirely new attitude," the bishops explicitly condemned aggressive wars and total war. (pars. 98–99). Asserting that the soldier contributes to peace by ensuring order, the bishops reminded Catholics that "in the Christian message peace is not merely the absence of war or the balance of power" (par. 101). Charity and justice are true peace, and they are achieved not by support of dictatorships but by true development as defined by Paul VI.[195] Turning to the issue of America's nuclear capability, the bishops repeated the message of *Gaudium et Spes,* condemning the "indiscriminate destruction of whole cities or vast areas with their inhabitants [as] a crime against God and man" (par. 105). They endorsed the Partial Test-Ban Treaty and the Non-Proliferation Treaty, condemned the antiballistic missile (ABM), the doctrine of nuclear superiority, and escalation, (pars. 106–13) and described the arms race as "an utterly treacherous trap for humanity, . . . which ensnares the poor to an intolerable degree."[196]

Turning to Vietnam, the bishops declared their opposition to the peacetime draft as an institution that only contributes to future wars, a position, they noted, once taken by Benedict XV.[197] Finally the bishops posed several questions about the war in Vietnam: Has the United States already crossed the point of proportionality that makes the war unjust? Can the United States now withdraw? Would the billions of dollars being spent on killing be better used on hospitals, schools, poverty programs, and positive works of social justice (pars. 137–38)? The bishops concluded that these are all valid moral questions and that Vietnam was providing several moral lessons. They considered the possibility

> that military power and technology do not suffice, even with the strongest resolve, to restore order or accomplish peace, [par. 140] [and that] evils such as undernutrition, economic frustration, social stagnation and political injustices, may be more readily attacked and corrected through non-military means than by military efforts to counteract the subversive forces bent on their exploitation [par. 141].

The bishops then turned to the responsibility of American Catholics to make peace. They declared, for the first time in U.S. history, that conscientious objectors—even selective conscientious objectors, who refuse to fight because of the injustice of a particular war—have a basis in modern Catholic teaching, especially after Vatican II (pars. 144–45, 150–51), and that unquestioning obedience "is not necessarily in conformity with the mind and heart of the Church" (par. 147). The prelates therefore declared that the Selective Service System must modify the draft law to include selective objection against particular wars considered unjust or immoral (par. 152), and that even if the SSS should refuse to act, Catholics must follow their consciences in refusing to serve (par. 153). They concluded that "the hour has indeed struck for 'conversion,'" for personal transformation, for interior renewal" (par. 155).

The bishops' attitudes followed the lead of Catholic opinion during the Vietnam years. Despite the image of Catholics as authoritarian, conservative, ultrapatriotic, and militaristic—an opinion based largely on the immigrant church—American Catholics were more critical of the Vietnam War than has often been supposed.[198] As early as 1965 *Continuum,* a Catholic periodical, condemned American plans for the bombing of Hanoi as immoral.[199] In 1967 the *National Catholic Reporter* called for an immediate pullout from Vietnam, draft resistance, conscientious objection, and tax resistance, as did *Commonweal* in 1968.[200] These periodicals represented the vanguard of the Catholic intelligentsia, but the Catholic press in general gradually shifted from avid support for the struggle to a call for negotiations as a way of ending it.[201]

General Catholic opinion followed this course. In 1967 Catholics ranked only below Jews in their opposition to Vietnam.[202] By 1970 more Catholics than Protestants were calling for withdrawal from Vietnam.[203] Catholic white collar groups most consistently opposed the war.[204]

By August 1970 the bishops were critical of U.S. policy toward the UN and the developing world and praised American overtures to the communist government of the Peoples' Republic of China.[205] In October 1971 they repeated Vatican II's call on Catholics to follow the dictates of conscience and declared that

> in the light of the Gospel and from an analysis of the Church's teaching on conscience, it is clear that a Catholic can be a conscientious objector to war in general or to a particular war "because of religious training and belief."[206]

The bishops again pressed the Selective Service System to authorize selective objection and to grant amnesty to draft resisters. The letter was approved by over two-thirds of the American prelates.[207]

By the fall of 1971, 10 percent of the hierarchy had made public statements condemning the war.[208] Finally in November 1971, the bishops condemned the war in Vietnam as unjust, its destructiveness far disproportionate to the good that was sought there, and called for its rapid conclusion, the rebuilding of Southeast Asia, pardons and amnesties for war resisters, the rehabilitation of veterans and prisoners of war, and forgiveness and reconciliation for all Americans.[209]

By the time the Vietnam War had ended a dialogue was beginning with the Catholic Church between its hierarchy and its people, between its pacifists and its just warriors. A new theology of peace had emerged and was being accepted by the hierarchy. The hopes of Dorothy Day, of Thomas Merton, and of thousands of young conscientious objectors had begun to be fulfilled. The 1970s and the 1980s would show the promise and the challenge of this new-found Catholic peace.

## THE CATHOLIC PEACE MOVEMENT TODAY

With the end of U.S. involvement in Vietnam, the Catholic peace movement, like the American peace movement in general, entered a period of inaction and critical self-appraisal. The November 1965 Federal Courthouse action in New York City was the last major peace rally that religious pacifist groups, including the Catholic Worker, directed.[210] From then on leadership passed to general coalitions of antiwar groups in which Catholics participated both as organizations and as individuals. The rising level of rhetoric and of direct actions troubled many in the Catholic peace movement who feared that nonviolent witness to the gospel was being lost amid a rush for effectiveness and for purely political opposition to the U.S. government.[211] While the Catholic pacifists had formed the nucleus of the Catholic peace movement, attracting a swirl of support as the Vietnam War ground to a halt, relatively few of the Catholics who participated were willing to undergo the radical personal conversion that peacemaking required. Thus with the end of the war, considerations of politics, personal career, and fashion drew the majority of those opponents of the war back into the mainstream of American culture and its indifference to matters of peace and justice.

Nevertheless, the length of the conflict, the active opposition by Catholic peace groups and individual peacemakers, the notoriety of the "great Catholic peace conspiracy," and the shift in official Catholic thought to an acceptance of pacifism and nonviolence as legitimate Catholic alternatives left the Catholic peace movement with a larger following than it had had after World War II and with better direction and morale. Many issues of the Vietnam era were still unresolved, and Catholics began to seriously reexamine their peace tradition, to press for reconciliation, for amnesty of draft resisters, for justice for Vietnam and for American veterans of the war, and for a critical approach to U.S. power around the world, to the draft, and to the still pressing issue of nuclear war. One of the most important concerns of Catholic activists was that a distinctly Catholic peace movement survive the coming of "peace" both to maintain the Catholic peace witness within American society and to complete the work of converting the American Catholic Church from its Constantinian alliance with power into a church of peacemakers.[212] This double campaign took many forms: the witness of individual Catholic prophets and teachers, of major peace groups like the Catholic Worker and the CPF, the creation of new groups like Pax Christi, and the continuing shift of official church teaching toward the gospel of peace.

## PROPHETS AND TEACHERS: THE BERRIGANS

In May 1968 a group of nine Catholic activists, including Daniel and Philip Berrigan, David Darst, Thomas and Marjorie Melville, George Mische, Mary Moylan, John Hogan, and Thomas Lewis, entered the Selective Service headquarters in Catonsville, Maryland, brought draft files outside, and burned them with napalm. The police waited until the nine had completed the Lord's Prayer and then handcuffed them and led them away.[213] The action, arrest, trial, and conviction of the Catonsville Nine issued in a new era in American and Catholic peace history. In October 1967 Philip Berrigan had led a similar raid on the draft offices in the Baltimore Customs House. The demonstrators had poured blood on draft records as a dramatic way of confronting the Pentagon and the American people with their war guilt.[214] The Baltimore action had also resulted in arrest, but the Catonsville case raised new issues and concerns. Daniel Berrigan succinctly explained the motives of the Catonsville Nine:

> When at what point will you say no to this war?
> We have chosen to say
> with the gift of our liberty
> if necessary our lives:
> the violence stops here
> the death stops here
> the suppression of the truth stops here
> this war stops here
> Redeem the times!
> The times are inexpressibly evil
> Christians pay conscious     indeed religious tribute
> to Caesar and Mars
> by the approval of overkill tactics     by brinkmanship
> by nuclear liturgies     by racism     by support of genocide.[215]

The Catonsville Nine took every precaution to avoid human injury, made their protest openly, and did not resist arrest but made it a form of nonviolent witness. Yet their illegal break-in and their destruction of property were seen by many to be forms of nonviolence that stretched the definition. Thomas Merton, while fully in accord with the idea of an active resistance, wondered whether the Catonsville Nine had crossed the line. He finally concluded that they had not.[216] Dorothy Day and the Catholic Worker lent them their full support.[217]

Despite the Catonsville Nine's eventual conviction for interfering with operations of the Selective Service and for destroying Selective Service and federal property, other actions quickly followed in Milwaukee and Chicago, and the media soon turned on to the new "Catholic Left."[218] In 1969 Catholic resisters had staged similar actions against private corporations in secret night actions, later surfacing to face arrest. In April 1970 Daniel Berrigan went underground to avoid arrest, emerging sporadically to give interviews, to embarrass the FBI, or to celebrate Mass with supporters. He was finally arrested in August.

The tactics produced serious splits within Catholic peace circles. Many condemned them as a serious departure from Gandhian openness and truth, closely approaching the "just revolution." They brought a repression from the Nixon administration that exceeded the seriousness of the actions.[219] They deviated from the type of commitment to nonviolence laid out by Dorothy Day and the Catholic Worker and such Catholic intellectuals as Gordon Zahn and James Douglass.[220] The Berrigans and the others involved in the actions claimed that their tactics were the only form of nonviolent witness to the horrors of mass destruction and sanitized madness that an American people immunized to every sight of brutality and destruction could respond to. The symbolism of the actions was not lost on the Pentagon or the administration, which reacted in shock and outrage to every ounce of blood poured with an almost ritual understanding of the actions' true witness. When Philip Berrigan, Sister Elizabeth McAlister, and five others were subsequently arraigned, tried, and acquitted of conspiracy in what was to become known as the Harrisburg Seven Trial,[221] Catholic resistance and government repression reached levels that exhausted the Catholic peace movement amid doubts over aims, tactics, and effectiveness.

By the 1980s, however, renewed concern over the immorality and apocalyptic destructiveness of nuclear weaponry led the Berrigans to take literally the call of the prophets Isaiah and Micah: "They shall beat their swords into plowshares, and their spears into pruning hooks" (Is 2:4; Mi 4:3). On September 9, 1980, eight persons, including Daniel and Philip Berrigan and Sister Ann Montgomery, entered the General Electric nuclear warhead plant in King of Prussia, Pennsylvania, and "disarmed" Mark 12A warheads. There followed a series of "Plowshares" actions:[222] ramming and "disarming" nuclear submarines in Groton, Connecticut, pouring blood in a GE nuclear warhead plant, "disarming" components of Cruise, Pershing, and MX missiles at the AVCO plant in Wilmington, Delaware. Elizabeth McAlister and others hammered and poured blood on a B-52 bomber armed with Cruise missiles at Griffiss Air Force Base on Thanksgiving Day 1983,[223] and on Easter of 1984 members of Plowshares poured blood and hammered on Pershing II components at the Martin Marietta plant in Orlando, Florida.

Clearly repudiating the secret tactics of the Vietnam era, the prophets offered themselves for arrest without resistance and affirmed their commitment to nonviolence, to God's law above human law. For them the outrage expressed by government officials at their hammering on warheads symbolizes the twin American evils: love of material things and the love of death. Charges that they have broken the law by destroying private property are dismissed as absurd since property in Catholic tradition is something that enhances life and contributes to the common good. It is the Pentagon and the arms producers who destroy property by misusing "the resources of God's earth" to create tools of destruction.[224]

Members of the Plowshares compare their acts to those of Old Testament prophets who smashed false gods and idols, the "gods of metal" (Ex 34:17) that America has made of nuclear warheads and missiles.[225] Acquitted in the King of Prussia action because of the unfairness of the trial,[226] the Plowshares activists face stiff prison sentences for their continued actions. Philip Berrigan may well spend the rest of his life behind bars.[227] Yet they have continued their witness and have won the support of laypeople and religious across the country and of such prominent churchmen as Archbishop Raymond Hunthausen.[228]

## INSTITUTIONAL PEACEMAKING: PAX CHRISTI

At the end of the Vietnam War the Catholic Worker and the CPF returned to their traditional peace and justice work. In 1973 Dorothy Day was arrested for the last time in Kern County, California, for her support of Ceasar Chavez and the United Farm Workers' nonviolent struggle for social justice.[229] They were soon joined by another Catholic peace group, Pax Christi.

Born at the end of World War II out of the desire of several French Catholics for reconciliation with the German people, Pax Christi had as its enthusiastic leader Bishop Pierre-Marie Théas of Lourdes.[230] Endorsed by Pius XII in 1948, the group spread all over Europe and to Australia.[231] Closely aligned with the Catholic hierarchy, Pax Christi was a Catholic internationalist organization that concentrated on disarmament, peace education, contacts with the Eastern Bloc, the arms race, and the arms trade. Although it was not specifically pacifist, the group reflected the church's gradual abandonment of the just-war theory after World War II.[232]

On his return from a European meeting of Pax Christi in 1957, Gordon Zahn attempted to found a chapter of the group in the United States. The American hierarchy, however, already had its own internationalist group, CAIP, which well served the needs of its still intimate alliance with U.S. military and foreign policy.[233] At the end of the Vietnam War, however, when the British PAX became an affiliate of Pax Christi International, the American PAX under Eileen Egan decided to make the same move and to affiliate with the international group. By then CAIP was dead, smothered by its own embrace of U.S. policy in Vietnam and discredited by its diehard adherence to the theory of the just war in the nuclear age. It was dissolved in 1967 when its functions were absorbed into the Commission for World Justice and Peace of the U.S. Catholic Conference.[234] Two bishops, Carroll T. Dozier of Memphis[235] and Thomas J. Gumbleton of Detroit, agreed to act as "moderators" for Pax Christi/USA, an arrangement that avoided the hierarchical control that characterized the European chapters and that had proven so compromising for CAIP.

The group got started in October 1973, but it was suspended because of staff and communications problems. In May 1975, however, at a meeting at Manhattan College in New York, Joseph Fahey, Dorothy Day, Tom Cornell, Eileen Egan, Gordon Zahn, and others re-formed Pax Christi.[236] They held a well-publicized national meeting in Dayton, Ohio, in November 1975.[237] The new Pax Christi maintained the internationalist and lobbying directions of PAX and of its predecessor CAIP but modified and amplified these in order to reflect the new outlook of Catholic peacemaking in the twentieth century. Committed to its role in the institutional church, respectful of the church's traditions, and sensitive to the majority of Catholics, Pax Christi's basic goal is to convert: to educate, conscienticize, and convert individual Catholics to peace and through them to make the Catholic Church an instrument of positive peacemaking.

Its goals range from continuing Vatican II's commitment to look at war with an entirely new attitude to allying with all groups committed to nonviolent peacemaking and to maintaining an alliance between pacifists and just warriors on certain key issues. These issues include supporting the UN and all efforts for a viable world government; critically examining nuclear arms, the federal budget, arms traffic, and disarmament; working for recognition of conscientious objection and selective conscientious objection; and furthering the role of women and the local community in making peace. Pax Christi places great emphasis on peace education.[238] It looks for alternatives to violence on all levels and has condemned ROTC and Junior ROTC as being clearly against Catholic principles.

While attempting to maintain a fragile balance between all segments of the Catholic peace movement in America, Pax Christi/USA seems gradually to be moving away from the just-war theory and toward pacifism as the only viable Catholic attitude.[239] By the time of the October 1981 Pax Christi conference in Richmond, Virginia, the group had 5,000 members, 46 of whom were bishops, and had openly begun its criticism of U.S. nuclear and conventional militarism.[240] It opened a Center on Conscience and War to counsel Catholics of draft age and may be one of the first Catholic agencies to qualify as an employer of conscientious objectors under a new draft law.[241] In June 1983 Pax Christi joined other religious groups in calling for an end to draft registration.[242]

## THE BISHOPS, THE BOMB, AND PEACE

The conversion of the American Catholic Church into a force for peace is nowhere more clearly seen than in the direction taken by the National Conference of Catholic Bishops since 1970. By the end of the war in Vietnam the American bishops had come to condemn U.S. participation there as unjust and to reaffirm the right, and the duty, of American Catholics to follow the dictates of their consciences, even if this involved direct disobedience to the Selective Service System.[243] By the late 1970s the bishops had taken two steps that reflected these changes: they opened their conferences to the participation of all clergy and laity on every level of the church;[244] and they moved decisively toward breaking with the U.S. government on the issues of nuclear arms, deterrence, and war and peace.

In October 1976, the Detroit Call to Action Conference took a radical position on disarmament, calling for the condemnation not only of the use or threatened use of nuclear weapons, but also of their production and possession. The pastoral letter that followed the conference officially recommended this position.[245] In 1978[246] and again in 1979[247] the bishops boldly supported SALT II. In 1980, in the face of national reaction to the Soviet invasion of Afghanistan and a political campaign that sought to use the draft as a test of loyalty and anticommunism, they again affirmed the Catholic right of conscientious objection and selective conscientious objection. They approved the general idea of draft registration, but they declared that the state must show convincing reasons for its particular action. Despite the approval, the bishops affirmed their opposition to the draft at the time, condemned a draft of women, and recommended that draft counseling be available in Catholic schools and agencies.[248]

The election of Ronald Reagan to the presidency, the deterioration of U.S.-Soviet relations, the return to the Cold War of the 1950s, and the crisis in Central America demonstrate the shift in U.S. Catholic attitudes to the state and to peace. In November 1982 the U.S. Catholic Conference issued its *Statement on Central America*.[249] Gone is the crusade zeal that marked the bishops' statements just before World War II and the just-war approval of the early stages of the war in Vietnam. Instead, the bishops affirm Vatican II, Medellín, Puebla, and the tradition of liberation and peace. They mourn the martyrdoms of Archbishop Oscar Romero and the four American churchwomen in El Salvador, and confirm the "special tie to our brother bishops and to the church in Central America" (p. 2). Noting that the Central American church is neither naive nor complacent about the threat of communism in the region, the bishops flatly refute U.S. government statements and declare that "the dominant challenge is the internal condition of poverty and the denial of basic human rights" (p. 3).

The American bishops declare their support for Oscar Romero's successor, Archbishop Rivera; they call for an end to U.S. military intervention in Central America, for a political solution to the region's problems, for asylum for political refugees,[250] and for an end to the deportations of Central American refugees (p. 4). The bishops voice concern over curtailment of human rights in Nicaragua under the Sandinistas, but they also oppose the Reagan administration's policy there, and they decry the abuses of human rights in neighboring Guatemala (pp. 4–6).

By the 1980s individual Catholic bishops had come to the forefront of Catholic witness and prophecy against war. Seattle's Bishop Raymund Hunthausen's dramatic adoption of tax resistance against the U.S. war machine in June 1981 sent shock waves across the country.[251] In July Bishop Kenny of Juneau, Alaska, declared that despite his patriotism and loyalty to the United States, "I will not fight for my country. . . . More and more I find myself in opposition to all military power. I am becoming what in common parlance is called a pacifist."[252] In August 1981 Amarillo's Bishop L. T. Matthiesen called on the United States to stop production of the neutron bomb and announced the establishment of a fund to ease the transition for workers who leave defense work in favor of peaceful production. This caused a furor in a region heavily involved in defense work.[253]

In their 1983 pastoral, *The Challenge of Peace: God's Promise and Our Response,*[254] the American bishops formalized these trends toward a theology and practice of peace. The pastoral underwent three drafts and intense debate inside and outside the church.[255] It has produced a revolution in American Catholic thinking on war and peace equal to that of Vatican II and the Pastoral Constitution *Gaudium et Spes.*

Condemned by some for not going far enough for peace, for affirming the church's accommodation to power and to the just-war tradition, it is condemned by others for going too far in the direction of pacifism.[256] The pastoral epitomizes the history and scope of the American Catholic dialogue of peacemaking. It is the first attempt at a synthesis of and compromise between the just-war and pacifist traditions within Catholic history, between the church's recognition of the nation-state and the international system and its defense of the rights of individual conscience, between its functions of prophetic denunciation and education and its role as an institution in American society. It combines the wisdom of the gospels (pars. 30–55), the Catholic tradition of positive peacemaking (pars. 56–70), *Pacem in Terris,* Vatican II, recent papal teaching, and the experience of recent American history.

The synthesis is revolutionary; for the first time in American Catholic history pacifism and "active nonviolence" are seen as both evangelical imitations of Christ and legitimate means of serving the *political* community, as means of Christian action as legitimate as military defense in the service of the nation (pars. 73–77). In the last analysis, however, the bishops admit that nonviolence "best reflects the call of Jesus both to love and to justice" (par. 78), even if Catholics live in a dangerous world of aggression and injustice.

The bishops evaluate the validity of both the just-war and the pacifist traditions in the modern world (pars. 80–110). Discussing the cornerstone of any just war, just cause and retribution, their fundamental attitude is clear and vindicates a Catholic tradition stretching from Erasmus to Thomas Merton. They note that war "is permissible only to confront a 'real and certain danger,' " but they declare that "if war of retribution was ever justifiable, the risks of modern war negate such a claim today" (par. 86). The excesses of undeclared U.S. wars, of national security state repression, and of certain revolutions, the disproportionate and indiscriminate destructiveness of modern total war all reinforce this view. The bishops then praise the lives of modern peacemakers: Gandhi, Martin Luther King, and Dorothy Day (par. 117), reiterate their support for conscientious objection and selective conscientious objection (par. 118), and confirm that pacifism has finally found its legitimate place alongside the just-war theory in a Catholic "theology of peace" (pars. 120–21).

The prelates next examine the immediate issues facing American Catholics. These include the duty of the church and of Catholics to discern the problems of peace; to speak out in the spirit of the gospel to reject nuclear war, the arms race, and the billions of dollars devoted to death while the hungry, the poor, the homeless, and the helpless have less and less; to realize that nuclear arms have made the nation-state obsolete as a means of defense; and to take up the Christian call to lead in educating for peace and in opposing the rhetoric of the warmakers and planners (pars. 122–41).

Essential to Christian witness is a critical examination of nuclear war, its strategies, the concept of first use, and of deterrence (pars. 142–99). The bishops find retaliation for nuclear attack and first use against conventional attack unjust on the basis of discrimination, proportionality, and reasonable success, stating flatly that "no Christian can rightfully carry out orders or policies aimed at killing noncombatants" (par. 148). On the practice of deterrence, they note that the peace brought by the balance of power is not really Christian peace (par. 168) and is more like the peace of terror imposed by the Pax Romana (par 172; see chapter 2 above). While they admit that deterrence is not fully moral and has not led to arms reductions in the past (pars. 195–99), the bishops accept Pope John Paul II's formula for deterrence not as an end in itself, but as a temporary transition to true disarmament (pars. 172–77).

After endorsing several arms control treaties and plans, backed by the Freeze Movement (pars. 188–91), the bishops call for international controls on arms and the arms race, the substitution of conventional for nuclear forces as a means of disarmament, and cast doubt on the validity of civil defense as a defensive option (pars. 200–220). They devote equal attention to the creation of nonviolent forms of defense and again assert their full legitimacy as Catholic options (pars. 221–25). Yet nonviolence is not simply another means of national defense against enemies, for the bishops call is plainly one of gospel peacemaking: the goal of nonviolence is to win the enemy over, despite the suffering, even the martyrdom involved in this struggle (pars. 226–27). No matter what the method, however, peacemaking depends on the consciences of the individuals who practice it (pars. 231–33).

The result of Catholic peacemaking is a new world order. The bishops describe this according to the traditional lines of Catholic internationalism (pars. 234–58; see also chapter 11), admitting the reality of the American-Soviet conflict (pars. 245–58), and then according to the church's approach since Vatican II, stressing the pressing reality of world interdependence (pars. 259–73), of peace as justice and development in the Third World, of the American obligation to share its wealth and resources, and of the moral question raised by the "massive distortion of resources" for armaments when so much of the world remains poor and helpless (par. 270).

The bishops' conclusions reflect the revolution in American Catholicism (pars. 274–339). The bishops define the church no longer as the hierarchical institution to be defended and obeyed, but above all as the "People of God" marked by their gospel imitation of Christ (par. 274). Yet these Christians now form a minority in a world and in an America that is clearly un-Christian. The Christian call to peacemaking therefore involves a new witness, a new sharing of Christ's cross "and that we must regard as normal even the path of persecution and the possibility of martyrdom" (pars. 276–78).

Christian witness must be assertive, it must not fear accusations of political interference when it speaks out on vital issues. It must revere life in all its forms and cannot accept violence in any form, whether from the oppression of poverty, abuse of human and civil rights, pornography, or abortion (pars. 284–89). Realizing that peace begins not with institutional pressure or authority, but from individual conversion, the bishops call for prayer and penance that can bring reconciliation (pars. 290–300). They then call for conversion among Catholics—clergy, educators, parents, youth, soldiers, men and women in the defense industry, scientists, those in the media, public officials, and Catholic citizens in general—to examine their consciences and to help build a new theology of peace, to choose professions carefully, to serve human beings, and to act on their consciences to change their lives away from hate and war and toward the positive works of peace (pars. 301–29).

In a world headed in the direction of war and destruction, peacemaking is no longer an optional choice for the Christian (pars. 332–33). It is not a counsel to perfection but an essential commandment. It is the challenge of peace, the promise of God's kingdom, the New Jerusalem of the apocalypse (par. 339). It must be the choice of every Catholic.

## CONCLUSIONS

By the 1980s the American Catholic Church had achieved a revolution in peacemaking, one marked by the reconciliation of opposing views and the synthesis of a new theology of peace. From a Constantinian alliance with power, condemned by a few isolated prophets, the American Catholic Church has come to embrace the full legitimacy of gospel peacemaking and has once again claimed its heritage and its challenge of peace, the call to peacemaking that Christ gave to his disciples: "Peace I leave with you; my peace I give to you" (Jn 14:27). Despite this, in the 1980s many American Catholics remain "completely unaware of the pacifist implications of their faith"[257] and of the revolutionary directions of their own church. Much has yet to be done.

# ABBREVIATIONS

| | |
|---|---|
| BS | *Bibliotheca sanctorum.* Istituto Giovanni XXIII della Pontificia Università Lateranense. 12 vols. Rome: Società Grafica Romana, 1961–1970. |
| Butler | Butler, Alban. *Butler's Lives of the Saints.* 4 vols. Edited by Donald Attwater and Herbert Thurston. New York: Kennedy, 1956. |
| CAH | *Cambridge Ancient History.* 2d rev. ed. in progress. 12 vols. New York: Cambridge University Press, 1923–. |
| CCSL | *Corpus Christianorum: Series Latina.* Turnhout, Paris: Brepols, 1953–. |
| CMH | *The Cambridge Medieval History.* 8 vols. New York: Cambridge University Press, 1913–1967. |
| CPG | *Clavis Patrum Graecorum.* Edited by Maurice Geerard. Turnhout, Paris: Brepols, 1974–. |
| CPL | *Clavis Patrum Latinorum.* Edited by Eligius Dekkers. Steinberg: St. Peter's Abbey, 1951–. |
| CSEL | *Corpus Scriptorum Ecclesiasticorum Latinorum.* 60 vols. Vienna: Akademie der Wissenschaften, 1866–1913. |
| DACL | *Dictionnaire d'archéologie chrétienne et de liturgie.* Edited by Fernand Cabrol, Henri Leclercq, and Henri Marrou. 15 vols. Paris: Letouzey et Ané, 1907–1953. |
| DMA | *Dictionary of the Middle Ages.* Edited by Joseph R. Strayer. New York: Charles Scribner's, 1982–. |
| DSAM | *Dictionnaire de spiritualité, ascetique, et mystique: Doctrine et histoire.* 10 vols. Paris: Mythe, 1937–. |
| DTC | *Dictionnaire de théologie catholique.* Edited by A. Vancant, E. Mangenot, and E. Amann. 15 vols. in 23, with supplements. Paris: Letouzey et Ané, 1903–1972. |
| EC | *Enciclopedia Cattolica.* 12 vols. Vatican City: Ente per l'Enciclopedia Cattolica, 1949–1954. |
| JB | *The Jerusalem Bible.* Garden City, N.Y.: Doubleday and Co., 1968. |
| LCC | *Library of Christian Classics.* Edited by J. Baille, J. T. MacNeill, and H. P. van Dusen. Philadelphia: Westminster, 1953–. |
| MGH, Scriptores | *Monumenta Germaniae historiae: Scriptores rerum Germanicarum.* Hanover: Gesellschaft für ältere deutsche Geschichtskunde, 1826–. |

| | |
|---|---|
| NCE | *The New Catholic Encyclopedia.* 15 vols. Washington, D.C.: Publisher's Guild, and New York: McGraw-Hill, 1967. |
| NCMH | *The New Cambridge Modern History.* 14 vols. New York: Cambridge University Press, 1964–1970. |
| NCR | *The National Catholic Reporter.* |
| NOP | *In the Name of Peace: Collective Statements of the United States Catholic Bishops on War and Peace 1919–1980.* Washington, D.C.: U.S. Catholic Conference, 1983. |
| Omnibus | Habig, Marion A., O.F.M., ed. *St. Francis of Assisi: Writings and Early Biographies. English Omnibus of the Sources for the Life of St. Francis.* Chicago: Franciscan Herald Press, 1973. |
| PG | *Patrologia cursus completus. Series Greca.* 161 vols. Edited by Jacques-Paul Migne. Paris: Migne, 1857–1934. |
| PL | *Patrologia cursus completus. Series Latina.* 221 vols. Edited by Jacques-Paul Migne. Paris: Migne, 1843–1890. |
| Previté-Orton | Previté-Orton, C. W. *The Shorter Cambridge Medieval History.* 2 vols. Cambridge: Cambridge University Press, 1966. |
| Recueils . . . Jean Bodin | *Paix: Recueils de la Société Jean Bodin.* Vols. 14 and 15 (1961). |
| RSV | *The Holy Bible.* Revised Standard Version. Cleveland and New York: The World Publishing Co., Meridian Books, 1962. |

# NOTES

## 1. A CATHOLIC DEFINITION OF PEACE

1. *Webster's Dictionary,* New Collegiate Edition (Springfield, Mass.: Merriam, 1981), 835.

2. This "implies freedom, not only from strife or contention, but from all disturbing influences." Ibid.

3. *Oxford English Dictionary* (OED), Compact Edition (New York: Oxford University Press, 1971), 2:581–83.

4. P.C. Curren, 11:37.

5. *OED,* 2:584.

6. Thus "to pacify" can also be taken to mean "to impose order" or "to impose silence." See *Webster's,* 815. Thus "pacification" in Vietnam, the systematic reduction of a countryside and a people to the silence of death, was an appropriate, if perverse, label for U.S. policy there.

7. *OED,* 584. As President Ronald Reagan dubbed that ultimate weapon for imposing an enforced order of lasting silence.

8. *OED,* 584.

9. *Webster's,* 815.

10. *Webster's,* 835.

11. Ibid. See also Charlton T. Lewis and Charles Short ed., *Oxford Latin Dictionary* (Oxford: Clarendon Press, 1966), 1320; Zampaglione, 133. See also Roscher, 3, 2: 1719–22.

12. *Webster's,* 835.

13. Zampaglione, 133.

14. Lewis and Short, 1320. See also Bainton, *Christian Attitudes,* 18.

15. Zampaglione, 133.

16. Foerster, et al., in *Theological Dictionary,* 401.

17. Zampaglione, 133.

18. See Harris, 10–19; and Hopkins, 11, 25–37. Hopkins notes that "right down to the end of the Republic Rome is best seen as a warrior state" (32).

19. Harris notes that "the Romans seem . . . to have conceived of *pax* as a condition that could only result from successful war" (35).

20. Harris (172) also puts forth the thesis that throughout its long history of essentially aggressive and imperialistic wars, Rome was always careful to maintain at least a pretext of a defensive and just war sanctioned with the proper religious rituals. See also Zampaglione, 133.

21. Zampaglione, 132.

22. Zampaglione, 132; Fenwick, 11:38–41.

23. For accounts of the *Pax Romana* see Petit; Imbert, 14 (1961): 303–19; and Waddy. Waddy's frankly apologetic work was written in the context of the Cold War.

24. Grant, *History,* 19. See also MacMullen, *Paganism,* 50–57. MacMullen says that even salvation was seen in terms of bodily well-being.

25. Grant, *History,* 19–20.

26. Ovid, *Metamorphoses* 11.624.

27. Seneca, *De consolatione ad Marciam* 19.5.

28. Zampaglione, 134.

29. V.xvi.48.

30. Zampaglione, 137; Harris, 2–3, 23–30, 33–35, 105–7. See Earl, 20–43, especially 20–21, 33–36.

31. *De providentia* IV.14.

32. *Discourses* III.xiii.9.

33. See Peebles, 2:436–57.

34. The Greek translation of the Hebrew Old Testament was completed in the third and second century B.C., supposedly in Alexandria (Egypt) by seventy-two scholars and called after them by the Latin word for seventy, Septuagint. See Skehan, 2:425–29.

35. This is the source of the English word "irenic," used to "describe attitudes and measures likely to allay dispute" (*Webster's*, 815), and of "irenics," the study of peace. See *America* 125 (Oct. 30, 1971): 336.

36. Beck and Brown, 776.

37. Rodriquez, 11:37–38; Beck and Brown, 776; Foerster, et al., *"Eirene,"* 401. See also McKenzie, 651–52.

38. Beck and Brown, 776.

39. Foerster, *"Eirene,"* 400–401.

40. Zampaglione, 27.

41. One cannot take the distinction too far, however. *Eirenopoios*, the Greek word for "peace-maker," could still be taken to mean the strong ruler, especially the Roman emperor, who imposed peace by force. See, for example, the description of Commodus in *Dio Cassius* 72.15.5; or Antony's speech on the murdered Caesar, 44.49.2. These, however, were written under the Roman Empire.

42. Foerster, *"Eirene,"* 402; Zampaglione, 134.

43. Rodriquez, 38; Zampaglione, 28.

44. Foerster, *"Eirene,"* 401.

45. Gross, 650.

46. Lines 230–37.

47. Zampaglione, 27.

48. See Bainton, *Christian Attitudes*, 17.

49. But only in a very limited external sense. It was not used until the Peripatetic School to include the whole of mankind. See Den Boer, 78.

50. The uses of the term to describe love of neighbor in Greek culture have been greatly exaggerated according to Den Boer (66–67).

51. Beck and Brown, 776.

52. Ibid.

53. Xavier Léon-Defour, ed. 412.

54. Gross, 648.

55. Zampaglione, 188.

56. Jos 21:44, 23:1; 1 Kgs 7:2; 3 Kgs 5:4; 1 Chr 22:9; Sir 47:53.

57. Jgs 6:23; Jer 34:4. See Léon-Dufour, 412.

58. Gn 15:15, 25:8. See Léon-Dufour, 412.

59. It did later develop this meaning. See Is 2:4, 9:4; Gross, 649.

60. 2 Kg 19:24, 30; 3 Kgs 22:27–28. See Jgs 8:7–9; Van der Ploeg and Hartman, col. 1783; and Gross, 648.

61. 2 Kgs 18:29; Is 32:18; Ez 7:25. See Zampaglione, 186.

62. Sir 26:2. See Van der Ploeg and Hartman, col. 1783; Rodriquez, 37.

63. Ps 71:3–4, 7. See Zampaglione, 187.

64. Ps 40:10; Jer. 20:10. See Léon-Dufour, p. 412.

65. Ex 18:23; 3 Kgs 5:4; Pss 75, 121, 124. See Van der Ploeg and Hartman, col. 1783; Léon-Dufour, 412.

66. Zampaglione, 186.

67. Zampaglione, 186–88; Foerster, *"Eirene,"* 402, 405–6; Gross, 648.

68. The texts are too numerous to cite here. See Beck and Brown, 778; Léon-Dufour, 412; Foerster, *"Eirene,"* 403.

69. Gross, 648.

70. Lv 26; Nm 6:22–26, 25:12. See Van der Ploeg and Hartman, col. 1783; Zampaglione, 187.

71. Is 11:1–9, 65:17–25. See Rodriquez, 38.

72. Lv 1:3–4; Ez 34:17–31, 37:23–28. See Foerster, *"Eirene,"* 403; Léon-Dufour, 412.

73. Pss 4:9, 111:6, 124:5, 127:6; Is 26:3. See Léon-Dufour, 412.

74. 2 Kgs 7:1–3; 1 Chr 22:9. See Léon-Dufour, 412.

75. Ps 84:9–11; Is 9:6, 32:17, 55:12, 57:19; Zach 8:12. See Zampaglione, p. 168.

76. Nm 6:24–27. See Beck and Brown, 778.

77. The texts are too numerous to cite here. See Beck and Brown, 778.

78. See articles by Cook, especially "The Fall and Rise of Judah" and "The Prophets of

Israel.'' See also Anderson, 226–331; and Moscati, 246–49, 256–61.

79. 1 Kgs 22:13–28; Jer 14:12–13, 23:9–40; Mal 3:1–5. See Léon-Dufour, 412–13.

80. Moscati, 237.

81. Jer 31:31–34. See Moscati, 256; and Anderson, 367–96.

82. See Albright, 306–8.

83. See 48:21, 57:21, 60:17.

84. 14:13, 28:8–9, 29:11, 33:9. See Léon-Dufour, 412–13.

85. 13:10–16, 34:25, 37:26–28. See Gross, 649; Foerster, *"Eirene,"* 404–5; and Léon-Dufour, 412–13.

86. Foerster, *"Eirene,"* 405; Léon-Dufour, 413.

87. Rodriquez, 38; Gross, 650; Van der Ploeg and Hartman, col. 1783; Léon-Dufour, 413.

88. Is 11:3–5, 32:15–18; Pss 71, 84:9–14. See Gross, 650.

89. Is 11:6–9, 35:9, 65:25; Ez 34:25; Hos 2:20. See Léon-Dufour, 413; Gross, 649; Van der Ploeg and Hartman, col. 1783.

90. Pss 45:9–12, 85:11–17; Is 2:2–4, 32:1–8; Zach 2:5–17.

91. Jer 31:33–34; Ez 36:24–27. See Gross, 650.

92. Pss 27:3, 33:15; Prv 12:20; Is 48:21.

93. See Foerster, *"Eirene,"* 409, and Beck and Brown, 779–80, for its expression in the eschatological expectations of the Essene community.

94. Beck and Brown, 782.

## 2. THE CONTEXT AND MESSAGE OF PEACE IN THE NEW TESTAMENT

1. *Roman History* II. cxxvi.

2. III.xiii.9. See also Lewis and Reinhold, eds., 80.

3. See chapter 1, p. 10; and Zampaglione, 134–35, 138–39.

4. Waddy, 26, 207–25; Petit, 104–21, 227–32.

5. See Harris, 2–3, 10–19; Lewis and Reinhold, 2:80.

6. Tacitus, *Agricola,* xxx, in H. Mattingly, ed., *Tacitus on Britain and Germany* (Baltimore: Penguin, 1967), 80.

7. Zampaglione, 135.

8. See Lewis and Short, 1997.

9. Earl, 21.

10. Earl, 20.

11. Harris, 123–30.

12. See Harris, 30; Earl, 32–35.

13. See Harris, 10–19, 33–34. Harris notes that "Absent from the quite long list of abstract terms to which the Romans of the third and second centuries are known to have paid communal attention, *concordia, salus, victoria, spes, fides, honos, mens, virtus, pietas,* and others—are *pax* and related ideas" (35).

14. See Harris, 33–34, 107; Earl, 32–35.

15. Harris, 35–38, 41–53. While Harris does note the judicial and religious formulae used to justify Roman wars, he dismisses these as pious fictions. See 163–75; and Hopkins, 28.

16. See Den Boer, 83–89; and MacMullen, *Roman Social Relations,* especially "Class," 88–120.

17. Den Boer, 83–89; and Nock, "Religious Developments." On Roman religion see the excellent study of Ferguson. *Religions of the Roman Empire,* 1–87; and the collection of sources in Frederick C. Grant, 3–50.

18. For a brief survey see Philippe Wolff, *Western Languages* A.D. *100–1500* (New York: McGraw-Hill, 1971), 29–44. See also W. D. Elcock, *The Romance Languages* (London: Farber and Farber, 1971), 17–39.

19. The classic work here is Aristotle's *Poetics* 2, in which he notes that high style alone is appropriate for aristocratic and heroic men; low style, satire, and comedy are fit for the lower classes. See also Erich Auerbach, *Mimesis: The Representation of Reality in Western Literature,* trans. Willard R. Trask (Princeton, N.J.: Princeton University Press, 1960), 21–23.

20. See Arnold Hauser, *The Social History of Art,* 3 vols. (New York: Vintage, 1951), 1:81–84, 107–10.

21. See Den Boer, 151–56.

22. See *Politics* I.5.35; I.6. For a survey of ancient opinion see Wiedemann, 1–35. The dan-

gerous and contentious fields of modern opinion have been surveyed by Wiedemann, (pp. viii–xi); and by Finley, 11–66.

23. Den Boer, 82; Hopkins, 131–32. See Finley (11) on the dangers inherent in the "volume and the polemical ferocity of the history of slavery."

24. See Hopkins, 119; Finley, 93–122.

25. Finley, 119.

26. Den Boer, 167–68.

27. Den Boer, 62–63. See also Bauer, 678; and Liddell and Scott, 647.

28. Den Boer, 89–90.

29. See Finley, 64–65.

30. See chapter 4, p. 46–47.

31. Seneca on Marcus Cato, quoted in Piper, 22–25.

32. Seneca, *De Beneficiis* IV.26. See Piper, 21–22.

33. *Discourses* I.22.36.

34. *Discourses* I.25.29, III.13.11. See Piper, 26.

35. See Piper, 23.

36. Ibid., 25.

37. See Den Boer, 72.

38. Stevenson and Momigliano, 850–51.

39. Ibid., 850.

40. See Den Boer, 62; Piper, 30–33.

41. See Den Boer, 62; Piper, 30–31.

42. See chapter 1, pp. 12–14.

43. The traditional interpretation of Christian ethics as quietistic has been summed up classically in Ernst Troeltsch, *The Social Teaching of the Christian Churches*, trans. Olive Wyon (New York: Harper and Row, 1960), especially 39–69. Reinhold Niebuhr has stated the modern position many times, most forcefully in *Moral Man and Immoral Society*.

44. See above, pp. 11–12, 19–20.

45. It is used 91 times in the New Testament, 24 times in the gospels alone. Only once (1 Pt 5:14) is *galene* used for the idea. See Beck and Brown, 780.

46. See Van der Ploeg, cols. 1783–84; Foerster, "*Eirene*," 411. The Septuagint uses 20 terms to translate *šālōm*, but the New Testament settles on *eirene*. See Gross, 650. For the influence of Scribal and Rabbinical traditions on the early church via the synagogues see Piper, 20.

47. Beck and Brown, 780.

48. Lk 14:32; Acts 12:20.

49. Lk 11:21; Acts 24:2.

50. 1 Cor 14:33.

51. Mt 10:34; Acts 7:26; Gal 5:22; Eph 4:3, Jas 3:18.

52. Mk 5:34; Lk 7:50. See Foerster (411) for further citations.

53. Lk 8:48.

54. Lk 7:50. See Léon-Dufour, 413.

55. Lk 1:79, 2:14, 19:42.

56. As in Acts 7:26; Rom 14:19; Gal 5:22; Eph 4:3; Heb 12:14; Jas 3:18; 1 Pet 3:11.

57. See Van der Ploeg, col. 1785; Rodriguez, 38.

58. See 1 Cor 1:3; 2 Cor 1:2; Gal 1:3; Eph 1:2; Phil 1:2; Col 1:2; 1 Tim 1:2; 2 Tim 1:2; Tit 1:4; Philem 3. See also Gross, 650.

59. Rom 14:17; 1 Cor 7:15. See Foerster, 416.

60. Mk 9:49; Rom 14:17, 15:13; 2 Cor 13:11; Col 3:15; 1 Pet 1:2; Jude 2. See Beck and Brown, 781.

61. See chapter 1, pp. 12–13.

62. Jn 14:27, 16:33; Eph 2:14–17; Heb 12:14. See Foerster, 414; Beck and Brown, 780–81; and "Paix," in DTC 2:3407–9, col. 3407.

63. Gal 3:23–29; Eph 2:14–22; Col 3–11. See Beck and Brown, 781.

64. Rom 5:1; 2 Cor 5:18–20; Eph 4:3; Col 1:19–20, 3:15. See Rodriquez, 38; Piper, 80–85; Zampaglione, 226–27; Léon-Dufour, 414.

65. Rom 5:1–6:14, 16:20; Col 1:19–20; Heb 13:20. See Foerster, 415–16; Rodriquez, 38; Léon-Dufour, 414; and Ferguson, *Politics of Love,* 47.

66. Lk 7:50, 8:48; Jn 14:27. See Rodriquez, 38.

67. See Beck and Brown, 780.

68. 783.

69. See Léon-Dufour, 414.
70. Lk 1:79, 2:14; Acts 10:36. See Rodriquez, 38.
71. See Beck and Brown, 780.
72. Beck and Brown, 783; Foerster, 413–14, 417.
73. Foerster, 413.
74. Rom 12:18, 14:17; 1 Cor 7:15; Eph 4:3; 2 Tim 2:22; Heb 12:14. See Foerster, 414; Gross, 651; Léon-Dufour, 414.
75. See Ferguson, *Politics,* 12–15.
76. Eph 4:3; 2 Tim 2:22; Heb 12:14; 1 Pet 3:11.
77. See Beck and Brown, 787; Léon-Dufour, 414.
78. 1 Pet 3:11. See Gross, 651.
79. Acts 24:2. See Léon-Dufour, 413.
80. This is the meaning of the story of the rich young man in Mk 10:17–31; the paradox of the camel passing through the needle's eye. See Piper, 78–79.
81. 2 Cor 1:3–7; Eph 1:2. See Rodriquez, 38.
82. For a general introduction see Lawlor. The term ''mystical'' derives from the twelfth century.
83. See Lasserre, 30, 54. See also Piper, 91.
84. Acts 10:36; Eph 2:17, 6:15. See Beck and Brown, 780.
85. Rom 15:33, 16:20; 1 Cor 14:33; 1 Thess 5:23; Heb 13:20.
86. Lk 2:14, 19:38. See Léon-Dufour, 413; Foerster, 414–15.
87. Acts 10:36; Phil 1:2; Col 1:20. See Van der Ploeg, col. 1784.
88. See Brock, *Roots of War Resistance,* 9, citing C. J. Cadoux; MacGregor, 37; Ferguson, *Politics,* viii; Lasserre, 55; and Merton, ''Peace,'' 12–19.
89. Lk 17:20–21; Jn 18:36. MacGregor (36) emphasizes that this does not mean that it is not *for* this world.
90. Jn 18:36. See Ferguson, *Politics,* 42.
91. Mt 25:31–46; See Ferguson, *Politics,* 49–50.
92. See Mt 12:18; Lk 1:69; Acts 3:13, 18, 24, 4:27, 30. See also Ps 21:1–19; Isa 42:1–4, 52:13–53:12.
93. Isa 7:14, 8:8; Mt 1:23.
94. Ps 71:7; Isa 9:1–6; Lk 2:11, 14; Heb 7:2.
95. Lk 9:52–56. See Ferguson, *Politics,* 22–23.
96. Mt 9:18–22, 27–33, 15:29–31; Mk 1:23–28, 3:1–5, 7:31–37; Lk 5:12–14; Jn 5:1–9.
97. Mt 5, 13:1–52; Mk 4; Lk 2:46–50, 6:17–49, 8:4–18, 11:1–13, 14:7–16:13.
98. Mt 9:1–2; Mk 2:1–5; Lk 5:18–20; Jn 8:1–11.
99. Mt 14:13–21, 15:32–39; Mk 6:34–44, 8:1–9; Lk 9:12–17; Jn 6:1–13.
100. Mk 5:22–43; Lk 8:40–56; Jn 11:1–44.
101. Mt 21:1–9; Mk 11:1–11; Lk 19:29–38; Jn 12:12–16.
102. Ps 17:23–27; Zach 9:9–10.
103. Rom 5:10–18.
104. See Auerbach, 41–49.
105. Mt 10:23, 12:15, 14:13; Mk 11:19; Lk 4:30; Jn 8:59, 10:39.
106. Mk 7:24; 14:12–16; Jn 7:1–10, 11:54.
107. Mt 10:12–14, 26:51–53; Lk 9:51–56, 22:49–53; Jn 18:11.
108. Acts 8:1, 4, 9:25, 30, 17:10–14.
109. Acts 4:3, 5:26, 41, 21:30–33.
110. Acts 7:54–60, 12:2–3, 14:18–19. Lasserre (31) notes that the equivalent of our word ''defense'' does not appear in the New Testament.
111. Mt 26:51–54; Lk 22:35–38, 49–51; Jn 18:10–11. See also Ferguson, *Politics,* 25; and Lasserre, 37.
112. Rom 14:17; Gal 5:22. See MacGregor, 102.
113. Mt 5:3–12. For a modern interpretation see Egan, ''Beatitudes,'' 169–87. Egan demonstrates the essential links between the Beatitudes and peace, emphasizing the meaning of ''blessed'' as ''happy in the here and now.''
114. 6:27–36. See Piper, 49; and Ferguson, *Politics,* 3–6.
115. See Piper, 169–70.
116. See McSorley, 5–20; and Ferguson, *Politics,* 3–6. MacGregor (11–12, 33–36) offers a slight shift in emphasis. For a review of the scholarship on the Sermon see Kissinger.
117. The verb, *eirenopoieo,* to make peace, appears only once, in Colossians 1:20, in the

same sense that Christ has made peace with God through his reconciliation of all creation. See Foerster, 420.

118. See Makarewicz.

119. As in 2 Cor 10:1; see also 1 Tim 3:3; 1 Pt 2:18; Jas 3:17. See Makarewicz (477) and MacGregor (108) for other texts associated with selflessness, humility, and meekness.

120. As in Philem 2:5–8, 4:5; Tit 3:2; Jas 3:17; and in this sense in 2 Cor 10:1.

121. P. 65.

122. His ideas were heavily influenced by Gandhi. See Merton, "Blessed are the Meek."

123. P. 62.

124. See 2 Cor 10:7–8; Philem 4:5; 1 Tim 3:3; Jas 3:17.

125. See Makarewicz, 477.

126. See also Lk 22:24–27; and MacGregor, 44–47.

127. See Ferguson, *Politics,* 6–8.

128. See also Mt 5:17–19; Mk 10:19; Lk 10:29; Jn 13:5; Gal 5:13, 6:2; 1 Jn 3:16–18.

129. See Piper, 94–97, 152; McSorley, 50–51. See also Furnish, especially 45–69.

130. *Polemos,* the Greek for "foe in battle," is not used in the New Testament. See Bauer, 331; and MacGregor, 47.

131. See 1 Cor 13; Lasserre, 35.

132. See McSorley, 5.

133. See Piper, 56–59, 128–29.

134. See Mt 5:46–47; Lasserre, 57–58; and Piper, 59.

135. Piper, 88.

136. Mt 5:45. See also Mt 6:14–15, 18:20, 35; Mk 11:25; Lk 6:35; and Piper, 62.

137. The unity and identity of the end and the means is central to the New Testament and is a key to pacifism and peacemaking today. See especially Merton, "A Tribute to Gandhi," in *Nonviolent Alternative,* 178–84.

138. See Piper, 87, 97–98.

139. Jer 31:31–34; 32:37–44.

140. Ezek 11:19, 36:26–32. See Piper, 60–61, 90; Lasserre, 23.

141. See Piper, 78–80, 160–61.

142. See Kirwin, 9:724.

143. Mt 4:1–11; Mk 1:12–13; Lk 4:1–13. The confrontation, of course, also had messianic implications. See MacGregor, 40, 46; and Frend, *Martyrdom,* 79–87.

144. For a general introduction see Schroeder. See also Piper, 76–77, 79; and Ferguson, *Politics,* 9–10.

145. See also Piper, 27, 63–64 for the Old Testament roots of Paul's words in Deuteronomy, Psalms, and Proverbs.

146. Lk 6:28. See Piper, 57.

147. See also 1 Cor 4:12; 1 Pet 3:9.

148. See also Mt 10:24–26, 28; Jn 15: 18–21; Philem 1:28; 1 Pet 2:18–25. See also Lasserre, 66.

149. See Piper, 129–30; Ferguson, *Politics,* 9–10.

150. See Piper, 98–99

151. Rom 13:12; 2 Cor 10:3–4; Eph 6:12.

152. See Ferguson, *Politics,* 49.

153. Lasserre, 65.

154. See Zampaglione's opinion (209–22) that New Testament peace resembles Stoic tranquility and is essentially an otherworldly ethic with no expectation of change.

155. See MacGregor, 73.

156. Mt 5:48. See Beck and Brown, 782.

157. Foerster, 419. See also Beck and Brown, 776–77.

158. Mt 19:27–30; Mk 10:30–31; Lk 13:30, 14–11, 18:14, Rom 5:7–9, 12:19–20. See Piper, 59, 87; Ferguson, *Politics,* 12; and MacGregor, 74–75.

### 3. PEACEMAKING IN THE EARLY CHURCH

1. As in Zeiller, 2:1155–59. See also Ryan.

2. See, for example, Hornus's account.

3. The approach was put into classical form by Reinhold Niebuhr in *Moral Man and Immoral Society.* H. Richard Niebuhr, in *Christ and Culture,* (New York: Harper and Row, 1956), espe-

cially in "The Christ of Culture" (83–115), sets out the main features of the tradition.

4. See Gero, 286, 288.

5. See, for example, Brock (*Roots of War Resistance*, 13), who claims that "Christian pacifism is submerged for nearly a millennium"; and Bainton (*Christian Attitudes*, 88–121), who notes that "the barbarians militarized Christianity." Helgeland ("Christians and the Roman Army") and Windass, "Early Christian Attitude" and *Christianity Versus Violence* also put forth this view.

6. The historiography on the topic up to 1965 has been summarized by Fontaine in "Christians and Military Service in the Early Church." See also Bainton, *Christian Attitudes*, 66–100; and von Campenhausen, "Military Service in the Early Church."

7. See the works of Zeiller, Hornus, Helgeland, and Gero cited.

8. The definition of the term used by the U.S. Selective Service System under Section 6 (j) of the Military Service Act is the exemption from requiring "any person to be subject to combatant training and service in the Armed Forces of the United States who, by reason of religious training and beliefs, is conscientiously opposed to participation in war in any form."

9. See chapter 1 above for my definition.

10. See M. Grant, *Rome*, 242–304, 377–94.

11. M. Grant, *Rome*, 305–33; Hauser, 1:101–20.

12. See Meeks, 9–23; Frend, *Martyrdom*, 236–67, 303–439; Baus, *Apostolic Community*, 217–29; Lebreton and Zeiller, 2:751–64, 791–806; H. Chadwick, 60–66; Harnack, xx–xxi; Tim Cornell and John Matthews, *Atlas of the Roman World* (New York: Facts on File, 1982), 177–79.

13. See Meeks, 9–73, especially 30–32; A. H. M. Jones, "Social Background," especially 20–21.

14. Peter Brown, *World*, 66.

15. Meeks, 74–84.

16. H. Chadwick, 41–53; Meeks, 111–39; Lebreton and Zeiller, 1:336–55, 478–500, 2:617–717, 1103–22; Baus, *Apostolic Community*, 146–53, 254–88, 346–89.

17. See Frend, *Martyrdom* 398–400; Jones, "Social Background," 26–27, 33, 37; Momigliano, "Christianity and the Decline of the Roman Empire," in *Conflict*, 1–16, especially 9.

18. Jones, "Social Background," 30–33; Frend, *Martyrdom*, 450–53.

19. The classic account is in Cumont. See also Harnack, 91–116; Nock, *Conversion*, 77–155, 210–27; Lebreton and Zeiller, 1:25–38; and Ferguson, *Religions*, 211–43.

20. H. Chadwick, 56–60.

21. Nock, *Conversion* 1–7; Brown, *World*, 64–66.

22. For John's Gospel and Gnostic support of Rome see R. E. Brown, especially 1082. For Paul's approval of the empire see 1 Tim 2:1–7; Tit 3:1. See also 1 Pet 2:13, 2:1–4, 3:1–3, 20:25; and Meeks, 169–70. See also Sherwin-White, "The Roman Citizenship" and "Aspects of Roman Citizenship," 172–93; Zampaglione, 229; Lebreton and Zeiller, 1:315–23; 2:1158; Bainton, *Early Christianity*, 51; and "The Early Church and War," especially 204–5; Hornus, 80–82; and Cadoux, *Early Christian Attitude*.

23. See MacGregor, 82, 86–87; Frend, *Martyrdom*, 94–95.

24. See, for example, Rom 14:10; 1 Thess 4:13–18, 5:1–8. See also Frend, *Martyrdom*, 96–97.

25. See Meeks, 177–78, 180–83.

26. Especially useful is the outline in Quispel. For an introduction see Siegman.

27. See Cohn, xiii–xvi. For a corrective view see Costa, 1–21, especially 1, 4, 17.

28. See Zampaglione, 216.

29. See McGinn, ed., 7–16.

30. Cohn, 1–7.

31. Frend, *Martyrdom*, 104–95. See also Quispel, 15–18.

32. Frend, *Martyrdom*, 193–96.

33. See Cohn, 7–16; McGinn, ed., 19–22.

34. See also Frend, *Martyrdom*, 361–65; Hornus, 43–45, 93–94. See Kelly (459–74) for Christian eschatology through Origen.

35. See Meeks, 164–69; Bainton, *Early Christianity*, 49–51.

36. See Harnack, 240–56.

37. As in 1 Cor 12. See R. Grant, *Early Christianity*, 36–43.

38. See Hornus, 98–103; Kelly, 192–93.

39. Brown, *World*, 66–67.

40. *Homilies on the Psalms* 48.1, 59.3; *Letter* 66.2.

41. H. Chadwick, 72. See also Hornus, 106–7.

42. See Hornus, 30–43, 95–96; Grant, *Early Christianity*, 35–36; Harnack, 300–312; Cochrane, 213–60.

43. Zampaglione, 227.

44. Dodds. (103) notes the multilevel nature of the struggle between paganism and Christianity.

45. Bainton, *Early Christianity*, 206–7.

46. See also Hornus, 16, 110–17; Egan, "Beatitudes," 177.

47. *Letter to the Ephesians* 13.2. See Lebreton and Zeiller, 1:420–32.

48. *Letter to the Ephesians* 10.1–3.

49. I.39. See Ferguson, *Politics*, 55–56; Lebreton and Zeiller, 1:541–71. Halton and Sider, 89–90.

50. Chapter 110.

51. 1 *Apology* 39.

52. Chapter 11. See Lebreton and Zeiller, 1:571–75.

53. *Embassy Concerning the Christians* 35. See Lebreton and Zeiller, 1:575–78.

54. See M. Grant, *Rome*, 353–76.

55. 25.5. For recent work see Halton and Sider, 112.

56. See Lebreton and Zeiller, 2:894–926; H. Chadwick, 94–100.

57. See Lebreton and Zeiller, 2:811–42; H. Chadwick, 90–93; Le Saint, 13:1019–22; and Halton and Sider, 115–21.

58. H. Chadwick, 92.

59. See Ferguson, *Politics*, 57–58; Bainton, "Early Church," 201–2, and *Christian Attitudes*, 68–69, 80–82; Zampaglione, 245–46; Frend, *Martyrdom*, 366.

60. *The Prescription Against Heretics* 7.

61. The phrase is H. Richard Niebuhr's. See *Christ and Culture*, 51–55.

62. *On Idolatry* 19.

63. 20.94. See also Frend, *Martyrdom*, 366–68.

64. *Against Marcion* 3.14. See Ferguson, *Politics*, 58.

65. See Lebreton and Zeiller, 2:744–46; H. Chadwick, 49–50, 87–89; Hornus, 161–66. The fourth-century *Canons of Hippolytus* also draw on this collection. See Hornus, 166–69; H. Chadwick, 264–65; Ferguson, *Politics*, 61. For recent work see Halton and Sider, 113–14.

66. Judging from his condemnation of Rome as the idol with the feet of clay in his *Commentary on Daniel* (II.12; IV.7), Hippolytus was just as strongly opposed to Roman civilization. He equates Rome with the Beast (III.8.9; IV.8. 7–8, 9.2) and urges disobedience to unjust laws (III.23.1–3). See Frend, *Martyrdom*, 375–76; Hornus, 46–47.

67. See II.16. The text appears in Bainton, *Early Christianity*, 152–53. The list is not restricted to professions involving violence but extends to other serious sins.

68. See Crouzel, 10:767–74; Lebreton and Zeiller, 2:927–86; H. Chadwick, 110–13. For recent work see Halton and Sider, 104–9. On Origen's pacifism see Cadoux, *Early Christian Attitude*, 129–47.

69. See VIII.65. See also Frend, *Martyrdom*, 396–97; Zampaglione, 256; Egan, 177; Cadoux, *Early Christian Attitude*, 210.

70. *Exhortation to Martyrdom* 5. See also *Against Celsus* II.45.

71. *Against Celsus* V.33.

72. *Against Celsus* VIII.73.

73. See Cadoux, *Early Christian Attitude*, 207–8; Zampaglione, 257; Helgeland, 152–53.

74. See Lebreton and Zeiller, 2:1035–41; Frend, *Martyrdom*, 400–403; Attwater, 159–60; Delaney, 228–29; Butler, 4:362–64; and BS 7:214–17.

75. Lebreton and Zeiller, 2:842–75; Delaney, 133–34; Attwater, 96–97; Butler, 3:561–67; BS 3:1260–78; H. Chadwick, 118–21. For recent work, see Halton and Sider, 122–24.

76. Chapter VII. Arnobius' opposition thus appears fundamental and is not based simply on a resistance to idolatry as Helgeland (15) asserts.

77. See M. Grant, 353–76, 394–419.

78. See H. Leclercq, "Paix de l'Église."

79. For example, Hornus, 200–212; and n. 56 above.

80. See Lebreton and Zeiller, 2:1090–93; McGinn, 17–24; Halton and Sider, 125–27.

81. *Divine Institutes* VI.20.15.

82. See Ferguson, *Politics*, 56–60; Egan, 176.

83. See McGinn, 17–24.

84. *Divine Institutes* VI.17.

85. VII. 15–16.
86. VII.27.
87. See chapter 2 above.
88. See Cumont, 196–211; Frend, *Martyrdom*, 104–26; Lebreton and Zeiller, 2:875–79. See also F. Grant, *Ancient Roman Religion*, 157–214; Ferguson, *Religions*, 88–98.
89. See Brown, *World*, 49–52.
90. See Frend, *Martyrdom*, 106–7; Lebreton and Zeiller, 1:30–34.
91. See Frend, *Martyrdom*, 118–19.
92. Brown, *World*, 52–53.
93. See Frend, *Martyrdom*, 6–10, 161–67, 221–25, 268–72; Harnack, 266–78; Baus, *Apostolic Community*, 125–37, 164–71, 389–96; Lebreton and Zeiller, 1:371–82, 384–96. See also Dodds, 111–16, and de Ste-Croix.
94. See Nock, *Conversion*, 204–8; Frend, *Martyrdom*, 252–57.
95. See Lebreton and Zeiller, 1:391–92; Frend, *Martyrdom*, 217–22; and Sherwin-White, *Letters of Pliny*, 691–712, for Book X, 96–97.
96. See de Ste-Croix, 24–26, 30; Ferguson, *Religions*, 233–34.
97. See Lebreton and Zeiller, 2:972–76; Baus, *Apostolic Community*, 164–71; and Frend's synopsis, 276–83.
98. Frend, *Martyrdom*, 483–85; Lebreton and Zeiller, 2:887–91.
99. *Meditations* XI. 3. See Moses Hadas, ed., *Essential Works of Stoicism* (New York: Bantam, 1961), 190. On voluntary martyrdom in the early church see de Ste-Croix, 21–24.
100. Bainton, *Early Christianity*, 24–27.
101. See Frend, *Martyrdom*, 427. The text is in Stevenson, *New Eusebius*, no. 227, pp. 260–63.
102. Frend, *Martyrdom*, 330–32.
103. See Frend, *Martyrdom*, 21–22, 59–62, 66–68; Nock, *Conversion*, 193. For source materials on the martyrs see Frend, *Martyrdom*, 572–77; and Musurillo, ed. For recent literature see Halton and Sider, 87–89.
104. See Nock, *Conversion*, 193, 200–201.
105. Dodds (132) notes that "Christianity . . . was judged to be worth living for because it was worth dying for." He adds that, in a way, martyrdom also offered "something worth living for" (135–36).
106. See Cunningham, ed., 5–6; Frend, *Martyrdom*, 197–201; Lebreton and Zeiller, 1:390–92, 420–32; Attwater, 176–77; BS 7:653–65. For recent work see Halton and Sider, 76–78.
107. See Bainton, *Early Christianity*, 91–96; Musurillo, 2–21; BS 10:985–89; Butler, 1:167–71; Attwater, 290–91. For recent work see Halton and Sider, 78.
108. See Lebreton and Zeiller, 1:284–99, 493–95; Frend, *Martyrdom*, 417; Brown (*Cult of the Saints*, 17–22) rejects any "two-tiered" theory that would relegate the veneration of the martyrs to a purely "popular" spirituality.
109. Frend, *Martyrdom*, 537; Lebreton and Zeiller, 1:515–19.
110. Nock, *Conversion*, 175–76, 194–201.
111. Frend, *Martyrdom*, 306.
112. See Harnack, 487–97.
113. Frend, *Martyrdom*, 516–21.
114. Frend, *Martyrdom*, ix.
115. See Momigliano, "Christianity and Decline." Momigliano notes, however, that this observation is "not . . . a simple return to Gibbon. Christianity produced a new style of life, created new loyalties, gave people new ambitions and new satisfactions."
116. For Catholic interpretations see Fontaine; and Zeiller.
117. See Helgeland, 156–57; Bainton, *Early Christianity*, 53; Ferguson, *Politics*, 61; Zampaglione, 234; Gero, 285; Hornus, 129–30. The author has not seen Sergio Tanzarella, "I cristiani e il servizio militare nella chiesa antica: Il problema dalle origini alla fine del II° secolo," *Asprenas* 31 (March 1984): 75–87.
118. Helgeland (157) notes that the issues of sources are too difficult to be analyzed in a short article. The evidence of the Christian Theban legion, supposedly sent to the Danube in 286, offers similar problems. See Frend's analysis in *Martyrdom* (486).
119. See M. Grant, *Rome*, 439; Zampaglione, 234; Gero, 289–91.
120. Jones, "Social Background," 24–25.
121. See M. Grant, *Rome*, 438–39.
122. Jones, "Social Background," 24–25.

123. Leclercq ("Militarisme," DACL 11:1108–81) found eleven such inscriptions. Helgeland, writing some twenty years later, reduced this number to seven, asserting in full contradiction of historical method that "more are undoubtedly from our time (before Constantine) but it is not possible to say which ones are" (161).

124. Hornus, 118–23; Gero, 285.

125. Zampaglione, 233, 243; see also Gero, 298.

126. Gero, 291. Frend, (*Martyrdom*, 319–23) shows that the Severan period was one of increasing persecution in which Christians seemed less likely to have been attracted to the army.

127. See also Zeiller (2:1158) for the assertion that these canons were neither binding nor representative of the "good sense of the people."

128. See Ferguson, *Politics*, 62–63.

129. See Hornus, 152–53.

130. See Cadoux, *Early Christian Attitude*, 256–57.

131. See Delehaye, *Les légendes grecques, 112; Passions* 236–318, especially 242–45.

132. Delehaye, *Passions*, 321–28.

133. See Erdmann, 14; Delehaye (*Légendes*, 113) also notes many military saints who were converted to peaceful ones.

134. See Leclercq, "Militarisme."

135. See Gero, 291–94; Hornus, 158–59.

136. MacMullen, *Soldier and Civilian*, v.

137. Helgeland (162–63) objects to this thesis and notes the dangers: "capturing terrorists, criminal investigation, finding missing persons, questioning suspects (torture), raiding houses in search of illegal weapons, collecting tariffs and tolls and spying." See Davies, who ennumerates these duties.

138. See Bainton, *Early Christianity*, 54–55, and *Christian Attitudes*, 79–81; Egan, 176; Lassere, 180–96.

139. See Hornus, 36–38.

140. The text reads: "ut qui in pace arma projiciunt excommunicentur." Von Hefele (1:185–86), notes the major lines of interpretation. See also Hornus, 172–74; and Hermann Dörries, 111–13. Unlike Hornus, Dörries sees no inconsistency in the declaration of Arles with previous Christian peacemaking. See also Munier, ed., in CCSL, 148, p. 9.

141. See M. Grant, *Rome,* 368–69.

142. See Musurillo, 240–44; Frend, *Martyrdom,* 442; BS 8:1181–82; Attwater, 231.

143. M. Grant, *Rome,* 297–98.

144. See Musurillo, 244–50; Siniscalco; Bainton, *Christian Attitudes,* 70. Egan, 175–76; Attwater, 239–40; Butler, 1:571–73; BS 9:25–26.

145. See Musurillo, 250–60; Attwater, 228; Delaney, 333; Butler, 4:220–21.

146. As in Helgeland, 158–59.

147. See Brock, *Roots,* 12; Hornus, 133–35.

148. See Frend, *Martyrdom,* 487.

149. Zeiller (1156) argues that the purge "on the threshold of the fourth century, is best proof that from the end of the second to that of the third century . . . a 'conscientious objection' was not felt by the majority." His argument from the fourth century back to the second and from a handful of known cases who were objectors to prove a majority of militarists follows no known law of evidence or logic. That Christians formed a minority in the army well into the fourth century is best supported by arguments such as that of Jones cited above.

150. See the exchange between Maximilian and his judge in which it is acknowledged that other Christians do serve.

151. See Frend, *Martyrdom,* 477–81.

152. See John Holland Smith, 21–34; and Ferguson, *Religions,* 88–98. Ferguson notes (95) that "so far as the government at Rome was concerned, the object of the imperial cult was political. 'The emperor was god," said Fustel de Coulanges, 'because he was emperor.' "

153. See Ferguson, *Politics,* 43; Hornus, 26–27, 136–40; Bainton, *Early Christianity,* 53; Gero, 294.

154. For these objections see Hornus, 176.

## 4. CHRISTIAN PEACE AND THE BARBARIANS

1. On these aspects see especially Dórries, 130–41; and Lebreton and Zeiller, 3:88–110.

2. See chapter 3.

3. See Zampaglione, 274; Hornus, 184.

4. See Brown, "Aspects"; Matthews; and Momigliano, "Christianity and Decline," 9–11.

5. *Codex Theodosianus* XVI.10.21. See Stevenson, *New Eusebius,* 263; Hornus, 183–85.

6. See Chadwick, *Early Church,* 163–65; Brown, *World,* 86–92, 132–35, 182–85; Baus, *Imperial Church,* 78–93; Dörries, 130–41, 197–223.

7. See chapter 3, p. 34, for St. Basil's use of this term.

8. See Renna, 146,1; 160,2.

9. See Renna, 146,2–148,2; Paradisi, 337–39.

10. See Renna, 146,1; 160,2; Paradisi, 333–35, 345–52, 358.

11. See Du Cange, 2: 229; and Bonnaud-Delamare, *L'Idée de paix,* 70–92.

12. See Gleiman, 120.

13. See Paradisi, 378–81; Du Cange, 229–30.

14. Renna, 145,2–146,1.

15. For general bibliography see McGuire; *Biblioteca Sanctorum* 1:945–90; Butler, 4:509–16; Rusch, 47–65; Attwater, 43–44; and Toporoski.

16. *On Psalm 45* 21; *On the Duties of Ministers* I.27.29; III.3.23. See Hillgarth, ed., 65–66.

17. *On Psalm 118* 1.

18. *Letter 51* 1–4, 6–14, 17; see his *Life* by the Deacon Paulinus in Hoare, 145–88, especially 167–68 (chap. 24).

19. See Hornus, 220–26.

20. See Cochrane, 22–23, 73–86.

21. *Sermon against Auxentius* 2; Cochrane, 73.

22. *Sermon against Auxentius* 9; Cochrane, 76.

23. *Sermon against Auxentius* 11–14; Cochrane, 76–79.

24. *Sermon against Auxentius* 29; Cochrane, 83.

25. Cochrane, 23.

26. See Zampaglione, 294.

27. Ibid.

28. The best introduction to Augustine is *Augustine of Hippo* by Peter R. L. Brown. See also Chadwick, *Early Church,* 216–35. For recent research see Synan. For a general discussion of Augustine's ideas on peace, see Bonnaud-Delamare, *L'Idee de paix,* 27–53.

29. See Zampaglione, 312–14; Paradisi, 337–45, 360–71.

30. See Augustine's *City of God,* 19.7, pp. 861–62.

31. *City of God* 5.22–25, pp. 216–21.

32. See Zampaglione, 306–7.

33. For a full discussion see Russell, *Just War;* Bainton (*Christian Attitudes,* 89–100) discusses the elements of the theory and the criteria for a just war, as does McCormick. For full summations see Hehir, "Just-War Ethic"; Shannon, *War or Peace?,* 15–39; and "The Development of the Just War Tradition," in *What Are They Saying About Peace and War?* 3–16; and Klassen. See also Zampaglione, 307–8; Egan, "Beatitudes," 180–82; and Finn, "Pacifism," especially p. 4.

34. See Brown, "St. Augustine's Attitude."

35. See Zampaglione, 309.

36. *City of God* 19.27, pp. 892–93.

37. See the comments of Thomas Merton in "Christian in World Crisis," 43.

38. *City of God* 19.26, p. 892.

39. See Paradisi, 337–39, 342–45.

40. *City of God* 19.11, p. 865. The theme of the City of God as the Apocalyptic Jerusalem, the *visio pacis* (vision of peace) as opposed to the "confusion" of Babylon-Rome, finds its place in Augustine's *Commentary on Psalm 64* (2) and *On the Religious Instruction of the Young* (20.36). Ladner (241–46) also shows its fundamentally pacifist usage in Origen's *Homily on Jeremiah* (9) and in Dionysius the Areopagite. The *visio pacis* thus establishes a precedent for the continuing nonviolent apocalyptic tradition that later emerges in the European opposition to the Crusades. See also Duby (*Three Orders,* 112–15) for the peaceful apocalyptic in Dionysius. See also chapter 7 below.

41. Zampaglione, 299.

42. *City of God* I. Preface, pp. 5–6. See also Ladner, 248–51.

43. See Ladner, 256–83.

44. See Frend, *Martyrdom,* xiii.

45. Setton, *Christian Attitudes;* Zampaglione, 271–72, 280–83. Zampaglione notes that chapter 11 of Dionysius' *On Divine Names* is a treatise on peace.

46. See Runciman, *History,* 1:83; Bainton, *Christian Attitudes,* 113–14.

47. Zampaglione, 287–88. See Rusch, 25–29.

48. See Rusch, 11–17; Laistner, 56–57; BS 7:719–27; Butler, 1:77–80; Attwater, 286–87.

49. Zampaglione, 286.

50. *Short Commentary on Psalm 121,* 11, PL 9:665B. See Zampaglione, 286.

51. See Rusch, 74–92; BS 6:1109–37; Butler, 3:686–93; Attwater, 185–86.

52. *Letter 14 to Heliodorus* 2. See Hornus, 309.

53. Zampaglione, 288.

54. *Commentary on the Gospel of Matthew* I.V, PL 26:34D. See Zampaglione, 288.

55. On early monasticism see Baus, "Early Christian Monasticism"; Chitty; Knowles, *Christian Monasticism,* 1–24.

56. See Chadwick, *Early Church,* 174–83; Bainton, *Early Church,* 71–73.

57. Knowles, *Christian Monasticism,* 10–12; Brown, *World,* 98–99.

58. See Frend, *Martyrdom,* 462–63, 548–50; Momigliano, "Christianity," 12; Brown, *World,* 98–99; Knowles, *Christian Monasticism,* 12.

59. See Brown, *World,* 101–2.

60. Momigliano, "Christianity," 12.

61. See BS 2:106–36; Butler, 1:104–9; Attwater, 49–50; Frend, *Martyrdom,* 463–67. For general background see Chitty, 1–45.

62. BS 10:10–21; Butler, 2:259–62; Attwater, 263.

63. Hornus, 76–78; McNeill, "Asceticism versus Militarism," 6.

64. Brown, *World,* 96–101.

65. Brown (*World,* 100–102) reminds us that spiritual factors and ascetic drives were essential motives for the movement.

66. See Momigliano, "Christianity," 12; Frend, *Martyrdom,* 462–63, 548–50; Brown, *World,* 98–101.

67. See Knowles, *Christian Monasticism,* 14–15; Brown, *World,* 96–100; Momigliano, "Christianity," 12; Frend, *Martyrdom,* 462–63, 548–50.

68. Frend, *Martyrdom,* 548–50.

69. Brown, *World,* 101–3; Frend, *Martyrdom,* 549. One must also, however, note the excesses of violence against the last vestiges of paganism committed by the monks. See, for example, Brown, *World,* 104; Frend, *Martyrdom,* 548–49; Stevenson, *New Eusebius,* 252; and Frazee.

70. Brown, *World,* 96–97.

71. Hillgarth, 16–17; Brown, *World,* 182–83.

72. Erdmann, 90.

73. On Western monasticism in this period see Knowles, *Christian Monasticism,* 25–48; Baus, "Latin Monasticism," 690–707; Duckett, *Monasticism;* McDermott, ed., *Monks, Bishops and Pagans;* and McNeill, "Asceticism."

74. His *Life,* by Sulpicius Severus, is presented in Hoare, 1–44. See also BS 8:1248–91; Butler, 4:310–13; and Attwater, 233–34.

75. Hoare, 13 (chap. 2).

76. See BS 8:1279–91.

77. Hoare, 14–15 (chap. 3).

78. Dörries (112–13) describes Martin as a Christian who performed peaceful police functions in the Roman army, but who later could not inflict violence in war.

79. Hoare, 16 (chap. 4).

80. Ibid.

81. Hoare, 17–29 (chaps. 5–14).

82. Hoare, 29 (chap. 15).

83. Sulpicius Severus, *Dialogue 2, Gallus* 4–8, in Hoare, 126–31.

84. Sulpicius Severus, *Chronicle* II.51. See Hornus, 150–51.

85. *Dialogue 2, Gallus* 4, in Hoare, 126–27.

86. See Erdmann, 14. Sulpicius' own critique of the idealization of violence in Homer in his *Life of St. Martin* I, Preface (Hoare, 11) anticipates that of Simone Weil in *The Iliad, or The Poem of Force* (Wallingford, Pa.: Pendle Hill, 1978) by some 1500 years.

87. See Hornus (143–47) for discussion.

88. McNeill, "Asceticism," 4–6.

89. Hoare, 308–9.

90. BS 12:1310–15; Butler, 3:275–76; Attwater, 335.

91. Hornus, 148–50.

92. Attwater, 335; Hillgarth, 17, 22–27.

93. For the essential link between monasticism and missionary work during this period see Baus and Ewig, especially 213–17; Vogt; Neill, 61–78; and Hillgarth.

94. See E.A. Thompson, especially 66.

95. See Brown, *World*, 112–13. For a general account see n. 1 above.

96. See H. Chadwick, 247–57; Hillgarth, 71; and Brown, *World*, 115–19.

97. Hillgarth, 71.

98. Brown, *World*, 12. See also Goffart, who seeks to revise the standard history of a massive destructive series of invasions.

99. See Hillgarth, 51–52; Baus and Ewig, 205–13, 225–26; Lebreton and Zeiller, 3:272–83.

100. The classic introduction is Bloch, 2:293–99. See also Painter, 7, 28–37; and Erdmann, 19.

101. Erdmann, 20.

102. Brown, *World*, 115–19.

103. Momigliano, "Christianity," 13–15.

104. See Laistner, 74–75; Rusch, 161–63.

105. *On the Governance of God* IV.4. See Frend, *Martyrdom*, 561.

106. *History Against the Pagans* VII.32.13. See E.A. Thompson, 67; Laistner, 73–74; and Rusch, 148–50.

107. *Sermon 106*, in Hillgarth, 54–55. See also *Maximi episcopi Taurinensis, collectionem sermonum*, ed. Almut Mutzenbecher (Turnholt: Brepols, 1962) (CCSL 23), 417. For his life see BS 9:68–72; and Butler, 2:640–41.

108. Erdmann, 20.

109. Le Bras, "Sociology," 51.

110. Hillgarth, 85.

111. Ibid.

112. Hillgarth, 69.

113. See Laistner, 75–76; and Rusch, 190–91.

114. II.31–33. See Hillgarth, 69–70.

115. See BS 10:156–62; Butler, 2:615–17; Attwater, 270–71; Rusch, 101–4; Laistner, 79–82.

116. *Carmen 26*, 245–59, 425–29. See Hillgarth, 66.

117. See Rusch, 160–62; Attwater, 173; BS 9:1202–3; Butler, 1:100–101. See Hilary of Arles, *Discourse on the Life of St. Honoratus*, in Hoare, 248–80.

118. I.8. See Hoare, 254.

119. VIII.37. See Hoare, 278.

120. Attwater, 223; BS 8:390–91; Butler, 3:207–8.

121. Bela Palanka in Serbia.

122. BS 9:893–97; Butler, 2:614–15; Attwater, 250.

123. *Carmen 17*.

124. E.A. Thompson, 65.

125. BS 11:965–71; Butler, 1:52–53; Attwater, 307. See also Duckett, 3–17. According to Danielou and Marrou (414) the case of Severinus was not rare.

126. Duckett, 7.

127. BS 6:232–36; Butler, 3:251–53; Attwater, 151. See Constantius of Lyons, *The Life of St. Germanus, Bishop of Auxerre*, in Hoare, 284–320.

128. Chapters 2–4, in Hoare, 287–90.

129. See Attwater, 151–52; *Life*, chapters 17–18, in Hoare, 300–301. This "Alleluia Victory" is recounted in Bede, *History of the English Church and People* I.20. Sullivan ("Carolingian Missionary," 729) remarks that hagiographical stories of miracles were often based on real works performed by Christians to aid the sick, poor, or oppressed. Howard Clark Kee (*Miracle in the Early Christian World* [New Haven, Conn.: Yale University Press, 1983]) argues that our interpretations of such miracles depends very much on understanding the intent behind the hagiographer's account. It may not be too off the mark to interpret Germanus' nonviolent confrontation with the Saxons and Picts as a miraculous victory when seen through the eyes of his contemporaries.

130. Constantius, chapter 19, in Hoare, 302.

131. Chapter 20, in Hoare, 302–3.

132. Chapter 19, in Hoare, 302.

133. Chapter 28, in Hoare, 308.
134. Ibid.
135. Hoare, 308–9.
136. Chapter 36, in Hoare 314–15. Delaney (211) notes that soon after Germanus' death Aetius did launch a second invasion of Armorica.
137. Hoare, 315.
138. See Hoare's introduction, 283.
139. BS 10:396–408; Butler, 1:612–17; Attwater, 265–66. See also R.P.C. Hanson, *The Life and Writings of the Historical Saint Patrick* (New York: Seabury, 1983).
140. Sections 1–3, 12, 14, 21. See Stevenson, *New Eusebius,* 356. See also Duckett, 66–69.
141. Stevenson, *New Eusebius,* 356.
142. See Butler, 1:28–30, Attwater, 147.
143. See BS 7:1232–80; Butler 2:67–70.
144. See Danielou and Marrou, 415.
145. *Epitoma chronicon.* See Stevenson, *New Eusebius,* 359; Laistner, 64, 75, 126, 165, 221, 310; Rusch, 158–61.
146. On Frankish Merovingian society in general see Lasko, *The Kingdom of the Franks.* On the progress of conversion during the period see Vogt, "The Missionary Work of the Latin Church."
147. BS 3:1148–50; Butler, 3:418–21; Attwater, 77.
148. See Butler, 3:419.
149. BS 9:900–902; Butler, 4:499–500; Attwater, 250.
150. BS 6:257–59; Butler, 2:410–11; Attwater, 152.
151. BS 7:217–22; Butler, 4:367–69; Rusch, 183–85.
152. See the abridged edition translated by Ernest Brehaut.
153. Gregory of Tours, *History* 9.20, pp. 212–18.
154. BS 8:1230–32; Butler, 1:636–37; Attwater, 233; Laistner, 116–19.
155. See Hillgarth, 53–63.
156. Hillgarth, 53.
157. BS 7:222–87; Butler, 1:566–71; Attwater, 157–58; Rusch, 171–77; Laistner, 103–11, 120–24, 142–46, 161–68, 210–12, 380–81. For his missionary activities and opposition to forced conversion see Sullivan, "Papacy," 47–51.
158. See Renna, 149,1; Bonnaud-Delamare, *L'idée de paix,* 60–61.
159. For details see Bede, *History* I.20–33, pp. 66–91; Sullivan, "Papacy," 52–66. Baus and Ewig (215) and Sullivan, "Papacy" (47) note that Gregory was probably the first missionary pope in the full sense, but that his personal direction of these missions should not be exaggerated.
160. Bede, *History* I.26, p. 70.
161. Ibid., p. 91.
162. Bede, *History* I.30, pp. 86–87.
163. BS 4:131; Butler, 2:270–71; Attwater, 93.
164. See Butler, 2:506–9; Attwater, 91–92; Duckett, 81–87.
165. See the text in Tierney, *Middle Ages,* 1:71–73.
166. See Neill, 77; Frantzen, *Literature,* 1–18, 27–39.
167. On the penitentials see Bieler, *Irish Penitentials,* and "Penitentials"; Le Bras, "Penitentials"; McNeill and Gamer'; Oakley; Vogel, *Le Pecheur;* and Watkins. See also the works of Allen J. Frantzen, most recently "Penitentials Attributed to Bede," all cited in the bibliography.
168. See McNeill and Gamer, 18–19.
169. See Hillgarth, 131; Watkins, 2:645; Vogel, 44–47.
170. Chapter 14, McNeill and Gamer, p. 78.
171. McNeill and Gamer, 169–70.
172. Chapters 6–9, McNeill and Gamer, p. 88; Vogel *Le Pecheur,* 53–54.
173. Chapter 23, McNeill and Gamer, p. 91; Frantzen, *Literature,* 36–38, 42.
174. See McNeill and Gamer, 249–50.
175. Ibid, 254; Frantzen, *Literature,* 21, 26–29, 36–37, 94–95.
176. McNeill and Gamer, 98–99, 107.
177. Ibid, 117–18.
178. Ibid., 179–82.
179. Chapters 3–4, McNeill and Gamer, p. 187.
180. I.2, McNeill and Gamer, p. 118.
181. XXVIII. 10, See McNeill and Gamer, pp. 139–40.
182. Ibid, 187; Frantzen, *Literature,* 76.

183. McNeill and Gamer, 155–57; Frantzen, *Literature*, 38–39, 43–44.

184. V.4, McNeill and Gamer, p. 166.

185. Hornus, 175. Frantzen (*Literature*, 76 and n.63) states that Egbert imposed no penance for killing in public war.

186. McNeill and Gamer, 217–21; Vogel, *Le Pecheur*, 77. For the controversy over attribution see Frantzen, "Penitentials Attributed to Bede." See also his *Literature*, 76.

187. See for example the *Burgundian Penitential* of c. 700–725, canons 2–3 (McNeill and Gamer, 273–74); the *Paris Penitential* of c. 750 (McNeill and Gamer, 279–80); and the Spanish *Penitential of Silos* of c. 800 (VI. 103, McNeill and Gamer, 285–86). See also Watkins, 2:627–28, 645; Frantzen, *Literature*, 101–104, 119–21; and "Significance."

188. Erdmann, 17; Haines, 380. Frantzen (*Literature*, 111–12) shows the dilemma inherent in imposing such penances when the combatants were such secular leaders as the sons of Louis the Pious.

189. See chapters 1–13, McNeill and Gamer, pp. 372–76; Bieler, *Irish Penitentials*, 136–37. See Frantzen (*Literature*, 39–49) for the influence on Irish law.

190. Canon 46, in Bieler, *Irish Penitentials*, 145.

191. McNeill and Gamer, 386. See Frantzen (*Literature*, 75–81, 125–26, 146–47) for the influence on Anglo-Saxon law.

192. See chapter 3, above.

193. Hornus, 188–89.

194. Hornus, 190.

195. Erdmann, 15; Hornus, 191. On Innocent's writings see Rusch, 5–7.

196. See Hornus, 191–94; Russell, *Just War*, 77.

197. See Le Bras, "Sociology," 53.

198. See chapter 5 below.

199. BS 4:108–20; Butler, 4:409–13; Attwater, 92–93. His *Life* by Jonas is translated in McDermott (75–113). See also Duckett, 89–121.

200. The phrase is Helen Waddell's (*The Wandering Scholars*, 37).

201. *Life*, chapters 33–34, in McDermott, 96.

202. Chapters 34–35, in McDermott, 96–98.

203. Chapters 36–37, in McDermott, 98–99.

204. Chapter 40, in McDermott, 100.

205. Chapter 48, in McDermott, 105.

206. Chapters 59–61, in McDermott, 112–13.

207. BS 12:62–64; Butler, 1:111–12; Attwater, 316.

208. BS 1:918–23; Butler, 1:263–64.

209. BS 7:1079–81; Butler, 3:579–80; Attwater, 214.

210. BS 10:144–48; Butler, 1:188; Attwater, 270.

211. BS 5:702–5; Butler, 3:367–68; Attwater, 282.

212. BS 2:971–72; Butler, 1:204–5; Attwater, 60.

213. BS 1:199–201; Butler, 3:625–26; Attwater, 30–31.

214. The text is printed in McNeill and Gamer, 135–36.

215. See chapter 5 below.

216. Attwater, 168.

217. BS 8:290–92; Butler, 1:686–88; Attwater, 222.

218. BS 3:308–20; Butler, 2:477–81; Attwater, 71–72. For recent scholarship see Reuter, ed.; and Powell. His *Life* by Willibald is printed in Talbot, 25–62. See also Sullivan, "Papacy," 71–80.

219. *Life*, chapter 8, in Talbot, 56.

220. See, for example, the *Letter of Daniel of Winchester*, dated 723/4, printed in Talbot (75–78), and in Barry, 1:274–76. See also Hillgarth, 135–36.

221. *Letter to Pope Zacharias on the Foundation of Fulda*, dated 751. See Talbot, 134–36; and Barry, 1:276–77.

222. *Letter of Pope Gregory III to Boniface*, dated 732, in Hillgarth, 137–38.

## 5. FROM CAROLINGIAN PEACE TO PEOPLE'S PEACE

1. Fichtenau, 65–78, 88; Ullmann, *Renaissance*, 1–8, 15–21; *Government*, 129.

2. Ullmann, *Renaissance*, 43–70.

3. Bonnaud-Delamare, *L'Idée de paix*, 91.

4. Renna, 152, 1–2; Bonnaud-Delamare, *L'Idée de paix,* 190–91; Fichtenau, 47–48.
5. Du Cange, 1:230; Fichtenau, 104–5.
6. Bonnaud-Delamare, *L'Idée de paix,* 179–80; Du Cange, 231; Ullmann, *History,* 57.
7. Bonnaud-Delamare, *L'Idée de paix,* 133.
8. See Ullmann, *Renaissance,* 60–61; *History,* 38–66.
9. Bonnaud-Delamare, *L'Idée de paix,* 89, 154–56, 195–96.
10. Ibid., 177.
11. Ibid., 178–89; see also Ullmann, *Renaissance* (29–42) for the Carolingian capitularies.
12. Bonnaud-Delamare, *L'Idée de paix,* 178–89; Renna, 153,1–2; Gleiman, 122.
13. Bonnaud-Delamare, *L'Idée de paix,* 115–17; Hornus, 193–94; Printz, 1–45; McNeill and Gamer, 388–89.
14. Because of its large land holdings and control over worker potential.
15. See Fichtenau, 130–34, 156–60; and Prinz.
16. Fichtenau, 62–65; Ullmann, *History,* and *Renaissance,* 135–42; and Hay, *Emergence,* 14–36.
17. Renna, 151,1.
18. Fichtenau, 62–66; Bonnaud-Delamare, *L'Idée de paix,* 163.
19. Bonnaud-Delamare, *L'Idée de paix,* 137–44; Ullmann, *Renaissance,* 171–73; Sullivan, "Carolingian Missionary and the Pagan," 730–34, "Papacy," 80–89; and Delaruelle, *L'Idée,* 1–23.
20. See Previté-Orton, 1:303–11; and Sullivan, "Early Medieval Missionary Activity" (23), "Carolingian Missionary and the Pagan" (278–84) for intellectuals' support of this method.
21. Bloch, 2:412.
22. Bonnaud-Delamare, *L'Idée de paix,* 169–71, 164–69.
23. Du Cange, 1:230–31.
24. Ibid.
25. Fichtenau, 171–76.
26. Bonnaud-Delamare, *L'Idée de paix,* 218–23, 263–95; Ullmann, *Renaissance,* 23–29.
27. Fichtenau, 93–103.
28. Bonnaud-Delamare, *L'Idée de paix,* 199–201.
29. MacKinney, 183, n. 1; Sullivan, "Early Medieval Missionary Activity," 23.
30. Despite Fichtenau's reservations (see p. 120).
31. *Epist. LXXIII ad Calvinum presbyterem,* PL 100:248D; Bonnaud-Delamare, *L'Idée de paix,* 199.
32. *Epist. LVI ad Calvinum presbyterem,* PL 100:225B; Bonnaud-Delamare, *L'Idée de paix,* 197.
33. *Epist. VIII ad Beorminum presbyterem,* PL 100:149A; Bonnaud-Delamare, *L'Idée de paix,* 199.
34. *Epist. XCI ad Arnonem,* PL 100:295D–296A; Bonnaud-Delamare, *L'Idée de paix,* 202.
35. *Diadema monachorum LXXXI,* PL 102:675C; Bonnaud-Delamare, *L'Idée de paix,* 202–3.
36. *Diadema monachorum XII,* PL 102:609A; *Via regia* 17, PL 102:957C–D; Bonnaud-Delamare, *L'Idée de paix,* 203–4.
37. *Commentarium in regulam S. Benedicti,* PL 102:710D; Bonnaud-Delamare, *L'Idée de paix,* 203.
38. *Expositio in Mattheum* 28; Bonnaud-Delamare, *L'Idée de paix,* 233–34.
39. *Expositio in Mattheum* III, PL 120:223–25; Bonnaud-Delamare, *L'Idée de paix,* 235.
40. *De exordis et incrementis rerum ecclesiasticorum* 23; Bonnaud-Delamare, *L'Idée de paix,* 235–36.
41. *De ecclesiastica disciplina* 3, PL 112:1236–37; Bonnaud-Delamare, *L'Idée de paix,* 239.
42. *Commentarium in libros Machabaeorum* I.12, PL 109:1197; Bonnaud-Delamare, *L'Idée de paix,* 239.
43. PL 125:953–56.
44. In his *Praeloquiorum de militibus* I.2, PL 136:149; Erdmann, 18.
45. Erdmann, 18.
46. *Adversus legem Gundobadi* 3, MGH, Epist. 5:161; Russell, *Just War,* 30.
47. For recent scholarship see Bishop, *Pope Nicholas I.*
48. Delaney, 370.
49. MGH, Epistolae, 6:568–600; see also Sullivan, "Khan Boris," and "Papacy," 93–94; and Latourette, *Expansion,* 2:241–49.
50. Sullivan, "Khan Boris," 128.

51. See Ferguson, *Politics,* 42.

52. Sullivan, "Khan Boris," 127–28.

53. Bonnaud-Delamare, *L'Idée de paix,* 218–23.

54. See Fuhrmann, 820–22; Fournier and Le Bras, 1:145–71.

55. See Bonnaud-Delamare, *L'Idée de paix,* 241–46.

56. Ibid., 248–52.

57. VI,I; Bonnaud-Delamare, *L'Idée de paix,* 249.

58. Bonnaud-Delamare, *L'Idée de paix,* 241–43.

59. Ullmann, *Government,* 167–89; Fournier and Le Bras, 1:171–83; Fuhrmann, 823.

60. For this analysis see Bonnaud-Delamare, *L'Idée de paix,* 253–59.

61. See Fournier and Le Bras, 1: 347–56.

62. The *Poenitentiale Hrabani,* PL 110:471–73. See Frantzen, "Significance," 414.

63. *Ecclesiastical Discipline* II:50. See McNeill and Gamer, 314, 317; and Erdmann, 17.

64. X.152; see Erdmann, 17; Bonnaud-Delamare, *L'Idée de paix,* 236; and Fournier and Le Bras, 2:55–85.

65. *Commentary on the Book of Judges* I.13, PL 108:1141.

66. Chap. 79, in McNeill and Gamer, 310; Russell, *Just War,* 31; Frantzen, *Literature,* 103–7, 130–33; "Significance," 413–14, 419.

67. Chap. 80.

68. VI.14; Russell, *Just War,* 31. See Frantzen, *Literature,* 132–33.

69. Chap. 11; Russell, *Just War,* 31.

70. Chap. 34; McNeill and Gamer, 317. See Frantzen, "Significance," 414–17.

71. VI.26, PL 140:770–71.

72. See Fournier and Le Bras, 1:364–420.

73. See Erdmann, 80–81.

74. *Corrector sive medicus* I.1–6; Vogel, *Le Pécheur,* 81.

75. Chap. 9; *Decretum* XIX:15, PL 140:952.

76. Vogel, *Le Pécheur,* 82; Erdmann, 81; Cowdrey, "Ermenfrid," 239–40.

77. PL 141:339–40.

78. *In publico bello;* see Cowdrey, "Ermenfrid," 240; Erdmann, 80; MacKinney, 189.

79. Erdmann, 77–78; Delaruelle, "Paix de Dieu," 57.

80. *De vera ac falsa poenitentia,* PL 11:1113–30.

81. Cowdrey, "Ermenfrid," 238, nn.3–4.

82. Ibid., 236.

83. *Poenitentiae institutio;* see Cowdrey, "Ermenfrid," 233–40.

84. Cowdrey, "Ermenfrid," 233, n.6.

85. Ibid., 238.

86. See Vogel, *Le Pécheur,* 119–28.

87. Art. 10, in Douglas and Greenway, 2:400.

88. Haines, 372.

89. *Leges Henrici Primi;* see Haines, 380.

90. See chapter 4, pp. 50–59.

91. McNeill, "Asceticism," 18–19.

92. Ibid., 11, quoting W. S. Davies. See also Bonnaud-Delamare, *L'Idée de paix,* 261–62.

93. Delaney, 37; BS 9:1098–1100.

94. Delaney, 230; Butler, 2:375–76; BS 7:495–96.

95. McNeill, "Asceticism," 15; Attwater, 149; Butler, 4:17–18.

96. Attwater, 299–300; Delaney, 437–38; Butler, 1:266–68; BS 11:65–84.

97. See chapter 6, p. 78.

98. Delaney, 474; Butler, 2:678–79; BS 12:196–97.

99. Erdmann, 68–71.

100. See Renna, 153,2; Duckett, 197–212; and works by Sullivan cited in the bibliography.

101. McNeill, "Asceticism," 14–15; Attwater, 258; Delaney, 377–78; Butler, 4:384–86; BS 9:1101–4.

102. PL 133:639–645; Erdmann, 87–88; Duby, *Three Orders,* 98.

103. Attwater, 174; Butler, 2:188–89; BS 12:752–56.

104. Erdmann, 88–89.

105. Delaney, 377; Attwater, 258; Butler, 1:12–14; BS 9:1116–19; McNeill, "Asceticism," 20–21.

106. See chapter 7, pp. 88–89.

107. See chapter 4, pp. 52–61.

108. Delaney, 199–200; Butler, 3:139–40; BS 5:529–31.

109. The sources disagree in assigning the blame: some lay it to the empress, others to the pagan Walcherens.

110. Runciman, *History,* 1:85; Attwater, 72; Delaney, 83–84; Butler, 2:585–86; BS 3:583–84.

111. Attwater, 313; Delaney, 462–63; Butler, 2:244–46; BS 11:1362–67.

112. See chapter 14, pp. 233–37.

113. For background see Previté-Orton, 1:225–44, 372–78; O'Callaghan, 91–115, especially 109–12.

114. Waltz, "Voluntary Martyr Movement," 153–55.

115. Cutler, "Spanish Martyrs' Movement," 321–22.

116. See Attwater, 121–22; Delaney, 171; Butler, 1:561–63; BS 5:218–19. Eulogius' works are printed in PL 115:731–870.

117. Waltz, "Voluntary Martyr Movement," 155.

118. Ibid.

119. Ibid., 156–57; Southern, 21–24.

120. Waltz, "Voluntary Martyr Movement," 156–59.

121. Attwater, 122; Waltz, "Voluntary Martyr Movement," 226–27; Cutler, "Spanish Martyr's Movement," 324.

122. Cutler, "Spanish Martyrs' Movement," 324–25.

123. Waltz, "Voluntary Martyr Movement," 227.

124. Ibid., 227–28.

125. Colbert, 148–66, 399.

126. Waltz, "Voluntary Martyr Movement," 228; Cutler, "Spanish Martyrs' Movement," 325–26.

127. See Cutler, "Spanish Martyrs' Movement," 330–31.

128. Attwater, 132.

129. Cutler, "Spanish Martyrs' Movement," 325.

130. Cutler, ibid., 325; Attwater, 92.

131. Attwater, 57.

132. Waltz, "Voluntary Martyr Movement," 228.

133. Attwater, 121–22; Cutler, "Spanish Martyrs' Movement," 326.

134. Waltz, "Voluntary Martyr Movement," 232–33.

135. Colbert, 1–2.

136. See Colbert, 6–18; Cutler, "Spanish Martyrs' Movement," 321, 327–32; Waltz, "Voluntary Martyr Movement," 226, 229–30.

137. See the bibliography.

138. See Bloch, 2:414; Bisson, 298; Callahan, "Adhemar," 22; Cowdrey, "Peace," 48.

139. See Bouard, 181–82; Bloch, 2:414; Cowdrey, "Peace," 53.

140. See the works by Töpfer, Hoffmann, and Huberti cited in the bibliography.

141. Ullmann, "Legislation."

142. Ibid., 4.

143. Rosenthal, 28–29, 39.

144. See Bisson, 292.

145. Fichtenau, 139–40.

146. Ibid., 144–56; Bonnaud-Delamare, "Institutions," 422, and *L'Idée de paix,* 282–95.

147. Callahan, "Adhemar," 21–22; Renna, 154,2; Delaruelle, "Paix de Dieu," 52; Russell, *Just War,* 29.

148. See above; see also Callahan, "Adhemar," 36–37.

149. Duby, "Laity," 124–27; Bisson, 292.

150. MacKinney, 182, 186.

151. Duby, *Three Orders,* 37–38.

152. Duby, *Three Orders,* 135; Callahan, "Adhemar," 28.

153. See Duval, 11; Erdmann, 60–68.

154. See Bisson, 190.

155. MacKinney, 185–87.

156. Callahan, "Adhemar"; Bonnaud-Delamare, "Institutions," 456–66; Cowdrey, "Peace," 45–46, 49–52.

157. See above, pp. 71–72.

158. *Principes, nobiles,* and the *vulgaris plebs;* see Cowdrey, "Peace," 46; Callahan, "Adhemar," 29.

159. For details see Callahan, "Adhemar," 28–30.

160. See Cowdrey, "Peace," 47. Bloch, 2:415, disagrees.

161. Callahan, "Adhemar," 30–36.

162. See Bloch, 1:145–238; Ganshof, *Feudalism,* 63–95; Duby, *Three Orders,* 28.

163. Bouard, 184.

164. See Duby, *Three Orders,* 39.

165. Duby, "Laity," 127.

166. Duby, *Three Orders,* 95–99; MacKinney, 186–87.

167. See Bloch, 2:416–17.

168. Cowdrey, "Peace," 46, 52; MacKinney, 204.

169. MacKinney, 182.

170. Cowdrey, "Peace," 48–50; Bisson, 292–93; Gleiman, 125–26.

171. Du Cange, 1:228.

172. Duby, *Three Orders,* 139, and "Laity," 130; Bisson, 292–93.

173. Delaruelle, "Paix de Dieu," 52–53.

174. See Bonnaud-Delamare, "Institutions"; Duby, *Three Orders,* 34–35; Töpfer, 21–27, 60–75; Callahan, "Adhemar," 26–28.

175. Cowdrey, "Peace," 52; Callahan, "Adhemar," 27.

176. Strubbe, 494–95; Hoffmann, 45–69; Callahan, "Adhemar," 27; Cowdrey, "Peace," 42; Duby, "Laity," 123.

177. Strubbe, 497–99; Duby, *Three Orders,* 137.

178. Bonnaud-Delamare, "Institutions," 448–51, 456–69; Callahan, "Adhemar," 29–36; Töpfer, 60–76.

179. Duby, "Laity," 123; Hoffmann, 62–64.

180. Hoffmann, 81–85; Runciman, *History,* 1:86.

181. Strubbe, 496; Kennelly, "Catalan Peace," 42; Hoffmann, 70–89.

182. Kennelly, "Catalan Peace," 44; Hoffmann, 98–102.

183. Kennelly, "Catalan Peace," 47–48.

184. See, for example, Hoffmann, 104–8; Duby, *Three Orders,* 185–87; MacKinney, 193; Bisson, 293.

185. Erdmann, 75–77. Duval (22–24) lists only four such expeditions.

186. Duby, "Laity," 132; Cowdrey, "Peace," 44–54.

187. See above, p. 65–66.

188. See Bisson; Cowdrey, "Peace," 58–63; Bloch, 2:418; Delaruelle, "Paix de Dieu," 54–55.

189. Bisson, 297; Kennelly, "Catalan Peace," 49–51; Bloch, 2:413.

190. Kennelly, "Catalan Peace," 50.

191. Bisson, 304.

192. See Duby, *Three Orders,* 136–38; MacKinney, 188; Bouard, 168–70, 176–80, 188; Joris, "Observations;" Gernhuber, "Staat und Landfrieden;" Hoffmann, 207–16; and Bisson, 291–98, 305–6.

193. Bisson, 291–93, 305–6.

194. See Du Cange, 1:229–30; Gleiman, 136.

195. Bouard, 182–83; Gleiman, 118–19; Delaruelle, "Paix de Dieu," 53.

196. See chapter 6, pp. 78.

197. Bouard, 168, MacKinney, 198.

198. See Duby, Bouard, 168

199. *Three Orders,* 16–20.

200. For this analysis see Duby, *Three Orders,* 23–34, 39, 138.

201. For analysis see Duby, *Three Orders,* 39, 45–46, 50–59.

202. See Haines, 372–74; Renna, 155,2; MacKinney, 193; Delaruelle, "Paix de Dieu," 56; Kennelly, "Towns."

## 6. THE ERA OF THE CRUSADES

1. See Duval, 35–38; Bloch, 2:312–19; Painter; Althoff; Delaruelle, "Paix de Dieu," and Herlihy, 281–344. Not all in the hierarchy followed this reaction. Bishop Hugh of Lincoln (1135–1200), for example, was a constant ally of the poor and the oppressed, and is well remembered

for his protection of the Jews. He was a tireless peacemaker who refused to pay war taxes and defied two kings to protect his people. See Attwater, 175–76.

2. On Bernard's peace ideas see Renna, 158,1–160,1; J. Leclercq, "Attitudes"; Lorson; and Delaruelle, "Paix de Dieu," 155–69.

3. For a basic introduction see Previté-Orton, 1:471–501; Brooke, 237–93; Heer, 1:94–196.

4. See the works of Rosenstock-Huessey, Tellenbach, B. Tierney, and S. Williams cited in the bibliography.

5. See Erdmann, 229–34, 258–59.

6. Ibid., 257.

7. See Attwater, 279–80, 300; Delaney, 404; Butler, 1:399–401; BS 10:554–74.

8. Renna, 154,1.

9. *Epistola ad Oldericum episcopum Firmanum*, PL 144:311–13; see Duval, 3–4; Pissard, 13–14.

10. *Epistola ad Alexandrum romanum pontificem*, PL 144:228; see Duval, 4.

11. See Haines, 380; MacKinney, 183,1.

12. See Delaruelle, "Paix de Dieu," 57–65; Mayer, *Crusades*, 9–40; MacKinney, 200–206; Cowdrey, "Peace," 56–58.

13. See the bibliography.

14. See W. Ferguson, *Renaissance*, 96–97.

15. I know of no systematic survey of Crusade historiography. See Brundage, *Crusades*.

16. Ibid., 1–6.

17. Paris: Victor Lecoffire.

18. See Brundage, *Crusades*, 28–29, 85–87.

19. Alphandéry, 2:273–89. For the survival and re-creation of these myths into the era of World War I, see Girouard, especially 19, 42–43, 281, 289.

20. By Leff, *Dissolution*, 119–20; and Chenu, especially 202–38.

21. See also Cracco, especially 91–92.

22. Manteuffel, 39–43; and Bligny.

23. See Little, *Religious Poverty;* Doyère; and Vicaire.

24. For general background see the collection of essays in *L'Eremetismo in Occidente nei secoli xi e xii.*

25. See the works of Michel Mollat, Wolff, Flood, Manselli, and Bolton cited in the bibliography.

26. See Jean Leclercq, "Aux origines bibliques," especially 40–41.

27. Bligny, 136.

28. See George; Manselli, "Evangelismo," and de Schampheleer.

29. See Schmitt.

30. Fonseca.

31. Bolton, "Paupertas," 96–97; and M. Mollat, "Hospitalité."

32. M. Mollat, "Pauvres," 87.

33. See Bligny, 146; M. Mollat, "Pauvres," 90.

34. Bligny, 135; E. Delaruelle, "Les Ermites," 226–31; and J. Leclercq, "Les Controverses."

35. See Little, "Evangelical Poverty."

36. See Grundmann, *Movimenti*, 1–134.

37. Clasen, 653.

38. See Lambert, 49–181; Leff, *Heresy*, 1:1–47.

39. See Herbert E. J. Cowdrey, *The Papacy, the Patarines, and the Church of Milan* (London: Transactions of the Royal Historical Society, 1968).

40. See Leff, *Heresy*, 2:452–85; M. Mollat, *Vaudois.*

41. See also Thouzellier; McDonnell; and Leff, *Heresy*, 2:445–52.

42. See Madaule, *Albigensian Crusade;* Evans, "Albigensian Crusade"; and Previté-Orton, 2:660–65.

43. See Haines, 373.

44. See Bloch, 1:145–238; Ganshof, *Feudalism*, 63–95.

45. See Grundmann, *Movimenti*, 65–74; Moorman, 41–42; Milano; and Laughlin.

46. This has been edited by Meersseman, *Dossier*, 276–82.

47. Ibid., 276–79.

48. See Grundmann, *Movimenti*, 135.

49. Laughlin, 234.
50. Milano, 754–55; Grundmann, *Movimenti,* 74.
51. See Meersseman, *Dossier,* 284–86.
52. Grundmann, *Movimenti,* 79–88.
53. Meersseman, *Dossier,* 282–84.
54. See Meersseman, *Dossier* (286–88), for their rule.
55. Grundmann, *Movimenti,* 84–88.
56. As Grundmann labeled it. See *Movimenti,* 63–134.
57. See the basic works on Francis and Franciscan history cited below.
58. Either on his way to join a campaign in southern Italy, or while in prison during a war between Assisi and Perugia. See *1 Cel.* 1,1–3; *2 Cel.* 1,1–2; *Leg. 3 Com.,* 2. For Martin see chapter 4, pp. 51–52. It is no coincidence that the Church of San Francesco at Assisi contains both the Martin and Francis life-cycles in frescoes. Francis is depicted repeating Martin's donation of his cloak to the beggar.
59. See *1 Cel.* 1,5; *2 Cel.* 1,7; *Leg. 3 Com.,* 6.
60. *1 Cel.* 1,4.
61. *1 Cel.* 1,19; *2 Cel.* 2,40, 42, 60, 162.
62. See *2 Cel.* 2,89–90; and G. K. Chesterton, *St. Francis of Assisi* (Garden City, NY: Doubleday, 1957), 66–82.
63. *1 Cel.* 1,15.
64. See McNeill, 25.
65. Daniel, *Franciscan Concept,* 54.
66. See Haines, 374.
67. *1 Cel.* 1,15. See also *1 Cel.* 1,10; Bonaventura, *Major Life,* Prologue, 1; 3,2; 3,7.
68. *2 Cel.* 2,8.
69. *Mirror of Perfection,* 101.
70. McNeill, 25; Thomas of Spalato, *Historia Salonitarum,* in Omnibus, 1601–2.
71. See, for example, the conversion of the soldier recounted in the *Little Flowers,* 17.
72. 1 *Cel.* 1, 15.
73. See *Rule of 1221* 9; *Testament* 1; *1 Cel.* 1,7; Bonaventura, *Major Life* I,1,5, *Leg. 3 Com.* 4; *Mirror of Perfection* 44, 58.
74. 17:15.
75. 3:10–14.
76. II:1.
77. II:1.
78. Section 1.
79. Chaps. 13, 15.
80. 10–11.
81. Chap. 23.
82. *Rule of 1221,* 17:5.
83. Ibid. 13,15.
84. See Duby, *Three Orders,* 13, 56–60, 81–119.
85. *1 Cel.* 2,6 makes this identification clear.
86. See McNeill, 25–26; Duval, 29.
87. *1 Cel.* 1,15. The Franciscan life of peace has been epitomized not only for Catholics, but for the entire world by the much quoted "Peace Prayer of St. Francis." Not his own work, this prayer actually came to light only in the twentieth century, but it has become so enshrined by usage that we have included it here:

Lord,
Make me an instrument of your peace:
Where there is hatred, let me sow love;
Where there is discord, harmony;
Where there is injury, pardon;
Where there is error, truth;
Where there is doubt, faith;
Where there is despair, hope;
Where there is darkness, light;
Where there is sadness, joy;

O Divine Master,
Grant that I may not so much seek:
To be consoled, as to console;
To be understood, as to understand;
To be loved, as to love.
For, it is in giving, that we receive;
It is in forgetting self, that we find ourselves;
It is in pardoning, that we are pardoned;
and
It is in dying, that we are born to eternal life.

For more details see Habig, *Francis of Assisi, Writer,* pp. 31–33; and Cajetan Esser, O.F.M., *Opuscula Sancti Patris Francisci Assisiensis,* Grottaferrata (Roma): Editiones Collegii S. Bonaventurae Ad Claras Aquas, 1978, p. 43, par. 24.

88. See Tugwell, 432–51; and Grundmann, *Movimenti,* 79–80.

89. See chapter 7, p. 92; and chapter 10, pp. 138–49.

90. *1 Cel.* 1,15. See Moorman, 40–45; Meersseman, *Dossier,* 1–11; and Hallack and Anson, ix–xix.

91. Duval, 29–30.

92. Moorman, 42.

93. Meersseman, *Dossier,* 89.

94. Ibid., 41. The English text is in Baldwin, 350–56; and Omnibus, 165–75.

95. See, for example, 7,27, which establishes a procedure for responding to political pressures.

96. Anywhere from 1221 to 1228. See Meersseman, *Dossier,* 42–43, 101; Moorman, 217; Duval, 31.

97. See Duval, 31; McNeill, 26.

98. Meersseman, *Dossier,* 42–47, 101; Duval, 31.

99. See Meersseman, *Dossier,* 47–67, 79, 116, 128–38, 174–77.

100. See Moorman, 43–45, 216–20; see also Haines, 373–74.

101. See Hartdegen, 95; Hallack and Anson; Moorman, 222–23, 426–28.

102. Moorman, 221.

103. Callaey's estimate, see Moorman, 418–21.

104. Moorman, 560.

105. Moorman, 222–23; Hallack and Anson, 48–52; Attwater, 113; Delaney, 158–59.

106. Moorman, 222–23; Hallack and Anson, 94–98; Attwater, 113–14; Delaney, 159.

107. See Hallack and Anson, 142–52; Attwater, 74; Delaney, 91–92; Butler, 4:54–59; BS 3:439–533; McNeill, 26.

108. See Tugwell, 29–31; Meersseman, *Dossier,* 13–38, 127, 143–58; Hartdegen, 95–96.

109. See Grundmann, *Movimenti,* 29–33.

110. The basic account is in the *Chronicle* of Salimbene de Adam. See the editions of O. Holder-Egger in MGH, Scriptores 32:70–80, and Scalia, 1:99–123.

111. See Previté-Orton, 2:682–89.

112. Cohn, 99–107.

113. See Salimbene da Adam, trans. and ed. G. G. Coulton, 21–29.

114. See Symonds, 56; and Fumigalli, "Alleluia."

115. Previté-Orton, 2:689.

116. See Frugoni "Flagellanti," especially 220; Scaramucci, ed., *Il Movimento dei Disciplinati;* Haines, 371; Meersseman, *Ordo Fraternitatis,* 1:45–512; Leff, *Heresy,* 2:485–93; Cohn, 124–48.

117. Attwater, 284.

118. Dante himself (*Inferno* XVIII, 28–33) testifies to the huge crowds clogging streets and bridges in the city during the jubilee of 1300; see Frugoni, "Giubileo," especially 78–121. On Venturino see Genaro (especially 388–92, 395) for the movement's apocalyptic expectations for the "restoration of peace of the whole of Italy," as a result of its "crusade." Venturino thus restored the word "peregrinatio" to its peaceful meaning. The term had been appropriated and perverted by the age's military Crusades. See above, pp. 93.

119. See Previté-Orton, 2:1076–79; and Denys Hay, *Europe,* 168–81.

120. For a good account of what follows see Webb, 243–53. See also Frugoni, "Devozione."

121. Webb, 250–51.

122. "Non viles quidem, sed urbis illius principes et notabiles mercatores." See Webb, 251.

123. Webb, 251.
124. This was the estimate of Ser Luca Dominici. While Frugoni ("Devozione," 246) warns against accepting so large a figure literally, he does conclude that the numbers involved were certainly grand.
125. Runciman, *History,* 1:285; Previté-Orton, 1:522.
126. Runciman, *History,* 2:291–92.
127. Ibid., 2:259.
128. H.E. Mayer, 138.
129. Runciman, *History,* 3:11, n.4.
130. H.E. Mayer, 142.
131. Runciman, *History,* 3:71.
132. Ibid., 3:113.
133. Ibid., 3:167.
134. Runciman, *History,* 3:413.

## 7. ALTERNATIVES TO THE CRUSADES

1. See chapter 5 above, pp. 69–71.
2. See Waltz's criticisms of Cutler's *Catholic Missions* and "First Crusade" in "Historical Perspectives."
3. Burns, 1389–92; Daniel, *Franciscan Concept,* 8, and "Apocalyptic Conversion," 127.
4. See Dunlop.
5. Waltz, "Perspectives," 183. See also chapter 5, pp. 67–68.
6. See Berry; and Kritzeck, 20–21, 23.
7. Daniel, "Apocalyptic Conversion," 127, and *Franciscan Concept,* 8; Kritzeck, 22–23; Southern, 37–40.
8. *Liber contra sectem sive haeresim Saracenorum* I, in Kritzeck, 231–32. This translation is in Daniel, *Franciscan Concept,* 8.
9. Kritzeck, 6–7.
10. Ibid., 21.
11. Kritzeck, 22.
12. Ibid., 20.
13. Ibid., 10–14.
14. See the text in Kritzeck, 220–91.
15. See Throop, *Crusades,* 122–23. The author has not seen Benjamin Z. Kedar, *Crusade and Mission* (Princeton, N.J.: Princeton University Press, 1984).
16. See Throop, *Crusades,* 288; Duval, 32–33; Daniel, *Franciscan Concept,* xiii–xiv, 27–29, 39–40.
17. See the comments of Steven Runciman in "The Decline of the Crusading Idea."
18. See *1 Cel.* 2,9; *2 Cel.* 2,98–99; Bonaventure, *Major Life,* 1.13,15; 2.1.
19. *Rule of 1223* 3,11,13; *Rule of 1221* 14.2.
20. See Daniel, *Franciscan Concept,* 26–34; and Stanislao da Campagnola, *L'Angelo del sesto sigillo e l'alter Christus* (Rome: Istituto Francescano di spiritualità, 1971).
21. See *1 Cel.* 1,20; Bonaventura, *Major Life,* 9.5–9.
22. *2 Cel.* 2,4.
23. Jacques de Vitry, *History of the Orient,* c.32, in Omnibus, 1609–13; see also Moorman, 226; Daniel, *Franciscan Concept,* 41–42.
24. Chapter 16; see also his commission to his disciples in *1 Cel.* 1,11, 15.
25. Chap. 12.
26. See Daniel, *Franciscan Concept,* 32, citing Bonaventure's *Collationes in Hexaemeron.*
27. Burns, 1395.
28. Daniel, *Franciscan Concept,* 48; Alphandéry, 2:228; Duval, 32–33.
29. See Moorman, 227–28.
30. See Moorman, 228–29; Daniel, *Franciscan Concept,* 43–45; Burns, 1396.
31. Moorman, 229–32.
32. See Muldoon, *Popes,* 36–45, 52–59; Latourette, 2:324–42.
33. See Dawson; Moorman, 232–35; Muldoon, *Popes,* 41–45, 59–97; Richard; and Latourette, 2:327–42.
34. Moorman, 235–39, 429–37; Daniel, *Franciscan Concept,* 110–12.
35. See Moorman, 434; E. Johnson; and Christiansen. For recent scholarship see Richard Spence,

"Pope Gregory IX and the Crusade on the Baltic," *Catholic Historical Review* 69, 1 (1983):1–19.

36. See Daniel, *Franciscan Concept*, 110–12, 118–26.

37. See Bacon, *Opus majus;* the text is edited in Bridges (3:120–22), translated by Burke (110–15).

38. See Daniel, *Franciscan Concept*, 61–63; Throop, *Crusades*, 111, 132–33; Alphandéry, 2:253; Latourette, 2:319–20; Southern, 52–61.

39. Bacon (Burke, 113; Bridges, 123).

40. Bacon (Burke, 111; Bridges, 121).

41. Bacon (Burke, 110; Bridges, 120–21).

42. Bacon (Burke, 111; Bridges, 121–22).

43. Ibid.

44. Bacon (Burke, 111; Bridges, 122).

45. See Hallack and Anson, 65–73; Moorman, 224–25, 230–32; Gibert, 125–48; Daniel, *Franciscan Concept*, 66–74; Peers.

46. Daniel, *Franciscan Concept*, 67–74; Burns, 1399–1400; Gibert, 129; Peers, 1–141.

47. Peers, 142–58; Gibert, 129.

48. Ibid., 192–319.

49. Ibid., 320–41.

50. Ibid., 364–75.

51. See Gibert; and Fermin de Urmeneta, "El pacifismo luliano," *Estudios lulianos* 2 (1958): 197–208.

52. See Atiya, 74–94.

53. See Moorman, 230–32; Atiya, 75–77.

54. Atiya, 54–55, 75–93.

55. Ibid., 86–87.

56. Peers, 342–58; Atiya, 85–86; Altaner, "Lullus"; Gibert, 130; and Musto, "Angelo Clareno," 216–17.

57. Translated in Hallack and Anson, 65. See also Gibert, 131–34.

58. See Peers, 159–91; and Lull, *Blanquerna*, especially 322–31; *Blanquerna* (Excerpts), 149–56; and Gibert, 144–45.

59. 80.1, "Gloria in excelsis Dei," Lull, *Blanquerna*, 323, and Blanquerna (Excerpts), 149–50.

60. Lull, *Blanquerna*, 331–39.

61. See Burns, 1400–10, 1433; Daniel, *Franciscan Concept*, 10–11.

62. See Joseph Dahmus, *Dictionary of Medieval Civilization* (New York: Macmillan, 1984), 227.

63. Throop, *Crusades*, 129–30; Alphandéry, 2:252–53; Russell, *Just War*, 132.

64. The *Summa contra Gentiles.*

65. See Muldoon, *Popes*, 43, 176; Aquinas, *Truth* (Anderson ed.) 2:13; Throop, *Crusades*, 131.

66. See Throop, *Crusades*, 115–30; Runciman, *History*, 3:340; Southern, 62–63.

67. Throop, *Crusades*, 119–20; Daniel, *Franciscan Concept*, 12.

68. See Duby, *Three Orders*, 22.

69. Runciman, *History*, 1:38–40; H.E. Mayer, 28; Brundage, *Canon Law*, 3–18.

70. H.E. Mayer, 13–14, 28; Runciman, *History*, 1:44–48.

71. H.E. Mayer, 12–13.

72. H.E. Mayer, 14; Porges, 1.

73. H.E. Mayer, 15; Porges, 1.

74. H.E. Mayer, 15, 30–32. See chapter 6, p. 78.

75. See Cohn, 33–52.

76. H.E. Meyer, 12–13; Cohn, 33–52.

77. Duby, "Laity," 132.

78. Duby, *Three Orders*, 199–200; Porges, 1–3.

79. See Runciman, *History*, 1:113–15, 121–44; H.E. Mayer, 55; Porges, 12–13. Cutler's attempt ("Conversion," 57–69) to make Peter into a peaceful missionary is unconvincing; one must agree with Waltz ("Perspectives," 177–85) that he stretches the meaning of missionary work too thin.

80. Porges, 9–15; see also chapter 6, pp. 86–87.

81. See Majorie Reeves, *The Influence of Prophesy;* and *Prophetic Future.*

82. See Reeves, *Prophetic Future,* 1–28; and the selections in McGinn, 97–148.
83. Daniel, "Apocalyptic Conversion," 132–36.
84. Reeves, *Influence,* 6–10; Southern, 40–42.
85. For this analysis see Daniel, "Apocalyptic Conversion," 136–39, 148–52.
86. See Reeves, *Influence,* 133–273; *Prophetic Future,* 29–58; McGinn, 149–81; Daniel, *Franciscan Concept,* 21–22, 76–98; "Apocalyptic Conversion"; Douie, 1–48.
87. See chapter 6 above, p. 83.
88. The phrase is E. R. Daniel's.
89. See Douie, 81–119; McGinn, 149–58, 173–81; and the works of Burr, Flood, and Olivi, *Lectura.*
90. Douie, 120–52; Davis; and Manselli, "L'Antichristo mystico," and "Olivi ed Ubertino."
91. See Douie, 49–80; von Auw, *Clareno et les Spirituels,* and *Epistole;* Berardini; and Musto, *Letters* and "Angelo Clareno."
92. See Daniel, *Franciscan Concept,* 21, 84–86, and "Apocalyptic Conversion," 140–54.
93. See Musto, "Angelo Clareno."
94. See chapter 6 above, p. 85.
95. Daniel, *Franciscan Concept,* 80, and "Apocalyptic Conversion," 143–44.
96. Daniel, "Apocalyptic Conversion," 143.
97. Throop, *Crusades,* 135.
98. See Throop, *Crusades,* 29–42, 382; and Wood, 11–73.
99. See Delaruelle, "Critique"; and the poetry of Peire Cardenal in Wood, 9–10, 84–89.
100. See Previté-Orton, 2:660–65; Madaule; and Evans.
101. Throop, *Crusades,* 139–40, 177.
102. At line 2769. See also Delaruelle, "Critique," 173–87.
103. Wood, 94–95.
104. Ibid., 5, 19–22, 28–29.
105. Ibid., 3–4, 26–27.
106. Albert C. Baugh with Kemp Malone in *The Literary History of England,* vol. 1, *The Middle Ages* (London: Routledge and Kegan Paul, 1967), 241.
107. See Baugh (241–45) and the edition by J. F. Goodridge (Baltimore: Penguin, 1968).
108. See Runciman, "Decline," 65; and Adams, "Pre-Renaissance".
109. See G. R. Owst, *Literature and Pulpit in Medieval England,* 2d ed. (New York: Barnes and Noble, 1961), especially 174, 330–38.
110. *Piers Plowman,* ed. Goodridge, 52–53. (see n. 107 above). For *Piers Plowman* as a nonviolent apocalyptic, looking forward to an age of peace and restoration, see Bloomfield, esp. 104,112.
111. Goodridge, 191–93. See Bloomfield, *Piers Plowman,* 112. (See n. 107 above.)
112. See the edition of Gower's *Confessio Amantis* by Terence Tiller (Baltimore: Penguin, 1963), 9–14; Baugh, 1:264–66.
113. Steinberg, 104.
114. Lines 2226–2626.
115. Tiller, 145–46 (see n. 112 above).
116. Lines 2226–41; Tiller, 144–45 (see n. 112 above).
117. See Egan, "Beatitudes," 169–87, for a modern restatement of this position.
118. Lines 2241–78; Tiller, 145–46 (see n. 112 above).
119. Lines 2305–2484; Tiller, 146–47 (see n. 112 above).
120. Lines 2490–2506; Tiller, 147 (see n. 112 above).
121. Throop, "Criticism," 381–82.
122. Throop, *Crusades,* 17–25.
123. See Tugwell, 31–35.
124. Throop, *Crusades,* 135–83; Daniel, *Franciscan Concept,* 11; Runciman, "Decline," 640–43.
125. Throop, *Crusades,* 135–39, 162–64.
126. Ibid., 151–62, 171–82; Alphandéry, 2:223–31.

## 8. THE PAPACY AS PEACEMAKER

1. See Ullmann, *Government,* 450, and "Papal Court"; G. Mollat, "Diplomatie"; Thomson, 98–103; and the works by Blet, Gaudemet, and Kyer.

2. A. Wynen, *Die päpstliche Diplomatie* (Freiburg: I. Brisgau, 1922), gives a broad history but concentrates on the modern period.

3. See Ganshof, *Middle Ages*, 60–63, 73–74.

4. Ganshof, *Middle Ages*, 56–77, 95–96; Gaudemet, 81–82, 89.

5. Ganshof, *Middle Ages*, 95–96; Gaudemet, 84–87; Ullmann, "Papal Court," 356–57.

6. Ganshof, *Middle Ages*, 234; Gaudemet, 105–6.

7. Ganshof, *Middle Ages*, 289–90; Gaudemet, 95–96; G. Mollat, "Diplomatie," 507–12; Thomson, 103; and the works by Kyer.

8. See Novacovitch (99–159) for examples of these.

9. Duval (58–63, 80) provides an example of such misguided efforts to paint papal politics as peacemaking.

10. See Beales, *Catholic Church*, 28–35; using Novacovitch.

11. See Bainton (*Christian Attitudes*, 116–17), who uses the same evidence.

12. Barraclough, 33; Sullivan, "Papacy," 48; Ganshof, *Middle Ages*, 15, 37, 51.

13. See Hallenbeck; Hill, 1:59–74; and chapters 4 and 5 above.

14. Ganshof, *Middle Ages*, 19–27, 37; Hill, 1:75–96.

15. The best account of the development of papal political theory during the period is Ullmann, *Government*.

16. See Duval, 7 and above.

17. Ullmann, *Government*, 190–209, especially 204; Ganshof, *Middle Ages*, 27; and Bishop, *Pope Nicholas I*; and Sullivan, "Papacy," 89–96.

18. Ullmann, *Government*, 204.

19. *Epistola* 16; Ullmann, *Government*, 211. See Sullivan, "Papacy," 96–98.

20. Ullmann, *Government*, 211.

21. See Duval, 76, and pp. 76–78 above.

22. Duval, 77.

23. See Russell, *Just War*, 183–86; Duval, 26–28; James T. Johnson, 42–45; Cowdrey, "Peace," 55; Hoffmann, 230–42; and Bisson, 295–96.

24. Duval, 78; Gaudemet, 82.

25. Gaudemet, 82.

26. Ibid., 83.

27. Ibid.

28. Gaudemet, 83; Ganshof, *Middle Ages*, 136.

29. Duval, 67; Gaudemet, 91.

30. Duval, 80.

31. Duval, 80; Gaudemet, 91–92.

32. Duval, 68–70.

33. Gaudemet, 91–92.

34. Gaudemet, 93; Ganshof, *Middle Ages*, 194.

35. Duval, 80–81; Gaudemet, 93.

36. Gaudemet, 93.

37. Ibid.

38. Duval, 74, 81; Gaudemet, 83–84, 89–90, 94–95; Novacovitch, 111–12.

39. Ganshof, *Middle Ages*, 316.

40. Ibid.

41. See G. Mollat, *Popes;* Renouard; and Hay, *Europe*, 267–79.

42. The best account of these years is Fliche and Martin, vol. 14. See also Hay, *Europe*, 279–91; and Previté-Orton, 2:953–62.

43. See Perroy; Hay, *Europe*, 153–60; G. Holmes, 83–94; and Previté-Orton, 2:876–79, 884–85, 977–86.

44. See Gruber, 191.

45. G. Mollat, *Popes*, 343. Hill (2:3–27) views this "papist" diplomacy as obstructionist.

46. Gruber, 197; Ganshof, *Middle Ages*, 315.

47. See G. Mollat, *Popes*, 3–8. For Clement and succeeding popes see Pastor, *History*, vol. 1.

48. G. Mollat, *Popes*, 5.

49. Ibid., 7.

50. Ibid.

51. Ibid., 68–69.

52. Ibid., 70–74.

53. Duval, 81–82; Gaudemet, 90.
54. G. Mollat, *Popes,* 9–25.
55. Duval, 74.
56. G. Mollat, *Popes,* 261–62.
57. Gaudemet, 99–100; Hill, 2:12.
58. Duval, 82; Gaudemet, 100.
59. Gaudemet, 100.
60. Duval, 253; Gaudemet, 100.
61. See G. Mollat, *Popes,* 252; Ganshof, *Middle Ages,* 292.
62. See G. Mollat, *Popes,* 26–36; Barraclough, 151–52. For a full account see Jenkins.
63. See Ladurie, xi–xvii; and Jenkins, 15–17, 117.
64. See chapter 4 above, pp. 47–48.
65. Barraclough, 151; see also G. Mollat, *Popes,* 110–119; Hill, 2:17; Jenkins, 81–82, for negative appraisals.
66. Jenkins, 18.
67. Perroy, 90; Jenkins, 9–13; Gaudemet, 101.
68. G. Mollat, *Popes,* 252; Perroy, 90–94; Jenkins, 25–57; Gruber, 192; Gaudemet, 101.
69. Jenkins, 32.
70. As, for example, Perroy, writing after World War II and the French humiliation of invasion and occupation. See his *Hundred Years War.*
71. See Gruber, 190.
72. Perroy, 102; Gruber, 193; Jenkins, 55–57.
73. Duval, 82; Perroy, 106; Gruber, 193; Jenkins, 64–65.
74. Jenkins, 66; Gaudemet, 95–96.
75. Jenkins, 72–74.
76. Jenkins, 77–78; Gaudemet, 101.
77. See G. Mollat, *Popes,* 37–43.
78. G. Mollat, *Popes,* 42; Duval, 82; Gaudemet, 102.
79. Perroy, 115–16; Gaudemet, 101; Gruber, 193–94.
80. Perroy, 127; Gruber, 194.
81. See G. Mollat, *Popes,* 44–51.
82. Gruber, 194–95. Perroy, 129, has a negative judgment of papal actions here.
83. Perroy, 130; Gaudemet, 102.
84. Perroy, 137; Gruber, 195–96.
85. Duval, 82; Perroy, 138–40; Ganshof, *Middle Ages,* 315.
86. G. Mollat, *Popes,* 52–58.
87. Duval, 82; Gruber, 196–97; Gaudemet, 103.
88. See G. Mollat, *Popes,* 59–63.
89. See Gruber, 198.
90. Duval, 83; Gaudemet, 104.
91. See Perroy, 166–68.
92. See G. Mollat, *Popes,* 62.
93. Perroy, 166–68; Gruber, 198–99; Gaudemet, 103; Ganshof, *Middle Ages,* 315.
94. Duval, 82–83.
95. Duval, 83–84; Perroy, 239–44.
96. Novacovitch, 133.
97. Ibid., 139–40.
98. Ibid., 140–43.
99. Gaudemet, 104; Perroy, 291–93.
100. Duval, 88.
101. Ibid.
102. Ibid., 89.
103. Ibid., 74.
104. See Ganshof, *Middle Ages,* 279.
105. For these activities see Mattingly, 74–76.
106. On the methods and institutions of papal diplomacy in this period see Ganshof, *Middle Ages,* 294–99; Jenkins, 79–80; and Thomson, 98–103.
107. See Duval, 74–75, 89–92; Mattingly, 30–38, 90–93.
108. See Duval, 94–98; Muldoon, *Popes,* 134–39; and Hale, *Renaissance Exploration,* 64–65. For the texts see Barry, 1:621–25.

109. J. T. Johnson, 59; Russell, *Just War*, 42–44.
110. See the works by J. T. Johnson, Vanderpol, Russell, Hehir, cited above and in chapter 4.
111. As J. T. Johnson has properly pointed out (p. 26).
112. J. T. Johnson, 27.
113. See chapter 4, pp. 48–49.
114. J. T. Johnson, 34–38; Russell, *Just War*, 5–8.
115. See J. T. Johnson, 26.
116. Ibid., 26, 42.
117. Ibid., 30.
118. Ibid., 21, 66–75.
119. See *Decretum,* Causa 23; J. T. Johnson, 35–38; Russell, *Just War,* 55–68.
120. See Russell, *Just War,* 101, 138–39.
121. See Hehir, "Just-War Ethic," 16; Russell, *Just War,* 141, 267–71; J. T. Johnson, 38–39.
122. J. T. Johnson, 48–49; Russell, *Just War,* 128–29, 219–20.
123. Russell, *Just War,* 68–69.
124. Ibid., 86–87.
125. Ibid., 104.
126. Ibid.
127. Ibid., 106–7.
128. See chapter 6.
129. Russell, *Just War,* 106.
130. Ibid., 132.
131. See for example, chapters 4 and 5, pp. 59, 63.
132. See chapter 6 above, pp. 84–87.
133. See Russell, *Just War,* 127–28.
134. Ibid., 145–55.
135. See Russell, "Innocent IV."
136. For what follows see Russell, *Just War,* 217–31.
137. See Knowles, *Evolution,* 165.
138. As Russell, *Just War,* 230–31, has noted.
139. Ibid., 218.
140. Baylor, 40–44.
141. Ibid., 45–49.
142. Potts, 85–89; Baylor, 40–49.
143. See Knowles, *Evolution,* 116–30; Leff, *Thought,* 107–14.
144. Baylor, 49–50.
145. Baylor, 49–50. See also Bainton, *Christian Attitudes,* 107.
146. Knowles, *Evolution,* 179–84; Leff, *Thought,* 129–30.
147. Potts, 91–93; Baylor, 52, 97–103.
148. See Baylor, 52–53.
149. *Treatise on Conscience* 2–4; Potts, 100–107.
150. See Baylor, 39, 54–68, 83–91, 96–105.
151. *Debated Questions on Truth* 17.2–4; Potts, 134–36.
152. Baylor, 68, 97–103.
153. Ibid., 83.
154. Ibid., 88–91.
155. Ibid., 104–5.
156. Ibid., 106.
157. Knowles, *Evolution,* 318–26; Leff, *Thought,* 279–94.
158. Baylor, 120–26.
159. Ibid., 134–36.
160. Ibid., 146, 152.
161. Ibid., 147.
162. Ibid., 143–44.
163. Ibid., 149.
164. Ibid., 185.
165. Ibid., 187–89.
166. See chapter 6, p. 84.

167. For background see Douie, 153–201; Paul; Leff, *Heresy,* 1:51–255; Tierney, *Infallibility,* 171–204; and the books referred to in chapter 7, nn. 89–93.
168. Leff, *Heresy,* 1:51–166.
169. See Tierney, *Ockham,* 28–29, and *Infallibility,* 205–37.
170. See Congar, "Olivi"; Paul, 239–45; Leff, *Heresy,* 1:100–139; and Tierney, *Infallibility,* 93–130.
171. See chapter 7, p. 94 above. See also von Auw, "Vraie Église"; and Musto, *Letters,* 26–34.
172. See Tierney, *Ockham,* 18–19.
173. See Musto, *Letters,* 32–33.
174. Tierney, *Ockham,* 35; and Musto, *Letters,* 32–33. See also Congar, "Devotion mariale."
175. Musto, *Letters,* 32–33.
176. See Letter 28, in Musto, *Letters,* 307–27; von Auw, *Epistole,* 141–54.
177. Musto, *Letters,* 440; von Auw, *Epistole,* 228.
178. Acts 5:29; Musto, *Letters,* 31–32.
179. Musto, *Letters,* 500; von Auw, *Epistole,* 265.
180. Musto, *Letters,* 284; von Auw, *Epistole,* 126.
181. Musto, *Letters,* 604; von Auw, *Epistole,* 326. See Paul, 230–31, for this parallel expressed by the Spiritual martyrs burned at Marseille in May 1318.
182. Musto, *Letters,* 284; von Auw, *Epistole,* 126.
183. See *Acta Sanctorum,* Junii 3, dies 15, 566–68, App. 25*–30*.

## 9. HUMANIST PEACEMAKERS

1. See Rice, 92–106; G. R. Elton, "Constitutional Development and Political Thought in Western Europe," in NCMH 2:438–63; Hale, *Europe,* 55–86.
2. See Bense, 168–69.
3. See Rice, 10–18, 98–99; Tracy, 3, 43–45; Hale, *Europe,* 87–100; "Public Opinion," 26–27, and "Armies."
4. Hale, "War and Violence," 4, 11–12, 20; J. T. Johnson, 66–75.
5. In *The Prince* (chapters 12–13). See also Tracy, 72–88 on the impact of mercenaries on the Low Countries.
6. For the following analysis see Hale, "Public Opinion," 21–25.
7. See, for example, Moorman, 369–585; Ozment, 73–134, 182–90; Grundmann, 147–70.
8. See Pierre Debognie, "Devotion Moderne," in DSAM 3 (Paris, 1957): 727–47; Ozment, 96–98; Post; and Hyma, *Christian Renaissance.* On the Third Orders see chapter 6, pp. 84–85.
9. See McCann, v–ix; Post; Hyma, 521–50.
10. See, for example, I:1, in McCann (pp. 17–18); I:25 (pp. 48–51); II:7–12 (pp. 59–71).
11. II:3, in McCann, 55–56.
12. III:25, in McCann, 105–6.
13. III:58, in McCann, 151.
14. III:54, in McCann, 143.
15. III:42, in McCann, 123–24; IV:13, in McCann, 178.
16. See Kristeller; Gilmore, 183–228; Rice, 66–91; Hans Baron, "Fifteenth Century Civilization and the Renaissance," in NCMH 1:50–75.
17. See Hexter, 63; Tracy, 8–9.
18. Hexter, 82; Adams, "Pre-Renaissance," 431, and Adams, *Valor,* 3–7.
19. See Adams, *Valor,* 223–26; Tracy, 23–69.
20. See Bainton, *Attitudes,* 128.
21. Adams, 93, 83–85. For negative appraisals of the Humanists' role see Hale, "Public Opinion," and "War and Violence"; and Lauro Martines, *Power and Imagination* (New York: Random House, Vintage, 1980), especially 241–76, 297–331.
22. See Letter 541 of 1517 in Erasmus, *Letters,* 4:261–68.
23. See Jayne; Harbison, 56–67; Hyma, *Youth,* 343–65; Kaufman, 55–110, especially 60–68.
24. Adams, *Valor,* 21. See also Chambers, 78–80.
25. Adams, *Valor,* 23.
26. Ibid.
27. Ibid. See chapter 2 above, pp. 26–27.
28. Adams, *Valor,* 55–61.
29. Ibid., 69–72.

30. Tracy, 32–33.
31. Adams, *Valor*, 88, 162; Chambers, 167–68.
32. Adams, *Valor*, 161–62, 175–76; Tracy, 50–54, 90–95.
33. For details of Thomas More's life see Chambers.
34. Greene and Dolan, 19–20; Adams, *Valor*, 172–73; Chambers, 154–56.
35. *Utopia*, Book I; Greene and Dolan, 48–49.
36. Ibid. See also Hexter, 86–93.
37. Adams, *Valor*, 221.
38. Adams, *Valor*, 213–15; Chambers, 208–9.
39. Adams, *Valor*, 240.
40. On his epitaph, in fact, he claimed it as his chief achievement and contribution. See Adams, *Valor*, 292–93; Chambers, 232–35.
41. Chambers, 236–90.
42. Ibid., 241–43.
43. See Chambers, 291–350; Greene and Dolan, 294–98.
44. See the texts in More, *Complete Works* 1; Greene and Dolan, 196–216, 232–34. See also Chambers, 265–82; Bense, 170; Adams, *Valor*, 275–76.
45. See Ligeia Gallagher, *More's Utopia and its Critics* (Chicago: Scott, Foresman, 1964).
46. Chambers, 127–29; Hexter, 78–79.
47. See Adams, *Valor*, 127–28; Chambers, 256–67. Hexter (45–50) criticizes this "medievalist" view.
48. Adams, *Valor*, 127–34; Chambers, 136–37.
49. See Hexter, 58, 103–5; Adams, *Valor*, 157.
50. Hexter, 51–57; Adams, *Valor*, 123; Chambers, 182–83; see Hale, "Public Opinion," 23–24, and "War and Violence," 18–20.
51. Greene and Dolan, 62, 71–72. In his obituary in 1984, Lord Somerset, tenth duke of Beaufort, was reported to have defended hunting as "the only thing that draws this country together—apart from war" (*Time*, Feb. 20, p. 84).
52. Adams, *Valor*, 76–79, 223–34; Chambers, 115–17; Greene and Dolan, 169–96.
53. Chambers, 182–83; 189–90; Adams, *Valor*, 234.
54. Greene and Dolan, 34–41. See also Adams, *Valor*, 125.
55. Greene and Dolan, 34.
56. Adams, *Valor*, 124–25.
57. Greene and Dolan, 38.
58. Ibid., 40–41.
59. Ibid., 76.
60. Ibid., 39.
61. Greene and Dolan, 33.
62. Ibid., 44; Adams, *Valor*, 123–24.
63. Greene and Dolan, 35.
64. Ibid., 44–45; Hexter, 48–49.
65. Greene and Dolan, 36.
66. Ibid., 45–46.
67. Ibid., 36.
68. Ibid., 81.
69. Ibid., 57–60, 71–72; Adams, *Valor*, 145.
70. Greene and Dolan, 81–86. See also Adams, *Valor*, 129–54.
71. Greene and Dolan, 68–69, 74–76, 86–87; Adams, *Valor*, 142.
72. See the text in More, *Dialogue of Comfort*.
73. See Adams, *Valor*, 301–3; More, *Dialogue of Comfort*, cxxi–cxxxi.
74. For what follows see More, *Dialogue of Comfort*, cvi–cvii, cxxi–cxxxiii.
75. Ibid., 317.
76. See the works by Gibert, Woodward, and Vives.
77. Vives, 23–32.
78. Vives, 1; Gibert, 149–51.
79. See Vives, 10–19; Adams, *Valor*, 189–90.
80. Vives, 24–28.
81. Vives, 29–32; Adams, *Valor*, 269–71.
82. See Vives, 32–36
83. For analysis see Adams, *Valor*, 189–94.

84. Ibid., 191.
85. Ibid., 201–2; Gibert, 151–52.
86. *De Europae statu ac tumultibus.* See Adams, *Valor,* 207; Gibert, 152–56.
87. Adams, *Valor,* 249.
88. *De Europae dissidiis et bello Turcico.* See Adams, *Valor,* 262–64; Gibert, 159–60.
89. *De pacificatione.* See Brachin, 254.
90. *De concordia et discordia in humano genere.* See Brachin, 254; Adams, *Valor,* 285–91; Gibert, 161–66.
91. See Adams, *Valor,* 286–88.
92. See Gibert, 165–66.
93. Adams, *Valor,* 286.
94. See Adams (*Valor,* 245–47) for Archbishop Warham's report of widespread opposition to Henry's war taxes.
95. *De subventione pauperum.*
96. See Adams, *Valor,* 250–51.
97. Ibid., 222, 231–33.
98. Ibid., 237–38.
99. Ibid., 297–98.
100. See Vives, 40–46.
101. See Adams, *Valor,* 238–39.
102. Vives, 128–37.
103. Nos. 349–52, Vives, p. 129.
104. Nos. 359–64, Vives, 130.
105. Nos. 382–87, Vives, 133.
106. Nos. 389–95, Vives, 133–34.
107. No. 392, Vives, 134.
108. See Renaudet, 157–61, 368–80.
109. *De bello et pace opusculum.* See Brachin, 255; Bense, 170–75.
110. Bense, 172–73.
111. See L. Delaruelle, *Budé;* Plattard, *Budé;* Renaudet, 284–88, 481–84; Simone, 85–89.
112. *De asse et partibus eius.* See Tracy, 39–42, 47; Simone, 85.
113. *De l'institution du prince.* See Tracy, 60–61.
114. *Oraison de la paix.* See Bense, 181–82.
115. Ceneau restricted this gift of peace to Christians. Turks, who were not heirs, were the legitimate objects of war. See Bense, 182.
116. For his early life see Bainton, *Erasmus,* 1–30, 78–97; Huizinga, 1–19, 62–78; Tracy, 13–14; Philips, *Erasmus,* 91–102.
117. Adams, *Valor,* 27. See also Brachin, 248.
118. Adams, *Valor,* 62–68; McConica, 449–51; Erasmus, *Letter to Anthony of Bergen,* 54.
119. Bainton, *Erasmus,* 110–24; Huizinga, 130–50.
120. Adams, *Valor,* 159–61.
121. Bainton, *Erasmus,* 129–82; Huizinga, 151–60; Dolan, 21–23; McConica, 462–63.
122. Bainton, *Erasmus,* 249–72; Huizinga, 179–87; Dolan, 22–23.
123. Bainton, *Erasmus,* 277–78; C. R. Thompson, *Ten Colloquies,* xxviii.
124. See Tracy's comments (5).
125. Adams, *Valor,* 26; Bainton, *Erasmus,* 14–19.
126. *Enchiridion militis Christiani.* See the text in Dolan, 24–93. See also Adams, *Valor,* 29–30; Bainton, *Erasmus,* 60–71; Philips, *Erasmus,* 46–54.
127. See the text in Dolan, 94–173.
128. For ancient and medieval antecedents, including Brant's *Ship of Fools,* see Dolan, 95–97, 161–66; and the Zeydel edition.
129. Dolan, 115.
130. Ibid., 158–59.
131. Dolan, 159. See also Adams, *Valor,* 50–51.
132. Dolan, 170–73; Adams, *Valor,* 50–51.
133. Dolan, 167.
134. Ibid., 170–73.
135. *Querela pacis.* For the text see Dolan, 174–208.
136. See Dolan, 174–75; Adams, *Valor,,* 164–65.
137. See Erasmus, *Education,* 7; Adams, *Valor,* 164–65; Brachin, 254.

138. See Dolan, 175–76; Adams, *Valor,* 166. For the literary form see Herding.
139. *Summa nostrae religionis pax est et unanimitas.* Dolan, 177.
140. See, for example, C. S. Lewis, *The Discarded Image* (New York: Cambridge University Press, 1967), especially 92–197.
141. Dolan, 178–80.
142. Ibid., 180–84.
143. Ibid., 189.
144. Ibid., 189.
145. Ibid., 190.
146. Ibid., 198–200.
147. Ibid., 203.
148. See Philips, *Adages,* ix–165, 296–300; Brachin, 253.
149. No. 3001; Philips, *Adages,* 298–300, 308–54. See Erasmus, *Education,* 7; Adams, *Valor,* 81–85, 90, 110–11, 322; Brachin, 253.
150. See Adams, 108–9.
151. See Hexter, 69–71.
152. Its traces can still be found in the opening sequences of Stanley Kubrick's film *2001: A Space Odyssey.*
153. Philips, *Adages,* 310–21; Adams, *Valor,* 47–53, 94–104, 254–56.
154. Philips, *Adages,* 323–24.
155. Ibid., 326.
156. Ibid., 321–22.
157. Ibid., 327–29.
158. Philips, *Adages,* 327–28.
159. Ibid., 335–51.
160. Ibid., 349.
161. Ibid., 352.
162. See Brachin, 259–60.
163. See, for example, *Against War,* Philips, *Adages,* 326.
164. See Tracy, 88–99.
165. See Adams, *Valor,* 256. The translation in Philips, *Adages* (335), is not as satisfactory.
166. Erasmus, *Education,* 226.
167. Ibid., 250.
168. See the Pascal edition; McConica provides a full bibliography on pp. 467–71. See also Adams, *Valor,* 36–37, 47–49, 72–73; Bainton, *Erasmus,* 103–9; Tracy, 27–29.
169. Pascal, 45–50.
170. Ibid., 50–55.
171. Ibid., 55–61.
172. Ibid., 61–71; McConica.
173. Pascal, 71–80.
174. Ibid., 80–89.
175. Ibid., 89.
176. Ibid., 90.
177. Thompson, *Ten Colloquies,* xxv–xxvii.
178. *Militaria.* See Thompson, *Colloquies,* 11–15.
179. *Militis et Carthusiani.* See Thompson, *Colloquies,* 127–33; Adams, *Valor,* 215–17.
180. Thompson, *Ten Colloquies,* 92–112.
181. Ibid., 120–29.
182. Ibid., 113–19. See also Adams, *Valor,* 276–82.
183. Thompson, *Colloquies,* 424–32.
184. Ibid., 425–28.
185. Ibid., 429.
186. Ibid., 430–32.
187. Brachin, 261–62.
188. See Tracy, 34–35.
189. Tracy, 17–20, 64; Adams, *Valor,* 30–31.
190. *Scarabeus aquilam quaerit,* in Philips, *Adages,* 229–65.
191. *Aut fatuum aut regem nasci oportere,* in Philips, *Adages,* 213–25.
192. *Spartam nactus es, hanc orna,* in Philips, *Adages,* 300–308.
193. Ibid., 269–300.

194. See Tracy, 35–39.
195. See Halkin, 109–11.
196. In his *On Mending the Peace of the Church,* in Dolan, 327–88.
197. See the edition in Erasmus, *Education,* and introductory comments (1–29). See also Adams, *Valor,* 112–16; Tracy, 51–63; Hardin, 153–62.
198. Brachin, 253–54; Erasmus, *Education,* 27–29.
199. See Adams, "Pre-Renaissance"; Hardin, 158–60.
200. Erasmus, *Education,* 178–79.
201. Mt 20:25–26; Erasmus, *Education,* 168.
202. Erasmus, *Education,* 168.
203. Ibid., 175–79.
204. Erasmus, *Education,* 155; Hardin, 161; Tracy, 65.
205. Erasmus, *Education,* 200; Adams, *Valor,* 29, 114–16, 170, 229–30.
206. Erasmus, *Education,* 143, 151–52, 226. See Tracy, 64.
207. Erasmus, *Education,* 251. See above for this theme in *Against War.*
208. Erasmus, *Education,* 255.
209. Ibid., 257.
210. Ibid., 249.
211. See chapter 8 above, pp. 104–6.
212. Erasmus, *Education,* 249.
213. Ibid., 251.
214. P. Mayer, 55.
215. Philips, *Adages,* 269–96, especially 280; Adams, *Valor,* 93.
216. *Letter,* in P. Mayer, 56.
217. Ibid.
218. Ibid., 59.
219. Philips, *Adages,* 339–40.
220. Ibid., 340–43.
221. Ibid., 344–48. See Adams, *Valor,* 106–7.
222. Ibid., 337.
223. Dolan, 184.
224. Ibid., 188.
225. Ibid., 192.
226. Halkin, 114; Philips, *Erasmus,* 146.
227. Philips, *Adages,* 113–15.
228. Thompson, *Ten Colloquies,* 115.
229. Brachin, 266, quoting Allen, Epist. 858, III, 371.
230. See Brachin, 266.
231. Hardin, 162–63. See also Erasmus, *Education,* 175–79.
232. Philips, *Adages,* 338; Brachin, 266.
233. See Erasmus, *Paul Volz,* 107–33.
234. Ibid., 123.
235. Philips, *Adages,* 338. See Adams, *Valor,* 254–55.
236. Philips (*Adages,* 114–15), rephrases this as Erasmus' "consciousness that to be categorical is to be unrealistic."
237. Ibid.
238. P. Mayer, 58. See Brachin, 268.
239. *Bulla absolutionis concilii Laterani cum decreto expeditionis in Turcas.* See Cytowska, 313.
240. Brachin, 268.
241. Adams, *Valor,* 171.
242. Erasmus, *Paul Volz,* 113.
243. Ibid., 114–15. See Adams, *Valor,* 174–75.
244. Erasmus, *Education,* 256.
245. Dolan, 196.
246. Philips, *Adages,* 344–46.
247. Ibid., 348.
248. Ibid., 347, quoting Eph 6:14–17.
249. Philips, *Adages,* 348. Adams, *Valor,* 108, 208–9.
250. Adams, *Valor,* 217.

251. *Ultissima consultatio de bello Turcis inferendo,* the 1530 edition reprinted in 1643, reissued by Karavis (Athens, 1974). See also the *Opera Omnia,* ed. J. Clericus, 10 vols. (Leyden, 1703–6 [LB]), 5:345–68.

252. See Adams, *Valor,* 298–99; Bense, 181; Cytowska, 313–21; Brachin, 266–68.

253. See Rummel, 16; Bense, 176–84; Adams, *Valor,* 271.

254. Erasmus, *Consultatio,* 86–87.

255. Ibid., 18–31.

256. Ibid., 75–76.

257. Ibid. 34–38, 60–65, 80–81.

258. Ibid., 34; Brachin, 266.

259. Erasmus, *Consultatio,* 88.

260. Ibid., 39.

261. Ibid., 1–16, 31–32, 80–81.

262. Ibid., 19, 49–54. See Brachin, 268; Cytowska, 319–20.

263. Erasmus, *Consultatio,* 49–50. See also Brachin, 268.

264. A point that he had already made in his *Handbook.* See Dolan, 73–74.

265. Erasmus, *Consultatio,* 69–74, 81–82.

266. Ibid., 78–80.

## 10. MISSIONARY PEACEMAKING

1. See Parry, *Hegemony,* 26–53; Hale, *Renaissance Exploration;* and Samuel Eliot Morison, *The European Discovery of America: The Southern Voyages,* A.D. *1492–1616* (New York: Oxford University Press, 1974).

2. Muldoon, "Papal Responsibility," 177–81.

3. Neill, 141.

4. Muldoon, "Papal Responsibility," 116, 182–84; Neill, 141–42. For the texts see Davenport, 1:56–78.

5. For summary accounts of the history of Catholic missions in the Third World see Neill; and Latourette, *Three Centuries.*

6. Latourette, 3:240–46; Neill, 140–41.

7. Latourette, 3:160–67; Neill, 168–69.

8. Latourette, 3:247–76, 285–92; Neill, 142–53.

9. Latourette, 3:300–306; Neill, 153–54.

10. Latourette, 3:307–21.

11. Latourette, 3:322–35; Neill, 153–62; and C. R. Boxer, *The Christian Century in Japan 1549–1650* (Berkeley and Los Angeles: University of California Press, 1969).

12. Latourette, 3:336–66; Neill, 162–67.

13. See Attwater, 141–42; Latourette, 3:252–55; Neill, 148–56.

14. Latourette, 3:259–61; Neill, 183–87.

15. Attwater, 198.

16. See chapter 4 above, pp. 57, 60–61.

17. See chapter 7 above, pp. 88–92.

18. For a basic account see Kennedy.

19. See Kennedy, 98–105, 109–32.

20. Ibid., 82–90.

21. Neill, 200–201.

22. See Neill, 201.

23. Attwater, 197–98.

24. Ibid., 51.

25. Ibid., 180.

26. Ibid., 296.

27. Ibid., 144.

28. Ibid., 84.

29. See Hanke, "Heat and Light," 293.

30. See chapter 5 above, pp. 62–63; Dussel, *History of the Church,* 37–38, 44–45.

31. See Simpson, xiii; Parry, "Spaniards in the New World," 1:430–44; "The New World," 2:564–65; Gibson, 48–67; Friede and Keen, 618; Hanke, *Spanish Struggle for Justice,* 19–20, 86–91.

32. Parry, "The New World," 2:582–83; Simpson, 159–71; Dussel, *History of the Church,* 41–42.
33. See Dussel, *History of the Church,* 35–43; Picón-Salas, 7–69.
34. Dussel, *History of the Church,* 38–39; Neill, 142, 178–82; Gibson, 76–78.
35. The story has been told many times. See Dussel, *History of the Church,* 44–47; Hanke, *Spanish Struggle for Justice,* 17–18, Neill, 170–71; Gibson, 75–77.
36. Quoted from Neill, 170–71.
37. Hanke, *Spanish Struggle for Justice,* 17.
38. Ibid., 8–10.
39. See Simpson, 16–28.
40. Hanke, *Spanish Struggle for Justice,* 23–30; Simpson, 29–38.
41. See Dussel, *History of the Church,* 44; Appendix II, 314.
42. For the best account see Bataillon.
43. *On Eating Fish.* See Adams, *Valor,* 253.
44. Gibert, 155.
45. See Bataillon, 1–75; Gibson, 69–71; Phelan, 43–44; Picón-Salas, 21–22; 46–51.
46. See Picón-Salas, 45–46.
47. Hanke, *Spanish Struggle for Justice,* 27–29.
48. See Simpson, 2–6.
49. Latourette, 3:136–41; Hanke, *Spanish Struggle for Justice,* 58–59.
50. M. G. Fernandez, 74–75.
51. See the works by Hanke cited, especially the bibliographies in *Spanish Struggle for Justice* (197–99) and *All Mankind,* 176–95; Friede and Keen, 3–63, 487–600; Latourette, 3:93–98.
52. For a good biographical sketch see M. G. Fernandez.
53. M. G. Fernandez, 70–74.
54. Ibid., 74–75.
55. See Cespedes, 81–99; Hanke, *Spanish Struggle for Justice,* 65.
56. M. G. Fernandez, 75–77; Picón-Salas, 21–22; Hanke, *Spanish Struggle for Justice,* 42–45; Simpson, 39–55.
57. Hanke, *Spanish Struggle for Justice,* 56–58.
58. For background see Parry, *Hegemony,* 149–50; Hanke, *All Peoples,* 13.
59. Hanke, *Spanish Struggle for Justice,* 45–47, 63.
60. Ibid., 42.
61. Ibid., 59–60.
62. Ibid., 59–60.
63. Hanke, *Spanish Struggle for Justice,* 61, 66–67; M. G. Fernandez, 77–82.
64. M. G. Fernandez, 82–87.
65. See Hanke, "Heat and Light," for his comments on Las Casas' ideological consistency.
66. Hanke, *Spanish Struggle for Justice,* 7.
67. Ibid., 72; M. G. Fernandez, 89.
68. Hanke, *Spanish Struggle for Justice,* 72–73. See also M. G. Fernandez, 88.
69. Hanke, *Spanish Struggle for Justice,* 77–81; and Biermann.
70. Gibson, 92–100; Parry, "The New World," 2:571–72.
71. See the Buffault edition.
72. Hanke, *Spanish Struggle for Justice,* 115–17.
73. Neill, 172–73; M. G. Fernandez, 92–103; Dussel, *History of the Church,* 52.
74. From Picón-Salas, 48.
75. See Hanke, *Spanish Struggle for Justice,* 156; M. G. Fernandez, 104–10.
76. Losada, 301.
77. See chapter 2, pp. 16–18.
78. Hanke, *Aristotle,* 14–17; *Spanish Struggle for Justice,* 113–14.
79. See Hanke, *All Mankind,* especially 73–112, and *Aristotle;* see also Losada for details.
80. See Hanke, *Aristotle,* 14–17.
81. See Hanke, *Spanish Struggle for Justice,* 11–13, 113–17; Losada.
82. Hanke, *Spanish Struggle for Justice,* 117.
83. Ibid., 129–30; M. G. Fernandez, 110–12.
84. Hanke, *Aristotle,* 86; M. G. Fernandez, 112–16.
85. See Keen; Hanke, "Heat and Light," 302.
86. Dussel, *History of the Church,* 315.
87. Hanke, *All Peoples,* 16.

88. See Simpson, 123–58; Gibson, 58–61.
89. See Simpson, 129–32; Hanke, *Spanish Struggle for Justice,* 83, 91–105; Latourette, 3:98–99; Parry, "The New World," 2:578–80; Neill, 172.
90. Hanke, *Spanish Struggle for Justice,* 102; Simpson, 132–40.
91. Simpson, 140.
92. Ibid., 145–58.
93. For a complete list see Dussel, *History of the Church,* 51.
94. For the following account of these bishops see Dussel, *History of the Church,* 52–55.
95. Latourette, 3:132.
96. Picón-Salas, 69.
97. Ibid., 15–16.
98. Ibid., 20–21; Hanke, *Spanish Struggle for Justice,* 31–36; Gibson, 38–40; and Verlinden.
99. Parry, "The New World," 2:588; Hanke, *Aristotle,* 86–88; *Spanish Struggle for Justice,* 130–46.
100. Dussel, *History of the Church,* 57.
101. Latourette, 3:317–21.
102. Hanke, *Spanish Struggle for Justice,* 156–58.
103. See Latourette, 3:318; Hanke, *Spanish Struggle for Justice,* 158–61.
104. See Ricard, 128–32.
105. Parry, "The New World," 2:565; Gibson, 68–73.
106. See Phelan, 46–47; and chapter 9, pp. 116–18, 123–27.
107. Simpson, 133–40.
108. Picón-Salas, 59; Parry, "The New World," 2:566.
109. Gibson, 71–72.
110. Ricard, 132.
111. See Dussel, *History of the Church,* 49; Latourette, 3:109; Simpson, 56–83, 159–71.
112. Picón-Salas, 19–20.
113. Dussel, *History of the Church,* 49; Latourette, 3:110, 120–21.
114. Dussel, *History of the Church,* 49.
115. Picón-Salas, 59.
116. Ibid., 62.
117. Dussel, *History of the Church,* 62–68.
118. Ricard, 83–108, 207–35.
119. Ibid., 155–61.
120. Picón-Salas, 57.
121. See his letter to Charles V of Jan. 2, 1555, in Simpson, 234–43; and Hanke, *Aristotle,* 21–22.
122. Phelan, 45–46.
123. Picón-Salas, 58–59.
124. See Latourette, 3:116–17; Gibson, 73–74; Neill, 174; Picón-Salas, 47–49.
125. For his support of a reformed *encomienda* see Simpson, 205–13.
126. Hanke, *Aristotle,* 19.
127. Parry, "The New World," 2:565.
128. Picón-Salas, 47–49.
129. Parry, "The New World," 2:570.
130. For the text of the letter see Simpson, 214–29.
131. Picón-Salas, 60–62; Phelan, 44; Gibson, 74.
132. He seems to have made marginal notes in a copy of the Froben, 1518 edition.
133. See Phelan, 26–81.
134. Ibid., 82–86.
135. Ibid., 56–58, 63–65.
136. Ibid., 58–59.
137. Ibid., 89–93.
138. Ibid., 96–97.
139. Ibid., 94.
140. Ibid., 62–63.
141. Ibid., 94.
142. Ibid., 50.
143. Picón-Salas, 119–20.
144. See Latourette, 3:121–28.

145. Attwater, 220; Delaney, 76–77; Butler, 4:72–74; BS 8:342–48.
146. Picón-Salas, 119.
147. Ibid., 121–22.
148. Picón-Salas, 119–20; Attwater, 140–41; Delaney, 459–60; BS 5:1241–44.
149. Latourette, 3:144–45; Picón-Salas, 119–20; Attwater, 278–79; Delaney, 121; Butler, 3:519–24; BS 10:818–21.
150. For brief accounts see Latourette, 3:110–11, 122–25, 143–44.
151. Caraman, 32–35.
152. See Picón-Salas, 131–33.
153. See Charles E. Ronan, *Francisco Javier Clavigero, S.J. (1731–1787)* (Rome: Jesuit Historical Institute, Chicago: Loyola University Press, 1977).
154. See Allan F. Deck, *Francisco Javier Alegre: A Study in Mexican Literary Criticism* (Rome: Jesuit Historical Institute, Tucson, Ariz.: Kino House, 1977).
155. See Picón-Salas, 137–41.
156. See above, p. 148.
157. Picón-Salas, 141.
158. Ibid., 139–40.
159. Dussel, *History of the Church,* 43.
160. Latourette, 3:112; Dussel, *History of the Church,* 62–64.
161. See, for example, Dussel, *History of the Church,* 58–61, 69–71.
162. Phelan, 83–84.
163. Neill, 175.
164. Picón-Salas, 77–84; Gibson, 78–81.
165. Neill, 175.
166. Picón-Salas, 72–74, 93–95.
167. A good account is in Caraman, *Lost Paradise.*
168. Caraman, 51–68.
169. Ibid., 69–81; Neill, 202–3.
170. Dussel, *History of the Church,* 60; Latourette, 3:156.

## 11. THE EBB TIDE OF CATHOLIC PEACEMAKING

1. See chapters 4–9.
2. See the comments of Lammers in Shannon, *War or Peace?* (93–95).
3. See Dunn, 128–73; Krieger, 1–13.
4. See chapter 9 above, pp. 110–35.
5. See Rice, 155–71; Dunn, 76–78.
6. Cragg, 12–18; Heyer, 14–34.
7. See Cragg, 219–33; Heyer, 32–34.
8. Cragg, 193–99; Heyer, 18–23.
9. Cragg, 18–24; Callahan and Higgs, 10, 48; Krieger, 284–90.
10. See Bokenkotter, 248–58; O. Chadwick, 255–64; O'Connell, 83–118; Rice, 142–46.
11. Bokenkotter, 251; Rice, 142–46.
12. Bokenkotter, 255; Steinberg, 261–62.
13. Bokenkotter, 251, 258.
14. Ibid., 264, 267–71.
15. See chapter 9 above, pp. 132–35.
16. See Bainton, *Christian Attitudes,* 152–72; Brock, *Pacifism in Europe.*
17. See chapters 6 and 7 above, pp. 81–86, 88–92.
18. See chapter 9 above, pp. 133–34.
19. O'Connell, 84–118; Bokenkotter, 248–55.
20. Cragg, 9–11.
21. Bokenkotter, 283–85; Cragg, 209–14.
22. See Callahan, "Spanish Church," 50; Rosa, 75; Bokenkotter, 298–305.
23. Bokenkotter, 314–26.
24. Bokenkotter, 327–39; Heyer, 183–94.
25. Cragg, 199–204; Callahan, and Higgs, 3–4; Hufton.
26. Rosa, 75–76.
27. Callahan, "Spanish Church," 38–41.
28. Higgs, 51–55.

29. Cragg, p. 206; Callahan, "Spanish Church," 3–4; Hufton, 22–24.
30. The phrase is that of Erasmus. See Erasmus, *Handbook of the Militant Christian*, 92.
31. Cragg, 204–5, 223–24.
32. See the comments of Higgs, 58–60; and Venard.
33. Callahan, "Spanish Church," 7.
34. Higgs, 62; Rosa, 73; Berenger, 101–3.
35. Callahan, "Spanish Church," 8; Heyer, 47–61.
36. See Cragg, 25–34; Bokenkotter, 276–79; Heyer, 70–82.
37. Hufton, 25–28; Callahan, "Spanish Church," 41–47; Higgs, 51–55, 61.
38. For examples of popular superstition, skepticism, and indifference see Ladurie, 288–356.
39. Hufton, 31.
40. See Attwater, 201–2; Butler, 3:280–87; BS 6:1040–45.
41. Steinberg, 307–8.; Bokenkotter, 436.
42. See Bataillon.
43. Simone, 97–136.
44. Brachin, 254.
45. See Rabelais, 22; Simone, 129–36; and Costa's interpretation of the work as a peaceful apocalyptic (107–38).
46. See Bainton, *Attitudes,* 129.
47. Cohen, 26–30.
48. Ibid., 28–30.
49. Chapters 25–51, in Rabelais, 94–148. See Stapfer, 367–69; and Costa, 115–19.
50. Chapter 25, in Rabelais, 94–95.
51. Chapter 33, in Rabelais, 109–13.
52. Chapter 32, in Rabelais, 107–9.
53. Chapters 28–29, in Rabelais, 101–3; Stapfer, 373.
54. Rabelais, 105.
55. Chapters 43–51, in Rabelais, 131–49; Stapfer, 374–75.
56. Chapter 46, in Rabelais, 138. See Stapfer, 371.
57. Chapters 23–34, in Rabelais, 245–80. See Costa, 128–29.
58. Chapter 1, in Rabelais, 290.
59. Rabelais, 292; Stapfer, 376–77.
60. Chapter 8, in Rabelais, 307–10.
61. Chapter 7, in Rabelais, 307.
62. Dunn, 211.
63. See Lange, *Internationalisme,* 1:213–14.
64. Montaigne, vii–xi.
65. See *Essays* II:19, "On Freedom of Conscience," in Montaigne, 506.
66. Montaigne, xi–xii.
67. I:5–6, in Montaigne, 16–19.
68. I:45, in Montaigne, 200; I:48, 209–15; II:9, 293–96; II:16, 475; II:34, 556–63. For a summation of his views see Armaingaud.
69. II:12, in Montaigne, 318–457.
70. Montaigne, 335.
71. Ibid., 348–49.
72. Ibid., 323.
73. Ibid., 325.
74. Ibid., 347–48.
75. Ibid., 323.
76. Ibid., 350.
77. See Erasmus, *Education,* 143, 151–52, 226, and chapter 9, pp. 129–30.
78. Montaigne, 468–71.
79. Numbers 291–94, 300–301, in Montaigne, 83–86. See Souleyman, 56–58.
80. See his reference to *The Soldier and the Carthusian* in No. 538, Pascal, 144–45. See C. R. Thompson, *Colloquies,* 128.
81. No. 291, in Pascal, 300.
82. Greene and Dolan, 81.
83. No. 294, in Pascal, 83–85.
84. See Cragg, 30, 33; Souleyman, 42–47; Eppstein, 266.
85. Eppstein, 266.

86. See Souleyman, 42–47.
87. See chapter 10, pp. 140–44.
88. See Souleyman, 159–61.
89. See chapter 8, pp. 97–104.
90. See chapter 9 above.
91. See chapter 7 above, pp. 93–94.
92. See Reeves, *Influence*, 306–92; *Prophetic Future*, 59–82.
93. Reeves, *Influence*, 395–428 and *Prophetic Future*, 59–82.
94. Reeves, *Influence*, 463–72, and *Prophetic Future*, 116–35.
95. *Glossa super Apocalypsim de statu ecclesie ab anno . . . MCCCCLXXXI usque ad finem mundi.* See Reeves, *Influence*, 463–64, and *Prophetic Future*, 124–25.
96. Printed in Piacenza in both Latin and Italian in 1569/70.
97. Reeves, *Influence*, 469–70; and *Prophetic Future*, 126.
98. See chapter 7, pp. 89–92.
99. Chapter 7, pp. 91–92.
100. Gibert, 138–44. See chapter 7 above, pp. 92.
101. *De monarchia.* See Dante Alighieri (Schneider edition) cited in the bibliography.
102. Dante Alighieri, ix.
103. Book I, in Dante, 3–23. See also Hembelen, 4–12, and Costa (40–83) for his interpretation of the *Purgatorio,* especially Cantos XXVII ff., as a peaceful apocalyptic.
104. Chapters 12–14, in Dante, 16–20.
105. In Book III, in Dante, 52–80.
106. See Gewirth's edition cited in the bibliography and his introduction, xix–xci.
107. See Dubois (Brandt edition) cited in bibliography. See also Hemleben, 1–3; Lange, *Internationalisme,* 1:90–107; Atiya, 47–73; Souleyman, 2–8; Vesnitch, 25–50.
108. Dubois, 3–10; Souleyman, 2–3.
109. Dubois, 6–8, 37; Souleyman, 3.
110. See Dubois, 62–63.
111. Hemleben, 1–3; Souleyman, 4.
112. Dubois, 43–47.
113. Ibid., 50–59; 115–42.
114. Chapter 3(IV), in Dubois, 74. See Souleyman, 5–6.
115. Chapters III, in Dubois, 71; 27 (XIV), 89, citing *Nicodemian Ethics* x, 7, 1177b, 8–10. See also Souleyman, 7.
116. Chapter III, in Dubois, 72.
117. Chapter 27, in Dubois, 88.
118. Ibid., 89.
119. Chapter 28, in Dubois, 89.
120. See Souleyman, 5–8; Hemleben, 8.
121. Chapters II–III, in Dubois, 69–71.
122. Chapters 12–13, in Dubois, 78–80; Souleyman, 7–8; Hemleben, 3.
123. Chapters 3 (IV)–7, in Dubois, 74–77.
124. Chapter 7, in Dubois, 77–78.
125. Chapter 29, in Dubois, 90–92.
126. Chapter 109 (LXVIII), in Dubois, 161–63.
127. Bainton, *Attitudes,* 178; Lammers, 94–95.
128. See articles by Benson and Muldoon cited in the bibliography.
129. See Truyol y Serra, 242–43.
130. Including J. T. Johnson, 150–71, especially 154–60; Hamilton, 111–13, 136–54; Hehir, "Just-War Ethic," 17; Eppstein, 65–123.
131. See Aguilar, 186–201; Brière; Grisel; Hamilton, 176–84; Muldoon, "Contribution"; Eppstein, 262–66; Scott; Truyol y Serra, 251–54.
132. See Scott; Aguilar; Grisel; McKenna; Lange, *Internationalisme,* 1:269–79; Eppstein, 261–62; Hamilton, 171–76; and Truyol y Serra.
133. See chapter 10, pp. 139–40.
134. See Hamilton, 171–74; and chapter 10, pp. 143–44.
135. Hamilton, 175; Muldoon, *Popes,* 147–50.
136. See chapter 10, pp. 140–41.
137. Hamilton, 176–80; Truyol y Serra, 251–52.
138. Hamilton, 175; see also chapter 10 above.

139. Hamilton, 110, 175–76; see also chapter 10 above.
140. *Theological Lectures.* See Vitoria (Nys edition) cited in the bibliography. See also Grisel, 307; McKenna, 727.
141. Hamilton, 120–22.
142. Hamilton, 122–24, 127–30; Hanke, *Spanish Struggle for Justice,* 150–52; Truyol y Serra, 268–69.
143. *De Indis* I, qu.11, prop.vi. See Hamilton, 124–26; Grisel, 318–19, Truyol y Serra, 269.
144. Grisel, 312–16.
145. Hamilton, 132–34.
146. See Truyol y Serra, 259; Aguilar, 209–11.
147. Truyol y Serra, 257–60; Aguilar, 197–98.
148. Truyol y Serra, 258.
149. Aguilar, 206, 219; Truyol y Serra, 161–63.
150. Aguilar, 208–9.
151. Truyol y Serra, 266–67.
152. Aguilar, 209–14; Grisel, 319.
153. Aguilar, 209–12.
154. Chapter 8, pp. 104–9.
155. *De iure belli,* qu.iv, prop.iii–iv, in Vitoria, 174; quoted from Hamilton, 148.
156. Ibid., qu.iv, prop.i, in Vitoria, 173; quoted from Hamilton, 150.
157. *Apology of Peace.* For what follows see Lange, *Internationalisme,* 1:328–36.
158. Hemleben, 21–29; Lange, *Internationalisme,* 1:398–433, and *Doctrine,* 232–41; Bainton, *Attitudes,* 180; Souleyman, 9–19.
159. See Crucé, *Nouveau Cynée* (Balch translation), cited in the bibliography; and "A Holy Resolve."
160. Hemleben, 21–22; Souleyman, 9–10, 14.
161. See Lange, *Internationalisme,* 1:407–8.
162. See Hemleben, 23–24.
163. Souleyman, 14–15.
164. Ibid., 11–12.
165. See above, p. 164.
166. P. Mayer, 68. See also above, p. 159.
167. Souleyman, 17.
168. P. Mayer, 68.
169. Ibid.
170. Hemleben, 29.
171. Souleyman, 18–19; Hemleben, 25.
172. Souleyman, 15; Hemleben, 25–26.
173. Hemleben, 26–28.
174. Ibid., 23.
175. *Projet de paix perpetuelle.* See Saint-Pierre (edition of M. C. Jacob) cited in the bibliography.
176. Lange, *Internationalisme,* 2:196–213, and *Doctrine,* 303–10; Hemleben, 56–64; Constantinescu-Bagdat, 2:108–70; Hayden, 942; Souleyman, 78–90.
177. Hayden, 942.
178. Lange, *Doctrine,* 303–10.
179. Hayden, 942.
180. See Hemleben, 57. For background see Krieger, 14–42.
181. Hemleben, 56–57. The 1738 edition, with supplements, appears in Saint-Pierre, 1–61.
182. Saint-Pierre, 18–20; Souleyman, 78.
183. Saint-Pierre, 24–26; Souleyman, 79–80.
184. For the text see Saint-Pierre, 21–31. For a summation see Souleyman, 81–90; Hemleben, 61–64.
185. Saint-Pierre, 27.
186. Ibid., 32, 34–36, 54.
187. Hemleben, 14–15.
188. See Brière, *L'Organization international,* 2:2–4.
189. See the introduction to Brière, "Conceptions," 4.
190. Constantinescu-Bagdat, 2:24–38.

## 12. THE LESSONS OF THE TWENTIETH CENTURY

1. See Sweeney, 15.
2. See Rhodes, *Power of Rome,* 15–66.
3. See chapter 11 above.
4. See Bokenkotter, 355.
5. See Borgese, 415.
6. See chapter 8, pp. 97–104; chapter 10, pp. 136–37, 141–42.
7. Beales, *History,* 132, 187; Fernessole, 51–65.
8. See Bokenkotter, 356–57; Rhodes, *Power of Rome,* 67–178.
9. Bokenkotter, 341.
10. See Vidler, 125–29, 143–47.
11. See Koenig, 1–109. See also Fernessole, 65–91.
12. Koenig, 52–81.
13. Acts 5:29. See *Sapientiae Christianae,* in Koenig, 49–51.
14. *Nostis Errorem,* in Koenig, 47–49; Flannery, *Pattern for Peace,* 1; J. J. Wright, 41.
15. Dec. 23, 1893; Koenig, 85–87.
16. Flannery, *Pattern for Peace,* 3. See also *Diuturnum,* in Koenig, 12–15; *Pervenuti* of March 19, 1902, in Flannery, *Pattern for Peace,* 5; Beales, *History,* 187.
17. See chapter 11; and Cardinal Rampolla's diplomatic notes, in Flannery, *Pattern for Peace,* 2–4.
18. As in Budapest in 1896 and Madrid in 1889. See Beales, *History,* 187; Koenig, 91.
19. Beales, *History,* 187; Koenig, 31–32.
20. Beales, *History,* 187.
21. Koenig, 17–18, 45–46.
22. See Rhodes, *Power of Rome,* 217–22; Fernessole, 91–111.
23. See the letter (Nov. 3, 1906) to the Fifteenth World Peace Conference held in Milan, in Koenig, 120–21; and the telegram to Archbishop Mora y del Rio of Mexico City (May 9, 1914), in Koenig, 123.
24. *Libenter abs te,* Jan. 11, 1911; Koenig, 122–23.
25. *Amplissimum Coetum,* March 27, 1905; Koenig, 112–13.
26. For Benedict's reign see Rhodes, *Power of Rome,* 223–48; Fernessole, 112–89.
27. See chapter 8, pp. 101–2.
28. See Bokenkotter, 398–99.
29. J. Derek Holmes, 13.
30. J. Derek Holmes, 7; Bokenkotter, 399.
31. *Pacem Dei Munus Pulcherrimum,* May 23, 1920; Flannery, *Pattern for Peace,* 17.
32. Koenig, 131; J. Derek Holmes, 3. See chapter 9, pp. 124–25.
33. Koenig, 132–38.
34. J. Derek Holmes, 6–7, 10; Beales, *History,* 301.
35. J. Derek Holmes, 3, 8.
36. Chapter 8, pp. 101–3.
37. See Koenig, 140–260; J. Derek Holmes, 7.
38. Bokenkotter, 400.
39. J. Derek Holmes, 3.
40. *Allorchè fummo* (July 28, 1915), in Flannery, *Pattern for Peace,* 9.
41. Flannery, *Pattern for Peace,* 9.
42. *Fuldae,* in Flannery, *Pattern for Peace,* 10.
43. See especially *Pacem Dei Munus Pulcherrimum,* in Koenig, 284–92; Flannery, *Pattern for Peace,* 17. See also Koenig, 261–317; Flannery, *Pattern for Peace,* 12–16.
44. J. Derek Holmes, 14–18.
45. Ibid., 19.
46. Ibid., 12.
47. *Des les Début* (Aug. 1, 1917) in Flannery, *Pattern for Peace,* 11. For details see Rhodes, *Power of Rome,* 239–48.
48. Flannery, *Pattern for Peace,* 11–12.
49. See, for example, Rhodes, *Vatican;* J. Derek Holmes, 33–168; and Delzell, including bibliography, 173–79; and Fernessole, 190–260.

50. Bokenkotter, 354.
51. *Con Vivo Piacere* (April 7, 1922) in Flannery, *Pattern for Peace*, 21.
52. Flannery, *Pattern for Peace*, 29.
53. *Nostis Qua Praecipue* (Dec. 18, 1924) in Flannery, *Pattern for Peace*, 33.
54. Dec. 23, 1922, in Koenig, 332–55; Flannery, *Pattern for Peace*, 22–28.
55. Flannery, *Pattern for Peace*, 28.
56. Gonella, 193.
57. Flannery, *Pattern for Peace*, 23.
58. Ibid., 25–27.
59. Ibid., 27. See also J. J. Wright, 42.
60. As in *Benedetto il Natale* (Dec. 24, 1930), Flannery, *Pattern for Peace*, 34–35; *Quadragesimo Anno* (May 15, 1931), Koenig, 397–446; Bokenkotter, 354; and *Divini Redemptoris* (March 17, 1937); J. J. Wright, 41.
61. "War and the Crisis of Language," in Zahn, *Nonviolent Alternative*, 234–47.
62. As with Sturzo's Popular Party or the reactionary Action Française. *Civiltà Cattolica* and *Osservatore Romano*, though critical of Fascist violence, showed even more concern with leftists. See Rhodes, *Vatican*, 103–11; J. Derek Holmes, 33–75, 83–91.
63. From that year on, in fact, it is "difficult to find an episcopal sermon or pastoral letter . . . that did not contain favorable references to the Duce." See J. Derek Holmes, 59.
64. As in open condemnations of the Fascist state for its attempts to coopt the activities of Catholic Action and to "educate for conquest", for its neopagan values and its persecution of individual clergy. See *Non Abbiamo Bisogno* (June 29, 1931), in Koenig, 446–48; J. Derek Holmes, 58–68.
65. See J. Derek Holmes, 68–70; Rhodes, *Vatican*, 69–77.
66. Helmreich, 103–13.
67. Ibid., 113–17; Lewy, 57–93.
68. See Helmreich, 240–56; J. Derek Holmes, 100–117; Rhodes, *Vatican*, 173–83.
69. See Helmreich, 257–73; Rhodes, *Vatican*, 185–93; Lewy, 258–67. See below, pp. 179–80.
70. Helmreich, 277–80; Lewy, 309–21.
71. Helmreich, 262–63, 269; Lewy, 313–16.
72. Rom 12:9–21. See chapter 2 above, pp. 26–27.
73. Flannery, *Pattern for Peace*, 38–45; Koenig, 498–510. See Rhodes, *Vatican*, 195–217; J. Derek Holmes, 111–13.
74. Flannery, *Pattern for Peace*, 44.
75. Helmreich, 280–83; J. Derek Holmes, 111.
76. Flannery, *Pattern for Peace*, 45–70; Koenig, 510–35.
77. Koenig, 539–40.
78. Koenig, 546–47.
79. Bokenkotter, 404.
80. J. Derek Holmes, 119–24; Rhodes, *Vatican*, 219–33; Bokenkotter, 405–410; Halecki, 26–93.
81. See Conway, "Silence," 79–108; and Ellsberg, 108–24.
82. Studies include Friedlander; Lewy, 242–51; Halecki; Helmreich; Delzell; Falconi; Graml; Littell and Locke; Rhodes, *Vatican*, 219–352.
83. See H. E. Cardinale, "The Contribution of the Holy See to World Peace in the Areas of Diplomacy, Development and Ecumenism,'" in Sweeney, 88–92; J. Derek Holmes, 152–68; Lewy, 268–308; Rhodes, *Vatican*, 337–52.
84. See his *Allocution to the College of Cardinals* (June 2, 1945) in Flannery, *Pattern for Peace*, 131–37; and *Vous Etes Venus* (Sept. 30, 1939), in Koenig, 589–91; Graham, "Vatican Peace Initiatives"; J. Derek Holmes, 127–40.
85. Koenig, 585; Flannery, *Pattern for Peace*, 76; J. Derek Holmes, 122.
86. See *C'est une Vive Satisfaction* (September 14), in Flannery, *Pattern for Peace*, 76–77.
87. See Flannery, *Pattern for Peace*, 77–98; Koenig, 592–615; J. Derek Holmes, 123–24; J.J. Wright, 42.
88. Flannery, *Pattern for Peace*, 80–81.
89. Ibid., 77–80, 93–94.
90. *D'une Nation Lointaine* (Nov. 10, 1939), in Flannery, *Pattern for Peace*, 98; *In Questo Giorno di Santà* (Dec. 24, 1939), in Flannery, *Pattern for Peace*, 100–101.
91. *Grazie Venerabili Fratelli* (Dec. 24, 1940), in Flannery, *Pattern for Peace*, 102–3.

92. See Christmas Address of 1939, J. Derek Holmes, 125.
93. Flannery, *Pattern for Peace*, 104–8; Koenig, 750–62; Gonella, 189.
94. Flannery, *Pattern for Peace*, 107.
95. See *Message to Cardinals* (Dec. 24, 1945), Flannery, *Pattern for Peace*, 141–45.
96. Flannery, *Pattern for Peace*, 119.
97. Ibid., 125.
98. Beales, *History*, 188; Bainton, *Attitudes*, 193.
99. Beales, *History*, 76, 133, 178–79.
100. Bokenkotter, 347–53; Vidler, *Social Catholicism;* D. J. Geaney, "Catholic Action," in NCE 3:262–63.
101. See above, pp. 170–77.
102. See above, p. 170.
103. Chickering, 304.
104. Chickering, 300, 310–11.
105. See Cooper.
106. Beales, *History*, 301–2.
107. J. Derek Holmes, 20.
108. Helmreich, 47–48.
109. Helmreich, 59–60, 102–3.
110. Rhodes, *Power of Rome*, 77–97; Helmreich, 54–55.
111. See above, pp. 174–75.
112. See Zahn, "Catholic Resistance?" 205–10; Wolf, 224.
113. Zahn, *German Catholics*, 179–80, 189–204; "Case," 255.
114. Chickering, 301–4; Conway, "Silence," 25–26.
115. Zahn, *German Catholics*, 3–8; "Case," 251–52.
116. Zahn, *German Catholics*, 102–3.
117. Ibid.
118. Zahn, *German Catholics*, 124, and "Case," 251.
119. Zahn, *German Catholics*, 124.
120. Zahn, "Case," 251–52.
121. Zahn, *German Catholics*, 54.
122. This incredible progression is clearly traced in Zahn, *German Catholics*, 60–82, 101–4.
123. See Zahn, "Catholic Resistance?" 203–5; Helmreich, 445.
124. Helmreich, 348, 467; J. Derek Holmes, 140; Zahn, "Catholic Resistance?" 205.
125. See von Oppen, 30–31; Lewy, 313–16.
126. Zahn, "Catholic Resistance?" 206–7; Helmreich, 286, 352–58, 365–67. See Pius XII's *Allocution to the College of Cardinals* (June 2, 1945), in Flannery, *Pattern for Peace*, 131–37.
127. Helmreich, 268.
128. See his *German Catholics*, and "Catholic Resistance?" 232–34.
129. Helmreich, 116–17.
130. Helmreich, 237; J. Derek Holmes, 102; Lewy, 3–56.
131. Helmreich, 237–40.
132. Ibid., 263.
133. Zahn, "Catholic Resistance?" 213. See also Lewy, 94–100.
134. Helmreich, 287.
135. Helmreich, 276; Zahn, "Catholic Resistance?" 214; Wolf, 203, 209; J. Derek Holmes, 107–9; Lewy, 100–159.
136. Helmreich, 294–95. See chapter 5, pp. 60–61.
137. Zahn, "Catholic Resistance?" 213.
138. Zahn, *German Catholics*, 35–39 and "Catholic Resistance?" 216–19.
139. See the careful analysis of this dynamic in Zahn, *German Catholics*, and "Catholic Resistance?" 232–34. See also Lewy, 224–42; Rhodes, *Vatican*, 293–98.
140. Zahn, "German Catholic Press," 211–14.
141. Statement by Cardinal von Galen; see Zahn, *German Catholics*, 86, and "Catholic Resistance?" 211. See also Lewy, 310–11.
142. See Zahn, *German Catholics*, 114, 125–31, 148–49, 152–63, and "Catholic Resistance?" 211–13; Lewy, 205–11.
143. See statement of Cardinal Gröber, in Zahn, "Case," 253–56, and *German Catholics*, 125; Lewy, 235.

144. See chapter 8, above, pp. 104–9; chapter 11, p. 164.
145. Zahn, "Catholic Resistance?" 228. See also "Case," 246–47.
146. See Zahn, "Catholic Resistance?" 234, "German Catholic Press," 208–10, and *German Catholics,* 195–204.
147. Zahn, "Catholic Resistance?" 226–27.
148. See Wolf, 225 and chapter 5, pp. 69–71.
149. J. Derek Holmes, 165–66.
150. J. Derek Holmes, 165; Rhodes, *Vatican,* 318–22.
151. Walker, 56.
152. See J. Derek Holmes, 164; Rhodes, *Vatican,* 315–18.
153. Fahey, "Pax Christi," 59. See chapter 15, pp. 259–60.
154. "Passivity," in Zahn, *Nonviolent Alternative,* 129–33.
155. Zahn, *German Catholics,* 83–100; von Oppen, 28–29; Helmreich, 359–61.
156. Helmreich, 297.
157. Von Oppen, 39–49.
158. Zahn, "Case," 247; Merton, "Martyr," 139–43.
159. Zahn, "Case," 247, *In Solitary Witness,* 4; J. Derek Holmes, 142–43.
160. See, for example, J. Derek Holmes, 142–49.
161. The main sources here are Gordon Zahn's *In Solitary Witness* and "In Praise." See also von Oppen, 49–53; Merton, "An Enemy of the State," 134–38.
162. See chapter 8, pp. 108–9, for the origins of this tradition.
163. Zahn, *In Solitary Witness,* 111–12.
164. Ibid., 41–48.
165. Ibid., 53–59.
166. Ibid., 61.
167. Ibid., 75–76, 151–71.
168. Ibid., 165. For the record of Christian soldiers refusing orders to fight see chapter 3, pp. 42–44.
169. Ibid., 76–90, 130, 132.
170. "Little Thoughts," in Zahn, *In Solitary Witness,* 200, 66. The similarity to medieval Franciscan statements is striking. See chapter 8, pp. 109.
171. "Bolshevism, or National Socialism?" in Zahn, *In Solitary Witness,* 223.
172. Ibid., 224, 101.
173. Zahn, *In Solitary Witness,* 237–38.
174. Merton, "Enemy of the State," 138.
175. For a general analysis see Guerry; and Halecki.
176. Flannery, *Pattern for Peace,* 281.
177. Ibid.
178. Easter Message (April 1, 1956), in Flannery, *Pattern for Peace,* 276–77.
179. See Wright, 42.
180. Flannery, *Pattern for Peace,* 126.
181. See the Christmas Broadcast (Dec. 23, 1956), in Flannery, *Pattern for Peace,* 285; J. Derek Holmes, 181–82; Gonella, 183–86.
182. See chapter 11 above, pp. 159–67.
183. Flannery, *Pattern for Peace,* 244.
184. Christmas Broadcast (Dec. 23, 1956), in Flannery, *Pattern for Peace,* 283. See also Christmas Broadcast (Dec. 22, 1957), in Flannery, 295.
185. Christmas Broadcast (Dec. 23, 1956), in Flannery, 283. See also Hehir, "Just-War Ethic," 17.
186. Flannery, *Pattern for Peace,* 284.
187. Christmas Broadcast (Dec. 24, 1944), in Flannery, *Pattern for Peace,* 126.
188. Christmas Broadcast (Dec. 24, 1954), in Flannery, *Pattern for Peace,* 242–43.
189. Address at St. Peter's Square (April 18, 1954), in Flannery, *Pattern for Peace,* 235.
190. Address to the World Medical Association (Sept. 30, 1954), in Flannery, 236. See also Hehir, "Just-War Ethic," 17; J. Derek Holmes, 183.
191. Flannery, *Pattern for Peace,* 236.
192. Ibid., 237.
193. Easter Message (April 1, 1956), in Flannery, *Pattern for Peace,* 277.
194. Christmas Broadcast (Dec. 24, 1955), in Flannery, *Pattern for Peace,* 272.

### 13. A CATHOLIC THEOLOGY OF PEACE

1. See J. Derek Holmes, 200–218.
2. See *Mater et Magistra*, par. 219, in O'Brien and Shannon, 103. See also Zahn, *Alternative*, 9.
3. *Mater et Magistra*, par. 236, in O'Brien and Shannon, 107.
4. Flannery, *Pattern for Peace*, 299–300.
5. See O'Brien and Shannon, 44–116.
6. Par. 159, in O'Brien and Shannon, 90; Flannery, *Pattern for Peace*, 311.
7. Par. 69, in O'Brien and Shannon, 67; Flannery, *Pattern for Peace*, 308–9; par. 161, in O'Brien and Shannon, 90; Flannery, 312.
8. Par. 69, in O'Brien and Shannon, 67; Flannery, *Pattern for Peace*, 308–9.
9. Pars. 203–4, in O'Brien and Shannon, 99–100; Flannery, *Pattern for Peace*, 320.
10. See chapter 9, pp. 115–16, 119–21, 127–30.
11. Sept. 10, 1961. See Flannery, *Pattern for Peace*, 322–26.
12. See O'Brien and Shannon, 117–70.
13. J. Derek Holmes, 201.
14. O'Brien and Shannon, 118.
15. Ibid., 120.
16. See Ibid., 119.
17. See chapter 9 above, pp. 129–30; chapter 11, pp. 162–64.
18. See, for example, T. M. Finn, "Peace, War"; and "Conditions of Peace," cited in the bibliography.
19. J. Derek Holmes, 203–12; Bokenkotter, 416.
20. See Bokenkotter, 411–24; Schuijt's and Coste's remarks in Vorgrimler, *Commentary*; McNeal, *Peace Movement*, 198–204.
21. For the texts see Abbott and Gallagher, 183–316; O'Brien and Shannon, 171–284.
22. Abbott and Gallagher, 289–308; O'Brien and Shannon, 259–76.
23. Par. 80, in Abbott, 293; in O'Brien and Shannon, 262. See Borgese, 417–18.
24. T. M. Finn, "Peace, War," 270–71; Bokenkotter, 429–30, 437–50.
25. T. M. Finn, "Peace, War," 271.
26. See T. M. Finn.
27. See Schuijt and Coste, 350; P. C. Curran, 37.
28. Schuijt and Coste, 348; T. M. Finn, "Peace, War," 271.
29. See J. J. Wright, 42–43.
30. See T. M. Finn, "Peace, War" 271; Schuijt and Coste, 349.
31. See T. M. Finn, "Peace, War," 272; Schuijt and Coste, 352–53.
32. See chapter 8 above, pp. 104–9.
33. See chapter 11 above, pp. 162–64.
34. T. M. Finn, "Peace, War," 272; Schuijt and Coste, 353–54. There have, of course, been many theologians and church historians who have expressed their private, unofficial, disapproval. See, for example, R. T. Powers and H. A. Freeman, "Conscientious Objection," in NCE 4:405–6.
35. Abbott and Gallagher, 292; O'Brien and Shannon, 262.
36. T. M. Finn, "Peace, War," 272–73.
37. Abbott and Gallagher, 293; O'Brien and Shannon, 262. See T. M. Finn, "Peace, War," 272.
38. Abbott and Gallagher, 294; O'Brien and Shannon, 263. The position is well based on papal teaching. See T. M. Finn, 273; Schuijt and Coste, 356–58; Borgese, 416; and chapter 12 above, pp. 184–86.
39. T. M. Finn, 274; Schuijt and Coste, 358–59.
40. Abbott and Gallagher, 295–96; O'Brien and Shannon, 265–66. See Schuijt and Coste, 360–61; T. M. Finn, 274–75.
41. Abbott and Gallagher, 297; O'Brien and Shannon, 266.
42. See Schuijt and Coste, 364–65.
43. Borgese, 415–16.
44. O'Brien, "American Catholic Opposition," 122; McNeal, *Peace Movement*, 205–6; Shannon, *War or Peace?*, x.

45. J. Finn, "Pacifism," 8.
46. See the statement of the bishops on the lay apostolate in the Introduction above.
47. Bokenkotter, 425–27; O'Brien, "American Catholic Opposition," 125.
48. Zahn, *In Solitary Witness,* 205; Bokenkotter, 429–30, 437–50.
49. See Bokenkotter, 416–24; J. Derek Holmes, 221–54.
50. Bokenkotter, 420; J. Derek Holmes, 245.
51. "Goodwill: The Key to Peace," *Vital Speeches* 33 (Jan. 15, 1967): 194–96; Graham, "Vatican Peace Initiatives," J. Derek Holmes, 247.
52. Stefan Swiezawski, "Excursus on Article 90: The Commission 'Iustitia et Pax,' " in Vorgrimler, *Commentary,* 5:382–83.
53. See, for example, "Pope Paul's Christmas Plea for Peace," *America* 114 (Jan. 8, 1966): 35; "Peace and Justice in the World: The Church's Contribution," *Vital Speeches* 38 (Feb. 15, 1972): 258–60; "No to Violence, Yes to Peace; Pope Paul's Message," *America* 138 (Jan. 7, 1978): 4.
54. "The Arms Race: It is to be Condemned Unreservedly," quoted in Fahey, "Pax Christi," 66–67. See also Finn, "Pacifism," 5.
55. See "Pope and Peace: Appeal Against Pacifism," *Christian Century* 85 (Jan. 3, 1968): 3; and comments by Richard McSorley, S.J., in *Commonweal* 87 (Feb. 2, 1968): 519, 547.
56. Hehir, "Just-War Ethic," 22; Fahey, "Pax Christi," 66.
57. O'Brien and Shannon, 307–46.
58. O'Brien and Shannon, 343–46; J. Derek Holmes, 244–47.
59. See below, pp. 215, 221–22, 223–24.
60. O'Brien and Shannon, 340.
61. Ibid., 309.
62. This account is taken from Borgese, 418–20.
63. For details see Leiper, 359–60.
64. III, precept. IV, par. 16.
65. See Wentworth, "COs in France," 6.
66. *The Reporter for Conscience Sake* 40:3 (April/May 1984): 3.
67. Ninety-seven percent Catholic. See *Information Please Almanac 1985,* (Boston: Houghton-Mifflin, 1984), 154.
68. Smyth, "Anti-War," 3.
69. Davidon, 8.
70. See "Spain Incarcerates Catholic CO."
71. See chapter 15, pp. 259–61.
72. See Davidon.
73. Smyth, "New Hope," 3.
74. A pro-CO committee was lead by Abbé Pierre, Albert Camus, Jean Cocteau, and Louis Lecoin. See Wentworth, "COs in France," 5.
75. Wentworth, "COs in France," 5.
76. See "Pacifists Win in France"; Wentworth, "COs in France," 5; and Hope and Young, *Struggle,* 59–60.
77. Wentworth, "COs in France," 6.
78. Wentworth, "COs in France," 6; and his "New Rights."
79. See Heneghan, Deedy, and Kaza articles.
80. Heneghan, 5.
81. See Heneghan, Kaza.
82. Heneghan, 7.
83. See McNeish, 19-26; the introductory comments by Justin Vitiello in *Creature,* ix–x; and chapter 9, pp 111.
84. McNeish, 27–31; Hope and Young, *Struggle,* 75–77.
85. McNeish, 32–40.
86. McNeish, 43–55; Hope and Young, *Struggle,* 77–78.
87. McNeish, 56–77; Hope and Young, *Struggle,* 78–84.
88. Hope and Young, *Struggle,* 84–86.
89. McNeish, 78–132; Hope and Young, *Struggle,* 87–89; McNeal, *Peace Movement,* 190; P. Mayer, 391, 398–99.
90. See P. Mayer, 398–99.
91. An ultraconservative and supporter of Spanish dictator Franco. See McNeish, 152–59, 234–36; Hope and Young, *Struggle,* 91.

92. McNeish, 160–95.
93. McNeish, 196–227.
94. Hope and Young, *Struggle,* 91.
95. See Dolci's *The Man Who Plays Alone,* which recounts the campaign against the Mafia; *Creature,* xiii; McNeish, 137–43; Hope and Young, *Struggle,* 91–100.
96. McNeish, 236–39.
97. Hope and Young, *Struggle,* 102–7. Overcoming the urge to violence, even in the name of change, is a central theme of Dolci's poetry. See "The Moon Lemon" of 1968/69 in *Creature,* especially p. 14.
98. McNeish, 240–43; *Creature,* xiv–xv.
99. *New York Times* (Oct. 30, 1977) 49:1.
100. Hope and Young, *Struggle,* 104. See below, pp. 227–231.
101. See chapter 4, pp. 50–52.
102. See chapter 4, pp. 57–61; chapter 5, pp. 67–68; chapter 6, pp. 81–85; chapter 7, pp. 88–92.
103. See chapter 15, pp. 249–52.
104. See chapter 6, pp. 80–85; chapter 7, pp. 92–94.
105. For details of his life see Hope and Young, *Struggle,* 44–45.
106. Hope and Young, *Struggle,* 56; Vasto, *Make Straight the Way of the Lord,* 253–54. For the community's organization see Hope and Young, *Struggle,* 51–58.
107. For the seven principles of the Arks' nonviolent life see Hope and Young, *Struggle,* 59.
108. Ibid., 58.
109. See above, pp. 197–98.
110. Hope and Young, *Struggle,* 61. See above, pp. 191–93.
111. Hope and Young, *Struggle,* 69–70.
112. Ibid., 61–63.
113. See Deutsch, 1–6.
114. See Tousley.
115. Deutsch, 17–19.
116. Ibid., 30–32.
117. Ibid., 49–53, 60.
118. Ibid., 69–72.
119. Ibid., 83–93.
120. See, for example, chapter 5, pp. 71–73; chapter 7, pp. 85–86.
121. Deutsch, 94–98.
122. Ibid., 6–12.
123. Ibid., 122–27.
124. Ibid., 111–12.
125. Ibid., 193–98.
126. Ibid., 42–43, 129–43.
127. See McKeown's comments, in Deutsch, 75–81.
128. Corrigan's comments, in Deutsch, 39–40, 48.
129. Ibid., 86.
130. Ibid., 134–39.
131. In McKeown's editorial for *The Northern Irish Fortnight* 14 (Jan. 1977), in Deutsch, 144–45.
132. Ibid., 60.
133. McDowell, 165.
134. Deutsch, 86.
135. Ibid., 159.
136. Ibid., 147–48.
137. Deutsch, 149–59; *Facts on File* (May 19, 1978), 373; McDowell.
138. Deutsch, 144–59, 172–74.
139. *New York Times* (March 2, 1980) 9:1; (Oct. 21, 1984), E10; McDowell, 165.
140. See Tousley; McDowell, 165.
141. Deutsch, 65–69.
142. As John XXIII noted in *Pacem in Terris* (par. 151), in O'Brien and Shannon, 161.
143. See chapter 3, pp. 38–40.
144. Weschler, 13–14; James E. Will, "The Power of the Polish Church," *Christian Century* 99 (Jan. 6, 1982): 5–6; "Poland, The Church vs. the State," *Newsweek* 99 (Feb. 15, 1982): 39–40; and Christopher Cviic, 92–108.

145. See Weschler, 28; "Pope and Emperor," *New Republic* 189 (July 18, 1983): 7–9.
146. Weschler, 30. For detailed analysis see Potel, 82–102.
147. MacShane, 96–101.
148. MacShane, 30–39; Weschler, 24–30; Persky and Flam, 15–22, 35–70.
149. Weschler, 74–76, 111.
150. See the works by Weschler; MacShane; Persky and Flam; Staniszkis; Touraine; and Brumberg cited in the bibliography.
151. See Persky and Flam, 17–18, 77, 95, 110; Weschler, 32–33.
152. MacShane, 95.
153. Ibid.
154. See Point 3, item 2 of the Gdansk Agreement, in Persky and Flam, 95.
155. See Cviic, 106–7.
156. Cviic, 106; MacShane, 96; "Pope and Emperor," 8 (see n. 145 above).
157. *Pacem in Terris*, pars. 86–100, in O'Brien and Shannon, 145–48. See Tischner, especially 1–5, 39–59, 71–75, 79–83.
158. *New Evolutionism*, in Persky and Flam, 64.
159. Ibid., 64–66. Others, including Staniszkis (92–93) and Touraine (69, 105), see the church as a moderating influence and Solidarity gradually moving from its orbit.
160. Persky and Flam, 63, 113–22.
161. Ibid., 119.
162. See the Program of the First National Congress, October 1981, in Persky and Flam, 205–6.
163. Interview with Prof. Bonislaw Geremek, an advisor to the Gdansk strikers in 1980. See Persky and Flam, 228.
164. See, for example, *The Book of Lech Walesa*, 54–55, 88–96, 102–5, 188–94, 200–201.
165. Weschler, 62–66; *Book of Lech Walesa*, 92–94.
166. Interview with Oriana Fallaci, in Persky and Flam, 100–105; *Book of Lech Walesa*, 102–5, 155–57.
167. Weschler, 44–46.
168. *Facts on File*, Oct. 5, 1983, 756; *Time* 122:17 (Oct. 17, 1983): 50.
169. Weschler, 107–8; Christopher Bobinski, "Polish Bishops: Talk, Don't Fight" (NCR 18:19 [March 12, 1982]), 2.
170. Weschler, 149–52.
171. Appeal by Stefan Bratkowski, in Persky and Flam, 246.
172. *We Are All Hostages*, in Persky and Flam, 255.
173. Weschler, 160–61. For analysis see Peter Hebblewaite, " 'Murder in the Cathedral' Echoes in Poland's Plans" (NCR 19 [Feb. 11, 1983]), 7; and "Pope and Emperor" (see n. 145 above).
174. See chapter 12, pp. 173–75, 177–80.
175. Weschler, 166–67.
176. As in his 1984 removal of a dissident priest from a suburban parish of Ursus, a major Solidarity center. See *Time* (March 26, 1984), 37. See also Weschler, 163–66.
177. Weschler, 115, 149, 166–68. See also Michnik's *We Are All Hostages*, in Persky and Flam, 225; *Facts on File* (March 7–15, 1984), 186–87; *Time* (March 19, 1984), 38.
178. Weschler, 166–67; "Pope and Emperor" (see n. 145 above).
179. Weschler, 187–93; John Kohan, "Poland: Marching Out of Step." (*Time* 123 [May 14, 1984]).
180. See Weschler, 188; Kohan, 28 (see note 179 above); "Faith, Prayer, Defiance," (*Newsweek* 101 [Jan. 27, 1983]), 38.
181. See *Facts on File* (June 23, 1983), 462, 525; Weschler, 189–90; Russell Watson, "Has Walesa Been Dumped?" (*Newsweek* 102 [July 11, 1983]), 30–31.
182. See Weschler, 190–91, also summarizing the views of Daniel Singer.
183. Weschler, 188–89.
184. Weschler, 189; *Facts on File* (June 18, 1983), 461–62.
185. See Weschler, and Singer's interpretation, 191–92.
186. Weschler, 193; Thomas E. Bird, "The Pope and Poland: And Now What? Resistance, Not Rebellion" (*Commonweal* 110:13 [July 15, 1983]), 390–92.
187. Weschler, 193–94.
188. See chapter 14 below, pp. 232–33.
189. From Lernoux, 431–32.
190. See above, p. 206–7.

191. Kohan, 36 (see n. 179 above).
192. See John Kohan, "Poland: A Nation Mourns a Martyred Priest," *Time* (Nov. 12, 1984), 58. See also *New York Times* (Oct. 29, 1984) A3:1–3; (Nov. 4, 1984), 1:3.
193. See Weschler, 203–4.

## 14. THE THIRD WORLD

1. See Chapter 10 above.
2. See Chapter 10, pp. 137–38.
3. *Information Please Almanac* (New York: A & W, 1982), 52.
4. Ibid., 191.
5. Ibid., 244.
6. Ibid., 156.
7. Lernoux, "Long Path," in Eagleson and Scharper, 16.
8. See Lernoux, 62, and below, pp. 233–37.
9. See Lernoux, 19–22.
10. See Comblin, *Church and the National Security State*, 56–78.
11. See de Gruchy, 240.
12. Hope and Young, *South African Churches*, 55.
13. Ibid., 55; de Grouchy, 97–98.
14. Regehr, 103–114, 150–52, 163–69; de Grouchy, 69–85. This view has been challenged. See, for example, Andre du Toit, "No Chosen People: The Myth of the Calvinist Origins of Afrikaner Nationalism and Race Ideology" (*American Historical Review* 88:4 [October 1983]), 920–52.
15. Hope and Young, *South African Churches*, 55; Regehr, 256; de Grouchy, 98–99.
16. See Walshe, 41.
17. See de Grouchy, 99; Walshe, 76.
18. See Regehr, 170–73.
19. Hope and Young, *South African Churches*, 56.
20. See chapter 13, pp. 193–95.
21. Regehr, 256–57; de Grouchy, 99.
22. Hope and Young, *South African Churches*, 158–59; Regehr, 258.
23. See Walshe, 71–72.
24. "Statement by the National Committee of Black Churchmen, June 13, 1969," in Cone and Wilmore, *Black Theology*, 100–102.
25. Regehr, 264–77.
26. Hope and Young, *South African Churches*, 76–82. See also Bosch; Cone and Wilmore, "Black Theology"; and Braxton.
27. Hope and Young, *South African Churches*, 159.
28. Ibid., 154; Regehr, 257.
29. Regehr, 15–21.
30. See Regehr, 268–75.
31. Hope and Young, *South African Churches*, 92; Regehr, 274–75.
32. Hope and Young, *South African Churches*, 163–66.
33. Ibid., 158; Regehr, 256. These efforts were not entirely successful. See Walshe, 142–43.
34. Hope and Young, *South African Churches*, 155–57; Regehr, 257–58.
35. Walshe, 77–78.
36. Walshe, 41–42, 76.
37. Hope and Young, *South African Churches*, 231–32.
38. Ibid., 253; "Catholics Defy Banning" (*Christian Century* 98 [July 15, 1981]), 729; and "South African Priest" (*Catholic Peace Fellowship Bulletin* [May 1984]), 12.
39. See chapter 10, pp. 136–37; Digan, 3–33.
40. With the 1975 Emergency in India, in fact, Japan was the only remaining functioning democracy in Asia. Digan, 32–33.
41. Ibid., 34–41.
42. Ibid., 50–53.
43. See below, pp. 220–22. See Digan, 54–56; Claver, "Prophesy," 357.
44. Digan, 54–56.
45. As, for example, in the 1979 meeting of the Ecumenical Association of Third World

Theologians, which saw Marxism and violence as unavoidable elements of liberation. See Digan, 89–90.

46. See Digan, 107.

47. Eighty-five percent. See *Information Please Almanac,* 244. (See n. 3 above).

48. Digan, 108–11; Giordano, 277; Claver, "Free," 144–45.

49. Typical of this trend is the career of Edicio de la Torre. See Digan, 92.

50. Claver, "Prophesy," 358.

51. Claver, "Prophesy," 358; Digan, 115.

52. Digan, 114–19; Claver, "Prophesy," 356.

53. Claver, "Prophesy," 358; Broad and Cavanaugh.

54. Claver, "Prophesy"; Bernas.

55. For a review of developments see Claver, "Prophesy," 354–56 and "Free," 144.

56. See Martin; and "Church of Both Right and Left."

57. Claver, "Prophesy," 356; Digan, 113.

58. Claver, "Prophesy," 356. See also Martin.

59. Digan, 145.

60. Claver, "Prophesy," 358.

61. See Ostling.

62. In its joint pastoral, "Dialogue for Peace." See Giordano, 226.

63. *Facts on File* (March 23, 1983), 416.

64. Ibid. (Aug. 5, 1983), 631.

65. Ibid. (Aug. 23, 1983), 637–38.

66. Ibid. (Aug. 27–31, 1983), 665.

67. Ibid., 757.

68. Ibid. (Sept. 22, 1983), 718.

69. Ibid. (Sept. 25, 1983), 757.

70. In November thirty-three business executives were charged with smuggling and hiding their foreign exchange earnings, a favorite Nazi charge against critics in the Catholic Church. See *Facts on File* (Sept. 23, 1983), 757; (Nov. 14, 1983), 996.

71. Ibid. (Sept. 23, 1983), 757.

72. Justice for Aquino, Justice for All.

73. *Facts on File* (Sept. 22, 1983), 718.

74. *Facts on File* (Jan. 6, 1984), 39; "Filipino Bishops Approve Boycott of Election," (*NCR* 20:14 [Jan. 27, 1984]), 3.

75. *Facts on File* (Feb. 29, 1984), 159, 239.

76. See Chapter 10 above.

77. For nineteenth- and twentieth-century developments see Dussel, *History of the Church,* 87–116.

78. See Comblin, *Church,* 64–78; Lernoux, "Long Path," 15–20.

79. See Dussel, *History of the Church,* 148–76, 194–222; Lernoux, *Cry;* Comblin, *Church;* and Lange and Iblacker.

80. Dussel, *History of the Church,* 129–32, 222. For the U.S. and European role in spreading and maintaining this repression see Lernoux, *Cry,* 280–310.

81. See Dussel, *History of the Church,* 119–20; Bokenkotter, 455.

82. Dussel, *History of the Church,* 87–116.

83. Bokenkotter, 455.

84. See pp. 184–95.

85. See, for example, his *Theology of Liberation* and "Liberation Praxis."

86. See "Liberation Theology."

87. See Boff, "Christ's Liberation."

88. See Segundo, "Capitalism versus Socialism."

89. Most especially his *Pedagogy of the Oppressed* (New York: Continuum, 1981).

90. O'Brien and Shannon, 541–46; Gutiérrez, *Liberation,* 33–37.

91. Gutiérrez, *Liberation,* 69–72.

92. O'Brien and Shannon, 542; Gutiérrez, *Theology of Liberation,* 3–15; Boff, "Christ's Liberation," 122–24; Segundo, "Capitalism versus Socialism"; Vidales, "Methodological Issues."

93. See chapter 9, pp. 110–35.

94. See chapter 6, pp. 80–85; chapter 7, pp. 89–92.

95. Gutiérrez, *Theology of Liberation,* 189–212. See also Dussel, "Historical and Philosophical Presuppositions."

96. Gutiérrez, *Theology of Liberation,* 149–87.

97. Ibid., 49–52, 255–72.

98. Ibid., 213–50. Dussel's analysis of the peaceful apocalyptic of liberation theology is almost Joachite. See *History of the Church,* 240–53, and chapter 7, pp. 92–94.

99. See McCann, 164–72, 197–200.

100. See Dussel, *History of the Church,* 240–42.

101. See Gutiérrez, *Theology of Liberation,* 156–57, 165, 190, 294–95.

102. See Gutiérrez, *Theology of Liberation,* 167–68, 305; Dussel, *History of the Church,* 113–14, 234; Boff, 107–9.

103. See Gutiérrez, *Theology of Liberation,* 21–33, 153–61, 114–19, 181–99, 213–50.

104. Ibid., 45–49, 272–76.

105. See Dussel, *History of the Church,* 175–76.

106. See McCann, 225–30; Segundo; J. Finn, "Pacifism," 12.

107. See Gutiérrez, *Theology of Liberation,* 108–9, 274–76; Ellacuria, 187–231.

108. See O'Brien and Shannon, 547 and the basic texts, 539–84; Dussel, *History of the Church,* 141–47. For criticisms of the bishops' ambiguous approach to liberation see McCann, 136–41.

109. Dussel, *History of the Church,* 113, 138–41; O'Brien and Shannon, 547, 559–60.

110. O'Brien and Shannon, 547.

111. Ibid., 549–60.

112. Ibid., 561–72.

113. See chapter 13, pp. 193–95.

114. *Populorum Progressio,* par. 26.

115. *Quadragesimo Anno,* May 15, 1931 (*Acta Apostolicae Sedis* 23 [1931]), 212.

116. Paul VI, *Homily of the Mass on Development Day,* Bogota, 23 August 1968.

117. As, for example, in the December 1977 call for just revolution by Gaspar Garcia Laviana. See Margaret Randall, *Christians in the Nicaraguan Revolution* (Vancouver: New Star, 1983), 26–29.

118. Paul VI, *Populorum Progressio,* par. 31.

119. Ibid.

120. See O'Brien and Shannon, 573–79.

121. Ibid., 577.

122. Gutiérrez, *Theology of Liberation,* 133–42.

123. See Dussel, *History of the Church,* 125, and above, pp. 219–20.

124. See Dussel, *History of the Church,* 166–69; Swomley, 136–43; Lernoux, *Cry,* 29–30. For bibliography see Dahlin, 145–49.

125. See Dussel, *History of the Church,* 115–22, 186–98, 211–16, 223.

126. See Gutiérrez, *Theology of Liberation,* 101–14; Dussel, *History of the Church,* 224–27. See also the books by Lernoux, Comblin, and Lange and Iblacker cited in the bibliography.

127. *New York Times* (June 20, 1984), D1:4.

128. See Hope and Young, *Struggle,* 110–11.

129. *Facts on File* (July 23, 1982), 520.

130. See Dussel, *History of the Church,* 148–54.

131. Lernoux, *Cry,* 33–34, 158–75, 191–200, 247–80, 313–32; Hope and Young, *Struggle,* 132–39; Comblin, 64–66; Dussel, *History of the Church,* 198–200; Lange and Iblacker, 37–43, 107–112, 114–27, 135–40.

132. Dussel, *History of the Church,* 148–50.

133. For what follows see De Broucker; Hope and Young, *Struggle,* 109–44; Dussel, *History of the Church,* 198–200; Lernoux, *Cry,* 307–8, 411–15, 423–26; and Camara's own *Revolution Through Peace.* For bibliography see Dahlin, 25–26, 179–88.

134. See Lernoux, *Cry,* 159.

135. See Hope and Young, *Struggle,* 111–12.

136. Hope and Young, *Struggle,* 113; McCann, 141–45.

137. Hope and Young, *Struggle,* 114.

138. See Hope and Young, *Struggle,* 114–15. See the summary of its history in Lernoux, *Cry,* 293–304; and Dussel, *History of the Church,* 148–49.

139. See Camara, 41–60.

140. Camara, 77–103; de Broucker, 79.

141. Hope and Young, *Struggle,* 118–19; Camara, 104–35.

142. Hope and Young, *Struggle,* 132.

143. De Broucker, 71.

144. Hope and Young, *Struggle,* 119–20.
145. De Broucker, 59–73.
146. Hope and Young, *Struggle,* 116–18.
147. Hope and Young, *Struggle,* 116–18. On these communities see Eagleson and Torres, especially "Final Document," 231–46.
148. See chapter 6, pp. 84–85.
149. Hope and Young, *Struggle,* 124–27.
150. Lernoux, "Long Path," 19.
151. See Camara, 133.
152. Ibid., 68–73.
153. See chapter 13, pp. 198–200.
154. Chapter 13, pp. 200–201.
155. Chapter 13, pp. 201–4.
156. Hope and Young, *Struggle,* 109.
157. Ibid., 139–40.
158. Hope and Young, *Struggle,* 139–40; de Broucker, 75–76.
159. Hope and Young, *Struggle,* 140.
160. See de Broucker, 75–76; Cuneen; Goss-Mayr.
161. Camara, 142.
162. Hope and Young, *Struggle,* 127–29. See Camara, 137.
163. Hope and Young, *Struggle,* 123, 127–28, 132–34; Lernoux, *Cry,* 247–80, 300–304.
164. Hope and Young, *Struggle,* 116–17.
165. Ibid., 123.
166. See chapter 12, pp. 174–75.
167. Lernoux, *Cry,* 300–301.
168. Ibid., 326–32.
169. Hope and Young, *Struggle,* 129–30; Lernoux, *Cry,* 255–57; Lange and Iblacker, 43–53.
170. See chapter 12, p. 175.
171. See Lange and Iblacker, 85–88, 91–92.
172. *Populorum Progressio,* par. 81, in O'Brien and Shannon, 341.
173. See *Facts on File* (Feb. 10, 1984), 97.
174. Ibid. (April 27, 1984), 296–97; *Time* (Jan. 28, 1985), 52.
175. For background see Esquivel, 3–6; Lernoux, *Cry,* 3–10, 43–48, 159–62; Lange and Iblacker, 73–78, 97–102, 112.
176. Estimates of the "disappeared" have ranged as high as 20,000. See *Facts on File* (Nov. 12, 1982), 848.
177. His report on the *Final Document on the War Against Subversion and Terrorism.* See *Facts on File* (May 6, 1983), 331.
178. $2,390 in 1980. *Information Please Almanac,* 148 (see n. 3 above).
179. See "Esquivel, Adolfo Perez"; and Esquivel, 1–3.
180. See Esquivel, 10, and jacket.
181. See Esquivel, 1–3, 10–15.
182. See chapter 6, pp. 83–84; chapter 7, pp. 89–90.
183. See chapter 13, pp. 200–201.
184. See chapter 15 below, pp. 249–252.
185. See below, pp. 230.
186. Esquivel, 8–9; "Esquivel, Adolfo Perez," 322–23.
187. Esquivel, 19; Lernoux, *Cry,* 137–41, and "Long Path," 17; Lange and Iblacker, 128–32.
188. On Proaño's activities on behalf of the Indians of the region, see Esquivel, 71–91; Lernoux, *Cry,* 146–47, 150–53, 436–37; Lange and Iblacker, 53–60. For an introduction see Proaño.
189. Esquivel, 7–9; "Esquivel, Adolfo Perez," 323.
190. Esquivel, 19–24.
191. See chapter 13, pp. 201–4.
192. "Esquivel, Adolfo Perez," 323.
193. For his ideas on nonviolence see Esquivel, 18–19, 26–35, 53.
194. See chapter 13, pp. 206–7.
195. Esquivel, 6. See Esquivel's acceptance speech, 137–38.
196. Ibid., 43–44.
197. See Robert F. Drinan, "Human Rights in Argentina" (*America* 145 [Oct. 10, 1981]),

198–200; "Self-Amnesty: A Military Pardon" (*Time* 122 [Oct. 3, 1983]), 40.

198. Esquivel, 44–48.

199. Ibid., 52.

200. See chapter 13, p. 203.

201. Esquivel, 54–57.

202. See Miguel Amador, "Silent Accomplices" (*Christian Century* 97 [Dec. 3, 1980]), 1180–81. For Esquivel's activities since the Nobel Prize see "Prize for Peace."

203. See Drinan (see n. 197 above).

204. See *Facts on File* (Dec. 10, 1982), 916; *Information Please Almanac 1985,* 149.

205. See Dussel, *History of the Church,* 222–29; and his "Current Events," in Eagleson and Torres, 77–102.

206. Dussel, *History of the Church,* 224.

207. *Nonviolence: A Power for Liberation,* in Esquivel, 117–34.

208. See *Commentary on Vatican II* 5:339.

209. *Education of the Christian Prince.* See chapter 9, p. 130.

210. *Nonviolence,* in Esquivel, 129–31.

211. See Lernoux, *Cry,* 409–59, and "Long Path," 3–27, especially 20–25; Dussel, *History of the Church,* 230–31.

212. See Dussel, *History of the Church,* 237–39, and the articles by Sobrino, Gremillion, and Brown in Eagleson and Scharper, 289–346.

213. See Eagleson and Scharper, 123–285.

214. See chapter 6, pp. 80–85; chapter 7, pp. 89–92.

215. *Gandium et Spes,* par. 78. See chapter 13, pp. 191–92.

216. Dussel, *History of the Church,* 235; Lernoux, *Cry,* 425–44, especially 431–32. See also chapter 13, pp. 207–9.

217. See chapter 13, pp. 204–9.

218. See above, pp. 214–19.

219. See chapter 4, pp. 60–61.

220. See chapter 5, pp. 68–69.

221. See Riding, 189–98; Berryman, *Religious Roots,* 91–161; and Montgomery.

222. See Brockman, 30–37.

223. Ibid., 37–45.

224. Ibid., 45–51; Lernoux, *Cry,* 61–69.

225. Brockman, 51.

226. Ibid., 1–5.

227. Lernoux, *Cry,* 72–73.

228. See Lernoux, *Cry.*

229. Brockman, 4–7.

230. Brockman, 8–10; Lernoux, *Cry,* 73–75; and Lange and Iblacker, 27–33.

231. See, for example, Brockman, 20–21, 119–20.

232. See chapter 12, p. 175.

233. Brockman, 55–59; Lernoux, *Cry,* 75–80.

234. Brockman, 21; Lernoux, *Cry,* 75–76.

235. Brockman, 27.

236. Brockman, 70–79. See also Lacefield, 198–203.

237. Brockman, 28–29; Lernoux, *Cry,* 61–62; Lange and Iblacker, 33–36.

238. Brockman, 59–65, 90–91.

239. Including that of American Catholics through an honorary degree awarded by Georgetown University President Timothy Healy, S.J. See Brockman, 94–95.

240. Brockman, 121–51.

241. Ibid., 127–40. On the theory of just revolution in El Salvador see "A Sign of Resurrection," in Gettleman, 206–10.

242. Brockman, 156.

243. Ibid., 176–77.

244. Ibid., 194.

245. Ibid., 200–210.

246. Ibid., 217.

247. Brockman, 218–23; Lange and Iblacker, 113–14.

248. Lernoux, *Cry,* xvii–xviii.

249. Ibid., xvi. Many of the death squads have been connected with D'Aubuisson. See James

Wallace, "A No-Win Election for U.S. in El Salvador" (*U.S. News & World Report*, March 26, 1984), 32; and Pyes.

250. Brockman, 223.

251. See Berryman, *Religious Roots*, 51–80; Teofilo Cabestrero, *Ministers of God, Ministers of the People*, translated by R. R. Barr (Maryknoll, N.Y.: Orbis, 1983); and Randall (see no. 117 above).

252. See, for example, Christine Gudorf, "The Quiet Strength of Liberation Theology" (*Commonweal* 111:12 [June 15, 1984]), 365–67; and Kenneth A. Briggs, "Catholic Liberals Defend Activism" (*New York Times*, June 25, 1984), A1, 8. Henry Kamm, "Vatican Censures Marxist Elements in New Theology" (*New York Times* [Sept. 4, 1984]), A1, 10; Walter Goodman, "Church's Activist Clergy: Rome Draws Line" (*New York Times*, [Sept. 6, 1984]), A1, 14; Henry Kamm, "Friar Defends Views at Vatican Session" (*New York Times* [Sept. 8, 1984]), A3; "Liberation Theology: Thy Kingdom Come, Here and Now," (*Economist* [Oct. 13, 1984]), 31–34; George Russell, "Taming the Liberation Theologians" (*Time* [Feb. 4, 1985]), 56, 59; and Richard N. Ostling, *"Si* to a Demanding Friend" (*Time* [Feb. 11, 1985]), 76.

## 15. CATHOLIC PEACEMAKING IN THE UNITED STATES

1. See chapter 5, pp. 62–63.
2. See chapter 11, pp. 153–56.
3. See chapters 3–4, pp. 31–61.
4. See chapter 5, pp. 69–71.
5. See chapters 6–7, pp. 81–85, 89–92.
6. See chapter 2, pp. 15–18.
7. See chapter 12, pp. 182–84.
8. See chapter 14, pp. 233–37.
9. See Hennessey, 36–54; Ellis, *American Catholicism*, 19–38, 45–47; *Colonial America*, 320–24, 344–59, 360–80.
10. Hennessey, 101–27; Ellis, *American Catholicism*, 53–61.
11. Bokenkotter, 378–90. See Hennessey, 172–203.
12. See chapter 11, pp. 154–56; Hennessey, 196–203; Bokenkotter, 390–91; Piehl, 25–55.
13. See Piehl, 49–55.
14. Bokenkotter, 341–55.
15. McNeal, *Peace Movement*, 3, 10–13.
16. See chapter 12, pp. 177–78.
17. McNeal, "Catholic Conscientious Objectors," 222.
18. September 1919, in NOP, 3–5.
19. See Conway, "Struggle for Peace," 29.
20. For the following account see McNeal, *Peace Movement*, 17–33, 47. See Flannery, "Catholic Association."
21. A priest and a professor at Catholic University active in Catholic social issues as the head of the U.S. church's Social Action Department and a strong proponent of the League of Nations. McNeal, *Peace Movement*, 11–17.
22. See chapter 11, pp. 154–56.
23. McNeal, *Peace Movement*, 17–23; Zahn, "Carrying Our Weight," 143.
24. See below, pp. 241–44; and McNeal, *Peace Movement*, 25–30.
25. Ibid., 28–29.
26. Ibid., 170–71.
27. Ibid., 114–16, 176.
28. Ibid., 172–74.
29. See Day, *Loaves and Fishes;* McNeal, *Peace Movement* 58–80; Miller, *Harsh and Dreadful Love;* and Piehl.
30. See Miller, *Dorothy Day;* Day's autobiography, *The Long Loneliness;* Day's essays in *By Little and Little;* and Piehl, 3–24. For a complete bibliography see Klejment and Klejment.
31. For her early life see Day, *Long Loneliness,* 9–83, 113–60; Miller, *Dorothy Day,* 1–226; McNeal, *Peace Movement,* 59–66.
32. Day, *Long Loneliness,* 169–81; *Loaves and Fishes,* 3–11, 93–102; McNeal, *Peace Movement,* 37–38, 66–69; Miller, *Harsh and Dreadful Love,* 17–32, 63–77, 113–26; and *Dorothy Day,* 227–48; Piehl, 57–66.
33. See Day, *Long Loneliness,* 182–204; *Loaves and Fishes,* 12–27; Miller, *Harsh and Dreadful*

*Love,* 63–77; *Dorothy Day,* 249–80; Piehl, 57–94; McNeal, *Peace Movement,* 38–42, 70.
34. See Day, *Loaves and Fishes,* 28–41; *Long Loneliness,* 204–35; Piehl, 95–96.
35. See Piehl, 109–112.
36. McNeal, *Peace Movement,* 38–39.
37. See Day, *Long Loneliness,* 263–73; Miller, *Harsh and Dreadful Love,* 154–70.
38. Hennessey, 272.
39. McNeal, *Peace Movement,* 39, 43; Piehl, 192–93; Miller, *Dorothy Day,* 313–16.
40. Reprinted in Day, *By Little and Little,* 77–78. See Miller, *Dorothy Day,* 314–15.
41. McNeal, *Peace Movement,* 48.
42. Ibid., 72–73, 83; Conley, 382; Piehl, 193.
43. McNeal, *Peace Movement,* 83; Piehl, 195.
44. McNeal, *Peace Movement,* 73.
45. Piehl, 193.
46. McNeal, *Peace Movement,* 41–43, 46–47, 87; Piehl, 195.
47. McNeal, *Peace Movement,* 84.
48. Piehl, 194–95. On Furfey see also Shannon, *What Are They Saying,* 59–62; McNeal, *Peace Movement,* 82–83.
49. McNeal, *Peace Movement,* 34–35, 44; Hennessey, 274–75.
50. McNeal, *Peace Movement,* 75–77, 90–93; Piehl, 195–98.
51. See Day, *Loaves and Fishes,* 60–64; Miller, *Harsh and Dreadful Love,* 216–35.
52. "National Catholic College Poll" (*America* 62 [Nov. 11, 1939]), 116–19; and 62 (Nov. 18, 1939), 144–47. See also McNeal, *Peace Movement,* 89–90.
53. Bainton, *Christian Attitudes,* 219.
54. See McNeal, *Peace Movement,* 47–49 for a class analysis of the appeal of these groups.
55. McNeal, *Peace Movement,* 86.
56. Pastoral of Nov. 14, 1941, Flannery, *Pattern for Peace,* 333–34; Nolan, 372–77.
57. *Victory and Peace,* Nov. 14, 1942, NOP, 7–9; Nolan, 380–84.
58. McNeal, *Peace Movement,* 88–90.
59. Ibid., 93–95, and "Catholic Conscientious Objectors," 222.
60. See Zahn, "Social Thought," 149–50.
61. Piehl, 199.
62. War resisters constituted one in six of all Federal prison inmates during the war.
63. McNeal, *Peace Movement,* 77–78.
64. Piehl, 199.
65. McNeal, *Peace Movement,* 85; Piehl, 200.
66. McNeal, *Peace Movement,* 98; Piehl, 200.
67. They provided the government with eight million man hours of free labor at a cost to the churches of $7 million. See McNeal, *Peace Movement,* 98.
68. Piehl, 200.
69. McNeal, *Peace Movement,* 103–4.
70. See McNeal, *Peace Movement,* 98–100; Piehl, 200–204; and especially Zahn, *Another Part.*
71. McNeal, *Peace Movement,* 101–2.
72. See *Another Part.* See also McNeal, *Peace Movement,* 98–108; Piehl, 201. For Zahn see Shannon, *What Are They Saying,* 79–81.
73. See Zahn's analysis in *Another Part,* 103–35.
74. See Piehl, 203.
75. McNeal, *Peace Movement,* 105; Piehl, 204–5; Zahn, *Another Part,* 240–41.
76. See McNeal, *Peace Movement,* 102–3.
77. See Day's essays, "Our Country Passes from Declared to Undeclared War," in Day, *By Little and Little,* 261–70; McNeal, *Peace Movement,* 81–82, 112–13.
78. "Current Moral Theology and Canon Law" (*Theological Studies* 2 [December 1941]), 551. See Shannon, *What Are They Saying,* 48–49.
79. *Theological Studies* 5 (September 1944). See Shannon, *What Are They Saying,* 48–53; McNeal, *Peace Movement,* 109–10; Bainton, *Christian Attitudes,* 233; Piehl, 202.
80. The balance between the justice of the means used and the just end.
81. McNeal, *Peace Movement,* 110–12.
82. See, for example, Gerald Kelly, S.J.'s advocacy of the use of atomic weapons in "the conflict between theistic, peace-seeking nations and atheistic, aggressive forces" (Shannon, *What Are They Saying,* 53–55).

83. Nov. 16, 1944, NOP, 11–16; Flannery, *Pattern for Peace,* 335–40; Nolan, 390–93.
84. See chapter 11, pp. 161–64.
85. See chapter 12, pp. 184–86.
86. *Between War and Peace,* Nov. 18, 1945, Flannery, *Pattern for Peace,* 346–50.
87. *Man and the Peace,* Nov. 17, 1946, Nolan, 398–402; Flannery, *Pattern for Peace,* 351–57, especially 356–57. The bishops recall the words of Bartolomé de las Casas. See chapter 10, pp. 140–44.
88. *Dignity of Man,* Nov. 21, 1953, Flannery, *Pattern for Peace,* 364–72.
89. *The Hope of Mankind,* Nov. 18, 1956, Flannery, *Pattern for Peace,* 375–78. The German Cardinal Faulhaber, later an avid supporter of the Nazi war effort, made the same statement in the 1930s. See chapter 12, pp. 178.
90. Nov. 19, 1959, NOP, 17–23; Flannery, *Pattern for Peace,* 386–90; Nolan, 515–19.
91. Flannery, *Pattern for Peace,* 390.
92. Nov. 19, 1960, Flannery, *Pattern for Peace,* 391.
93. See chapter 12, pp. 187–91.
94. See McNeal, *Peace Movement,* 123–24; Piehl, 204–5; Miller, *Dorothy Day,* 372–79, and *Harsh and Dreadful Love,* 216–35.
95. See above, pp. 240–41, 243–44.
96. McNeal, *Peace Movement,* 123, 181; Piehl, 204–5.
97. McNeal, *Peace Movement,* 177–79; Piehl, 205–8; Miller, *Harsh and Dreadful Love,* 236–65.
98. Piehl, 207.
99. See Day, *Loaves and Fishes,* 103–117; Miller, *Harsh and Dreadful Love,* 266–301; McNeal, *Peace Movement,* 184–90; Piehl, 210–16; and Hennacy, *Autobiography.*
100. See Hennacy, 128–78; Piehl, 210–13.
101. See chapter 13, pp. 198–200.
102. Hennacy, 195–303.
103. Conway, "Struggle for Power," 19–20.
104. See McNeal, *Peace Movement,* 185–87; Piehl, 214–15; Zahn, "Appreciation," in Merton, *Nonviolent Alternative,* xv; Cornell, "Witness," 204.
105. McNeal, *Peace Movement,* 188–90; Piehl, 213.
106. On the revival of pacifism see Lammers, "Catholic Ethics and Pacifism," in Shannon, *War or Peace?,* 96–103.
107. See Piehl, 216–17.
108. McNeal, *Peace Movement,* 174–75.
109. Ibid., 191–93.
110. See Furlong; Merton, *Nonviolent Alternative,* including Gordon Zahn's introduction; Zahn, "Thomas Merton"; Forest, "Thomas Merton's Struggle"; and McNeal, *Peace Movement,* 126–68. For bibliography see Breit.
111. New York: Harcourt, Brace, 1948. See Furlong, 3–79, 153–79.
112. McNeal, *Peace Movement,* 127–28; Forest, "Thomas Merton's Struggle," 16; Zahn, "Thomas Merton," 56.
113. See McNeal, *Peace Movement,* 128. For these years see Furlong, 80–152, 180–250.
114. See, for example, chapter 4, pp. 50–61; chapter 6, 81–85; chapter 7, pp. 89–92.
115. See Zahn, "Thomas Merton," 59–60; Forest, "Thomas Merton's Struggle," 25–32.
116. Preface to the Japanese edition of *No Man Is An Island,* quoted in Forest, "Thomas Merton's Struggle," 33–34.
117. See chapter 9, pp. 117–18.
118. See chapter 9, pp. 131–32.
119. See for example, "Target Equals City," in Zahn, *Nonviolent Alternative,* 94–102. See also Forest, "Thomas Merton's Struggle," 15–16.
120. See Shannon, *What Are They Saying,* 65–69.
121. See "Christianity and Defense in the Nuclear Age," in Merton, *Nonviolent Alternative,* 88–94; "Target Equals City," in ibid., 101. See also McNeal, *Peace Movement,* 135–36.
122. Merton, *Nonviolent Alternative,* 160–62.
123. See Merton, "Peace: Christian Duties and Perspectives," in *Nonviolent Alternative,* 12–19; McNeal, *Peace Movement,* 132–33; and Zahn, "Appreciation," in Merton, *Nonviolent Alternative,* xiii, xvi–xvii.
124. See Zahn, "An Appreciation," in Merton, *Nonviolent Alternative,* xii–xiii; Forest, "Thomas Merton's Struggle," 21.

125. See "The Christian in World Crisis," in Merton, *Nonviolent Alternative*, 52–53; McNeal, *Peace Movement*, 150.

126. McNeal, *Peace Movement*, 151, quoting Merton's *Seeds of Destruction* (New York: Farrar, Straus & Giroux, 1964), 122.

127. "Christian in World Crisis," in Merton, *Nonviolent Alternative*, 20–28; "Peace: Christian Duties," in ibid., 17.

128. "Christian in World Crisis," in Merton, *Nonviolent Alternative*, 28–29.

129. Merton, *Nonviolent Alternative*, 56.

130. Ibid., 36.

131. See McNeal, *Peace Movement*, 140; Zahn, "Appreciation," xvii–xix (see n. 124 above).

132. See "The Machine Gun in the Fallout Shelter," in Merton, *Nonviolent Alternative*, 104; "Christian in World Crisis," in ibid., 32–34.

133. See Forest, "Thomas Merton's Struggle," 36; McNeal, *Peace Movement*, 146.

134. "The Christian in World Crisis," in Merton, *Nonviolent Alternative*, 24–28; McNeal, *Peace Movement*, 151–53. For similar sentiments in Erasmus, see chapter 9, pp. 129–30.

135. "Faith and Violence," in Merton, *Nonviolent Alternative*, 186–92.

136. See chapter 4, p. 49.

137. "Faith and Violence," in Merton, *Nonviolent Alternative*, 188–89.

138. Ibid., 190.

139. "Peace: Christian Duties and Perspectives," in Merton, *Nonviolent Alternative*, 19.

140. "The Christian in World Crisis," 60–61 (see n. 128 above).

141. McNeal, *Peace Movement*, 154–56, 159. See chapter 3, pp. 33–34; chapter 4, pp. 49–50; chapter 7, pp. 92–94.

142. See for example, "A Tribute to Gandhi," in Merton, *Nonviolent Alternative*, 178–84. See McNeal, *Peace Movement*, 147–49.

143. "Peace and Revolution: A Footnote from *Ulysses*," in Merton, *Nonviolent Alternative*, 75.

144. Ibid.

145. See John 14:27.

146. "Faith and Violence," in Merton, *Nonviolent Alternative*, 192.

147. "Blessed Are the Meek: The Christian Roots of Nonviolence," in Merton, *Nonviolent Alternative*, 208. See also "Note for *Ave Maria*," in ibid., 233; and the comments of Forest, "Thomas Merton's Struggle," 37; and Zahn, "Thomas Merton," 72.

148. "Blessed Are the Meek," in Merton, *Nonviolent Alternative*, 208–18.

149. Ibid., 209.

150. Matthew 5:3–4. See chapter 2, pp. 21–23.

151. By an accidental electrocution while on a visit to Bangkok, Thailand. See Furlong, 318–22.

152. See Vorgrimler, *Commentary on the Documents of Vatican II*, vol. 5, especially 75–76, 339–46; Bokenkotter, 418–20; Yzermans, 183–269.

153. See chapter 13, pp. 191–93.

154. See Borgese, 416–17.

155. McNeal, *Peace Movement*, 201–2.

156. Borgese, 416–17; Vorgrimler, 5:344–45.

157. See Yzermans, 217–18, 254–55; McNeal, *Peace Movement*, 198–206; Borgese, 416–17.

158. Yzermans, 220–21.

159. For the American role see McNeal, *Peace Movement*, 194–99; Piehl, 224–29; Miller, *Dorothy Day*, 480–81.

160. See Day's "A Prayer for Peace," in *By Little and Little*, 331–36.

161. See chapter 13, pp. 201.

162. As expressed in his *Public Laws of the Church* (Rome 1947). See McNeal, *Peace Movement*, 198; Merton, "Christian Ethics and Nuclear War," in *Nonviolent Alternative*, 86, and Vorgrimler, 5:339–40.

163. McNeal, *Peace Movement*, 204; Yzermans, 217–19, 254–55.

164. McNeal, *Peace Movement*, 203–4.

165. Piehl, 227. See Miller, *Harsh and Dreadful Love*, 302–49 for CW activities during the 1960s.

166. On the Berrigans see McNeal, *Peace Movement*, 246–99; Deedy, *Apologies;* Gray, 66–95; and Shannon, *What Are They Saying*, 69–73 on Daniel.

167. Forest, "Thomas Merton's Struggle," 40; McNeal, *Peace Movement*, 161–62, 220–22; O'Brien, "American Catholic Opposition," 137–38; Piehl, 234–36.

168. McNeal, *Peace Movement*, 188, 222–23.

169. Ibid., 223; Piehl, 231.

170. See McNeal, *Peace Movement*, 223–25; Piehl, 231–32; O'Brien, "American Catholic Opposition," 131; Cornell, "Witness," 209.

171. McNeal, *Peace Movement*, 224.

172. See Day's essays, "The Fear of Our Enemies," in *By Little and Little*, 321–23, and "War Without Weapons," in ibid., 326–29; O'Brien, "American Catholic Opposition," 131; McNeal, *Peace Movement*, 187–88.

173. Piehl, 232; Forest, "Thomas Merton's Struggle," 43–46; *Newsweek* 66 (Nov. 22, 1965), 71.

174. Forest, "Thomas Merton's Struggle," 45–46; Piehl, 232.

175. For Day's reaction see Miller, *Dorothy Day*, 482–83.

176. Borgese, 420–21.

177. Piehl, 233.

178. McNeal, *Peace Movement*, 264; Borgese, 421.

179. McNeal, *Peace Movement*, 234–35, and "Catholic Conscientious Objectors," 222.

180. See, for example, Bainton, *Christian Attitudes*, 85–135; "Pacifism," in NCE 10:856.

181. See Zahn, *Solitary Witness*, 199–206, and "In Praise," 145.

182. McNeal, *Peace Movement*, 218. See Furfey's criticisms of this stance in Shannon, *What Are They Saying*, 60–61.

183. O'Brien, "American Catholic Opposition," 126.

184. Saigon, Christmas Eve, 1966. See McEoin, 159.

185. Manila, Dec. 28, 1966. See McEoin.

186. Lubic, Philippines, Dec. 29, 1966. See McEoin. For Dorothy Day's criticisms see "In Peace Is My Bitterness Most Bitter," in Day, *By Little and Little*, 337–39.

187. See McNeal, *Peace Movement*, 232–33.

188. Nov. 18, 1966. See NOP 25–29.

189. O'Brien, "American Catholic Opposition," 126–27.

190. See NOP 31–32.

191. Forest, "Thomas Merton's Struggle," 19. Day, in "A Prayer for Peace" (*By Little and Little*, 334), praises the cardinal's respect for freedom of conscience and speech and asserts that she would have obeyed his order to fall silent.

192. O'Brien, "American Catholic Opposition," 128–31.

193. See Shannon, *What Are They Saying*, 35–37. For the text see O'Brien and Shannon, 421–67; Nolan, 697–705.

194. See O'Brien and Shannon, 421–22; Nolan, 701–2.

195. See chapter 13, pp. 193–95.

196. Par. 106, quoting *Pastoral Constitution*, par. 81.

197. Par. 123. See chapter 12, pp. 171–83.

198. See O'Brien, "American Catholic Opposition," 120–21.

199. Summer 1965, inside cover. See O'Brien, "American Catholic Opposition," 125.

200. Ibid., 133–35.

201. See Deedy, "Catholic Press," 121–31.

202. They averaged 27 percent opposed, Jews 48 percent opposed, and Western European Protestants, 17 percent. See Greeley, 101, Table 5:7; O'Brien, "American Catholic Opposition," 147. On greater Catholic opposition to war in general see Greeley, 96. On Catholic opposition to hand guns see Greeley, 99.

203. Given a choice of withdrawal/victory in Vietnam, Anglo-Saxon Protestants recorded 40/36, Catholics, 51/30. See Greeley, 98.

204. Northern white opposition divided along the following lines, Protestant/Catholic: blue collar 50%/47%, clerical 32%/38%, professional 39%/52%. See Greeley, 99–100.

205. *Human Solidarity*, April 1970, in NOP, 47–51.

206. *Declaration on Conscientious Objection and Selective Conscientious Objection*, Oct. 21, 1971, in NOP, 53–57.

207. "American Catholic Bishops Support Selective Conscientious Objection" (*Christian Century* 88 [Nov. 10, 1971]), 1320.

208. O'Brien, "American Catholic Opposition," 128–31.

209. *Resolution on Southeast Asia*, November 1971, in NOP, 59–62.

210. See Piehl, 232.

211. See McNeal, *Peace Movement*, 235–36; Piehl, 232–39; Merton, "Blessed Are the Meek," 208–18.

212. For an analysis of these challenges see Zahn, "Future"; and Conley, "Catholic Pacifism."

213. McNeal, *Peace Movement*, 241–44, 269–73; Gray, 45–228; and Berrigan, *Trial of the Catonsville Nine*.

214. See McNeal, *Peace Movement*, 265–69.

215. Berrigan, 94–95.

216. Zahn, "Thomas Merton," 73.

217. Gray, 50–56.

218. McNeal, *Peace Movement*, 272. See Meconis.

219. See McNeal, *Peace Movement*, 273–82.

220. See Cornell, "Witness," 210; O'Brien, "American Catholic Opposition," 138–39.

221. See McNeal, *Peace Movement*, 283–93; O'Rourke.

222. See *CPF Bulletin*, May 1984, 4–5; "Civil Disobedience: A Catalyst for Disarmament" (*CPF Peace Education Supplement* 5); Plowshares, *The Hammer Has to Fall*; Jim Schwartz, "A Conspiracy of Conscience," *The Nation*, Dec. 8, 1984; and "Plowshares Update," *The Nation*, Jan. 19, 1985.

223. See McAlister, "For Love of the Children"; Plowshares, *Hammer Has to Fall* 32–36; *CPF Bulletin* (May 1984), 5.

224. Grace, 13.

225. Plowshares, *Hammer Has to Fall*, 12–16.

226. Ibid., 50–54.

227. Grace, 13.

228. See "In Support of Protestors," in Plowshares, *Hammer Has to Fall*, 8–11.

229. See Miller, *Dorothy Day*, 500. On Chavez as a Christian peacemaker see Hope and Young, *Struggle*, 147–82; Conley, 383.

230. See chapter 12, pp. 182.

231. See Fahey, "Pax Christi," in Shannon, *War or Peace?*, 60–61.

232. Fahey, "Pax Christi," 68; van Allen, 613.

233. See Zahn, "Carrying Our Weight," 143.

234. See Zahn, "Carrying Our Weight," 143–44; Fahey, "Pax Christi," 61–62; McNeal, *Peace Movement*, 229, 309–11; McCloskey, "CAIP," and "Farewell to CAIP."

235. For a summary of Dozier's views of peace see his "Peace: Gift and Task."

236. See Zahn, "Carrying Our Weight," 144–45.

237. See Gilhooley, "Pax Christi"; van Allen.

238. See Graham, "Pax Christi," 35.

239. See Fahey, "Pax Christi," 63–70.

240. Jones, "Pax Christi Conference."

241. See *Reporter for Conscience Sake* 39:4 (April 1982): 27.

242. *Reporter for Conscience Sake* 30:6 (June 1983): 2.

243. As for selective conscientious objection, see above p. 256.

244. See, for example, U.S. Catholic Conference, *A Call to Action*, especially Appendix, 160–66.

245. U.S. Catholic Conference, *To Live in Jesus Christ*. See J. Finn, "Pacifism," 9; and Shannon, *What Are They Saying*, 37–38.

246. *The Gospel of Peace and the Danger of War* (Feb. 15, 1978), in NOP, 69–71. In 1976 Cardinal Krol of Philadelphia had already endorsed the treaty. See Shannon, *What Are They Saying*, 39–42.

247. *SALT II: A Statement of Support* (Sept. 6, 1979), in NOP, 73–82.

248. *Statement on Registration and Conscription for Military Service* (Feb. 14, 1980), in NOP, 83–86.

249. Dated Nov. 19, 1981, published Washington, D.C., 1982. For Latin American developments see chapter 14.

250. Church support for refugees, including asylum, continued into 1985, despite Reagan administration moves to prosecute lay and church people. See *New York Times*, April 1, 1984; *Fellowship* (July–August 1984), 34; *Time* (July 9, 1984), 68; *New York Times* (Jan. 15, 22, 24–25, 1985).

251. For the text see "Faith and Disarmament," in *U.S. Bishops Speak*, 1–2. See also Shan-

non, *What Are They Saying*, 92–95; and NCR 18:14 (Feb. 5, 1982), 1, 27.

252. "The Way of Jesus," in *U.S. Bishops Speak*, 4.

253. "The Production and Stockpiling of the Neutron Bomb," in *U.S. Bishops Speak*, 4; Shannon, *What Are They Saying*, 91–92.

254. I follow the edition published by the Daughters of St. Paul. See also Murnion, 245–335; Castelli, 185–276.

255. See, for example, Castelli; Shannon, *What Are They Saying*, 85–89, 101–9; and the reviews by Richard McSorley, S.J., in the *Reporter for Conscience Sake* 40:1 (January 1983), 6–8; and 40:5 (May 1983), 8.

256. See Cornell, "War and Peace Pastoral."

257. Zahn, "Appreciation," in *Alternative to War*, xxvii.

# BIBLIOGRAPHY

## PRIMARY SOURCES

Abbott, Walter M., and Joseph Gallagher, eds. *Documents of Vatican II*. New York: Guild, America, and Association Presses, 1966.

*The Ante-Nicene Library*. 10 vols. Grand Rapids, Mich.: Eerdmans, 1951–1953.

Aquinas, Thomas. *On the Truth of the Catholic Faith (Summa contra Gentiles)*. Edited and translated by Anton Pegis and James F. Anderson. 2 vols. Garden City, N.Y.: Doubleday, 1960.

Augustine of Hippo. *The City of God*. Translated by Henry Bettenson and edited by David Knowles. New York: Pelican, 1977.

Bacon, Roger. *Opus majus ad Clementem quartem*. Edited by J. H. Bridges. Oxford: Oxford University Press, 1900.

———. *Opus majus*. Translated by Robert B. Burke. New York: Russell and Russell, 1962.

Bainton, Roland H., ed. *Early Christianity*. New York: Van Nostrand, 1960.

Baldwin, Marshall W., ed. *Christianity through the Thirteenth Century*. New York: Harper and Row, 1970.

Barry, Colman J., O.S.B., ed. *Readings in Church History*. Vol. 1, *From Pentecost to the Protestant Revolt*. Westminster, Md.: Newman Press, 1966.

Bede. *A History of the English Church and People*. Translated by Leo Sherley-Price. Baltimore: Penguin, 1965.

Berrigan, Daniel, S.J. *The Trial of the Catonsville Nine*. Boston: Beacon Press, 1970.

Bieler, Ludwig, ed. *The Irish Penitentials*. Vol. 5 of *Scriptores Latini Hiberniae*. Dublin: Institute for Advanced Studies, 1963.

Boff, Leonardo. "Christ's Liberation via Oppression: An Attempt at Theological Construction from the Standpoint of Latin America." In Gibellini, 100–132.

Bonaventure. *The Life of St. Francis (Legenda maior)*. In *Bonaventure*, translated and edited by Ewert Cousins. New York: Paulist, 1978.

Brant, Sebastian. *The Ship of Fools*. Translated and edited by Edwin H. Zeydel. New York: Dover, 1962.

Camara, Helder. *Revolution Through Peace*. Translated by Amparo McLean and edited by Ruth Nanada Anshen. New York: Harper and Row, 1971.

*The Catholic Worker*. New York, 1933–.

Cone, James H., and Gayraud S. Wilmore, eds. *Black Theology: A Documentary History 1966–1979*. Maryknoll, N.Y.: Orbis, 1979.

*Corpus Christianorum: Series Latina* (CCSL). Turnhout, Paris: Brepols, 1953–.

*Corpus Scriptorum Ecclesiasticorum Latinorum* (CSEL). 60 vols. Vienna: Akademie der Wissenschaften, 1866–1913.

Coulton, G. G., trans. and ed. *From St. Francis to Dante: Translations from the Chronicle of the Franciscan Salimbene (1221–88)*. Translation of *Chronicon* by Salimbene da Adam. Philadelphia: University of Pennsylvania Press, 1972.

Crucé, Emeric. *Le Nouveau Cynée*. Translated by Thomas W. Balch. Philadelphia: Allen, Lane, and Scott, 1909.

———. "A Holy Resolve." In P. Mayer, ed., *The Pacifist Conscience*, 68–70.

Cunningham, Agnes, S.S.C.M., ed. *The Early Church and the State*. Philadelphia: Fortress, 1982.

Dante Alighieri. *On World Government (De Monarchia)*. Translated by Herbert W. Schneider, introduction by Dino Bigongiari. Indianapolis and New York: Bobbs Merrill, 1957.

Davenport, Frances G., ed. *European Treaties Bearing on the History of the United States and Its Dependencies to 1648*. 4 vols. Washington, D.C.: Carnegie Institution, 1917–1937. Reprinted Gloucester, Mass.: Peter Smith, 1967.

Dawson, Christopher, ed. *Mission to Asia*, New York: Harper and Row, 1966.

Day, Dorothy. *By Little and Little: The Selected Writings of Dorothy Day*. Edited by Robert Ellsberg. New York: Alfred A. Knopf, 1983.

———. *Loaves and Fishes*. San Francisco: Harper and Row, 1983.

———. *The Long Loneliness*. New York: Harper and Row, 1952. Reissued San Francisco: Harper and Row, 1983.

Dolan, John P., ed. *The Essential Erasmus*. New York: Mentor-Omega, 1964.

Dolci, Danilo. *Creature of Creatures: Selected Poems*. Translated by Justin Vitiello. Saratoga, Calif.: Anma Libri, 1980.

———. *The Man Who Plays Alone*. New York: Pantheon, 1968.

———. "Trial Statement." From *Outlaws*, in P. Mayer, *Pacifist Conscience*, 391–401.

Douglas, David C., and George W. Greenway. *English Historical Documents*. vol. 2. New York: Oxford University Press, 1968.

Dozier, Carol T. "Peace: Gift and Task: A Pastoral Letter." *Commonweal* 95 (Dec. 24, 1971): 289, 294–300.

Dubois, Pierre. *The Recovery of the Holy Land*. Translated, with introduction and notes by Walther I. Brandt. New York: Columbia University Press, 1956.

Eagleson, John, and Philip Scharper, eds. *Puebla and Beyond*. Translated by John Drury. Maryknoll, N.Y.: Orbis, 1980.

Eagleson, John, and Sergio Torres, eds. *The Challenge of Basic Christian Communities*. Maryknoll, N.Y.: Orbis, 1981.

Ellacuria, Ignacio. *Freedom Made Flesh: The Mission of Christ and His Church*. Translated by John Drury. Maryknoll, N.Y.: Orbis, 1976.

Erasmus, Desiderius. *The Adages of Erasmus*. Edited by Margaret Mann Philips. Cambridge: Cambridge University Press, 1968.

———. *Charon*. In Thompson, ed., *Ten Colloquies*, 113–19.

———. *The Collected Works of Erasmus*. Toronto: University of Toronto Press, 1974–.

———. *The Colloquies of Erasmus*. Translated and edited by Craig R. Thompson. Chicago: University of Chicago Press, 1965.

———. *The Complaint of Peace*. In Dolan 1964, 174–204.

———. *Consultatio de bello Turcis inferendo*. Athens: Karavia, 1974. Reprint of the 1643 edition of the *Ultissima Consultatio*.

———. *Cyclops, or the Gospel Bearer*. In Thompson, *Ten Colloquies*, 120–29.

———. *The Education of a Christian Prince*. Translated and edited by Lester K. Born. New York: Columbia University Press, 1968.

———. *Erasmus Against War*. In Erasmus, *Adages*, 308–53.

———. *Erasmus: Ten Colloquies*. Edited by Craig R. Thompson. Indianapolis and New York: Bobbs-Merrill, 1957.

———. *The Essential Erasmus*. Edited by John P. Dolan. New York: Mentor-Omega, 1964.

———. *The Funeral*. In Thompson, ed., *Ten Colloquies*, 92–112.

———. *The Grub Pursues the Eagle*. In Erasmus, *Adages*, 229–65.

———. *The Handbook of the Militant Christian*. In Dolan, ed., 24–93.

———. *The Ignoble Knight*. In Thompson, ed., *Colloquies*, 424–32.

———. *The Julius Exclusus of Erasmus*. Translated by Paul Pascal. Bloomington, Ind.: Indiana University Press, 1968.

———. *Letter to Anthony of Bergen*. In P. Mayer, *Pacifist Conscience*, 53–59.

———. *Letter to Paul Volz*. In *Desiderius Erasmus: Christian Humanism and the Reformation*, edited by John C. Olin, 107–33. New York: Harper and Row, 1965.

———. *Letters*. In *The Correspondence of Erasmus*, translated and edited by R. A. B. Mynors and D. F. S. Thomson. 6 vols. In *The Collected Works of Erasmus*, 1974–.

———. *Military Affairs*. In Thompson, ed., *Colloquies*, 11–15.

———. *The Praise of Folly*. In Dolan, *Erasmus*, 94–173.

———. *Sileni Alcibiades*. In Erasmus, *Adages*, 269–300.

———. *The Soldier and the Carthusian*. In Thompson, *Colloquies*, 127–33.

Esquivel, Adolfo Perez. *Christ in a Poncho*. Edited by Charles Antoine, and translated by Robert R. Barr. Maryknoll, N.Y.: Orbis, 1983.

Eulogius of Cordova. *Memoriale sanctorum libri III*. PL 115:731–870.

*Fathers of the Church: A New Translation*. 68 vols. New York: CIMA, 1947–.

Ferguson, John. *Greek and Roman Religion: A Source Book*. Park Ridge, N.J.: Noyes, 1980.

Flannery, Harry W., ed. *Pattern for Peace: Catholic Statements on International Order*. Westminster, Md.: Newman, 1962.

Francis of Assisi. *Francis of Assisi: Writer*. Chicago: Franciscan Herald Press, 1983.

————. *Francis and Clare: The Complete Works*. Translated by Regis J. Armstrong, O.F.M. Cap., and Ignatius Brady, O.F.M.. New York: Paulist, 1982.

————. *St. Francis of Assisi: Writings and Early Biographies. English Omnibus of the Sources for the Life of St. Francis* (Omnibus). Edited by Marion A. Habig, O.F.M. Chicago: Franciscan Herald Press, 1973.

Galilea, Segundo. "Liberation Theology and New Tasks Facing Christians." In Gibellini, 163–83.

Gibellini, Rosino, ed. *Frontiers of Theology in Latin America*. Translated by John Drury. Maryknoll, N.Y.: Orbis, 1979.

Goffart, Walter, ed. *Barbarians and Romans A.D. 418–584*. Princeton, N.J.: Princeton University Press, 1980.

Greene, James J., and John P. Dolan, eds. *The Essential Thomas More*. New York: Mentor-Omega, 1967.

Gregory of Tours. *History of the Franks*. Translated and edited by Ernest Brehaut. New York: Norton, 1969.

Gutiérrez, Gustavo. "Liberation Praxis and Christian Faith." In Gibellini, 1–33.

————. *A Theology of Liberation*. Translated and edited by Caridad Inda and John Eagleson. Maryknoll, N.Y.: Orbis, 1973.

Hennacy, Ammon. *The Autobiography of a Catholic Anarchist*. New York: Catholic Worker, 1954.

Hillgarth, J. N., ed. *The Conversion of Western Europe, 300–750*. Englewood Cliffs, N.J.: Prentice-Hall, 1969.

Hoare, F. R., trans. and ed. *Sulpicius Severus et al.: The Western Fathers*. New York: Harper and Row, 1965.

Hunthausen, Most Rev. Raymond. "Faith and Disarmament." In *U.S. Bishops Speak against Nuclear Arms*, 1–2.

Kenny, Most Rev. Michael. "The Way of Jesus." In *U.S. Bishops Speak against Nuclear Arms*, 4.

Kidd, Beresford J., ed. *Documents Illustrative of the Early Church*. 2 vols. New York: Macmillan, 1920–1923.

Koenig, Harry C., ed. *Principles of Peace: Selections from Papal Documents: Leo XIII to Pius XII*. Washington, D.C.: National Catholic Welfare Conference, 1943.

Las Casas, Bartolomé de. *The Devastation of the Indies: A Brief Account*. Translated by Herma Buffault. New York: Seabury, 1974.

————. *History of the Indies*. Translated and edited by Andree Collard. New York: Harper and Row, 1971.

————. *In Defense of the Indians*. Translated, edited, and annotated by Stafford Poole, C.M. DeKalb, Ill.: Northern Illinois University Press, 1974.

Lewis, Naphtali, and Meyer Reinhold, eds. *Roman Civilization*. 2 vols. New York: Harper and Row, 1966.

*Library of Christian Classics* (LCC). Edited by J. Baille, J. T. MacNeill, and H. P. van Dusen, eds. Philadelphia: Westminster, 1953–.

Lull, Ramon. *Blanquerna: A Thirteenth-Century Romance*. Edited by E. Allison Peers. London: Jarrold's, 1926.

————. Excerpted in *Late Medieval Mysticism*, edited by Ray C. Petry, 142–69. Philadelphia: Westminster Press, 1957.

McDermott, William C., ed. *Monks, Bishops and Pagans*. Rev. ed. Philadelphia: University of Pennsylvania Press, 1981.

McGinn, Bernard, ed. *Apocalyptic Spirituality*. New York: Paulist Press, 1979.

McNeill, John T., and Helena M. Gamer, eds. *Medieval Handbooks of Penance*. New York: Columbia University Press, 1938.

Marsiglio of Padua. *The Defender of Peace (Defensor pacis)*. Translated and edited by Alan Gewirth. New York: Harper and Row, 1967.

Matthiesen, Most Rev. Leroy T. "The Production and Stockpiling of the Neutron Bomb." In *U.S. Bishops Speak against Nuclear Arms*, 4.

Maurin, Peter. *Easy Essays*. New York: Sheed and Ward, 1936. Reissued Chicago. Franciscan Herald Press, 1977.

Mayer, Peter, ed. *The Pacifist Conscience.* Harmondsworth: Penguin, 1966.

Merton, Thomas. "Blessed Are the Meek: The Christian Roots of Nonviolence." In Zahn, *Nonviolent Alternative,* 208–18.

———. "The Christian in World Crisis: Reflections on the Moral Climate of the 1960s." In Zahn, *Nonviolent Alternative,* 20–62.

———. "An Enemy of the State." In Zahn, *Nonviolent Alternative,* 134–38.

———. "A Martyr for Peace and Unity: Father Max Josef Metzger (1887–1944)." In Zahn, *Nonviolent Alternative,* 139–43.

———. *The Nonviolent Alternative.* Rev. ed. of *Thomas Merton on Peace.* Edited by Gordon Zahn. New York: Farrar, Straus, Giroux, 1980.

———. "Passivity and Abuse of Authority." In Zahn, *Nonviolent Alternative,* 129–33.

———. "Peace: Christian Duties and Perspectives." In Zahn, *Nonviolent Alternative,* 12–19.

Montaigne, Michel Eyquem de. *The Complete Essays.* Translated by Donald M. Frame. Stanford, Calif.: Stanford University Press, 1958.

*Monumenta Germaniae historiae: Scriptores rerum Germanicarum* (MGH, Scriptores). Hanover: Gesellschaft für ältere deutsche Geschichtskunde, 1826–.

More, Thomas. *A Dialogue Concerning Heresies.* Edited by Thomas M. C. Lawlor, Germain Marc'hadour, and Richard C. Marius. Vol. 6 of *The Yale Edition of the Complete Works of Thomas More* (1981).

———. *A Dialogue of Comfort against Tribulation.* Edited by Louis L. Martz and Frank Manley. Vol. 12 of *The Yale Thomas More.* New Haven, Conn.: Yale University Press, 1976.

———. *The Essential Thomas More,* selected and edited by James J. Greene and John P. Dolan. New York: Mentor-Omega, 1967.

———. *Utopia.* In *The Essential Thomas More,* 23–96.

Munier, C., ed. *Concilia Galliae A. 314–A. 506.* Turnholt: Brepols, 1963.

Musurillo, Herbert A., S.J., ed. *The Acts of the Christian Martyrs.* Oxford: Clarendon Press, 1972.

Nolan, Hugh J., ed. *Pastoral Letters of the American Hierarchy 1792–1970.* Huntington, Ind.: Our Sunday Visitor, 1971.

O'Brien, David J., and Thomas A. Shannon, eds. *Renewing the Earth: Catholic Documents on Peace, Justice and Liberation.* Garden City, N.Y.: Image Books, 1977.

Olivi, Peter John. *Peter Olivi's Rule Commentary.* Edited by David Flood. Weisbaden: F. Steiner, 1972.

———. *La "Lectura super Apocalipsim" di Pietro di Giovanni Olivi.* Edited by Raoul Manselli. Rome: Istituto Storico Italiano per il Medioevo, 1955.

Pascal, Blaise. *Pensées.* Introduction by T. S. Eliot. New York: Dutton, 1958.

*Patrologia cursus completus. Series Greca* (PG). 161 vols. Edited by Jacques-Paul Migne. Paris: Migne, 1857–1934.

*Patrologia cursus completus. Series Latina* (PL). 221 vols. Edited by Jacques-Paul Migne. Paris: Migne, 1843–1890.

Persky, Stan, and Henry Flam, eds. *The Solidarity Sourcebook.* Vancouver: New Star, 1982.

Philips, Margaret Mann, ed. *The Adages of Erasmus.* Cambridge: Cambridge University Press, 1968.

Plowshares. *For Swords into Plowshares, The Hammer Has to Fall.* Piscataway, N.J.: Plowshares Press, 1984.

Quinn, Most Rev. John R. "The Very Survival of the Human Race Is at Stake." In *U.S. Bishops Speak against Nuclear Arms,* 3.

Rabelais, François. *The Histories of Gargantua and Pantagruel.* Translated by J. M. Cohen. Baltimore, Md.: Penguin, 1969.

Saint-Pierre, Charles Irenée Castel de. *A Project for Perpetual Peace.* In *Peace Projects of the Eighteenth Century,* edited by M. C. Jacob, 1–61. New York: Garland, 1974.

Salimbene da Adam. *Chronicon.* Translated and edited by G. G. Coulton. *From St. Francis to Dante: Translations from the Chronicle of the Franciscan Salimbene (1221–88).* Philadelphia: University of Pennsylvania Press, 1972.

———. *Chronicon.* Edited by O. Holder-Egger. In MGH, Scriptores, vol. 32.

———. *Chronicon.* Edited by Giuseppi Scalia. 2 vols. Bari: Laterza, 1966.

Schaefer, Mary C., ed. *A Papal Peace Mosaic 1878–1936: Excerpts from the Messages of Popes Leo XIII, Pius X, Benedict XV, and Pius XI.* Washington, D.C.: CAIP, 1936.

Segundo, Juan Luis. "Capitalism versus Socialism: Crux Theologica." In Gibellini, 240–59.

*A Select Library of Nicene and Post-Nicene Fathers of the Christian Church.* Edited by Philip Schaff and Henry Wall. 28 vols. Grand Rapids, Mich.: Eerdmans, 1952–1956.

Stevenson, James, ed. *Creeds, Councils, and Controversies: Documents Illustrative of the History of the Church* A.D. *337–461.* London: S.P.C.K., 1966.

——. *A New Eusebius: Documents Illustrative of the History of the Church to* A.D. *337.* London: S.P.C.K., 1960.

Talbot, C. H., ed. *The Anglo-Saxon Missionaries in Germany.* London: Sheed and Ward, 1981.

Thomas à Kempis. *Of the Imitation of Christ.* Edited by Abbot Justin McCann. New York: Mentor-Omega, 1962.

Thompson, Craig R., trans. and ed. *The Colloquies of Erasmus.* Chicago: University of Chicago Press, 1965.

Thompson, Craig R., ed. *Erasmus: Ten Colloquies.* Indianapolis and New York: Bobbs-Merrill, 1957.

Tierney, Brian, ed. *The Crisis of Church and State 1050–1300.* Englewood Cliffs, N.J.: Prentice-Hall, 1964.

——. *The Middle Ages.* Vol. 1, *Sources of Medieval History.* 3d ed. New York: Alfred A. Knopf, 1978.

Tischner, Josef. *The Spirit of Solidarity.* Translated by Marek B. Zaleski and Benjamin Fiore, S.J. San Francisco: Harper and Row, 1982.

Torres, Sergio, and John Eagleson, eds. *Theology in the Americas.* Maryknoll, N.Y.: Orbis, 1976.

Tugwell, Simon, O.P., ed. *The Early Dominicans.* New York: Paulist, 1982.

*U.S. Bishops Speak against Nuclear Arms.* Catholic Peace Fellowship, Peace Education Supplement 4.

U. S. Catholic Conference. *A Call to Action: An Agenda for the Catholic Community.* Washington, D.C., 1976.

——. *The Challenge of Peace: God's Promise and Our Response.* Washington, D.C., 1983. Also published in Castelli, 185–276, and by the Daughters of St. Paul, Boston, 1983.

——. *In the Name of Peace: Collective Statements of the United States Catholic Bishops on War and Peace 1919–1980* (NOP). Washington, D.C., 1983.

——. *Statement on Central America.* Washington, D.C., 1982.

——. *Statement on Registration and Conscription for Military Service.* In NOP (Feb. 14, 1980), 83–86.

——. *To Live in Jesus Christ: A Pastoral Reflection on the Moral Life.* Washington, D.C., 1976.

Vasto, Lanzo del. *Make Straight the Way of the Lord.* New York: Alfred A. Knopf, 1974.

Vidales, Raul. "Methodological Issues in Liberation Theology." *Frontiers,* 34–57.

Vitoria, Francisco de. *De Indis et de iure belli relectiones.* Edited by Ernest Nys, and translated by John P. Bate. Washington, D.C.: Carnegie Institution, 1917. Reprinted Dobbs Ferry, N.Y.: Oceana, 1964.

Vives, Juan Luis. *Introduction to Wisdom: A Renaissance Textbook.* Edited by Marian Leona Tobriner, S.N.J.M. New York: Columbia University Press, 1968.

Wright, Frederick Adam, ed. *Fathers of the Church: Tertullian, Cyprian, Arnobius, Lactantius, Ambrose, Jerome, Augustine.* New York: Dutton, 1929.

## SECONDARY WORKS

Adams, Robert T. *The Better Part of Valor: More, Erasmus, Colet, and Vives on Humanism, War and Peace 1496–1535.* Seattle, Wash.: University of Washington Press, 1962.

——. "Pre-Renaissance Courtly Propaganda for Peace in English Literature." *Papers of the Michigan Academy* 32 (1946–48): 431–46.

Aguilar, José Manuel de. *The Law of Nations and the Salamanca School of Theology.* Washington, D.C.: Spanish Embassy, 1947.

Albright, William Foxwell. *From the Stone Age to Christianity.* 2d ed. Garden City, N.Y.: Doubleday, 1957.

Allegro, John Marco. *The Chosen People: A Study of Jewish History from the Time of the Exile to the Revolt of Bar Kocheba.* London: Hodder and Stoughton, 1971.

Allen, John. "The Bishops' Letter: Challenge . . . What Response?" *The Objector* 4:1 (Sept. 1, 1983): 4.

Alphandéry, Paul. *La Chrétienté et l'idée de croisade.* 2 vols. Paris: Albin Michel, 1954–1959.

Altaner, Berthold. *Patrology.* Translated by Hilda C. Graff. Westminster, Md.: Herder and Herder, 1960.

————. "Raymundus Lullus und der Sprächenkanon des Konzils von Vienne." *Historisches Jahrbuch* 52 (1933): 190–219.

Althoff, Gerd. "Nunc fiant Christi milites, qui dudum extiterunt raptores. Zur Entstehung von Rittertum und Ritterethos." *Saeculum* 32 (4, 1981): 317–33.

"American Catholic Bishops Support Selective Conscientious Objection." *Christian Century* 88 (Nov. 10, 1971): 1320.

Anderson, Bernhard W. *Understanding the Old Testament.* Englewood Cliffs, N.J.: Prentice-Hall, 1975.

Armaingaud, N. "Montaigne et la guerre." *Revue politique et parlementaire* 98 (1919):81–86, 186–96, 304–315.

Arnaldi, Francesco, and Maria Turriani. "Pax." In *Latinitatis italicae Medii Aevi unde ab A. CDLXXVI usque ad A. MXXII Lexicon imperfectum,* 2:219. Brussels: Union Academique Internationale, 1936–.

Atiya, Aziz S. *The Crusade in the Later Middle Ages.* 2d ed. London: Butler and Tanner, 1938. Reprinted New York: Kraus, 1965.

Attwater, Donald. *The Penguin Dictionary of Saints.* New York: Penguin, 1976.

Auerbach, Erich. *Mimesis: The Representation of Reality in Western Literature.* Translated by Willard R. Trask. Princeton, N.J.: Princeton University Press, 1960.

Bainton, Roland H. *Christian Attitudes toward War and Peace.* Nashville, Tenn.: Abingdon Press, 1980.

————. "The Early Church and War." *Harvard Theological Review* 39 (1946): 189–213.

————. *Erasmus of Christendom.* New York: Charles Scribner's, 1969.

Bark, William Carroll. *The Origins of the Medieval World.* Stanford, Calif.: Stanford University Press, 1966.

Barnes, Timothy D. *Constantine and Eusebius.* Cambridge, Mass.: Harvard University Press, 1981.

Baron, Salo Wittmayer. *A Social and Religious History of the Jews.* 17 vols. New York: Columbia University Press, 1952–1976.

Barraclough, Geoffrey. *The Medieval Papacy.* New York: Norton, 1979.

Barrett, Charles Kingsley. *The New Testament Background.* New York: Harper and Row, 1961.

Bataillon, Marcel. *Erasme et l'Espagne.* Paris: Droz, 1937.

Bauer, W. *A Greek-English Lexicon of the New Testament.* Chicago: University of Chicago Press, 1979.

Baus, Karl. "Early Christian Monasticism: Development and Expansion in the East, 337–73." In Baus, *Imperial Church,* 337–73.

————. *From the Apostolic Community to Constantine.* Vol. 1 of Jedin and Dolan.

————. *The Imperial Church from Constantine to the Early Middle Ages.* Vol. 2 of Jedin and Dolan. Translated by Anselm Biggs. New York: Seabury, 1980.

————. "Latin Monasticism from the Mid-Fifth Century to the End of the Seventh Century." In Baus, *Imperial Church,* 690–707.

————. "The Monasticism of the Latin West." In Baus, *Imperial Church,* 374–92.

Baus, Karl, and Eugen Ewig. "Missionary Activity of the Church." In Baus, *Imperial Church,* 181–230.

Baylor, Michael George. *Conscience in Late Scholasticism and the Young Luther.* Ann Arbor, Mich.: University Microfilms, 1971.

Beales, Arthur C. F. *The Catholic Church and International Order.* Harmondsworth: Penguin, 1941.

————. *The History of Peace.* London: G. Bell, and New York: Dial, 1931.

Beck, H., and C. Brown. "Peace." *New International Dictionary of New Testament Theology* 2:776–83.

Bense, Walter F. "Paris Theologians on War and Peace, 1521–1529." *Church History* 41 (1972): 168–85.

Benson, Robert L. "Medieval Canonistic Origins of the Debate on the Usefulness of the Spanish Conquest." In Chiappelli, 1:327–34.

Berardini, Lorenzo, O.F.M. Conv. *Frate Angelo Chiarino alla luce della storia.* Osimo: Pax et Bonum, 1964.

Berenger, Jean. "The Austrian Church." In Callahan and Higgs, 88–105.

Bernas, Joaquin G. "Empowering the Powerless." *America* 145 (Dec. 26, 1981): 414.

Berry, Virginia. "Peter the Venerable and the Crusades." In Constable and Kritzeck, 141–62.

Berryman, Philip E. "Latin American Liberation Theology." In Torres and Eagleson, 20–83.

————. *The Religious Roots of Rebellion: Christians in Central American Revolutions.* Maryknoll, N.Y.: Orbis, 1984.

*Bibliotheca Sanctorum* (BS). Istituto Giovanni XXIII della Pontificia Università Lateranense. 12 vols. Rome: Società Grafica Romana, 1961–1970.

Bieler, Ludwig. "Penitentials." In NCE 11:86–87.

Biermann, Benno M. "Bartolomé de Las Casas and Verapaz." In Friede and Keen, 443–84.

Bishop, Jane C. *Pope Nicholas I and the First Age of Papal Independence.* Ph. D. Dissertation. Columbia University, 1980.

"Bishops: Catholic Personnel Must Look at Own Role in Nuclear Warfare." *The Objector* 3:3 (Dec. 1982): 5–6.

"Bishops, the COs and Amnesty." *America* 125 (Sept. 4, 1971): 108.

Bisson, Thomas N. "The Organized Peace in Southern France and Catalonia c. 1140–c. 1233." *American Historical Review* 82:2 (1977): 290–311.

Blet, P. "La Représentation pontificale de Gregoire I à Gregoire XIII." *Divinitas* 19 (1975): 335–52.

Bligny, Bernard. "Monachisme et pauvreté au xii$^e$ siècle." In *La Povertà del secolo xii et Francesco d'Assisi,* 99–147. Atti del II Convegno Internazionale. Società Internazionale di Studi Francescani, Assisi, 1975.

Bloch, Marc. *Feudal Society.* Translated by L. A. Manyon. 2 vols. Chicago: University of Chicago Press, 1965.

Bloomfield, Morton W. *Piers Plowman as a Fourteenth-Century Apocalypse.* New Brunswick, N.J.: Rutgers University Press, 1962.

Bokenkotter, Thomas. *A Concise History of the Catholic Church.* Rev. ed. Garden City, N.Y.: Doubleday, 1979.

Bolton, Brenda M. "Innocent III's Treatment of the Humiliati." *Studies in Church History* 8 (Cambridge, 1972): 73–82.

———. "*Paupertas Christi:* Old Wealth and New Poverty in the Twelfth Century." In *Renaissance and Renewal in Christian History,* 95–103. Oxford: Basil Blackwell, 1977.

Bonnaud-Delamare, Roger. "Fondement des institutions de paix au xi$^e$ siècle." In *Mélanges d'histoire du Moyen Âge dédiés à la mémoire de Louis Halphen.* Paris: Press Universitaire, 1951.

———. *L'Idée de paix à l'époque Carolingienne.* Paris: Domat-Montchrétien, 1939.

———. "Les Institutions de paix en Aquitaine au xi$^e$ siècle." *Recueils . . . Jean Bodin* 14 (1961): 415–87.

———. "La Paix d'Amiens et de Corbie au xi$^e$ siècle." *Revue du Nord* 38 (150) (1956): 167–78.

*The Book of Lech Walesa.* New York: Simon and Schuster, 1982.

Borgese, E. M. "Vatican II: Anathema upon War: Cases of Italian Conscientious Objectors." *Nation* 202 (April 11, 1966): 415–21.

Bosch, David J. "Currents and Crosscurrents in South African Black Theology." In Cone and Wilmore, 220–37.

Bouard, M. "Sur les origines de la trêve de Dieu en Normandie." *Annales de Normandie* 9 (1959): 168–89.

Boussard, Jacques. *The Civilization of Charlemagne.* New York: McGraw-Hill, 1968.

Brachin, Pierre. "*Vox clamantis in deserto:* Reflexions sur le pacifisme d'Erasme." In *Colloquia Erasmiana Turonensia,* edited by Jean-Claude Margolin, 1:247–76. 2 vols. Toronto: University of Toronto Press, 1972.

Braxton, Edward. "Toward a Black Catholic Theology." In Cone and Wilmore, 325–28.

Breit, Marquita, ed. and comp., *Thomas Merton: A Bibliography.* Metuchen, N.J.: Scarecrow, 1974.

Breunig, Charles. *The Age of Revolution and Reaction, 1789–1850.* New York: Norton, 1971.

Brière, Yves de la. "Conceptions du droit international chez les théologiens catholiques." In *Les Grands Systèmes de politique internationale* by C. Dupuis. Paris: Carnegie Endowment for International Peace, 1930.

———. *Église et paix.* Paris: Flammarion, 1932.

———. *L'Organization international du monde contemporain et la papauté souveraine.* 3 vols. Paris: Editions Spes, 1924–1930.

Broad, Robin, and John Cavanaugh. "The Philippines: Government Hits Church in Waves of Repression." *NCR* 19:19 (March 4, 1983): 1, 8.

Broadhead, Meg. "War is Sweet to Those Who Have Not Tried It." *Catholic Worker* 45, 1 (Jan. 1979): 8.

Brock, Peter. *Pacifism in Europe to 1914.* Princeton, N.J.: Princeton University Press, 1972.

———. *Pacifism in the United States from the Colonial Era to the First World War.* Princeton, N.J.: Princeton University Press, 1968.

──────. *The Roots of War Resistance: Pacifism from the Early Church to Tolstoy.* Nyack, N.Y.: Fellowship of Reconciliation, 1981.

Brockman, James R. *The Word Remains: A Life of Oscar Romero.* Maryknoll, N.Y.: Orbis, 1983.

Brooke, Christopher. *Europe in the Central Middle Ages, 962–1154.* New York: Holt, Rinehart and Winston, 1964.

Brown, Peter R. L. "Aspects of the Christianization of the Roman Aristocracy." In Brown, *Religion and Society,* 161–82.

──────. *Augustine of Hippo.* London: Faber and Faber, 1967.

──────. *The Cult of the Saints: Its Rise and Function in Latin Christianity.* Chicago: University of Chicago Press, 1981.

──────. *The Making of Late Antiquity.* Cambridge, Mass.: Harvard University Press, 1978.

──────. *Religion and Society in the Age of St. Augustine.* London: Faber and Faber, 1972.

──────. "St. Augustine's Attitude to Religious Coercion." In Brown, *Religion and Society,* 260–78.

──────. *The World of Late Antiquity.* New York: Harcourt Brace, 1971.

Brown, R. E. "John, Gospel According to St." In NCE 7:1080–88.

Bruce, F. F. *New Testament History.* Garden City, N.Y.: Doubleday, 1971.

Brumberg, Abraham, ed. *Poland: Genesis of a Revolution.* New York: Random House, 1983.

Brundage, James A., ed. *The Crusades: Motives and Achievements.* Boston: D. C. Heath, 1964.

──────. *Medieval Canon Law and the Crusader.* Madison, Wis.: University of Wisconsin Press, 1969.

Bultmann, Rudolf. *Primitive Christianity in its Contemporary Setting.* New York: Meridien, 1956.

Burns, R. I. "Christian-Islamic Confrontation in the West: The Thirteenth Century Dream of Conversion." *American Historical Review* 76 (1971): 1386–1434.

Burr, David. *The Persecution of Peter Olivi.* Philadelphia: American Philosophical Society, 1976.

Butler, Alban. *Butler's Lives of the Saints.* 4 vols. Edited by Donald Attwater and Herbert Thurston. New York: Kennedy, 1956.

Cadoux, Cecil J. *The Early Christian Attitude to War.* New York: Seabury, 1982.

──────. *The Early Church and the World.* Edinburgh: Clark, 1955.

Callahan, Daniel F. "Adhemar de Chabannes et la paix de Dieu." *Annales du Midi* 89,1: 131 (1977):21–43.

Callahan, William J. "The Spanish Church." In Callahan and Higgs, 34–50.

Callahan, William J., and David Higgs, eds. *Church and Society in Catholic Europe of the Eighteenth Century.* New York: Cambridge University Press, 1979.

*Cambridge Ancient History* (CAH). 2d rev. ed. in progress. 12 vols. New York: Cambridge University Press, 1923–.

*The Cambridge Medieval History* (CMH). 8 vols. New York: Cambridge University Press, 1913–1967.

Caraman, Philip. *The Lost Paradise: The Jesuit Republic in South America.* New York: Seabury, 1976.

Carroll, Berenice, and Clinton Fink. *Peace and War: Guide to Bibliographies.* New York: ABC-Clio, 1982.

Castelli, Jim. *The Bishops and the Bomb.* Garden City, N.Y.: Doubleday-Image, 1983.

"Catholic Pacifism: Pax Christi." *America* 131 (Dec. 14, 1974): 379–80.

"Catholic Worker, R. A. LaPorte Burns Self to Death," *Newsweek* 66 (Nov. 22, 1965): 71.

"Catholics and Peace." *Commonweal* 95 (Jan. 7, 1972): 315–16.

Cespedes, Guillermo. *Latin America: The Early Years.* New York: Alfred A. Knopf, 1974.

Chadwick, Henry. *The Early Church.* Baltimore, Md.: Penguin, 1967.

Chadwick, Owen. *The Reformation.* New York: Penguin, 1979.

Chambers, R. W. *Thomas More.* Ann Arbor, Mich.: University of Michigan Press, 1962.

Chapiro, José. *Erasmus and Our Struggle for Peace.* Boston: Beacon Press, 1950.

Chatfield, Charles. *For Peace and Justice: Pacifism in America, 1914–1941.* Boston: Beacon Press, 1973.

──────. *Peace Movements in America.* New York: Schocken, 1973.

Chenu, M.-D., O.P. *Nature, Man, and Society in the Twelfth Century.* Translated and edited by Jerome Taylor and Lester K. Little. Chicago: University of Chicago Press, 1979.

Chiappelli, Fredi, ed. *First Images of America: The Impact of the New World on the Old.* 2 vols. Berkeley and Los Angeles: University of California Press, 1976.

Chickering, Roger P. "The Peace Movement and the Religious Community in Germany 1900–1914." *Church History* 38 (1969): 300–311.

Chitty, Derwas J. *The Desert a City*. Oxford: Basil Blackwell, 1966.
Christiansen, Eric. *The Northern Crusades*. Minneapolis: University of Minnesota Press, 1980.
*The Church and the Arms Race*. Cambridge, Mass.: Pax Christi, 1977.
"Church of Both Right and Left Suffers . . . Splits." NCR 19: 41 (Sept. 16, 1983): 6–7, 9.
Clasen, Sophronius, O.F.M. "Poverty Movement." In NCE 11:652–53.
Claver, Francisco F. "Free Even in Enslavement. The Philippines: Yesterday, Today, Tomorrow." *Commonweal* 111 (March 9, 1984): 141–45.
————. "Prophesy or Accommodation: The Dilemma of a Discerning Church." *America* 142 (April 26, 1980): 354–56.
*Clavis Patrum Graecorum* (CPG). Edited by Maurice Geerard. Turnhout, Paris: Brepols, 1974–.
*Clavis Patrum Latinorum* (CPL). Edited by Eligius Dekkers. Steinberg: St. Peter's Abbey, 1951–.
Cochrane, Charles N. *Christianity and Classical Culture*. New York: Oxford University Press, 1957.
Coffman, J. "CO and the Draft: Bibliography." *Library* 94 (May 15, 1969): 2059–65.
Cohn, Norman. *The Pursuit of the Millennium*. New York: Harper and Row, 1961.
Colbert, Edward P. *The Martyrs of Cordoba (850–859): A Study of the Sources*. Washington, D.C.: Catholic University, 1962.
Comblin, José. *The Church and the National Security State*. Maryknoll, N.Y.: Orbis, 1979.
Comblin, Joseph. *Théologie de la paix*. 2 vols. Paris: Éditions universitaires, 1960–1963.
"Conditions of Peace: Concerning John XXIII's Recent Encyclical." *America* 109 (July 13, 1963): 38.
Cone, James H., and Gayraud S. Wilmore. "Black Theology: Considerations for Dialogue, Critique, and Integration." In Cone and Wilmore *Documentary*, 463–76.
Congar, Yves M.-J. "Incidence ecclésiologique d'un thème de dévotion mariale." *Mélanges de Science Religieuse* 7 (1950): 277–92.
————. "Les Positions ecclésiologiques de Pierre Jean Olivi." In *Franciscains d'Oc*, 155–65.
Conley, J. J. "Catholic Pacifism in America." *America* 131 (Dec. 14, 1974): 381–83.
Connery, J. R. "Law and Conscience." *America* 122 (Feb. 21, 1970): 178–81.
Constable, Giles, and James Kritzeck, eds. *Petrus Venerabilis 1156–1956*. Rome: Studia Anselmiana, 1956.
Constantinescu-Bagdat, Elise. *Études d'histoire pacifique*. 2 vols. Paris: Les Presses Universitaires de France, 1924–1925.
*Conversione al cristianesimo nell'Europa dell'alto medioevo*. Spoleto: Centro italiano di studi sull'alto medioevo, 1967.
Conway, John S. "The Silence of Pope Pius XII." In Delzell, 79–108.
————. "The Struggle for Peace between the Wars: A Chapter from the History of the Western Churches." *Ecumenical Review* 35 (Jan. 1983): 25–40.
Cook, Stanley A. "The Fall and Rise of Judah." CAH 3 (1965): 388–414.
————. "Israel and the Neighboring States." CAH 3 (1965): 354–87.
————. "Israel before the Prophets." CAH 3 (1965): 416–57.
————. "The Prophets of Israel." CAH 3 (1965): 458–99.
Cooper, Sandi E. "The Guns of August and the Doves of Italy: Intervention and Internationalism." *Peace and Change* 7,1–2 (1981): 29–44.
Cornell, Thomas. "The Catholic Church and Witness against War." In Shannon, *War or Peace?*, 200–213.
————. "War and Peace Pastoral." *Catholic Peace Fellowship Bulletin* (March 1983): 1–2.
Costa, Dennis. *Irenic Apocalypse: Some Uses of Apocalyptic in Dante, Petrarch and Rabelais*. Vol. 21, Stanford French and Italian Studies. Saratoga, Calif.: Anma Libri, 1981.
Courtois, C. "L'Évolution du monachisme en Gaule de St. Martin à St. Columban." In *Il monachesimo*, 47–72.
Cowdrey, H. E. J. "Bishop Ermenfrid of Sion and the Penitential Ordinance following the Battle of Hastings." *Journal of Ecclesiastical History* 20 (1969): 225–42.
————. "The Peace and Truce of God." *Past and Present* 46 (1970): 49–56.
Cracco, G. "La Spiritualità italiana del Tre-Quattrocento: Linee interpretative." *Studia Patavina* 18 (1971): 74–116.
Cragg, Gerald R. *The Church and the Age of Reason, 1648–1789*. New York: Penguin, 1981.
Crouzel, H. "Origen." In NCE 10:767–74.
Cumont, Franz. *Oriental Religions in Roman Paganism*. New York: Dover, 1956.
Cuneen, Sally. "The Good News from Latin America." *Christian Century* 98 (Jan. 7, 1981): 5.

Curran, C. E. "Epikeia." In NCE 5:476–77.

Curran, P. C. "Peace." In NCE 11:36–37.

Cutler, Allan. "The First Crusade and the Idea of Conversion." *Muslim World* 58 (1968): 57–71, 155–64.

———. "The Ninth-Century Spanish Martyrs' Movement and the Origins of Western Christian Missions to the Muslims." *Muslim World* 55 (1965): 321–39.

Cviic, Christopher. "The Church." In Brumberg, 92–108.

Cytowska, Maria. "Erasme et les Turcs." *Eos* 62 (1974): 311–21.

Dahlin, Therrin C., et al. *The Catholic Left in Latin America: A Comprehensive Bibliography.* Boston: G. K. Hall, 1981.

Daniel, E. Randolf. "Apocalyptic Conversion: The Joachite Alternative to the Crusades." *Traditio* 25 (1969): 127–54.

———. *The Franciscan Concept of Mission in the High Middle Ages.* Lexington, Ky.: University Press of Kentucky, 1975.

Danielou, J., S.J., and Henri Marrou. *The First Six Hundred Years.* Translated by Vincent Cronin. New York: McGraw-Hill, 1964.

Daube, David. *Civil Disobedience in Antiquity.* Edinburgh: Edinburgh University Press, 1972.

Davidon, A. M. "International War Resisters: Spain." *The Progressive* 40 (October 1976): 8–9.

Davies, R. W. "Police Work in Roman Times." *History Today* 18 (1968): 700–707.

Davis, Charles T. "Le Pape Jean XXII et les Spirituels, Ubertin de Casale." In *Franciscains d'Oc,* 263–83.

De Broucker, Jose. *Dom Helder Camara: The Violence of a Peacemaker.* Translated by Herma Briffault. Maryknoll, N.Y.: Orbis, 1970.

Deedy, John G. *Apologies Good Friends: An Interim Biography of Daniel Berrigan.* Chicago: Fides Claretian, 1981.

———. "At Ease: Status in West Germany." *Commonweal* 103 (June 4, 1976): 354.

———. "The Catholic Press and Vietnam." in Quigley, 121–31.

De Gruchy, John W. *The Church Struggle in South Africa.* Grand Rapids, Mich.: Eerdmans, 1979.

Delaney, John J. *Pocket Dictionary of Saints.* Garden City, N.Y.: Doubleday, 1983.

Delaruelle, Étienne. "La Critique de la guerre sainte dans la litterature méridionale." In Delaruelle, *Paix de Dieu,* 128–39.

———. "Les Ermites et la spiritualité populaire." In the collection *L'Eremetismo in Occidente nei secoli xi e xii.* Milan: Centro di Studi Medievali, 1965.

———. *L'Idée de croisade au Moyen Âge,* 1–23. Turin: Bottega d'Erasmo, 1980.

———. "Paix de Dieu et croisade dans la chrétienté du xiie siècle." In *Paix de Dieu et guerre sainte en Languedoc au xiiie siècle,* 51–71. Cahiers de Fanjeaux 4, Toulouse: Privat, 1969. Reprinted in Delaruelle, *L'Idée de croisade,* 233–53.

Delaruelle, Louis. *Études sur l'humanisme français: Guillaume Budé.* Paris: H. Champion, 1907.

Delehaye, Hippolyte. *Les Légendes grecques des saints militaires.* Paris: A. Picard, 1909.

———. *The Legends of the Saints.* Translated by Donald Attwater. New York: Fordham University Press, 1962.

———. *Les Origines du culte des martyrs.* Brussels: Société des Bollandists, 1912.

———. *Les Passions des martyrs et les genres litteraires.* Brussels: Societé des Bollandists, 1921.

Delzell, Charles F., ed. *The Papacy and Totalitarianism between the Two World Wars.* New York: John Wiley, 1974.

Den Boer, Willem. *Private Morality in Greece and Rome.* Leiden: Brill, 1979.

Deutsch, Richard. *Mairead Corrigan–Betty Williams.* Woodbury, N. Y.: Barrons, 1977.

*Dictionary of the Middle Ages* (DMA). Edited by Joseph R. Strayer. New York: Charles Scribner's, 1982–.

*Dictionnaire d'archéologie Chrétienne et de liturgie* (DACL). Edited by Fernand Cabrol, Henri Leclercq, and Henri Marrou. 15 vols. Paris: Letouzey et Ané, 1907–1953.

*Dictionnaire de spiritualité, ascetique, et mystique: Doctrine et histoire.* 10 vols. Paris: Mythe, 1937–.

*Dictionnaire de théologie Catholique* (DTC). Edited by A. Vancant, E. Mangenot, and E. Amann. 15 vols. in 23, with supplements. Paris: Letouzey et Ané, 1903–1972.

Digan, Parig. *Churches in Contestation: Asian Christian Social Protest.* Maryknoll, N.Y.: Orbis, 1984.

Dodds, E. R. *Pagan and Christian in an Age of Anxiety.* New York: Norton, 1965.

Donfried, Kare P., ed. *The Romans Debate.* Minneapolis: Augsburg Publishing, 1977.

Dörries, Hermann. *Constantine the Great*. Translated by Roland H. Bainton. New York: Harper and Row, 1972.

Dougherty, James E. "The Christian and Nuclear Pacifism." *Catholic World* 198 (March 1964): 336–46.

Douglas, James W. *The Non-Violent Cross: A Theology of Revolution and Peace*. New York: Macmillan, 1968.

Douie, Decima L. *The Nature and the Effect of the Heresy of the Fraticelli*. Manchester: University of Manchester Press, 1932. Reprinted New York: AMS, 1978.

Doyère, P. "Eremitisme en Occident." In DSAM (fasc. 28–29), t.4, pt. 1 (1960), cols. 953–70.

Duby, Georges. "Laity and the Peace of God." In *The Chivalrous Society: Essays by Georges Duby*, translated by Cynthia Postan, 123–33. London: Edward Arnold, and Berkeley, Calif.: University of California Press, 1977.

———. *The Three Orders: Feudal Society Imagined*. Chicago: University of Chicago Press, 1980.

Du Cange, Charles Du Fresne. "Pax." In *Glossarium mediae et infimae latinitatis*, 2:228–31. 10 vols. Paris: Osmont, 1937–1938.

Duckett, Eleanor Shipley. *Gateway to the Middle Ages: Monasticism*. Ann Arbor, Mich.: University of Michigan Press, 1971.

Dunlop, D. M. "A Christian Mission to Muslim Spain in the Eleventh Century." *Al-Andalus* 17 (1952): 259–310.

Dunn, Richard S. *The Age of Religious Wars, 1559–1689*. New York: Norton, 1970.

Dussel, Enrique. "Current Events in Latin America." In Eagleson and Torres, 77–102.

———. "Historical and Philosophical Presuppositions of Latin American Theology." Gibellini, 184–212.

———. *History and Theology of Liberation: A Latin American Perspective*. Translated by John Drury. Maryknoll, N.Y.: Orbis, 1976.

———. *A History of the Church in Latin America: Colonialism to Liberation 1492–1979*. 3d ed. Translated by Alan Neely. Grand Rapids, Mich.: Eerdmans, 1981.

Duval, Frederic Victor. *De la paix de Dieu à la paix de fer*. Paris: Paillard, 1923.

Earl, Donald C. *The Moral and Political Tradition of Rome*. Ithaca, N.Y.: Cornell University Press, 1967.

Egan, Eileen. "The Beatitudes, The Works of Mercy, and Pacifism." In Shannon, *War or Peace?*, 169–87.

———. *The Catholic CO: The Right to Refuse to Kill*. Cambridge, Mass.: Pax Christi, 1981.

Eissfeldt, O. "The Hebrew Kingdom." CAH 2 (1975): 537–605.

Ellis, John Tracy. *American Catholicism*. 2d rev. ed. Chicago: University of Chicago Press, 1969.

———. *Catholics in Colonial America*. Baltimore, Md.: Helicon, 1965.

———. "United States of America." In NCE 14:425–48.

Ellis, Marc. *Peter Maurin: Prophet of the Twentieth Century*. New York: Paulist, 1981.

Ellsberg, Patricia Marx. "An Interview with Rolf Hochhuth." In Delzell, 108–24.

*Enciclopedia Cattolica* (EC). 12 vols. Vatican City: Ente per l'Enciclopedia Cattolica, 1949–1954.

Eppstein, John. *The Catholic Tradition of the Law of Nations*. Washington, D.C.: Carnegie Endowment, 1935.

*Erasmus in English*. Annual newsletter published by the University of Toronto Press, 1970–.

Erdmann, C. *The Origin of the Idea of Crusade*. Translated by Marshall W. Baldwin and Walter Goffart. Princeton, N.J.: Princeton University Press, 1977.

*L'eremetismo in Occidente nei secoli xi e xii*. Miscellanea del Centro di Studi Medioevali. Vol. 4. Milan: Università Cattolica del Sacro Cuore, 1965.

"Esquivel, Adolfo Perez." In *Current Biography Yearbook*, 321–24. New York: H. H. Wilson, 1981.

Evans, Austin P. "The Albigensian Crusade." In Setton, *Crusades* 3:277–324.

Fahey, Joseph. "Pax Christi." In Shannon, *War or Peace?*, 59–71.

———. "Toward a Theology of Peace." *Catholic World* 213 (May 1971): 64–68.

Falconi, Carlo. *The Silence of Pius XII*. Translated by Bernard Wall. Boston: Little, Brown, 1970.

"Farewell to CAIP." *America* 120 (May 24, 1969): 609–10.

Fenwick, C. G. "Peace, International." In NCE 11:38–41.

Ferguson, John. *The Politics of Love: The New Testament and Nonviolent Revolution*. Nyack, N.Y.: Fellowship of Reconciliation, 1979.

———. *The Religions of the Roman Empire*. Ithaca, N.Y.: Cornell University Press, 1970.

———. *War and Peace in the World's Religions*. Nyack, N.Y.: Fellowship of Reconciliation, 1977.

Ferguson, Wallace K. *The Renaissance in Historical Thought.* Boston: Houghton Mifflin, 1948.
Fernandez, J. A. "Erasmus on the Just War." *Journal of the History of Ideas* 34 (1973): 209–26.
Fernandez, Manuel Gimenez. "Fray Bartolomé de Las Casas: A Biographical Sketch." In Friede and Keen, 67–125.
Fernessole, Pierre. *La papauté et la paix du monde de Gregoire XVI à Pie XI.* Paris: Beauchesne, 1948.
Fichtenau, Heinrich. *The Carolingian Empire.* Translated by Peter Munz. New York: Harper and Row, 1964.
Finley, Moses I. *Ancient Slavery and Modern Ideology.* New York: Penguin, 1983.
Finn, James. "Pacifism and Justifiable War." In Shannon, *War or Peace?*, 3–14.
Finn, Thomas M., C.S.P. "Peace, War and the Vatican Council." *Catholic World* 203 (August 1966): 270–75.
Fitzmyer, J. A. "Romans, Epistle to the." In NCE 12:635–39.
Flannery, Harry W. "Catholic Association for International Peace (CAIP)." In NCE 3:264.
Fliche, A., and V. Martin, eds. *Histoire de l'Église depuis les origines jusqu'à nos jours.* Paris: Bloud and Gay, 1934–.
Flood, David, O.F.M., ed. *Poverty in the Middle Ages.* Werl, Westfalia: D. Coelde, 1975.
Foerster, W., et al. "*Eirene,*" in *Theological Dictionary of the New Testament,* edited by Gerhard Kittel, translated and edited by Geoffrey W. Bromley, 2:400–420. Grand Rapids, Mich.: Eerdmans, 1976.
———. *From the Exile to Christ: A Historical Introduction to Palestinian Judaism.* Translated by Gordon E. Harris. Philadelphia: Fortress, 1964.
Fonseca, Cosimo D. "La Povertà nelle sillogi canonicali del xiiº secolo: fatti istituzionali e implicazioni ideologiche." In *La Povertà del secolo xii,* 149–77.
Fontaine, J. "Christians and Military Service in the Early Church." Translated by T. Westow. *Concilium* 7 (1965): 107–119.
Forest, James. *Catholics and Conscientious Objection.* New York: Catholic Peace Fellowship, 1981.
———. "No Longer Alone: The Catholic Peace Movement." In Quigley, 139–49.
———. "Thomas Merton's Struggle with Peacemaking." In Twomey, 15–54.
Fournier, Paul E. L., and Gabriel Le Bras. *Histoire des collections canoniques en Occident depuis les Fausses Décrétales jus qu'au Décret de Gratien.* 2 vols. Paris: Sirey, 1931.
*Franciscains d'Oc: Les Spirituels ca. 1280–1324.* Cahiers de Fanjeaux 10, Toulouse: Privat, 1975.
Frantzen, Allen J. *The Literature of Penance in Anglo-Saxon England.* New Brunswick, N.J.: Rutgers University Press, 1983.
———. "The Penitentials Attributed to Bede." *Speculum* 58, 3 (1983): 573–95.
———. "The Significance of the Frankish Penitentials." *Journal of Ecclesiastical History* 30 (1979): 409–21.
———. "The Tradition of Penitentials in Anglo-Saxon England." *Anglo-Saxon England* 11 (1982): 23–56.
Frazee, Charles A. "Late Roman and Byzantine Legislation on the Monastic Life from the Fourth to the Eighth Centuries." *Church History* 51 (Sept. 1982): 263–79.
Frend, W. H. C. *The Early Church.* Philadelphia: Fortress, 1982.
———. *Martyrdom and Persecution in the Early Church.* Rev. ed. Grand Rapids, Mich.: Baker House, 1981.
Freyne, Sean. *The World of the New Testament.* Wilmington, Del.: Glazier, 1980.
Friede, Juan. "Las Casas and Indigenism in the Sixteenth Century." In Friede and Keen, 127–234.
Friede, Juan, and Benjamin Keen, eds. *Bartolomé de Las Casas in History.* DeKalb, Ill.: Northern Illinois University Press, 1971.
Friedlander, Saul. *Pius XII and the Third Reich.* New York: Alfred A. Knopf, 1966.
Friedrich, C.-J. "Guerre et paix d'après Erasme et Kant." *Colloquia Erasmiana* 1:277–83.
Frugoni, Arsenio. "La devozione dei Bianchi del 1399." In *L'Attesa dell'età nuova nella spiritualità della fine del medioevo,* 232–48. Todi: Centro di Studi sulla Spiritualità del Medioevo, 1962.
———. "Il Giubileo di Bonifacio VIII." *Bulletino del Istituto Storico Italiano per il Medioevo* (BISI) 62 (1950): 1–121.
———. "Sui flagellanti del 1260." BISI 75 (1963): 211–37.
Fuhrmann, H. "False Decretals (Pseudo-Isidorian Forgeries)." In NCE 5:820–24.

Fumigalli, Vito. "In margine all' 'Alleluia' del 1233." BISI 80 (1968): 257–72.

Furfey, Paul Hanley. "The Civilian COs." In Shannon, *War or Peace?*, 188–99.

Furlong, Monica. *Merton: A Biography*. San Francisco: Harper and Row, 1980.

Furnish, V. P. *The Love Command in the New Testament*. Nashville, Tenn.: Abingdon, 1972.

Ganshof, F. L. *Feudalism*. Translated by Philip Grierson. New York: Longmans, 1952.

———. *Histoire des relations internationales I: Le Moyen Âge*. Paris: Hachette, 1953. (Translated by Remy I. Hall. *The Middle Ages*, New York: Harper and Row, 1970.)

Gaudemet, Jean. "Le Rôle de la papauté dans le règlement des conflits entre états aux xiii<sup>e</sup> et xiv<sup>e</sup> siècles." *Recueils . . . Jean Bodin* 15 (1961): 79–106. Reprinted in *La société ecclésiastique dans l'occident médiéval*, by Jean Gaudemet, 79–106. London: Variorum Reprints, 1980.

Genaro, Clara. "Venturino da Bergamo e la peregrinatio romana del 1335." In *Studi sul medioevo cristiano offerti a R. Morghen*, 375–406. I. Rome: Instituto Storico Italiano per il Medioevo, 1974.

George, A., ed. *La pauvreté évangélique*. Paris: Éditions du Cerf, 1970.

Gernhuber, Joachim. "Staat und Landfrieden im deutschen Reich des Mittelalters." *Recueils . . . Jean Bodin* 15 (1961): 27–78.

Gero, S. " 'Miles gloriosus': The Church and Military Service according to Tertullian." *Church History* 39 (1970): 285–98.

Gettleman, Marvin E., et al., eds. *El Salvador: Central America in the New Cold War*. New York: Grove, 1982.

Gibert, Rafael. "Lulio y Vives sobre la paz." *Recueils . . . Jean Bodin* 15 (1961): 125–70.

Gibson, Charles. *Spain in America*. New York: Harper and Row, 1966.

Gihooley, J. J. "Pax Christi/U.S.A.: Out of the Ashes; National Assembly." *America* 133 (Dec. 27, 1975): 458–60.

Gilmore, Myron. *The World of Humanism 1453–1517*. New York: Harper and Row, 1952.

Giordano, Pasquale T., S.J. "The Philippine Church: Exercising Her Prophetic Role to a Nation in Crisis." *New Catholic World* 226 (Sept.–Oct. 1983): 226–28.

Girouard, Mark. *The Return to Camelot: Chivalry and the English Gentleman*. New Haven, Conn.: Yale University Press, 1981.

Gleiman, L. "Some Remarks on the Origins of the Treuga Dei." *Études d'histoire litteraire et doctrinale*, Publications 17 (1962): 117–37. Montréal: Université de Montréal, Institut d'Études Médiévales.

Gonella, Guido. *The Papacy and World Peace: A Study of the Christmas Messages of Pope Pius XII*. London: Hollis and Carter, 1945.

Gorgen, Carol. *Catholic Conscientious Objectors*. San Francisco: Allied Printing, 1963.

Goss-Mayr, Hildegard. "Choosing Means Toward a Just End." *Fellowship* 49:10–11 (Oct.–Nov. 1983): 5, 27.

Grace, Tom. "Living on the Front Lines." *Fellowship* 49:4 (April 1983): 11–13.

Graham, R. A. "Pax Christi." In NCE 11:34–35.

———. "Vatican Peace Initiatives." *America* 114 (March 26, 1966): 416.

Graml, Hermann, H. Mommsen, H. Reichhardt, and E. Wolf. *The German Resistance to Hitler*. Berkeley, Calif.: University of California Press, 1970.

Grant, Frederick C. *Ancient Roman Religion*. New York: Liberal Arts Press, 1957.

Grant, Michael. *History of Rome*. New York: Charles Scribner's, 1978.

Grant, Robert M. *Augustus to Constantine: The Thrust of the Christian Movement into the Roman World*. New York: Harper and Row, 1970.

———. *Early Christianity and Society*. San Francisco: Harper and Row, 1977.

———. *A Historical Introduction to the New Testament*. New York: Harper and Row, 1963.

Gray, Francine du Plessix. *Divine Disobedience: Profiles in Catholic Radicalism*. New York: Alfred A. Knopf, 1970.

Greeley, Andrew M. *The American Catholic: A Select Portrait*. New York: Harper and Row, 1977.

Grisel, Étienne. "The Beginnings of International Law and General Public Law Doctrine: Francisco de Vitoria's *De Indis prior*." In Chiappelli, 1:305–25.

Gross, Heinrich. "Peace." In *Encyclopedia of Biblical Theology: The Complete Sacramentum Verbi*, edited by Johannes Baptist Bauer, 3:648–51. 3 vols. New York: Herder and Herder, 1970.

Gruber, John. "Peace Negotiations of the Avignonese Popes." *Catholic Historical Review* 19 (1933–34): 190–99.

Grundmann, Herbert. *Religiöse Bewegungen im Mittelalter*. Darmstadt: Wissenschafliche Buchgesellschaft, 1961. Translated with new introduction as *Movimenti religiosi nel Medioevo*. Bologna: Mulino, 1974.

Guerry, Emile M. *The Popes and World Government*. Translated by G. J. Roettger. Baltimore: Helicon, 1964.

Gumbleton, Thomas J. "The Role of the Peacemaker." In Shannon, *War or Peace?*, 214–29.

Haines, Keith. "Attitudes and Impediments to Pacifism in Medieval Europe." *Journal of Medieval History* 7 (1981): 369–88.

Hale, J. R. "Armies, Navies, and the Art of War." In NCMH 2:481–509.

———. *Renaissance Exploration*. New York: Norton, 1968.

———. *Renaissance Europe 1480–1520*. London: Fontana, 1973.

———. "Sixteenth-Century Explanations of War and Violence." *Past and Present* 51 (1971): 3–26.

———. "War and Public Opinion in the Fifteenth and Sixteenth Centuries." *Past and Present* 22 (1962): 18–35.

Halecki, Oscar, with James F. Murray. *Eugenio Pacelli: Pope of Peace*. New York: Creative Age Press, 1951.

Halkin, Léon-E. "Erasme et la politique des rois." In Herding and Stüpperich, 109–18.

Hallack, Cecily, and P. F. Anson. *These Made Peace*. Paterson, N.J.: St. Anthony Guild, 1957.

Hallenbeck, Jan T. "Instances of Peace in Eighth-Century Lombard–Papal Relations." *Archivum Historiae Pontificae* 18 (1980): 41–56.

Halton, Thomas P., and Robert D. Sider. "A Decade of Patristic Scholarship 1970–1979." *Classical World* 76 (Nov.–Dec. 1982): 67–127.

Hamilton, Bernice. *Political Thought in Sixteenth-Century Spain: A Study of the Political Ideas of Vitoria, De Soto, Suarez, and Molina*. Oxford: Clarendon Press, 1963.

Hanke, Lewis. *All Mankind Is One*. DeKalb, Ill.: Northern Illinois University Press, 1974.

———. *All the Peoples of the World Are One*. Minneapolis: University of Minnesota Press, 1970.

———. *Aristotle and the American Indians*. London: Hollis and Carter, 1959.

———. *Bartolomé de Las Casas*. The Hague: Nijhoff, 1951.

———. "More Heat and Some Light on the Spanish Struggle for Justice in the Conquest of America." *Hispanic American Historical Review* 44 (1964): 293–340.

———. *The Spanish Struggle for Justice in the Conquest of America*. Philadelphia: University of Pennsylvania Press, 1949.

Harbison, E. Harris. *The Christian Scholar in the Age of the Reformation*. New York: Charles Scribner's, 1956.

Hardin, Richard F. "The Literary Conventions of Erasmus' *Education of a Christian Prince:* Advice and Aphorism." *Renaissance Quarterly* 35 (1982): 151–63.

Harnack, Adolf. *The Mission and Expansion of Christianity in the First Three Centuries*. Translated and edited by James Moffatt. New York: Harper and Row, 1962.

Harris, William V. *War and Imperialism in Republican Rome 327–70 B.C.* Oxford: Clarendon Press, 1979.

Hartdegen, S. "Third Orders." In NCE 14:93–96.

Hay, Denys. *Europe in the Fourteenth and Fifteenth Centuries*. New York: Holt, Rinehart and Winston, 1966.

———. *Europe: The Emergence of an Idea*. New York: Harper and Row, 1966.

Hayden, J. M. "Saint-Pierre, Charles Irenée Castel de." In NCE 12:942.

Heer, Friedrich. *The Intellectual History of Europe*. 2 vols. Garden City, N.Y.: Doubleday, 1968.

Hefele, Karl Josef von. *A History of the Councils of the Church*. 5 vols. Edinburgh: Clark, 1883–1896. Reprinted New York: AMS, 1972.

Hehir, J. Bryan. "The Catholic Church and the Arms Race." *Worldview* 21 (July–August 1978): 13–18.

———. "The Just-War Ethic and Catholic Theology: Dynamics of Change and Continuity." In Shannon, *War or Peace?*, 15–39.

Helgeland, J. "Christians and the Roman Army, A.D. 173–337." *Church History* 43 (1974): 149–63, 200.

Helmreich, Ernst C. *The German Churches under Hitler*. Detroit: Wayne State University Press, 1979.

Hemleben, Sylvester John. *Plans for World Peace through Six Centuries*. Chicago: University of Chicago Press, 1943.

Heneghan, T. "COs or Cheap Labor: West Germany." *Commonweal* 105 (Jan. 6, 1978): 5–7.

Hennessey, James, S.J. *American Catholics: A History of the Roman Catholic Community in the United States*. New York: Oxford University Press, 1981.

Henriot, P. J. "American Bishops and Conscientious Objectors." *America* 120 (Jan. 4, 1969): 17–19.

Herding, Otto. "Humanistische Friedensideen am Beispiel zweier Friedenklagen." In Herding and Stüpperich, 7–34.

Herding, Otto, and Robert Stüpperich, eds. *Die Humanisten in ihrer politischen und sozialen Umwelt*. Boppard-am-Rhein: Harald Boldt Verlag, 1976.

Herlihy, David. *The History of Feudalism*. New York: Harper and Row, 1970.

Hexter, Jack N. *The Vision of Politics on the Eve of the Reformation*. New York: Basic Books, 1973.

Heyer, F. *The Catholic Church from 1648 to 1870*. London: Black, 1969.

Higgs, David. "The Portuguese Church." In Callahan and Higgs, 51–65.

Hill, David J. *A History of Diplomacy in the International Development of Europe*. 3 vols. New York: Longmans, 1905–1914.

Hinnebusch, William A. *History of the Dominican Order*. New York: Alba House, 1973.

Hoffmann, Harmut. *Gottesfriede und Treuga Dei*. In MGH, Scriptores, vol. 20. Stuttgart: Hiersmann, 1964.

Holmes, Arthur F. *War and Christian Ethics*. Grand Rapids, Mich.: Baker House, 1975.

Holmes, George. *Europe: Hierarchy and Revolt 1320–1450*. London: Fontana, 1975.

Holmes, J. Derek. *The Papacy in the Modern World*. New York: Crossroad, 1981.

Hope, Marjorie, and James Young. *The South African Churches in a Revolutionary Situation*. Maryknoll, N.Y.: Orbis, 1983.

———. *The Struggle for Humanity*. Maryknoll, N.Y.: Orbis, 1979.

Hopkins, Keith. *Conquerors and Slaves: Sociological Studies in Roman History*. Vol. 1. New York: Cambridge University Press, 1977.

Hornus, Jean-Michel. *It Is Not Lawful for Me to Fight: Early Christian Attitudes toward War*. Scottsdale, Pa.: Herald Press, 1980.

Huberti, Ludwig. *Die Entwicklung des Gottesfriedens im Frankreich*. Ansbach: Brugel, 1891.

Hubrecht, George. "La juste guerre dans la doctrine chrétienne, des origines au milieu du xviᵉ siècle." *Recueils . . . Jean Bodin* 15 (1961): 107–25.

Hufton, Olwen. "The French Church." In Callahan and Higgs, 13–33.

Huizinga, Johan. *Erasmus and the Age of Reformation*. New York: Harper and Row, 1957.

Hyma, Albert. *The Christian Renaissance*. Hamden, Conn.: Archon Books, 1965.

———. *The Youth of Erasmus*. Ann Arbor, Mich.: University of Michigan Press, 1968.

Imbert, Jean. "Pax Romana." *Recueils . . . Jean Bodin* 14 (1961): 303–19.

"Irenics: The Study of Peace." *America* 125 (Oct. 30, 1971): 336.

Jayne, Sears R. *John Colet and Marsiglio Ficino*. Oxford: Oxford University Press, 1963.

Jedin, Hubert, and John Dolan, eds. *Handbook of Church History (History of the Church)*. New York: Herder and Herder, Seabury Press, 1965–.

Jenkins, Helen. *Papal Efforts for Peace under Benedict XII, 1334–1342*. Philadelphia: Ph.D. Dissertation, University of Pennsylvania, 1933.

Johnson, E. "The German Crusade in the Baltic." In Setton, *Crusades* 3:545–85.

Johnson, James T. *Ideology, Reason, and the Limitation of War: Religious and Secular Concepts 1200–1740*. Princeton, N.J.: Princeton University Press, 1975.

Jones, A. H. M. *Constantine and the Conversion of Europe*. New York: Collier, 1962.

———. *The Later Roman Empire, 284–602: A Social and Administrative Survey*. 3 vols. Norman, Okla.: University of Oklahoma Press, 1964.

———. "The Social Background of the Struggle between Paganism and Christianity." In Momigliano, *Conflict*, 17–37.

Jones, Arthur. "Pax Christi Conference Records Historic Change." *The Reporter for Conscience Sake* 38, 12 (December 1981): 1–2.

Joris, André. "Observations sur la proclamation de la trêve de Dieu à Liège à la fin du xiᵉ siècle." *Recueils . . . Jean Bodin* 14 (1961): 503–45.

Kaufman, Peter Iver. *Augustinian Piety and Catholic Reform: Augustine, Colet, and Erasmus*. Macon, Ga.: Mercer University Press, 1982.

Kaza, J. "West Germany's COs." *New Leader* 61 (Feb. 27, 1978): 3.

Keen, Benjamin. "Approaches to Las Casas, 1535–1970." In Friede and Keen, 3–63.

Kelly, J. N. D. *Early Christian Doctrines*. 2d ed. London: Adam & Charles Black, 1960.

Kennedy, J. H. *Jesuit and Savage in New France.* New Haven, Conn.: Yale University Press, 1950.

Kennelly, Karen. "Catalan Peace and Truce Assemblies." *Studies in Medieval Culture* 5 (1975): 41–51.

———. "Medieval Towns and the Peace of God." *Medievalia et Humanistica* 15 (1963): 35–53. 53.

Kirkpatrick, Frederick A. *The Spanish Conquistadors.* 2d ed. New York: Barnes and Noble, 1967.

Kirwin, G. F. "Metanoia." In NCE 9:724.

Kissinger, Warren S. *The Sermon on the Mount: A History of Interpretation and Bibliography.* Metuchen, N.J.: ATLA Bibliography Series, 1975.

Kittel, Gerhard. *Theological Dictionary of the New Testament.* Translated and edited by Geoffrey W. Bromley. Grand Rapids, Mich.: Eerdmans, 1976.

Klassen, Walter. "The Doctrine of the Just War in the West: A Summary." *Peace Research Reviews* VII-6, 1978.

Klejment, Anne, and Alice Klejment. *Dorothy Day and the Catholic Worker: A Bibliography and Index.* New York: Garland, 1985.

Knowles, David. *Christian Monasticism.* New York: McGraw-Hill, 1969.

———. *The Evolution of Medieval Thought.* New York: Vintage, 1962.

Koester, Helmut. *History and Literature of Early Christianity.* Philadelphia: Fortress, 1982.

Krieger, Leonard. *Kings and Philosophers, 1689–1789.* New York: Norton, 1970.

Kristeller, Paul Oskar. *Renaissance Thought.* New York: Harper and Row, 1961.

Kritzeck, James. *Peter the Venerable and Islam,* vol. 23. Princeton, N.J.: Princeton Oriental Studies, 1964.

Kuttner, Stephan, ed. *Proceedings of the Fourth International Congress of Medieval Canon Law.* Vatican City: Bibliotheca Apostolica Vaticana, 1976.

Kyer, Clifford Ian. *"Legatus* and *nuntius* as Used to Denote Papal Envoys: 1245–1378." *Mediaeval Studies* 40 (1978): 473–77.

———. *The Papal Legate and the "Solemn" Papal Nuncio, 1243–1378: The Changing Pattern of Papal Representation.* Toronto: Ph.D. Dissertation, University of Toronto, 1979.

Lacefield, Patrick. "Oscar Romero: Archbishop of the Poor." In Gettleman, 198–203.

Ladner, Gerhart B. *The Idea of Reform: Its Impact on Christian Thought and Action in the Age of the Fathers.* Rev. ed. New York: Harper and Row, 1967.

Ladurie, Emmanuel L. *Montaillou: The Promised Land of Error.* New York: Random House, Vintage Books, 1979.

Laistner, M. L. W. *Thought and Letters in Western Europe,* A.D. *500 to 900.* Ithaca, N.Y.: Cornell University Press, 1966.

Lambert, Malcolm. *Medieval Heresy: Popular Movements From Bogomil to Hus.* New York: Holmes and Meier, 1977.

Lammers, Stephen E. "Roman Catholic Social Ethics and Pacifism." In Shannon, *War or Peace?,* 93–103.

Lange, Christian Louis. *Histoire de la doctrine pacifique.* The Hague: Academy of International Law, 1927.

———. *Histoire de l'internationalisme.* 3 vols. Kristiania (Oslo): H. Aschenhoug, 1919–1963.

Lange, Martin, and Reinhold Iblacker, eds. *Witnesses of Hope.* Translated by William E. Jerman. Maryknoll, N.Y.: Orbis, 1981.

Lassere, Jean. *War and the Gospel.* Translated by Oliver Coburn. Scottsdale, Pa.: Herald Press, 1962.

Lasko, Peter. *The Kingdom of the Franks.* New York: McGraw-Hill, 1971.

Latourette, Kenneth S. *History of the Expansion of Christianity.* 7 vols. New York: Harper and Row, 1937–1945.

———. *The Thousand Years of Uncertainty,* A.D. *500–* A.D. *1500.* Vol. 2 of Latourette, *History.* Reprinted Grand Rapids, Mich.: Zondervan, 1976.

———. *Three Centuries of Advances,* A.D. *1500–*A.D. *1800.* Vol. 3 of Latourette, *History.* New York: Harper and Row, 1939.

Laughlin, M. F. "Humiliati." In NCE 7:234.

Lawler, F. X. "Mystical Body of Christ." In NCE 10:166–70.

Le Bras, Gabriel. "Pénitentiels." In DTC 12:1160–79.

———. "The Sociology of the Church in the Early Middle Ages." In Thrupp, 47–57.

Lebreton, Jules, S. J., and Jacques Zeiller. *History of the Primitive Church.* Translated by Ernest C. Messenger. 3 vols. New York: Macmillan, 1944–1948.

Leclercq, Henri. "Militarisme." In DACL 11:1108–81.

———. "Paix." In DACL 3,1:465–83.

———. "Paix de l'Église." In DACL 3,1:483–99.

Leclercq, Jean, O.S.B. "Aux origines bibliques du vocabulaire de la pauvreté." In Mollat, *Etudes,* 1:35–43.

———. "Les Controverses sur la pauvreté du Christ." In Mollat, *Études,* 1:45–55.

———. "Saint Bernard's Attitude towards War." *Studies in Cistercian History* 2 (1975): 1–39.

Leff, Gordon. *The Dissolution of the Medieval Outlook: An Essay on Intellectual and Spiritual Change in the Fourteenth Century.* New York: Harper and Row, 1976.

———. *Heresy in the Later Middle Ages.* 2 vols. New York: Barnes and Noble, 1967.

———. *Medieval Thought.* Baltimore, Md.: Penguin, 1968.

Leitzmann, H. *A History of the Early Church.* Translated by B. L. Woolf. Cleveland: World, 1961.

Leiper, G. A. "Letter from Italy." *Christian Century* 79 (March 21, 1962): 359–60.

Léon-Dufour, Xavier. "Peace." In *Dictionary of Biblical Theology,* Translated and edited by P. Joseph Cahill, 411–14. 2d ed. New York: Seabury, 1973.

Lernoux, Penny. *Cry of the People.* New York: Penguin, 1982.

Le Saint, W. "Tertullian." In NCE 13:1019–22.

Lewy, Guenter. *The Catholic Church and Nazi Germany.* New York: McGraw-Hill, 1964.

Liddell, Henry George, and Robert Scott. *A Greek-English Lexicon.* Oxford: Clarendon Press, 1968.

Littell, Franklin H., and Hubert G. Locke. *The German Church Struggle and the Holocaust.* Detroit: Wayne State University Press, 1974.

Little, Lester K. "Evangelical Poverty, the New Money Economy, and Violence." In Flood, 11–26.

———. *Religious Poverty and Profit Economy in Medieval Europe.* Ithaca, N.Y.: Cornell University Press, 1978.

Livermore, H. V. "Portuguese Expansion." In NCMH 1:420–30.

Lockhart, James, and Stuart B. Schwartz. *Early Latin America.* New York: Cambridge University Press, 1983.

Lohse, Eduard. *The New Testament Environment.* Translated by John E. Steely. Nashville, Tenn.: Abingdon, 1976.

Long, Edward L. *War and Conscience in America.* Philadelphia: Westminster, 1968.

Lorson, Pierre, S. J. "Saint Bernard devant la guerre et la paix." *Nouvelle Revue Théologique* 75 (1953): 785–803.

Losada, Angel. "The Controversy between Sepulveda and Las Casas in the Junta of Valladolid." In Friede and Keen, 279–307.

McCann, Dennis P. *Christian Realism and Liberation Theology.* Maryknoll, N.Y.: Orbis, 1981.

McCloskey, P. W. "CAIP: What is its Future?" *Commonweal* 87 (Nov. 17, 1967): 194–95.

McConica, James K., C.S.B. "Erasmus and the 'Julius': A Humanist Reflects on the Church." In Trinkaus and Oberman, 444–77.

McCormick, R. A. "War, Morality of." In NCE 14:802–7.

McDonnell, E. W. *The Beguines and Beghards in Medieval Culture.* New Brunswick, N.J.: Rutgers University Press, 1954.

McDowell, Michael H. C. "Post-Nobel Decline: Peace People Fall on Hard Times." *Commonweal* 107 (March 28, 1980): 164–65.

McEoin, Gary. "The European Church and the War." In Quigley, 151–62.

MacGregor, C. H. C. *The New Testament Basis of Pacifism.* Nyack, N.Y.: Fellowship of Reconciliation, 1968.

McGuire, M. R. P. "Ambrose, St." In NCE 1:372–5.

McKenna, C. H. "Vitoria, Francisco de." In NCE 14:727–28.

McKenzie, John L., S.J. "Peace." In *Dictionary of the Bible,* by John L. McKenzie, 651–52. Milwaukee: Bruce, 1965.

MacKinney, Loren C. "The People and Public Opinion in the Eleventh-Century Peace Movement." *Speculum* 5 (1930): 181–206.

McKitterick, Rosamond. *The Frankish Kingdoms under the Carolingians 751–987.* New York and London: Longmans, 1983.

MacMullen, Ramsay. *Constantine.* New York: Dial, 1969.

———. *Paganism in the Roman Empire.* New Haven, Conn.: Yale University Press, 1981.

——. *Roman Social Relations 50 B.C. to A.D. 284*. New Haven, Conn.: Yale University Press, 1974.

——. *Soldier and Civilian in the Later Roman Empire*. Cambridge, Mass.: Harvard University Press, 1963.

McNeal, Patricia. *The American Catholic Peace Movement 1928–1972*. New York: Arno, 1978.

——. "Catholic Conscientious Objectors during World War II." *Catholic Historical Review* 61 (April 1975): 219–42.

McNeill, John T. "Asceticism versus Militarism in the Middle Ages." *Church History* 5 (1936): 3–28.

McNeish, James. *Fire Under the Ashes: The Life of Danilo Dolci*. London: Holder and Stoughton, 1965.

McReavy, L. L. "Pacifism." In NCE 10:855–57.

MacShane, Denis. *Solidarity*. Nottingham: Spokesman, 1981.

McSorley, Richard, S.J. *New Testament Basis of Peacemaking*. Washington, D.C.: Georgetown University Center for Peace Studies, 1979.

Madaule, Jacques. *The Albigensian Crusade*. Translated by Barbara Wall. New York: Fordham University Press, 1967.

Makarewicz, S. "Epikeia (in the Bible)." In NCE 5:476–77.

Maly, Eugene H. *Romans*. Wilmington, Del.: Glazier, 1979.

Manselli, Raoul. "L'Antichristo mistico, Pietro di Giovanni Olivi, Ubertino da Casale, e i papi del loro tempo." *Collectanea Franciscana* 47 (1977): 5–25.

——. "Evangelismo e povertà." In Manselli, ed., *Povertà*, 9–41.

——. "Pietro di Giovanni Olivi ed Ubertino da Casale." *Studi Medievali* ser. 3, 6–2 (1965): 95–122.

Manselli, Raoul, ed. *Povertà e ricchezza nella spiritualità dei secoli xi e xii*. Todi: Centro di studi sulla spiritualità medievale, 1969.

Manteuffel, Tadeusz.. *Naissance d'une hérésie: Les adeptes de la pauvreté volontaire au Moyen Âge*. Translated from the Polish by Anna Posner. Paris: Mouton, 1970.

Marchand, C. Roland. *The American Peace Movement and Social Reform 1898–1918*. Princeton, N.J.: Princeton University Press, 1973.

Markus, Robert A. *Christianity in the Roman World*. New York: Charles Scribner's, 1974.

Martin, Earl S. "Cardinal Opposes Repression, Revolution." NCR 16:37 (Aug. 15, 1980): 7.

Matthews, John Frederick. *Western Aristocracies and Imperial Court, A.D. 364–425*. Oxford: Clarendon Press, 1975.

Mattingly, Garrett. *Renaissance Diplomacy*. Baltimore, Md.: Penguin, 1964.

Mayer, Hans Eberhard. *The Crusades*. New York: Oxford, 1972.

Meconis, Charles A. *With Clumsy Grace: The American Catholic Left 1961–1975*. New York: Seabury-Continuum, 1979.

Meeks, Wayne A. *The First Urban Christians: The Social World of the Apostle Paul*. New Haven, Conn.: Yale University Press, 1983.

Meersseman, Giles G., O.P. *Dossier sur l'ordre de la Pénitence au xiiiᵉ siècle*. Fribourg: Éditions Universitaires, 1961.

——. *Ordo Fraternitatis: Confraternitate e pietà dei laici nel medioevo*. Rome: Italia Sacra, 1977.

Milano, Ilarino da, O.F.M. Cap. "Umiliati." In EC 12:754–56.

Miller, William D. *Dorothy Day: A Biography*. San Francisco: Harper and Row, 1982.

——. *A Harsh and Dreadful Love: Dorothy Day and the Catholic Worker Movement*. New York: Liveright, 1973.

Mollat, Guillaume. "La Diplomatie pontificale au xivᵉ siècle." In *Mélanges Louis Halphen*, 507–12. Paris: Presses Universitaires, 1951.

——. *The Popes at Avignon*. New York: Thomas Nelson, 1963.

Mollat, Michel. "Hospitalité et assistance au début du xiiiᵉ siècle." In Flood, 37–51.

——. "Pauvres et pauvreté dans le monde médiéval." In *La Povertà nel secolo xii*, 79–97.

——. "Les Pauvres et la société médiévale." In *Rapports du xiiiᵉ Congrès International des sciences historiques* 1 (Moscow, 1973), 162–80.

——. *Vaudois languedociens et Pauvres Catholiques*. Cahiers de Fanjeaux 2, Toulouse: Privat, 1967.

Mollat, Michel, ed. *Études sur l'histoire de la pauvreté: Moyen Age–xviᵉ siècle*. 2 vols. Paris: La Sorbonne, 1974.

Mollat, Michel, with Philippe Wolff. *The Popular Revolutions of the Late Middle Ages*. Translated by A. L. Lytton-Sells. London: Allen and Unwin, 1973.

Momigliano, Arnaldo. "Christianity and the Decline of the Roman Empire." In Momigliano, *Conflict*, 1–19.

———. "Herod of Judaea." CAH 10 (1966): 316–39.

Momigliano, Arnaldo, ed. *The Conflict between Paganism and Christianity in the Fourth Century.* Oxford: Clarendon Press, 1963.

*Il Monachesimo nell'alto medioevo e la formazione della civiltà occidentale.* Spoleto: Centro italiano di studi sull'alto medioevo, 1957.

Montgomery, Tommie Sue. *Revolution in El Salvador.* Boulder, Colo.: Westview, 1982.

Moorman, John. *A History of the Franciscan Order from Its Origins to the Year 1517.* Oxford: Clarendon Press, 1968.

Moose, G. L. "Changes in Religious Thought." In NCMH 4:169–201.

Moscati, Sabatino. *The Face of the Ancient Orient.* Garden City, N.Y.: Doubleday, 1962.

Moss, H. St. L. B. *The Birth of the Middle Ages.* New York: Oxford University Press, 1961.

Muldoon, James M. "The Contribution of the Medieval Canon Lawyer to the Formation of International Law." *Traditio* 28 (1972): 483–97.

———. "A Fifteenth-Century Application of the Canonistic Theory of the Just War." In Kuttner, 467–82.

———. "Papal Responsibility for the Infidel: Another Look at Alexander VI's *Inter caetera.*" *Catholic Historical Review* 64 (1978): 168–84.

———. *Popes, Lawyers, and Infidels: The Church and the Non-Christian World 1250–1550.* Philadelphia: University of Pennsylvania Press, 1979.

Murnion, Philip J. *Catholics and Nuclear War: A Commentary on The Challenge of Peace.* New York: Crossroad, 1983.

Murphy, R. T. A. "Luke, Gospel According to." In NCE, 1067–73.

Musto, Ronald G. "Angelo Clareno, O.F.M.: Fourteenth-Century Translator of the Greek Fathers." *Archivum Franciscanum Historicum* 76 (1983): 215–38, 589–645.

———. *The Letters of Angelo Clareno, O.F.M. (c. 1250–1337).* Ph.D. Dissertation, Columbia University, 1977.

Neill, Stephen. *A History of Christian Missions.* New York: Penguin, 1980.

*The New Cambridge Modern History* (NCMH). 14 vols. New York: Cambridge University Press, 1964–1970.

———. *The Renaissance 1493–1520.* Vol. 1 of NCMH, edited by Denys Hay. New York: Cambridge University Press, 1975.

———. *The Reformation 1520–1559.* Vol. 2 of NCMH, edited by G. R. Elton. New York: Cambridge University Press, 1975.

———. *The Decline of Spain and the Thirty Years War, 1606–48/59.* Vol. 4 of NCMH, edited by J. F. Cooper. New York: Cambridge University Press, 1970.

*The New Catholic Encyclopedia* (NCE). 15 vols. Washington, D.C.: Publisher's Guild, and New York: McGraw-Hill, 1967.

Niebuhr, H. Richard. *Christ and Culture.* New York: Harper and Row, 1956.

Niebuhr, Reinhold. *Moral Man and Immoral Society.* New York: Charles Scribner's, 1960.

Nock, A. D. *Conversion: The Old and the New in Religion from Alexander the Great to Augustine of Hippo.* New York: Oxford University Press, 1965.

———. "Religious Developments from the Close of the Republic to the Death of Nero." CAH 10 (1966): 465–511.

Noth, Martin. *The Old Testament World.* Translated by Victor I. Gruhn. Philadelphia: Fortress Press, 1964.

Novacovitch, Mileta. *Les Compromis et les arbitrages internationaux du xii^e au xv^e siècle.* Paris: A. Pedone, 1905.

Oakley, Francis. *The Western Church in the Later Middle Ages.* Ithaca, N.Y.: Cornell University Press, 1979.

Oakley, T. P. "Cultural Affiliations of Early Ireland in the Penitentials." *Speculum* 8 (1933): 489–500.

O'Brien, David J. "American Catholic Opposition to the Vietnam War: A Preliminary Assessment." In Shannon, *War or Peace?*, 119–50.

———. "Catholic Peace Movement Lives!" *America* 130 (May 4, 1974): 342–43.

O'Callaghan, Joseph F. *A History of Medieval Spain.* Ithaca, N.Y.: Cornell University Press, 1975.

O'Connell, Marvin R. *The Counter Reformation, 1560–1610.* New York: Harper and Row, 1974.

Onclin, Willy. "L'Idée de la société internationale en Europe occidentale avant Grotius." *Recueils . . . Jean Bodin* 15 (1961): 219–40.

O'Rourke, William. *The Harrisburg Seven and the New Catholic Left.* New York: Crowell, 1972.

Ostling, R. N. "Mission to the East." *Time* 117 (March 2, 1981): 34–36.

Ozment, Steven. *The Age of Reform 1250–1550.* New Haven, Conn.: Yale University Press, 1980.

"Pacem in Terris and Vietnam." *Christianity Today* 12 (Jan. 5, 1968): 39.

"Pacifists Win in France." *Christian Century* 79 (July 11, 1962): 856.

Painter, Sidney. *French Chivalry.* Ithaca, N.Y.: Cornell University Press, 1965.

"Paix." In DTC, Tables Générales 2:3407–9.

*Paix: Recueils de la Société Jean Bodin (Recueils . . . Jean Bodin).* Vols. 14 and 15 (1961).

Palms, C. L. "Peace and the Catholic Conscience." *Catholic World* 203 (June 1966): 145–52.

Paradisi, Bruno. "L'Organization de la Paix aux iv$^e$ et v$^e$ siècles." *Recueils . . . Jean Bodin* 14 (1961): 321–95.

Parry, J. H. *The Establishment of the European Hegemony.* New York: Harper and Row, 1966.

———. "Spaniards in the New World." In NCMH 1:430–44.

———. "The New World, 1521–1580." In NCMH 2:562–90.

Pastor, Ludwig. *The History of the Popes.* 40 vols. St. Louis, Mo.: B. Herder, 1938–1969.

Paul, Jacques. "Les Spirituels, l'église et la papauté." In *Chi erano gli Spirituali, Atti del III Convegno Internazionale,* 221–62. Assisi: Società Internazionale di Studi Francescani, 1976.

Peebles, B. M. "Bible, IV, 13: Latin Version." In NCE 2:436–57.

Peers, E. Allison. *Ramon Lull.* London: S.P.C.K., 1929.

Pennington, Kenneth. "Bartolomé de Las Casas and the Tradition of Medieval Law." *Church History* 39 (1970): 149–61.

Perroy, Edouard. *The Hundred Years War.* New York: Capricorn, 1965.

Petit, Paul. *Pax Romana.* Translated by James Willis. Berkeley, Calif.: University of California Press, 1976.

Pfeiffer, Robert H. *Introduction to the Old Testament.* New York: Harper and Row, 1948.

Phelan, John Leddy. *The Millennial Kingdom of the Franciscans in the New World.* Berkeley and Los Angeles: University of California Press, 1956. Revised 1970.

"Philippines (Special Issue)." NCR 19:41 (Sept. 16, 1983).

Philips, Margaret Mann. *Erasmus and the Northern Renaissance.* London: English Universities Press, 1967.

Picón-Salas, Mariano. *A Cultural History of Spanish America.* Translated by Irving A. Leonard. Berkeley, Los Angeles, and London: University of California Press, 1962.

Piehl, Mel. *Breaking Bread: The Catholic Worker and the Origin of Catholic Radicalism in America.* Philadelphia: Temple University Press, 1982.

Piper, John. *Love Your Enemies: Jesus' Love Command in the Synoptic Gospels and in the Early Christian Paraenesis.* Cambridge: Cambridge University Press, 1979.

Pisani, J. "Conscientious Objection: No Longer Un-Catholic." *Christian Century* 88 (July 21, 1971): 876–78.

Pissard, Hippolyte. *La Guerre sainte en pays chrétien.* Paris: A. Picard, 1912. Reprinted New York: AMS, 1980.

Plattard, Jean. *Guillaume Budé, 1468–1540, et les origines de l'humanisme français.* Paris: Les Belles Lettres, 1966.

"Plowshares Actions." *CPF Bulletin* (May 1984): 4–5.

Polner, M. "No Jew nor Catholic Need Apply." *Commonweal* 90 (June 20, 1969): 386–87.

Porges, W. "The Clergy, the Poor, and the Non-Combatants on the First Crusade." *Speculum* 21 (1946): 1–23.

Post, Regnerus R. *The Modern Devotion: Confrontation with Reformation and Humanism.* Leiden: Brill, 1968.

Potel, Jean-Yves. *The Promise of Solidarity.* New York: Praeger, 1982.

Potts, Timothy C. *Conscience in Medieval Philosophy.* New York: Cambridge University Press, 1980.

Powell, James M. "Boniface, St." In DMA 2:321–32.

Powers, R. T., and H. A. Freeman. "Conscientious Objectors." In NCE 4:204–6.

Preaux, Claire. "La Paix a l'époque hellenistique." In *Receuils . . . Jean Bodin* 14 (1961): 227–301.

Previté-Orton, C. W. *The Shorter Cambridge Medieval History.* 2 vols. Cambridge: Cambridge University Press, 1966.

Prinz, Friedrich. *Klerus und Krieg im Früheren Mittelalter.* Stuttgart: Hiersmann, 1971.

"The Prize for Peace Doesn't Always Lead to It." *New York Times,* Oct. 21, 1984.

Proaño, Leonidas. "The Church and Politics in Ecuador." *Concilium* 71 (1972): 99–105.

Pyes, Craig. "Who Killed Archbishop Romero? D'Aubuisson's Role." *The Nation* 239:11 (Oct. 13, 1984): 337, 350–54.

Quasten, Johannes. *Patrologia*. 3 vols. Westminster, Md.: Newman, 1960.

Quigley, Thomas E., ed. *American Catholics and Vietnam*. Grand Rapids, Mich.: Eerdmans, 1968.

Quispel, Gilles. *The Secret Book of Revelation*. New York: McGraw-Hill, 1979.

Reeves, Marjorie. *The Influence of Prophesy in the Later Middle Ages*. Oxford: Clarendon Press, 1969.

———. *Joachim of Fiore and the Prophetic Future*. London: S.P.C.K., 1976.

Regehr, Ernie. *Perceptions of Apartheid: The Churches and Political Change in South Africa*. Scottsdale, Pa.: Herald Press, and Kitchener, Ontario: Between the Lines, 1979.

Renaudet, Augustin. *Préréforme et humanisme à Paris*. 2d ed. Paris: Libraire d'Argences, 1953.

Renna, Thomas. "The Idea of Peace in the West, 500–1150." *Journal of Medieval History* 6:2 (1980): 143–67.

Renouard, Yves. *The Avignon Papacy, 1305–1404*. Translated by Denis Bethell. Hamden, Conn.: Archon, 1970.

Reuter, Timothy, ed. *The Greatest Englishman*. Exeter: Paternoster, 1980.

Rhodes, Anthony. *The Power of Rome in the Twentieth Century: The Vatican in the Age of Liberal Democracies 1870–1922*. New York: Franklin Watts, 1983.

———. *The Vatican in the Age of the Dictators, 1922–1945*. New York: Holt, Rinehart and Winston, 1974.

Ricard, Robert. *The Spiritual Conquest of Mexico: An Essay on the Apostolate and Evangelizing Methods of the Mendicant Orders in New Spain, 1523–1572*. Berkeley and Los Angeles: University of California Press, 1966.

Rice, Eugene F., Jr. *The Foundations of Early Modern Europe, 1460–1559*. New York: Norton, 1970.

Richard, Jean. *La Papauté et les missions d'Orient au Moyen Âge (xiiiᵉ–xvᵉ siècles)*. Rome: École Française de Rome, 1977.

Riding, Alan. "The Cross and the Sword in Latin America." In Gettleman, 189–98.

Riga, Peter J. *A Guide to Pacem in Terris for Students*. New York: Paulist, 1964.

———. "Selective Conscientious Objection: Progress Report." *Catholic World* 211 (July 1970): 161–65.

Rodriquez, M. "Peace (in the Bible)." In NCE 11:37–38.

Roemer, William F., and John Tracy Ellis. *The Catholic Church and Peace Efforts*. Washington, D.C.: Catholic Association for International Peace, 1934.

Rosa, Mario. "The Italian Churches." In Callahan and Higgs, 66–76.

Roscher, Wilhelm Heinrich. "Pax." In *Ausführliches Lexicon der griechischen und romischen Mythologie*, III, 2:1719–22. 6 vols. in 9. Hildesheim: Olms, 1965.

Rosenstock-Huessey, Eugen. *The Driving Power of Western Civilization*. Boston: Beacon Press, 1950.

Rosenthal, J. T. "The Public Assembly in the Time of Louis the Pious." *Traditio* 20 (1964): 25–40.

Rummel, Erika. "A Reader's Guide to Erasmus Controversies." *Erasmus in English* 12 (1983): 13–19.

Runciman, Steven. "The Decline of the Crusading Idea." In *Relazioni del xᵒ congresso internazionale di scienze storiche*, 3: 637–52. Florence: International Congress of Historical Sciences, 1955.

———. *A History of the Crusades*. 3 vols. New York: Harper and Row, 1964–1967.

Rusch, William G. *The Later Latin Fathers*. London: Duckworth, 1977.

Russell, Frederick H. "Innocent IV's Proposal to Limit Warfare." In Kuttner, 383–99.

———. *The Just War in the Middle Ages*. New York: Cambridge University Press, 1975.

Ryan, E. A., S. J. "The Rejection of Military Service by Christians." *Theological Studies* 13 (1952): 1–32.

Ste-Croix, G. de. "Why Were the Early Christians Persecuted?" *Past and Present* 26 (1963): 6–38.

Sandmel, Samuel. *Judaism and Christian Beginnings*. New York: Oxford University Press, 1978.

Scaramucci, Lodovico, ed. *Il Movimento dei Disciplinati nel settimo centenario dal suo inizio*. 3 vols. Perugia: Deputazione di storia patria per l'Umbria, 1962.

Schampheleer, Jacques de. "La Pauvreté évangélique." *Études Franciscains* 18, 46 (1968): 173–85.

Schmitt, Clément, O.F.M. "Les Citations bibliques et canoniques dans les traités médiévaux sur la pauvreté, xiv$^e$–xv$^e$s." *Études sur pauvreté* 2:547–60.

Schoeck, R. J. "Colet, John." In NCE 3:990–91.

Schroeder, F. "Paul, Apostle, St." In NCE 11:1–12.

Schuijt, William J., and René Coste. "History and Commentary of *Gaudium et Spes,* pt. II, chap. V." In Vorgrimler 5:328–69.

Scott, James Brown. *The Catholic Conception of International Law.* Washington, D.C.: Georgetown University Press, 1934.

"Selective Objectors and the Court." *America* 123 (July 11, 1970): 6.

Setton, Kenneth Meyer. *Christian Attitudes towards the Emperor in the Fourth Century.* New York: Columbia University Press, 1941.

Setton, Kenneth Meyer, ed. *A History of the Crusades.* 5 vols. Madison, Wis.: University of Wisconsin Press, 1955–1983.

Shannon, Thomas A., ed. *War or Peace? The Search for New Answers.* Maryknoll, N.Y.: Orbis, 1982.

———. *What Are They Saying about Peace and War?* New York: Paulist Press, 1983.

Sheehan, Arthur. *Peter Maurin, Gay Believer: The Biography of an Unusual and Saintly Man.* Garden City, N.Y.: Hanover House, 1959.

Sheerin, J. B. "Must Conscientious Objectors be Pacifists?" *Catholic World* 206 (January 1968): 146–47.

Sherwin-White, Adrian N. *The Letters of Pliny: A Historical and Social Commentary.* Oxford: Clarendon Press, 1968.

———. *Roman Society and Roman Law in the New Testament.* Oxford: Clarendon, 1963.

Siegman, E. F. "Apocalypse, Book of." In NCE 1:654–59.

"A Sign of Resurrection in El Salvador." In Gettleman, 206–10.

Simone, Franco. *The French Renaissance.* Translated by H. Gaston Hall. London: Macmillan, 1969.

Simpson, Lesley Byrd. *The Encomienda in New Spain.* Berkeley, Los Angeles, and London: University of California Press, 1966. Reprinted 1982.

Siniscalco, Paolo. *Massimiliano: Un obiettore di coscienza del tardo impero. Studi sulla "Passio S. Maximiliani."* Turin: Paravia, 1974.

Skehan, P. W. "Bible, IV, 5: Septuagint." In NCE 2:425–29.

Smallwood, E. Mary. *The Jews under Roman Rule.* Leiden: Brill, 1976.

Smith, John Holland. *The Death of Classical Paganism.* New York: Charles Scribner's, 1976.

Smith, Michael Auckland. *The Church Under Siege.* Downers Grove, Ill.: Inter-Varsity, 1976.

Smyth, Philip. "Anti-War Feeling Growing in Belgium." *CCCO News Notes* 35,2 (Summer 1983): 3.

———. "New Hope for Spanish COs." *CCCO News Notes* 35,1 (Spring 1983): 3.

Solon, Paul D. "Popular Response to Standing Military Forces in Fifteenth-Century France." *Studies in the Renaissance* 19 (1972): 78–111.

Souleyman, Elizabeth V. *The Vision of World Peace in Seventeenth and Eighteenth Century France.* New York: G. P. Putnam's, 1941.

Southern, Richard W. *Western Views of Islam in the Middle Ages.* Cambridge, Mass.: Harvard University Press, 1962.

"Spain Incarcerates Catholic CO." *Christian Century* 88 (May 12, 1971): 585.

Staniszkis, Jadwiga. *Poland's Self-Limiting Revolution.* Princeton, N.J.: Princeton University Press, 1984.

Stapfer, Paul. "Les Idées de Rabelais sur la guerre." *Bibliotheque Universelle et Revue Suisse* (3d ser.) 40 (1888): 367–79.

Steinberg, S. H. *Five Hundred Years of Printing.* Baltimore: Penguin, 1974.

Stevenson, G. "The Imperial Administration." CAH 10 (1966): 182–216.

Stevenson, G., and Arnaldo Momigliano. "Rebellion within the Empire." CAH 10 (1966): 840–65.

Strattmann, Franziscus. *War and Christianity Today.* Translated by John Doebele. London: Blackfriars, 1956.

Strubbe, E. I. "La Paix de Dieu dans le Nord de la France." *Recueils . . . Jean Bodin* 14 (1961): 489–501.

Sullivan, Richard. "The Carolingian Missionary and the Pagan." *Speculum* 28 (1953): 705–40.

———. "Carolingian Missionary Theories." *Catholic Historical Review* 42 (1956–57): 273–95.

———. "Early Medieval Missionary Activity: A Comparative Study of Eastern and Western Methods." *Church History* 23 (1954): 17–35.

———. "Khan Boris and the Conversion of Bulgaria: A Case Study of the Impact of Christianity on a Barbarian Society." *Studies in Medieval and Renaissance History* 3 (1966): 53–139.

———. "The Papacy and Missionary Activity in the Early Middle Ages." *Mediaeval Studies* 17 (1955): 46–106.

Sweeney, Francis, S. J., ed. *The Vatican and World Peace: A Boston College Symposium.* Gerrards Cross: Smythe, 1970.

Swomley, John M. *Liberation Ethics.* New York: Macmillan, 1972.

Symonds, J. A. "Religious Revivals in Medieval Italy." *Cornhill* 31 (181) (Jan. 1875): 54–64.

Synan, Edward A. "Augustine of Hippo, Saint." In DMA 1:646–59.

Tellenbach, Gerd. *Church, State and Christian Society at the Time of the Investiture Contest.* Translated by R. F. Bennett. New York: Harper and Row, 1970.

Thompson, E. A. "Christianity and the Northern Barbarians." In Momigliano, *Conflict,* 56–78.

Thomson, John A. F. *Popes and Princes 1417–1517.* London: Allen & Unwin, 1980.

Thouzellier, Christine. *Catharisme et Valdéisme en Languedoc à la fin du xii^e et au début du xiii^e siècle.* Louvain: Nauwelaerts, 1969.

Throop, Palmer A., "Criticism of Papal Crusade Policy in Old French and Provençal." *Speculum* 13 (1938): 379–412.

———. *Criticism of the Crusades: A Study of Public Opinion and Crusade Propaganda.* Amsterdam: Swets and Zeitlinger, 1940.

Thrupp, Sylvia, ed. *Early Medieval Society.* New York: Appleton-Century-Crofts, 1967.

Tierney, Brian. *Ockham, the Conciliar Theory, and the Canonists.* Philadelphia: Fortress, 1971.

———. *Origins of Papal Infallibility 1150–1350.* Leiden: Brill, 1972.

Töpfer, Bernhard. *Volk und Kirche zur Zeit der beginnenden Gottesfriedensbewegung im Frankreich.* Berlin: Rutten and Loening, 1957.

Toporoski, Richard. "Ambrose, St." In DMA 1:230–32.

Touraine, Alain, et al., eds. *The Analysis of a Social Movement: Poland 1980–1981.* New York: Cambridge University Press, 1983.

Tousley, Ben. "Small Candles of Peace in Northern Ireland." *Fellowship* 49,12 (Dec. 1983): 7–10, 22.

Tracy, James. *The Politics of Erasmus: A Pacifist Intellectual and His Political Milieu.* Toronto: University of Toronto Press, 1978.

Trinkaus, Charles, and Heiko Oberman, eds. *The Pursuit of Holiness in Late Medieval and Renaissance Religion.* Leiden: Brill, 1974.

True, Michael. "Persisters for Peace: Catholic Peace Movement." *Commonweal* 100 (April 26, 1974): 180–81.

Truhlar, K. V. "Obedience." In NCE 10:602–6.

Truyol y Serra, Antonio. "La Conception de la paix chez Vitoria et les classiques espagnols du droit des gens." *Recueils . . . Jean Bodin* 15 (1961): 241–73.

Twomey, Gerard, ed. *Thomas Merton: Prophet in the Belly of a Paradox.* New York: Paulist Press, 1978.

Ullmann, Walter. *The Carolingian Renaissance and the Idea of Kingship.* New York: Barnes and Noble, 1969.

———. *The Growth of Papal Government in the Middle Ages.* 3d ed. London: Methuen, 1970.

———. *A History of Political Thought in the Middle Ages.* Baltimore, Md.: Penguin, 1965.

———. "The Medieval Papal Court as an International Tribunal." *Virginia Journal for International Law* 11 (1971): 356–71.

———. "Public Welfare and Social Legislation in Early Medieval Councils." *Studies in Church History* 7 (Cambridge, 1971): 1–39.

Van Allen, R. "Pax Christi in Dayton: International Peace Movement." *Commonweal* 102 (Dec. 19, 1975): 612–14.

Van der Ploeg, J., O.P., and Louis F. Hartman, C.S.S.R., trans. "Peace." In *Encyclopedic Dictionary of the Bible,* translated and edited by Louis F. Hartman, cols. 1782–84. New York: McGraw-Hill, 1963.

Vanderpol, Alfred. *La Doctrine scholastique du droit de guerre.* Paris: A. Pedone, 1919.

Venard, Marc. "Popular Religion in the Eighteenth Century." In Callahan and Higgs, 138–54.

Verlinden, Charles. "La 'Requerimiento' et la 'paix coloniale' dans l'empire espagnol d'Amerique." *Recueils . . . Jean Bodin* 15 (1961): 397–414.

Vesnitch, R. M. "Deux precurseurs français du pacifisme et de l'arbitrage internationale." *Revue d'Histoire Diplomatique* 25 (1911): 23–78.

Vicaire, Marie-Humbert. *L'Imitation des Apôtres: moines, chanoines, mendiants (iv<sup>e</sup>–xiii<sup>e</sup> siècles).* Paris: Éditions du Cerf, 1963.

Vidler, Alec R. *A Century of Social Catholicism.* London: S.P.C.K., 1964.

———. *The Church in an Age of Revolution.* New York: Penguin, 1961.

Vogel, C. "Les Pèlerinages pénitentiels." *Revue des Sciences Réligieuses* 38 (1964): 113–45.

———. *Le Pécheur et la pénitence au Moyen Âge.* Paris: Éditions du Cerf, 1969.

Vogt, Hermann Josef. "The Missionary Work of the Latin Church." In Baus, *Imperial Church,* 517–601.

Von Auw, Lydia. *Angeli Clareni Opera.* Vol. 1, *Epistole.* Rome: Istituto Storico Italiano per il Medioevo, 1980.

———. *Angelo Clareno et les Spirituels italiens.* Rome: Edizioni di Storia e Letteratura, 1979.

———. "La Vraie Église d'après les lettres d'Angelo Clareno." In *L'Attesa dell'età nuova nella spiritualità della fine del Medioevo,* 433–42. Todi: Centro di studi sulla spiritualità medievale, 1962.

Von Campenhausen, Hans. "Military Service in the Early Church." In *Tradition and Life in the Church,* 160–70. Philadelphia: Fortress, 1968.

Von Oppen, Beate Ruhm. *Religion and Resistance to Nazism.* Princeton, N.J.: Center for International Studies, Princeton University Press, 1971.

Vorgrimler, Herbert, ed. *Commentary on the Documents of Vatican II.* Vol. 5, *Pastoral Constitution of the Church in the Modern World.* New York: Herder and Herder, 1969.

Waddell, Helen. *The Wandering Scholars.* Garden City, N.Y.: Doubleday, 1961.

Waddy, L. H. *Pax Romana and World Peace.* New York: Norton, 1954.

Walker, Lawrence D. "Priests vs. Nazis in the Diocese of Limbourg, 1934: The Confessional Factor." *Historical Social Research—Historische Sozialforschung* 23 (July 1982): 55–65.

Wallbank, F. W. *The Hellenistic World.* Cambridge, Mass.: Harvard University Press, 1982.

Wallis, Jim. *Peacemakers: Christian Voices from the New Abolitionist Movement.* San Francisco: Harper and Row, 1983.

Walshe, Peter. *Church vs. State in South Africa.* Maryknoll, N.Y.: Orbis, 1983.

Waltz, James. "Historical Perspectives on 'Early Missions to the Muslims': A Response to Allan Cutler." *Muslim World* 61 (1971): 170–86.

———. "The Significance of the Voluntary Martyr Movement of Ninth-Century Cordoba." *Muslim World* 60 (1970): 143–59, 226–36.

Watkins, Oscar D. *A History of Penance.* 2 vols. London: Longmans, 1920.

Webb, Diana M. "Penitence and Peace-Making in City and Contado: The *Bianchi* of 1399." *Studies in Church History* 16 (1979): 243–56.

Wentworth, Cedric. "COs in France." *The Objector* 3,2 (Oct. 1982): 5–6.

———, "New Rights for French COs." *The Objector* 4,1 (Sept. 1, 1983):3.

Wentzlaff-Eggebert, Friedrich-W. *Kreuzzugsdichtung des Mittelalters.* Berlin: De Gruyter, 1960.

Weschler, Lawrence. *The Passion of Poland.* New York: Pantheon, 1984.

Wiedemann, Thomas. *Greek and Roman Slavery.* Baltimore, Md.: Johns Hopkins, 1981.

Williams, C. "Conscience: 3. In Theology." In NCE 4:198–202.

Williams, Schafer, ed. *The Gregorian Epoch.* Boston: D. C. Heath, 1967.

Windass, Stanley. *Christianity versus Violence: A Social and Historical Study of War and Christianity.* London: Sheed and Ward, 1964.

———. "The Early Christian Attitude to War." *Irish Theological Quarterly* 29 (1962): 235–45.

Wittner, Lawrence. *Rebels Against War: The American Peace Movement 1941–1960.* New York: Columbia University Press, 1969.

Wohlhaupter, Eugen. *Studien zur Rechtsgeschichte der Gottes und Landfrieden im Spanien.* Heidelberg: Winter, 1933.

Wolf, Ernst. "Political and Moral Motives Behind the Resistance." In Graml, et al., 193–234.

Wolff, Philippe. *Western Languages A.D. 100–1500.* New York: McGraw-Hill, 1971.

Wood, Mary M. *The Spirit of Protest in Old French Literature.* New York: Columbia University Press, 1917. Reprinted New York: AMS, 1983.

Woodward, William H. *Studies in Education during the Age of the Renaissance, 1400–1600.* New York: Columbia University Press, 1967.

Wright, J. J. "Peace: Modern Papal Teaching." In NCE 11:41–45.

Yzermans, Vincent A., ed. *American Participation in the Second Vatican Council.* New York: Sheed and Ward, 1967.

Zahn, Gordon. *An Alternative to War*. New York: Council on Religion and International Affairs, 1963.

———. *Another Part of the War: The Camp Simon Story*. Amherst, Mass.: University of Massachusetts Press, 1979.

———. "Carrying Our Weight in the Catholic Peace Movement." *America* 133 (Sept. 20, 1975): 143–46.

———. "The Case for Christian Dissent." In Zahn, *War, Conscience and Dissent*, 243–63.

———. "Catholic Conscientious Objection in the United States." In Zahn, *War, Conscience and Dissent*, 145–59.

———. "Catholic Resistance? A Yes and a No." In Littell, 203–37.

———. "Conscientious Objection in Nazi Germany: Martyrdom, 1943." In Zahn, *War, Conscience and Dissent*, 177–91.

———. "Future of the Catholic Peace Movement." *Commonweal* 99 (Dec. 28, 1973): 337–42.

———. "The German Catholic Press and Hitler's Wars." In Zahn, *War, Conscience and Dissent*, 204–29.

———. *German Catholics and Hilter's Wars: A Study in Social Control*. New York: Sheed and Ward, 1962.

———. "In Praise of Individual Witness: F. Jaegerstaetter's Refusal to Serve in the Nazi Army." *America* 129 (Sept. 8, 1973): 141–45.

———. *In Solitary Witness: The Life and Death of Franz Jaegerstaetter*. Collegeville, Minn.: Liturgical Press, 1964. Reissued 1977.

———. "The Social Thought of the Catholic Conscientious Objector." In Zahn, *War, Conscience and Dissent*, 160–76.

———. "Thomas Merton: Reluctant Pacifist." In Twomey, 55–79.

———. *War, Conscience and Dissent*. New York: Hawthorne, 1967.

Zahn, Gordon. ed. *The Nonviolent Alternative*. Rev. ed. of *Thomas Merton on Peace*. New York: Farrar, Straus, Giroux, 1980.

Zampaglione, Gerardo. *The Idea of Peace in Antiquity*. Translated by Richard Dunn. Notre Dame, Ind.: University of Notre Dame Press, 1973.

Zeiller, Jacques. "The Question of Military Service." In Lebreton and Zeiller, 2:1155–79.

# INDEX

## Other Orbis Titles . . .

### OF WAR AND LOVE
#### by Dorothee Sölle
In this moving and beautifully written volume of poetry and prose, Dorothee Sölle cries out against war and violence citing a number of situations and attitudes she sees as fostering them—the arms race, oppression in Latin America, racism, and sexism. She asks Christians to voice their oppositions to war and its underlying causes and to respond through a measure of nonviolent resistence.

"*Of War and Love* is a book like a banner, a book like a broadsheet. Dorothee Sölle is that rare human: a theologian who is not afraid to be loud and faithful and lucid about unmentionable topics."                    *Daniel Berrigan, S.J.*

**no. 350-3**                    **172pp. pbk.**                    **$7.95**

### REVOLUTIONARY PATIENCE
#### by Dorothee Sölle
A collection of 26 fervent poems that attempt to make sense, in light of the gospel, of a world brutally scarred by oppression.

". . . full of precise emotions, powerfully evoked. And full of challenges to human complacency."                    *Sojourners*

German theologian Dorothee Sölle divides her time between New York City, where she teaches as Union Theological Seminary, and Hamburg.

**no. 439-9**                    **82pp. pbk.**                    **$5.95**

### JUSTICE AND PEACE EDUCATION
#### Models for College and University Faculty
#### edited by David M. Johnson
A collection of models for integrating justice and peace concerns into courses in various disciplines ranging from the humanities, the social sciences, and inter-disciplinary studies to business, management, and engineering. Based on the practical educational and research experience of professors in U.S. Catholic colleges and universities, each model includes a course syllabus, a list of

required texts for students, and suggested readings for faculty. The result is an intelligent, pragmatic manual for educators seeking to promote a more just and peaceful world. Contributors include Monika Hellwig, William Byron, David O'Brien, Marie Augusta Neal, Thomas Shannon, and Suzanne Toton.

"A remarkable array of authors and a really sophisticated approach in which peace and justice themes are introduced without despoiling the inner integrity of the various disciplines." *Padraic O'Hare, Boston College*

". . . should be a standard resource for all who seek to introduce peace studies into higher eductation." *Betty Reardon, Teachers College,*
*Columbia University*

**no. 247-7**            **256pp. pbk.**            **$16.95**

## PARENTING FOR PEACE AND JUSTICE
### by Kathleen and James McGinnis

How do parents act for justice without sacrificing their own children? How do they build family community without isolating themselves from the world? In this practical and insightful volume, Kathleen and James McGinnis address these and many other problems families may encounter in their effort to integrate social and family ministry. Topics discussed include stewardship, nonviolence both in and outside the family, promoting sexual equality in the family, multiculturalizing family life, and inviting children to participate in social action.

"The guide is filled with exercises, readings, and worksheets to supplement the reading of the book and make its contents all the more real in our lives. This combination is indispensable for educators and families alike."

*Religious Education*

Kathleen and James McGinnis are staff members of the Institute for Peace and Justice in St. Louis and the parents of three children.

**no. 376-1**            **143pp. pbk.**            **$6.95**

## WAR OR PEACE?
### The Search for New Answers
### *edited by Thomas A. Shannon*

A collection of 13 essays that address the issues of both pacifism and just-war theory with respect to ethical theory, political strategy, and the responsibility of individuals and the community.

". . . an invaluable aid to understanding this most serious problem." *America*

"Shannon's book will be a strong resource to introduce students to the issues without theological pretentiousness or denominational provincialism."

*Mission Focus*

**no. 750-9**            **256pp. pbk.**            **$9.95**

## SOCIAL ANALYSIS
### Linking Faith and Justice
*by Joe Holland and Peter Henriot*

This study describes the task of social analysis and its relevance to social justice action. According to Joe Holland and Peter Henriot, the way people see a problem determines how they will respond to it. Social analysis is a result of "seeing a wider picture" of the problem—exploring structural issues, examining causal linkages, identifying key factors, and tracing long term trends. This approach, they assert, will initiate action capable of affecting profound social change. The book provides illustrations of analytical approaches to various problems and explores the suggestions and questions they raise for pastoral response.

". . . a provocative essay that is particularly valuable in highlighting the role of the social sciences in effective applications of faith values." *Sociological Analysis*

Peter Henriot and Joe Holland are director and staff member, respectively, of the Center of Concern, Washington, D.C.

no. 462-3                                118pp. pbk.                                $6.95


## THIRD WORLD RESOURCE DIRECTORY
### A Guide to Organizations and Publications
*edited by Thomas Fenton & Mary Heffron*

A comprehensive guide which lists and describes hundreds of resources for educators, committed church and political activists, and other concerned citizens interested in Third World issues. The directory is divided into two parts: by area and by issues. The areas include Third World, Africa, Asia and the Pacific, Latin America and the Caribbean, and the Middle East. The issues addressed are Food, Hunger, Agribusiness, Human Rights, Militarism, Peace, Disarmament, Transnational Corporations, and Women. Resources include organizations, books, periodicals, pamphlets and articles, films, slideshows, videotapes, and simulation games. Comprehensively cross referenced and indexed.

". . . there is no other source that provides such a wealth of information."

*Choice*

no. 509-3                                304pp. pbk.                                $17.95


## CRY JUSTICE!
### Prayers, Meditations, and Readings from South Africa
*by John de Gruchy*
### Preface by Bishop Desmond Tutu

John de Gruchy has collected 31 sets of readings from scripture, poetry, personal testimonies, and a variety of other historical and contemporary materials that chronicle the journey of Christian faith amid the struggle against apartheid. *Cry Justice!* begins with the author's penetrating essay on the relationship between prayer and politics, spirituality and social transformation. Interspersed with African linocuts and songs from the African churches, the book concludes with an Agape or "love-feast."

This is an exciting resource for community reflection, discussion, personal devotions, sermons, and worship in any region of the world

"In this struggle for justice, peace, and reconciliation the Christian resources are ultimately spiritual. We are thankful that John de Gruchy has illustrated this to be the case." *Desmond Tutu, Bishop of Johannesburg*

John de Gruchy, a native South African, is Professor of Religious Studies at the University of Cape Town and an ordained minister in the United Congregational Church of Southern Africa.

**no. 223-X**                        **264pp. pbk.**                        **$6.95**


## THE GOSPEL OF PEACE AND JUSTICE
### Catholic Social Teaching Since Pope John
***edited by Joseph Gremillion***

"This source book and survey of social problems contains 22 documents—encyclicals, conciliar decrees, and papal and episcopal addresses—which have appeared during the reigns of Pope John XXIII and Paul VI. Gremillion introduces them with a 140 page outline of the world situation today, the role the Catholic Church has played and should play in promoting justice and peace, and the development of papal thought on these questions." *Theology Digest*

"Gremillion's study is not just four star work, it is four star plus. It should be preached, studied, meditated, and read. It is without equal. It is a must for anyone seeking to live the social Gospel." *Religious Media Today*

**no. 166-7**                        **637pp. pbk.**                        **$14.95**